D1328189

An Introduction to MODERN ECONOMIC THEORY

By Basil J. Moore

Intended specifically for the more well prepared student, this textbook has been written out of the conviction that introductory texts in economics must try *not* to survey the whole of economics. It is the author's belief that conventional elementary texts attempt to cover too much territory and frequently leave the student with little command over the relatively few central principles on which a fundamental economic understanding is based. *An Introduction to Modern Economic Theory* departs from the approach of existing large texts by presenting the central ideas of economic theory clearly and concisely, and by making intensive use of simple diagrammatical presentations rather than complicated mathematical equations.

Says Professor Moore, "Rather than slowly plowing through a huge 1,000-page watered-down encyclopedia, supplemented by study guides, student workbooks, and snippets gathered in 'collected readings,' the student will find it more satisfying intellectually, more flexible for changing current interests, and more compatible with the civilizing ideal of a liberal education first to develop an elementary understanding of the central principles of economic analysis and then to consider the contrasting thought of a number of able men. . . .

An understanding of these central principles of modern economic analysis, combined with selected statistics to provide a summary profile of the economy, should enable the student to comprehend and assess current economic developments with some perspective, and to respond with an increased level of critical sophistication to policy proposals, political justifications, and popular interpretations. . . .

Continued on Back Flap

AN INTRODUCTION TO MODERN ECONOMIC THEORY

Basil J. Moore

 The Free Press, New York
Collier–Macmillan Publishers, London

TEXAS SOUTHMOST COLLEGE LIBRARY
1825 MAY STREET, FT. BROWN
BROWNSVILLE, TEXAS 78520

For Jessica

Copyright © 1973 by THE FREE PRESS
A Division of Macmillan Publishing Co., Inc.
Printed in the United States of America
All rights reserved. No part of this book may be
reproduced or transmitted in any form or by any
means, electronic or mechanical, including photo-
copying, recording, or by any information storage
and retrieval system, without permission in writing from the Publisher.

THE FREE PRESS
A Division of Macmillan Publishing Co., Inc.

Collier–Macmillan Canada Ltd.

Library of Congress Catalog Card Number: 77–96708

printing number
1 2 3 4 5 6 7 8 9 10

contents

manifesto to the student

A colleague, commenting on a preliminary draft of this manuscript, remarked that upon reading the preface he thought he had encountered a swinging book by an angry young man — but on reading the text he found that the author was over thirty after all. But I am not so far over that I cannot vividly remember the trauma and regret of crossing that particular boundary line.

Many of you are suspicious of the old categories of left and right. But the fundamental division of mankind does not hinge on the question of generation, or of age. The watershed is the attitude to social justice, the empathy with humanity. As Bertrand Russell summed it up in his autobiography:

Three passions, simple but overwhelmingly strong, have governed my life — the longing for love, the search for knowledge, and unbearable pity for the suffering of mankind. These passions, like great winds, have blown me hither and thither over a deep ocean of anguish.

Such passions, when pursued with spirit and generosity, lead to the charge of immaturity whatever one's age. If the hat fits, put it on. I, as many of my friends, resonate to the urging of your generation for social justice, the noble and instinctive predisposition to defend all those categories of people who are being oppressed.

The current college generation has a record of dissent and progress that reflects a deep and genuine concern for mankind. You have, with a refreshing naïveté, stubbornly refused to admit that demonstrable wrongs should be allowed to persist merely because they have been hallowed by history. But you have not been equally impressive in defining and demonstrating better institutions and organizations than the ones you have rejected. And how could you? The best will in the world can accomplish little if objective analysis of the problem is faulty. Revolutions are not made by passion or injustice alone. Confrontation, escalation, and conflict, as political techniques without a program, eventually slow the pace of change as they provoke resistance and disillusionment and lead to a choice for order in response to the interplay of force and counterforce. As *The Bhagavadgita* puts it:

For the uncontrolled there is no wisdom, nor for the uncontrolled is there the power of concentration, and for him without concentration there is no peace. And for the unpeaceful, how can there be happiness?

The university can and must play a crucial role in harnessing and shaping the energy, enthusiasm, and humanism of your generation to the task of creatively modifying old forms to accommodate new conditions, in building institutions we again can honor. Economics, properly taught, is an important means to this end. This is the chief reason I have written this book.

You will have to judge for yourselves the truth of these assertions. In the following chapters I have tried to tell it like it is, to the best of my ability. Learn how the economy works, who makes its decisions, who owns it, where and why it falls down. Then go out and try to beat it on its own terms. Or to change it. Its future, like your own, is up to you.

preface to the instructor

The first question any writer of an introductory economics book must face, in view of the glut of texts on the market, is "Why yet another?" It might be best to begin with a disclaimer. This book makes no attempt to compete directly with any of the conventional elementary texts currently available. In a monopolistic competitive market, it represents one attempt at radical product differentiation.

SCOPE

My own teaching experience has gradually led me to the conviction that an introductory course must try *not* to survey the whole of economics. In this process, I have become increasingly dissatisfied with the encyclopedic text as a genre for introductory economics courses.

The fundamental weakness of such texts is that they lead the instructor and the student to attempt to cover too much territory. Although the best are ably written and researched, each chapter replete with a carefully balanced menu of principle, example, historical illustration, and anecdote, the student all too frequently derives very little solid intellectual sustenance. The final examination, subsequent courses, and conversation demonstrate distressingly little command over the relatively few central principles on which an elementary economic understanding is based.

This has been the case at Wesleyan even for some of our best and most idealistic students, who with their increasing concern and involvement in social problems ought to benefit enormously from an economist's way of looking at things. These same young men and women occasionally admit with chagrin to spending as much time with introductory economics as with all their other courses combined. As one result, introductory economics has a reputation for being extremely demanding. Another consequence of this anticipated low benefit-cost ratio is that students vote with their feet.

This book has been written out of the conviction that an introduction to economic analysis can and should be presented in a way that is not intrinsically particularly difficult, no more so than, for example, introductory government or French, yet is at the same time worthwhile, exciting, and relevant. An interesting and rewarding subject, at which few will excel but which all can understand and appreciate. I have deliberately chosen to discard much formal theoretical ballast in this presentation, to emphasize a select few analytical fundamentals at the expense of scope and technical training. As Professor Samuelson once remarked, students of economics are like athletes carefully trained for a race they never run.

Only by the application of economic analysis intensively in a few selected areas does the introductory student learn to see an economic problem as one of costs and benefits, with both allocation and distribution implications, and to develop some appreciation and respect for the spirit of thinking in an analytical and objective way about issues that more typically are decided on the basis of vested interests and inherited prejudices.

Rather than slowly plowing through a huge 1,000-page watered-down encyclopedia, supplemented by study guides, student workbooks, and snippets gathered in "collected readings," the student will find it enormously more satisfying intellectually, more flexible for changing current interests, and more compatible with the civilizing ideal of a liberal education first to develop an elementary understanding of the central principles of economic analysis and then to consider the thought of a number of contrasting and able men, as expressed in a succinct, provocative, and successful book. The present brief introduction to the fundamentals of economic analysis will permit an instructor to assign a number of selected paperbacks and explore selected topics in depth. A bibliography of recommended paperbacks is presented at the end of each section.

CONTENT

With this goal in mind, I have attempted to develop as clearly, rigorously, and concisely as possible a brief introduction to modern economic theory. It contains little application to economic policy, only glimpses at economic history and the development of doctrine and, insofar as was humanly consistent with authorial vanity, no padding.

Mathematics at the level of algebra or calculus has, with the exception of a few footnotes and appendices, been avoided throughout. A large proportion of students continue to have a block against anything that looks vaguely mathematical. Just as importantly, formal mathematical presentation is in no way essential to a clear understanding of basic economic concepts and analysis. There are no important ideas in economics that cannot be expressed in clear English. On the other hand, extensive use is made of simple diagrammatic presentation. It has been my experience that diagrams, unlike equations, can be understood and mastered by students with quite limited mathematical aptitude or background. Once the fundamental notion of a relationship between two or more variables is grasped, all that deductive economic analysis can generally conclude — that is, whether the association is positive or negative and in some cases whether it is increasing or decreasing — can be illustrated simply and concisely on a diagram.

This book is based on my introductory economics lectures at Wesleyan as they have developed over the past twelve years. The book has been used in class and has undergone intensive revision and reorganization. Ample use has been made of appendices, where more difficult or advanced material may be detoured without interrupting the cumulative development of the argument. It is my hope that this introduction may prove useful for students continuing in economics beyond the elementary course: senior majors finally master at a deeper level of understanding the core concepts of the introductory course. For this purpose it is important that nothing be introduced that must later, amid misgivings and confusion, be unlearned as incorrect.

The presentation and development in Part II of household and business behavior as building blocks for both micro and macro theory has compelling logical advantages. In addition to permitting flexibility of sequence in the coverage of subsequent material, it provides an analytical integration of static and dynamic aspects of household and firm behavior, conventionally wrenched apart and considered in two artifically separated micro and macro sections. Household consumption and saving behavior is developed directly from the theory of demand, and business investment behavior from the theory of the firm.

I have attempted to incorporate where appropriate the most important recent advances of modern economic theory. Because of my own professional interests in financial theory, the strongest and most novel aspect of the book is its emphasis on uncertainty and the interrelation of income, wealth, and financial variables. This is introduced at the beginning in the analysis of household behavior, where saving is treated as the demand to accumulate assets, portfolio considerations are developed, and the concepts of "lifetime" or "permanent" income and consumption follow naturally and directly. In the analysis of business behavior, investment expenditures are treated as the adjustment of actual to desired asset stocks, so that the importance of speed of adjustment is easily understood.

In the micro section the formal theory of the firm under certainty is covered only in its bare essentials, while considerable effort has been put into the analysis of market power. The emphasis on wealth accounts and the relation between tangible and financial asset stocks and income flows are used to develop the theory of distribution between labor and property income. The government sector incorporates recent advances in public finance with reference to the theory of collective choice and of public goods.

In the macro section the interrelation between real and financial variables is presented as a natural and logical development from behavioral foundations. The role of financial assets and financial intermediaries is carefully developed. Banks are treated as one particular type of intermediary, and the disequilibrium adjustment consequent upon monetary disturbance becomes a straightforward application of portfolio analysis. Changes in the high-powered money stock, whether through monetary or fiscal operations, are presented as the centerpiece in the management of aggregate demand. It is a much less Keynesian (though perhaps more Keynes') book than I would have written several years ago, particularly with regard to income-expenditure analysis and the relative effectiveness of monetary and fiscal policy. An entire chapter is devoted to consideration of the conflict between inflation and unemployment and to incomes policy as the major stabilization issue facing modern governments.

VALUES

Another distinctive aspect of the book concerns the issue of "relevance" and the attitude to social and institutional change herein exhibited. I have not attempted to hide my own political preferences. For this engagement I make no apologies. Students increasingly want to be shown that economics can speak to the most pressing social problems of our contemporary world. Most professional economists today are primarily involved in the construction of theoretical models, the collection of empirical data, and the statistical testing of hypotheses. Another task of equal validity for the social scientist, that of social critic, reformer, and gadfly is less well attended. Yet an intellectual may be described as one whose most essential job depends on resistance to his society. Consideration of radical structural change may be utopian, in that immediate enactment is not to be expected, yet practical and pragmatic in being directed toward desperately real problems of our human community. Besides, the set of the "politically feasible" is subject to frequent shifts.

The questions considered by economists are, by and large, those for which their concepts and methods are analytically suited. Broader problems, comprising what used to be termed "political economy," which may well be more important from the viewpoint of social welfare — for example, the quality of work and leisure, exploitation, imperialism, waste, aesthetics, individual dignity and freedom, institutional authority, and legitimacy — have largely been ignored by economists. This is not because such questions are considered unimportant, but because economists cannot easily measure or analyze them in an objective or determinate manner. I have not hesitated to raise some of these questions in an attempt to show how economic analysis, through its comprehension of economic behavior, may enrich public discussion and contribute to the exploration and solution of broader social problems. It is thoroughly possible for an economist to be engaged in the application of his analysis in the role of social critic without compromising his scientific integrity and dispassion as a theorist.

FACTS

The availability of empirical data also tends to predetermine the questions selected for analysis. Consider the central question concerning the relationship between economic and political power. This has long been considered an unfashionable topic by economists, in part because of the dominance of a business ideology that shapes the agenda of questions for research and discussion, in part because of the "softness" of the subject and its analytical intractability (what is *power* and how is it to be measured?) and in part simply to the absence of data on the distribution of wealth ownership and control.

As a result, it has been possible for most economists to continue to view the economy as fundamentally competitive and governed by impersonal market forces, in which case there appears little scope for the exercise of personal or class power and influence. Yet it is a stubborn fact that the fifty largest industrial corporations in the United States account for nearly half of all industrial profits.

Available data on the distribution of wealth ownership are shockingly incomplete. We do at least know that three quarters of total corporate stock and one third of the total wealth are owned by the wealthiest 1 percent of American households. At the other end of the scale, Afro-Americans and other minority groups, constituting 15 percent of the population, own less than 1 percent of total wealth. But although the broad contours are visible, the existing degree of concentration of wealth is not widely known, or even generally mentioned in polite circles. The author of one popular 800-page text, for example, devotes half of one page to a discussion of the distribution of wealth, in which no statistics intrude. He presents a Lorenz curve to show that wealth ownershp is "less concentrated" in the United States than in England, without deigning to mention that in England 1 percent of the population owns one half of the total wealth.

As a further distinctive feature of this book, I have provided contemporary statistical material pertaining to the key topics considered in each chapter. Although such an approach might be considered out of place in a short introduction to economic theory, I have chosen this approach for two reasons.

As a heuristic technique it is important to illustrate that economic theory does not stand in splendid isolation as an intellectual structure, but represents our attempts to discover and make sense out of patterns in observed behavior. The student is shown how hypotheses emerge from examination of empirical data and how they are continually tested by confrontation with new evidence. By starting the inquiry with empirical data on aspects of economic life, the theory is developed not for its own sake but as an attempt to explain questions raised by the statistical material.

The availability of a comprehensive statistical summary is convenient to the instructor and useful to the student. Because much empirical evidence is not easily accessible, its collection requires considerable legwork on the part of the instructor and student. In consequence, students in introductory economics courses gain little empirical acquaintance with the dominant contours of their economy.

An attitude of intellectual fairness, of respect for logic and for facts, are essential if the idealistic aspirations and moral concern of today's radical generation of students are to have substantive social impact. Economics, after all, does try to deal with maximizing the welfare of individuals as members of society. Its ultimate aim is "doing good," as students should be encouraged to perceive; but it attempts to do so in an analytical and unsentimental way. To this end, the student requires a few important facts and a sense of how to go about looking for relevant facts with respect to any particular problem.

An understanding of the central principles of modern economic analysis, combined with selected statistics to provide a summary profile of the economy, should enable the student to comprehend and assess current economic developments with some perspective and to respond with an increased level of critical sophistication to policy proposals, political justifications, and popular interpretations. Perhaps the greatest problem now facing capitalist and socialist countries alike is that of political representation and responsibility in a world of large-scale organization. In the face of the enormous pressures of technology and population, the best and probably the only hope for individual freedom and human development in a satisfying environment remains an alert, well-informed, and discriminating electorate. Here lies the role and relevance of economics in a liberal education.

I would like to thank a select number of Wesleyan colleagues who in various ways have maintained me in this enterprise. William Barber, Stanley Lebergott, Michael Lovell, and Richard Miller have each commented on various chapters. Mrs. Joan Halberg and Mrs. Chris Kenny cheerfully typed never-ending drafts. The detailed comments and criticisms of two anonymous readers have been taken seriously and appreciated.

The time and energy to write a book comes in part out of one's family life, and I have promised my wife Karin and my sons Robin and Martin to try to rebalance my account.

I dedicate this book to my daughter Jessica, who liked to see her name in print.

list of figures

list of scatter diagrams

The unquestioned life is not worth living.

SOCRATES

We dance around in a ring and suppose
But the secret sits in the middle and knows.

ROBERT FROST

PART ONE

INTRODUCTION

economics

OF ALL THE QUACKS that ever quacked, political economists are the loudest. Instead of telling us what is meant by one's country, by what causes men are happy, moral, religious, or the contrary, they tell us how flannel jackets are exchanged for pork hams, and speak much of the land last taken into cultivation.
— *THOMAS CARLYLE*

THE STUDY OF ECONOMICS does not seem to require any specialised gifts of an unusually high order. Is it not, intellectually regarded, a very easy subject compared with the higher branches of philosophy and pure science? Yet good, or even competent, economists are the rarest of birds. An easy subject at which very few excel! The paradox finds its explanation, perhaps, in that the master-economist must possess a rare combination of gifts. He must reach a high standard in several different directions, and must combine talents not often found together. He must be mathematician, historian, statesman, philosopher—in some degree. He must understand symbols and speak in words. He must contemplate the particular in terms of the general, and touch abstract and concrete in the same flight of thought. He must study the present in the light of the past for the purposes of the future. No part of man's nature or his institutions must lie entirely outside his regard. He must be purposeful and disinterested in a simultaneous mood; as aloof and incorruptible as an artist, yet sometimes as near the earth as a politician.
— *JOHN MAYNARD KEYNES*

THE SCOPE OF ECONOMICS

The Social Sciences

Economics is the study of the material means of satisfying human needs. As such it is but one of a number of disciplines that study man and society. Each deals selectively with only certain aspects of human behavior, and the boundaries between them are somewhat arbitrary. The growth of knowledge has led to increased specialization in all fields of study, simply because of the limits of human intelligence. Though our concern may be global in its extent, the problems on which we work must ordinarily be problems of detail. In spite of the dangers of compartmentalization — there is sad truth to the definition of a specialist as someone who knows more and more about less and less — there is no other way to find out about the world.

But is society a branch of physics? The answer of an economist must be, "to a limited extent, yes." All science is concerned with the discovery of the repeatable patterns of dependence in which various aspects of the subject stand to one another. There are enough regularities in social behavior to permit the discovery of "laws" that describe its movements and enable its prediction. In economics these regularities are grounded on one side in the processes of production, which describe the relationships between inputs and outputs of economic goods, and on the other in the behavior of economic actors — buyers, sellers, businesses, consumers, workers, owners — each of whom is seeking to realize certain goals.

It must at once be said that it is impossible to reduce the richness of the real world to the simple functional relationships of economic models. The vagaries and complexities of economic events and human behavior are such as to limit severely the predictive power of economic theory. But then physicists are not very successful at predicting the behavior of a falling leaf. It must never be forgotten that, as economics is a social science, at the basis of all economic theory is the human being.

Scarcity

Economics is conventionally described as the study of the allocation of scarce means among competing ends. The dominant element in all economic problems is the pervasive and inescapable fact of *scarcity*. If goods were not scarce it would not be necessary to consider how they are to be produced. All men could have all of everything they want and would not be forced to choose how best to allocate available resources among alternative uses. Economists would occupy roughly the same position in a world without scarcity as doctors in a world of Christian Scientists.

But goods are scarce and wants are unlimited in every society. Consider what would happen if all goods were declared free and everyone were permitted to take everything he wanted. There would not be enough to go around, and some individuals would remain unsatisfied. It would then be necessary to impose some system of rationing, or man's relation to man would rapidly become extremely unpleasant.

This fundamental fact of scarcity holds even the richest of societies in its grip. Tax receipts out of a growing national income currently yield the United States government about $20 billion a year in increased revenue at existing tax rates. Against this "growth dividend" may be placed the estimated additional annual costs of existing and proposed federal programs recommended as urgently desirable by one or another government task forces.

1.	Already authorized expenditure and welfare programs	$10 billion
2.	Proposed tax cuts and reforms	$10 billion
3.	New civilian programs in education, health, urban development, environment, transportation, manpower	$40 billion
4.	New defense programs held essential to national security	$ 5 to $50 billion
5.	New initiatives advanced as alternatives to existing approaches: negative income tax, revenue sharing, guaranteed employment, urban development bank, volunteer army	$30 to $80 billion
	Total	$95 to $190 billion

For years ahead, in the richest country in the world, any growth dividend will be dwarfed by the magnitude of the vast and pressing needs facing the government to combat poverty, develop human resources, and improve the physical environment. Social priorities must somehow be determined and difficult choices made. This is what economics is all about.

It has become fashionable to argue that because of the current scientific revolution in technology scarcity, if not yet dead, will soon be a problem of the past and that affluence is the problem of the future. It is true that at current growth rates per-capita real income is doubling every generation and that such rapid rates of growth have never before been experienced. The power of compound interest is indeed impressive, but it cuts both ways. There are undesirable effects of disposing of the residuals from mass production and consumption into the environment. While the costs to society are negligible for a small population or in an economically undeveloped setting, they become progressively more important as population rises and the level of output increases. This fact lies behind the increasing public concern about environmental pollution. Spaceship Earth is ultimately a closed system, in which there are no mines or sewers and everything must be recycled. The great plain is becoming a closed sphere.

Choice

Economics is about human needs and the limited means of satisfying them. Because of the pervasive character of scarcity, there is an economic dimension to all aspects of human behavior where choice is involved — behavior as diverse as going to work, winning an election, or composing a love letter.

Economics has also been defined as the science of choice. But such a definition is too encompassing, for choice is involved in all purposeful behavior. Life always forces us to choose, and each choice conditions the next by shaping the new situation we confront and the beliefs and values with which we confront it. Economics is confined to the problems of choice among *material* means of satisfying human wants, where some type of production and distribution is possible.

Noneconomic Goods

Goods may be defined as being any objects capable of satisfying human wants. But most goods do not exist in any external sense. Man has intellectual and emotional as well as material needs, and it is difficult to say that one is more important than the other. Wisdom, justice, freedom, love, honor, courage, and beauty are all objects of desire and are all conducive to human satisfaction. Behavior concerned with nonmaterial means and ends is in some ultimate sense vastly more important than economics — as Ruskin said, there is no good but life.

Unfortunately there exists no known technology and little agreement on the processes by which intellectual and emotional wants are satisfied. Noneconomic goods cannot be produced or distributed anywhere on earth. As a result, the analysis of such goods is beyond the professional skills of an economist. Economics fails to deal explicitly with noneconomic goods not because it in any way denies their importance, but because the satisfaction of intellectual and emotional goals is vastly more elusive and difficult to analyze.

Men living in society have various economic needs — food, clothing, shelter, recreation, and many others. All are social in the sense that they are conditioned by the complex set of factors that constitute what is called the culture of a society. Even biological needs such as food take on specific forms and character in different societies.

Economics does not consider whether it is possible to establish a hierarchy of human needs, at least after the biological minimum necessary to sustain life has been satisfied. Status, honor, power, love are not less important or even less powerful motives of human behavior than hunger and gain in any total view of man, nor less conducive to human happiness. The omission of such considerations, while difficult to remedy, is a critical limitation of economics as a guide to the good society.

Economic Goods

Economic goods are material objects that are desired and scarce and could conceivably be bought or sold in a market. Economic goods encompass all things that are not free and are capable of being produced or distributed to satisfy human needs.

Given the fact that resources are limited, only some limited total quantity of economic goods can be produced. To increase the production of one good requires more resources and so leaves fewer resources available for the production of other goods. The cost of an economic good may therefore be measured in terms of the other goods given up to produce it. This is termed *opportunity cost*. It represents the best — most highly valued — opportunities that must be given up in order to have more of any economic good.

The restriction of economic analysis to economic wants and economic goods unfortunately eliminates love letters from our inquiry. Nevertheless an understanding of a few fundamental economic principles, in addition to answering questions such as why some things are cheap and others dear, why some men are rich and others poor, can provide an insight into broad arenas of social behavior. Economic analysis is currently being applied intensively in areas previously considered the provinces of the politician, the lawyer, the military, and the historian.

Economists are frequently considered rather tough-minded in matters of social policy. They are forever pointing out to people that you cannot have your cake and eat it too. Nevertheless it is not true, as Oscar Wilde is reported to have said, that an economist is a man who knows the price of everything and the value of nothing. In fact the converse is more likely to be the case. A man cannot be a good economist if he is nothing else. This is fundamentally because noneconomic goods, though largely beyond the grasp of economic analysis, cannot be ignored in the application of economics to life.

Free Goods

There are some goods that are economic but that were long thought beyond the province of economics. The view of the moon over the ocean, the sound of stillness in the desert, the beauty of a mountain sunset are all desirable goods. Yet they were long regarded as *free,* in the sense that they are not provided by man and nothing must be sacrificed in order that they may be consumed.

As anyone who has travelled through America or Europe knows to his distress, the quality of free goods can be soiled by man and his things. As production, consumption, and population increase, many goods that were once free are free no longer. Resources must now be given up to preserve or restore what was once taken for granted — even the very air we breathe.

Even in paradise where, as is well known, all goods are free, time is required to enjoy them. (Most free goods require sacrifice of other resources in addition to time if they are to be consumed. Tourism represents in part travel in order to enjoy free goods — mountains, beaches, architecture, and people.) If life is short, even the best things in life are not really free. The economist, in his insistence that everything has its cost, is hardly the life of the party.

Consumption and Production

Because economists are concerned with increasing human welfare, there is an implicit assumption, which underlies most economic policy recommendations, that the increased satisfaction of material wants is a good thing. Modern economics largely ignores the direct effects of production on welfare and concentrates on the satisfaction derived from consumption. Except for a few ascetics, more economic goods are generally regarded as having a favorable effect on the ability to realize noneconomic ends.

It [money] is the most important thing in the world. It represents health, strength, honour, generosity, and beauty as conspicuously and undeniably as the want of it represents illness, weakness, disgrace, meanness, and ugliness. It is only when it is cheapened to worthlessness for some, and made impossibly dear to others, that it becomes a curse.[1]

But the activity of work itself involves satisfaction and dissatisfaction. People spend just as much time in the role of producers as in the role of consumers. It is difficult to demonstrate how and by how much the production and distribution of economic goods involve an increase or impairment in the realization of emotional and intellectual human needs. Clearly, enormous personal satisfaction is derived from creative activity and even from simple shopping, while debilitating dissatisfaction follows from dull and repetitive tasks. Marx alone made the process of production central to his analysis, and argued that under capitalist conditions of production the worker is increasingly rendered powerless, isolated, and self-estranged, and so is turned into a dehumanized appendage of the machine and the system.

It [capitalism] transforms the worker into a cripple, a monster, by forcing him to develop some specialized dexterity at the cost of a world of productive impulses and faculties. . . . Having been rendered incapable of following his natural bent to make something independently, the manufacturing worker can only develop productive activity as an appurtenance of the capitalist workshop. Just as it was written upon the brow of the chosen people that they were Jehovah's property, so does the division of labor brand the manufacturing worker as the property of capital.[2]

The response that work is entered into voluntarily and presumably is preferred to the alternatives does not consider how the available alternatives have shifted with the process of industrialization. An important critic has argued that modern life has become "one-dimensional" since alternatives are no longer really perceived.

ALLOCATION AND DISTRIBUTION

Economic goods have been defined as all scarce things that can be produced and distributed for the satisfaction of human needs. As a result all economies, no matter how they are organized, must somehow provide an answer to two questions:

1. What goods are to be produced and in what way?
2. To whom are these goods to be distributed?

1. G. B. Shaw, quoted in Maurice Colbourne, *The Real Bernard Shaw*, p. 284.
2. Karl Marx, *Capital*, vol. 1, chap. 12.

Production

Production is the human activity or labor that adapts things to human needs. The material objects used with labor in the production process—machines, buildings, trucks, raw materials, and the like—are called *capital*, and, except for natural resources such as land and minerals, have required past labor time for their production. Labor and capital are termed *factors of production*. The relationship between current inputs of labor and capital in the production process and the future output of economic goods is termed the *production function*. All economic goods produced may be divided into *consumer goods*, which are used directly to satisfy human needs, and *producer goods*, which are added to the stock of capital and used to produce additional economic goods.

Allocation

All economic behavior has an allocational implication. If resources are limited, more production of one good necessarily implies less production of other goods. Cost in economics is viewed as opportunities foregone, the sacrificed alternatives implicit in not producing something else. This concept of *opportunity cost* is illustrated in Goering's Law: "We cannot have both guns and butter," although what he actually said was "Guns will make us powerful; butter will only make us fat."

Production Possibilities

The central fact that economic goods are limited, so that more of one entails less of another may be represented simply on a diagram. In Figure 1-1 the quantities of consumer goods—such as food, shelter, clothing—a society is capable of producing are measured on the horizontal axis. The quantities of capital goods—such as machines used to produce consumer goods or other machines — are measured on the vertical axis. The curve *AB* represents the maximum alternative amounts of consumption and capital goods that a society is capable of producing at a particular time. This curve is termed the society's *production possibility frontier.*

Figure 1-1 expresses in a compact way a great deal of information. If all of the society's resources were devoted to producing consumer goods, the maximum quantity that could be produced is represented by the distance *OB*. Similarly, *OA* shows the maximum amount of capital goods that could be produced, if all resources were devoted to capital goods production. Alternatively, it is possible to produce both consumption goods and capital goods, but only in the quantities shown along the production possibility frontier.

Suppose the economy were initially at the point *B* and desired to move to the point *C* in order to provide capital goods for future production. Figure 1-1 shows that it must give up or *trade off* an amount *EB* of consumer goods in order to get *OD* of cap-

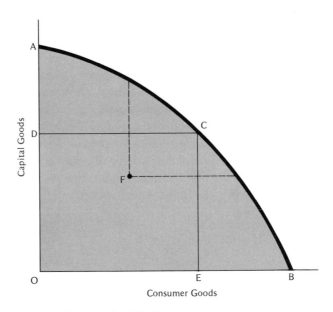

Figure 1-1 Production Possibility Frontier

ital goods. The cost to society of *EC* capital goods is thus the *EB* of consumer goods that must be given up. This cost may be represented by the ratio *EB/EC*, the cost in consumer goods per unit of capital goods, which so long as *AB* is not a straight line, will change for different combinations along the production possibility frontier of consumer and capital goods. This concept of *social opportunity cost,* the cost to society in terms of the alternatives foregone, plays a central role in economic analysis.

The production possibility frontier of Figure 1-1 is intended to represent the maximum amounts of consumption and capital goods that the society can produce, given its stock of resources and technology. The shaded area within the frontier may be viewed as the set of all attainable goods. The economy may not be operating on its production possibility frontier. It may, for example, be producing only the combination *F*. Points such as *F* within the shaded area are termed *inefficient,* because they are clearly dominated by all points to the northeast, which contain more of one or both goods. Such inefficient operation may be due to the fact that some resources are unemployed or are being used for the wrong task. Productive efficiency requires that the economy be operating on its production frontier.

Distribution

All economic behavior has a distributional as well as an allocational implication. Some goods, called public goods, can be enjoyed by everyone. But for most goods, as the Duchess in *Alice in Wonderland* expounded, "The more there is of yours the less there is of mine." Once goods are produced, it must be decided by whom they are to be enjoyed. Although it is not logically necessary, in all societies the question of distribution is related to the question of production. The communist distributive ethic, "From each according to his abilities, to each according to his needs," has never yet been put into practice for an entire economy, largely because of the problem of incentives.

In a socialist economy the questions of allocation and distribution are answered by a government planning board that determines the mix of goods to be produced and sets the wages and salaries of different workers. In a capitalist economy the government plays a much less active role, and the *price system* operates both to allocate resources and to distribute income. No single group is responsible for deciding how resources ought to be allocated or income to be distributed. The workings of private markets, reflecting the individual decisions of millions of households and firms, participating as buyers and sellers in thousands of markets, operate as if guided "by an invisible hand" to decide the questions of what goods are to be produced, how they are to be produced, and who is to enjoy them.

An understanding of the manner in which the market system allocates resources, determines the total level of output, and distributes income is one of the main intellectual achievements of modern economics. Briefly, what goods are produced is determined by demand and ultimately by the dollar votes of consumers. The question of the proportion of consumer goods to capital goods produced and therefore the rate at which the stock of capital goods is accumulated and the productive capacity of the economy grows depend on the proportion of their income that individual wealth owners choose to consume or save. How goods are produced is determined by the cost of alternative methods of production. An important social function of competition among producers is to assure that costs will be kept to a minimum, because when one producer discovers a cheaper way, others must follow or lose their market. The distribution of goods is determined by the ownership of factors of production. Income is distributed by the market as a payment for the services of labor and capital. As will be shown, the distribution of wealth ownership, and therefore of income from property, is extremely unequal in virtually all capitalist societies. Consumers with larger wealth and income have greater purchasing power and so more dollar votes. In contrast to the communist ethic, the capitalist distributive ethic is, "to each according to what he and the factors of production that he owns can get."

The Circular Flow of Income and Output

The process of production and distribution of economic goods involves continual repetition of certain activities. It is because of the repetitive nature of such behavior that it is possible to observe patterns of regularity that are susceptible of generalization.

Specialization and the division of labor result in a vast increase in labor's productivity. The decisions of what and how much to produce and what and how much to consume are as a result undertaken separately by individuals and firms. This separation of production and consumption creates a problem of coordination. In a price system these decisions are connected and interrelated by a system of markets, as shown in a simplified way by the circular flow diagram of Figure 1-2.

In product markets, households in the role of consumers buy goods and services from firms in return for dollars. In factor markets, households in the role of factor owners sell the services of labor and capital to firms in return for dollars. Sales of goods and services in the product markets yield revenue to firms. This revenue is in turn distributed as income to the owners of the labor and capital employed by the firm. Income received in the factor markets by households is spent again on commodities in the product markets. All goods sold by one firm to another are referred to as *intermediate* goods in this process.

In both product and factor markets supply and demand determine the prices at which goods and services are exchanged. These prices and the profits they imply at the same time serve as signals to sellers to allocate resources to those markets where prices and profits are relatively high. A disturbance in one market leads to ramifications that produce disturbances in other markets. The price system may be likened to a gigantic computer that registers the demand and supply of millions of different economic units and then determines the price at which markets will be cleared.

THEORY, VALUES, AND POLICY

Theory Versus Practice

Students of economics never tire of raising, although teachers of economics sometimes tire of hearing, the following objection: "That is all very well in theory, but it doesn't work out that way in practice." If the speaker is challenged as to what does "work out" in practice, he will invariably respond with another *theory*.

It is essential to be quite clear on this point at the outset. Theorizing is simply a systematic attempt to understand the world about us, that "big, buzzing, blooming

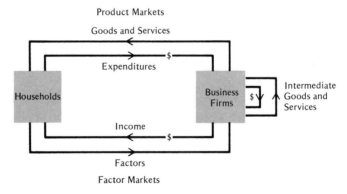

Figure 1-2 Circular Flow of Income and Output

confusion," as William James called it. Because one factor is critically scarce, the limited human intellect, it is necessary to simplify, and in the process to distort, in order to understand. All analysis necessarily involves abstraction and simplification.

The object of all intellectual inquiry is the discovery of significant relationships within the subject matter under investigation. The essence of theorizing is to select some key aspects of reality and then put them together in a cunning way to provide a model of reality itself.

A theory ordinarily consists of a set of definitions stating the meanings of various terms, a set of assumptions defining the conditions under which the theory is to apply, and one or more hypotheses about behavior. These hypotheses are deduced from the assumptions. If the hypotheses lead to predictions that can be tested against empirical observations, it may then be concluded whether the theory is refuted by the facts or is consistent with the facts.

Mental Experiments

Unfortunately for cumulative scientific progress, it is not generally feasible in the social sciences to conduct controlled laboratory experiments to test a particular theory. To the extent that it is not possible to conduct statistical tests or controlled experiments which hold all other relevant factors constant, the social scientist is forced to resort to "mental experiments." Since his subject is man and not molecules, he can appeal to introspection and empathy to explain social behavior. Rather than pushing someone who cannot swim overboard at night in mid-Atlantic, it is plausible to conduct a mental experiment and suppose the probable outcome of such a hypothetical event.

Although such hypothesizing is frequently necessary, the power of this method is subject to substantial limitations. So long as the outcomes of mental experiments are not subject to operational empirical refutation, it is difficult to discriminate between alternative explanations.

Whether or not they are aware of it, most people spend much of their waking adult life engaged in and theorizing about economic behavior. The advantage this fact gives the student is that everyone has some familiarity with and understanding of the subject matter of economics. The disadvantage is that most people have developed their own common-sense or intuitive explanations of what they have observed. These explanations often conflict with the results of systematic investigation of the same problems.

One characteristic of economics is that it is necessary for a beginning student to *unlearn* a great deal, including some things that many people ordinarily take for granted as self-evident. For example, what is true òr desirable for one individual is not necessarily true or desirable for a group or a collective. To accept a proposition as generally valid because it is valid in a particular case is called the *fallacy of composition,* a fallacy which appears frequently in popular discussion. Here are a few common illustrations:

1. An individual whose indebtedness grows continually will eventually face bankruptcy, but this does not generally apply to a government.
2. One farmer can increase his income by working harder and increasing his output, but if all farmers do so, their income will fall.
3. One individual or firm can increase its holdings of money, but all individuals and firms together cannot.

Another common error, not unknown among economists, is to deduce causation from correlation, that is, from a sequence observed in the past. In a world as rich in historical variety as our own and in an economy as large as the American, one can find an example that may appear to support almost anything. But one swallow does not make a summer. The study of economics leads one to become highly critical of reasoning by example or by analogy. Personal experience as well as common sense often provides completely wrong answers.

Positive and Normative Statements

Economic theory is an attempt to explain economic behavior by isolating certain significant behavioral relationships, patterns, and regularities. As such, economic analysis is non-normative or *positive*, that is, it is intended as an *objective statement* of behavior, which may be refuted by empirical evidence. A number of the most interesting economic issues, however, are not positive but *normative*, concerned not with explanation but with justification, approval, or condemnation of particular circumstances or behavior. "That picture is pink" is a positive or descriptive statement, which may be refuted by empirical evidence. "That picture is good" is a normative statement or *value judgment* and is not refutable by empirical verification. Value judgments ordinarily have an implicit positive component — "that picture has the characteristics *A*, *B*, *C*, and *D*" — and an implicit normative component — "the characteristics *A*, *B*, *C*, and *D* are good." Normative statements reveal how the speaker feels about the picture and are frequently also intended to persuade the hearer to agree.

Positive statements concern what *is;* normative statements concern what *ought to be*. Disagreement over positive statements may in principle be settled by an appeal to facts. Normative statements make a judgment about what is desirable or undesirable, and disagreement can never be settled merely by appeal to facts. As Hume pointed out long ago, it is logically impossible to deduce normative statements from positive assumptions. With practice, one becomes sensitive to when an "is" in an argument subtly changes to an "ought."

Many attributes or aspects of economic behavior — such as the Puritan ethic of hard work and thrift, the goal of living within one's means and rapidly paying off one's debts, the phenomena of inflation, high interest rates, welfare payments, and waste — have in some people's minds strong normative associations. Such events are considered desirable or undesirable per se. A number of components of popular belief — the "burden" of government debt, the competition of "cheap" foreign labor, and the "evil" of inflation — conflict and interfere with an understanding and acceptance of the conclusions of economic analysis.

Economics for the most part has not developed a special vocabulary of its own. It is thus critically important to distinguish carefully the definition of some common words as they are used in economic analysis: equilibrium, disequilibrium, saving, investment, capital, money, income, property, monopoly, competition. These words all carry a freight of meanings and emotional association in everyday conversation quite different from their economic denotation.

Analysis and Policy

The conscious attempt to preformulate behavioral rules is termed *policy*. All individuals, institutions, and governments pursue a multiplicity of policies simultaneously. Even the decision not to act is a policy decision.

Any policy action has two aspects, the *ends* to be achieved and the *means* by which these ends are to be realized. Economic analysis can explore the consequences of actual and proposed policies by studying the relation between ends and means. Will the means chosen achieve the goals? Are there other policies that would achieve the desired objectives at lower cost? What side effects on other objectives and goals are associated with a particular policy?

Positive economics does not provide a basis for passing judgment on the ends themselves, but it can attempt to point out the trade-offs between different social goals involved in any policy action. The principle of opportunity cost means that more of one objective implies less of another. The decision-maker must somehow decide on a set of priorities in order to determine how much of one is worth sacrificing to get more of another.

The major social impact of science has been due to its increased ability to *control* the environment, which has followed from the increased ability to predict the outcomes of any action. The unanticipated wider consequences of technological advance, for example, environmental pollution and resource depletion, have frequently been unsatisfactory from a humanist perspective. Now that man increasingly has the means available to determine the course of his future, he must increasingly accept the widened responsibility for planning that future.

To the extent that unquantifiable experience is relegated to the shadowy realm of "value judgments," the consequence is to free the natural and social sciences from all accountability to ethical and moral standards and consequences. Scientists who as professionals choose to ignore important social problems and consequences, because they cannot handle ethical implications "rigorously," have led to the charge of irresponsibility against "objective" scholarship. The fact that science cannot itself alone determine policy goals and objectives does not imply that normative issues are unimportant, nor that they may be neglected by scientists. It is possible to take wider considerations into account without substituting emotion for analysis and without becoming a social evangelist.

THE INSTITUTIONAL FRAMEWORK

Although the price system can operate in a socialist economy, where factors of production are publicly owned and production is undertaken for use and not for private gain, this book is chiefly concerned with the behavior of capitalist economies based on private property rights and production for profit. Capitalism is sometimes termed the *private enterprise* or *free market* system, which terms refer to the institutional facts of private property, free and voluntary contracts, and production for private profit.

An economy such as America's is termed a *mixed economy* because it includes private property, public ownership, and an intermediate range consisting of private institutions in which property, although private, cannot be used for the personal advantage of the owners. However, the private sector still accounts for the dominant share (80 percent) of economic output; and in this sector profit — the excess of revenues over costs — is the central motive that causes factors to be offered and allocated and goods and services to be produced.

Conflict

Conflict is inescapably bound to the human condition. It derives fundamentally from the scarcity of economic goods relative to unlimited human wants. When tastes differ for public goods consumed by all, the satisfaction of one taste may make the satisfaction of another impossible, regardless of the resources available. Only in Utopia would it be possible to find an order so harmonious that conflict is eliminated. The concept of *justice* is correlative with the problem of conflict — what criteria exist to judge between conflicting claims once force is repudiated? The most central ethical idea of justice, as explored by Socrates in the *Republic,* in fact founded on an economic conception, that of exchange or *quid pro quo,* "to each what he deserves." But what does he deserve?

Exchange was regarded by Adam Smith as stemming from a "natural human propensity to truck and barter." An economic system with specialization in production and private property cannot operate without markets where economic exchange can occur. Prices, the ratio at which exchange occurs, will depend on the relative bargaining power of buyer and seller.

Competition on a free market is one of an enormous variety of techniques for resolving human conflict. Although it is beyond the purpose of this book to explore in depth the ethics involved in private ownership, one great virtue of a competitive market is that social cooperation is achieved with considerable individual freedom, without legal or physical coercion of one individual by another. *Voluntary exchange* has been incisively described as a form of *systematized bribery,* where individual inducement occurs through the offer of gain. Exchange that is not free, informed, or impartial — for example, as occurs in the presence of violence, coercion, fraud, or favoritism — is not generally considered fair. The Goddess of Justice sits blindfolded before her scales.

Voluntary economic exchange must be mutually advantageous or it would not occur. But voluntary exchange does not, in general, benefit both parties *equally*. To take an extreme case, the North American Indians who were hooked on firewater by fur traders and voluntarily bartered their beaver skins, land, and women for a bottle of cheap rum would not be regarded by everyone as having come out ahead.

To be meaningful, freedom of choice must imply that *similar alternatives* are available to both parties, and similar alternatives are unlikely to coexist with severely dissimilar material circumstances. The distribution of economic and market power determines the extent to which the outcome of exchange favors one or the other party. The idea of equality under the law is made a mockery when individual circumstances differ widely. Rich and poor alike are forbidden to sleep in the public parks. Legal prohibitions on choice must be compared with the constraints forced upon individuals by economic necessity. *Freedom* in a positive sense refers not to the absence of legal coercion, but to the ability to realize one's desires, to do what one wants. Circumstances as well as other individuals coerce, and much of such coercion is avoidable.

Private Property

Private property rights entitle an owner to dispose of his property as he pleases and to exclude others from the use of it. His range of freedom is necessarily limited, in that he may not interfere with the property rights of others. The state as the ultimate coercive power defines and enforces these property rights through its legislative, judicial, and law enforcement processes. Within these rules of the game established by the state, private parties are free to make any contract they wish, and the state will adjudicate differences and determine penalties for breach of contract.

Property rights are not rights belonging to property. They are rights of people to use goods and, as such, describe codes of behavior or relations between people. Each man forfeits the right to steal from others and in return is himself guaranteed security against theft. Property rights are neither absolute nor self-evident propositions but are man-made, creatures of the state. It is not always recognized that in the absence of the state to guarantee order and to outlaw force, private property rights would not exist.

Even what a person has produced by his individual toil, unaided by anyone, he cannot keep, unless by permission of society. Not only can society take it from him, individuals could and would take it from him, if society only remained passive; if it didn't interfere *en masse*, or employ and pay people for the purpose of preventing him from being disturbed in the possession.[3]

The institutional rules of private property are conventionally regarded as given for economic analysis. Nevertheless, the substance of private property rights and the meaning of possession have changed dramatically over time, and differ substantially

3. John Stuart Mill, *Principles of Political Economy*, bk. II, chap. 1.

TEXAS SOUTHMOST COLLEGE LIBRARY.
1825 M/. S...T, FT. BROWN
BROWNSVILLE, TEXAS   78520

among countries. Access to beaches is a public right by law in France and Mexico. In forests and farmlands in Sweden, England, and Germany, there is a public right of trespass. Private ownership does not in this case confer exclusivity to the owner for all types of use. In less developed countries, and in all earlier societies, a number of individuals typically share common use-rights to land. These use-rights are based on custom and are nontransferable by sale. Private property thus refers to a complex interrelated set of rights and responsibilities.

The term "property" cannot be defined except by defining all the activities which individuals and the community are at liberty or are required to do or not to do, with reference to the object claimed as property.[4]

The rights of disposal over goods conferred by the private property concept is limited. One man may not throw his rock through another man's window. As a society develops technologically and its population density increases, the effects of individual behavior increasingly impinge on the behavior of others. In consequence of such *externalities* associated with the greater interdependence of individuals in modern societies, the scope of private property rights has been narrowed. For example, individuals living in cities today are no longer permitted to do as they wish with their own land, but are restricted from raising pigs or burning refuse in their gardens or building a structure different from that in a prescribed code.

The Rules of the Game

The state as the ultimate authority for private property bars certain behavior such as theft, force, and fraud, enforces property rights, and defines the punishment for civil damages. Where the costs of defining and enforcing property rights are high — as is the case with air, noise, water, and broadcasting — they will be weakly defined or nonexistent. .

The power of property, in particular the power creditors have over debtors, is entirely dependent on the law. Over time, as the franchise has been extended more widely to non-property-owning groups, punishments for crimes against property have been relaxed and the power of creditors over debtors gradually reduced. Theft is no longer a capital offense, or punished by cutting off a hand, and indentured servants and debtor's prisons have disappeared. Wide areas of voluntary contracts among persons have been made illegal or restricted on social grounds, — child and female labor, maximum hours worked, minimum wages, and discriminatory employment practices. Since slavery was abolished, labor income cannot be capitalized into private property and transferred by sale.

One of the most important problems for the state is to determine what rules of the game are most conducive to social welfare. Because the answer will change with the level of technology, there is usually a lag between legislation and the conditions that brought it forth. Fraud, robbery, and gambling are discouraged by most states, in part because resources devoted to them do not increase the total amount of econom-

4. John R. Commons, *Institutional Economics, Its Place in Political Economy* (New York, 1934), p. 74.

ic goods and services available (except in so far as individuals receive satisfaction from gambling) and so are not socially productive behavior. Just as football would be a different game if five downs were permitted, the particular rules of the economic game determine the extent to which private interest and social interest coincide, and the quality of private and social life.

Viewed in this light, public and private ownership of property are not two logically opposite extremes of social institutions. There is rather an infinity of points along a spectrum of individual authority to dispose of things, more or less restrained by the community acting collectively.

The Evolution of Capitalism

Just as property rights are continually changing, as the courts redefine what rights of use and disposition will be enforced, so capitalism itself is an evolving system. Although property rights appear to be about things, they are ultimately about relations among men.

$$\text{Men} \longleftrightarrow \text{Things} \longleftrightarrow \text{Men}$$

Because men do not work in isolation, production always involves certain social relations. The relations of production are determined by the underlying technology of production and in turn shape the social and economic relations between men. As Marx put it succinctly in *The Poverty of Philosophy,* "The hand mill gives you society with the feudal lord, the steam mill society with the industrial capitalist."

Private property, like any institution, is ultimately justifiable only in so far as it performs a useful social function. The essential function of private ownership is to provide an incentive to production and accumulation. Selfishness and acquisitiveness are common and powerful human traits. People take care of their personal property in a way that they do not apply to the property of others. "The magic of property turns sand into gold."

This clear economic function of private property in the production process tends to obscure the fact that it simultaneously represents a system of privilege in the distribution process. To the Marxian view, as capital represents past labor time, all income stems ultimately from labor, so that all property (nonlabor) income represents exploitation. The excess of what a man can produce above what is needed to feed and clothe him and his family represents a kind of *surplus.* For Marx all history is a record of class struggle between workers, who own no property, and owners of property, who do no work, for the disposition of this surplus.

In the feudal economy much of the surplus was seized by force by the feudal lord, to whom the peasant owed certain dues (known as *corvée*). With the development of the market, forced labor (seizure) gradually disappeared, and capital appeared as a legal "personage," claiming its rightful share of the increment in production attributable to it. Unlike feudalism, capitalism proclaims that all men have equal rights before the law. But the distributive results may be identical. If the lord now owns the land and the capital with which the peasant works, he may receive the same surplus as before, but in the form of property income — interest, rents, and profits. Because property is only receiving a market rent for its contribution to the productive process, and everyone is free to own property, the exploitation of one man by another appears to have disappeared. The veil is pulled down further when the peasant owns his own house and tools directly and merely pays interest on his mortgage. Interest is the price paid for the rental of generalized purchasing power, and the lord now merely owns pieces of paper, which also may be purchased openly by anyone.

It is not private property per se but *concentration of the private ownership* of wealth that produces this result. If all property or claims to property were owned equally, the ethical verdict would be very different. Concentration of ownership by some implies lack of ownership by others. When a few own, the rest work for those that own, whether they know it or not.

It is interesting to inquire as to the origins of private property. Thorsten Veblen argued that the origins of ownership, the right of one person to the fruits of another's labor, was to be found in a particular choice item of primitive war plunder and "tenure by prowess" — women. First you own the person and then you naturally own what the person produces. Similarly, as labor cannot produce without the use of capital, denial of equal right to the use of capital may be regarded as denial of the right of labor to its own produce. It is the injustice inherent in the concentration of private property, its monopolization in a few hands, which its critics find so offensive. Henry George, in *Progress and Poverty,* put it as follows:

Consider for a moment the utter absurdity of the titles by which we permit to be gravely passed from John Doe to Richard Roe the right exclusively to possess the earth, giving absolute dominion as against all others. In California our land titles go back to the Supreme Government of Mexico, who took from the Spanish King, who took from the Pope, when he by a stroke of the pen divided lands yet to be discovered between the Spanish or Portuguese — or if you please they rest upon conquest. In the eastern states they go back to treaties with Indians and grants from English kings; in Louisiana to the government of France; in Florida to the government of Spain; while in England they go back to the Norman conquerors. Everywhere, not to a right which obliges, but to a force which compels. And when a title rests but on force, no complaint can be made when force annuls it. Whenever the people having the power choose to annul those titles, no objection can be made in the name of justice. . . . And to this manifest absurdity does the recognition of individual right to land come when carried to its ultimate — that any one human being, could he concentrate in himself the individual rights to the land of any country, could expel therefrom all the rest of its inhabitants; and could he thus concentrate the individual rights to the whole surface of the globe, he alone of all the teeming population of the earth would have the right to live.

APPENDIX: METHODOLOGY

Causality

A theory is tested by its ability to predict or its consistency with empirical evidence, not by the realism of its assumptions. The assumptions made by a theory are a way of simplifying and abstracting from reality in order to concentrate on the factors considered most important for a particular question.

The terms *theory, hypothesis, explanation, model,* and *law* are all broadly synonymous and refer simply to a particular assertion or story about the world. Unlike fictional stories, these scientific stories are subject to an elaborate process of tests to see if they in fact conform to what may be observed in the world.

The term *causality* is used loosely to refer to the chain of events described or predicted by a theory. Strictly speaking, the term *cause* or *law* is a shorthand way of denoting the existence of an observed invariant sequence of events—whenever *A* happens, *B* follows—for which an explanation has been offered that to date appears consistent with observed reality.

When a large number of factors are involved, it is frequently misleading or impossible to distinguish a direct causal sequence, in the sense of a unidirectional process from *A* to *B* to *C*. When variables are interrelated and interdependent in a complex way, the shorthand notion of causality is no longer appropriate. The terms *explanatory variable* and *dependent variable* are used in economic discussion to indicate such relationships.

With a new story or theory, reality is comprehended in a different way. Unfortunately man is a prisoner of his theoretical preconceptions. To quote William Sumner, "The educated classes are victims of the phrase." This makes it extremely difficult, after one has long been in the habit of looking at the world in a particular way, to break out of one's conventional vision. It is in part for this reason that science progresses by generations and that youth is able to make such brilliant and innovative contributions. It has been observed that most scholars live for most of their lives on the ideas originally conceived in their glorious and fertile third decade.

Scientific Method

Theories are an attempt to answer the question: Why? There may be, and in principle there always exist, more than one competing explanation for any observed phenomenon. In order to determine which explanation is superior, theories must be tested by evidence. The process of systematic confrontation of theory with fact is called the *scientific method.*

A student trained in economics will gradually get into the habit of asking, "What is the evidence required to support that conclusion?" This capacity for careful, informed, effective criticism is the process by which science progresses. It is also the essence of an educated mind.

Providing that a theory is internally consistent (correct on grounds of logic), is it possible to find evidence of observations that refute it? Strictly speaking, theories can never be proved correct but can only be disproved or refuted. The scientist appeals to evidence, rather than to authority or introspection or definition. One of the most difficult tasks for a social scientist, and one which requires a high degree of creativity, is to pose a question bearing on a problem in such a way that it can be answered by reference to evidence.

It is often extremely difficult to reject a theory as inconsistent with factual observations when many things are happening at once and thus the "true" explanatory variables are unknown. The development of a new hypothesis is often the outcome of a fascinating and inspired creative process, a "Eureka!" sensation. But the quality of the sensation unfortunately does not prove that the hypothesis is correct.

The ultimate test of a theory is its ability successfully to predict future events. In general theories are abandoned when they cannot explain evidence or predict consequences better than the best alternative. This alternative may be another competing theory, or it may be simply a naïve model: "Next year will be (or will change) just like this year." Any developing science is continually rejecting some of its theories and accumulating evidence that cannot be explained by any existing theory. With regard to forecasting ability it is never possible to know in advance how a statement will describe future data, but only how well it fits available data. Particularly in the social sciences, it is never absolutely certain that the future will be like the past. When a theory is not refuted by contradictory evidence, yields accurate predictions of future events, and is consistent with other accepted explanations of related phenomena, it gradually becomes accepted as corroborated within the corpus of a discipline. This is the scientific meaning of truth!

Controlled Experiments

In the natural sciences it is possible to conduct laboratory experiments in which only specified variables are allowed to change, while everything else is held constant. In this way a natural scientist is able to generate evidence for or against a hypothesis.

In the real world, where many things are happening at the same time, it is ordinarily not possible to find a situation in which all but one or a few selected variables are constant. As a result, in the social sciences, unless controlled experimentation is possible, it may be extremely difficult to refute a particular explanation. Consequently there may coexist over long periods a number of alternative theories, some or all mutually contradictory, each purporting to explain the same set of events.

This situation is characteristic of all the social sciences, but it is generally more serious for disciplines dealing with nonquantifiable aspects of social behavior, where it is more difficult to measure the magnitude of various explanatory factors. A historian may outline a set of relationships that led up to the Second World War or the Industrial Revolution. But he will be unable to put relative weights on them or to demonstrate that other explanations are invalid. As a result, different historians or sociologists or political scientists will isolate and emphasize different phenomena in reconstructing the same event. To the extent that a situation verges on the unique rather than belonging to the general, explanations are merely speculative statements, which cannot be refuted by appeal to empirical evidence.

Quantification

Under these circumstances, one might ask whether it is possible at all to have a science of human behavior. Free will is difficult to reconcile with inexorable laws.

To answer this question, it is important to distinguish the behavior of individuals ' from that of groups. Individual behavior is very difficult to predict, because a very large number of economic and noneconomic considerations are likely to be operative. But for a group, many of the random forces affecting individuals tend to offset one another. The behavior of groups can as a result be predicted with much higher probability than can the behavior of individuals.

This important fact is termed the *law of large numbers.* All factual statements about the world are subject to error. But if this error is due to the fact that a large number of random variables are affecting individual observations, its distribution will follow what is called a *normal curve of error* and can be estimated by statistical techniques. As the size of the group or the number of observations is increased, individual errors will tend to cancel out. As a result, the behavior of the group can be predicted with a high degree of probability and confidence, even though the margin of error in predicting the behavior of a particular individual may be very large. Some philosophers of epistemology have argued that the truth value of any empirical statement can only be defined in probabilistic terms.

History, with all its uniqueness, has long been the only laboratory of the social scientist. With the revolutionary development of statistical techniques, social scientists have recently devoted increasing attention to the statistical analysis of historical evidence and to the construction of controlled experiments and pilot projects to test and measure the significance of empirical hypotheses. A variety of statistical tests have been developed to determine whether a quantitative hypothesis is consistent with an observed set of data and to determine the confidence that may be placed in its numerical estimates. The decision to accept or reject a hypothesis is subject to error, but this error can to some extent be controlled.

The age of quantification is now full upon us. We are now armed with a bulging arsenal of techniques of quantitative analysis and of power — as compared to untrained common sense — comparable to the displacement of archers by cannon.[5]

5. George Stigler, "The Economist and the State," *American Economic Review,* March, 1956.

demand and supply

WISDOM, WHOSE LESSONS have been represented as so hard to learn by those who were never at her school, only teaches us to extend a simple maxim universally known. And this is, not to buy at too dear a price.

— *HENRY FIELDING*

KNOWING HOW TO SIMPLIFY one's description of reality without neglecting anything essential is the most important part of the economist's art.

— *JAMES DUESENBERRY*

Someone once said that a parrot could be taught to be an economist by learning to repeat the words *supply* and *demand*. Skillfully applied, these two elementary concepts do possess considerable explanatory power. Once they are understood, the forces determining the price of economic goods in competitive markets may be explained.

This chapter, after developing the underlying notion of a functional relationship, provides an introduction to demand and supply behavior and shows how supply and demand interact to determine price in competitive markets. Because the proof of the pudding is in the eating, the chapter closes with an application of these simple tools to some contemporary economic problems.

FUNCTIONAL RELATIONSHIPS

In the economic as in the astronomic universe everything is related to everything else. Economic theory, by simplifying and abstracting in order to reveal regular behavioral relationships, provides a method for perceiving reality. Facts alone never speak for themselves; they must always be interpreted in order to answer the question "Why."

"The theory of economics does not furnish a body of settled conclusions immediately applicable to policy. It is a method rather than a doctrine, an apparatus of the mind, a technique of thinking which helps its possessor to draw correct conclusions."[1]

Economics has an advantage over other social sciences in the relative ease with which its subject matter can be ordered and measured. Relationships between different variables may therefore be more precisely specified.

The term *function* is used to describe a relationship between two or more variables. There is a relationship between, for example, human weight and height, or education and income. Once a relationship has been identified, knowledge of one set of variables will yield information about the magnitude of another set of variables. It is conventional to refer to the first set of variables as *explanatory* or *independent* and to the remaining variables as *explained* or *dependent*. These terms do not necessarily imply a particular direction of causality or even the existence of any unidirectional cause-effect relationship. Education affects one's future income but the income of one's parents affects the level of education attained. A functional relationship simply describes a postulated or observed association between two or more variables. Knowledge of one variable then permits one to know something about the magnitude of the other.

A functional relationship is termed *positive* if larger (smaller) magnitudes of one variable are associated with larger (smaller) magnitudes of the other variable. The quantity of a commodity purchased by a consumer is ordinarily positively related to a consumer's income. A functional relationship is termed *negative* if larger mag-

---

1. John Maynard Keynes, Introduction to D. H. Robertson, *The Control of Industry* (New York, 1923).

nitudes of one variable are associated with smaller magnitudes of the other. The quantity of a commodity purchased by a consumer is ordinarily negatively related to the price of the commodity.

Postulating the existence of a functional relationship between two variables represents an attempt to abstract from reality in order to isolate which variables are most important, that is, have most explanatory power. It does not imply that other unspecified variables have no effect. This assumption is sometimes indicated by the Latin expression *ceteris paribus,* which means "other things being equal." If a consumer's income, wealth, tastes, expectations, and everything else remain unchanged, *ceteris paribus* the quantity of a commodity demanded will be inversely related to the price of the commodity.

DEMAND

The Meaning of Demand in Economics

The law of demand describes the behavior of buyers. Demand has a particular connotation in economics that differs from its colloquial use. The phrase *demand for a good* denotes that someone is willing and able to pay for the commodity or service in question. *Demand* in economics is what might colloquially be termed "effective demand" and is not a synonym for needs, desires, or wants.

A very large number of forces may be expected to influence the quantity of any commodity demanded. Those few singled out for analysis as most important are called the determinants of demand. The chief of these are the price of the commodity, the price of other commodities, the level of income and wealth, and tastes and preferences.

The factors affecting the quantity demanded may be expressed symbolically by the following function:

$$Q_i = f(P_i, P_n, Y, W, T)$$

This equation simply states concisely that the quantity of the ith commodity demanded (Q_i) is some function ($f()$) of its own price (P_i), the price of other goods (P_n), income (Y), wealth (W), and tastes (T). To complete the specification it is necessary to stipulate the time period over which each variable is measured. Demand may denote flow of services over a particular period, or may refer to a stock at a moment of time. Because an indefinitely large number of factors affect the demad for every commodity, any simplified formulation will be only approximate and its predictions subject to error.

The Law of Demand

While the quantity demanded of any particular commodity is a function of many variables, the price of the commodity is frequently singled out as the most important determinant.

If all determinants of the quantity demanded other than the good's own price (other prices, income, wealth, tastes, expectations) remain constant, the quantity demanded of the commodity can be formulated as a simple function of price. The *law of demand* states that *quantity demanded and price charged are inversely related; ceteris paribus,* quantity demanded is a decreasing function of price. The higher the price, the smaller the quantity demanded. Conversely, the lower the price, the larger the quantity demanded. The law of demand states nothing about the quantitative magnitude of the association but only that the direction of the relationship is inverse.

The law of demand holds because, as the price falls, existing buyers decide to add to their purchases and new buyers enter the market. The reasons for this will be developed in the next chapter from the general theory of household behavior.

The relationship between price and quantity demanded may be described by a *demand schedule,* as shown in Table 2-1. The term *demand* by convention denotes the entire demand schedule, not a single quantity. The demand schedule in column 2 of Table 2-1 shows the quantities of the good (Q) that a particular consumer would demand at different prices (P). The market demand schedule is constructed as the sum of all individual demand schedules of market participants. It shows what hypothetical quantities would be demanded at each price by all buyers in the market. If there were 1,000 individuals, each with identical tastes and incomes, the market demand schedule would simply be this multiple of the individual demand schedule, as shown in column 3.

Table 2-1   DEMAND SCHEDULE

	Individual Demand	Market Demand
Price (P)	Number of Units (Q)	Number of Units (Q)
100	5	5,000
90	6	6,000
80	8	8,000
70	10	10,000
60	13	13,000
50	16	16,000
40	20	20,000
30	24	24,000

The transition from a demand schedule to a *demand curve* is very simple. On a diagram, quantity demanded per period of time is measured on the horizontal axis, and price per unit on the vertical axis. Each pair of related points of the demand schedule may then be plotted on this diagram. When the points are connected by a smooth line, the slope of the line will be negative, that is sloping downward to the right. This demand curve (D) is shown in Figure 2-1.

It is essential to be able to translate graphic presentation into words. Figure 2-1 shows that a rise in price from P_1 to P_2 results in a negative *change in the quantity demanded* from Q_1 to Q_2. The amount of the change will depend on the slope of the curve. The demand curve is drawn with reference to a particular period of time. For most commodities, the responsiveness of quantity demanded to a change in price

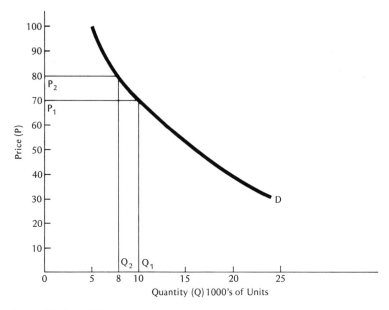

Figure 2-1 Demand Curve

will be greater the longer the period of time considered. Buyers do not adjust immediately to a change in price. Learning takes time.

Providing other things remain constant, the position of the demand curve itself will not shift when price changes. The term *change in demand* is used to refer to a shift in the entire demand schedule caused by a change in other variables. For example, an increase in income or tastes will generally result in an increased demand and so a rightward shift in the entire demand curve. Such an increase is shown in Figure 2-2 by the shift in the demand curve from D_0 to D_1. Similarly, a change in the price of another good may result in an increase or decrease in demand, depending on whether the other good is a substitute (margarine for butter) or a complement (butter and bread) to the good in question. The demand curve will remain stable only if the *ceteris paribus* assumption holds.

Elasticity of Demand

Goods differ in the degree to which the quantity demanded varies in response to a change in price. The term *elasticity* has been devised to measure this responsiveness. A demand curve is termed *elastic* if the quantity demanded changes by a large amount relative to the change in price. Demand is termed *inelastic* if the quantity supplied or demanded changes by a small amount relative to the change in price.

The single most important factor determining the elasticity of demand for a particular commodity is the extent to which substitutes are available. The greater and closer the number of substitutes, the more elastic the demand. In addition inexpensive commodities (such as salt and tooth paste) have more inelastic demand than

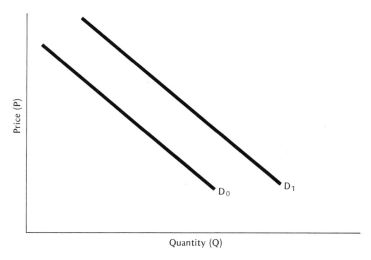

Figure 2-2 Shift in Demand

expensive commodities. Because their total cost represents a very small fraction of the consumer's income, even a large proportionate change in their prices appears inconsequential. Similarly, demand by the rich is more inelastic than demand by the poor for any particular commodity, as its cost accounts for a smaller proportion of a larger budget.

The longer the period of time considered, the more elastic is the demand curve. for any commodity. Time is required to learn about the price changes, to explore and develop tastes, and to adjust consumption patterns in accordance with the new set of prices. Where durable goods are involved, individuals may wait until existing goods are worn out before adjusting their expenditures. Because there are costs of gathering information and of making decisions, considerable inertia and lagged response exist in economic behavior.

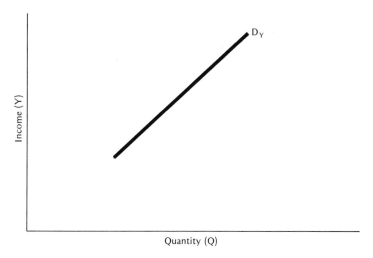

Figure 2-3 Income Demand Curve

Income Demand

There is nothing singular about the negative demand relationship between price and quantity demanded. It is also possible to draw an *income demand curve* that shows the relationship between income and quantity demanded. In this case it is price that is assumed to remain constant in the *ceteris paribus* box.

An income demand curve (D_y) is illustrated in Figure 2-3. The income demand relationship will ordinarily have a positive slope. An increase in income increases the quantity demanded. When the slope is negative the commodity is termed an *inferior good,* for which quantity demanded decreases as incomes rise. Potatoes and margarine are inferior goods at relatively high income levels.

SUPPLY

On the other side of the market the supply relationship summarizes the behavior of sellers. For most commodities, the higher the price the greater will be the quantity supplied, as is illustrated in Figure 2-4 by the supply curve (*S*). By convention, a *change in supply* denotes a shift of the entire curve, while a movement along the curve is referred to as a *change in the quantity supplied.*

Supply and Costs

The total supply curve of a commodity is the summation of the supply curves of individual producers. Goods and services are supplied in expectation of profit, which is simply the difference between total revenues and total costs. The supply curve of Figure 2-4 is based on the cost curves to suppliers of producing these goods.

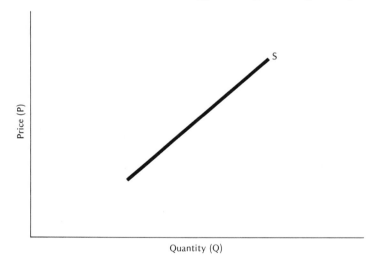

Figure 2-4 Supply Curve

The cost of production and sales consists of the prices of the factors of production — labor, capital, and raw materials — used up in the production and selling process. The quantity of factors required to produce any particular output depends on their productivity, which in turn depends on the quality of the factor inputs, the amounts used, and the technology by which they are combined. The relationship between factor inputs and units of output is termed the *production function.*

Unlike the law of demand, the positive relationship between quantity supplied and price described by the supply relationship is not general. In competitive markets, quantities supplied by sellers are related to their costs of production. As the quantity produced varies, so may the per-unit cost of producing these goods. Ordinarily average costs rise as more is produced, but average costs may remain constant or even fall as output is increased. It is thus possible for a supply curve to be horizontal or downward sloping, depending on the conditions of production and the period of time considered.

Elasticity of Supply

The concept of elasticity is also used to measure the responsiveness of the quantity supplied to a change in price. It is important to specify the time period to which a supply relationship applies. The longer the period of time considered the more elastic the supply curve becomes. This variability reflects the fact that supply adjustment by producers to a change in price cannot occur instantaneously but must be spread out over some period of time, depending upon the conditions of production. For some goods the supply cannot be varied even over the long run, and the supply curve will be a vertical line.

If markets are not perfectly competitive, individual producers will be able to influence the price at which they sell their commodity. In such cases it is not possible to draw a supply curve. As will be shown, the quantity supplied is then not related uniquely to price but will depend on the nature of the demand curve faced by sellers processing market power.

MARKET PRICE

Demand and supply relationships together explain how the prices of commodities bought and sold in competitive markets are determined. The analysis of the determination of the price of economic goods is termed the *theory of value.*

Markets

The following analysis applies to the determination of a commodity's price in a particular market. A market may be defined as an area over which buyers and sellers are in touch with one another and transportation costs are sufficiently low that the prices of similar articles tend to equality. A market may be defined rigorously as an area over which the same good will sell at a single price. In practice it is often difficult to define precisely a particular commodity and market, particularly when close substitutes exist. Most goods are in some sense substitutes for many other goods. The definition of a commodity refers to a gap in this chain of substitutes.

The geographic area that comprises a market varies widely for different commodities. For some goods that are perishable or have high transportation costs relative to their cost of production (flowers or bricks), the market is local or regional. For other goods whose transportation costs are relatively low (wheat, automobiles, or corporate stocks and bonds), the market is national or even international.

Equilibrium Price

In Figure 2-5 the supply and demand curves for a particular commodity are drawn on the same diagram. It is not possible to state at what price exchanges initially occur. But whatever the initial level of prices, the price toward which market exchanges will tend is P_E, where the supply and demand curves intersect. Only at P_E is the quantity demanded by buyers equal to the quantity supplied by sellers. At all other prices buyers or sellers have an incentive to change their behavior in an attempt to move toward their demand or supply curves. P_E is termed the *equilibrium price*, where *equilibrium* is defined as a situation in which there is no tendency to change.

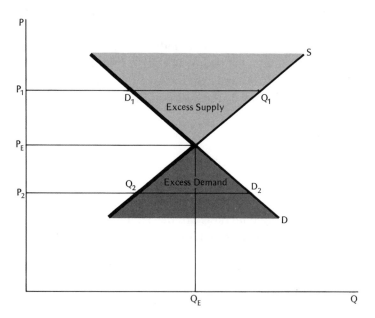

Figure 2-5 Equilibrium Price

This movement toward equilibrium may be shown as follows: Suppose that the market price is temporarily above the equilibrium price, e.g., P_1. As shown in Figure 2-5, at this higher price (P_1) the quantity supplied (Q_1) exceeds the quantity demanded (D_1). At that price there exists an *excess supply* of Q_1-D_1. Some sellers will be unable to find a buyer at the price P_1. As a result unsatisfied sellers will offer to sell for slightly less, and the market price will tend to fall. At a lower price the quantity demanded will increase and the quantity supplied will decrease, reducing the excess supply. As long as excess supply exists, this process will continue. The market price will fall until eventually the equilibrium position E is attained.

Alternatively, suppose the market price is temporarily below the equilibrium level, e.g., P_2. There is then an *excess demand* of D_2-Q_2, as the quantity of goods demanded (D_2) exceeds the quantity supplied (Q_2). Some buyers will then be unable to get the goods they demand at the price P_2. As a result unsatisfied buyers will offer to pay a slightly higher price. The market price will continue to rise so long as excess demand exists. Only when the equilibrium position E is reached is excess demand eliminated.

In Figure 2-5 the equilibrium position E represents the only price at which sellers are on their supply schedules and buyers are simultaneously on their demand schedules. At all other prices either buyers or sellers would be dissatisfied, that is, not on their demand or supply schedules and unable to buy or sell their preferred quantity. Moreover they would be able to improve their position by further trading, and so have an incentive to bid prices up or down. At E they may still be desperately unhappy about the price, but they are unable to better their position by further exchange. As shown by the heavy line, Q_E represents the maximum quantity that will be voluntarily exchanged. At higher prices less will be demanded; at lower prices less will be supplied.

Equilibrium as an Analytic Concept

The concept of *equilibrium* plays a central role in economic analysis. It is defined generally as a situation of a market, a household, a firm, or an economy from which there is no tendency to change within the time period considered. It is thus a position of balance, the position toward which an economic unit or system is tending.

An equilibrium position represents a conceptual event, like a pendulum lying at rest. It is not intended as a description of real world circumstances but as a conceptual tool, a method of analyzing the outcomes of real world situations. Equilibrium or disequilibrium have no normative implications. They are neither good nor bad but *value neutral,* an analytical construct.

Economic markets or participants may never actually reach an equilibrium position. If variables are continually changing and speeds of adjustment are sluggish, they may remain perpetually in disequilibrium. Nevertheless the concept of equilibrium represents a fruitful analytic technique. It permits the investigator to define the position toward which a decision unit or a system is tending, given the initial conditions and behavioral reactions.

Change in Supply and Demand

Whenever the nonprice determinants affecting the demand or supply curves change, there will be a new equilibrium position. In Figure 2-6 such an occurrence is represented by a shift in the supply curve from S_0 to S_1 to S_2, resulting in a new equilibrium price and quantity. If the demand curve remains constant as shown in Figure 2-6, shifts in the supply curve trace out points along the demand relationship.

An equilibrium price and quantity are only analytically determinate if the demand and supply schedules are *independent* of one another. If the increase in supply in Figure 2-6 were to provoke an unknown responsive shift in the demand relationship, it would not be possible to determine the new price or even to state whether it would be higher or lower. Because in the real world many things are changing at once, supply and demand curves frequently shift together. As a result it is difficult to estimate demand or supply relationships from observed market prices and sales.

Figure 2-6 shows that, in general, neither demand nor supply alone is sufficient to explain the value of economic goods. Both are necessary, like the two blades of a scissors. However, for those goods for which the supply is fixed (the quantity of land or old masters), competitive price is determined entirely by demand. As shown in Figure 2-7 with a vertical (perfectly inelastic) supply curve, a rise in demand increases the price from zero to P_1 to P_2.

Conversely, for those goods for which the supply can be increased indefinitely at

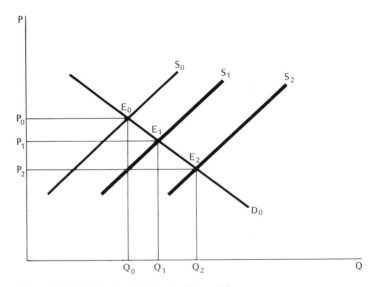

Figure 2-6 Shift in Supply with Constant Demand Curve

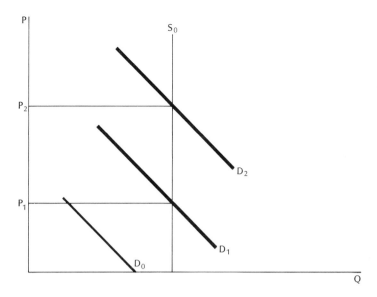

Figure 2-7 Determination of Price with Perfectly Inelastic Supply

a constant cost, (pins or post cards), competitive price is determined entirely by supply. As shown in Figure 2-8 with a horizontal (perfectly elastic) supply curve, changes in demand affect only the quantity produced and sold.

APPLICATIONS

The economic concepts of supply and demand are merely useful initial categories for ordering and analyzing the magnitude of forces impinging on the market value of

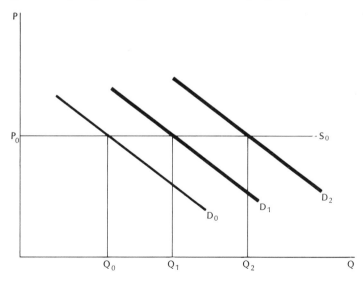

Figure 2-8 Determination of Quantity with Perfectly Elastic Supply

economic goods. Yet even the simple tools forged in this chapter possess considerable explanatory power. Consider the following examples.

Luxuries in Trade

Nationals of a country frequently complain that much of their highest quality products are exported, while lower quality goods remain for domestic consumption. The best Canadian bacon, Colombian coffee, California grapes, and Argentinian beef are produced for export. Why is this?

It is not due generally to the higher incomes or more refined tastes of consumers in the importing countries, but to rational consumer behavior. Assume that tastes and incomes were identical in all countries and that costs of production are such that the best grade of Canadian bacon costs 75 cents a pound, while the lowest grade can be produced for 25 cents a pound. Assume further that transportation and distribution costs to Europe are 25 cents a pound. As a result, the highest quality bacon is three times as expensive as the lowest quality bacon in Canada but only twice as expensive in Europe. Europeans, faced with a lower price of choice bacon *relative* to inferior bacon, will demand relatively more choice bacon than Canadians.

The same argument explains why someone visiting New York for a weekend is more likely to buy expensive seats to the theater than to go to a movie, compared with people who live in New York.

Stock Prices

Stock markets are surrounded by an undeserved mystique. Corporate stocks are merely pieces of paper representing a legal title to future dividends declared by a corporation. They are traded in national markets where, because of the large volume of transactions, individual buyers or sellers ordinarily cannot affect the market price.

Largely because of tax considerations, most corporations rely on internal funds (retained earnings) rather than the issue of new shares to finance their plant and equipment expenditures. The total number of shares of stock issued by General Motors Corporation, for example, typically remains constant, as is shown by the vertical supply curve S_0 in Figure 2-9.

Given the number of G.M. shares outstanding, the price per share will depend on the total demand on the part of investors to hold G.M. stock. The lower the price, the greater the quantity demanded, as is shown in Figure 2-9 by the demand curve D. The quantity of G.M. stock demanded depends on investor expectations of the size, growth, and variability of future G.M. earnings and dividends, plus more general factors such as the outlook for corporate profits, the behavior of other stocks, and the rate of growth of the economy.

At any moment in time, different individuals have different expectations of

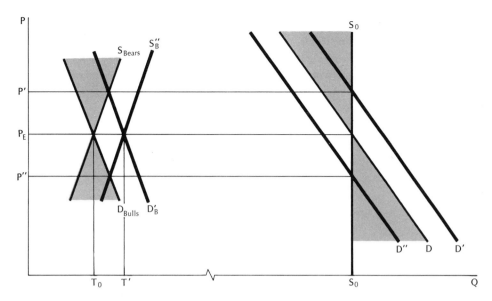

Figure 2-9 Determination of Stock Prices

G.M.'s future performance. Some individuals (termed *bulls,*) who are optimistic about G.M.'s prospects desire to add to their holdings on any given day and to add more when the current market price is lower. Other individuals (termed *bears*) who are pessimistic about G.M. at current prices desire to reduce their holdings on any given day and to sell more when the current market price is higher. Their demand and supply offer curves, illustrated in Figure 2-9, are compiled as buy-and-sell orders in the book of the "specialist" who trades G.M. stock on the floor of the exchange.

After consulting his order book, the specialist will set a price he estimates will clear the market by satisfying all would-be buyers and sellers. If the supply and demand curves of the bulls and the bears intersect at the market price existing at the close of the previous day, there will be no change in the price of G.M. stock, even though there may be a large volume of transactions (T_0). Ordinarily this will not be the case, and the price at which G.M. stock is traded for the day (P_E) will adjust to equate the quantities demanded and supplied by bulls and bears.

As may be seen from Figure 2-9, the total demand to hold G.M. stock (D) differs from the quantity of stock available (S_0) by the excess of bear demand over bull supply. The difference $D_B - S_B$ is shaded in the diagram and is exactly equal to the difference $D - S_0$. An increased demand for stock by bulls (a rightward shift in D_{Bulls} to D'_B) will raise the current market price to P'. An increased supply of stock by bears (a rightward shift to S''_B and a leftward shift to D'') will lower the current market price to P''. An equal increase in supply and demand will raise the volume of transactions (T') but leave price unchanged.

The price of G.M. stock will in this way adjust every trading day to clear the market so that the total quantity of G.M. stock demanded by investors is exactly equal to the quantity of stock available. Because the quantity of stock outstanding is constant, shifts in demand due to shifts in investor optimism or pessimism must necessarily result in a change in stock prices. While one investor can increase or reduce his holdings of G.M. stock, so long as the total supply does not change investors as a whole cannot. If everyone wants to sell, the price must fall until investors are willing to hold the existing quantity.

Differences of opinion make a horse-race. With widespread disagreement concerning the future of G.M., there will be heavy trading, yet there may be little or no change in price. Conversely, with generalized optimism or pessimism, a very large change in price may occur with little or even no trading.

A Change in Demand for Agricultural Commodities

Suppose that oranges are traded in competitive markets. An increase in demand for oranges by housewives — due for example, to an increased appreciation of the effects of vitamin C — will initially result in a higher price of oranges. This process is illustrated in Figure 2-10 as an increase in price from P_0 to P_1.

Retailers, wholesalers, shippers, and growers each hold inventories of oranges to act as a cushion or buffer against short-run changes in demand. Total inventories may be equal to several months' sales. As a result of the existence of these inventories at various stages, the rise in price will characteristically appear to be due to an increase in costs rather than to an increase in demand. Consider the following scenario:

Housewives increase their consumption of oranges at the current price, thus depleting retail inventories. After a period of time retailers increase their orders from wholesalers in order to restore their inventories. Wholesalers and shippers in turn

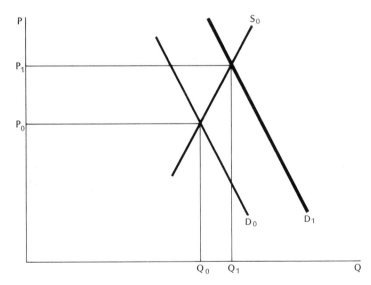

Figure 2-10 An Increase in Demand for Oranges

attempt to adjust their inventories by directing their buyers to purchase more oranges from growers. But only a limited amount of oranges is ripening at any one time. With all shippers desiring to increase their purchases, some will raise their offers in order to persuade growers to sell to them rather than to some other shipper. The higher price paid by shippers will force them to raise the price they charge to wholesalers, in order to protect their markup. In turn wholesalers will raise the price charged to retailers, who will then charge a higher price to customers.

Retailers can and if pressed will argue that they have not attempted in any way to exploit the increased consumer demand for oranges, and wholesalers and shippers can say the same. They have raised their prices only in response to a rise in their costs. Orange growers now enjoy higher incomes, as shown by the larger rectangle P_1Q_1 in Figure 2-10. In response they are likely to plant more orange trees, and new growers may be attracted into the now more profitable orange-growing industry. But the supply of oranges cannot increase overnight. An additional result of the increase in demand has been to transfer and redistribute real income away from consumers to producers of oranges. This story illustrates the dual function that prices perform in a market economy: to allocate resources and to distribute income.

If an economist is to be analytically superior to a parrot, he must be able to look behind demand and supply relationships. Economics is a method rather than a doctrine, and supply and demand represent initial questions rather than final answers. Why have these particular quantities and not others been demanded and offered? Why do the curves have these slopes? How does the nature of the market on which goods are traded affect the price at which exchange occurs? To this end it is first necessary to develop a general understanding of the economic behavior of households and business firms, the chief actors on the economic stage.

APPENDIX: ELASTICITY, TIME, AND ADDITIONAL APPLICATIONS

Elasticity

Different goods vary in the degree to which the quantity demanded or supplied varies in response to a change in price. The concept of *elasticity* is used to measure this responsiveness. Elasticity refers to movement along a particular curve in response to a change in price and not to shifts in the curve in response to changes in other variables.

Elasticity is defined as the proportionate change in quantity divided by the proportionate change in price. By convention negative signs are ignored, and elasticity is defined as a positive number. This may be stated as follows:

$$E = \frac{\Delta Q/Q}{\Delta P/P} = \frac{\Delta Q}{\Delta P} \cdot \frac{P}{Q} \qquad \text{(where } \Delta \text{ denotes } change \ in.)$$

Diagramatically it is convenient to represent an elastic curve as relatively flat and an inelastic curve as relatively steep. Elasticity is, however, not the same as the inverse of the slope of the curve $\left(\dfrac{\Delta Q}{\Delta P}\right)$. The steepness or slope of the same relationship will appear to vary in different diagrams, depending on the scale in which quantities are measured.

Because it is defined in terms of proportionate or percentage change, elasticity avoids dimensional arbitrariness. As the definition states, elasticity is equal to the inverse of the slope of the curve, multiplied by the ratio of price over quantity. This definition implies that a straight line with a constant slope will have differing elasticity at different points, as long as it does not go through the origin.

When the coefficient of elasticity is zero, demand or supply is termed *perfectly inelastic*. As shown in Figure 2-11, a curve that is perfectly inelastic throughout its length may be represented by a vertical straight line. There is no response in the quantity demanded or supplied to a change in price. If the coefficient of elasticity is less than one, supply or demand is termed *inelastic*.

When the coefficient of elasticity is equal to one, it is called *unit elasticity*. Unit elasticity implies that a change in price will result in an identical proportionate change in quantity. As shown in Figure 2-11a, a demand curve of unit elasticity throughout is represented by a rectangular hyperbola. A supply curve of unit elasticity is represented by a straight line of any slope that passes through the origin.

If the coefficient of elasticity is greater than one, demand or supply is termed *elastic*. When the coefficient of elasticity is infinite, the curve is called *perfectly elastic*. A curve that is perfectly elastic throughout its length may be represented by a horizontal straight line.

The elasticity of demand determines how the total amount spent by purchasers on a commodity will vary in response to a change in price. Total expenditure for the commodity is simply the product of price paid multiplied by quantity purchased and may be represented by the area of the rectangle PQ under the demand curves in Figure 2-11a. If the elasticity of demand is unity $(E=1)$, total expenditure is constant as the price changes. If demand is elastic $(E>1)$, total expenditure will in-

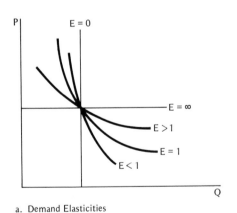

a. Demand Elasticities

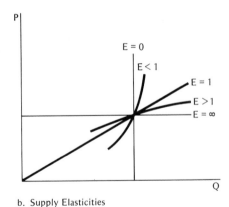

b. Supply Elasticities

Figure 2-11 The Elasticity of Demand and Supply Curves

crease as the price falls and decline as the price rises. If demand is inelastic ($E < 1$), total expenditure will decline as the price falls and increase in response to a rise in price.

This relationship is particularly important for buyers or sellers possessing market power, that is, ability to affect the market price. If demand is inelastic, firms can always increase total revenues by raising prices. Trade unions can increase the total wage bill by bargaining for higher wages. An inelastic demand implies that the proportionate fall in the quantity demanded by purchasers will be less than the proportionate rise in the total price paid.

Time

The treatment of time is a difficult problem in economics. As a first step it is useful to distinguish *static analysis* and *dynamic analysis*.

Static analysis abstracts from time entirely. It asks the question: "What result or solution would occur as a result of a certain initial set of assumptions?" Comparative static analysis essentially compares two final equilibrium situations, after a period of time long enough to permit certain stipulated responses to occur.

Dynamic analysis, on the other hand, is concerned with behavior over time. Household savings and business investment behavior are intrinsically concerned with the future. Dynamic analysis is more difficult and complicated than static analysis, because expectations and uncertainty must be taken into account.

In the case of most commodities, producers are able to respond to a change in market price only after some lag, depending on their period of production. For certain agricultural commodities — oranges, coffee, meat — this lag is relatively well defined as the period of time required to grow a particular commodity. It takes, for example, five years for a newly planted rubber tree to reach maturity.

Assume that the supply of an agricultural commodity in the current period (t) is functionally related to the market price of the commodity in the previous period ($t-1$), where the length of the period is equal to the period of production. Under such circumstances there will be a tendency for price to fluctuate over time.

The cyclical behavior of price over time is illustrated in Figure 2-12. Depending on the elasticity of supply response and the expectations of producers these cycles will be diminishing, constant, or even increasing. This *cobweb theorem*, as it is called, explains part of the observed price fluctuations in many agricultural products.

In practice unstable cobwebs with ever-increasing fluctuations do not occur, largely because of the action of *speculators*. If the good can be stored, speculators will not permit the present market price to fall very far below the level of prices they expect in the future. By buying at a low price and selling at a high price speculators, attracted by private profit prospects and willing to bear the risk of an uncertain future, operate to dampen market fluctuations. For most agricultural commodities,

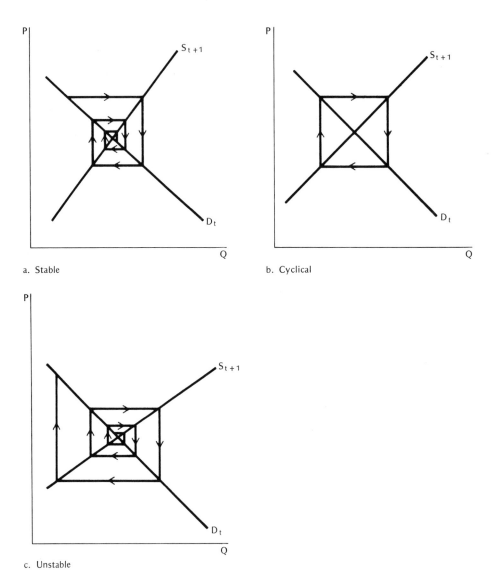

a. Stable

b. Cyclical

c. Unstable

Figure 2-12 Cobweb Cycles

organized *futures* markets exist that serve to stabilize prices and reallocate consumption over time. Governments may also operate to stabilize prices in exactly the same manner.

Time is also important for the behavior of buyers. Once expectations of the future are taken into account, the very law of demand may be reversed. If a current increase in price leads to expectations of future price increases, it may induce buyers to purchase more in the present. Conversely a reduction in price, if it leads to the expectation of future reductions, may lead buyers to purchase less in the present. It makes a great deal of difference whether a current change in price is expected to be permanent, to continue, or to be reversed in the future.

Additional Applications

The Effects of Quotas   Consider again the orange market. Since oranges are traded internationally, an increased domestic demand for oranges can be met by increased imports. Assume that foreign oranges are good substitutes for domestic oranges and that the world price of oranges is not affected by a moderate increase in imports by any one country. The supply of imported oranges may then be regarded as perfectly elastic at the world price.

This supply of imports is shown in Figure 2-13 as the horizontal straight line S_M at the world price P_W. The total supply curve, the quantity supplied at different prices, then becomes the heavy line $S_D S_M$, where $S_D S_D$ represents domestic supply. In this case an increase in demand from D_0 to D_1 will not result in any increase in price but will be met by an increase in imports from M_0 to M_1.

Now suppose that domestic orange growers persuade the government to pass a law restricting foreign imports to protect domestic growers from "unfair" competition. A *quota* is established, equal for example to the initial level of imports M_0. The supply curve then becomes heavy line $S_D S_M$ in Figure 2-14. After the import quota M_0 has been filled, additional oranges can be supplied only by domestic producers.

In such circumstances the increase in demand causes orange prices to rise from P_W to P_1. The shaded area measures the increased cost of the quota to consumers. The effect of a quota is thus analogous to a hidden tax paid by consumers to producers.

The cross-hatched rectangle within the shaded area is received by orange importers who are able to buy M_0 oranges at the world price P_W and sell them at the domestic price P_1. It represents the total value of possession of a quota. These valuable quotas are ordinarily not auctioned off but distributed according to other criteria. As a result, importers have an incentive to spend large sums to influence the quota-determining process. Not surprisingly this leads subtly or openly to the corruption of public officials.

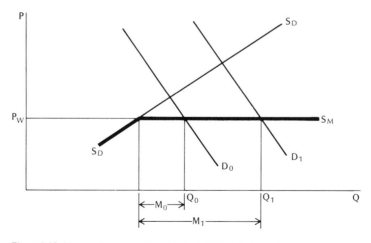

Figure 2-13 Increase in Demand Leading to an Increase in Imports

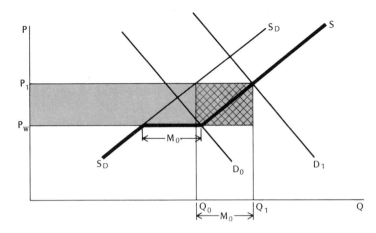

Figure 2-14 Increase in Demand with a Quota Restricting Imports

An Increase in the Supply of Agricultural Commodities   Now suppose that as a result of an unusually favorable harvest there is a large increase in the domestic supply of oranges. This case is represented in Figure 2-15 by a rightward shift in the supply curve from S_0 to S_1.

The result is to reduce the price of oranges and increase the quantity sold. But if, as shown in Figure 2-15, the demand for oranges is inelastic, the quantity purchased increases by a smaller proportion than the fall in price. In consequence of the increased supply, the total income received by orange growers falls from $P_0 Q_0$ to the shaded area $P_1 Q_1$. The result of the increase in supply has been to transfer real income away from orange growers to consumers.

If growers are able to export oranges freely, the domestic price cannot fall below the world price. The demand curve becomes heavy line $D_D D_X$ in Figure 2-16. The quantity X_1 will be exported and growers' total income will rise.

However, other countries may have quotas, closing off export markets. Under

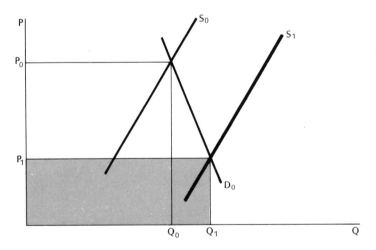

Figure 2-15 An Increase in Supply with Inelastic Demand

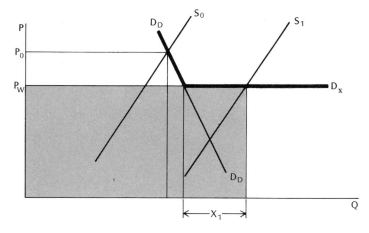

Figure 2-16 An Increase in Supply Leading to an Increase in Exports

such conditions growers may attempt to persuade the government to protect the income of orange growers. The government may enforce crop restrictions, limiting the amount of oranges that can be grown and shifting the supply curve in Figure 2-16 leftward. Alternatively, the government may support the domestic price at some predetermined level. In this case the government offers to purchase at the support price all oranges not demanded by domestic consumers. If the support price is set above the market equilibrium price, the government will be forced to stockpile oranges.

Price Controls Governments frequently set a minimum price at which goods may be sold, as in the case of farm price-support policy or minimum-wage legislation. Such a minimum price will be effective only if it is *above* the equilibrium market price. This situation is illustrated in Figure 2-17. Surpluses will develop, since

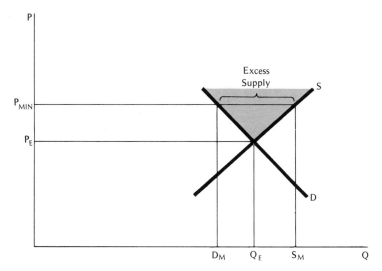

Figure 2-17 Price Controls: Minimum Price

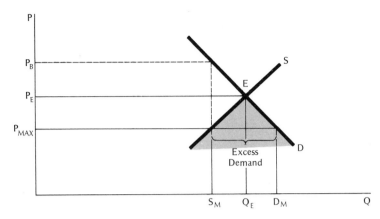

Figure 2-18 Price Controls: Maximum Price

at the floor price (P_{MIN}) the quantity supplied exceeds the quantity demanded.

In the case of agricultural goods, surpluses must be taken off the market and either destroyed or dumped abroad by the government if they are not to depress the domestic price. If demand is inelastic, government price supports will raise the amount spent by consumers; and total farm income will rise ($P_M D_M > P_E Q_E$).

In the case of labor, minimum wage legislation will put some people out of work and so harm some of those it intends to help. Unemployed workers will drive down wage rates in noncovered industries. If the demand for labor is inelastic, minimum wage legislation will increase the total wage bill going to workers ($P_M D_M > P_E Q_E$), even though some workers now unemployed or in noncovered jobs are made worse off.

Governments frequently also set a maximum price at which a commodity may be bought and sold. Such prices are typically justified as protection for consumers in special circumstances (wartime scarcity of goods, or rent controls in time of housing shortage). They will be effective only if the ceiling is set *below* the market equilibrium price. When the imposed maximum price (P_{MAX}) is less than the equilibrium price, a shortage will develop. As shown in Figure 2-18, excess demand for the good is created as people desire to buy more than is available at the existing price. One result is to transfer income from producers to consumers, as the amount spent ($P_M S_M$) is less than would be the case in the absence of controls.

Price ceilings do not resolve the fundamental economic problem of *to whom* available supplies will be distributed. Various nonprice allocation devices must therefore be resorted to — queuing, barter, favoritism (pretty girls having an advantage over plain girls), rationing, and other forms of nonprice discrimination among customers. A black market may also develop in which producers or consumers are bribed by buyers to sell goods illegally at a price above the government's ceiling. Buyers might willingly pay the price P_B for the quantity S_M, but, as not all goods produced will be sold on the black market, the black market price may considerably exceed P_B.

Excise Taxes   A final example of analytical insight shed by the simple tools of supply and demand is the question of excise taxation. Assume that the government imposes a value-added tax of 30 percent on each unit of a commodity sold. Who pays the tax, the consumers or the producers? How much will the market price increase as a result of the tax? What determines the total tax revenue that will be received by the government? Few individuals could answer these questions correctly without some previous study of economics.

Assume that underlying supply conditions initially remain unchanged. In order for suppliers to receive the same after-tax price for any given quantity sold, the market price must exceed the price that sellers receive by the amount of the tax. The effect of such a tax may thus be shown diagramatically in Figure 2-19 by a vertical upward shift of the supply curve by 30 percent, the amount of the tax.

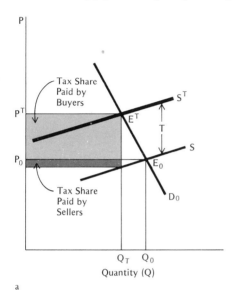

a

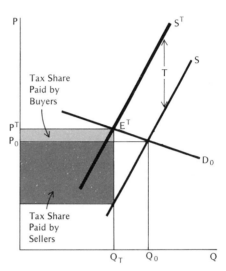

b

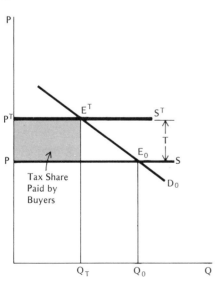

c

Figure 2-19 Figure Commodity Taxation

In Figure 2-19 the shaded areas represent total tax receipts. Figure 2-19 reveals that the extent to which the tax will be paid by buyers and sellers will depend on the relative elasticities of the supply and demand curves. If *demand is inelastic,* as shown in Figure 2-19a, consumers pay the major part of the tax, compared to the pretax price. If *supply is inelastic,* as illustrated in Figure 2-19b, producers pay the major part of the tax.

If the government desires to raise revenue, it should tax those commodities for which both supply and demand are inelastic. A tax on commodities for which either supply or demand is elastic will result in a large reduction in the quantity demanded and supplied, and therefore in sales volume, the base on which the tax is levied, and so tax receipts.

The increase in market price in the short run will ordinarily be less than the tax rate of 30 percent, as shown in Figure 2-19, parts a and b. Only for the case in which supply is perfectly elastic, as represented by the horizontal line in Figure 2-19c, or demand is perfectly inelastic, will the market price increase by the full amount of the tax.

BIBLIOGRAPHY OF SELECTED PAPERBACKS: PART ONE

A. Classics

Commons, J. R., *Legal Foundations of Capitalism,* University of Wisconsin Press.
Keynes, J. M., *The General Theory of Employment, Interest, and Money,* Harcourt, Brace & World.
Knight, F. H., *Risk, Uncertainty and Profit,* Harper & Row.
Malthus, T. R.,*On Population: Three Essays,* New American Library.
Marx, K., *Capital,* 3 volumes, International Publishing Company.
Smith, A., *Inquiry into the Nature and Causes of the Wealth of Nations,* 2 volumes, Irwin.
Veblen, T., *Theory of the Leisure Class,* New American Library.

B. History of Economic Doctrine

Barber, W. J., *History of Economic Thought,* Penguin.
Heilbroner, R. L., *Worldly Philosophers,* Simon and Schuster.
Myrdal, G., *Political Elements in the Development of Economic Theory,* Simon and Schuster.
Schumpeter, J. A., *Ten Great Economists: From Marx to Keynes,* Oxford University Press.

C. General Interest

Dowd, D. F., *Modern Economic Problems in Historical Perspective,* Heath.
Friedman, M., *Capitalism and Freedom,* University of Chicago Press.
Galbraith, J. K., *Economics and the Art of Controversy,* Random House.
—— *The Affluent Society,* Houghton Mifflin.

Heilbroner, R. L., *"Making of Economic Society,"* Prentice Hall.

_____ *Between Capitalism and Socialism,* Random House.

Keynes, J. M., *Essays on Persuasion,* Norton.

Landes, D. S., ed., *Rise of Capitalism,* Macmillan.

—— *Unbound Prometheus: Technological Change and Industrial Development in Western Europe from 1750 to the Present,* Cambridge University Press.

Robinson, J., *Economic Philosophy,* Doubleday.

—— *Economics: An Awkward Corner,* Random House.

—— *Freedom and Necessity,* Random House.

Tawney, R. H., *Acquisitive Society,* Harcourt, Brace & World.

—— *Religion and the Rise of Capitalism,* New American Library.

Toynbee, A., *Industrial Revolution,* Beacon Press.

PART TWO

HOUSEHOLD AND FIRM BEHAVIOR

household economic behavior: static analysis

IT IS THIS ACCURSED PRACTICE of ever considering only what seems expedient for the occasion, disjointed from all principle or enlarged systems of action, of never listening to the true and unerring instincts of our better nature, which has led the colder-hearted men to the study of political economy.

—*SAMUEL TAYLOR COLERIDGE*

ECONOMIC MAN IS A CLOD, heroic man is a fool, but somewhere between the clod and the fool, human man, if the expression may be pardoned, steers his tottering way.

—*KENNETH BOULDING*

The present chapter attempts to explain the central principles behind household demand for goods in product markets and supply of labor and capital services in factor markets. In Chapter 2 it was simply asserted that the quantity of goods households demand is negatively related to the price charged, so that demand curves are downward-sloping to the right. Why? Why in particular does the market value of a commodity often appear unrelated to its intrinsic human value or usefulness? Why is water cheap while diamonds are dear?

THE RATIONALITY MODEL

Consumption behavior is an instance of decision-making, of choosing among alternatives. In order to understand household behavior, it is necessary first to inquire into the motivation behind household decisions.

The fundamental unit of behavior for economic analysis is the individual. All group actions represent the outcomes of individual decisions. Attribution in everyday conversation of goals and actions to groups really refers to the goals and actions of some or all individuals making up these groups. Neither a nation, a community, a corporation, nor a family can brush its teeth. There is no national interest. Economics takes an individualistic approach to economic behavior as an analytic point of departure. This does not of course depreciate the importance of society and culture in shaping individual values, preferences, and motivations.

Utility-Maximizing Behavior

The assumption of *rational self-interest* lies at the core of economic analysis. *Goods* were previously defined as any object of human want or desire. Each individual will now be assumed to prefer more of any good to less, and to act in a way consistent with this preference. This assumption is conventionally termed *utility-maximizing* behavior, although utility cannot be measured directly by any operation.

The *rationality model* proceeds from the assumption that the behavior of individuals as economic actors, whatever their role, can be understood as an attempt to act in their own self-interest. Once the content of self-interest is stated and defined, this formulation is no longer tautological and empty of empirical content. The general procedure is to determine what arguments enter into the *utility function* of different economic units and then to develop an explanation of their behavior, assuming that individuals act to maximize their self-interest.

The postulate of rationality is not intended to be descriptive of the decision-making process, in the sense of asserting that individuals consciously perform complicated mental calculations in determining their actions. It states rather that individuals by and large behave *as if* they were purposeful, *as if* they attempted to maximize certain objectives. The hypothesis of optimizing individual behavior is consistent with observed regular and predictable patterns of response to specified choices and changes in the environment.

To the extent that behavior is truly random, there are no patterns to be found, and no explanation is possible. Our ignorance is then complete.

The assumption of utility-maximizing behavior permits a number of powerful mathematical tools to be applied in the analysis of economic behavior. In order to maximize utility, the decision-maker must focus on the situation at the *margin*. What are the effects of consuming or producing one unit more or less? Does an incremental change in behavior increase or reduce the utility of the economic unit? (The techniques of calculus are designed to answer just such questions.) The concept of optimizing behavior, whether applied to households, firms, governments, or voters, plays a central role in economic model-building.

Benevolence and Malevolence

Utility maximization must not be interpreted as a narrow hedonistic model of human behavior. It does not imply that all men are rational, selfish, greedy, calculating, or unconcerned with the interests of others. Arguments included in the utility functions of economic units may include the well-being of other individuals and short-run or long-run considerations and will vary widely over time and place. Nevertheless the strength of idealistic and altruistic motives is often exaggerated. Most economic behavior can be explained with reference to a rather narrow definition of self-interest.

It is not from the benevolence of the butcher, the brewer, or the baker, that we expect our dinner, but from their regard to their own interest. We address ourselves, not to their humanity but to their self-love, and never talk to them of our own necessities but of their own advantages.[1]

Certainty and Uncertainty

The simplest models of individual behavior are based on the assumption of *perfect certainty*. Market participants are assumed to know all the information relevant to making a rational decision, including perfect foresight of the future as well as perfect knowledge of the past and the present. This analytical simplification is very convenient and somewhat similar to the assumption of a frictionless state in physics. It is justified on the grounds not of realism but of tractability. If the assumption of perfect certainty is not made, the outcomes of the analysis are dependent on the particular and much more complex assumptions posited concerning unknown expectations.

1. Adam Smith, *The Wealth of Nations,* book I, chap. 2.

There are a number of areas dealing explicitly with behavior concerning the future in which the assumption of certainty implies quite unsatisfactory results. It then becomes necessary to recognize explicitly the fact that observed behavior can be understood only as a response to an uncertain future. The introduction of uncertainty always complicates economic analysis and makes it more difficult to reach general conclusions. One of the most challenging tasks facing economists today is the systematic introduction of uncertainty into the whole corpus of economic theory.

HOUSEHOLD DEMAND FOR GOODS AND SERVICES

Table 3-1 presents the amount and composition of household expenditures for different classes of consumption goods. The first fact to be noted is that households do not devote all their expenditure to a particular good but allocate their purchases among many different commodities. Not surprisingly the total amount spent on goods and services increases with the level of household income. The composition of consumption expenditures also changes with income level. For some classes of goods such as food and housing the proportion of total expenditure falls substantially at higher levels of income. For other goods such as clothing, recreation, education, and travel the proportion rises substantially for higher income groups. How can these phenomena be accounted for?

Consumption is not an end in itself. The purpose of consumption is not to consume but to enjoy the services that goods yield. Consumers will be assumed to act as if they attempt to maximize the utility or satisfaction from available alternatives. As different households have different tastes and preferences, the satisfaction enjoyed from the consumption of any particular good may be expected to differ widely among households. But each household will adjust its purchases among goods to maximize its expected utility from consumption.

The first and obvious fact that households choose to allocate their purchases in many directions may be explained by the principle of diminishing marginal utility.

Diminishing Marginal Utility

The law of *diminishing marginal utility* was formulated independently and nearly simultaneously by economists in England, Germany, and France in the 1870s. They postulated that consumers experience *utility* or satisfaction from ownership and consumption of economic goods. Utility was regarded as a quantifiable entity, measurable on a cardinal scale, which implies that increments of utility yielded by economic goods can be compared in magnitude by the person who experiences them.

Under these assumptions, *marginal utility* may be defined as the addition to total utility or satisfaction that a consumer derives from one additional unit of a commodity. The law of diminishing marginal utility states that in general the more a person

Expenditure Categories	Money Income After Taxes									
	All Families		$1,000–1,999		$4,000–4,999		$7,500–9,999		$15,000 and over	
	Dollars	Percent	Dollars	Percent	Dollars	Percent	Dollars	Percent	Dollars	Percent
Food	1,235	24	533	30	1,125	23	1,766	24	2,720	19
Tobacco	91	2	36	2	94	2	125	2	140	1
Alcoholic Beverages	78	2	17	1	67	1	121	2	259	2
Housing	1,461	29	626	35	1,271	29	2,043	28	4,205	30
Clothing	518	10	119	7	420	9	830	11	1,745	12
Medical Care	340	7	156	9	293	7	469	6	878	6
Recreation	200	4	38	2	161	4	327	4	665	5
Education	53	1	5	—	26	1	83	1	395	3
Automobile	693	14	113	6	664	15	1,117	15	1,589	11
Other Travel	77	2	26	1	62	1	105	1	459	3
Total Expenditures for Current Consumptions	5,047	100	1,781	100	4,428	100	7,416	100	14,208	100

Source: Consumer Expenditures and Income, Bureau of Labor Statistics, Department of Labor.

has of any one thing, the smaller the utility he derives from an additional unit of it. It was concluded that behind the observable law of demand — the lower the price at which a thing is offered, the greater the quantity demanded — lies this fundamental diminishing marginal utility relationship. Diamonds are dear because they are scarce and their marginal utility high. Water is cheap because it is plentiful and its marginal utility low.

This law of diminishing marginal utility was based essentially on introspection, on what one knows about one's own mind. Outside observers can never measure a man's utility the way they can measure the length of his nose. But, on the assumption that consumers behave rationally to maximize total expected utility, the price paid for each economic good represents an indirect measure of its utility at the margin.

The price paid for goods may be taken as an indirect money measure of desire. In order to use it as an indirect measure of utility, it is necessary to assume that a man's desire for a thing is proportionate to the utility he expects to get from it and that the utility he does get is equal to the utility he expects to get. It was acknowledged that neither of these assumptions would always hold for every decision of every individual. Nevertheless, as a generalization of household behavior, they were held to be approximately satisfied.

The Condition for Utility Maximization

If a consumer acts to maximize total utility from his expenditures, he will distribute his purchases so that the utility received from the last dollar spent on each commodity he buys is equal. Unless this condition is satisfied, the consumer could always increase his total utility by transferring a dollar from a commodity for which the marginal utility of a dollar spent is lower to another commodity for which the marginal utility is higher.

Alternatively stated, utility maximization requires that the marginal utility of each commodity consumed be proportional to its price, so that for all goods the ratio of their prices equals the ratio of their marginal utilities.

Stated formally:

$$\frac{MU_A}{P_A} = \frac{MU_B}{P_B} \qquad \text{or} \qquad \frac{MU_A}{MU_B} = \frac{P_A}{P_B},$$

where A and B can represent any two goods in the consumer's budget.

Each consumer will therefore adjust his consumption until the price paid for any good indirectly measures the marginal utility derived from it. Because consumers have different tastes and incomes but pay the same price, this condition for utility maximization can be satisfied only if individuals with different tastes consume different amounts of the same good.

Figure 3-1 presents the marginal utility schedules of two individuals, X and Y, derived from the consumption of the same good. (The marginal utility of money is

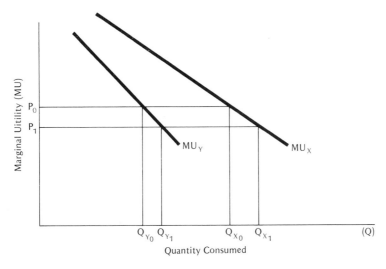

Figure 3-1 Diminishing Marginal Utility

assumed constant.) Individual X receives greater satisfaction from this good than does Y, and as a result X consumes more. But for each consumer, price is an indirect measure of the *marginal* utility received.

The Effect of a Change in Price

The condition for utility maximization, that individuals adjust their purchases of all goods until their expected marginal utilities are proportional to their prices, leads to testable predictions about household behavior. As shown in Figure 3-1, households, assuming no change in tastes, will increase the amount purchased of any good in response to a fall in its price (from P_0 to P_1) relative to the price of other goods. Consumers will thus tend to substitute relatively cheaper goods for relatively more expensive goods.

The responsiveness of the quantity demanded to a change in price will vary for different commodities. It will depend, as shown in Figure 3-1, on how rapidly marginal utility diminishes as more is consumed and on how the curves shift. The existence of substitute and complementary goods implies that marginal utility curves are not independent. Changes in the consumption of substitute or complementary goods shift the marginal utility derived from a particular good downward or upward.

Table 3-2 presents economists' estimates of the price elasticity of demand for selected commodities, that is, the responsiveness of demand to a change in price. Most broad classes of goods are characterized by an inelastic demand, particularly staple foodstuffs. Some individual goods, such as different kinds of meat, appear to be close substitutes for one another. The demand for gas and oil is inelastic in the short run because of the existence of the complementary good, automobiles. Demand elasticities increase the longer the time period considered. Gas and oil constitute only a small part of the total cost of driving a car, but over a period of time with higher gasoline prices, consumers would purchase cars with lower gasoline consumption, and the quantity of gasoline demanded would fall.

Table 3-2 ESTIMATES OF PRICE AND INCOME ELASTICITIES

Commodity	Price Elasticity	Income Elasticity
Beef	−0.9	0.5
Veal	−1.6	0.6
Pork	−0.7	0.3
Chicken	−1.1	0.4
Butter	−0.8	0.3
Milk	−0.3	0.2
Fruit	−0.6	0.4
Potatoes	−0.2	0.1
Cereals and Baking Products	−0.2	0.0
All Foods	−0.3	0.3
Household Appliances	−0.6	1.5
Electricity	−0.6	3.5
Medical Care	−0.3	7.4
Legal Services	−0.5	0.3
Automobile Repair	−0.4	1.3
Gasoline and Oil	−0.2	1.7
Taxicabs	−0.5	0.7
Airline Travel	−0.1	4.5
Flowers	−0.5	2.2
Toys	−0.6	1.5
Jewelry and Watches	−0.4	1.7
Automobiles	−0.6	1.5
Refrigerators	−1.0	1.2
Housing	−0.9	0.9

Source: Estimates 1–10, George Brandow, *Interrelations Among Demand for Farm Products and Implications for Control of Market Supply,* Pennsylvania, 1961; Estimates 11–21, H. S. Houthakker and L. Taylor, *Consumer Demand in the United States, 1929–70* Cambridge 1966; Estimates 22–24, Arnold Harberger, *The Demand for Durable Goods,* Chicago, 1960.

The Effect of a Change in Income

The maximum amount of goods a consumer can command, given their market prices, is limited by the level of his income, supplemented by his ability to borrow and to sell some of his existing assets. This limit is termed his *budget constraint.*

In response to an increase in money income, households are observed to increase their purchases of all goods. As may be seen from Figure 3-1, for the case in which tastes (the *MU* curve) and prices (the price line) remain constant, this phenomenon implies that the marginal utility of money must have fallen as income increases. An increase in money income with prices constant is thus equivalent to a proportional reduction in the price of all goods. As incomes rise, goods are purchased that previously were regarded as too expensive. The alternative hypothetical case, that tastes grow systematically with income to shift the marginal utility curves upward, also occurs. The more we have, the more we want.

As revealed in Table 3-1, total consumption expenditures follow consumer money income. The higher the income, the greater the expenditure on all classes of consumption goods. But the composition of expenditure changes markedly, depending on how rapidly marginal utility diminishes for different goods as more are consumed.

Table 3-2 also presents estimates of the income elasticity of demand for selected commodities. The low income elasticity for food is consistent with the observed fall in food purchases as a proportion of household budgets at higher levels of income. Other goods, such as medical care and airline travel, are characterized by high income elasticities. A proportionate rise in income results in a much greater proportionate rise in expenditures on these commodities. Such goods represent growth industries.

Objections to Marginal Utility

A number of objections have been raised to the theory of diminishing marginal utility. The most fundamental is the argument that utility cannot be measured, even by the consumer himself, because it possesses merely *ordinal* rather than *cardinal* dimensions. It may be possible to establish a ranking, to say that one good is preferred to another, but not to determine by *how much* it is preferred. No one has yet devised a way of measuring utility operationally. Because it is not possible to measure the absolute amount of utility experienced but only to order it in terms of greater or less, the case is made that it would be preferable not to use the concept of diminishing marginal utility at all.

Further, utility is not a function of a single commodity. The utility derived from the consumption of one commodity is not independent but related to the amounts of other commodities consumed by the individual and by other individuals. As a result, the utility curves do not stay put. Similarly, the utility derived from any given income is related to the level of income received by others. Utility is relative and interdependent. No man is an island.

These objections have considerable force. As will be shown in the chapter appendix, through the use of indifference analysis it is possible to derive the same conclusions about consumption behavior without making any assumptions as to the measurability, comparability, or independence of utility. However, economists of the nineteenth century were concerned with the measurement of utility because they wanted to say something about *economic welfare*. They believed firmly that the law of diminishing marginal utility applied to total income as well as to individual commodities. It follows that the marginal utility of money declines as an individual's money income increases. This conclusion was used to justify a more egalitarian income-redistribution policy from rich to poor. On utilitarian grounds such a redistribution would increase total utility, "the greatest good for the greatest number."

Economists have since recognized that it is not possible to draw any strictly scientific conclusions from interpersonal comparisons of utility. Even if it is accepted (although it cannot be proved) that the marginal utility of income falls as income increases, the fact remains that individuals are different, and the utilities of two individuals cannot be compared. A rich man may be a more efficient utility-producing machine than a poor man. After all, he has had much more practice. It cannot be demonstrated that a transfer of income from rich to poor will result in a greater increase in utility to the poor man than the reduction in utility experienced by the rich man.

It is frequently said that progressive income taxation is based on the law of diminishing marginal utility. But if the marginal utility of money does not fall as income increases, a rich man must enjoy more total satisfaction than a poor man. On these grounds redistribution of income in the direction of greater equality might be desired, even in the face of evidence of increasing marginal utility, as an attempt to reduce vast disparities in total utility enjoyed by differently favored individuals who share a common humanity.

The Existence of Stable Preferences

The underlying assumptions necessary for utility maximization as a model of consumer behavior have been challenged from all sides. The assumption that tastes are given is clearly contrary to evidence. Many purchases appear to be made on impulse as if tastes and preferences were not known or well defined, and many kinds of expenditures are habitual. Consumers are strongly influenced by the behavior of others. As income levels rise, the share of goods in the category of discretionary purchases increases. Persuaded and sometimes manipulated by advertising, and in the process misled as to the satisfaction that goods create, individuals are often observed to buy things they don't need, and later discover they don't want.

Compulsive, impulsive, and habitual buying obviously occur. Many consumers act irrationally, in the sense of not weighing alternatives to maximize utility. Yet for most goods tastes are not ephemeral nor indefinitely malleable. Consumers must choose. They are observed to deliberate among alternatives, and their choices are consistent with the assumption of a fairly stable set of preferences. Households in the aggregate, constrained by a limited income and faced with a set of prices, do respond to changes in these variables with a systematic regularity that is consistent with the model. The theory of optimizing behavior appears justified as a simplified approximation to reality that yields successful predictions for certain questions.

Nevertheless, to the extent that preferences and tastes are acquired and so are at least in part created by the productive system that satisfies them, it is difficult to maintain that demand is an indirect measure of utility received. "We want what we get" is not the same thing as "we get what we want." The relation between market demand and utility is extremely tenuous. These objections must be taken seriously in any normative evaluation of the price system as an institution for providing economic goods. If consumers really do not know what they want, they will do a poor job of signaling to the economic system what is to be produced.

HOUSEHOLD SUPPLY OF PRODUCTIVE FACTORS

Households get the income with which they purchase goods by selling the services of factors of production that they own. It is conventional to distinguish two broad types of factors of production, labor and capital. The income received from the sale of labor services is termed wages and salaries. Property income received by the owners of capital consists of profits, rent, interest, dividends, and capital gains.

Labor

Labor is the most important factor of production and receives the largest share of income. In most countries labor income accounts for from one half to four fifths of total income received.

Modern governments no longer permit their citizens freedom of contract to buy or sell themselves or others. Only in a slave economy is human capital marketable as an asset. As a result, labor as a capital good can only be rented by the period, so that only the services of labor can be bought and sold. The forces determining the market value of different types and quality of labor services are examined in Chapter 8.

The quantity of labor offered by households in the aggregate is relatively inelastic in the short run to the level of wage rates. Higher wages raise the price of leisure (its opportunity cost in terms of work), which tends to reduce the consumption of leisure and to increase the amount of labor offered. At the same time, higher wages result in higher incomes and induce households to buy more of all things, including leisure, and so act to reduce the amount of labor offered. At relatively high wage rates the income effect tends to dominate and the quantity of labor offered to decline. As a result, as shown in Figure 3-2, the supply curve of labor over this range may be backward-bending. As indicated by the dashed lines, there is little evidence on the behavior of the curve over extreme wage values.

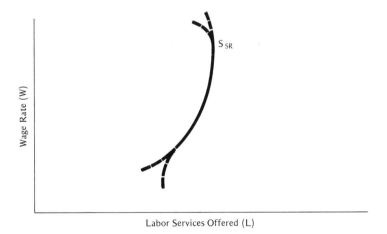

Figure 3-2 Short-Run Supply of Labor

Capital

Property income is derived ultimately from payments for the services of nonlabor factors of production — real capital goods and natural resources. Households ordinarily do not own real capital assets directly, with the exception of consumer durables, but hold ownership claims against business units in the form of financial assets. As a result property income takes many different forms.

Property income in the form of profits, rent, interest, and dividends accounts for from one-quarter to one half of total income in different countries. If capital gains are included in the definition of income, the property share is somewhat larger. Ownership of property is extremely unequally distributed among households in most capitalist economies. In the United States, the richest 5 percent of households owns more than half of total household net wealth. At the other end of the scale, the poorest half of all households owns less than 5 percent of total wealth.[2]

Household saving preferences, the ultimate source of increments to the stock of private wealth, are relatively inelastic with respect to expected rates of return, at least over the experienced range. A large proportion of total saving is undertaken by business firms and received by household stockowners in the form of capital gains. In the short run the total stock of capital owned and supplied by households is very inelastic, as is shown by the short-run supply curve S_{SR} in Figure 3-3.

As will be shown in the next chapter, households may choose to spend their wealth on consumption. Poorer households must be paid some income return as an inducement to reduce current consumption and add to their asset holdings out of current income. Rich households whose wealth already exceeds their expected lifetime consumption may continue to save even at zero or negative income return, due to the satisfaction from asset ownership and accumulation. There presumably exist some level of return sufficiently low (it may be negative) and some level of

2. See Table 10-5.

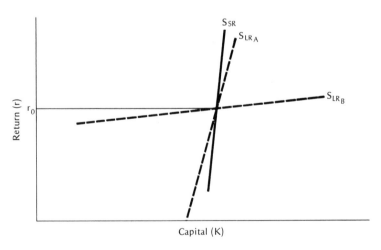

Figure 3-3 Short-Run and Long-Run Supply of Capital

wealth sufficiently high at which households on balance would choose to dissave rather than to accumulate additional assets.

Unfortunately there exists very little evidence concerning the interest elasticity of households' supply of savings schedule in the long run. This ignorance, the range of which is indicated by the dashed lines $S_{LR\,A}$ and $S_{LR\,B}$ in Figure 3-3, plays a critical role in discussions concerning the functional nature of private property income as a reward to ownership. If the curve follows the dashed line S_{LR_A}, a reduction in the existing return to property owners would not substantially reduce the supply of capital or the level of income in the economy. If the curve follows the relationship $S_{LR\,B}$, something approaching the existing reward to ownership must be paid over the long run in order to maintain the stock of capital intact.

APPENDIX: INDIFFERENCE ANALYSIS

Indifference curve analysis was developed early in the twentieth century as a technique by which downward-sloping demand curves could be derived without any assumption as to the cardinal measurability or independence of utility. By the use of indifference maps to describe tastes and preferences it is possible to dispense with utility entirely. Indifference analysis is based on a much weaker assumption: a consumer is simply able to prefer one combination of goods to another or, if he cannot rank one above the other, is indifferent between them.

Indifference Curves

Preferences or tastes are the starting point for indifference analysis. It is first necessary to postulate that the consumer has some existing set of preferences for different goods. In Figure 3-4, units of any two economic goods A and B are measured on the

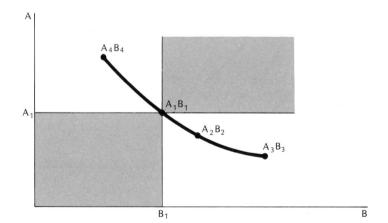

Figure 3-4 Derivation of an Indifference Curve

horizontal and vertical axis. Consider any one combination of A and B, for example, $A_1 B_1$. In Figure 3-4, vertical and horizontal lines have been drawn through this point. The combination $A_1 B_1$ is preferred to all combinations enclosed by the shaded rectangle formed with the origin, because it contains more of one or both goods. It is dominated by all combinations formed by the shaded rectangle away from the origin, as they each contain more on one or both goods.

Whether the combination $A_1 B_1$ is preferred to other combinations in the unshaded areas, each containing more of one good and less of the other, will depend on the consumer's tastes. But in general there exists some other combination (e.g., $A_2 B_2$) compared to which the consumer is indifferent. The smaller quantity of A ($A_1 - A_2$) is exactly offset by the greater quantity of B ($B_2 - B_1$). It is then possible to visualize a whole set of combinations in the nonshaded areas among which the consumer is indifferent — $A_3 B_3$ or $A_4 B_4$; for example. If these combinations are connected, the resulting line is termed an indifference curve.

Because the initial combination $A_1 B_1$ in Figure 3-4 was chosen arbitrarily, it is possible to find in the same way an indifference curve for any other combination of goods. In this manner a whole set of indifference curves can be constructed, as has been done in Figure 3-5. Each curve reflects the consumer's preferences by connecting a series of combinations of A and B among which he is indifferent. By definition, each point on a higher indifference curve is preferable to any point on a lower indifference curve. The set of indifference curves describing the preferences of a consumer is termed an *indifference map*.

Figure 3-5 makes no assumption about how much one bundle of goods is preferred to another. Utility may be regarded as being represented by a third axis, coming at right angles out of the diagram. The set of indifference curves may then be visualized as contour lines traced out upon a three-dimensional "hill of pleasure" utility surface, viewed as if seen from above. But the dimensions of this third axis remain unspecified.

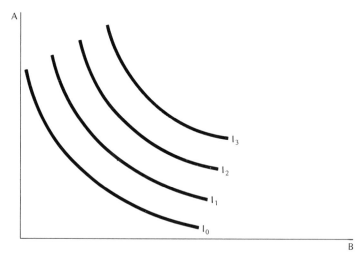

Figure 3-5 Indifference Curves

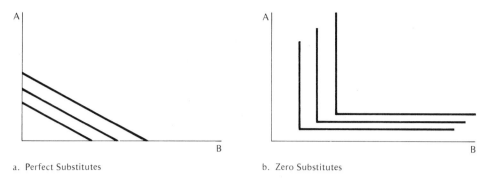

a. Perfect Substitutes   b. Zero Substitutes

Figure 3-6 Shape of Indifference Curves

Indifference curves are downward sloping as long as an additional unit of each good yields some positive satisfaction. Only if more of one good produced disutility (sometimes termed a *negative* good) would the indifference curves slope upward. By definition, indifference curves cannot intersect; that would mean that consumers were indifferent among all points on two intersecting indifferences curves.

Indifference curves are ordinarily drawn convex to the origin, reflecting the fact that as the consumption of one good is reduced, greater amounts of the other good are ordinarily required to leave the consumer equally well off. The slope of an indifference curve at any point is termed the *marginal rate of substitution* of one good for another. As individual indifference curves become flatter, the closer are the two goods to being substitutes for one another. Goods that are perfect substitutes may be represented by straight line indifference curves, meaning that constant amounts of the other good are sufficient to leave the consumer indifferent as one good is reduced. At the other extreme, goods that are zero substitutes (i.e., perfect complements) may be represented by a series of right-angled lines. These two extremes are represented in Figure 3-6.

Budget Restraint

An indifference map describes only the *tastes* of an individual. In order to determine the quantities of different commodities that he will demand, it is necessary to introduce *income* and *prices.* Assuming that the consumer's money income (Y_0) and the price of good A (P_{A_0}) and good B (P_{B_0}) are given, a budget equation may be constructed showing the maximum amounts of the two goods that he is able to purchase:

$$Y_0 = P_{A_0} \cdot A + P_{B_0} \cdot B.$$

The budget restraint or consumption possibility line ($C_0 C_0$) is seen in Figure 3-7. If he spends all of his income on good A and nothing on B, he can purchase Y_0/P_{A_0} units of A. If he spends all of his income on good B and buys none of A, he can buy Y_0/P_{B_0} units of B. Or he can purchase any combination on the straight line between these points. The slope of the budget line is the ratio of the prices (P_{B_0}/P_{A_0}).

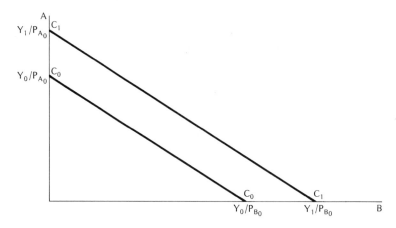

Figure 3-7 Consumption Possibility Lines

The distance of the budget line ($C_0 C_0$) from the origin is determined by the consumer's real income; that is, his money income (Y_0) divided by the prices of the goods he purchases. An increase in money income from Y_0 to Y_1, will shift the budget line outwards, if prices do not increase proportionally.

Consumer Equilibrium

To maximize total satisfaction, a consumer will attempt to reach his highest possible indifference curve. As shown in Figure 3-8, which combines Figures 3-6 and 3-7 and assumes that the consumer spends his entire income on two goods, this position will be at E_0, the highest indifference curve reached on the budget line. At this point of tangency the slope of the indifference curve is equal to the slope of the budget line, i.e., to the ratio of the prices. Because the slope of an indifference curve

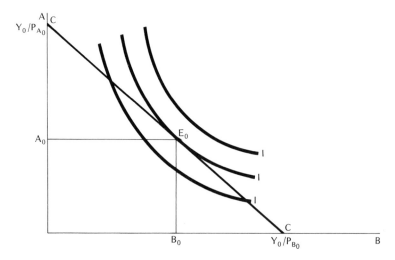

Figure 3-8 Consumer Equilibrium

68 HOUSEHOLD AND FIRM BEHAVIOR

at any point, termed the *marginal rate of substitution,* may be regarded as the ratio of the marginal utilities derived from the two commodities, this condition parallels the earlier condition for utility maximization under the assumption of cardinal utility.

To derive the demand curve for good B, let good A represent all other goods, so that the consumer by definition spends all his income on the two commodities. (This treatment is necessary because the graphical presentation is confined to two dimensions.) Now allow the price of good B to vary, holding the prices of other goods (P_{A_0}), income (Y_0), and tastes constant. As shown in Figure 3-9 as the price of B falls to P_{B_1}, P_{B_2}, ... P_{B_n}, the budget constraint line CC becomes flatter. Individuals adjust their purchases in order to move along the new budget line to reach a higher indifference curve.

As the price line is given all possible slopes, all points on the demand curve may be obtained. These equilibrium points trace out the demand curve DD, which may then be plotted in the usual manner, relating price to quantity demanded, as shown in Figure 3-10. Each point on a demand curve thus represents the consumer's preferred position, given his tastes, income, and the prices with which he is faced.

A similar analysis may be used to examine a change in income. A change in income results in an upward or downward shift in the budget constraint line CC but does not change its slope. The extent to which consumption of A and B increases as income is increased depends on the shape of the indifference map.

Four possible shapes of the income demand curve are shown in Figure 3-11. In

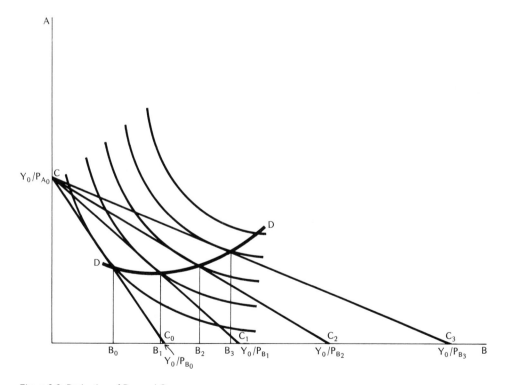

Figure 3-9 Derivation of Demand Curve

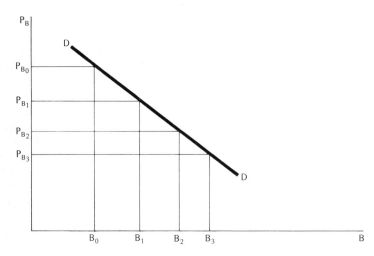

Figure 3-10 Demand Curve

Figure 3-11a the income elasticity of demand for B exceeds unity; in Figure 3-11b it is equal to unity; in Figure 3-11c it is less than unity. In Figure 3-11d the amount of B consumed falls as income increases, which illustrates the case of so-called *inferior goods.*

Income Effect and Substitution Effect

Indifference curve analysis permits the effects of a change in price on quantity demanded to be broken down into two component effects, the *income effect* and the *substitution effect.* In Figure 3-12, in response to a fall in price from P_{A_1} to P_{A_2}, the consumer moves from consuming A_1 to consuming A_2. A hypothetical budget line may now be drawn parallel to the new budget line, but through the old combination of commodities consumed E_1, thus holding real income constant. The consumer would adjust his consumption to consume A^* if he were faced by this hypothetical budget line.

The total effect of a price reduction on quantity demand from A_1 to A_2 may then be visualized as in part due to a pure *income effect,* the change from A^* to A_2. As a result of the fall in the price of A the consumer's real income has in effect been increased.

The effect of price reduction is also in part due to a pure *substitution effect,* the movement from A_1 to A^*. With the same real income (defined as the ability to buy the initial combination E_1), if one good is relatively cheaper, the consumer will adjust his consumption to buy more of the cheaper good.

The substitution effect will always induce the consumer to buy more of the relatively cheaper good. The amount will depend on the slope of his indifference curves, determined by the extent to which close substitutes are available. The income effect will ordinarily induce him to buy more of all goods, including the good A whose price has fallen, as shown in Figure 3-12. But if A is an inferior good, with an income elasticity of demand less than zero, the income effect will induce him to buy less.

It is conceivable that a strong income effect could more than offset a weak substitution effect, in which case the demand curve will be *positively* sloped over some range. Such a situation is termed the *Giffen paradox*. It has been applied to situations such as the demand for potatoes in Ireland during the great famine, but there is little empirical evidence that a positively sloped demand curve has ever actually been observed.

Objections

The apparently plausible assumption that consumers either are able to rank alternatives or are indifferent between them is, in fact, not always applicable. Many decisions are not resolvable in this way.

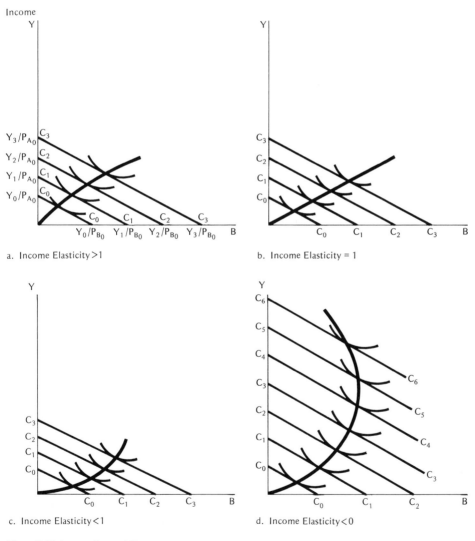

Figure 3-11 Income Demand Curves

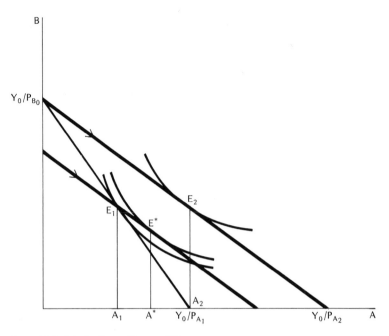

Figure 3-12 Substitution and Income Effects

Consider a decision in which a large amount of uncertainty is involved; for example, should one marry A or B or buy stock X or Y? One is undecided, unable to choose, yet one is definitely not indifferent, no matter how long he or she dithers. Pavlov induced neurotic behavior in his dogs by presenting them with uncertain alternatives. An ellipse meant food, a circle meant an electric shock. As the ellipses got fatter and the circles thinner, the dogs become more and more neurotic. Fortunately, although some individuals may agonize this way over a new car or house, most consumption decisions are not of this sort.

Obviously consumers do not actually attempt to estimate their indifference curves. It would not be fruitful, though it might be amusing, to question housewives as to their marginal rates of substitution between goods. Indifference analysis, like marginal utility analysis, is not intended as a description of the decision processes but as a simplified explanation that yields predictions of the outcomes of consumer behavior. Custom, rules of thumb, inertia, ignorance, and indivisibilities are all part of household behavior. Nevertheless, considering consumers as a whole, the theory provides a useful approximation of consumer behavior. Consumers must chose between alternatives and, by and large, they do behave as if they have a reasonably well-defined set of preferences.

The Independence of Preferences

Observations of human behavior provide convincing evidence that individuals have a kind of "cognitive map" by which they internally represent the external world. But just as there are innumerable ways of mapping the same territory, there are innumerable ways of developing a psychological representation. No man can be a perfectly impartial observer of the reality that confronts him. "The empiricist," said Santayana, "thinks he believes only what he sees—but he is much better at believing than at seeing."

While beliefs are based on induction (past observations) and construction (deductive theorizing), they are also based on analogy and, very frequently, on authority (experts, propaganda, advertising), particularly when no external referent is evident and uncertainty prevails. As a result, values, which are conceptually distinct (what is good?) influence beliefs (what exists, what is possible) and conversely. Values, like beliefs, reside neither in external objects nor within the person; rather, they emerge from *interaction* between a person and a portion of his environment. As every mountain climber knows, the extent to which the fruits of hard work are appreciated depends in part upon how hard the work was.

Because values are bi-directional concepts that inhere neither in persons nor in objects, changes in situations bring about changes in value orderings. The economist's assumption in the concept of utility that tastes and values are given eliminates much of this complexity but ignores the systematic interrelation, as the question of where values come from is excluded. There is abundant psychological evidence that value and moral development is the outcome of a social process and that value-biasing of beliefs is the rule rather than the exception. A major goal of contemporary psychological research is to specify the variables in the development of values and the transformation of beliefs. Tastes are indeed a subject for discussion. (We spend most of our time doing little else.) They are also a subject for analysis. As everyone must construct beliefs from meager information, the biasing process is universal. We can never share the full reality that events carry with them. As William James put it, man's hopes and beliefs are based more upon the unseen than the seen.

household economic behavior:
dynamic analysis

IT WAS A CONSUMING VEXATION to my father that my mother never asked the meaning of a thing she did not understand.

—*LAURENCE STERN*

WITH REGARD TO THEIR CHOICE of premises, it is not always easy to tell when a professor of the dismal science is making a joke.

— *CUNNINGHAM*

The previous chapter concluded that utility maximizing consumers allocate their expenditure among individual goods until the ratio of the prices of all goods is equal to the ratio of their marginal utilities or marginal rates of substitution. The analysis was static throughout; it simply assumed that all income was spent on economic goods. Once considerations of the future are introduced, it is necessary to recognize that rational consumers will be concerned with future as well as present satisfaction. The services yielded by some goods (assets) are spread out over long periods of time. Households must therefore decide on the proportion of their current income they will devote to asset accumulation. This chapter considers the forces that determine household demand for current consumption goods and services and household demand to save and accumulate assets.

HOUSEHOLD CONSUMPTION AND SAVING BEHAVIOR

All real economic goods produced by an economy may be divided into two types: consumption goods and investment goods. *Consumption goods* are goods consumed and used up within the period of analysis. *Investment goods* are goods produced but not consumed within the period. This distinction is important because investment goods yield their services over some future period and thus permit an increase of output and consumption in the future.

Saving is defined as the proportion of income earned within any period that is not spent on consumption goods:

$$S \equiv Y - C$$

As saving represents income earned but not spent to purchase consumption goods, such income must be devoted to the accumulation of assets and so result in an increase in the consumer's wealth. Saving thus represents the demand to accumulate assets, i.e., long-lived economic goods.

Lifetime Utility, Income, and Consumption

Utility is derived from future as well as present consumption. Optimizing consumers may be assumed to act to maximize expected utility over their entire lifetimes. This hypothesis is consistent with evidence on household spending behavior.

Table 4-1 shows how household income and consumption vary with the age of the consumer. Household income is not constant over the life cycle but rises with age to some peak earning level and then gradually declines, falling off sharply after retirement. Households consume a larger portion of their current income in those years when their income is below their lifetime average and a smaller proportion during the peak earning years. Saving is used to build up a buffer of assets to smooth out the impact of changes in income on consumption. In this way households spread con-

Table 4-1 HOUSEHOLD INCOME AND CONSUMPTION BY AGE OF HEAD OF HOUSEHOLD, 1960–61

Age of Family Head	Money Income After Taxes	Expenditures for Current Consumption	Consumption Expenditures as Percent of Money Income	Net Change in Assets and Liabilities	Percentage of all Families	Average Age of Family Head
Under 25	4234	4317	102	−121	4.8	22
25–34	5730	5458	95	159	18.5	30
35–44	6752	6223	92	231	22.1	39
45–54	6687	5925	89	302	19.7	49
55–64	5340	4576	86	289	15.9	59
65–74	3695	3220	87	125	13.1	69
75 and older	2566	2347	91	40	5.9	80

Source: Survey of Consumer Finances, Board of Governors, Federal Reserve System.

sumption more evenly over their entire lifetimes. This fact is consistent with the existence of some *lifetime utility function.*

In Figure 4-1 income and consumption are measured on the vertical axis and the age of the household unit is measured on the horizontal axis. Saving represents the difference between income and consumption. The distance *OW* represents the household's expected working life, and the distance *WR* its expected retirement horizon. Lifetime income and consumption paths are shown by the curves *YY* and *CC.*

Households deficit spend and go into debt when they are young to accumulate durable assets such as houses, cars, furniture, and appliances. They then save to accumulate financial assets and a positive net worth to finance consumption spending during their retirement years. In Table 4-1, older households as a group did not dissave in their retirement. Individuals also save during their working lifetimes to provide bequests for their children. In this case utility extends beyond the lifetime of a single individual.

The dissaving of retired households operates to offset the positive saving of other households in their working life. Total saving by the household sector is thus positively related and extremely sensitive to the rate of growth of population and per capita income. Given these variables, total household saving will be a relatively stable proportion of total household income over time.

Lifetime Wealth

Saving necessarily increases household net wealth. This consequence is shown in Figure 4-2, in which the income and consumption streams of Figure 4-1 are cumulated over time. The household is represented as starting life with initial net wealth B_0 and as planning its lifetime consumption in such a way as to leave some positive terminal bequest B_1.

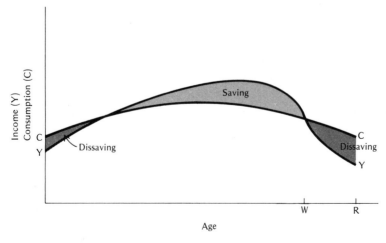

Figure 4-1 Lifetime Income, Consumption, and Saving

The hypothesis that households attempt to maximize some lifetime utility function implies that present household consumption expenditures are based on some expectation of lifetime income and future consumption needs. Providing households can borrow or have assets to expend, temporary changes in the level of current income will have a small effect on current consumption, except insofar as they affect expectations of lifetime income. Short-run changes in current income will result primarily in fluctuations in current saving and net wealth, which act as a buffer to stabilize consumption expenditures over a household's lifetime.

The effect of short-run increases and decreases in current income on household consumption, saving, and wealth is shown in Figure 4-3, which reproduces the lifetime income consumption and wealth relationships of Figure 4-2. For simplicity of graphical presentation, planned consumption is shown as evenly spread over the household's entire expected lifetime, and both initial wealth and target bequest are assumed to be zero. In the period (t_0) in which the change in income (ΔY) occurs, consumption is only slightly affected. The main effect falls on current saving and total wealth.

An Aggregate Consumption Function

Aggregate consumption expenditure is simply the aggregate of all individual household expenditures on consumption goods. Just as an indefinitely large number of factors influence the quantity of any individual commodity demanded, an indefinitely large number of forces determine total consumption expenditures. Relative prices of different consumption goods play a major role in determining the quantity demanded of any individual good. They are much less important in determining aggregate consumption expenditures, as changes in relative prices tend to cancel each other in their effects on total expenditure for consumption. The previous evidence and analysis suggest that the most important determinants of aggregate consumption expenditures will be the level and growth rate of the households' lifetime incomes and the distribution of the households in different phases of their life cycles. Other determinants will be the size and composition of the existing stock of assets and debts, the expected return to wealth ownership, desired target bequests to the next generation, and the multitude of factors that affect consumption expectations and attitudes toward thrift.

The hypothesis that present consumption is some function of lifetime income, wealth, asset returns, and tastes may be formulated by the following functional relationship:

$C = C(Y, W, r, T)$

The relevant magnitudes for consumption behavior are the anticipated values of future income, wealth, returns, and consumption needs in the mind of the household decision-maker. Unfortunately these subjective expected values are never directly measurable. A central difficulty in the empirical analysis of economic behavior

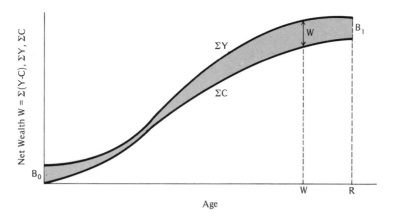

Figure 4-2 Lifetime Wealth

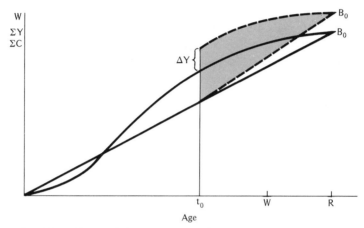

a. Unanticipated Increase in Income

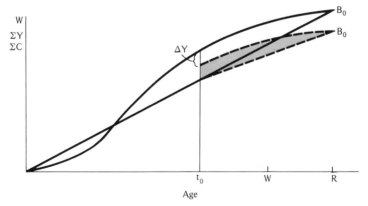

b. Unanticipated Decrease in Income

Figure 4-3 The Effect of Short-Run Changes in Income on Lifetime Consumption,
Saving, and Net Wealth

thus arises. The theoretically relevant variables are ordinarily not identical to the variables for which it is possible to obtain direct evidence. Much effort in empirical research must be devoted to the search for "proxy" variables that can be used successfully to represent the theoretically appropriate but not operationally measurable variables.

Long-Run Consumption Behavior

Over the long run the relationship between household disposable income and household consumption would be expected to remain reasonably stable. This hypothesis is supported by the data in Diagram 4-1, which shows relationship between these variables for the postwar period in the United States.

Diagram 4-1, termed a *scatter diagram,* shows graphically the relationship between the two variables. Each point represents the value of the two variables for a particular observation. If no relationship is apparent, the scatter diagram will be diffuse and cloudlike. In Diagram 4-1 a strong positive relationship between income and consumption at different points in time is observed. This relationship, summarized by the straight line drawn through the center of the scatter, describes the *long-run consumption function.*

The long-run consumption function in Diagram 4-1 is a straight line through the

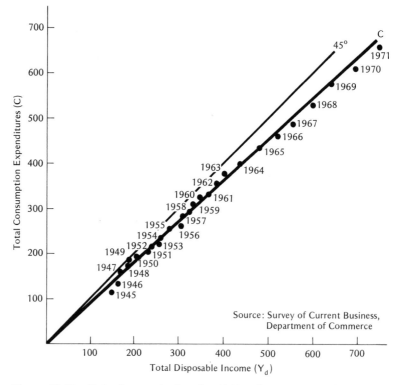

Diagram 4-1 Time Series Consumption Function, 1945-71 (Billions of Dollars)

origin with a slope of .93, which indicates that, on the average, 93 per cent of household disposable income was spent on consumption goods and 7 per cent was saved. The ratio of *total consumption* to *total income* is termed the *average propensity to consume* (APC = C/Y).

The *marginal propensity to consume* is defined as the *change in consumption* associated with a *change in income* (MPC = $\Delta C/\Delta Y$). It is represented by the *slope* of the consumption function. Over the long run, the average and marginal long-run propensities to consume were identical. Proportionate changes in income resulted over the long run in equal proportionate changes in consumption and savings.

Short-Run Consumption Behavior

The relationship between changes in income and changes in consumption is flatter and much less stable in the short run, as is illustrated in Diagram 4-2, which plots annual changes in disposable income and in consumption over the same period. In addition to changes in current income, it appears that a large number of other forces affect the change in consumption spending from year to year, as indicated by the number of points located off the line drawn to summarize the central relationship.

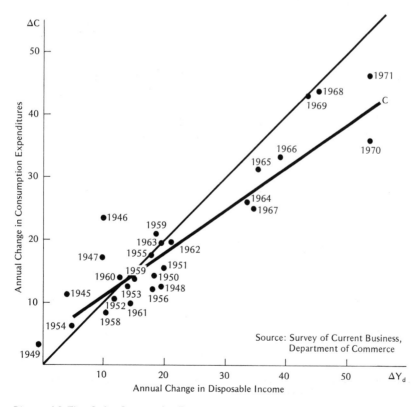

Diagram 4-2 Time Series Consumption Function 1945-71 (Annual Changes, Billions of Dollars)

HOUSEHOLD ECONOMIC BEHAVIOR: DYNAMIC ANALYSIS **81**

In Diagram 4-2, the slope of the short-run consumption function is flatter than the slope of the long-run consumption function of Diagram 4-1. In the short run the marginal propensity to consume out of income is lower, and less than the average propensity to consume.

With quarterly data the relationship between changes in disposable income and changes in consumption is even looser, as shown in Diagram 4-3, in which quarterly changes in consumption and income are plotted for the last four years of the period. Although there is a slight suggestion of a positive relationship in the extreme values, for all but seven quarters consumption increased within a relatively narrow range, between $5 and $12 billion per quarter. These changes appear to be largely independent of the accompanying change in disposable income. Changes in household *willingness* to spend in the short run are largely independent of changes in household *ability* to spend.

It may be concluded that in the short run changes in disposable income ordinarily generate much smaller changes in current consumption expenditure than in the long run. This is summarized in Figure 4-4, which presents the short-run relationships of consumption expenditure and saving to disposable income. Saving is defined as all income not consumed. The saving function is therefore constructed from the difference between the consumption function and the 45-degree line. At the income level

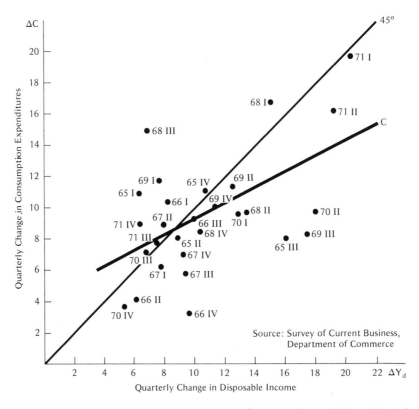

Diagram 4-3 Time Series Consumption Function 1965-71 (Quarterly Changes, Billions of Dollars) (Seasonally Adjusted Annual Rate)

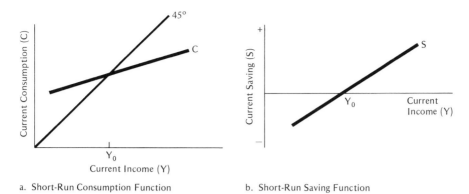

a. Short-Run Consumption Function   b. Short-Run Saving Function

Figure 4-4 Short-Run Consumption and Saving Behavior

where the consumption function crosses the 45-degree line, saving is zero. The short-run average propensity to save rises with income, because the marginal propensity to save exceeds the average propensity to save.

The lifetime income hypothesis is consistent with this empirical evidence of household consumption behavior. The flatter slope of the short-run consumption function is due to the fact that household consumption is dependent on the level of expected lifetime income, which changes only gradually and erratically with changes in current income and expectations. An average of past consumption and income, approximately weighted and adjusted for trend, provides a much better explanatory variable for current consumption than does current income. It may be regarded as a proxy for permanent income. This relationship suggests why the observed association between short-term changes in current income and consumption is extremely weak, while the longer-run relationship is quite stable.

DIFFERENCES IN HOUSEHOLD CONSUMPTION AND SAVING BEHAVIOR

The amount of wealth owned and income received varies widely among households. Household income is received from various sources: wages, salaries, interest, dividends, rent, and capital gains. Similarly, household wealth is held in various forms, each with different rates of return. Households differ in age, number of children, education, and a wide variety of noneconomic characteristics that affect needs and tastes and so influence consumption and saving behavior. In developing a theory to predict heterogeneous household consumption expenditure, each of these explanatory variables must be included and where necessary disaggregated.

Cross-Section Consumption Behavior

Table 4-2 presents data on the relationship between income and consumption for selected types of household units in the United States. As may be seen, households

Table 4-2   HOUSEHOLD CONSUMPTION EXPENDITURE BY TYPE HOUSEHOLD, 1960–61

Type of Household	Average Money Income and Consumption Expenditures					Family Characteristics		
	Money Income After Taxes	Net change in Assets and Liabili- ties	Expenditures for Current Consumption	Consumption Expenditures on Percent of Money Income	Percent of all Families	Average Age of Family Head	Average Education of Family Head (Year)	Percent Nonwhite
All Families (mean)	5,557	199	5,047	91	100	48	10	11
Money Income After Taxes								
Under $1,000	535	−722	1,276	239	3.7	66	6	17
$1,000– 1,999	1,521	−201	1,781	117	10.2	61	7	23
$2,000– 2,999	2,507	−181	2,670	107	11.1	54	8	18
$3,000– 3,999	3,515	−193	3,636	103	11.8	48	9	15
$4,000– 4,999	4,505	−4	4,428	98	13.3	44	10	10
$5,000– 5,999	5,491	69	5,172	94	12.7	43	11	8
$6,000– 7,499	6,707	210	6,125	91	15.1	43	11	6
$7,500– 9,999	8,554	524	7,416	87	13.4	44	12	4
$10,000–14,999	11,723	1099	9,521	81	6.8	47	13	4
$15,000–and over	21,926	5158	14,208	65	2.0	51	14	1
Education of Family Head (Years)								
8 or less	3,956	86	3,657	92	36.5	56	6	16
9–12	5,786	162	5,338	92	43.1	44	11	9
13–16	7,518	383	6,666	89	16.4	43	15	4
Over 16	9,709	874	7,992	82	4.0	42	17	3
Color of Family Head								
White	5,772	220	5,219	90	89.3	48	10	0
Black	3,584	—	3,465	97	9.6	47	8	100

Source: Survey of Consumer Finances, Board of Governors, Federal Reserve Board.

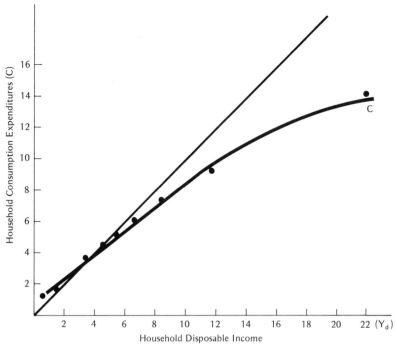

Source: Table 4-2

Diagram 4-4 Cross-Section Consumption Function, 1960-61 (Thousands of Dollars)

with higher incomes spend larger amounts on consumption, but their average and marginal propensities to consume declines.

This relationship between household consumption and income level at one point in time is plotted in Diagram 4-4. It is termed a *cross-section consumption function*. As may be seen, the slope of the consumption function (the marginal propensity to consume) declines at upper income levels. The cross-section consumption function of Diagram 4-4 shows how consumption expenditures are related to income levels at any one time. Each point on the curve represents average consumption expenditures for all households within that income class.

The converse relationship between income level and household saving is presented in Table 4-3. The average and marginal propensities to save rise with income level. As shown, in 1961 saving was significantly negative at lower income levels, rising to nearly 30 percent of income for income units earning over $15,000.

Because of dissaving by lower-income households, a very large proportion of total household saving is accounted for by upper income groups. As shown in Table 4-3, the richest 15 percent of households accounted for more than half of total household saving, while the poorest 50 percent of households accounted for only about 10 percent of total saving. Unrealized capital gains are not included in money income as reported. Because capital gains are concentrated in the upper income groups, saving including capital gains is much more highly concentrated.

As may be seen from Table 4-2, a multitude of economic and noneconomic factors

Table 4-3 HOUSEHOLD SAVING BY INCOME LEVEL

Income Class	1961-62 Average Money Income After Taxes in Dollars	1961-62 Average Savings in Dollars	1961-62 As Percent of Income	1963 Percentage of Consumer Units	1963 Percentage of Aggregate Saving
All Consumer Units (mean)	5,557	498	9.0	100.0	100.0
Under $1,000	535	−691	−129	8.3	−4.1
$ 1,000–$ 1,999	1,519	−172	−11	10.3	−3.5
$ 2,000–$ 2,999	2,507	− 93	− 4	9.4	3.4
$ 3,000–$ 3,999	3,515	− 45	− 1	11.4	6.2
$ 4,000–$ 4,999	4,504	232	5	10.9	9.7
$ 5,000–$ 5,999	5,491	370	7	10.1	8.9
$ 6,000–$ 7,499	6,707	598	9	12.3	11.8
$ 7,500–$ 9,999	8,554	1,036	12	14.8	22.7
$10,000–$14,999	11,723	1,787	15	9.3	28.1
$15,000–and over	21,926	6,335	29	3.2	16.7

Number of Units (Millions) 1963 . . . 57.9
Amount of Saving (Billions) 1963 . . . $56.2

Source: Survey of Consumer Finances, Board of Governors, Federal Reserve System.

such as wealth, education, expectations, occupation, location, and ethnic group also affect consumption expenditures. Consumption expenditures and saving by individual households in any income class would be represented by a wide scatter of points above and below the curves in Diagram 4-4.

SAVING, INVESTMENT, AND THE DEMAND FOR ASSETS

Saving is defined as the proportion of income not spent on current consumption:

$$S \equiv Y - C$$

Income not spent for consumption goods must be used to accumulate assets or to retire debt. There are no other alternatives to consumption expenditures. As a result, saving also represents the demand to acquire assets or to repay debt.

This can be illustrated in a simplified balance sheet. The economic unit's total assets are listed on the left-hand side and total liabilities on the right-hand side. The difference, total assets minus total liabilities, is termed *net worth* and represents the economic unit's *net equity* or net wealth ownership.

Balance Sheet

Financial Assets	X	Total Liabilities	X
Real Assets	X	Net Worth	X
		Total Liabilities	
Total Assets	XX	plus Net Worth	XX

Purchasing power to acquire additional assets may come from borrowing, which results in an increase in liabilities, or from saving, which results in an increase in net worth. As a balance sheet must always balance, savings, which results in an increase in net worth, necessarily must also result in an increase in total assets and/or a reduction in debt.

Assets refer to all goods that are long-lived and so yield their stream of services over some future period. Assets are of two types, real and financial.

Real Assets

Real assets refer to all economic goods that yield a valuable stream of future service in kind. Land, producer durable goods (plant, equipment), consumer durable goods (houses, homes, automobiles) — each represents different types of real assets. Real assets constitute the productive capital of an economy and increase the amount of real goods and services that the economy can produce and enjoy now and in the future.

Some real assets are demanded for the direct consumption services in kind that they yield, as in the case of consumer durables and houses. Others are demanded for the production services that they yield, as in the case of business plant, equipment, and inventories, which when combined with labor produce saleable commodities.

Financial Assets

Financial assets are simply pieces of paper that represent a legally enforceable promise by the issuer to pay money or its equivalent in the future. They record a loan of purchasing power by lenders and a claim against borrowers. For every financial asset owned by economic units there is a corresponding financial liability owed by other economic units. As a result, for the economy as a whole total financial assets equal total financial liabilities. Financial assets do not add to the real productive wealth or output of an economy but affect a transfer of income from asset issuers to asset owners. They play a crucial role in the saving, investment, and wealth ownership process in capitalist economies. The savings of asset purchasers are made available through the capital market to finance the investment spending of asset issuers.

Financial assets are demanded for their expected future return, which is received in money and in various nonmonetary services-in-kind. They are issued to provide debtor economic units with greater present purchasing power than their current income. There exist a wide variety of financial assets in developed capitalist economies. Notes, bonds, and mortgages are issued by households, businesses, and governments; currency, demand deposits, saving deposits, insurance policies, and pension claims are issued by government and private financial institutions; and equities are issued by business corporations.

Investment and Saving

For purposes of economic analysis, the term *investment* denotes only the accumulation of *currently produced real assets* by an economic unit. This definition differs from the colloquial meaning of investment that includes the accumulation of financial assets — for example, investment in common stocks.

The reason for this distinction is that for the economy as a whole, unlike an individual wealth-owner, the accumulation of financial assets does not represent an increase in real capital or wealth. An increase in financial assets owned by some units is always and necessarily accompanied by a reduction in the financial assets owned or an increase in the liabilities owed by other economic units. Financial assets represent claims of one economic unit against another. Similarly, the accumulation of existing (previously produced or nonproduceable) real assets merely represents a transfer of ownership, not a net addition to the economy's stock of real capital.

Saving thus represents all additions to net worth, which imply real and/or financial asset accumulation and/or debt reduction. Investment refers only to the accumulation of currently produced real assets by an economic unit. The accumulation of financial assets and previously existing real assets is a form of saving by the economic unit in question.

Human Capital

All wealth represents the *discounted present value* (see Chapter 9) of expected future income streams. Different types of income are discounted at various rates, depending on the degree of uncertainty surrounding the expectations and the marketability of the income-producing asset.

As labor cannot be bought and sold as an asset in a nonslave economy, but only the services of labor can be exchanged, the present value of expected future labor income (human capital) does not appear in conventional balance sheets. Although households cannot put up their human capital as collateral for a loan, the value of human capital, as reflected in their expected lifetime labor income, exerts an important influence on household spending behavior.

Expenditure on education and training can be regarded as an investment in human capital insofar as it increases the future expected labor income. Human capital is thus a kind of intangible asset that increases labor productivity and therefore the real wealth of the possessor. Educated workers enter the labor force with large amounts of human capital, which increases their ability and willingness to consume.

The Demand for Assets

Economic activity is a kind of game, and assets represent the chips. All assets represent a generalized store of value insofar as they can be sold and exchanged for other things. Total wealth enters household utility functions by providing a command against future commodities, a reserve against contingencies, power, prestige, and satisfaction from ownership.

Table 4-4 presents the chief categories of real and financial assets owned and debts owed by households in the United States at selected dates. There have been large fluctuations in the level of household balance sheets, particularly during the depression of the 1930s and World War II. But over the long run the proportions have exhibited considerable stability, with households preferring to hold about two thirds of their wealth in the form of financial assets. The ratio of debt to assets has increased over the post war period from 5 to 12 percent. In 1968 the total value of household assets exceeded $3000 billion, of which about $1000 billion was in real assets.

The composition of household wealth portfolios varies considerably by wealth level. As shown in Table 4-5, wealthier households hold a smaller proportion of their

Balance Sheet Item	1900 Dollars	1900 Percent	1929 Dollars	1929 Percent	1933 Dollars	1933 Percent	1945 Dollars	1945 Percent	1958 Dollars	1958 Percent	1968 Dollars	1968 Percent
Tangible Assets												
Residential Structures	15.2	25	79.4	18	61.7	20	123.7	20	346.8	22	567.1	17
Land	7.5	12	33.8	8	24.6	8	28.3	5	92.2	6	250.9	7
Consumer Durables	5.2	8	38.4	9	23.8	8	41.0	7	164.7	10	233.8	7
Total	29.1	47	157.6	35	115.2	37	200.1	32	632.0	39	1051.8	31
Financial Assets												
Currency and Demand Deposits	1.5	2	8.6	2	11.2	4	49.9	8	61.4	4	107.4	3
Other Bank Deposits	3.4	6	30.5	7	25.8	8	52.8	8	140.6	9	355.1	11
Life Insurance Reserves	1.4	2	15.8	4	8.9	3	41.0	7	99.7	6	} 465.6	} 14
Pension and Retirement Funds	—	—	1.9	—	3.4	1	28.0	4	93.5	6		
Mortgages	3.8	6	17.1	4	13.3	4	10.5	2	27.3	2	34.5	1
Bonds and Notes	4.4	7	36.8	8	40.9	13	80.0	13	94.5	6	114.2	3
Common and Preferred Stock	10.7	17	138.3	31	57.1	18	111.6	18	343.0	21	828.0	25
Total	32.4	53	290.5	65	195.4	63	422.6	68	969.8	61	2312.0	69
Liabilities												
Consumer Debt	.5	1	6.4	1	3.2	1	5.4	1	44.8	3 }	161.4	5
Loans	1.2	2	15.4	3	9.8	3	6.1	1	12.7	1 }		
Mortgages	2.6	4	18.0	4	14.6	5	18.5	3	117.0	7	241.1	7
Total	4.5	7	41.8	9	29.4	9	30.5	5	176.3	11	409.8	12
Net Worth	57.0	93	406.2	91	281.3	91	592.2	95	1,425.5	89	2954.0	88
Total Assets, Total Liabilities plus Net Worth	61.5	100	448.1	100	310.6	100	622.7	100	1,609.9	100	3363.8	100

Source: 1900–1958: Raymond Goldsmith, Robert Lipsey, Morris Mendelson, Studies in the National Balance Sheet of the United States, Vol. II, Table III-1. 1968: Institutional Investor Study Report of the Securities and Exchange Commission Supplementary Volume I (Washington, 1971), Table IB-2.

wealth in the form of real assets, homes, and automobiles and a much larger proportion in financial assets. Investment assets, primarily corporate stock, rise substantially as a proportion of total wealth as wealth level rises. Liquid assets, currency, and demand and savings deposits fall as a proportion of total portfolios as total wealth increases.

Household demand to hold wealth in different asset forms is based on the same general principles applicable to the demand for other commodities. Individual assets have widely different nonmonetary services-in-kind associated with them. Consumption services are derived directly from ownership of a home, a car, and a painting; exchange convenience (means of payment) from currency and demand deposits; income, liquidity, and security from claims against a variety of financial institutions; and dividends and anticipated capital gains from corporate stock.

The total stock of assets that a household demands will depend on the household's initial wealth and income, its expected future income relative to its expected future consumption needs, the return, both pecuniary and nonpecuniary, expected from asset ownership, and the costs of borrowing. The higher the return assets are expected to yield, the greater the future income and the amount of future goods and services that can be consumed for any given amount of saving and sacrifice of consumption in the present. *Ceteris paribus,* a reduction in the market price of an asset (a rise in its expected rate of return) will increase the amount of that asset demanded in household portfolios.

Risk and Diversification

In an uncertain world wealth owners cannot know exactly their future income, life horizon, needs, or the return that various assets will yield over the future. In some periods the actual return may be lower than the expected return. Wealth owners generally are adverse to bearing risk, a fact which may be explained as due to the diminishing marginal utility of income. A full purse is not so good as an empty one is bad.

Because of their superior marketability and lower risk, financial assets dominate most real assets as a store of value in household portfolios. As shown in Tables 4-4 and 4-5, rather than put all their eggs in one basket and hold the financial asset with the highest expected return, households chose to hold many different assets. Portfolio *diversification* enables wealth owners to reduce risk and render less probable the likelihood and extent that an unexpected unfavorable event will reduce their future income and wealth. Diversification at the same time implies some sacrifice of gain.

As a result, in addition to expected return the demand for assets is related to the risk of unfavorable outcomes. A reduction in an asset's expected risk, in particular the degree to which its return is likely to decline with that of other assets, will raise the amount of that asset demanded for wealth portfolios.

Wealth owners have some *preferred portfolio composition* of different assets.

Table 4-5 HOUSEHOLD WEALTH PORTFOLIOS BY WEALTH LEVEL (CONSUMER UNITS, 1962): MEAN DOLLAR AMOUNTS AND PERCENTAGE OF TOTAL WEALTH

				Real Assets			
	Total Wealth		Own Home		Automobile		Business, Profession (Farm and Nonfarm)
	Mean	Percent	Mean	Percent	Mean	Percent	Mean	Percent
All Units	20,982	100	5,653	27	644	3	3,881	18
Size of Wealth								
$1–999	396	100	40	10	190	48	9	2
$1,000–4,999	2,721	100	1,298	48	445	16	83	3
$5,000–9,999	7,267	100	4,260	59	614	8	625	9
$10,000–24,999	16,047	100	8,852	55	850	5	1,499	9
$25,000–49,999	35,191	100	12,991	37	1,134	3	6,644	19
$50,000–99,999	68,980	100	14,167	21	1,499	2	16,719	24
$100,000–199,999	132,790	100	22,790	17	2,232	2	22,938	17
$200,000–499,999	300,355	100	25,889	9	2,326	1	72,516	24
$500,000 and over	1,260,667	100	56,232	4	2,679	*	295,035	23

*Less than 1/2 of 1 Percent

Source: Survey of Consumer Finances, Board of Governors, Federal Reserve System.

This preferred portfolio will vary for different wealth owners, depending on their preferences, future needs, and attitude toward risk. It will also vary with asset prices, expected return, and risk.

There is considerable empirical evidence that households adjust their portfolio holdings only gradually in response to a change in asset return-risk differentials. This *speed of adjustment* will depend on the costs of transactions, information, and decision-making involved in asset management. As a result, a considerable period of time is likely to elapse before a household reaches a new position of portfolio equilibrium in response to a change in tastes or in asset return-risk opportunities.

APPENDIX: ACCOUNTING, INDIFFERENCE ANALYSIS, AND CONSUMPTION

The relationship between saving, investment, consumption, and changes in an economic unit's wealth can be better understood with the aid of some fundamental accounting concepts.

It is important to distinguish two dimensions by which economic variables may be measured — flows and stocks. *Flows* refer to phenomena that occur over periods of time. Income, consumption, investment, production, and sales are flow magnitudes, and all have a time dimension, a quantity per month or per year. *Stocks* refer to phenomena existing at a moment of time. Wealth, capital, land, population, money, bonds, equities and all assets are stock magnitudes, quantities existing at a moment of time. Flow magnitudes enter the income and expenditure statement of

Financial Assets					
Portfolio of Liquid Assets		Portfolio of Investment Assets		Miscellaneous Assets (Trust Funds)	
Mean	Percent	Mean	Percent	Mean	Percent
2,675	13	7,013	33	1,116	5
134	34	14	4	9	2
701	26	170	6	25	1
1,227	17	440	6	100	1
2,624	16	2,054	13	168	1
6,371	18	7,518	21	533	2
10,858	16	24,556	36	1,181	2
18,808	14	64,127	48	1,894	1
21,007	7	169,052	56	9,564	3
46,094	4	628,271	50	232,355	18

economic units, while stock magnitudes enter the balance sheet of an economic unit. If a stock exists, the net flow represents the rate at which the stock is changing over time.

Prices are neither stocks nor flows but ratios. Prices express relative market values of different goods, the number of units of one that can be exchanged for another. With n different goods, each good would have n-1 different exchange ratios or prices, one for each other good, resulting in n^{n-1} different prices. The price of all goods is calculated in terms of a single common good, which forms the unit of account. This good is conventionally an asset that serves as money. Money refers to those assets generally accepted as a means of payment for all other goods.

Balance Sheet

A *balance sheet* presents a financial picture of the total stock of all assets owned and all debts owed by an economic unit at a particular moment in time. The difference between total assets and total liabilities is defined as the economic unit's net worth.

1. Net Worth $\equiv$ Total Assets $-$ Total Liabilities

$$NW \equiv A - L$$

Rearranging,

2. Total Assets $\equiv$ Total Liabilities $+$ Net Worth

$$A \equiv L + NW$$

Equations 1 and 2 are the fundamental *balance sheet identity,* the reason that balance sheets must always balance. The identity sign ≡ indicates that the equality holds by definition, whatever the value of the variables. It follows that a change in assets must always be accompanied by an identical change in liabilities and net worth:

$$\Delta A \equiv \Delta L + \Delta NW$$

BALANCE SHEET

Assets			Total Liabilities and Net Worth	
Financial Assets (FA)			Liabilities (L)	
Cash	100		Debt	500
Bonds	200			
Equities	300	600		
Real Assets (RA)			Net Worth (NW)	1,000
Real Estate	400			
Durable Goods	500	900		
Total Assets (A)		$1,500	Total Liabilities and Net Worth	$1,500

Saving as the Change in Net Worth

Saving was defined as current income not spent on current consumption:

Saving ≡ Income − Consumption, or

3. $S \equiv Y - C$

But income not consumed must be used to accumulate assets or to retire debt. As is seen from the fundamental balance sheet equation, saving, the demand to acquire assets or to repay debt, is identically equal to the change in net worth from the beginning of the period to the end of the period:

4. $S \equiv \Delta A - \Delta L \equiv \Delta NW$

As seen from the balance sheet identity, borrowing, the issue of debt, permits economic units to accumulate assets in excess of their current saving. Rewriting Equation 4, we have:

5. $\Delta L = \Delta A - \Delta NW = \Delta A - S$

Deficit and Surplus Spending Behavior

Saving, investment, and borrowing decisions all affect an economic unit's balance sheet and are sometimes referred to as capital account transactions.

The net accumulation of real assets (ΔRA) may be financed out of current saving (ΔNW), new borrowing (ΔL), or out of past savings by the sale of previously accumulated financial assets $(-\Delta FA)$.Only the accumulation of currently produced real assets is defined as investment spending, since the purchase of previously existing assets does not add to the economy's capital stock, but merely represents a transfer of ownership.

6. $\quad \Delta RA \equiv (\Delta NW + \Delta L - \Delta FA)$

The accumulation of financial assets has no special term in economic analysis but is simply one component of saving.

7. $\quad S \equiv \Delta NW \equiv (\Delta RA + \Delta FA - \Delta L)$

As seen from Equation 6, an economic unit is able to spend for real asset accumulation a greater amount than it saves only by borrowing or by the sale of existing assets. Such economic units are termed *deficit spenders,* as their total current expenditure for consumption and investment goods exceeds their current income.

8. $\quad (C + I) - Y \equiv (I - S) \equiv (\Delta L - \Delta FA) > 0$

Economic units that invest less than they save are termed *surplus spenders,* as their total current expenditure for consumption and investment goods is less than their current income. Current surpluses may be devoted either to the accumulation of financial assets or to the reduction of outstanding debts.

9. $\quad Y - (C + I) \equiv (S - I) \equiv (\Delta FA - \Delta L) > 0$

Household units in the aggregate are surplus-spending units, while business and government units in the aggregate are deficit-spending units. As will later be demonstrated, surplus-spending households purchase the financial assets issued by deficit-spending business and government units. In this way the savings of households are mobilized through the financial markets to finance the investment spending of business and government units.

Depreciation

Assets are simply economic goods that possess durability and yield their services over some period of time. As a result, the particular goods defined as consumption goods and treated as consumed and used up during a given period will determine the measured magnitudes of consumption, saving, and investment. It is very difficult to establish the future life span of many goods; it is more so for services. The dividing line between consumption (short-lived) and investment (long-lived) goods is necessarily arbitrary.

The purchase of consumer durable goods (automobiles, appliances, houses) has both a consumption and an investment component. The consumption component is the value of the services enjoyed during the period. The amount of an asset used up over a particular period is termed *depreciation.*

The purchase of a new car valued at $3,000, with an expected lifetime of six years, represents both a consumption and an investment expenditure. If the car is assumed to depreciate by an equal amount each year, $500 of the automobile's value is used up each year during the life of the car. In the year of purchase the consumer would have invested and saved $2,500 in an automobile. Because of the practical difficulty of estimating the value of outstanding stocks and rates of depreciation, most durable consumer goods (houses are the important exception) are treated in the national income accounts as consumption goods, as if they were fully consumed in the year of purchase.

In the case of business investment in plant and equipment it is necessary to calculate depreciation expense, the amount used up in the period, in order to determine the total cost of producing economic goods. Depreciation expenses are estimated

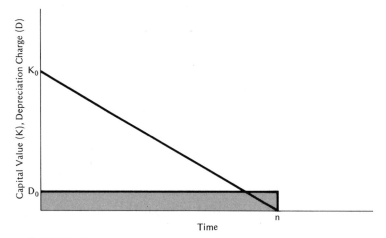

a. Straight-Line Depreciation

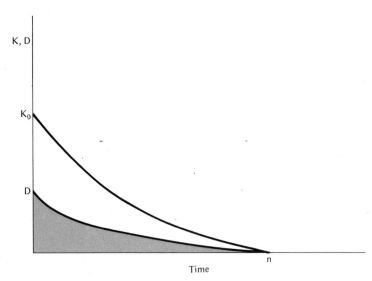

b. Accelerated Depreciation

Figure 4-5 The Estimation of Depreciation and Capital Value

rather arbitrarily by calculating the expected lifetime of the capital good and then writing off as depreciation some amount each year.

Figure 4-5 presents graphically two common approaches to estimating depreciation. With *straight-line* depreciation (Figure 4-5a) a constant amount of depreciation (D_0) is charged each year over the entire lifetime (n) of the investment good. With *accelerated* depreciation (Figure 4-5b) a constant proportion of the outstanding value of the asset is charged as depreciation each year. With accelerated depreciation the charge is higher in the initial years and declines as the good ages.

Indifference Analysis Applied to Saving Behavior

Indifference analysis can be applied fruitfully to saving behavior and the demand for assets. The assumption of indifference analysis that all income is spent and the consumer is on his budget restraint line is valid only if assets are included as one good.

The devotion of present income to the accumulation of assets permits a household to consume greater amounts in the future. Conversely borrowing permits greater consumption in the present at the expense of future consumption. The higher the return that assets offer, the greater the future income and amount of future goods and services that can be consumed for any given amount of saving and foregone consumption in the present. Assets also yield satisfaction from nonpecuniary returns, such as prestige and influence accruing to their owner.

The total stock of assets that a household demands will depend in part on the relationship between its present and its expected future income relative to its present and expected future needs, and the return expected from asset ownership. In this way relative prices affect aggregate consumption and saving expenditure.

Relative price effects are illustrated in Figure 4-6 for a simple two-period model, in which present income (Y_P) and consumption (C_P) are measured on the horizontal axis and future income (Y_F) and consumption (C_F) on the vertical axis. The indifference curves (I) represent preferences between present and future consumption. The slope of the consumption possibility line (BB) through the point P ($Y_P Y_F$) represents the price of future goods in terms of present goods. It is equal to one plus the rate of return on assets (r_0). The extension of the budget line BB leftward from the point $Y_P Y_F$ reflects the fact that present income may be saved and spent in the future. The extension of the budget line BB rightward from the point $Y_P Y_F$ reflects the fact that future income may be discounted and spent in the present. These operations of compound interest and discount relating present and future will be developed in Chapter 9.

Saving is the difference between present income and consumption ($Y_P - C_P$). Figure 4-6 illustrates that there are an indefinitely large number of possible combinations of present and future income ($Y_P Y_F$), all on the same consumption possibility line BB. Given preferences between present and future consumption, which determine the shape of the indifference curves, current saving will be greater the

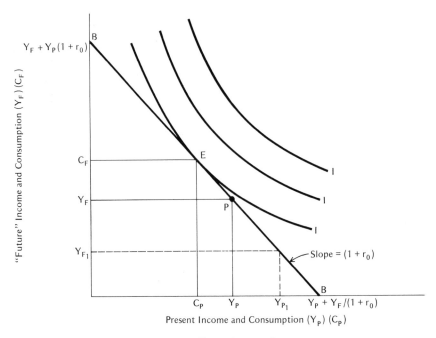

Figure 4-6 Interest Rates and Present Versus Future Consumption

larger is present income (Y_{P_1}) relative to expected future income (Y_{F_1}). Consumption is not a regular proportion of current income but of lifetime income.

Interest Inelasticity of Saving

The higher the rate of return on assets (r) the steeper the budget line BB, which reflects the fact that more future income can be enjoyed from present saving, more future goods consumed by foregoing consumption of present goods, and fewer present goods enjoyed by the sacrifice of future goods. It is in this sense that *the rate of return is the price of time*.

In Figure 4-7, with a higher rate of return (r_1), the budget line becomes B_1B_1. The household chooses the new combination of present and future goods $(C_{P_1} C_{F_1})$, with larger future consumption but nearly the same present consumption. Whether present consumption (and present saving) will increase or decrease in response to a change in return will depend on the tastes (the shape of the indifference map) and the location of P, the relationship between present and future income.

Higher rates of return on assets may be regarded as raising the price of present consumption in terms of future consumption. The *substitution effect* thus tends to induce people, in response to a rise in asset returns, to consume less present goods relative to future goods, that is, to save a greater proportion of their present income. But higher returns on assets also increase expected real income in the future. The *income effect* of higher returns tends to induce people to consume more of both

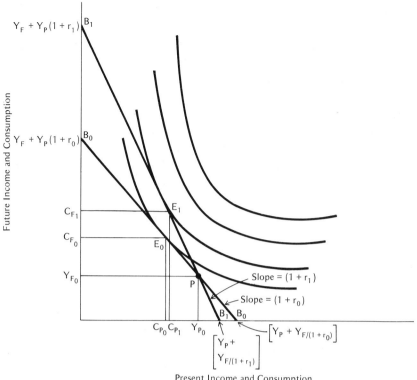

Figure 4-7 The Effect of a Change in Interest Rates

present and future goods and so to reduce current saving. The income effect will be greater the higher the ratio of present to expected future income, that is, the lower the position of the point P on the BB line.

Most empirical studies indicate that saving is relatively inelastic to changes in the return on assets. The substitution and income effects of a change in the rate of return on assets thus tend largely to offset one another, as illustrated in Figure 4-7.

Reconciliation of Cross-section and Time Series Consumption Behavior

On the basis of cross-section studies of household behavior, economists first believed that consumption was closely related to the level of household income as illustrated in Diagram 4-4. If this were indeed the "true" relationship, it would imply that, as disposable income rises over time with an economy's growth and more and more households move into higher income levels, the aggregate average propensity to consume would fall and the aggregate average propensity to save would rise. Household saving would rise as a proportion of current income. Many economists and others believed there would be a continual problem of under-consumption in mature economies.

In fact, as shown by the behavior of consumption and income over time illustrated in Diagrams 4-1 and 4-2, the cross-section relationship does not hold over time. The average propensities to consume and save remain remarkably constant over long periods of time. In the short run, changes in consumption are not related to changes in income in the manner in which the cross-section consumption function implies. As a result, the hypothesis that consumption was a function only of the absolute level of current income had to be abandoned.

The concept of permanent or lifetime income was shown to provide an explanation of the observed short-run and long-run relationship between consumption and income. This explanation holds irrespective of the shape of the cross-section consumption function. It was only gradually realized that the observed relation between consumption and income of households at different *levels* of income does not imply the logically distinct proposition that aggregate household consumption spending will follow this same relationship in response to *changes* in aggregate income.

There remains the question of explaining observed cross-section consumption and saving behavior. Why should the rich consume a smaller proportion of their income than the poor? If lifetime income is the appropriate determinant, it would seem necessary to introduce systematic differences in expectations, tastes, or risks to explain why rich and poor should not consume the same constant proportion of their lifetime incomes.

One explanation lies in the fact that consumption is relatively insensitive to short-run changes in income. At any moment in time the distribution of measured income among households does not reflect the distribution of lifetime income. Many households with high measured incomes, particularly those in their peak working years, are currently enjoying transitory income above their permanent lifetime level. Conversely, many households with low measured incomes, in particular the young and the old, are currently experiencing negative transitory income below their lifetime

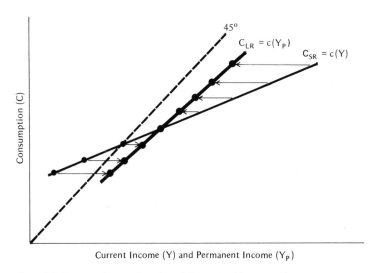

Current Income (Y) and Permanent Income (Y_P)

Figure 4-8 Consumption as a Function of Current and Permanent Income

income levels. As shown in Figure 4-8, the cross-section relationship would become more like the long-run relationship if permanent rather than measured income, which includes a positive or negative transitory income component, were measured on the horizontal axis. Current consumption expenditures must also be adjusted for the purchase and depreciation of consumer durables in order to equal permanent consumption.

A related explanation is the relative income hypothesis. Neither the absolute level of measured or permanent income may be the relevant concept determining the proportion of income consumed; rather the *relative* position in the income array. Living standards, expectations, and the very definition of subsistence and opulence are governed by the income and consumption of others in the same society. The current poverty level of $3,000 per year in the United States would be considered wildest luxury by families in most less-developed countries, where per capita income, in terms of United States dollars, is less than $100 per year.

The observed high average propensity to consume of low-income groups and the high average propensity to save of high-income groups are associated not with low or high *absolute* levels of income but with the fact that such incomes are low or high *relative* to the rest of the population. Even though household income may rise dramatically over time, the rich and poor will always be with us so long as income is not distributed equally. This relative income hypothesis or "keeping up with the Jones's" effect explains the upward shift in the cross-section consumption function over time, as shown in Figure 4-9. Each point on the long-run consumption function may be regarded as the average aggregate propensity to consume of different cross-section functions.

Another explanation for the flatter slope of the cross-section consumption function

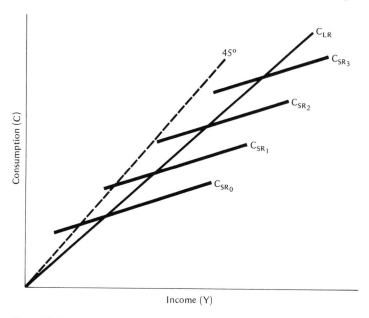

Figure 4-9 Upward Shifting of the Short-Run Consumption Function over Time

and its upward shift over time follows from the fact that consumption expenditures are affected by many variables in addition to disposable income. Demographic factors, such as the size, age distribution and rate of growth of the population, its occupational and geographic structure, the level and composition of wealth, and a wide range of sociological and historical factors affect consumption behavior. As these underlying variables have changed over time, the short-run consumption function has shifted upward.

Economists have included a large number of such explanatory variables in addition to income and wealth in an effort to explain household consumption behavior. Unfortunately these factors all tend to be dominated by strong trend movements. This phenomenon is known in statistics as the problem of *multicolinearity*. It is extremely difficult to discriminate among alternative explanatory variables when each is moving in parallel directions simultaneously.

These explanations are not sufficient to explain the observed very high saving ratios of the very rich, whose wealth already exceeds their expected lifetime consumption. These high savings ratios are due in part to the sheer difficulty of consuming very large amounts. The very wealthy must hire personal secretaries just to manage and advise them on consumption decisions. Even capital-intensive consumption takes energy and time. The relatively high level of saving of the very rich may be explained by the extension of the concept of lifetime income and utility onto the next generation. For the rich, since the return on wealth does not grow as do wages, the amount of wealth owned must increase to maintain one's heirs relatively as well off as oneself. In a growing economy workers' children will be better off than their parents even if they inherit no property, particularly if they have been given an education. Finally, satisfaction comes from asset ownership *per se,* irrespective of whether the assets are used up or consumed in the period. As works of art yield utility without depreciating and may even appreciate in value, so do many forms of real and financial assets. Satisfaction comes from playing the economic game, and not just from consumption. Less charitably expressed, pride, greed, acquisitiveness, and upward-striving to achieve success, power, and status are widely observed traits of human behavior.

the behavior
of business firms:
static analysis

THE INTELLECTUAL DISCIPLINE of economics itself becomes technicized. Technical economic analysis is substituted for the older political economy, included in which was a major concern with the moral structure of economic activity. Thus doctrine is converted into procedure. In this sphere as in others, the technicians form a closed fraternity with their own esoteric vocabulary. Moreover, they are concerned only with what is, as distinct from what ought to be.

—ROBERT K. MERTON
Introduction to *The Technological
Society* by Jacques Ellul

GRANT ME THE SERENITY to accept the things I cannot change, courage to change the things I can, and wisdom to know the difference.

—REINHOLD NIEBUHR

Business firms derive their income from the sale in product markets of goods and services to households and other business firms. With the income received from these sales they purchase labor and capital in factor markets. This chapter develops the central principles behind the supply of goods by business firms and their demand for productive factors.

PROFIT MAXIMIZATION

Utility Functions

Household economic behavior was interpreted as an attempt to maximize utility from consumption and wealth over some expected lifetime. Business behavior may also be viewed as an attempt on the part of business decision-makers to maximize some utility function. In capitalist economies business firms are owned ultimately by households. But it is the managers who determine a firm's policy, shaping the recurring operating decisions with regard to products, prices, sales, technology, and growth. The relationship between managers' and owners' utility functions varies widely, depending on the firm's scale and organization. For small owner-managed firms the two will be identical. At the other extreme, managers of large, widely held corporations may have a utility function that diverges sharply from that of their stockholders.

Perfect Certainty

For some short-run behavior, principally production and pricing decisions, the analysis of business behavior may as a first approximation be carried out under the assumption of perfect certainty. Assuming for the present that managers of business firms act in the interests of the owners, *profit maximization* may be regarded as the central goal of business behavior. Under certainty wealth owners always prefer a higher to a lower return on their investments.

The profit-maximizing *firm* of economic theory must not be confused with real-world firms. The profit-maximizing firm represents a theoretical abstraction that has proven useful for the analysis of certain types of business behavior. It provides an answer to the question: How would businessmen act to achieve greatest profits under a particular set of circumstances? It does *not* purport to be a descriptive model of how all real-world business managements actually behave.

Businessmen sometimes deny vehemently that they attempt to maximize profits. In part the controversy arises out of differences in the definition of *profits,* which is used in a different sense by businessmen and economists. The businessman's definition of profit or loss refers to recorded transactions in a particular year. The economist's definition of profits is a long-run definition that includes all future effects of decisions. Such a long-run definition of profits is not operationally useful to businessmen who must somehow judge their current performance. The concept of long-run profits may be given operational meaning by examining the effects of business decisions on the market value of the firm.

Economists are more successful in explaining and predicting industry and market behavior where, as in the case of the consumer, the law of large numbers operates. The profit maximization hypothesis provides better predictions when applied to industries composed of large numbers of firms than when applied to individual firms or industries with only a few sellers. This is true not because such businessmen are particularly selfish or callous to considerations of the public interest but because under competitive circumstances — sincere or self-serving protestations of serving the diverse interests of customers, employees, stockholders, and society notwithstanding — business firms have little choice but to act *as if* they were attempting to maximize profits. (Even in concentrated industries, whenever these vague interests conflict the dispute is likely to be resolved in favor of self-interest.)

The rule that marginal cost be made equal to marginal revenue is a normative one that describes how businessmen *should* act in order to maximize profits. The fact that the hypothesis leads to successful prediction of business behavior suggests that, for certain types of decisions, it is also a reasonably accurate approximation of how businessmen *do* act. Nevertheless, many real-world firms behave in a nonoptimizing or satisficing manner and follow simplified rules of thumb inconsistent with profit maximization. Such behavior may be the rational response to the high costs of information collection and decision-making under uncertainty. Real-world firms never know exactly their marginal costs and marginal revenue curves, whose calculation might be very expensive.

For many questions in which time is a central factor (investment, growth, and financial behavior), the assumption of perfect certainty is unacceptable even as a first approximation, and uncertainty must explicitly be recognized. Objectives additional to profit maximization and the question of the extent to which managers may have interests that diverge from those of owners will be considered in the next chapter.

Business firms must decide what to supply, and find the technology to produce it at the lowest cost. On the basis of estimates of demand they must then make price and quantity decisions. Because firms are centrally concerned with profits (the excess of revenues over costs) it is necessary to see how these concepts are derived.

COST CURVES

Cost in economics refers to *opportunity cost,* the best alternatives given up or foregone by choosing one particular thing. In business usage *cost* refers to cash disbursements, the actual money cost incurred for a particular thing, with some adjustments for accrued but unpaid obligations and depreciation. From the point of view of economic analysis there is an opportunity cost irrespective of whether money is actually paid out or liabilities are incurred for the cost of factors owned by the business unit. Cost depends on the alternatives considered. A factor of production, such as land, may have one opportunity cost to a firm, another to an industry, and still another cost from the point of view of the economy as a whole.

Production Function

For simplicity, a firm will be treated in this discussion as if it hired inputs to produce only a single product. The physical relationship between factor inputs and the resulting output of goods and services is termed a *production function.* It specifies for a given level of technology the changes in output associated with a change in factor inputs.

The most important general characteristic of production relationships is known as the *law of diminishing returns.* It may be stated as follows: If in the production of a commodity all factor inputs are increased, output will rise by the same proportion, with any given level of technology. But if one factor input is increased, other factor inputs remaining constant, total output will increase, but after a certain point at a progressively diminishing rate. It is due to the operation of the law of diminishing returns that all the world's wheat cannot be grown in a single flowerpot, no matter how much fertilizer and labor are applied.

This production relationship is shown in Figure 5-1, in which the variable factor labor is measured on the horizontal axis, total output on the vertical axis, and at least one factor, for example land, is assumed fixed. With a larger amount of the fixed factor, the production function *OY* would shift upwards to *OY'*. A similar upward shift would occur with an improvement in technology.

Marginal Product

The *marginal physical product* or more simply the *marginal product* of a factor of production is defined as the addition to total product resulting from the employment

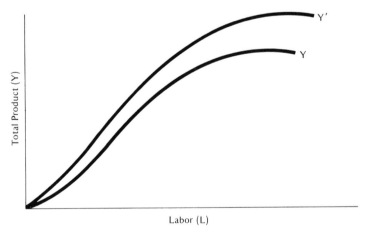

Figure 5-1 Production Function

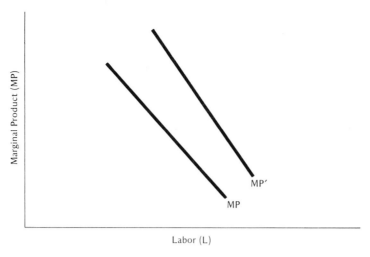

Figure 5-2 Marginal Product

of one extra unit of the factor, all other factors being held constant. It is thus the slope of the total product curve of Figure 5-1. The law of diminishing returns states that a factor's marginal product will decline as more units of that factor are used in production, when other factors remain constant. Equal increments of a factor will result in decreasing increments to total product, other factors being held constant. The marginal product of any factor will thus in general be downward sloping. A shift in the production function such as shown in Figure 5-2 would cause a shift in each factor's marginal product curve, by an amount depending on the change in the factor's marginal product at different levels of input.

Total Cost

Firms are typically confronted with a large number of alternative techniques for producing a particular product. Given the price of various factors, a profit-maximizing firm will attempt to find the technology that permits it to produce any desired output at minimum cost. These least-cost factor combinations for producing any given output make up a firm's total cost curve (TC). This curve is shown in Figure 5-3, where total output (Q) is measured on the horizontal axis and total cost in dollars is measured on the vertical axis.

While there are in general a large number of ways of producing any given output, assume that each point on the total cost relationship represents the *least-cost factor combination* to produce the particular output. There are thus an indefinitely large number of cost curves lying above TC in Figure 5-3, but it is assumed that the firm has chosen the lowest-cost production technique available.

It is convenient for short-run analysis to distinguish between *fixed costs* (sometimes called overhead costs) and *variable costs.* In Figure 5-3 total cost is divided into total fixed cost (TFC) and total variable costs (TVC). Fixed costs do not change in

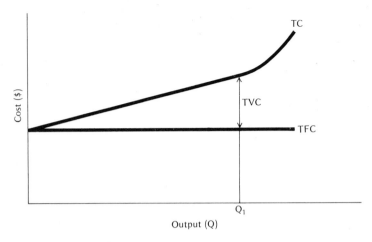

Figure 5-3 Total Cost Curves

total amount as the volume of total output is changed. Fixed costs refer to all the costs of plant, rent, depreciation, interest, maintenance, and administration that are invariant to output.

Variable costs, comprising most labor and raw materials costs, refer to the costs that do change in amount as the level of total output is changed. As shown in Figure 5-3, after some point (Q_1) variable costs rise more rapidly as it becomes increasingly difficult to increase output with a plant of a given size. The law of diminishing returns is as central for production behavior as the law of diminishing marginal utility is for consumption.

Average Cost

From the total cost curve of Figure 5-3, it is possible to derive the firm's average or unit cost curves, which are shown in Figure 5-4. Average cost or unit cost is defined simply as the corresponding total cost divided by the number of units produced.

Average fixed cost $\quad AFC = \dfrac{TFC}{Q}$

Average variable cost $\quad AVC = \dfrac{TVC}{Q}$

Average (total) cost $\quad AC = ATC = \dfrac{TC}{Q}$

Average fixed costs per unit fall continuously as output increases, because the total fixed costs are spread over a larger volume of output. The average fixed-cost curve is a rectangular hyperbola, because the area under the curve at every point is constant and equal to total fixed costs. (The behavior of average fixed costs may be represented by the slope of a line drawn from the origin to every point on the total fixed-cost curve in Figure 5-3.)

Average variable costs are typically constant over a substantial range and then rise as the firm reaches the capacity limits for which the particular plant was designed. Increasing output beyond this point is increasingly expensive as more men and materials are hired with a given stock of plant and equipment and diminishing returns set in. (The behavior of average variable costs may be represented by the slope of a line drawn from the intersection point on the vertical axis where total variable costs are zero to any point on the total variable-cost curve in Figure 5-3.)

Average total costs or simply average costs equal the sum of average fixed costs plus average variable costs. The average total cost curve in Figure 5-4 is drawn as U-shaped. Characteristically, average total costs fall over the initial range of output (because of the fall in average fixed costs), are broadly constant over some intermediate range for which the plant was intended, and then rise as full capacity is approached and average variable costs rise. (The behavior of average costs may be represented by the slope of a line drawn from the origin to every point on the total cost curve in Figure 5-3.)

Long-Run Cost

The cost curves of Figures 5-3 and 5-4 are *short-run curves,* as they refer to a particular plant size. In the long run it is possible to vary the size of plant. Such a change is shown in Figure 5-5, in which a long-run average-cost curve (AC_{LR}) or envelope curve has been constructed to show the lowest achievable cost of producing increasing levels of output with *different plant sizes.*

The minimum cost point of a particular plant size is not necessarily the least cost at which that volume of output can be produced. (Compare AC_1 and AC_2 in Figure 5-5.) It may be cheaper to build a larger plant with lower average costs and operate

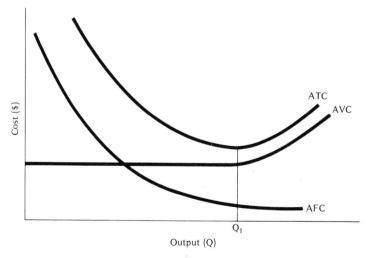

Figure 5-4 Average Cost Curves

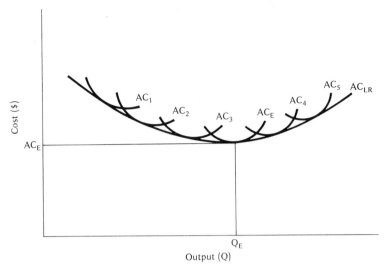

Figure 5-5 Long-Run Average Cost Curve

it at less than full capacity than to build a smaller plant and operate it at capacity. In the long run, when all factors can be varied, including plant size, there are no fixed costs; in the long run all costs are variable.

Returns to Scale

The shape of the long-run cost curve depends on the significance of economies and diseconomies of scale. The concept of *increasing returns to scale*, or *economies of scale*, describes a situation in which average costs fall as plant size is increased. Economies of scale are characteristic of all mass-production industries. They are in part attributable to purely technical considerations. (Over some range, storage volume increases with the cube of the size of the container, whereas storage costs increase only with the square of the size of the storage tank; a motor of 1,000 H.P. is not 1,000 times as expensive as a 1 H.P. motor.) Economies of scale also arise from increased division of labor, increased specialization, and longer production runs, all of which raise factor productivity as the volume of output is expanded.

Constant returns to scale describes a situation in which average productivity and therefore average cost are invariant to the size of the plant. *Decreasing returns to scale, or diseconomies of scale,* refers to a situation in which average costs rise with plant size. In such situations large plants will have a lower average factor productivity and higher average costs than small plants.

Diseconomies of scale set in as the scale of operations expands and the difficulties of coordination, information, and efficient decision making increase. These organizational diseconomies tend increasingly to offset the force of technical economies as the scale of operations is increased. Depending on the strength of these two factors the most efficient size of firm and plant will vary greatly among different industries.

SUPPLY PRICE AND MARKET STRUCTURE

Just as demand in economics denotes willingness and ability to pay the market price for a commodity, supply denotes willingness and ability to offer a particular quantity of the good or service in return for payment at the market price. As in the case of demand, it is important to distinguish between the *quantity supplied* and the *supply schedule*. The term *supply* is frequently used alone to refer to the latter, so that by "change in supply" is meant a shift of the supply curve.

The foregoing analyses of production relationships and the derivation of cost curves apply generally to firms operating in all types of markets. But cost alone does not determine the price that the firm will charge. The supply schedule shows the relationship between the quantity supplied and price. The supply curve is governed solely by cost considerations only if the firm is faced with a price over which it cannot exercise control. Otherwise the price it will charge will depend on its costs and on the demand curve for its product.

Absence of seller control over price exists only under a very limited set of circumstances that make up what is known as *perfect competition*. Perfect competition refers to a market situation which includes a large number of buyers and sellers, each so small relative to the total that no one individual can influence the price; absence of collusion; a homogeneous product so that buyers do not prefer the product of one firm to that of another; and free entry into and exit out of the market by all participants.

The concept of a firm or industry supply curve thus applies strictly only to perfectly competitive markets, where firms are faced with an infinitely elastic demand for their product at the existing market price. Such firms have only to decide the quantity to be produced. In all other situations the demand curve faced by a firm is downward sloping, so that the firm has some control over the price it may charge. The firm then has an additional decision: What price should it charge to maximize profits? Such a firm is a *price maker* rather than a *price taker*.

Whenever a firm has market power to influence price, it is not possible to determine a firm's supply schedule from cost information alone. A unique supply schedule, relating amount supplied to price charged, no longer exists. Given its cost relationships, the price a firm charges and the amount it supplies will depend on the characteristics of the demand curve for its products. The forces governing business pricing and output decisions under different market conditions are considered in Chapter 7, but the general relationship between supply price and costs may be briefly outlined.

Profits

The total revenues (TR) of a business firm are derived from its sales receipts from goods and services sold. They are equal to the price of each unit of output (P) multiplied by the number of units sold (Q): $TR = P$ times Q.

Price is thus equal to average revenue: $P = \dfrac{TR}{Q} = AR$

The total costs (TC) of a business firm are derived from all costs incurred in producing a particular output. Total cost is equal to the price of different inputs times the quantity of inputs used.

Profits (Π) are defined as the excess of total revenue (TR) above total costs (TC). If total costs exceed total revenue, profits are negative and the business realizes a loss.

$\Pi = TR - TC$

Total profits are also equal to average profit per unit times the number of units sold.

$$\Pi = \frac{\Pi}{Q} \times Q = \left(\frac{TR}{Q} - \frac{TC}{Q} \right) Q = (P - AC) Q$$

Cost and Supply Price

In the short run, the minimum price at which the firm will be willing to supply output must at least cover its average variable costs. If this is not the case the firm would prefer to shut down. If it shuts down it must still meet its fixed costs, and so incur a loss. But if it cannot cover even its variable costs, its loss would be larger from producing than from shutting down.

In the longer run if the firm is to stay in business it must be able to sell its output at a price which exceeds its average variable costs by a sufficient margin to cover all its total fixed costs, including at least some "normal" rate of profit on the capital invested in the business. While in the short run the minimum price at which it is willing to supply goods is its average variable costs, in the longer run it must cover all its costs, including the cost of the capital that it uses. In the long run all costs are variable, and its minimum supply price is its average total cost. If revenues are below this minimum level, the firm must eventually leave the industry. The factors determining the normal rate of profits are considered in Part III. If a firm possesses market power, it may be able to set a price markup over costs above this level so as to realize abnormally high or monopoly profits.

The relationship of costs (including profit) to price is illustrated in Figure 5-6, in which the firm's supply price is shown as the firm's average variable-cost curve plus a markup of price over unit costs sufficient to yield the firm some target level of profits. Average variable costs are typically falling and then fairly constant over some wide range of output, after which they increase as plant capacity is approached. Once the firm's supply price is set, the quantity that it can sell will depend, as shown in Figure 5-6, on the demand curve facing the firm.

The degree of market power possessed by a firm may be measured by the elasticity of the demand curve for its product. Firms with inelastic demand curves such as shown in Figure 5-6a will be able to charge a higher price, that is a greater markup over costs, and so enjoy a higher level of profits. Firms with highly elastic demand curves such as shown in Figure 5-6b will realize a smaller profit markup. For firms in perfectly competitive markets the demand curve is a horizontal straight line at

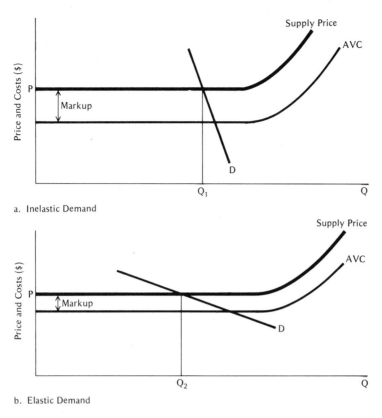

a. Inelastic Demand

b. Elastic Demand

Figure 5-6 Supply Price and Average Variable Costs

the existing market price. Such firms are price takers and have no influence over price. They must simply decide the quantity they will produce, can earn only normal profits, and will always produce on rising segments of their average variable-costs curve. The manner in which a firm's profit markup of price over average costs is related to its degree of market power is examined in Chapter 7.

The industry supply curve is simply the sum of the amount each individual firm chooses to supply. It thus depends on the level and shape of the individual firms' average cost and supply-price curves and on the number of firms in the industry. An increase in the number of firms will increase the total amount supplied, reducing the market price if demand remains unchanged. This case would be reflected in a leftward shift in the demand curve of Figure 5-6 facing each individual firm in the industry. Similarly a reduction in costs, due for example to improved technology, will shift the average cost and supply price curves downward. If profit margins remain unchanged, price will fall and sales will increase.

Profit Maximization

In the short run supply price will be based on average variable costs plus some unspecified markup to cover overhead costs and profits, the magnitude of which will depend on the degree of market power possessed by the firm. In the long run supply price must cover average total costs including at least normal profits on capital.

The relationship between average costs and supply price, and so the size of the markup, can be explained by the attempt of firms possessing market power to maximize profits. Profits are defined as the excess of total revenue over total costs. Profit maximization therefore requires that the firm find that level of output, and charge that price, for which the difference between total revenue and total costs are maximized.

For a firm faced by a downward-sloping demand curve, additional sales can be made only by lowering price. Total revenue, price times quantity, will thus increase with quantity sold but increase at a diminishing rate and eventually decline. Total costs in contrast increase with output and after some point grow at an increasing rate, because of diminishing returns and rising unit costs. These relationships are illustrated in Figure 5-7. Total revenue and total costs are measured on the vertical axis. Total profits at every output are equal to the vertical distance $TR - TC$. The point B where $TC = TR$ is termed the *break-even* point. At all outputs below this level the firm will make a loss.

In order to maximize profits, businessmen must attempt to find that output (Q_m) at which the difference between total revenue and total cost is maximized (Π_m). As shown in Figure 5-7, this profit-maximizing output must satisfy the condition that at that output the slope of the total revenue curve is equal to the slope of the total cost curve. At all outputs below this level (e.g., Q_1) total profits are less than Π_M and the firm could increase its profits by producing and selling more. Similarly, at all outputs above this level (e.g., Q_2) total profits are less than Π_M and the firm could increase its profits by producing and selling less.

The change in total cost from producing one more unit of output is termed *marginal cost*; $MC = \Delta TC$. Similarly the change in total revenue from selling one more

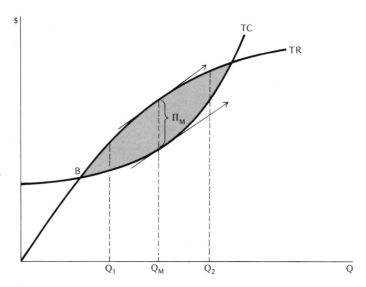

Figure 5-7 Profit Maximization

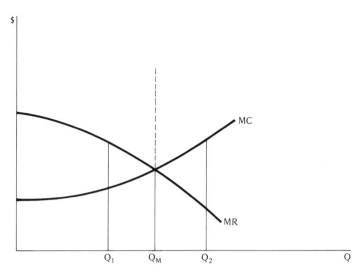

Figure 5-8 Marginal Revenue and Marginal Cost

unit of output is defined as *marginal revenue; MR* $= \Delta TR$. These concepts define the rate of change (slope) of the corresponding total curve. As illustrated in Figure 5-8, the necessary condition for profit maximization is that marginal revenue be equal to marginal cost.

If marginal revenue is greater than marginal cost (e.g., at Q_1) the firm can increase total profits by producing and selling an additional unit. What it adds to total revenue will be greater than what it adds to total cost. Conversely if marginal revenue is less than marginal cost (e.g., at Q_2) the firm can increase total profits by producing one unit less. The reduction in total revenue is then less than the reduction in total cost. Only when marginal revenue and marginal cost are equal (Q_M) can no further improvements in profits be realized. Thus in order to maximize profits firms must know by how much an additional unit raises costs and revenues.

If the firm is operating in a perfectly competitive market, it has no control over price and must take the ruling market price as given. Because it can sell any amount at this price, its total revenue curve in Figure 5-7 will be a straight line, with a slope equal to the market price, and its marginal revenue curve in Figure 5-8 will be a horizontal straight line. For such firms marginal revenue is equal to price, and profit maximization requires finding that level of output where price equals marginal cost ($P = MC$).

DEMAND FOR FACTORS OF PRODUCTION

The demand by firms for productive factors is derived indirectly from household and firm demand for the goods and services that the factors produce. The nature of this derived demand depends on technological relationships that govern the productivity of different factors. Firms demand factors of production not for their own sake but for the value of the economic goods that they can produce when combined with other factors. For this reason firm demand for factors of production is sometimes termed a *derived demand*.

Profit-maximizing firms will continue to hire any factor as long as the marginal cost of the factor is less than the value of what that factor contributes to total revenue. Until this limit is reached, hiring one more unit of the factor adds more to total revenue than it adds to total cost.

In perfect competition the increase in total revenue from hiring one additional unit of the factor is the value of the factor's marginal product, that is, the factor's marginal physical product (MP, the number of units of the commodity attributable to it) times the market price of the product (P). The increase in total cost of hiring one additional factor is the factor's price (P_F). Therefore the demand curve for a factor—the quantity that will be demanded at different factor prices—in perfectly competitive markets is the value of the factor's marginal product ($VMP = MP \times P$). The firm will hire (demand) any factor so long as the value of what that factor produces (its VMP) is greater than the factor's cost (its price P_F). In imperfect competition a factor's marginal revenue product will be below the value of its marginal product. Because more units can be sold only by lowering the market price of all units, marginal revenue is less than price ($MRP = MP \times MR$).

An individual firm's factor-demand curve is shown in Figure 5-9. It is downward sloping in accordance with the law of diminishing returns. In imperfect competition the demand curve for the factor will slope downward more steeply, to the extent that marginal revenue is less than the price of the commodity. The total demand for any particular factor is derived by summing up each individual firm's demand curve for that factor.

The slope of a firm's derived demand curve for a factor will depend on the demand for the goods produced by the factor and on the characteristics of the produc-

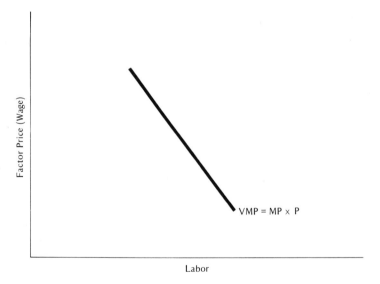

Figure 5-9 Factor Demand

tion relationship. The more inelastic the demand for the product, the more inelastic the derived demand for the factors producing it. The smaller the possibility of substituting other factors for this factor, the more inelastic will be its demand. The more rapidly diminishing returns set in, the more inelastic will be the demand curve for the factor. The smaller the proportion of total costs spent on a productive factor, the more inelastic the demand for the factor will tend to be, as a change in its price will then not substantially affect total costs of production. To have a strong bargaining position, a factor should represent a small fraction of total costs, yet be critical in the production process.

APPENDIX: THE PRODUCTION FUNCTION

A production function describes the technological relationship between inputs of productive factors and the resulting output of goods and services. Consider the two factors, labor (L) and capital (K). A production function may be formulated: $Y = T(L,K)$. This states that total output (Y) is some function (T) of the inputs of labor (L) and capital (K). The function by which they are combined (T) represents a particular level of technology. It is this technological relationship that lies behind the cost and supply curves of individual firms.

There are three important dimensions of the production-function relationship: diminishing returns, factor substitution, and returns to scale.

Diminishing Returns

A production function (T_0) exhibiting the law of diminishing returns is shown in Figure 5-10, where labor (L) is the variable factor and capital (K_0) is the fixed factor. With larger fixed amounts of capital, K_1, K_2, K_3, the productivity of labor inputs would increase and, as shown in Figure 5-10, the production function $T_0(K_1)$, $T_0(K_2)$, $T_0(K_3)$ would shift outward and upward.

Improvements in technology represent new ways of combining factor inputs to produce the same output more efficiently with fewer factors. They effectuate some upward shift in the production function, witness the dashed line $T_1(K_0)$ in Figure 5-10. The same factor inputs can now produce a greater output. The extent of the shift will depend on the type of technical change experienced, whether it is primarily labor saving or capital saving.

The *average product* of a factor of production is defined as total product divided by the number of units of the factor. A factor's *marginal product* is defined as the change in total product resulting from one additional unit of the productive factor. The law of diminishing returns states that a factor's marginal product after a point will decline and eventually become negative.

The relationship among total product, average product, and marginal product is shown in Figure 5-11. A factor's marginal product is represented by the slope of

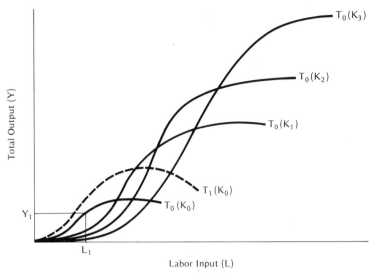

Figure 5-10 Production Functions

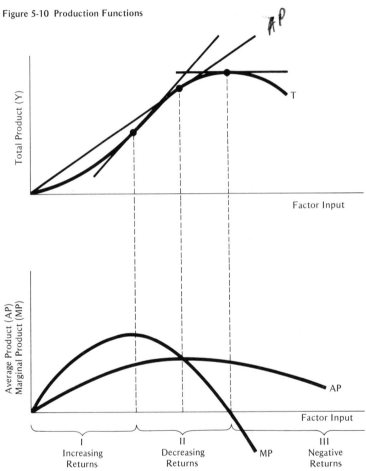

Figure 5-11 Relations among Total Product, Average Product, and Marginal Product

the production function at any point. Average product is the slope of a line drawn through the origin. When marginal product is zero, total product is at a maximum. Average product rises when marginal product exceeds average product and falls when marginal product is less than average product.

As shown in Figure 5-11 the production relationship may in general be divided into three phases: increasing returns, decreasing returns, and negative returns. Firms will never produce in the range of increasing returns, as this phase implies that the marginal productivity of another factor is negative, so that larger output could be produced using smaller amounts of this other factor. (As shown in Figure 5-10, the output Y_1 can be produced most efficiently with (K_0) of capital, since with larger quantities of capital and the same amount of labor (L_1) output is actually lower, i.e., the marginal product of capital is negative.) Firms will never produce in the range of negative returns; as a result, production occurs only in the phase of decreasing returns to each factor.

Factor Substitution

It is ordinarily possible to use different combinations of factor inputs to produce any given output. *Factor substitution* also involves a kind of law of diminishing returns, which may be formulated as follows: As successive quantities of one input are used in substitution for another factor in the production process, after some point other factor inputs can be withdrawn only at a diminishing rate if total output is to remain constant.

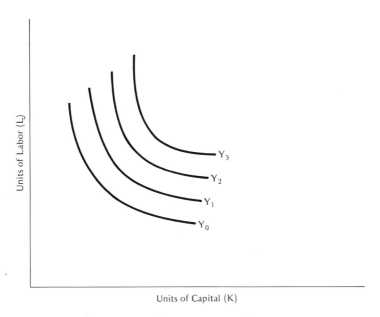

Figure 5-12 Equal Product Curves (Production Isoquants)

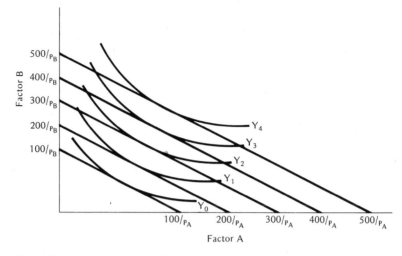

Figure 5-13 Least-Cost Factor Combination

The degree to which factors are substitutable for one another is shown graphically in Figure 5-12 by the use of *equal-product curves* or *production isoquants* Y_0 Y_1, Y_2, Y_3. The greater the degree of substitutability of one factor for another, the flatter are the production isoquants. If variable proportions do not exist, so that one factor cannot be substituted for another, production isoquants become right-angled straight lines. This extreme case is known as *fixed proportions.*

In the case in which factor proportions are truly fixed, it is impossible to determine a factor's marginal product. In the short run the possibilities of factor substitution in many industries may be small, as the plant and equipment for a particular technique of production have already been constructed. Even in this period overtime, shift work, and changes in factor quality typically permit some variability in factor proportions. In the longer run the possibility of factor substitution increases, as new techniques can be developed to take advantage of relatively cheap productive factors.

The least-cost factor combination may be determined for any output by drawing an *equal-cost line,* which is similar to the budget line in indifference theory. As shown in Figure 5-13, given the factor prices each equal-cost line describes the different combinations of factors that may be purchased for a given cost. The *least-cost factor combination* is found for a particular output where the *lowest equal-cost curve is tangent to the production isoquant* for that output. Because the slope of the equal-cost curve is equal to the ratio of the factor prices, the condition for minimum-cost production is that the ratio of factor prices be equal to the ratio of factor marginal products:

$$\frac{P_A}{P_B} = \frac{MP_A}{MP_B}$$

Scale Economies and Diseconomies

The third dimension of the production function involves the relationship between a proportionate change in *all* inputs and the resulting change in total output. This relationship is described as *returns to scale.*

Constant returns to scale occur in the situation in which a proportionate increase in all factors of production results in the same proportionate increase in total output. Decreasing returns to scale occur in the situation in which a proportionate increase in all factors of production results in a less than proportionate increase in total output. Increasing returns occur in situations in which an increase in all factors by any given proportion results in an increase in total output by a greater proportion. Increasing returns (economies of scale) are particularly important in many industries where the most productive and least-cost techniques require a large volume of output. It is inefficient to build a small steel mill or automobile factory. These three possibilities are illustrated graphically in Figure 5-14.

Production Surface

It is interesting to recognize that the production function relationship may be regarded as a surface in several dimensions. These relationships are represented three-dimensionally in Figure 5-15.

Looking at Figure 5-10, one can visualize a third axis coming out of the page at a right angle from the origin. On this axis is measured inputs of the other productive factor, capital. A production surface of three dimensions may then be envisioned

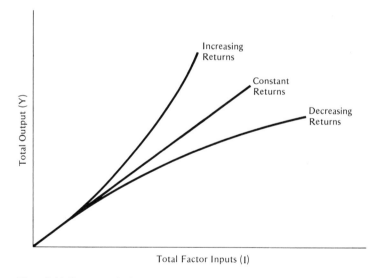

Figure 5-14 Returns to Scale

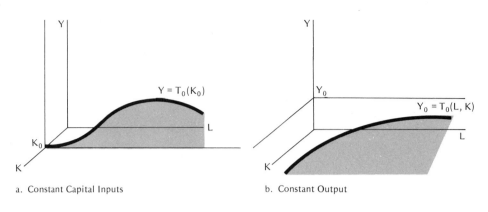

a. Constant Capital Inputs

b. Constant Output

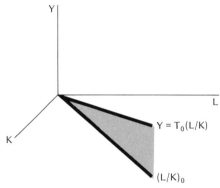

c. Constant Relative Factor Inputs

Figure 5-15 Cross Sections of the Production Function

rising out of the page. Figure 5-10 may now be seen to represent cross sections of this surface, as shown in Figure 5-15a, produced by slicing the surface by a vertical plane perpendicular to this third axis at various distances, each representing different constant amounts (K_1, K_2, K_3) of the other factor of production, capital.

Figure 5-12 represents the contours formed when the three-dimensional production surface is cut by horizontal planes at various constant levels of total output Y_0, Y_1, Y_2, Y_3. As shown in Figure 5-15b these contours represent the production surface as viewed from above, similar to the indifference curves described earlier as contours of a utility surface.

Finally Figure 5-14 describes the contour formed when the production function is intercepted by a vertical plane drawn through the origin at an angle equal to some constant proportion of the two productive factors. As shown in Figure 5-15c for the case of constant returns, it represents a view of the same production surface seen from the side.

When n factors are considered, the production function becomes a surface in $n + 1$ dimensions. It is not possible to visualize such a surface geometrically, but it may be handled algebraically in a manner exactly analogous to the case of two factors.

the behavior of business firms: dynamic analysis

FOR MY PART, I think that Capitalism, wisely managed, can probably be made more efficient for attaining economic ends than any alternatives system yet in sight, but that in itself it is in many ways extremely objectionable. Our problem is to work out a social organization which shall be as efficient as possible without offending our notions of a satisfactory way of life.

—JOHN MAYNARD KEYNES

AS THE PUBLIC CHARACTER of the mature corporation comes to be recognized, attention will doubtless focus on the position of the stockholder in this corporation. He is anomalous. He is a passive and functionless figure, remarkable only in his capacity to share, without effort or even without appreciable risk, in the gains from the growth by which the technostructure measures its success. No grant of feudal privilege has ever equalled for effortless return that of the grandparent who bought and endowed his descendants with a thousand shares of General Motors or General Electric. The beneficiaries of this foresight have become and remain rich by no exercise of effort and intelligence beyond the decision to do nothing, embracing as it did the decision not to sell.

—JOHN KENNETH GALBRAITH

The preceding chapter considered the production and output decisions of business firms in individual markets. Under conditions of certainty the goal of business behavior was assumed to be simply profit maximization for the owners.

Once uncertainty is recognized, businessmen can no longer be assumed to know exactly their technological possibilities, costs, and demand relationships. The single-valued cost and revenue curves of certainty analysis become fuzzy and dissolve into wide bands, representing some subjective probability distribution of expected values. The degree of uncertainty surrounding future outcomes can be reduced, but only at the considerable cost of collecting and processing information. Rules of thumb become rational approximations to economize on the costs of decision-making.

In the short run business firms operate with some historically given stock of plant and equipment. Over time, businessmen must decide what new plants to build for the production of what commodities, and how to finance these investment expenditures. In addition to present profits, in an uncertain world they must also consider expected future profits, their rate of growth, and the risk of ruin. This chapter is concerned with these dynamic aspects of business behavior. As in the case of households, when decisions over time are involved, much economic behavior can be understood only as a response to the fact of uncertainty. The simplifying assumption of perfect certainty must regrettably be discarded.

VALUE MAXIMIZATION UNDER UNCERTAINTY

Business Corporations

Business firms occur in a variety of legal forms with enormous differences in size, as illustrated in Table 6-1. Most firms are small. In the United States, nearly 90 percent of all firms have fewer than 10 employees. Most small firms are sole proprietorships or partnerships, in which the owner-managers have unlimited liability for all debts incurred by the firm.

While only about 12 percent of all firms are incorporated, this proportion rises to 100 percent as size of firm increases. In the United States, corporations account for about 80 percent of all privately produced goods and services. Corporations account for 85 to 98 percent of all the business in important sectors such as manufacturing, mining, transportation, utilities, and finance. Proprietorships and partnerships are most important in agriculture, construction, trade, and services.

The most important feature of corporations is the limited liability of their owners. Should the company be declared bankrupt, the personal liability of any shareholder is limited to the amount he has actually invested in the purchase of shares. This safeguard enormously reduces the risk of wealth ownership in corporations in comparison with proprietorships and partnerships.

The corporate form enables large amounts of capital to be collected from many individuals. Each stockowner receives a *pro rata* share (proportional to the number of his shares) of the firm's profits, either as dividends or as capital gains if earnings

Table 6-1 BUSINESS FIRMS BY FORM AND INDUSTRY, 1963

	Total		Sole Proprietorships				Partnerships				Corporations			
	Number	Sales	Number		Sales		Number		Sales		Number		Sales	
	Millions	Billions of Dollars	Millions	Percent of Total	Billions of Dollars	Percent of Total	Millions	Percent of Total	Billions of Dollars	Percent of Total	Millions	Percent of Total	Billions of Dollars	Percent of Total
All Industries	11.3	1,202.2	9.1	80	181.6	15	0.9	8	71.8	6	1.3	12	948.8	79
By Industry														
Agriculture, Forestry, and Fisheries	3.4	42.2	3.3	97	30.0	71	0.1	3	4.7	11	0.02	0.5	7.5	18
Mining	0.05	14.3	0.03	60	1.0	7	0.01	20	0.9	6	0.01	20	12.4	87
Construction	0.86	67.9	0.7	81	16.3	24	0.06	8	6.9	10	0.1	11	44.7	66
Manufacturing	0.44	431.8	0.2	45	6.4	1	0.04	10	6.1	1	0.2	45	419.3	98
Transportation and Public Utilities	0.38	81.8	0.3	79	5.0	6	0.02	5	1.1	1	0.06	16	75.7	93
Wholesale and Retail Trade	2.5	428.2	1.8	72	89.8	20	0.3	12	35.5	8	0.4	16	302.9	72
Finance, Insurance, and Real Estate	1.1	67.0	0.5	46	5.5	8	0.2	18	5.5	8	0.4	36	56.0	84
Services	2.6	68.2	2.2	84	27.1	40	0.2	8	11.1	16	0.2	8	30.0	44

Source: Treasury Department, Internal Revenue Service.

are retained. This method of assembling capital permits large-scale organization of production. The size of the largest corporation is staggering. Several American corporations have annual sales exceeding the total national revenue of most countries of the world. Because a corporation is a separate legal entity, the death or withdrawal of any owner does not terminate its existence. As a result corporations, like countries, can live forever.

Separation of Ownership and Control

One important aspect of the corporate form of organization is that owners do not have to concern themselves with the administration of their property. The functions of ownership and control have been sheared apart. Most stockowners have little direct ability to influence the corporation's policy, should they so desire.

Stockholder votes are weighted in proportion to shares held. Stockholders owning only a few shares have an insignificant effect on the voting outcome. Stockholder meetings are hardly a model of democratic decision-making. Few stockholders bother to vote and, if they do, they characteristically give a proxy vote to the directors in office. Corporate decisions are not made by so much as made for the majority of shareowners. As a result of this separation of ownership and control, shareholders dissatisfied with the performance of a corporation usually will sell their shares rather than attempt directly to change management policy. Stockholders would rather switch than fight.

Minority Control

In most public corporations ownership of shares is distributed over a large number of individual shareholders. At the same time stockholdings are highly concentrated, with a small proportion of total stockholders owning a sizable proportion of total stock. It has been estimated that 5 percent of the households own about 95 percent of all stock held by the household sector. Under such circumstances dominant groups owning a minority of the total stock frequently are able to control a majority of the voting shares, and thus exercise effective control over the policy of the directors.

There is formidable evidence that interlocking directorships exist on a large scale. In all capitalist economies a relatively small number of individuals, constituting what is sometimes termed the corporate elite, hold directorships in many corporations. Interlocking directorships extend the influence of dominant groups throughout many sectors of the economy. While this situation is important for the distribution of personal power, there is little evidence that common directors exert significant influence in altering firm behavior from what it would be if no such interlocking existed. Minority control is important for outcomes only to the extent the controlling minority have interests different from the majority.

Management Control

The extent to which directors exercise effective control over management is the subject of considerable dispute. Stockholders elect the directors, who in turn appoint the managers. Directors are supposed to represent stockholders' interests in determining the broad policies that management merely carries out. But in order to run a large corporation a full-time professional management group must be given broad powers of decision. Although legally they are the employees of the stockholders, within wide limits the "technocracy" exercise effective control over corporate policy, and are able to perpetuate themselves in office. So long as directors have confidence in the management they typically accept and ratify management's proposals.

Firm behavior was interpreted as the maximization of a utility function by business decision-makers. Once the possibility of managerial independence is admitted the question must be faced of whose utility function is being maximized. The self-interest of management at several points appears to diverge from the self-interest of owners. It is true that managers are themselves typically sizable stockholders, their shares frequently having been acquired as a result of bonuses and stock options. Thus they have considerable personal incentive to reflect stockholder interest. Nevertheless, on a number of questions there appears to be conflict. Salaries, bonuses, prestige, security, retention of control, sales volume, and the good life all may be expected to enter importantly into the utility function of business managers, even if they conflict directly with stockholder self-interest.

Value Maximization under Uncertainty

In a world of uncertainty the goal of profit maximization must be reformulated. Assume that managers always attempt to follow the normative rule to act only in the interests of the stockholders. Once time is introduced, managers must somehow decide questions that affect not only the level of profits and dividends, but their rate of growth over time, and the uncertainty of alternative future income streams. Lower profits today may be required for higher profits tomorrow. A policy of profit maximization may involve running a greater risk of unfavorable outcomes. Under such conditions the simple rule of profit maximization breaks down. How is the normative rule of acting in shareholder interest to be formulated?

Wealth owners *ceteris paribus* prefer higher to lower returns on their investment. They are also adverse to bearing risk and prefer present to future income. Attitudes toward risk and valuation of future income differ among individual investors depending on their needs and tastes. These diverse investor preferences enter into investor demand for assets and are reflected in the market price of different securities. All holders of a particular asset, irrespective of its characteristics and investor preferences, would be made better off if its price should rise and worse off if its price should fall. Managers acting in the interests of existing shareholders will therefore pursue only those policies whose effect is to raise the value of the corporation's stock. *Share price maximization* becomes the normative goal of business behavior under uncertainty.

This policy provides managers with an operative rule by which to judge all decisions. Whether the question affects the rate of growth of the corporation, the riskiness of profits, the volume of investment expenditures, the share of the market, the level of research and development, the type of financing, or the rate of product innovation, the criterion is always the same: Undertake only if the effect is expected to raise the market price of the corporation's stock. Stockholder attitudes and preferences among return, risk, and growth on their investments need not be ascertained directly. They are already incorporated in the market's valuation of the corporation's stock.

CAPITAL STOCK

In order to produce goods and services, firms require some stock of plant, equipment, and inventories of raw materials and goods in process. These real capital goods raise the productivity of labor and so increase the amount of goods and services that workers can produce. The term *capital stock* will be used to refer to all these real capital goods.

Businesses also hold stocks of financial assets, primarily money, liquid assets, and trade credit. Financial assets are demanded in some proportion to the level and variability of total transactions and wealth. Business total assets are financed in part by the issue of liabilities—trade debt, bank loans, notes, bonds, and mortgages—in part by saving (depreciation allowances and retained earnings) and to a smaller extent by the new issue of equities.

Table 6-2 presents a summary of the balance sheets of nonfinancial business corporations. Tangible assets accounted for slightly more than two thirds and financial assets slightly less than one third of total assets over the period. The ratio of liabilities to total assets was more variable, rising to over 60 percent in the great depression and falling and then rising in the postwar period to 45 percent. As business debts are fixed in money value, changes in the general price level and so in the price of capital goods result in an inverse change in the ratio of debt to the value of total assets. In 1968 the value of total business assets exceeded $1000 billion.

The Marginal Productivity of Capital

Capital goods are demanded by business firms because of their contribution to the total value of goods and services produced. The return on capital goods is conventionally expressed as an annual percentage of market value. As capital consists of heterogeneous types of "machines," each produced with different amounts of labor over different past periods, there are very difficult problems involved in its valuation. Putting these measurement problems to one side, the return on real capital

Table 6-2 NONFINANCIAL CORPORATIONS, BALANCE SHEETS, 1900–1968 (BILLIONS OF DOLLARS AND PERCENT OF TOTAL ASSETS)

	1900		1929		1933		1945		1958		1968	
	Dollars	Percent	Dollars	Percent	Dollars	Percent	Dollars	Percent	Dollars	Percent	Dollars	Percent
Tangible Assets												
Nonresidential Structures	18.3	57	99.3	53	75.3	58	54.4	24	180.8	26	272.4	24
Land							20.0	9	63.5	9	102.9	9
Producer durables							33.9	15	145.5	21	233.3	21
Total	21.1	66	121.3	65	89.1	69	142.8	64	489.4	71	757.9	68
Financial Assets												
Currency and Demand Deposits	2.0	6	7.4	4	5.6	4	19.7	9	33.3	5	28.1	3
Trade Credit	3.9	12	21.9	12	15.9	12	22.7	10	83.4	12	213.3	19
Securities	—		4.3	2	3.5	3	21.2	9	21.9	3	18.5	2
Total	11.1	34	64.4	35	39.9	31	80.6	36	196.7	29	357.3	32
Liabilities												
Trade Debt	3.1	10	16.0	9	11.9	9	19.7	9	68.8	10	222.1	20
Bank Loans	1.4	4	9.4	5	5.2	4	6.4	3	25.9	4	67.3	6
Mortgages	.8	2	11.2	6	9.7	8	7.9	4	29.7	4	136.8	12
Bonds and Notes	7.1	22	36.3	20	35.6	28	23.6	11	69.7	10		
Total	15.0	47	96.3	52	79.5	62	88.3	40	257.1	37	499.9	45
Net Worth	17.1	53	89.5	48	49.5	38	135.1	60	429.5	63	615.3	55
Total Assets or Liabilities plus Net Worth	32.2	100	185.8	100	129.0	100	223.4	100	686.6	100	1115.2	100

Business holdings of stock of other corporations have been omitted.

Source: 1900–1958 Raymond Goldsmith, Robert Lipsey, Morris Mendelson, *Studies in the National Balance Sheet of the United States,* Volume 2, Princeton, 1963. 1968 *Institutional Investor Study Report of the Securities and Exchange Commission* Supplementary Volume I (Washington, 1971), Table 1B-4.

(r_K) may be viewed as governed by its marginal revenue product, the contribution of additional units of capital goods to the value of total output.

Capital, like all productive factors, is subject to the law of diminishing returns. Given the labor force and the level of technology, increases in the stock of capital result in diminishing increments in the quantity of goods produced and so in the marginal product of capital. This relationship is shown in Figure 6-1. The total capital stock is measured on the horizontal axis, and the value of the marginal product of capital, expressed as a percentage rate of return, is measured on the vertical axis. The marginal productivity of capital schedule may be drawn for an individual firm or for the economy as a whole. The return on capital will depend on the quantity and quality of labor with which it is to be combined.

The Desired Capital Stock

The stock of plant and equipment desired by business firms will depend on the expected volume of sales. It will also depend on technological considerations, which determine the productivity of different capital goods, and on the cost of labor and capital as factors of production, as firms attempt to substitute factors to find the lowest cost technique for producing goods and services. A relative increase in the price of any factor will reduce the quantity demanded.

The total capital stock (K^*) that business firms desire to own in any period (t) may now be formulated as some function of the expected level of sales or output (Y), the return on capital goods (r_K), the cost of finance (r_F), the cost of labor (w), the state of technology (T), and the general climate of expectations concerning the future (E).

1. $K^* = f\ (Y,\ r_K,\ r_F,\ w,\ T,\ E)$

This desired capital stock represents the amount of plant and equipment that maximizes the present value of the business. A change in any of these variables will

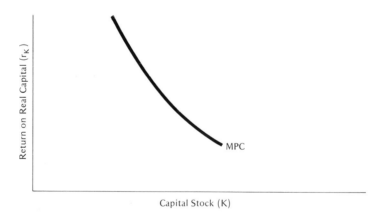

Figure 6-1 Marginal Productivity of Capital

change the stock of capital that businessmen desire to hold. A rise in the expected return on capital goods (r_K) will raise the desired capital stock. A rise in the cost of finance (r_F) will reduce the stock of capital that businessmen want to hold. A rise in the cost of labor (w) will increase the desired capital stock as businessmen substitute capital for labor in the production process.

The Capital–Output Ratio

The stock of capital desired by business firms is directly related to the expected level of output. The ratio of the stock of real capital to the value of annual output is termed the *capital-output ratio* (K/Y). Estimates of the value of the total capital stock, capital per worker, the ratio of capital stock to output, and the ratio of changes in capital stock to changes in output are presented in Table 6-3. Because of changes in the price level, in the relative price of different capital goods, and in technology, it is very difficult to measure the value of the existing capital stock. Although the particular magnitude of the ratio is sensitive to how capital is measured, its level appears to have fallen significantly, from over three to under two, over the period considered. The marginal capital output ratio ($\Delta K/\Delta Y$) fell even more substantially over the period.

Table 6-3   CAPITAL AND OUTPUT, 1869–1955

Year	Value of Total Net Capital Stock (K) (Billions of Dollars)	Capital per Worker (K/L) (Dollars)*	Capital–Output Ratio (K/O)*	Marginal Capital–Output Ratio (ΔK/ΔO)*
1869	27	2,110	3.5	2.3
1889	68	3,060	3.4	4.9
1909	165	4,410	3.6	4.3
1929	306	6,330	3.5	9.6
1939	319	6,040	3.9	0.7
1946	347	6,450	2.5	1.8
1955	442	6,740	2.5	

*Ten-year average
Source: Simon Kuznets, *Capital in the American Economy*, Princeton, 1961.

Because of differences in technology the desired ratio of capital to output varies widely by industry. Some industries, where least-cost production is highly capital-intensive (railroads, electric plants, and oil refineries) have very large values of capital relative to the value of annual production. At the other extreme are industries where least-cost techniques are highly labor-intensive (women's garments, barber and restaurant services) and the value of capital stock is very low relative to the value of annual output. The aggregate capital-output ratios for the economy as a whole presented in Table 6-3 may be regarded as a weighted average of different industry capital-output ratios.

Technological considerations determine some range of capital requirements for different industries. But this range is substantial, and wide variations in desired capital-output ratios are possible in response to changes in the cost of labor and capital. Plant and equipment may be of heavy or light construction, new or old machines may be used, utilization may be at a high or low level of capacity, and more or less capital intensive techniques of production may be adopted.

THE COST OF FINANCE

The desired stock of plant, equipment, and inventories that corporations want to own is inversely related to the cost they must pay for finance. Firms are owned ultimately by households. As shown in Table 6-2, nonfinancial corporations have financed most of their total assets through equity finance (primarily retained earnings), while debt finance accounted for about one third of total assets accumulation.

Perfect Certainty

In a world of perfect certainty the cost of finance to a firm would be perfectly elastic at the market rate of interest (r_B). If the firm could borrow or lend indefinite amounts at this rate, it would continue to acquire capital goods as long as their expected return at the margin exceeded the interest rate.

The determination of the desired capital stock under perfect certainty is shown in Figure 6-2. The cost of finance schedule is a horizontal straight line at the market rate of interest on "bonds" (r_B). The demand for capital schedule is downward-sloping, governed by the expected marginal productivity of capital (r_K).

The stock of capital desired (K^*) under such circumstances would be independent of the size of business retained earnings and of business net worth. If their desired capital stock exceeded their net worth, firms would simply borrow the excess at the

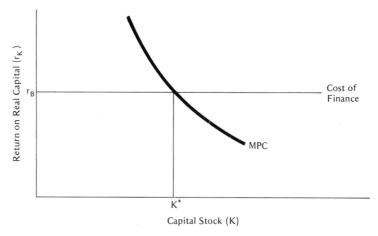

Figure 6-2 Desired Capital Stock Under Perfect Certainty

market rate of interest. If their desired capital stock were less than their net worth, they would simply lend the excess at the market rate of interest.

The Cost of Finance under Uncertainty

In a world of uncertainty the cost of finance to a business firm is no longer infinitely elastic at the market rate of interest. Firms issue different types of financial assets. The volume of finance any particular firm can raise and so the amount of real assets it can own is limited. At least after some point more financial assets can be sold only at a lower price and a higher rate of return. The cost of alternative sources of finance under uncertainty is illustrated in Figure 6-3, in which cost (r_F) is measured as a percentage rate of return on the vertical axis and total financing in dollars on the horizontal axis.

Alternative sources of finance have different costs. The low cost of depreciation funds is due to the fact that they are tax deductible. As a corporation attempts to raise additional loans or to issue additional bonds, it must at least after some point sell them for a lower price and pay a progressively higher rate of interest. As the ratio of firm debt to total assets and interest payments to total income rises, so does the possible risk of default. As borrowing increases, risk-averting lenders become increasingly reluctant to supply additional finance, even at higher interest rates. Similarly, the demand for a corporation's stock is downward-sloping. Existing stockholders must be induced to buy larger amounts, or new stockholders be persuaded or enticed to become owners, by lowering the price. As a corporation issues additional shares it can sell them only at a lower price with a progressively higher rate of return. The amount of debt issued also affects the return and risk and therefore the price of the corporation's stock. As a result the costs of different sources of finance

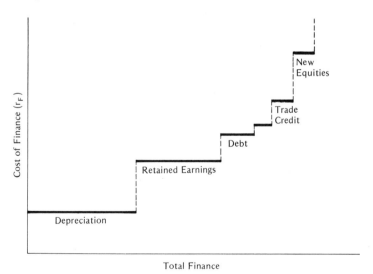

Figure 6-3 Cost of Alternative Sources of Finance

shown in Figure 6-3 are not independent of the amount of finance raised. After some point the costs of additional finance become increasingly expensive as wealth owners are unwilling to extend further financing at any price.

Corporate Financial Policy

The cost of finance under uncertainty is governed by the price at which the corporation is able to sell its financial assets, that is, the costs it must pay for different sources of funds. In an attempt to raise funds as cheaply as possible, corporations finance asset accumulation through the issue of a variety of financial instruments, each tailored to the preferences of different investors.

Corporate financial policy must attempt to determine the optimal mix of debt and equity finance, internally or externally generated, that will result in the lowest cost of finance schedule to the firm. By varying the proportion of earnings retained, the ratio of debt to equity, and the type of debt and equity securities issued, corporate financial managers are able to affect the average cost of finance to the corporation. The resulting cost of finance schedule is shown in Figure 6-4. It represents a weighted average of the costs of different sources of finance. As in the production cost curves of the previous chapter, there are an indefinite number of cost of finance curves for a corporation lying above the least-cost curve shown in Figure 6-4.

As reflected in Table 6-2, corporations, like households, maintain some preferred proportion of debt and equity finance to total assets. The mix chosen reflects their estimate of the lowest cost of finance. Firms with different investment-return opportunities will locate at different points on their cost of finance schedules with a different mix of financial assets. The shape and position of the cost of finance curve for a particular corporation will depend on the market's evaluation of its future prospects. Expectations must necessarily be based largely on past performance,

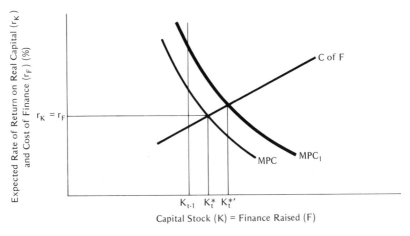

Figure 6-4 Desired Capital Stock under Uncertainty

existing stocks of assets and debts, existing managerial talents, and the sales and profit prospects for the industry.[1]

INVESTMENT BEHAVIOR

The Desired Capital Stock

A management acting in the interests of its shareholders will accumulate capital assets only as long as the effect is to raise the price of the corporation's stock. Given the expected future dividend stream from share ownership, the market price of the corporation's stock determines the rate of return received by stockholders on their investment (Chapter 9). This rate governs the cost of finance to the corporation. Capital accumulation will raise the price of the corporation's stock only if the expected rate of return on new investment exceeds the rate of return earned by stockholders. The return on corporate stock is thus the cutoff rate of return on new investment, the minimum required rate of return that a corporation must earn on the assets it acquires.

The determination of the desired capital stock under uncertainty is illustrated in Figure 6-4. The marginal productivity of capital schedule and the cost of finance schedule are superimposed on the same diagram. The desired capital stock is equal to K^*, at which point the cost of finance is equal to the real rate of return on capital. Firms acting in the interests of stockholders will accumulate capital goods up to the point where the expected return on capital (r_K) is equal to the cost of finance (r_F). Real assets with a return below the cutoff rate r_F will reduce the value of the corporation's stock. As the corporation always has the option of purchasing its own shares or those of other corporations, in the interests of its stockholders it should never acquire projects with a return below this opportunity cost of finance.

Shifts in the return expected on capital goods—due, for example, to a change in technology, in the growth of sales, or in the general climate of business expectations—shift the revenue productivity of capital schedule upward or downward (e.g., to MPC_1 in Figure 6-4). Similarly, changes in the price and return on financial assets result in an upward or downward shift in the cost of finance schedule. Changes in the availability of finance are frequently associated with changes in the price and return on financial assets. In this case a horizontal and a vertical displacement of the cost of finance schedule occur simultaneously.

---

1. This cost of finance schedule is widely termed the *cost of capital schedule.* This terminology is confusing, as the term *capital* is being required to bear two quite different meanings. In its first meaning capital denotes the stock of tangible assets, the plant, equipment, and inventories used in the production process (real capital). These assets have a market price or cost to the firm and also an expected return. In its second meaning capital denotes the supply of purchasing power to firms, which permits them as intermediate wealth owners to own and administer real capital goods and services (financial capital). This supply of purchasing power will henceforth be termed *finance,* so that *capital* may be confined to the stock of tangible assets used to raise the productivity of labor in the production process.

Investment as Stock-Adjustment Behavior

Firms have some *desired* stock of capital goods at the end of any period (K^*_t), depending on their sales expectations and on their choice of least-cost technology. In general this will not be equal to the *actual* stock of plant and equipment owned by the firm at the beginning of the period (K_{t-1}). The firm will attempt to reduce the discrepancy between its desired and its actual capital stock ($K^*_t - K_{t-1}$). This process of adjusting actual capital stocks towards their desired levels is the motive behind business investment behavior. Net investment represents simply the net accumulation of capital goods over some period of time.

$$I_t = (K_t - K_{t-1})$$

Investment takes time and is surrounded by very considerable uncertainty. A decision to invest in plant and equipment this year will not result in an expansion in productive capacity until perhaps several years in the future. Specialized capital goods must be ordered, and they then may require a considerable gestation period before they are produced. Once made, investment decisions are largely irreversible. Used capital goods can be resold only at substantial loss.

It follows that in a market economy investment is always something of a gamble, an act of faith regarding the future. When a businessman guesses incorrectly, the penalties can be enormous. If he decides to expand capacity and his market does not grow proportionately, he will be saddled with expensive unused plant and equipment. If his market expands by a greater extent than his capacity, he will loose out to his competitors. If he invests in new machinery that is rendered unprofitable and obsolete by innovations in technology, he will suffer a severe capital loss. Investment decisions are fraught with risk. Nevertheless they are the seed corn of the firm.

Psychologists have established that the time taken to make a decision is related to its importance and the degree of uncertainty. Businessmen attempt to move circumspectly, to keep as many options open as possible. Difficult decisions are temporized and spread out to allow additional information to be collected. Rome was not built in a day, and neither was a modern corporation. In any period firms will attempt to close only a portion of the gap between their desired and their actual capital stock.

Nevertheless investment expenditures are highly volatile, fluctuating widely from one year to the next, because investment is an adjustment process of actual to desired capital stocks. The desired capital stock depends on the expected future course of sales, and the climate of business expectations is extremely susceptible to waves of optimism or pessimism. Given the degree of ignorance concerning the future, blind confidence or "animal spirits" on the part of businessmen play an important role in investment behavior. Suppose sales were first expected to increase by 5 percent next year, and this estimate was then revised upward to 10 percent. If the desired capital stock were raised by the same proportion (10 percent) the size of the *gap* between desired and actual stocks would increase not by 5 but by 100 percent.

Similarly, any reduction in the level of the desired capital stock will result in a much larger reduction in the gap between desired and actual stocks.

The Demand for Investment

The portion of the gap between desired and actual capital stocks that firms desire to close in any period represents their demand for investment goods. Over any period a firm is faced with a number of investment opportunities. Management must estimate the expected rate of return on each of these projects.[2] It may then be envisaged as ranking its existing investment opportunities by descending order of expected rates of return. This array of projects constitutes the firm's *investment demand function* as shown in Figure 6-5, where the expected rate of return on investment projects is measured on the vertical axis and the volume of investment expenditure on the horizontal axis.

The desired capital stock, and so the return expected on new investment projects, will shift upward or downward with changes in the general climate of expectations concerning future sales. Even small changes in desired capital stock (e.g., from K^*_t to $K^*_t{}'$ in Figure 6-4) will result in very large changes in the gap between desired and actual stocks, and so in the investment demand schedule (e.g., from I_D to I_D' of Figure 6-5), even if managers plan to close only a portion of the total gap within the period.

Gross and Net Investment

Gross business investment refers to total expenditures on currently produced plant, equipment, and inventory over some period of time, conventionally one year. Over

2. The calculation of the expected rate of return on an investment is described in Chapter 9.

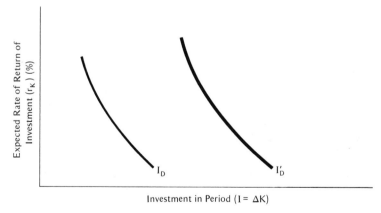

Figure 6-5 Demand for Investment Goods

Table 6-4 NONFINANCIAL CORPORATE INVESTMENT EXPENDITURE AND DEPRECIATION, 1946-71 (BILLIONS OF DOLLARS)

Year	Nonfinancial Corporate Gross Investment (Purchase of Physical Assets)	Depreciation (Capital Consumption Allowances)	Net Corporate Investment (1—2)	Ratio: Depreciation Corporate Investment (2/1)	Change in Gross Corporate Investment	Change in Gross National Product (GNP)
1946	17.9	4.6	13.3	.26	10* (est.)	−3.4
1947	17.2	5.7	11.5	.33	0.7	22.8
1948	20.3	6.8	13.5	.33	3.1	26.3
1949	15.3	7.8	7.5	.51	−5.0	−1.1
1950	24.1	8.6	15.5	.36	8.8	28.3
1951	29.9	10.0	19.9	.33	5.8	43.6
1952	24.4	11.2	13.2	.46	−5.5	17.1
1953	24.6	12.9	11.7	.52	0.2	19.1
1954	21.6	14.6	7.0	.67	−3.0	.2
1955	31.5	17.0	14.5	.54	9.9	33.2
1956	35.9	18.4	17.5	.51	4.4	21.2
1957	34.7	20.3	14.4	.58	−1.2	21.9
1958	27.3	21.4	5.9	.78	−7.4	6.2
1959	36.9	22.9	14.0	.62	9.6	36.4
1960	39.0	24.2	14.8	.62	2.1	20.0
1961	36.7	25.4	11.3	.69	3.7	16.4
1962	44.0	29.2	14.8	.66	7.3	40.2
1963	45.6	30.8	14.8	.68	1.6	30.2
1964	52.1	32.8	19.3	.63	6.5	41.9
1965	62.8	35.2	27.6	.56	10.7	52.5
1966	77.1	38.2	38.9	.50	14.3	65.0
1967	72.0	41.5	30.5	.58	−5.1	44.0
1968	76.2	45.1	31.1	.59	4.2	70.3
1969	84.0	49.9	34.1	.59	7.8	66.1
1970	84.6	52.7	31.9	.63	0.6	46.1
1971	85.2	57.3	27.9	.67	0.6	74.0

Source: "Flow of Funds," Board of Governors, Federal Reserve System; GNP; Department of Commerce.

time a firm's existing capital stock is continually wearing out and depreciating in value. The estimated decline in the value of the capital stock is a cost chargeable to current production and is termed *depreciation. Net investment* is defined as gross investment minus depreciation. It is equal to the net change in the capital stock from one period to the next.

Table 6-4 presents corporate investment expenditures and depreciation allowances over the postwar period. As may be seen, investment expenditures varied substantially from one year to the next and were extremely sensitive to the rate of growth of Gross National Product. As depreciation allowances grow smoothly, large increases in investment spending such as occurred in 1965, 1966, and 1969 must be financed from other sources.

Depreciation allowances accounted for from one half to two thirds of gross investment. As it is impossible to determine precisely the value of the capital stock used up in any period, charges for depreciation represent a rough estimate at best and depend on the conventions by which depreciation is calculated. Because depreciation expenses reduce taxable income and taxes paid, profitable firms have an incentive to increase their depreciation allowances to the maximum permitted by the government in order to reduce their tax liabilities. The rise in the ratio of depreciation to gross investment shown in Table 6-4 is due largely to more liberal provisions to calculate depreciation as a taxable expense. Reported depreciation is based on the original historical cost of the capital stock, so that in periods of rising prices depreciation allowances may understate the true current replacement cost of capital used up in production.

In addition to wear and tear, technological change reduces the lifetime use and value of existing capital equipment. This loss of value is termed *obsolescence.* A particular machine may not be fully depreciated in the sense of being physically worn out, and it may not be fully paid for. Nevertheless it may become obsolete and be scrapped because a newer, more efficient piece of equipment can produce the same output at lower cost. Whenever the average cost of the new equipment is less than the marginal cost of producing with the old equipment, the firm can raise profits by replacing obsolete capital goods. Because it is very difficult to estimate the rate of obsolescence, firms typically use a conservatively short estimate of the life of capital goods when calculating the expected return on new investment projects.

Sources of Funds

Businesses must always somehow finance any additions to their stock of assets. They may do this internally, through depreciation allowances and retained earnings, or externally, by new borrowing and the issue of debt and equity securities.

Table 6-5 presents the sources of funds (increases in liabilities and net worth) for nonfinancial corporations over the postwar period. The proportion of internal financing rose substantially, largely because of the rise in depreciation allowances. New issues of corporate stock were a small proportion both of total sources and of

Table 6-5 NONFINANCIAL CORPORATIONS, SOURCES OF FUNDS, 1946–71 (BILLIONS OF DOLLARS)

	Internal Sources		External Sources					Ratio of External to Total Sources
Year	Total Internal	Undistributed Profits	Total External	Stocks	Bonds & Mortgages	Bank & Other loans	Total Sources	
1946	7.8	8.5	10.9	1.1	2.5	3.7	18.8	.58
1947	12.6	12.8	15.9	1.2	4.4	2.8	28.5	.56
1948	18.7	14.0	9.7	1.0	5.4	0.1	28.3	.34
1949	19.1	9.5	0.5	1.3	3.8	−2.0	19.6	.03
1950	17.9	14.3	24.0	1.4	2.5	3.5	41.9	.57
1951	19.9	11.1	19.6	1.9	4.1	4.5	39.5	.50
1952	21.2	9.0	11.0	2.3	5.6	1.6	32.1	.34
1953	21.1	9.3	9.2	1.8	4.2	−0.2	30.3	.30
1954	23.3	9.0	5.9	1.6	5.1	−0.7	29.3	.20
1955	29.2	13.9	25.1	1.9	4.6	4.0	54.2	.46
1956	28.9	13.2	18.5	2.3	5.2	5.4	47.5	.39
1957	30.6	11.8	12.8	2.4	7.9	1.7	43.3	.29
1958	29.5	8.3	14.7	2.1	8.6	−0.5	44.2	.33
1959	35.0	12.6	22.9	2.2	6.0	3.2	57.9	.40
1960	34.4	10.0	13.7	1.6	6.0	3.8	48.1	.28
1961	35.6	10.2	21.0	2.5	8.5	1.3	56.6	.37
1962	41.8	12.4	23.1	0.6	9.1	3.0	64.9	.36
1963	43.9	13.6	23.2	−0.3	8.8	3.9	67.1	.35
1964	50.5	18.3	21.3	1.4	7.6	4.7	71.8	.30
1965	56.6	21.3	36.5	0.0	9.3	11.2	93.1	.39
1966	61.2	22.9	39.4	1.2	14.4	9.6	100.6	.39
1967	61.5	19.0	37.3	2.3	19.2	8.2	98.8	.38
1968	61.7	17.5	48.1	0.8	18.7	12.9	109.8	.44
1969	60.8	13.6	56.9	4.3	16.9	19.1	117.7	.49
1970	59.1	8.4	43.4	6.8	25.6	7.5	102.5	.42
1971	67.1	11.9	59.6	13.4	30.6	4.5	126.7	.47

Source: "Flow of Funds," Board of Governors, Federal Reserve System.

external sources, as corporations relied increasingly on internal funds to provide equity finance. With the fall in undistributed profits in 1969 and 1970, external financing, in particular new stock issues, increased sharply.

The amount of investment undertaken in any period is always constrained by the cost and availability of new financing to the firm. This is represented by the upward-sloping supply of funds schedule in Figure 6-6.

The short-run (flow) supply of funds schedule is at first flat but, beyond some normal amount, determined by the size and profitability of the firm, rises much more steeply than the long-run (stock) cost of finance schedule of Figure 6-4. In any period additional funds can be raised after some point only at sharply increasing cost. The volume of depreciation allowances, retained earnings, and "normal" credit lines determine the length of the horizontal portion of the supply of funds schedule. As a corporation attempts to raise additional external finance by the issue of new loans, bonds, and stock, these financial assets can only be sold by promising creditors a higher return. By extending the mix of sources to obtain additional higher-cost external financing, the average cost of finance is increased. As liabilities increase

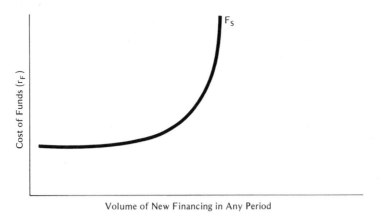

Figure 6-6 Supply of Funds Schedule

beyond some point lenders will be unwilling to grant more credit, even at every high rates of return, as they are concerned about the riskiness of their investments. The schedule then becomes vertical.

Investment Expenditure

It is at last possible to summarize the factors affecting the volume of business investment in any period. Total investment spending undertaken will depend on the demand for investment relative to the position of the supply of funds schedule. These relationships are shown in Figure 6-7, which combines Figures 6-5 and 6-6. Corporations will continue to invest as long as the expected return from capital accumulation exceeds their cost of funds.

The relative importance of demand and financial forces in affecting investment spending will depend on where the demand for investment curve and the supply

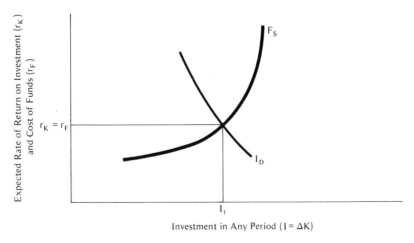

Figure 6-7 Determination of Investment Spending

of funds curve intersect. If the intersection occurs over the range where the supply of funds schedule is relatively flat, as in Figure 6-8a, changes in investment spending will be determined primarily by shifts in the demand for investment schedule. If the intersection occurs over the range where the supply of funds schedule is rising steeply, as in Figure 6-8b, even large shifts in the demand for investment and in the expected rate of return on capital goods will result in only small changes in investment spending, which is constrained by the cost and availability of funds.

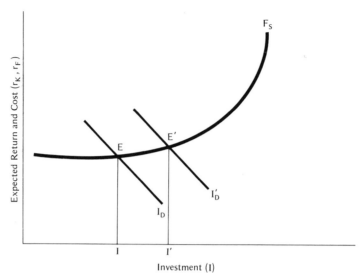

a. Demand Dominant

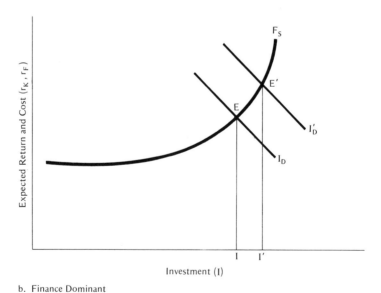

b. Finance Dominant

Figure 6-8 The Effects of a Shift in Investment Demand

Changes in the volume of funds that can be raised at any particular price and return result in a shift in the cost of funds schedule. As may be seen from Figure 6-9, the extent that investment expenditures respond will again depend on the intersection point.

Changes in the market price and therefore in the return on financial assets result in a vertical displacement of the supply of funds schedule. As shown in Figure 6-9a, if the intersection occurs over the range where the supply funds schedule is not vertical, it will affect investment spending. The amount that investment expenditure changes depends on return elasticity of the investment demand curve.

Changes in depreciation allowances, retained earnings, and the quantity of funds available in the financial markets result in a horizontal displacement of the supply

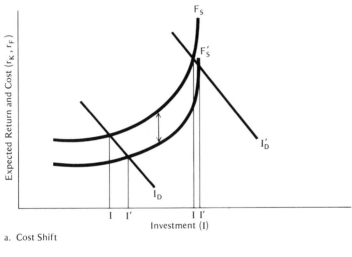

a. Cost Shift

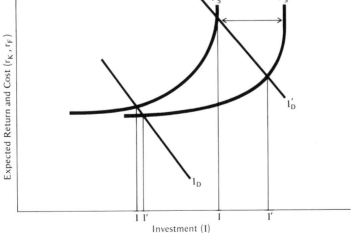

b. Availability Shift

Figure 6-9 The Effects of a Shift in the Cost and Availability of Funds

of funds schedule. As shown in Figure 6-9b, this change will affect investment expenditure whenever the initial intersection point is not over the horizontal section of the supply of funds schedule.

In periods when funds are readily available, demand factors (shifts in expected sales) dominate investment spending as shown in Figure 6-8a. In periods when funds are tight, shifts in the availability of funds dominate investment spending as shown in Figure 6-9b.

Because in the real world both the demand for investment and the supply of funds schedule are continually shifting, it is extremely difficult to estimate empirically the return elasticity of the investment demand function. For short-lived projects, inventories and rapidly depreciating equipment, investment demand appears inelastic to changes in the cost of funds. But for long-lived projects, plant, structures, and housing, the return elasticity of investment demand appears substantial. At very low costs of funds a large number of investment projects with long expected future earning lifetimes become profitable.

APPENDIX: THE STOCK MARKET, ACCOUNTING STATEMENTS, AND THE ACCELERATOR

The Discipline of the Stock Markets

The capital markets operate to constrain the discretionary power of corporate management. Even managers of giant corporations, largely independent of direct stockholder control, may find their freedom severely constrained by the discipline of the market. First they must meet their payroll and make a profit, or the corporation and their jobs will disappear. Competition in product markets weeds out grossly inefficient firms and serves as a stimulus to cost reduction.

Within this primary constraint to survive, managers cannot stray too far from stockholder preferences, because corporate performance is reflected in the market value of a corporation's stock. Consider the question of how rapidly the corporation ought to grow. In Figure 6-10 the corporation's per-share dividends (D) are measured on the vertical axis, while the rate of growth of dividends (g) is measured on the horizontal axis.

Share prices are determined in the financial markets by the expected level, stability, and rate of growth of corporate dividends. For a particular corporation the stock market's valuation of return and growth may be represented by the set of equal-share-price curves SS. Higher dividends and higher growth are always desirable. To maintain the same share price, a lower level of present dividends must be compensated for by a more rapid expected growth rate of future dividends.

Uncertainty that present growth rates can be maintained in the future increases with the rate of growth attained. Similarly, the risk of future capital loss increases as the price-dividend ratio of rapidly growing corporations rises. As a result the SS

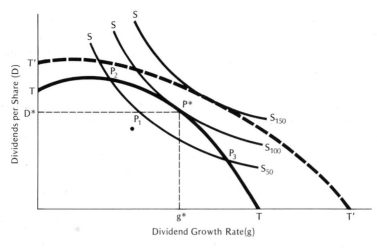

Figure 6-10 Market Valuation of a Business Corporation

curves flatten at higher growth rates. The slope of the curves represents how the financial market values growth in comparison with return. Greater valuation of future growth would cause the set of *SS* curves to become steeper. Corporations with different risk prospects will have different share prices for any combination of dividends and growth.

Managers in general are able to increase a firm's rate of growth, after some point at least, only by reducing the level of its current dividends. To grow more rapidly a firm must devote a larger amount of resources to research and development expenditures, product innovation, and advertising. A firm may also be able to increase its market share by cutting prices. It may retain and reinvest larger amounts of its profits by reducing the amount of dividends paid out. Or it may increase the number of shares outstanding. All of these techniques to raise the growth rate reduce current dividend levels per share.

The tradeoff relationship between dividends and growth rate for a particular firm is represented in Figure 6-10 by the curve *TT*. It will vary among different firms depending on their profit and growth opportunities. For firms with more attractive growth prospects the trade-off relationship will be flatter (e.g., *T'T'*), while for firms with limited growth prospects it will fall more steeply.

Corporate managers whose goal is maximization of the value of the corporation's stock will move to the point *P** on their dividend-growth possibility curve in Figure 6-10, where it is tangent to the highest equal share price curve ($100). As managers do not know with certainty the shape of the corporation's potential *TT* relationship, these decisions are the fighting point in corporate board rooms, the decisions on which management careers are made or broken.

This analysis reveals the potential importance of stock market discipline. Suppose the management is sleepy and inefficient and operates at a point far within its potential dividend-growth possibilities (e.g., at P_1). Or suppose the managers are tradition-oriented, or value highly the rewards of a comfortable life, and locate at the low growth position P_2. Alternatively managers may prefer a very rapid growth of the corporation, because of expected resultant higher salaries, greater power and responsibility, and a larger sense of achievement and status; and they may locate at the position P_3.

Managers preferring less rapid or more rapid growth than their stockholders will adopt a policy that may be represented along the corporation's possibility curve TT. As management preferences diverge increasingly from those of the stockholders, this position is located at increasing distances from P^*, and the market price of the corporation's stock falls progressively below its maximum potential value. A similar consequence occurs for inefficient managements that settle for positions within the TT frontier.

Under such circumstances the management becomes more and more subject to stockholder rebellion. Disenchantment grows as stockholders compare the performance of their stock unfavorably with that of competitors. Dividends or growth may have to be raised to keep the stockholders from braying too loudly at the door. Just as importantly, the management becomes increasingly exposed to a take-over bid from other corporations or minority stockholders. There is a market for corporate control. When a stock is selling substantially below its potential level, other managers or investors increasingly anticipate a profitable investment opportunity. If they are able to buy control at a low price, they can change the policy and then reap large capital gains on their investment. This indirect financial market discipline serves to prevent managers from straying too far from the policy P^* where stockowner interests are best served, even if stockholder direct influence over management policy is ineffective.

In the real world in addition to private corporations there are a variety of private nonprofit and public corporations, in which the property rights of "owners" are more or less severely circumscribed. For such institutions profit maximization is ordinarily an inappropriate formulation of their goals. Nevertheless they do have objectives, more or less quantifiable, and their managers may similarly be regarded as attempting to maximize some utility function. A critically important difference between nonprofit institutions (government agencies, universities, or foundations) and private corporations is that there exists no stock market on which the performance of the former is continually being evaluated and through which institutional control may be transferred. As a result, inefficient managements and suboptimum policies may persist with little external pressure for correction.

Interrelation Between Income Statements and Balance Sheets

An income statement refers to flow relationships. It records the income received by an economic unit over a particular period of time, conventionally one year, and the expenses that were incurred in producing that income. The difference between income and expenses for a business unit represent its profits.

FIRM A: SIMPLIFIED INCOME STATEMENT FOR THE YEAR 2000

Total Sales Receipts	$1,000	
Increase in inventories	100	$1,100
Total Costs of Production and Sales		
Wages and Salaries	$ 300	
Raw Materials	200	
Depreciation	100	
Interest and Rent	100	$ 700
Gross Profits		400
Taxes		200
Net Profits		200
Dividends		100
Retained Earnings: Transferred to Surplus		$ 100

The amount of saving or retained earnings always results in an equal change in the net worth of the economic unit over the period. Depreciation charges, recorded as a current expense even if no cash outflows are incurred, reduce the valuation of assets as recorded in the balance sheet. New investment and borrowing are capital account transactions. They do not appear in the income statement except as they affect current income and expenses.

As described earlier, a balance sheet represents a financial picture of an economic unit at a moment of time. It refers to stock relationships and is derived from the fundamental identity equating net worth to the difference between total assets and total liabilities.

A firm's total assets are financed in part by borrowing (debt finance) and in part by capital supplied by owners of the firm (equity finance). As shown in the simplified balance-sheet statements, earnings retained by the firm result in an identical increase in net worth ($100) over the period. This increase represents internal equity finance by the firm.

FIRM A: SIMPLIFIED BALANCE SHEET STATEMENT, DECEMBER 31, 1999

Assets			Liabilities and Net Worth	
Cash		$ 200	Accounts Payable	$ 100
Accounts Receivable		100	Bank Loans	200
Securities		400	Bonds	200
Inventory		100	Net Worth	
Plant and Equipment	1,000		Surplus	1,000
Reserve for De-				
preciation	300	700		
			Total Liabilities	
Total Assets		$1,500	and Net Worth	$1,500

FIRM A: SIMPLIFIED BALANCE SHEET STATEMENT, DECEMBER 31, 2000

Assets			Liabilities and Net Worth	
Cash		$ 100	Accounts Payable	$ 200
Accounts Receivable		100	Bank Loans	300
Securities		200	Bonds	400
Inventory		200	Net Worth	
Plant and Equipment	1,800		Surplus	1,100
Reserve for Depreciation	400	1,400		
			Total Liabilities	
Total Assets		$2,000	and Net Worth	$2,000

The effect of internal equity finance is as if the managers paid out all the profits as dividends and then sold new shares to existing stockholders for $100. As the number of shares outstanding did not change, the effect of internal finance is to raise the market price of outstanding shares. The extent to which share values increase, in particular whether the increase in values is greater or less than $100, will depend on the return earned by the firm on the new investment relative to the return received by stockholders from share ownership. If the stock market values the firm's additional earning prospects highly, the value of the firm's share will rise by much more than the $100 of retentions.

The depreciation expense of $100 shown in the income statement represents the estimated reduction over the year in the market value of the firm's plant and equipment. This estimate is charged as an expense against current operations but, unlike other expenses, it does not involve a cash payment outside the firm. Transfers to the depreciation reserve reduce the balance sheet value of plant and equipment.

The reserve for depreciation is not held as a specific actual reserve of cash or securities. Additions to the reserve for depreciation are represented elsewhere in the balance sheet, in the form of net increments to total assets or reductions in total debt owed. If the depreciation expense had not be charged, profits and net worth would have been $100 greater. But this accounting would involve an overestimation of profits, as these assets must someday be replaced. It is a more accurate presentation of the economic facts to write down the value of the depreciated assets.

The increase in inventories was treated similarly to sales in the income statement. Goods produced but not sold during the period are reflected in the increase of inventories in the balance sheet. Had these goods been sold, they would have resulted in an increase in cash or accounts receivable.

From comparison of the balance sheets for the years 1999 and 2000 it may be inferred that the firm made investment expenditures of $800 for plant and equipment during the year 2000. As these transactions did not affect current earnings or expenses, they did not appear in the income statement and did not affect current profits. One half of these investment expenditures was financed externally by borrowing, in the form of an increase in accounts payable ($100), bank loans, ($100), and bonds outstanding ($200). The other half was financed internally out of current retained earnings ($100), depreciation ($100), and past saving, as reflected in the reduction of security holdings ($200).

Business investment expenditures characteristically exceed business depreciation charges and retained earnings, so that business firms in most periods choose to raise some funds externally. When investment expectations are pessimistic, business firms will choose to invest less than their current retained earnings and depreciation. They will then use the surplus to pay off debts or to acquire financial assets.

Speed of Adjustment and the Accelerator

In any short period firms attempt to close only a portion of the gap between desired and actual capital stock. Empirical studies suggest that the speed of adjustment of actual to desired stocks is very slow, with adjustment behavior being distributed over several years. As the desired capital stock is continually changing, in a growing economy equilibrium between actual and desired capital stock is ordinarily never achieved. The actual investment expenditures undertaken in any period are in response to decisions made and conditions ruling in previous periods. Decisions taken in this period in the light of present evidence have their effect on investment spending and output in future periods, when conditions may have radically changed.

This view of investment spending as adaptive stock-adjustment behavior distributed over some period of time may be formulated more precisely. In any particular period — for example, one year — only some portion λ of the gap between desired and actual capital stock will be closed.

1. $I_t = \lambda (K^*_t - K_{t-1})$

where $1 > \lambda > 0$ (where $>$ means "greater than or equal to")

The constant λ may be termed the *speed of adjustment* coefficient. If $\lambda = 1$, all of the adjustment is completed over the period. If $\lambda = 0$, none of the adjustment is completed.

In addition to expected sales, the desired capital stock is a function of the return on capital goods (r_K), the cost of finance (r_F), the cost of labor (w), technology (T), and the general climate of investor expectations.

2. $K^*_t = f (Y, r_K, r_F, w, T, e)$

Substituting in equation 1: $I_t = \lambda f (Y, r_K, r_F, w, T, E) - \lambda K_{t-1}$

This relationship shows that the higher the level of the capital stock at the beginning of the period (K_{t-1}) relative to future needs, the smaller will be desired net investment as additions to that stock. Investment will thus be much greater in a rapidly growing economy. Increases in the cost of finance (r_F) reduce the desired capital stock and raise the required rate of return on new investment projects.

In order to maintain its capital stock intact, so as to be able to produce as much next period as it can produce this period, a firm must undertake sufficient investment expenditures to replace the capital stock that has worn out over the period. If it does not, net investment will be negative and the capital stock will decline. The volume of replacement investment expenditures in any period will thus be related to the quantity and age of the existing capital stock.

In order to be able to increase its future output, a firm must first increase its productive capacity and so its stock of real capital assets. Assume for simplicity that the desired capital stock (K^*) in any period (t) is simply some function of expected sales or output in that period (Y_t):

1. $K^*_t = f(Y_t)$.

The same relationship will hold in the next period:

2. $K^*_{t+1} = f(Y_{t+1})$.

Subtracting Equation 1 from Equation 2, we have:

3. $K^*_{t+1} - K^*_t = f(Y_{t+1} - Y_t) = f(\Delta Y_t)$.

The change in the desired capital stock is then some function of the change in sales or output. Suppose that firms were always to invest to maintain their actual capital stock equal to their desired capital stock ($K^*_t = K_t$, and $K^*_{t+1} = K_{t-1}$). In this case, with very rapid speeds of adjustment ($\lambda = 1$), the actual change in the capital stock from one period to the next (the *level* of net investment) becomes some function of the *rate* at which sales and output are expected to increase:

4. $I_t = (K^*_{t+1} - K^*_t) = f(\Delta Y_t)$.

For the case in which the ratio of capital to output was always constant ($K/Y = k$), the desired stock of capital would grow at the same rate as the growth of expected sales:

5. $\Delta K^*/K^* = \Delta Y/Y$.

As long as actual net investment in every period always equals the change in the desired capital stock ($I_t = \Delta K^*_t$), the level of net investment would simply equal the capital-output ratio times the change in output:

6. $I_t = k\Delta Y_t = K_t(\Delta Y/Y)_t$.

This rigid relationship between the level of net investment and the rate of growth of sales is termed the *accelerator principle*. As an explanation of the forces affecting investment demand it yields some interesting insights into the instability of business net-investment spending observed in Tables 6-4 and 6-5.

To the extent the capital-output ratio is constant, a constant *rate of growth* of sales will result in a constant *level* of investment. It follows that an increase in the rate of growth of sales will produce an *accelerated* increase in the level of investment demand. Conversely, a reduction merely in the rate of growth of sales will result in an *accelerated* reduction or even an absolute fall in the level of investment.

These relationships and the resulting instability of investment demand can be illustrated in a numerical example. Assume $K/Y = 10$, capital life $= 20$ years, an age structure of existing capital goods evenly distributed over time, and no technological change. A 10 percent increase in sales in period 2 results in a 200 percent increase in investment spending. This rate of growth of sales is required to maintain investment spending at this level. When the rate of growth of sales declines, as occurs in period 4, the level of investment falls absolutely.

Time Period	Sales	%Δ	Capital Stock	%Δ	Gross Investment	%Δ	Depreciation	Net Investment
0	1,000	0	10,000	0	500	0	500	0
1	1,000	0	10,000	0	500	0	500	0
2	1,100	+10	11,000	+10	1,500	+ 200	500	+1,000
3	1,200	+9	12,000	+9	1,500	0	500	+1,000
4	1,250	+4	12,500	+4	1,000	−33	500	+500
5	1,250	0	12,500	0	500	−50	500	0
6	1,000	−20	12,000	−4	0	−100	500	−500

In response to a fall in sales in period 6, firms can reduce the capital stock only by not replacing depreciated capital goods. As a result, excess capacity is easily created by a drop in sales. To the extent that excess capacity exists, an increase in sales in future periods need not induce gross investment demand. Firms may merely reactivate previously idle plant and equipment.

The ability of business firms to vary the ratio of capital to output even in the short run dulls the power of the accelerator relationship. But it does suggest that the rate of growth of an economy and changes in this rate of growth exert a most important influence on the volume of investment demand. Investment must be greater as a proportion of income in economies that are growing more rapidly merely to maintain any given capital–output ratio.

BIBLIOGRAPHY OF SELECTED PAPERBACKS: PART TWO

Baran, P. and Sweezy, P., *Monopoly Capital: An Essay on the American Economic and Social Order*, Monthy Review.

Barlow, R., *et al*, *Economic Behavior of the Affluent*, Brookings Institution.

Berle, A. and Means, G., *Modern Corporation and Private Property*, Harcourt Brace.

Gilboy, E. W., *Primer on the Economics of Consumption*, Random House.

Horowitz, D. (Ed.) *Corporations and the Cold War*, Monthly Review.

Marris, R., *Economic Theory of Managerial Capitalism*, Basic Books.

Mermelstein, D. (Ed.) *Economics: Mainstream Readings and Radical Critiques*, Random House.

Robinson, J., *Economic Heresies*, Basic Books.

PART THREE

MICROECONOMICS

competition and market power in product markets

THE INTERESTS OF THE DEALERS in any particular branch of trade or manufacture is always in some respects different from, and even opposite to, that of the public. To widen the market and to narrow the competition is always the interest of the dealers. To widen the market may frequently be agreeable enough to the interest of the public, but to narrow the competition must always be against it and can serve only to enable the dealers, by raising their profits above what they would naturally be, to levy for their own benefit, an absurd tax upon the rest of their fellow citizens. . . .

PEOPLE OF THE SAME TRADE seldom meet together, even for merriment and diversion, but the conversation ends in a conspiracy against the public, or in some contrivance to raise prices.

—*ADAM SMITH*

Part Two examined the forces behind household demand and business firms' supply of goods and services. The present chapter considers how the characteristics of the markets in which goods and services are exchanged affect the determination of their prices.

Types of Markets

A market is a group of buyers and sellers who are in contact with one another for the purpose of buying and selling a particular commodity. Markets vary enormously in their scope, physical arrangements, and conventional procedures for buying and selling. In most markets sellers nominate the price and are obliged, often legally, to sell to all comers. The buyer's market power inheres in his decision to buy or not to buy. He may pick and choose among commodities and discriminate among sellers, without any such restrictions or obligations as are imposed on seller.

As is shown in Table 7-1, manufacturing accounts for less than 30 percent of the value of all income and output, while trade, finance, and services account for nearly 40 percent. These shares vary widely in different countries, with agriculture accounting for the major share in less-developed countries.

Table 7-1   NATIONAL INCOME ORIGINATING BY INDUSTRY GROUP, 1963–70

Industry Group	1963 Billions of Dollars	1963 Percent	1970 Billions of Dollars	1970 Percent
Agriculture, Forestry, and Fishing	19	3.9	24	3.1
Mining and Construction	30	6.2	49	6.2
Manufacturing	144	30.0	218	27.3
Transportation, Communications and Public Utilities	40	8.3	61	7.6
Wholesale and Retail Trade	73	15.2	122	15.3
Finance, Insurance, and Real Estate	53	11.0	87	10.9
Services	54	11.3	103	13.0
Government	65	13.5	127	159
Rest of the World	3	0.6	5	0.6
Total All Industries (National Income at Factor Cost)	481	100.0	796	100.0

Source: Survey of Current Business, U.S. Department of Commerce.

Business output is highly concentrated. Table 7-2 shows that the smallest firms, making up 60 percent of all corporations, account for only 2 percent of total corporate assets and 1 percent of profits. Firms with assets over $150 million represented only one tenth of 1 percent of all firms, but accounted for nearly 60 percent of total assets and more than 60 percent of total profits.

Individual markets differ widely in their degree of concentration. Markets may be

Table 7-2 BUSINESS CORPORATIONS BY ASSET SIZE, 1963 (BILLIONS OF DOLLARS)

Measures of Concentration All Industries	Total	Under $100,000		$100,000–$999,999		Asset Size Class $1–$24.9 million		$25–$99.9 million		$150–$249.9 million		Over $250 million	
		Absolute	Percent of Total	Absolute	Percent of Total	Absolute	Percent of Total	Absolute	Percent of Total	Absolute	Percent of Total	Absolute	Percent of Total
Number of Firms (1,000's)	1,323	795	60	451	34	72	5	3.9	0.3	1.0	0.07	0.7	0.05
Total Assets	1,480	27	2	130	9	286	19	184	12	149	10	705	48
Total Sales	1,008	67	7	230	23	244	24	99	10	79	8	288	29
Net Profits	54.1	0.4	1	5.1	9	9.4	17	6.0	11	5.1	9	28.1	52

Source: Treasury Department, Internal Revenue Service.

157

classified into two broad types — perfectly competitive and imperfectly competitive. Perfect competition refers to markets in which neither buyers nor sellers have any ability to influence the market price. Imperfect competition refers to the whole range of market structures other than perfect competition in which buyers or sellers possess the power to affect price.

This distinction is critically important because behind market supply and demand behavior lies the motivation on the part of firms and households to act in their own self-interest. Given the fundamental conflict of interest between buyer and seller, the existence of market power permits sellers or buyers to influence the price in their favor.

There are many kinds of market situations in which market power exists. For analytical simplicity, it is convenient to focus attention on three general types of imperfect markets — monopoly, oligopoly, and monopolistic competition. Most real-world markets fall somewhere within the spectrum between perfect competition at one end and perfect monopoly at the other.

PERFECT COMPETITION

Absence of Market Power

In perfectly competitive markets, firms are faced with an infinitely elastic demand for their product at the going market price. Such firms have no market power and must take the price as established in the market. The demand curve for their product, as shown in Figure 7-1, is a horizontal straight line.

Marginal revenue is defined as the change in total revenue brought about by a change in quantity. In perfect competition it is equal to the price received for the additional unit sold, that is, the existing market price. As total revenue increases at a constant rate as output is expanded, only rising costs limit the amount produced. For this reason perfect competition is incompatible with economies of scale in production.

Conditions For Perfect Competition

A perfectly competitive market exists only when the following conditions exist:
1. A sufficiently *large number of buyers and sellers*, each acting independently, so that no one of them can perceptibly influence total supply and therefore the market price.
2. A *homogeneous product*, such that buyers are indifferent among the outputs of different producers.
3. *Free entry* into and exit out of the industry, so that no buyers or sellers are excluded or captive.
4. *Perfect information*, making all buyers and sellers aware of all opportunities.

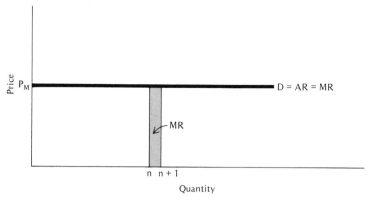

Figure 7-1 Demand in Perfect Competition

Many industries are characterized by a large number of small firms: agricultural commodities, services, trade. As indicated in Table 7-1, nearly 30 percent of the national income of the economy comes from such sectors. Nevertheless, only agriculture and some organized exchanges fit reasonably closely all of the requirements for competitive markets. An individual wheat farmer cannot affect the price of wheat; his only decision concerns how much and what kind of wheat he should grow. In virtually all other industries firms sell slightly differentiated products, have some influence over their price, or restrict entry and exit by government policies. The conditions necessary for perfect competition are thus highly restrictive and unrealistic. But the analysis of perfectly competitive markets is not intended primarily as an approximate description of real-world economies. *Perfect competition* represents a standard of economic performance, a yardstick against which real-world markets may be compared.

The equilibrium price in perfectly competitive markets is determined at the level where buyers are on their demand curves and sellers are on their supply curves. Until this price is established, excess demand or excess supply on the part of unsatisfied buyers or sellers will cause prices to rise or fall. As the concept of equilibrium has an implicit time dimension, it is useful to distinguish three different time periods with reference to supply behavior: market period, short run, and long run.

Market Period

Market period is defined as a period of time sufficiently short that supply is determined entirely by the stock of goods on hand and cannot be altered by current production. Total industry supply is the sum of the supplies produced by all the sum of individual sellers, as illustrated in Figure 7-2.

The equilibrium price (P_0) is determined at the level where quantity demanded is equal to the fixed stock in existence, that is, sufficient to clear the market. Price in the market period may be above or below the average costs of production. This divergence may be considerable for perishable commodities for which inventories

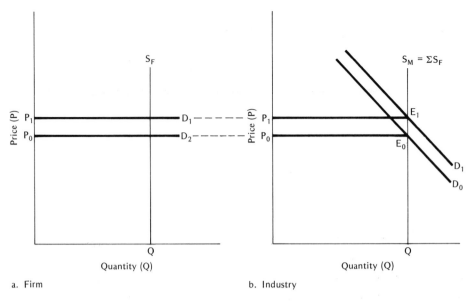

Figure 7-2 Market Period Supply Curves

cannot be held, and for durable commodities for which existing stocks are very large relative to current production. With a given supply, changes in price are determined entirely by shifts in the demand curve (e.g., from D_0 to D_1).

For commodities for which further production is not possible (land, antiques, or works of art) this market period analysis is the end of the story of competitive price determination. For commodities for which production is possible but accumulated stocks are large relative to current production (houses, gold, money, bonds, and equities) the market period is very long. Price is governed continuously by the market period relationships of Figure 7-2, in such a way as to equate quantity demanded with the existing stock available.

Short Run

The *short run* is defined as the period of time long enough to permit suppliers to vary their output within the limits of their existing capacity, but too short to permit them to vary the size of their plants or to enter or leave the industry.

For profit maximization a firm in a competitive market will produce at the output for which the market price is equal to marginal cost. Unless this is the case, the firm could raise its profits by producing more when $P > MC$ or by producing less when $P < MC$. The firm's supply curve is simply its marginal cost curve above the shutdown point, as price must at least exceed average variable costs if the firm is to produce at all. The industry short-run supply curve is the horizontal sum of the individual firm supply curves. The determination of short-run equilibrium price in competitive markets is illustrated in Figure 7-3.

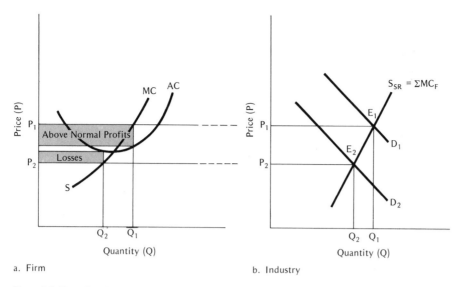

a. Firm   b. Industry

Figure 7-3 Short-Run Supply Curves

The short-run equilibrium price may be greater (P_1) or less than (P_2) the firm's average cost of production. The average cost curve in Figure 7-3 includes the opportunity costs of all factors of production used by the firm, even if, as is the case with owned factors, no cash payment is involved. Normal profits on capital invested are thus included in the definition of average costs. Normal profits are simply the cost of finance discussed in the previous chapter, and differ among firms and industries because of differences in risk and growth rates.

If market price in the short run lies above the minimum point on the average cost curve (e.g., P_1 in Figure 7-3), firms in the industry will earn greater than normal profits. If market price in the short run lies below the minimum point of the average cost curve (e.g., P_2 in Figure 7-3), firms will earn less than normal profits.

Changes in price in the short run are determined largely by shifts in the demand curve, as existing industry capacity is fixed. The extent to which price will rise or fall in response to shifts in demand will depend on the elasticity of the short-run supply curve, the extent to which producers are able to vary output without adjusting the size of their capital stock. Nevertheless price will always be equal to marginal cost $(P = MC)$ as long as firms attempt to maximize profits.

Long Run

The *long run* is defined as a period of time long enough that firms are able to change the size of their existing plants and to enter or leave the industry. In the long run, supply is much more elastic than in the short run. Each firm in the long run will move to its most efficient plant size. If average costs continued to fall, because of scale economies as output increases, firms would continue to expand in size and the conditions for perfect competition would no longer be satisfied. As a result, competi-

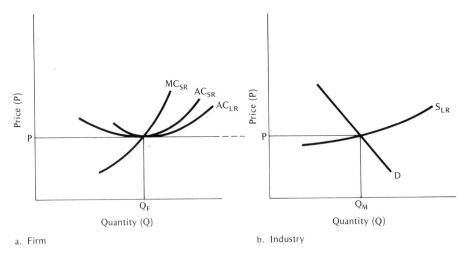

a. Firm b. Industry

Figure 7-4 Long-Run Competitive Equilibrium

tive markets require that the long run average cost curves of all firms be U-shaped, and that the output of the most efficient plant be small relative to total industry sales.

Because firms can enter or leave the industry, the long-run industry supply is the summation of the least-cost output of each individual firm's long-run average cost curve. If in Figure 7-4 there were 1,000 firms in the industry, each producing OQ_F at the price OP, the total market supply OQ_M would equal 1,000 Q_F

Firms will enter the industry if profits are above normal and leave the industry if profits are below normal. The number of firms in the industry will be in equilibrium when each firm is earning only normal profits. Assuming no barriers to entry, the normal profit rate, the level necessary to induce firms neither to enter nor to leave the industry, is equal to the market cost of finance.

Profit rates act as a red or green light to force resources out of or attract resources into an industry. Profits thus perform the fundamental role of allocating resources in a market economy. The answer to the question of what is to be produced is what is more profitable!

In the long run, as shown in Figure 7-4, price is equal to both marginal and average cost of production $(P = MC = AC)$. Each firm will operate with its most efficient plant size and at the minimum point on its average cost curve.

The long-run industry supply curve will ordinarily be upward sloping, as drawn in Figure 7-4. As more firms enter an industry, they increase the demand for, and so drive up the price of, those productive factors specific to the industry, thereby shifting upward the cost curves of each firm. An increase in the demand for wheat will lead to a rise in the price of land on which wheat is grown, raising the cost of producing wheat.[1] The determination of rent is considered in Chapter 9.

1. To the extent that the entry of additional firms results in lowering the cost curve of each firm in the industry by introducing economies *external* to each firm — for example, the development of a specialized transportation or credit system or a supply of trained workers — the long-run supply curve could slope downward.

By raising the productivity of labor and capital, an improvement in technology has the effect of shifting cost and supply curves, and so price, downward. As time is needed before the new processes are fully adapted, if demand and technology are continually changing the long-run equilibrium price may never actually be realized in practice. Nevertheless, it represents a useful analytical concept as the price toward which the system is tending over the long run.

The Behavior of Price Over Time

The effects of a shift in demand on equilibrium price are illustrated in Figure 7-5. Consider an initial position of long-run equilibrium (E_0). As shown in Figure 7-5a, a rise in demand from D_0 to D_1 results in a rise in price to $P_1{}^M$ in the market period. Over the short run, the price falls to $P_1{}^{SR}$ as firms respond to the higher price by

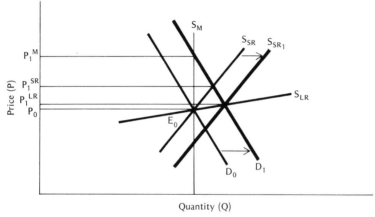

a. An Increase in Demand

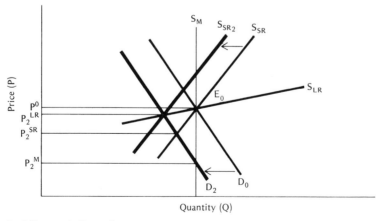

b. A Decrease in Demand

Figure 7-5 The Effects of a Change in Demand

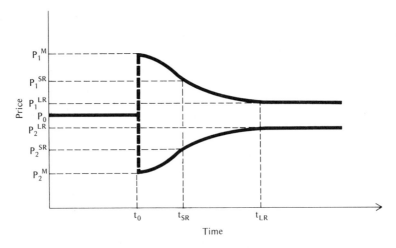

Figure 7-6 Behavior of Price over Time

increasing output. The price falls further in the long run to $P_1{}^{LR}$ as new firms enter the industry, shifting the short-run supply curve outward to S_{SR_1}. Conversely, as shown in Figure 7-5b, a fall in demand from D_0 to D_2 results in a fall in price to $P_2{}^M$ in the market period. The equilibrium price rises to $P_2{}^{SR}$ in the short run, as firms reduce output, and rises further to $P_2{}^{LR}$ in the long run as unprofitable firms leave the industry, shifting the short-run supply curve inward.

The behavior of price over time in response to a change in demand is illustrated in Figure 7-6, where time is measured on the horizontal axis. Demand is assumed to increase from D_0 to D_1, or to fall to D_2, at time t_0. Over the short run, price adjusts as firms raise or lower the output produced with a plant of a given size. Over the long run, supply is much more elastic as new plants are built or old plants abandoned as firms enter or leave the industry. The time period required for long-run adjustment to be completed will differ in different markets, depending on the capital investments required.

In the short run, changes in demand result primarily in a change in price. In the long run, changes in demand result primarily in a change in quantity. Supply price in the long run is determined solely by average costs of production. In the extreme case in which the long-run supply curve is perfectly elastic, price in the long run will return to its initial equilibrium value. Shifts in demand in the long run then affect only the quantity produced and sold and have no effect on price.

MONOPOLY

Monopoly denotes a market situation in which there is only one seller. It is at the opposite end of the spectrum from perfect competition. Like perfect competition, it is a theoretical concept, useful primarily for analytical purposes of comparison rather than as a description of reality. As the monopolist is the sole seller, his demand curve is the total market demand curve. Few markets are perfectly monopolistic in this sense. The closest examples are so called *natural* monopolies: transportation, communications, power, and water. These are all areas in which public regulation of prices is well established or firms are owned and operated by the government.

Market Power

A monopolist, faced by a downward-sloping demand curve, can set the price at which his product is sold. Monopolists thus possess market power: they are *price-makers* rather than *price-takers*. Price and sales are interdependent; once the price is chosen, the quantity that can be sold for any given demand curve is determined.

Even with one seller the amount of market power depends on the elasticity of demand for the good in question. Alternatives of one form or another exist for virtually all commodities. Railroads compete with airlines, trucking companies, and automobiles; aluminum producers compete with producers of other metals, glass, and plastics. The definition of a product is, in certain cases, extremely difficult to draw. A *good* refers essentially to a gap in the chain of substitutes. For many goods this gap may be quite small. All firms have a monopoly in the supply of their own services. Yet while alternatives are abundant, they are rarely perfect substitutes, if only because of differences in location and convenience. Few firms are faced with a perfectly elastic demand curve.

Marginal Revenue

With a downward-sloping demand curve, increased sales can be achieved by lowering price. Total revenue, equal to price times quantity, is equal to the area under the demand curve at any point.

Marginal revenue, the change in total revenue from the sale of an additional unit, will always be less than price. As shown in Figure 7-7, total revenue will increase by the gain in revenue from selling one additional unit, which is equal to the price of the unit sold. But total revenue will fall by the loss in revenue on all the previous number of units sold, which are now sold at a lower price. Marginal revenue, the net change in total revenue, may be regarded as the gain in revenue from increased sales minus the loss in revenue from reduced prices, shown by the cross-hatched area in Figure 7-7.

As more goods are sold, the loss in total revenue from a reduction in the price of goods sold will increase. As a result marginal revenue will be increasingly below price. For a straight line demand curve, the marginal revenue curve is the straight line formed by bisecting the horizontal distance from the demand curve to the vertical axis.[1]

The condition for *profit maximization* is equality of marginal cost and marginal

1. See Appendix to this chapter.

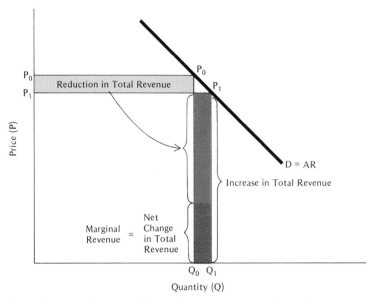

Figure 7-7 Average Revenue and Marginal Revenue in Imperfect Competition

revenue. If he knows the demand curve, the monopolist will set a price so that the quantity demanded will be the output for which marginal cost is equal to marginal revenue, a point shown as P_M in Figure 7-8. The difference between price and average cost per unit represents monopoly profit per unit. Total monopoly profits are equal to the shaded rectangle of profit per unit times quantity sold.

Providing that other firms cannot enter the monopolized industry, the monopolist can earn these above-normal monopoly profits permanently. The short- and long-run solutions are identical. The amount of monopoly profits will depend on the elas-

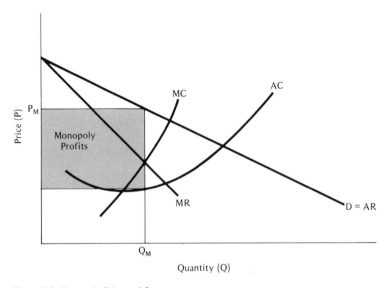

Figure 7-8 Monopoly Price and Output

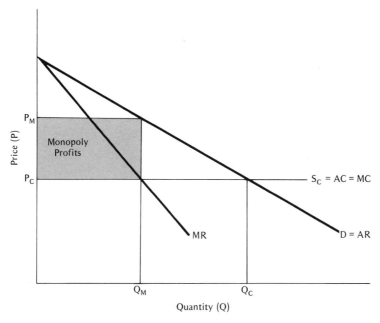

Figure 7-9 Comparison of Monopoly and Competitive Outcomes

ticity of the demand curve, which is determined by the closeness of substitutes for the product in question. The more substitutes available, the more elastic and flatter the demand curve and the flatter and higher the position of the marginal revenue curve.

Monopoly may arise as the result of concerted action by a number of producers. Consider the simplified situation shown in Figure 7-9. With a perfectly competitive market and a horizontal long-run industry supply curve, the competitive price and output are shown as P_C and Q_C. Now assume that all individual producers get together to form and enforce a cartel, with a single marketing board to determine industry price and quantity. To maximize industry profits, the cartel will set a price at which marginal cost equals marginal revenue for the industry. The extent to which the cartel price P_M is greater than the competitive price P_C and output is reduced depends, as may be seen, on the elasticity of the supply and demand curve for the commodity in question. In the present example with constant costs, monopoly output will be exactly one half of the competitive output, irrespective of the elasticity of demand. With increasing costs, monopoly output would be more than one half of competitive output.

Comparison of Monopoly and Competitive Outputs

The difference between the monopolistic and the perfectly competitive solution are now clearly exposed. First, *too little is produced* under monopoly as compared to the perfectly competitive outcome, because price always exceeds marginal cost. This price may be difficult to maintain. Individual firms in the cartel have an incentive to shade prices slightly to increase their profits. Similarly, new firms will be attracted and may undersell cartel members. Government enforcement is thus ordinarily necessary if the cartel is not to disintegrate.

Second, as a result of market power, *the distribution of income is changed* away from buyers toward sellers, the recipients of monopoly rents. Supply price exceeds average costs of production even in the long run. Monopoly income of sellers must then be distributed between owners of labor (wages) and owners of capital (profits).

The markup of price over average costs may be viewed as analogous to a tax on consumers through which monopoly income is created and diverted to producers through the restriction of output. Such profits have no function from a social point of view, as they are not a payment for any socially useful productive service but a return for a contrived scarcity. Such payments are a form of *rent,* a payment to a factor in excess of that required to call forth the supply.

Third, in the absence of competition there is no external stimulus to force producers to produce with the lowest-cost, most efficient factor combination. Costs may rise or the quality of the product or service offered may fall without the monopolists being punished by the market.

Natural Monopoly

Natural monopoly refers to market situations in which, because of substantial scale economies, a single producer is the most efficient way of producing the commodity. Whenever the least-cost technique involves very substantial capital equipment, fixed costs are high relative to variable costs, and average costs fall as output is increased. When average cost is falling, marginal cost must necessarily be below average cost.

Economies of scale are ordinarily exhausted after some large level of output is reached. Whether this leads to natural monopoly depends on the market's size. In Figure 7-10 the average cost curve is drawn as declining throughout, up to the

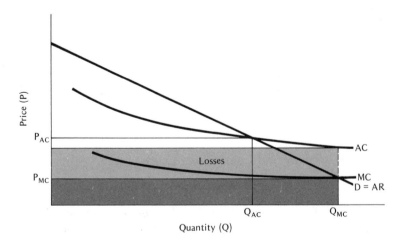

Figure 7-10 Price Regulation of a Natural Monopoly

industry demand curve, indicating strong economies of scale. An example would be a public utility providing electricity, gas, water, or telephone service to a particular area.

Regulation of Monopolies

In virtually all countries the prices that private natural monopolies may charge are regulated by the government. In many countries natural monopolies are publicly owned and operated. Nevertheless huge private fortunes have been made from ownership of monopolies, many of which still exist.

Regulatory authorities typically adopt an *average cost* pricing policy. The regulated price (P_{AC}) is established, as shown in Figure 7-10, at a level at which the average cost curve cuts the demand curve. At this price, owners of the monopoly can earn only normal profits or a "fair" return on their investment. *Fair return* is defined by the regulatory authorities as some rate of return on invested capital.

The amount of regulated profits will thus depend on what is meant by a fair rate of return and on how capital is valued. Original cost is the most widely used method of capital valuation. Valuation by replacement or reproduction cost would permit regulated companies to earn windfall profits and a much higher return on their original investment whenever the prices of capital goods rise. Table 7-3 presents total assets, sales, net profits, and rate of return on equity of the largest public utilities for recent years.

Under average-cost pricing, the price charged exceeds the marginal cost of providing the commodity. As shown in Figure 7-10, too little is produced (Q_{AC}) compared to the competitive ideal (Q_{MC}). To satisfy the competitive solution, regulatory authorities would have to adopt marginal cost pricing. However, when average cost is declining, a policy of setting price equal to marginal cost (P_{MC}) would imply losses. Because marginal costs are less than average costs, total revenue ($P_{MC} Q_{MC}$), shaded in Figure 7-10, would be less than total costs. The firm would go out of business rather than continue to produce. These losses could be made up by a government subsidy to the monopolist derived from government revenues. This has the redistributive effect that taxpayers at large subsidize consumers of the commodity, unless somehow the tax can be levied only on consumers.

Table 7-3   ASSETS, SALES, AND PROFIT RATES OF FIFTY LARGEST PUBLIC UTILITY COMPANIES, 1965–70 (BILLIONS OF DOLLARS)

Assets, Sales, and Profits	1965	1966	1967	1968	1969	1970
Total Assets (book value)	84.3	90.7	98.6	106.8	117.6	131.8
Operating Revenue	26.6	28.8	31.1	33.9	37.3	40.7
Net Income	4.0	4.3	4.6	4.7	5.0	5.2
Invested Capital	43.0	42.2	44.9	47.2	49.9	53.7
Net Income as Percent of Invested Capital	9.3	10.3	10.2	9.9	10.0	9.7
Net Income as Percent of Invested Capital for Largest 500 Industrial Corporations	13.0	13.2	11.3	11.7	11.5	9.6

Source: The Fortune Directory.

Government provision of public goods at a zero price in situations where marginal cost is close to zero—for example, roads, bridges, parks—represents one solution to this problem. Fixed costs are paid out of tax receipts. The ideal single-price solution on allocational and distributional grounds is to charge the competitive price equal to marginal cost (P_{MC}) and then to make up overhead or fixed costs by a flat fee, allocated among consumers in proportion to the benefit they derive from the commodity. Unfortunately in the absence of a market it is very difficult to estimate such benefits.

OLIGOPOLY

Oligopoly refers to market situations in which output is concentrated among a few sellers. The essential characteristic of oligopoly is that each firm in setting its own administered price must take into consideration the behavior and probable response of its competitors.

Concentration

A market structure dominated by a few large sellers is characteristic of many manufacturing industries in the United States. Two-thirds of all manufacturing industries have been described as concentrated or highly concentrated. Table 7-4 presents the proportion of total sales accounted for by the largest four firms, along with average profit rates earned, in all American manufacturing industries.

The concentration ratio depends on how narrowly an industry is defined. Concentration ratios increased in nine of these industries over the decade from 1954 to 1963, and fell in seven. Increases in concentration are impeded by antitrust laws and appear to have slowed down to a glacial accretion. Nevertheless, as a result of the growth in conglomerate mergers among firms operating in different industries, the share of total output accounted for by the largest corporations is increasing. In 1968 the 50 largest manufacturing corporations accounted for approximately one third of all manufacturing sales and assets and 40 percent of all profits. The 200 largest manufacturing corporations accounted for two thirds of all sales and assets and three quarters of total industry profits. This is approximately the same share that the largest 1,000 manufacturing corporations accounted for in 1941.

Mutual Interdependence and the Theory of Games

Oligopolistic markets are particularly difficult to analyze, since the outcome depends on competitor response and interaction. In many oligopolistic markets there may be no single analytically determinate price and output equilibrium solution. Given the

Table 7-4 MANUFACTURING CORPORATIONS: PROPORTION OF SALES ACCOUNTED FOR BY FOUR LARGEST FIRMS AND INDUSTRY PROFIT RATE, 1954–64

Industry Class	Percent of Value of Shipments of 4 Largest Firms [1]		Industry Profit Rate [2]
	1954	1963	Average 1962–1964
Tobacco Manufacturers	76	82	13.3
Transportation Equipment	69	77	15.3
Primary Metal Industries	57	50	7.5
Instruments and Related Products	43	46	12.8
Electrical Machinery	48	45	10.4
Chemicals and Allied Products	43	45	13.2
Rubber and Plastic Products	55	38	9.8
Stone, Clay and Glass Products	45	38	9.0
Petroleum and Coal Products	35	35	10.9
Machinery (except electrical)	33	35	10.4
Food and Kindred Products	34	34	9.3
Textile Mill Products	25	33	6.9
Paper and Allied Products	22	32	8.5
Miscellaneous Manufacturing	21	29	9.6
Fabricated Metal Products	27	23	8.8
Leather and Leather Products	26	22	8.1
Furniture and Fixtures	18	18	8.7
Printing and Publishing	17	17	10.6
Lumber and Wood Products	10	14	7.9
Apparel and Related Products	14	9	9.6

1. Concentration ratios—weighted average of 4-digit industries.
2. Profit rate: Total profits after taxes as percent of stockholder's equity.

Sources: Federal Trade Commission and Securities and Exchange Commission, *Quarterly Financial Report for Manufacturing Corporations;* Subcommittee on Antitrust and Monopoly, U.S. Senate, *Concentration Ratios in Manufacturing Industry 1963.*

market structure, the outcome will vary in each case in a manner impossible to predict, depending on the strategies adopted.

An understanding of the rich possibilities inherent in situations of mutual interdependence may be carried further with the aid of game theory. Consider the problem of oligopolistic pricing strategy. An oligopolist can either raise his price, leave it unchanged, or lower it. In response, his rivals can choose to raise their price, leave it unchanged, or lower it. This situation may be presented by a three-by-three *payoff matrix* listing all possible combinations of an oligopolist's action and his rival's reaction with respect to a change in price. The oligopolist's options are represented by the three rows of the matrix. His rivals' responses are represented by the three columns of the matrix.

In order to determine the payoffs for each of the nine possible combinations, it is necessary to make some assumptions about the market. Assume that total market demand for the product is inelastic, and that oligopolists have not reached a perfect cartel solution of maximizing joint profits. If the oligopolist raises his price and his rivals follow, the oligopolists' profits will rise. If the oligopolist lowers his price and his rivals follow, his profits will fall. If his rivals do not follow a rise in his price, the oligopolist's profits will fall. If his rivals do not follow a reduction in his price, the oligopolist's profits will rise.

On the basis of these assumptions, it is possible to fill in all the cells in the matrix: (+) refers to an increase in profits, (−) a reduction in profits, and (0) refers to no change.

PAYOFF MATRIX:

Rival's Price Reaction

		Raise	No change	Lower
	Raise	1 +	2 −	3 −
Oligopolist's price action	No change	4 +	5 0	6 −
	Lower	7 +	8 +	9 −

This payoff matrix reveals the essential nature of oligopolistic markets. An oligopolist's profits are determined not by his behavior alone but also by the behavior of his rivals. As a result of this interdependence, the actions of an oligopolist will depend on his anticipation of how his rivals will react to his own behavior.

Suppose first that the oligopolist is a price leader, as will typically be the case in markets dominated by one very large producer. The smaller firms follow the leader's action, anxious not to antagonize their larger competitor. In this case, the oligopolist is faced with only three of the nine possibilities — cells 1, 5, and 9.

Recognizing these probable consequences, the price leader will clearly choose cell 1 and raise his price. In response the other firms also raise their prices. The price leader will continue to raise his price in such a situation until his profits are maximized.

Under such circumstances, firms in the industry behave as if they were a collective monopoly, even though there is no overt agreement among competitors. All that is required is tacit agreement to a policy of price leadership. Recognizing these consequences, rivals have little incentive to pursue an independent policy but every incentive to follow a conscious parallelism of action. It is not even necessary for the same firm always to be the price leader in response to a change in conditions. This situation has been termed *barometric price leadership.*

The phenomenon of price leadership is very common in oligopolistic markets. The fewer the number of companies and the more similar their cost curves, the more robust is tacit leadership behavior. The largest firms, if economies of scale are important, provide a price umbrella under which the smaller firms can survive. Because they fear antitrust action, they almost never attempt to drive out competitors, or even to increase their market shares.

Now suppose that there is no tacit leadership agreement among competitors. The oligopolist is quite uncertain of how his rivals will behave if he keeps his price unchanged. If he lowers his price, his rivals may lower their price or keep it constant but they are unlikely to raise their price in response. If he raises his price, his rivals may raise their price or keep it constant but are unlikely to respond by lowering their prices. Under these circumstances, cells 2 and 6, and 4 and 8 now become possibilities, in addition to cells 1, 5, and 9. Only cells 3 and 7 are excluded.

If the oligopolist is a risk avoider and desires to avoid losses, he will be careful not to choose a policy that will cause his rivals to lower their prices. As seen by the right-hand column of the matrix, if rivals take this action, the oligopolist can only lose. As seen by the left-hand column, he will be best off if he can somehow induce his rivals to raise their prices.

His best policy is tentatively to raise his own price, which may encourage his rivals to raise their prices or to leave them unchanged. But at least it discourages rivals from lowering their prices, as they may do if he reduces his price or leaves it unchanged. If his rivals do not change their prices, he will incur a reduction in profits. But in this event, he can avoid a permanent reduction by again reducing his price. In this case he moves from cell 2 to cell 5, in which case he is no worse off than he was at the beginning.

To minimize his chance of unfavorable outcomes, the safest policy thus is again to raise his own price. The result is similar to price leadership. The industry outcome would again tend, but more hesitantly, toward that of monopoly price and output.

Finally, suppose that all the cells in the matrix represent a possibility. The expected gains in the first column are not all equal nor are the expected losses in the third column. The oligopolist will place a different subjective probability on the occurence of each response. His optimum strategy in this case will depend on his estimate of the various payoffs and the probability of their occurence. It will also depend on his attitude toward risk — for example, whether he decides to minimize his chance of loss or to maximize his chance of gain.

An aggressive oligopolist, confident of his cost, service, or product advantages, may choose the bottom-row strategy of lowering his price, in the expectation that the benefits of outcomes 7 and 8 will outweigh the risks of outcome 9 and that he has a good chance to increase his profits by capturing a larger share of the market.

Collusion

In the face of uncertainty, oligopolistic firms have a strong incentive to seek effective collusion, the gains from which will be directly related to their distance from the monopoly price and output position. Rather than competing for buyers and keeping prices down, they could coordinate their offers and keep prices up. The large potential gain is a persistent lure inducing sellers to seek collusion. The same argument applies to collusion among buyers.

Nevertheless, there are formidable obstacles to successful collusion even in the absence of legal prohibitions. As firms are not identical, there will always be conflict of interest among sellers with regard to an "equitable" division of the market. As price will exceed marginal cost, each member will have a private interest to violate the agreement secretly, to chisel in order to increase his sales and profits. Buyers will have an incentive to play one seller against the other. How can the group police the collusion, particularly with regard to nonprice competition? It is interesting to note that sealed-bid government buying reduces the industry costs of enforcement of collusion, and it is here that most cases of effective collusion have been prosecuted. There is also the freeloader problem. Any sellers left out of the collusion reap the advantage of a higher price and yet are able to sell all they are able. Outsiders are a powerful force tending to break up the cartel.

Even if all these obstacles are overcome and every existing seller induced to join an effective collusion, new producers would be attracted into the industry by the prospects of high prices and profits. High costs of capital facilities delay entry and make effective collusion more likely. But expensive capital facilities also increase the probable loss to existing producers if new firms are induced to enter. Finally, it is important to remember substitute commodities. Over the long run, their sales will increase in proportion to the effectiveness of the collusion in raising prices, and total sales and profits of the cartel will tend to fall.

Private price-fixing agreements, explicit market collusion, and private enforcement of collusion are, with the exception of labor services, illegal in the United States, though not in most other countries. Under such legislation it is more difficult for oligopolists to arrive at the monopoly price and output that would jointly maximize industry profits.

Table 7-4 provides suggestive evidence that the difficulty of reaching the industry profit-maximizing price through tacit collusion and parallel action is reduced as the number of competitors decreases. Profit rates tend to be higher in more highly concentrated industries. In markets with many sellers, — for example, agricultural goods — effective collusion is ordinarily possible only with government enforcement of collusion and restraints on entry.

Price Inflexibility

Prices in oligopolistic industries tend to be relatively inflexible both downward and upward in response to short-run shifts in cost and demand. One explanation of the observed inflexibility of prices in oligopolistic markets is that individual oligopolists anticipate that their competitors will be more likely to respond to and match any *price reduction* that they make, but will be less likely or may not respond at all to *any price increases*. This situation, which corresponds to cells 2, 5, and 9 in the payoff matrix, is illustrated in Figure 7-11.

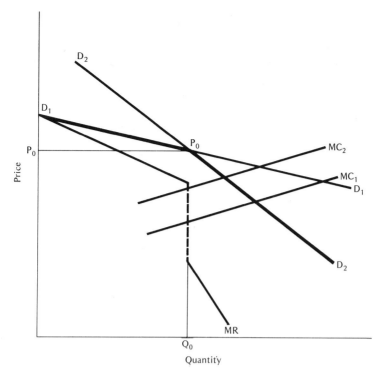

Figure 7-11 Kinked Demand Curve under Oligopoly

Under such circumstances the demand curve as viewed by the oligopolist becomes "kinked" at the going market price P_0. D_1D_1 is the demand curve faced by the firm if all other firms hold their price constant. D_2D_2 is the demand curve faced by the firm if all other firms change their prices in the same proportion. If oligopolists anticipate that their competitors will match any price cuts but not respond to price increases, the demand curve becomes the heavy shaded line $D_1P_0D_2$. This case results in a large discontinuity in the marginal revenue curve at the existing price and output.

In such situations a shift in costs (for example, from MC_1 to MC_2 in Figure 7-11) will not induce a firm to change its price and output as long as costs remain within this discontinuity of the marginal revenue curve. If the changes in cost are known to be general to all firms in the industry, such as a change in taxes, labor costs, or raw material prices, the expected position of the kink may change and a new level of prices be established.

Target Profit Pricing

Dominant firms in concentrated markets typically describe their price behavior as *target-profit* or *average-cost pricing* rather than profit maximization. This process is illustrated in Figure 7-12. Total revenue and costs are measured on the vertical axis and total output on the horizontal axis.

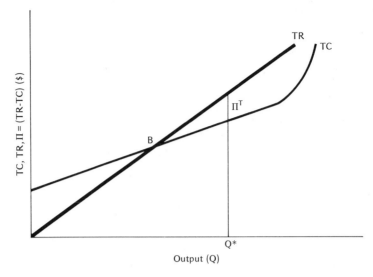

Figure 7-12 Target-Profit Pricing

A price is set sufficiently above average costs to yield some target rate of profit (Π^T) — for example, 15 or 20 percent return on capital invested — with a certain conservatively estimated level of capacity utilization (Q^*). The administered price chosen determines the slope of the total revenue curve, and also the profits for any particular level of sales. If sales exceed their estimated volume (Q^*), actual profits will be above the target level. If sales are less than anticipated, actual profits will be below target.

Table 7-5 TARGET AND ACTUAL PROFIT RATES FOR SELECTED
CORPORATIONS

Company	Principal Price Goal	Rate of Return on Investment after Taxes (Average 1947–55)
Alcoa	20% on investment before taxes, higher on new products (about 10% effective rate after taxes)	13.8
General Electric	20% on investment (after taxes); 7% on sales (after taxes)	21.4
General Foods	33⅓% gross margin: ("⅓ to make, ⅓ to sell, and ⅓ for profit"); expectation of realizing target only on new products	12.2
General Motors	20% on investment (after taxes)	26.0
International Harvester	10% on investment (after taxes)	8.9
Johns-Manville	Return on investment greater than last 15-year average (about 15% after taxes); higher target for new products	14.9
U.S. Steel	8% on investment (after taxes)	10.3

Source: R. F. Lanzillotti, "Pricing Objectives in Large Corporations," *The American Economic Review* December, 1958.

Table 7-5 presents target-profit rates and profit rates actually realized for a number of important American corporations. As may be seen, there are very wide differences among corporations both in target and realized profit rates. Neither the kinked demand curve of Figure 7-11 nor the target-profit pricing curve of Figure 7-12 explains why profits are observed to be higher for some corporations and industries than for others. Granted that prices in oligopolistic markets are administered and are likely to be relatively inflexible, what determines the target-profit rate, the level of the kink, and so the size of the markup over average costs?

Empirical studies reveal that the performance of oligopolistic firms is related to the structure of the markets in which they operate. Diagram 7-1 presents a scatter diagram of the data in Table 7-4 relating observed profit rates to industry concentration ratios. Profit rates actually realized are higher in more concentrated industries (in which concentration is defined as the proportion of industry sales accounted for

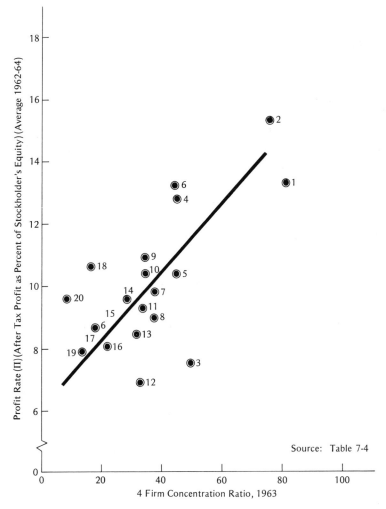

Diagram 7-1 Profit Rates and Concentration Ratios, 1962-64

by the largest four firms). The modifications to this relationship appear to be those concentrated industries producing largely homogeneous products and those less concentrated industries producing highly differentiated products.

Profit rates have also been found to be positively related to firm size, the growth of industry sales, and the relative size of advertising expenditures. Advertising expenses serve to render the demand for the firm's products more inelastic, to raise the entry barriers to other firms, and to increase the degree of market power. Profit rates are inversely related to the cross-elasticity of the demand curve faced by individual firms, that is, the extent to which substitutes are available.

The empirical evidence thus suggests that target rates of profit and so the markup of price over average costs are set at different levels by different firms according to the degree of market power possessed. Fear of government antitrust action, concern for public opinion, and worries over longer-run profit maximization may dissuade firms from maximizing short-run profits. But although firms may be satisfied with a target rate of profit rather than maximum profits, the level of profits regarded as satisfactory varies widely, depending largely on the amount of market power possessed by the firm.

Product Differentiation

Oligopolistic markets may further be distinguished according to whether the product is *homogeneous* or *differentiated.* In the case of homogeneous products, sometimes termed *pure* oligopoly, price cuts will increase one firms' sales at the expense of others. The more homogeneous the product, the more elastic the demand curve facing an individual firm. Whenever fixed costs are so large that average costs and price are high relative to marginal costs, there will be a strong temptation toward price-cutting by individual firms. Cost differences may induce relatively efficient producers to engage in price reduction to increase their shares of the market. Lower-cost firms are likely to be uncooperative with regard to tacit price and market agreements. The effectiveness of price competition in the case of homogeneous products may prevent market leaders from setting prices very far above average costs. Such an outcome has been termed *workable* competition. As noted, profit rates are lower in concentrated industries producing homogeneous products.

When products are heterogeneous, price cuts are less effective and firms have a stronger incentive to engage in nonprice competition through product differentiation, service appeal, and sales promotion. Nonprice competition represents an attempt to shift outward and steepen the demand curve faced by each firm. If the demand curve becomes more inelastic, the amount of market power possessed by the firm is increased. Nonprice attempts to increase sales cannot be matched as quickly or as easily by other firms as can overt price reduction. As a result, with heterogeneous products there appears frequently to be a sort of gentlemen's agreement among firms not to cut prices but to compete in terms of service, advertising, and innovation of new products, particularly if each firm believes that the total industry demand curve is inelastic.

To the extent that consumers prefer a wide variety of goods, product differentiation is not undesirable. A higher price may be paid voluntarily for the luxury of greater choice. This is true only to the extent that consumers have the option to purchase standard items at low prices, without differentiation and service extras, which is typically not the case.

Advertising

Advertising plays two roles in economic markets. The first is an *informational* role of providing consumers with more knowledge about different products. In this role it makes markets more perfect by reducing ignorance and uncertainty. The second is a *persuasive* role of attempting to cultivate and shape consumer preferences for particular products. Such advertising may create new tastes, but it may also merely shift demand from one similar product to another. Each producer may be forced to advertise merely to maintain his current market share in the face of advertising by his competitors. In the United States advertising costs for cosmetics, drugs, alcohol and soaps are 10 percent or more of the value of total sales. The effect is to add to total costs without adding an equal increase in total benefits.

Advertising in the United States provides the main revenue of the mass media: television, radio, newspapers, and magazines. As a result, consumers pay for their entertainment indirectly as part of the price they pay for the advertised products. There is no direct connection between the price consumers would be willing to pay directly for such entertainment and the price they actually if indirectly do pay. Television programs will be profitable if sponsorship sufficiently increases sales for the advertised products, not because entertainment demand for the programs covers their costs.

The exercise by giant firms of their market power to raise prices above costs of production is a kind of indirect tax levied by producers on consumers. Many firms allocate a part of their profits to expenditures in the public interest such as public affairs, education, cultural activities, or charity. Nevertheless, critics argue that such power has no legitimacy on democratic grounds. Taxation without representation is not more justified when undertaken by private governments.

The superior financial base of large corporations that rests on this market power, and so their ability to tax consumers, has the unintended result that business influence indirectly yet powerfully shapes social values, the scope of public debate, and the directions followed by many other institutions in the society. This dominance of the corporate viewpoint is particularly apparent in the mass media. While the printed media have at least the tradition of the separation of advertising from editorial content, in broadcasting the two are tied together under sponsor control. A magazine in the United States ordinarily would never consider permitting an advertiser to buy two separate pages and then to tell the editor what subject and viewpoint were to be placed between his pages. Yet this is exactly the manner in which most television time is sold at present.

MONOPOLISTIC COMPETITION

Monopolistic competition refers to market situations in which there are a large number of producers and entry into the industry is relatively free. But unlike perfectly competitive markets, the output of each individual seller is differentiated, so that buyers are not indifferent among the products of different sellers. As a result, each individual firm is faced by a downward-sloping demand curve and has some market power over the price at which it can sell its product. Each firm is able to influence its demand curve by product differentiation, advertising, and services offered. As there are a large number of firms, competitors' reaction to a change in a company's pricing policy is much less than in the case of oligopoly. Figure 7-13 summarizes the demand curves faced by firms in monopolistic competition compared to other market structures.

Assuming entry into the industry is free, in the long run excess profits tend to be eliminated. This situation is shown in Figure 7-14. As long as firms are making above normal profits (e.g., with the demand curve D_1), other firms have an incentive to enter the market. As a result, some customers are bid away, reducing the demand curve toward D_0. In the long run, price is driven down to the level P_0, at which level each firm is making just normal profits.

Excess Capacity

In monopolistic competitive markets, each firm is operating at *less* than its most efficient least-cost output (Q_{MIN} in Figure 7-14). This follows necessarily, assuming that firms set prices so as to equate marginal revenue and marginal cost, as the demand curve is downward sloping. Each firm is operating with excess capacity,

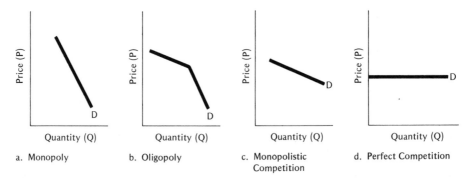

Figure 7-13 Demand Curves Faced by Firms in Different Markets

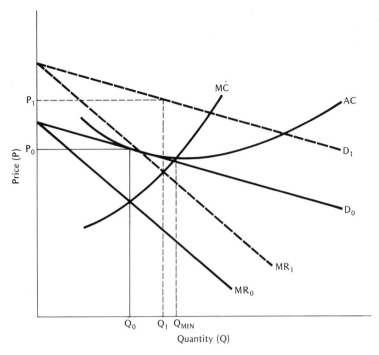

Figure 7-14 Price and Output under Monopolistic Competition

but no firm is able to move to the output at which average costs are at a minimum. There are too many firms in the industry, in the sense that the same output could be produced with fewer firms. The larger number of firms does provide customers with greater convenience and product differentiation.

Although no firm is making greater than normal profits, price exceeds marginal cost. As a result, the economy does not get as much of these goods as would be produced compared to the perfectly competitive solution. Monopolistic competition represents a misallocation of resources and economic waste to the extent that greater product differentiation occurs than consumers would desire, if they had the choice. It provides an explanation of the high costs of distribution in the United States, where every sixth worker is a middleman. The druggists' association has estimated that only one third of employee time is spent in selling, and one third in simply waiting for customers to come in. This situation is characteristic of many small retail businesses.

Nonprice Competition

Firms in perfectly competitive markets will never engage in advertising and non-price competition, as they can sell as much as they want at the going price. This is not the case for monopolistic competition. Advertising and product differentiation may enable a firm to raise the demand for its product and reduce the elasticity of this demand (for example, to D_1 in Figure 7-14). The result will be to permit the firm to charge a price and maintain a volume of sales that yields larger short-run profits. This increase holds even if entry is free and other firms are attracted into the market by the prospect of above-average profits. These new firms may capture a share of the customers of existing firms, shifting their demand curve leftward. But it pays to spend money on advertising in an attempt to stay ahead. In relatively small markets, discontinuities may be such that there is not sufficient business to justify the entry of another firm. In such cases, above-normal profits for existing firms may persist indefinitely, even though entry is free. Profit rates in a number of less concentrated manufacturing industries producing differentiated products were presented in Table 7-4. As may be seen, profit rates are frequently one third to one quarter lower than in more concentrated industries.

Government Restraints on Competition

Monopolistic competition characterizes most services and trades, such as barbers, repairmen, lawyers, retail stores, restaurants, gas stations. These industries are characterized by a large number of firms, each eking out a more or less profitable existence, with little or no rents, and each operating with excess capacity. Entry is free, profits are generally low, and firm mortality is high.

As these areas account for more than one third of total income and there are a large number of individual producers in these industries, they have considerable political power. Small businesses are given preferential treatment by the government in many ways.

In many service industries entry is restricted by licensing requirements, which are usually justified in terms of quality protection in the interests of the consumer. Their effect is always to raise prices by restricting supply.

In trade the government has enacted *fair trade* laws that limit the ability of larger firms, chain stores, and discount houses to act competitively with and so undersell the small retailer. Ironically, these laws are classified as antitrust laws, but their effect is to protect competitors from the rigors of competition.

Patents, copyrights, and trademarks all represent legal grants of monopoly to producer interests. In view of the prevalence of such policies, many economists have argued that the net effect of government intervention is probably to reduce the overall degree of competition in private markets.

APPENDIX: THE RELATIONSHIP BETWEEN ELASTICITY, MARGINAL REVENUE, AND TOTAL REVENUE

In perfect competition the demand curve faced by each producer is a horizontal straight line at the market price. The elasticity of demand is infinite. Total revenue may be represented by the area under the curve at any point. As sales are increased,

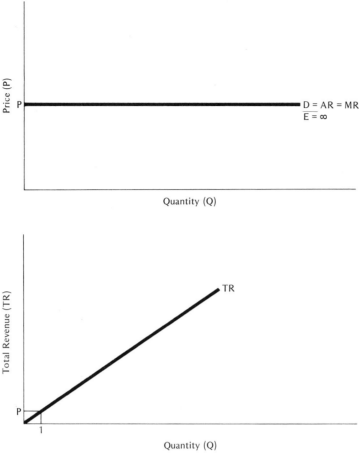

Figure 7-15 Relationship between Price, Marginal Revenue, and Total Revenue under Perfect Competition

marginal revenue, defined as the change in total revenue, is always equal to the revenue received on the additional unit sold, the prevailing market price. Total revenue may then be represented as a straight line through the origin with a slope equal to market price. These relationships are illustrated in Figure 7-15.

In imperfect competition, firms are faced by a downward-sloping demand curve. Total revenue may again be represented by the area under the curve at any point. The marginal revenue curve is a straight line through the y intercept bisecting the horizontal to a straight-line demand curve. If q units are sold at price P, and the price has to fall by ΔP in order to sell one more unit, then $MR = P - q\Delta P$.

Total revenue may then be represented by a parabola through the origin. Total revenue will rise initially as more goods are sold and reach a maximum where marginal revenue is zero. After this point, it will decline. These relationships are illustrated in Figure 7-16.

The elasticity of a straight-line demand curve will vary along its length. When elasticity is greater than unity (elastic), a reduction in price will raise total revenue.

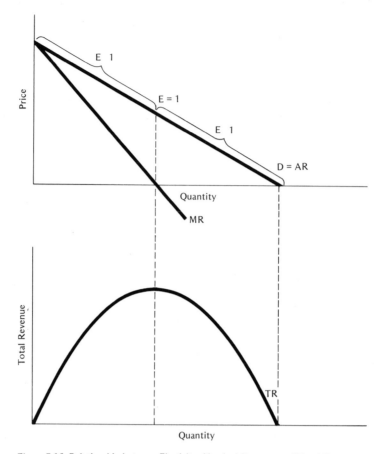

Figure 7-16 Relationship between Elasticity, Marginal Revenue, and Total Revenue under Imperfect Competition

The proportionate increase in quantity is greater than the proportionate reduction in price. When elasticity is less than unity (inelastic), a reduction in price will reduce total revenue. Firms possessing market power will never produce over the inelastic range of their demand curves. As seen in Figure 7-16, over this entire range marginal revenue is negative. Firms could always increase total revenue and profits by raising price and selling less, even if it meant throwing the excess output away.

There is an important relationship between marginal and average. When marginal is below average, the average is falling. When marginal is equal to average, the average is constant. When marginal exceeds average, the average is rising. The marginal increment pulls down the average if it is below the average, pulls up the average if it is above the average, and, leaves the average unchanged if it is equal to the average. Marginal-cost curves thus always intersect average-cost curves at their lowest point.

For straight-line demand curves, the marginal revenue curve bisects the horizontal from the vertical axis to the demand curve. This may be shown as follows. Take any point P on the straight-line demand curve D shown in Figure 7-17. What is the

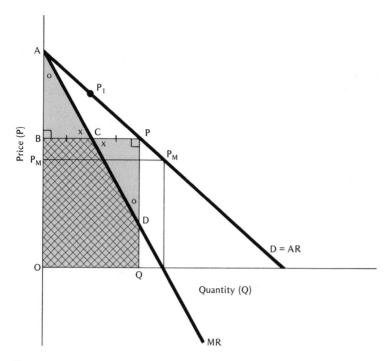

Figure 7-17 Derivation of Marginal Revenue from Average Revenue

marginal revenue corresponding to that point? Draw in a marginal revenue curve *MR* from *A* somewhere below the demand curve. At the point *P*, total revenue is equal to price times quantity, the area of the rectangle *BPQO*. Total revenue is also equal to the total area under the marginal revenue curve to point *Q* (*ADQO*), because marginal revenue is defined as the change in total revenue, and the area under the marginal revenue curve is the sum of the changes in total revenue from zero to its present value.

It follows that the area of the triangle *ABC* must equal the area of the triangle *CPD*. As these triangles are congruent, they must be identical, so that *BC = CP*. The marginal revenue curve must bisect the horizontal. At the price *P*, marginal revenue is the amount *QD*. As *DP =BA*, it is equal to price (*QP*) minus the distance *BA*.

The same analysis holds for any other point (e.g., P_1) on the demand curve. At the price P_M marginal revenue is zero and total revenue is at a maximum. After that point marginal revenue is negative, and total revenue falls.

Multiproduct Firms

As product differentiation increases, it becomes more difficult to define the terms *product* and *market*. A market was defined earlier as the area over which a particular product sells for a single price. Product differentiation blurs this definition, as it results in situations in which a multitude of slightly differing products sell at slightly different prices.

The nature and extent of the market typically vary widely for different products sold by a single multiproduct firm, as do the nature and scope of the markets in which a firm purchases different factors of production. Profit rates earned on different products sold by a single multiproduct firm are likely to differ widely. Actual profit rates as reported are a weighted average of different rates earned on different goods.

This situation is shown in Figure 7-18. It is assumed for simplicity that marginal costs are constant and equal for each product. Figure 7-18 may also be interpreted to represent price discrimination, in which the firm charges a different price for the same product in different separable markets, according to the elasticity of demand in each market.

Under these circumstances it is difficult to determine the industry in which multiproduct corporations are to be classified. This consideration is important for social policy with regard to mergers. As a means of reducing risk through diversification, merger may be attractive to stockholders, tending to raise the price of their shares. But because individual firm income statements are pooled, it is virtually impossible to judge the effects of the merger on performance in particular markets. Firms can decide at will for bookkeeping purposes at which stage of their operation they wish to record profits.

How is effective collusive agreement among separate firms different from the pooling of wealth into a larger corporation? If one is undesirable, why not the other? The courts in the United States have moved to stop mergers of firms in the same industry in all cases in which the effect is judged likely to reduce competition. The case of conglomerate mergers of firms in different industries has proved more difficult.

A firm resulting from the merger of two firms which are neither rivals nor customers of each other is termed a conglomerate. In such cases it is difficult to see how their ability to restrict supply in product markets, or demand in factor markets, which is what market power is all about, is affected. Merger may eliminate a poten-

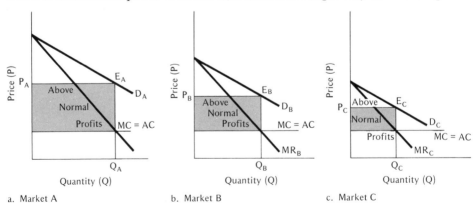

a. Market A   b. Market B   c. Market C

Figure 7-18 Product Differentiation and Price Discrimination

tial entrant to the market. The scope for favoritism, reciprocity, mutual forebearance from competition, preferred channels, and compartmentalization of the economy is increased. If there are real economies in management or advantages in the allocation of investment funds among a wider set of opportunities, such advantages represent efficiencies that are in the public as well as the private interest. Conglomerates have been held undesirable on political grounds, as tending to increase the concentration of economic resources in fewer hands.

In view of the desirability of decentralized economic power, it has been argued that before any merger is permitted, the prospective merger partners ought to be required to demonstrate that the probable effects of the merger will be in the public interest because of cost, technological, or marketing advantages leading to increased sales and lower prices. For antitrust policy, if voluntary collusion is deemed undesirable, prospective and even existing conglomerates may be assumed guilty until proved innocent. Bigness may be asked to justify itself in terms of efficiency and not solely by its ability to generate monopoly profits.

Price Discrimination

Discriminatory pricing is an alternative solution to the monopoly pricing problem. Price discrimination denotes charging different customers different prices for the same commodity. It is possible only when elasticities of demand differ and customers are unable to resell the commodity. Regulatory authorities frequently establish a price structure in which different classes of buyers are charged different unit prices, depending on the elasticity of their demand curve. Railroad tariffs are a classic case of discriminatory pricing.

Perfect price discrimination is defined as that situation in which each customer is charged a different price in proportion to the amount he is willing to pay for a particular unit of the good or service. If a different price could be charged for each unit

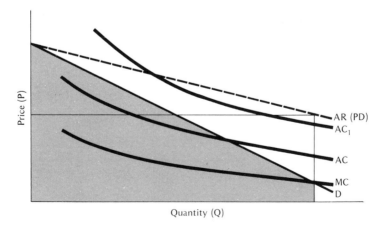

Figure 7-19 Perfect Price Discrimination

sold, total revenue for any output would be represented by the total area under the demand curve, which is shaded in Figure 7-19. For this case of perfect price discrimination, an average revenue curve ((AR_{PD})) may be constructed such that the demand curve becomes its marginal revenue curve. Price discrimination permits a larger quantity to be produced and sold than under a single price yielding the same profit rate.

The possibility of price discrimination may enable projects to become profitable that would not otherwise be undertaken, except with a government subsidy. In Figure 7-19 a product whose average costs are AC_1 would be produced privately only if price discrimination were possible. As a result of such price discrimination, both buyers and sellers are better off than if the good did not exist.

competition and market power in factor markets I: labor

HE WHO by any exertion of mind or body adds to the aggregate of enjoyable wealth, increases the sum of human knowledge or gives to human life higher elevation or greater fullness —he is, in the large meaning of the words, a "producer," a "workingman," a "laborer," and is honestly earning honest wages. But he who without doing aught to make mankind richer, wiser, better, happier, lives on the toil of others—he, no matter by what name of honor he may be called, or how lustily the priests of Mammon may swing their censers before him, is in the last analysis but a beggarman or a thief.

—HENRY GEORGE

God made the bees,
And the bees make honey.
The Miller's man does all the work,
But the Miller makes the money.
—ENGLISH NURSERY RHYME

This chapter explains the economic forces that determine wage rates and the share of labor income in a capitalist economy.

Factors of Production

The term *factors of production* refers to those original productive factors that lie behind all goods and services produced. While machines and intermediate goods are factors of production for a particular firm, they are themselves produced by other firms and their individual prices are determined as explained in the previous chapter.

For analytical purposes two main categories of ultimate factors of production may be distinguished, *labor* and *capital*. Labor denotes the human labor time devoted to the production and exchange of economic goods. Capital denotes the existing stock of all tangible assets that increase the output of labor in the production process. Capital goods are used because they increase the productivity of labor and so add to the value of total output. For some purposes it is useful to consider human capital: the stock of real resources embodied in the education, training, and skills of the labor force.

In capitalist economies productive factors are ultimately owned by private households and rented by them to firms, governments, and other individuals. Total income may be divided exhaustively between *labor income* received by workers and *property income* received by owners of capital.

As shown in Table 8-1, hourly money wage rates have more than tripled over the last twenty-five years. Labor income forms the largest component of total income received, with wages and salaries currently accounting in the United States for about 75 percent of national income. Proprietors' and professionals' income comprises a component of labor income as payment for the owner's own services, as well as a payment for the capital owned by the business. It has declined with the decline of individual proprietorships and the growth of the corporate form of business organization.

The share of total income received by labor varies from less than one half to more than three quarters in the national income statistics of different countries. In many countries this share appears to have exhibited considerable stability over time. In order to explain what determines the share of labor income in an economy it is first necessary to understand the forces that govern the wage level, the structure of wages, and the level of employment.

THE DETERMINATION OF WAGES IN PERFECTLY COMPETITIVE MARKETS

For analytical simplicity consider the case in which all workers are identical, labor mobility is perfect, and all jobs are equally desirable. Under these assumptions all workers receive the same wage. The question of differential wage rates may be side-stepped, and the analysis may proceed in terms of a single wage rate. (As long as

Table 8-1 WAGE RATE, LABOR INCOME, AND LABOR'S SHARE, 1945–71 (BILLIONS OF DOLLARS AND PERCENT OF PERSONAL INCOME)

Year	Wage Rate (Manufacturing) Dollars/hour	Compensation of Employees (Wages and Salary)		Business and Professional Income		Farm Proprietor's Income		Total Compensation of Employees as Percent of National Income
		Dollars	Percent	Dollars	Percent	Dollars	Percent	
1945	1.02	117.5	69	19.2	11	12.2	7	68
1946	1.07	112.0	63	21.6	12	14.9	8	65
1947	1.22	123.0	64	20.3	11	15.2	8	65
1948	1.33	135.3	64	22.7	11	17.5	8	63
1949	1.38	134.6	65	22.6	11	12.7	6	65
1950	1.44	146.7	64	24.0	11	13.5	6	64
1951	1.56	171.0	67	26.1	10	15.8	6	65
1952	1.65	185.1	68	27.1	10	15.0	6	67
1953	1.74	198.3	69	27.5	10	13.0	5	69
1954	1.78	196.5	68	27.6	10	12.4	4	69
1955	1.86	211.3	68	30.3	10	11.4	4	68
1956	1.95	227.8	68	31.3	9	11.4	3	69
1957	2.05	238.7	68	32.8	9	11.3	3	70
1958	2.11	239.9	66	33.2	9	13.4	4	70
1959	2.19	258.2	67	35.1	9	11.4	3	70
1960	2.26	270.8	68	34.2	9	12.0	3	71
1961	2.32	278.1	67	35.6	9	12.8	3	71
1962	2.39	296.1	67	37.1	8	13.0	3	71
1963	2.46	311.1	67	37.9	8	13.1	3	71
1964	2.53	333.7	67	40.2	8	12.1	2	71
1965	2.61	358.9	67	42.4	8	14.8	3	70
1966	2.72	394.6	67	44.8	8	15.9	3	70
1967	2.83	423.4	67	46.3	7	14.4	2	72
1968	3.01	463.5	68	47.8	7	15.1	2	72
1969	3.19	509.6	68	50.3	7	16.8	2	73
1970	3.36	541.4	67	51.0	6	15.8	2	75
1971	3.57	574.2	67	52.1	6	16.3	2	75

Source: Department of Commerce, Office of Business Economics; Wage Rate: Department of Labor, Bureau of Labor Statistics.

relative wage rates do not change, the wage rate for the economy as a whole may be regarded as a weighted average of different wage rates actually existing, and the analysis may be carried over to the case of heterogeneous labor.)

The wage rate paid for homogeneous labor inputs in a perfectly competitive labor market would be determined by the quantity of labor demanded by employers and the quantity of labor supplied by households. In a nonslave economy, only the services of labor can be bought and sold. Labor as a capital good can be rented, but in general the capitalized present value of labor services cannot be exchanged (professional athletes excepted).

The Demand for Labor

As developed in Chapter 5, in perfectly competitive markets business firms' derived demand for labor would be the value of labor's marginal product. As shown in Fig-

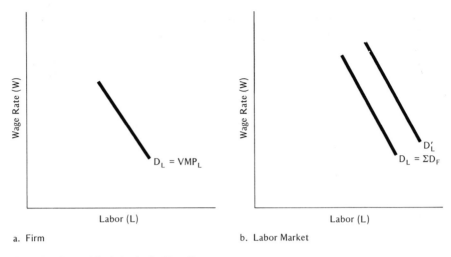

a. Firm   b. Labor Market

Figure 8-1 Demand for Labor in the Short Run

ure 8-1, the demand curve for labor (D_L) is downward sloping, according to the law of diminishing returns. Given the stock of capital and the level of technology, as more labor is hired its marginal product declines.

In competitive markets the value of labor's marginal product is the marginal physical product of labor times the price of the goods and services produced. The total demand for labor in the economy is simply the sum of all individual firm's demand for labor.

The position of the demand curve for labor D_L in Figure 8-1 is defined by the marginal productivity of labor. This in turn will depend on the stock of reproducible capital in the economy, the endowment of natural resources, the level of technology, and the skill and training of the labor force. Increases in any of these variables would raise the productivity of labor and shift the demand curve upward (e.g., to D'_L). In developed countries where the productivity of labor is high, the demand curve for labor will be higher than in less developed countries where labor productivity is lower.

The Supply of Labor in the Short Run

It is now necessary to examine the supply curve of labor. How does the amount of labor offered vary with the wage rate paid? As was the case with commodities, it is necessary to distinguish short-run and long-run supply relationships.

Rational households will continue to supply labor as long as the marginal utility of income earned exceeds the marginal disutility of work plus the marginal utility of leisure. Empirical studies indicate that over most of the observed range, the total supply curve of labor in the short run is positive but relatively inelastic with respect to the real wage rate. This implies that a slightly greater quantity of labor will be offered at higher wage rates.

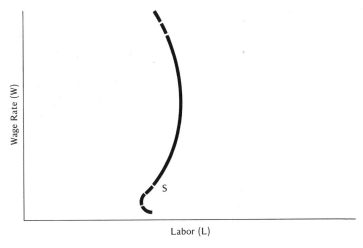

Figure 8-2 Supply Curve of Labor in the Short Run

In the short run the size of the population and the degree of effort and skill embodied in the labor force may be assumed constant. The quantity of labor supplied will then vary with the labor force participation rate — that is, the proportion of the total population of working age in the labor force — and the proportion of the labor force employed. The number of hours worked per week, holidays and vacations per year, and worker participation rates by sex and age are to a large extent historically determined in the short run. Nevertheless, considerable possibility of voluntary short-run variation occurs through overtime, sick leave, moonlighting, and withdrawal from or entry into the labor force. The supply of labor by married women, for example, is relatively elastic.

As shown in Figure 8-2, the quantity of labor supplied in the short run is observed to decrease for relatively large increases in wage rates. This phenomenon is termed the *backward-bending supply curve* of labor. For relatively large reductions of real wage rates the supply curve also appears to become negatively sloped, although little empirical evidence exists for this case.

Labor force participation rates, and therefore the quantity of labor supplied, are functionally related to many other variables in addition to the wage rate. One of the most important of these is the probability of finding employment.

The Wage Rate and Labor's Share

The wage rate paid to labor will tend toward the level where both employers and workers are on their demand and supply curves. This equilibrium wage rate and volume of employment is shown in Figure 8-3b. In a perfectly competitive labor market involuntary unemployment is impossible, as wages will adjust to clear the market and eliminate excess supply or excess demand for labor. At all higher wage rates there will be an excess supply of labor: involuntarily unemployed workers endeavor-

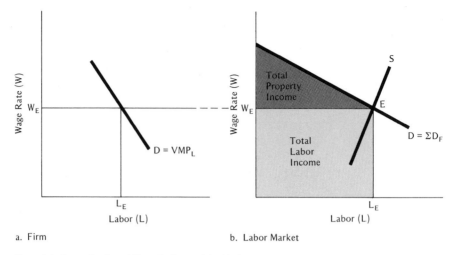

Figure 8-3 Determination of Wages in Competitive Markets

ing to sell their services will bid down wage rates. At all lower wage rates there will be an excess demand for labor: dissatisfied employers attempting to attract additional workers will bid up wage rates.

An individual firm in competitive labor markets will be faced by a perfectly elastic supply curve of labor at the going market wage rate, as shown in Figure 8-3a. The wage rate will equal the value of labor's marginal product.

The total wage bill is represented by the rectangle $W_E L_E$. As the area under the value of labor's marginal product curve to any input equals the value of total product,[1] the shaded triangle represents the residual share of income accruing to property.

The Supply of Labor in the Long Run

In the long run the supply of labor is more elastic with respect to the real wage rate. The size and composition of the population, institutional constraints, work habits and attitudes, and the capital embodied in the labor force can all vary over time.

Following Malthus, most nineteenth-century classical economists believed in the so-called *iron law of wages,* which states that in the long run the supply of labor will tend to increase whenever real wages are above some subsistence level. Alternatively expressed, the long-run supply curve of labor (S_{LR}) is perfectly elastic at a subsistence level of wages (W_S). This situation is illustrated in Figure 8-4. An increase in demand for labor might temporarily raise wage rates (e.g., from W_s to W_1). But over the long run the supply of workers would increase, reducing wages again toward subsistence.

Some classical economists, such as Ricardo and Mill, argued that this *subsistence*

1. The value of total product is equal to the sum of the additions to the value of total product made by each worker employed.

level was culturally determined. As a result, the long-run supply curve would be upward sloping, as conventional standards of subsistence and poverty adjusted upward over time. By a kind of ratchet effect, once workers had experienced a higher real wage (W_1), their concept of subsistence could rise to W'_S. The long-run supply curve becomes the dashed line $S^*_{L\,LR}$ in Figure 8-4.

Marx also argued that an iron law of wages would operate under capitalism to keep wages in the long run near the subsistence level. But his argument was not based on the vulgar Malthusian premise that workers would breed excessively whenever wages exceeded subsistence. For Marx the iron law of wages operated because dynamic technical change under capitalism generated a continuous pressure to substitute capital for labor. This pressure would be accentuated whenever wage rates tended to rise. As a result, over time the demand curve for labor would shift leftward relative to the supply of labor, and a reserve army of unemployed would be maintained, milling outside the factory gates to keep wages at a near subsistence level. This prediction of worker immiserization has not been borne out by history.

Economics was long termed the dismal science because most economists were pessimistic concerning the possibility of a sustained increase in real wages. Real wages in Europe did not in fact increase significantly in the first half of the nineteenth century, although this is still an issue of historical dispute. This was due in part to the force of Malthusian population pressure with the decline in mortality rates.

In a competitive economy the course of real wages over time may be viewed as the outcome of a race between the rate of technical change and tangible and human capital accumulation, which shift the demand for labor curve outward and so tend to raise real wages, and the rate of population growth, which shifts the supply curve

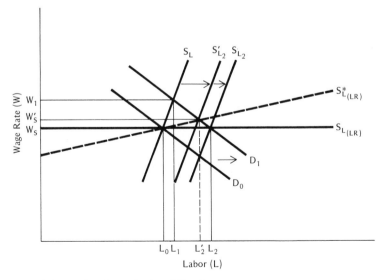

Figure 8-4 Long-Run Determination of Wage Rates

outward and so tends to lower real wages. Ultimately the governing factor is the behavior of the supply of labor. In many less-developed countries, Malthusian population forces are currently dominant.

Economists are now much less confident of their ability to predict the long-run behavior of the labor supply. The work week has fallen dramatically over the last one hundred years, apparently in response to the rise in real income. But it has fallen very little in the last thirty years. The postwar baby boom was not foreseen. A large number of imperfectly understood demographic forces influence the growth of the labor force — age of marriage, family planning, education, social attitudes to children and work — in addition to the direct influence of real income and consumption on fertility and mortality rates. Economists have been forced to regard the long-run growth of the labor supply as largely exogenous (determined outside their model) and taken as given for purposes of analysis.

THE DETERMINATION OF WAGES IN IMPERFECTLY COMPETITIVE MARKETS

Recognition that product and factor markets are not perfectly competitive necessitates a change in the foregoing analysis. In imperfectly competitive markets, the contribution of an additional worker to a firm's total profits is less than the value of the additional goods and services he produces.

Imperfectly Competitive Product Markets

Consider first the case of imperfectly competitive product markets, while retaining the assumption that labor markets are perfectly competitive. The change in total revenue resulting from a change in employment of one unit of a productive factor is termed the factor's *marginal revenue product*. In perfect competition, firms are faced with a perfectly elastic demand curve for their product. As they can sell additional units of output at the same price, a factor's marginal revenue product is simply the factor's marginal physical product times the market price of current output, i.e., *the value of the factor's marginal product*.

Firms operating in imperfectly competitive product markets are faced by a downward-sloping demand curve for their product. Marginal revenue is less than the price of the additional unit sold, because the firm must reduce its price on previous units sold in order to increase sales. In imperfect competition, a factor's marginal revenue product is equal to the marginal physical product of the factor times the *marginal revenue* from additional units sold. This amount is always less than the price to the extent the demand curve faced by the firm is less than perfectly elastic. The demand curve for labor in perfectly competitive (D_c) and imperfectly competitive (D_M) product markets is illustrated in Figure 8-5.

Figure 8-5 shows that for any given wage rate (W_0) firms possessing market power will hire less labor (L_M) than firms in competitive markets (L_C), given the

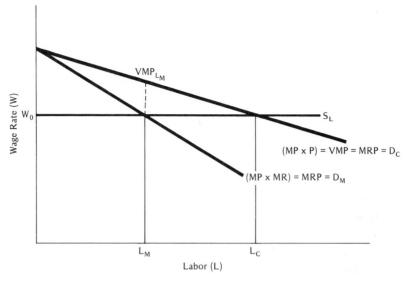

Figure 8-5 Demand for Labor in Perfectly and Imperfectly Competitive Product Markets

same factor-productivity schedules and industry demand schedule. This case reflects the fact that under imperfect competition output is restricted relative to the perfectly competitive outcome, and the quantity of factors demanded is therefore lower. Labor is paid a wage lower than the value of its marginal product in imperfect competition.

Lower aggregate demand for labor in an economy in which firms possess market power would result in less employment and a lower level of output, providing that the supply curve of labor is not perfectly inelastic. As shown in Figures 8-6a and 8-6b, it would also result in a lower level of wages, unless the supply curve of labor

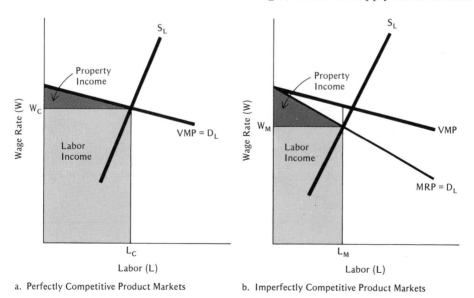

a. Perfectly Competitive Product Markets   b. Imperfectly Competitive Product Markets

Figure 8-6 Wage Rate Determination in Perfectly Competitive Labor Markets

COMPETITION AND MARKET POWER IN FACTOR MARKETS I: LABOR **197**

to the economy were perfectly elastic. The behavior of labor's share of total income will depend on the elasticity of the demand and supply curves for labor and capital. The more inelastic the supply of labor, the greater the fall in wages and labor's share in an imperfectly competitive economy.

Imperfectly Competitive Factor Markets

Now consider the case of factor markets that are imperfectly competitive because of market power of employers (buyers). Individual firms are faced by an upward-sloping supply curve of labor. The wage rate is no longer given: firms are able to hire more workers only by offering an increase in wages paid. This would be the case for a large factory operating in a small town or local labor market, or for employer collusion to keep wages down. The marginal cost of hiring additional workers now exceeds the wage rate paid, because the firm must pay increased wages to all workers previously hired.

This situation is shown in Figure 8-7 for a firm operating in perfectly competitive product markets. For a straight-line supply (average cost) curve, the marginal cost curve is again drawn through the y intercept to bisect the horizontal distance to the supply curve. The firm will continue to hire workers only as long as the marginal cost of labor is less than labor's marginal revenue product.

Market power in labor markets causes firms to reduce the amount of labor hired (L_M) relative to perfectly competitive labor markets (L_C) and to pay a wage rate (W_M) below the value of labor's marginal product (VMP_{L_M}). The marginal revenue product of labor is no longer the firm's demand for labor curve. In imperfectly competitive labor markets the quantity of labor demanded depends on the elasticity of the supply curve of labor facing the firm.

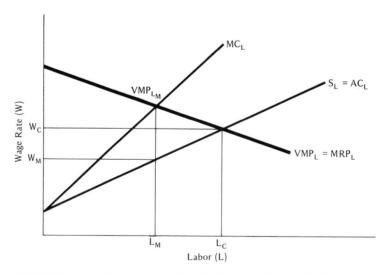

Figure 8-7 Wage Rate Determination in Imperfectly Competitive Labor Markets and Perfectly Competitive Product Markets

Market power of buyers, as distinct from sellers, is termed *monopsony power.* The fact that workers are many and employers few and that workers must work in order to live while employers may wait and live off their capital suggests that, in the absence of unions, owners of capital have greater bargaining power than owners of labor whenever competition is imperfect.

Imperfectly Competitive Product and Factor Markets

It is now possible to consider the more complex case in which firms possess market power in both product and factor markets. This situation is shown in Figure 8-8. The firm will hire labor only so long as the marginal revenue product of labor exceeds the marginal cost of labor. The wage rate paid (W_M) will be less than the value of labor's marginal product by the distance AB, because of the firm's market power in buying labor, plus the distance BC, because of the firm's market power in selling its product. The quantity of labor employed (L_M) and wage rates paid (W_M) will be less than would occur with perfect competition only in factor markets (L_{FC}, W_{FC}), with perfect competition only in product markets (L_{PC}, W_{PC}), and with perfect competition in both product and factor markets (L_C, W_C).

The marginal productivity theory of income distribution as it applies to the determination of wage rates and labor's share of total income may now be briefly summarized. The accumulated stock of real and human capital, the labor force, and the state of technology determine in the short run the productivity of labor and capital as factors of production. In competitive product markets the demand for labor and

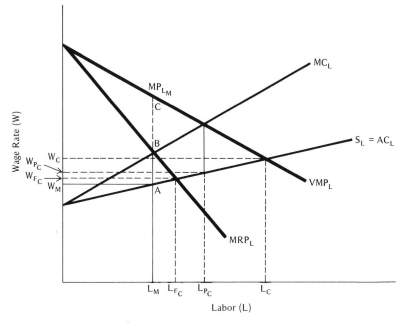

Figure 8-8 Wage Rate Determination in Imperfectly Competitive Product and Labor Markets

capital will be equal to the value of their marginal products. In competitive labor markets, the wage rate will adjust to clear the labor market, so that the quantity of labor demanded equals the quantity of labor supplied. This outcome is shown in Figure 8-9a.

The cumulative area under the marginal revenue product of labor curve from the vertical axis to any input of labor is equal to the value of total product. As a result, the analysis simultaneously determines the share of total income between labor and capital. Total wages are represented by the area of the rectangle ($W_0 L_0$). The residual area under the marginal revenue product curve, shaded in Figure 8-9a, represents the amount of total income accruing as property income to the owners of capital.

In imperfectly competitive product markets, the demand for labor would be lower and equal to labor's marginal revenue product, as illustrated in Figure 8-9b. As a result, *ceteris paribus*, the wage rate W_1, the amount of employment L_1, and/or the share of income received by labor would be lower. As may be seen from Figure 8-9b, the extent that wages, employment, or labor's share declines will depend on the elasticity of the supply of labor function. The more inelastic the supply of labor (e.g., S'_L), the lower the wage rate and labor's share but the smaller the fall in the level of employment and output compared to the perfectly competitive outcome. The outcome will also depend on the shape of the demand curve for labor, which is governed by the elasticity of substitution between labor and capital. The more inelastic the demand for labor, the lower will be wage rates and labor's share.

In the case of *imperfectly competitive labor and product markets,* as shown in Figure 8-9c, *ceteris paribus* the wage rate W_2, employment L_2, and labor's share will be still lower. The outcome will again depend on the slopes of the supply and demand curves for labor, as revealed by inspection of Figure 8-9c. In this case, firms are able to exercise their market power in both product and factor markets to turn the distribution of income in their favor.

Exploitation and Justice

Exploitation is sometimes defined in economics as payment to a factor of production of a price below the value of its marginal product. As may be seen from Figure 8-9, exploitation occurs whenever product or factor markets are imperfectly competitive. In Figure 8-9c the degree of exploitation (AC) is due in part to firm market power in factor markets (AB), and in part to firm market power in product markets (BC).

Exploitation is a term with obvious normative connotations. Used in its technical economic sense, it may appear to imply that payment equal to the value of a factor's marginal product is somehow "fair" or "just." This is a normative statement or value judgment and, as such, cannot be supported by objective economic analysis.

It is often argued that the proposition "To each according to what he creates" represents a just and simple principle on which any equitable distribution of income

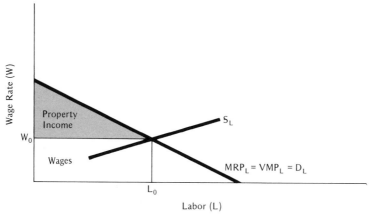

a. Perfect Competition in All Markets

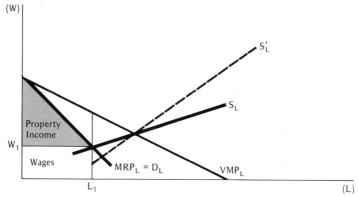

b. Imperfectly Competitive Product Markets

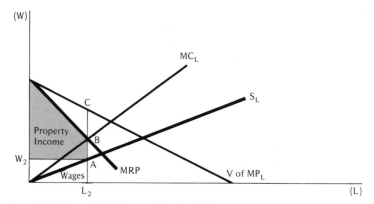

c. Imperfectly Competitive Labor and Product Markets

Figure 8-9 The Determination of Labor and Property Shares

must be based; any society that departs from this rule condones institutional robbery. This argument has a long and lustrous intellectual tradition. It was once regarded as a kind of natural law and the moral basis of private property. It was a short step for economists to conclude that perfectly competitive markets distribute income fairly and equitably.

While most traditional definitions of justice are based on some underlying concept of exchange, many would disagree with this particular definition. It is directly challenged by the socialist ethic "'From each according to his ability, to each according to his need." Less directly it is challenged by the Christian ethic of love. The problem of which precept is better or more humane is a question of ethics and, as such, cannot be answered by economic theory.

Even if the principle "To each according to what he creates" is accepted as a desirable moral precept, it does not follow that it is satisfied even in a perfectly competitive capitalist system. How did property owners get their property in the first place? If the answer is through inheritance, force, or luck, and not by their own production, the rule is violated and property owners themselves would appear to be the agents of institutional robbery. Most real capital goods, apart from unimproved national resources, represent the embodiment of past labor time.

Each worker or unit of capital, even in perfectly competitive markets, does not receive the value of what he or it personally contributes but rather the value of what one more worker or unit of capital would add to production, if all other factors were held constant. This is logically not the same as his own contribution to production. Where several factors cooperate in production, it is generally impossible to divide total production into the amounts contributed by each factor. In the conception of children, whose contribution is greater, the man's or the woman's? In the production of wine, whose contribution is greater, the man's or the land's? To answer this question with a story about the contribution of an additional man's efforts may be entertaining, but strictly irrelevant.

Finally, even accepting marginal productivity theory, property owners under capitalism receive a reward not for what they produce but for what the things that they own produce. Property income is received as a reward to ownership, not to the contribution of owners. As a result, the precept "To each according to what he creates" can hardly be used as a moral justification for the system of private property. Marx argued that all unearned (property) income represents exploitation of labor.

LABOR UNIONS AND COLLECTIVE BARGAINING

In view of the predominant market power possessed by employers in labor markets, workers have attempted to combine to increase their own bargaining position. The response of business was to resist, not infrequently by force. Labor troublemakers for centuries were beaten, dismissed, and blacklisted, which meant that other employers would not hire them. The response of governments, largely representative of business interests, was until recently a bloody history of arrests, imprisonments, and police suppression of worker strikes, picketing, and organizing activities.

In the United States workers did not win the right to organize and bargain collectively until the depression of the 1930s, when public sentiment turned dramatically against big business. The steel industry maintained a twelve-hour day and a seven-day week until 1924. The last "massacre" of strikers occured as recently as 1937, when more than one hundred unarmed workers were killed or wounded by Chicago police.

Labor Collusion

Labor collusion gives workers market power in factor markets. By bargaining collectively, workers are able to offer firms an all-or-nothing price for their services. For this reason, the right to strike — that is, to withhold their services completely — is critical to the union's bargaining position.

Collective bargaining affects the shape of the supply curve of labor as viewed by business firms. Rather than upward-sloping, the supply curve of labor to the firm becomes horizontal at the negotiated wage rate. Under such circumstances, the wage rate and the volume of unemployment become indeterminate over some range. The outcome will depend on the relative bargaining strength of labor and management, their goals and priorities, and the strategy selected.

This situation is illustrated in Figure 8-10, in which S_L and MC_L represent the supply curve and marginal cost curve for labor in the absence of a union. Under such circumstances the firm would hire L_0 workers, where the marginal cost of labor equals its marginal revenue product, and pay the wage rate W_0. Exploitation would be the difference between the value of labor's marginal product (VMP_{L_0}) and the wage rate paid (W_0). The effect of collective bargaining by workers through a union is to produce a perfectly elastic supply curve of labor to the firm at the negotiated wage rate, up to the supply of labor available. At the negotiated rate W_2 the supply curve of labor to the firm becomes the dashed horizontal and then upward-sloping line shown in Figure 8-10. The marginal cost of labor is constant and equal to average cost so long as workers are available at the collectively determined rate.

The Indeterminacy of Collective Bargaining

As the negotiated rate rises from W_0 to W_1, both wages and employment will increase. Over this range, workers can succeed in getting *both* higher wages and more jobs. To the extent that government minimum wages apply to such situations, they effectuate a reduction in the exploitation of workers unable to organize effectively, yet do not decrease employment. Wage increases beyond W_1 can be realized in general only by accepting lower levels of employment.

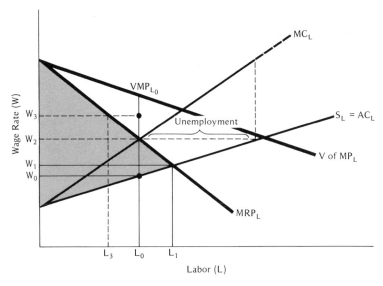

Figure 8-10 Collective Bargaining

For any particular level of employment below the maximum L_1, the outcome of the wage bargain is indeterminate. In such circumstances there is no determinate economic explanation of the share of income going to labor and capital. As shown by the shaded area in Figure 8-10, the limits will lie somewhere between the maximum the firm will be willing to pay (labor's marginal revenue product) and the minimum workers will accept (the supply curve of labor). At the initial level of employment L_0, this range of indeterminacy lies between W_0 and W_2. At all wage rates within this range both wages and employment are higher than in the nonunion case.

If workers succeed in bargaining for the rate W_2, they will have eliminated all exploitation due to the firm's market power in labor markets. They can capture the difference between the value of labor's marginal product and labor's marginal revenue product — i.e., exploitation due to the firm's market power in product markets — only if they can *simultaneously* bargain for the wage rate and the level of employment (e.g., W_3 and L_0). Otherwise, higher wage rates (e.g., W_3) can be realized only with a lower amount of employment (L_3) and fewer jobs for union members. As seen from Figure 8-10, in general, if profit rates remain unchanged, higher wages result in greater unemployment of labor. At any wage rate, unemployment is equal to the excess of labor supplied over labor demanded.

The outcome of the collective bargaining process is in part a question of strategy and will depend on the relative bargaining strength of labor and management. Labor's bargaining power is importantly influenced by the amount of unemployment prevailing in the economy and by the current level of profits. The attitude and goals of the union — in particular its trade-off between number employed, wage rates, and nonpecuniary benefits — are also important. Union officials may be regarded as maximizing some utility function that includes wage rate, volume of employment, job security, work conditions, grievance procedures, and a large number of other variables.

One of the most important benefits of unions is to provide workers with protection against unfair labor practices, that is, to limit management power to discriminate, discipline, hire, and fire individual workers. Before the existence of unions, the power of employers over their workers was largely unconstrained and, while at best paternal, was typically authoritarian and not infrequently corrupt. Another important benefit of unions has been to permit labor interests to have greater political influence in shaping government policy.

Labor's Share

The share of labor and profits in income depends in the long run on the nature of technological change and the degree of factor substitution that determine the ratio of capital to output, and the supply price of labor and capital. In the short run, firms possessing market power in product markets but not previously maximizing profits may be able to pass on wage increases to consumers in the form of higher prices and so protect their profit share. Firms following average-cost or target-profit pricing will be able to pass on cost increases completely and suffer no reduction in profits only if they were not previously charging a price at which profits were maximized. Under these circumstances, unions will be unable to increase the share of income going to workers. Wage demands will result instead in a higher level of prices and a lower real value of worker money wages. The so-called cost-push inflation that results is the by-product of this conflict over distributive shares.

In the United States less than one third of the labor force is unionized and only about one quarter of these unions have substantial market power, as in craft and building trades, railroads, shipping, and mining. It has been estimated that workers in unions with relatively strong bargaining positions have succeeded on the average in raising their wages by as much as one fifth over what they would have been in the absence of unions. This benefit appears to have been gained largely at the expense of other workers, as labor's total share of national income has increased only slightly, and at the expense of those property owners and fixed income claimants unable to protect their real income from inflation.

AUTOMATION

Given the degree of market power and the rate of growth of the capital stock and the labor force, the behavior of wage rates over time will depend on the nature of technical change, in particular the extent to which it is capital-saving or labor-saving.

Automation is a term used loosely to refer to strongly labor-saving technical change resulting in the replacement of workers by capital. The effect of automation is to shift leftward and steepen the marginal revenue product curve of labor. Given the capital stock, the marginal product of the first workers employed is very high, but the marginal productivity falls rapidly as more workers are hired, as is shown in Figure 8-11 by the shift from MRP_0 to MRP_1. In competitive labor markets, this would *reduce* the equilibrium wage rate (e.g., from W_0 to W_1) even though the *average* productivity of labor increased. The share of total income received by labor would fall and property income would increase as a proportion of the total. This result may be intuitively understood by considering the extreme case of a completely automated economy in which machines produce the entire output, in which case all income accrues to the owners of property.

If wages were inflexible downward and remained at W_0, the result would be an increase in unemployment to AE_0 and a fall in the share of income going to labor. Depending on their market power, unions might be able to protect labor's share by collective bargaining, as is shown in Figure 8-11 by a rise in the wage rate (e.g., to W_2). But this protection of labor's share in total income can, under these circumstances, be achieved only at the expense of even greater unemployment of labor (BC).

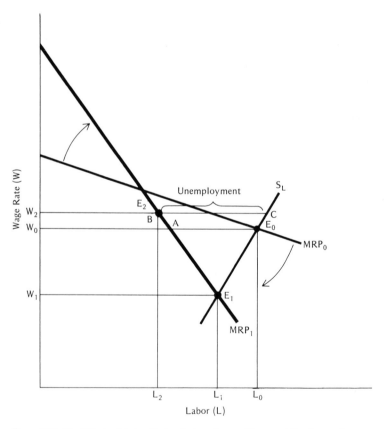

Figure 8-11 The Effects of Labor-Saving Automation on Wages and Employment

Technological Unemployment

The effect of technological change on wages and unemployment depends critically on whether the growth of the capital stock is sufficient to absorb workers released from production plus new entrants into the labor force. Marx argued that labor-saving technical change would result in a reserve army of unemployed workers, tending to keep wage rates at subsistence. In fact technical change has been capital-saving as well as labor-saving. The resulting rise in the productivity of capital, by reducing the stock of capital required to produce any given output, has operated to raise the demand for labor per unit of capital. Full employment has been possible with rising real wage rates. As the distribution of income between labor and property has remained relatively stable, it would seem that experienced technological change has not on balance been predominantly labor-saving. As an economy's real income increases, a growing proportion of the labor force is employed in the service sector, where automation is more difficult and productivity grows at a slower pace.

THE STRUCTURE OF WAGE RATES

The simplifying assumptions of homogeneous labor, homogeneous jobs, and perfect mobility may now be removed. Once differences in the quality of labor and in the disutility of work are recognized it is no longer possible to speak in terms of a *single* wage rate. There will then exist a whole family or *structure* of wage rates, each for a different type of labor or occupation. Not all of these rates will move together. The

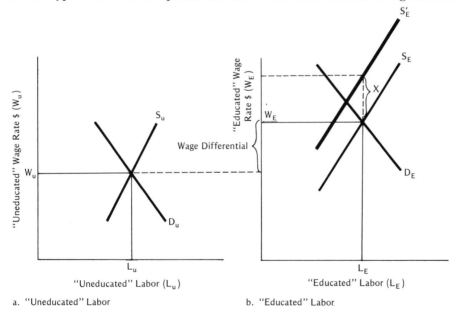

Figure 8-12 Relative Wage Rates

markets for coal miners, professional football players and economics professors are only distantly interrelated.

The forces determining the wage structure may again be analyzed in terms of supply and demand. Consider the case in which only two kinds of labor exist, educated and uneducated, but all jobs are alike in their nonpecuniary rewards. In competitive markets the wage rate received by each group will differ according to their relative marginal productivities. As shown in Figure 8-12, this in turn is determined by the position of the demand curve for their services relative to the quantity of labor supplied.

The ranking of selected occupations in the United States by income decile is presented in Table 8-2. The high relative positions of electricians, plumbers, locomotive firemen, engineers, and conductors appear to be attributable to union power. Table 8-3 presents more aggregated data on wage rates. As indicated by comparison between 1958 and 1966, the occupational wage structure exhibits considerable stability over time.

Table 8-2   SELECTED OCCUPATIONS RANKED BY MEDIAN INCOME, 1959
(OCCUPATION RANKED BY MEDIAN WAGE OR SALARY INCOME
IN 1959)

Lowest Tenth
 Messengers
 Charmen, Janitors, and Porters
 Waiters, Bartenders, and Counter Workers
 Fishermen
 Lumbermen
 Laborers (lumber, textile, trade)
Second Tenth
 Clergymen
 Apprentices
 Operatives (apparel, textile, leather, etc.)
 Barbers, Beauticians, and Manicurists
 Laborers (food, stone, machinery)
Third Tenth
 Drivers (bus, taxi, and truck)
 Laborers (paper, metal, railroad)
Fourth Tenth
 Musicians and Music Teachers
 Stenographers, Typists, and Secretaries
 Bakers
 Carpenters
 Sailors and Deck Hands
Fifth Tenth
 Mechanics and Repairmen
 Operatives (machinery)
Sixth Tenth
 Social, Welfare, and Recreation Workers
 Salaried Managers (eating and drinking places)
 Salesmen and Sales Clerks
 Operatives (paper, rubber, transportation equipment)

Table 8-2 SELECTED OCCUPATIONS RANKED BY MEDIAN INCOME, 1959
(OCCUPATION RANKED BY MEDIAN WAGE OR SALARY INCOME
IN 1959) (Cont'd)

Seventh Tenth
    Sports Instructors, Athletes, Entertainers
    Teachers
    Salaried Managers (personal services)
    Real Estate Agents and Brokers
    Policemen, Sheriffs, and Marshalls

Eighth Tenth
    Salaried Managers (retail trade)
    Compositors and Typesetters
    Machinists, Millwrights, and Toolmakers
    Firemen, Fire Protection

Ninth Tenth
    Artists and Art Teachers
    Designers and Draftsmen
    Pharmacists
    Postmasters
    Electricians, Plumbers
    Foremen (construction, manufacturing)
    Locomotive Firemen

Tenth Tenth
    Authors, Editors, and Reporters
    Chemists
    College Presidents, Professors, Instructors (n.e.c.)
    Conductors (railroad)
    Salaried Managers (manufacturing, finance, transportation, trade)
    Locomotive Engineers

Source: Census of Population, 1960.

Table 8-3 OCCUPATIONAL WAGE STRUCTURE, 1958, 1966

| *Year-'round Male Workers* | *Dollars and Percent of Median Earnings* | | | |
| | *1958* | | *1966* | |
	Dollars	*Percent*	*Dollars*	*Percent*
Professional, Technical, and Kindred Workers				
Self-employed	11,231	230	14,880	217
Salaried	6,514	133	8,958	131
Teachers	5,651	116	7,629	111
Managers, Officials and Proprietors	5,909	121	8,826	129
Chemical and Kindred Workers	4,864	100	6,542	95
Sales Workers	5,371	110	7,553	110
Craftsmen, Foremen, and Kindred Workers	5,346	109	7,161	104
Operative and Kindred Workers	4,502	92	6,135	89
Service Workers (except private household)	3,961	81	5,117	75
Laborers (except farm and mine)	3,732	76	5,133	75
Farm Laborers and Foremen	1,479	30	2,576	38
Farmers and Farm Managers	1,878	32	3,547	52
Total with earnings (Median)	4,888	100	6,856	100

Source: Department of Commerce, Bureau of the Census, *Current Population Reports.*

Equalizing Differentials

Observed differences in relative wage rates are attributable in part to differences in nonmonetary rewards associated with different occupations. But differential wage rates would occur even if all labor were homogeneous and perfectly mobile. People are attracted to a particular occupation not only by the pecuniary rewards but also by the satisfaction they expect to derive from the work itself.

Jobs that are relatively dirty, dangerous, tedious, irregular, or of low social prestige have low or negative nonmonetary rewards. As a result, a higher money income is required to offset the negative psychic income and induce workers to offer their services. Conversely jobs that are clean, secure, or challenging, with opportunities for creativity, freedom, leisure, influence, and high prestige have positive pecuniary rewards. A lower money wage is sufficient to call forth a supply of labor due to the positive psychic income. Money wage differences due to difference in nonmonetary rewards have been termed *equalizing* wage differentials. As costs and prices are based only on pecuniary rewards, the marginal product of labor will exceed or fall short of the total return to labor.

Occupations requiring education are generally regarded as more attractive than uneducated occupations in terms of the nonpecuniary rewards from work. The value attached to such psychic income will vary among different workers according to their preferences. Assume that the differential average pecuniary value of such nonmonetary rewards to workers in educated jobs is X dollars, as measured by the wage increase required to compensate them and induce them to move into uneducated jobs. As shown in Figure 8-12b, this factor shifts up the supply function by this amount, because the reward to labor in educated jobs includes both pecuniary and nonpecuniary components. Total differentials are larger than observed pecuniary differentials. The distribution of real income is thus absolutely more unequal once real income is redefined to include nonpecuniary benefits. Whether it is relatively more unequal than pecuniary income depends on whether nonpecuniary differentials are greater or less than pecuniary differentials among occupations.

As shown in Figure 8-12b the value of labor's marginal product in educated jobs is less than the value of the total reward to labor. Too much of such goods are produced, even under perfect competition, in the limited sense that the total value of output could be increased by reallocating labor until the value of its marginal product is equal to its wage rate.

Another important equalizing wage differential lies in the fact that different jobs require highly diverse educational and training attainments. Differences in labor productivity are in part explainable as a return to educational investment in human capital. Such differences must be reflected in differential wage rates to induce individuals to undertake the costs involved in training and education. The most important of these costs is the opportunity cost of labor time spent in years of education and training, the income foregone by not working. Doctors have a shorter working life than office workers.

Table 8-4 EDUCATION AND ANNUAL LIFETIME INCOME, 1966 (MALES 25 YEARS AND OLDER)

	Total	Elementary		High School		College	
		Less than 8 years	8 years	1–3 years	4 years	1–3 years	4 or more years
Mean Income in 1966 Dollars	6,908	3,520	4,867	6,294	7,494	8,783	11,739
Estimated Lifetime Income in 1966 Dollars	320,700	188,600	246,500	283,700	340,500	394,000	541,900
Estimated Lifetime Income in 1959 Dollars White		157,000	191,000	221,000	253,000	301,000	427,000
Nonwhite		95,000	123,000	132,000	151,000	162,000	215,000
Nonwhite as Percent of White		61	64	60	60	54	50

Source: U.S. Bureau of the Census.

Wages and salaries as reported include an important component of property income, the return to investment in human capital. As shown in Table 8-4, a comparison of lifetime incomes suggests that the present value of a college education in the United States may be as high as several hundred thousand dollars. Part of the observed differences are due to differences in labor quality.

Investment in human capital is becoming increasingly important in developed economies. It is in this sense that workers in mature capitalist economies are becoming "peoples' capitalists." Should this trend continue, wage and salary income may be expected to rise as a portion of total output and ownership of tangible assets recede in importance relative to ownership of human capital.

Nonequalizing Differentials

If nonmonetary differences alone accounted for differential wage rates among jobs, the more unpleasant jobs would be the more highly paid. As may be seen from examination of Tables 8-2 and 8-3, the exact opposite is observed. As a result the distribution of real income, monetary plus nonmonetary, is probably more unequal than the distribution of money income alone. These differences are termed nonequalizing wage differentials.

Nonequalizing wage differentials are due to the fact that labor is not homogeneous, opportunities are not equal, and mobility is not perfect. The resulting wage differences are generated by differences in productivity among individual workers, differences in taste for leisure and other psychic income, and unequal market power possessed by different types of labor. A substantial part of the observed differences in income among occupations presented in Table 8-2 is attributable to differences in labor's bargaining strength, either against employers or with employers against consumers, in imperfectly competitive markets.

Natural differences in the quality of labor are substantial. Individuals differ in their innate abilities, aptitudes, skills, and motivation. These distributions presumably follow a normal curve, similar to the distribution of height, weight, and other physical characteristics.

Unequal chances to develop one's capacities due to prejudice and differences in environment are a reinforcing social cause of nonequalizing differentials. There are substantial social as distinct from natural barriers to the free mobility of labor: color, religion, class, geography, sex. To the extent that access to a particular occupation is artificially restricted, worker productivity and therefore wages will be higher in that market and lower in other markets as a result of the artificially contrived scarcity. This is shown by the dashed supply curves S_{E_1} and S_{U_1} in Figure 8-13, relative to the supply of educated and uneducated labor (S_E and S_U) in the absence of artificial barriers.

Differences in wage rates lead to differences in income. In countries where class, religious, or racial differences are significant and upward mobility is restricted, the labor force is composed of separate noncompeting groups. These groups are segre-

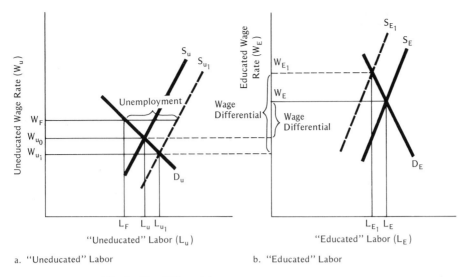

Figure 8-13 Factors Affecting Wage Differentials

gated not by natural ability but by ethnic background, religion, race, or class. Differences in access to and successful performance in the educational escalator among different groups play a critical role in shaping the supply of individuals among different occupations. White males enjoy 99 percent of all jobs paying over $25,000 per year in the U.S. Income differences by religion and color in the United States are summarized in Tables 8-5 and 8-6. Many of the differences in Table 8-5 are due to differences in geographic distribution. As may be seen from Table 8-6, the relative increase in nonwhite income was much greater in the North and West than in the South, but within each region the relative as well as the absolute gap between whites and nonwhites increased over the period.

Table 8-5 INCOME DIFFERENCES BY
RELIGION, 1953–55

Income Level	Protestant	Catholic	Jewish
Under $2,000	19	12	9
$2,000–$3,999	32	30	18
$4,000–$4,999	17	20	12
$5,000–$7,499	20	25	32
$7,500–$10,000	6	8	11
Over $10,000	5	5	19

Source: Donald Bogue, *The Population of the United States* (The Free Press, 1959).

In most countries the relative wage structure among different occupations has exhibited considerable stability over long periods of time. Relative demand has grown at different rates, which suggests that nonwage variables — in particular the ease of attaining employment and differential unemployment rates — play an important role in the allocation of workers among occupations.

Table 8-6 INCOME DIFFERENCES BY COLOR, 1950–60

| | Individuals born in 1915–24 | | |
Region, Education, and Color	Age 25–34 in 1950	Age 35–44 in 1960	Percent Increase
North and West			
White			
Total	3,848	6,776	76
Elementary: Less than 8 years	2,905	4,409	52
8 years	3,272	5,004	53
High School: 1–3 years	3,628	5,817	60
4 years	4,003	6,609	65
College: 1–3 years	4,205	8,169	94
4 years or more	4,898	11,530	135
Nonwhite			
Total	2,711	4,309	59
Elementary: Less than 8 years	2,460	3,548	44
8 years	2,633	3,905	48
High School: 1–3 years	2,695	4,242	57
4 years	2,932	4,731	61
College: 1–3 years	3,060	5,047	65
4 years or more	3,355	7,062	110
South			
White			
Total	3,327	5,778	74
Elementary: Less than 8 years	2,229	3,418	53
8 years	2,786	4,304	54
High School: 1–3 years	3,300	5,141	56
4 years	3,841	6,096	59
College: 1–3 years	4,109	7,602	85
4 years or more	5,063	10,547	108
Nonwhite			
Total	1,725	2,585	50
Elementary: Less than 8 years	1,516	2,132	41
8 years	1,858	2,699	45
High School: 1–3 years	2,003	2,900	45
4 years	2,241	3,304	47
College: 1–3 years	2,248	3,657	63
4 years or more	2,900	5,313	83

1963 Median Income

Occupation	Percent of Occupation that is Nonwhite	White	Nonwhite	Median Earnings NW/W
Professional and Technical	2.5	6,693	4,563	.68
Managers, Officials, and Proprietors	1.4	6,719	3,869	.58
Clerical Workers	5.9	4,848	4,072	.84
Sales Workers	1.6	5,036	2,809	.56
Craftsmen and Foremen	4.2	5,316	3,480	.65
Farmers and Farm Managers	6.5	2,324	788	.34

Source: U.S. Bureau of the Census.

A Just Wage

The observed stability in the wage structure may be evidence of the power of competition and self-interest. It may also be due in part to the widely held underlying concept of a *just wage*. Workers, unlike other productive factors, are also individuals, sharing equally in a common humanity and, in democratic governments, possessing equal political votes. The fundamental human desire for social justice is reflected in the appeal to equity in the wage structure, typically expressed in the thought that supply and demand relations alone ought not to determine wage rates. There is a general consensus that wage differentials ought not to be "too" large and that there is some minimum floor level of wages, related to the average level of income in a society, to which all men are entitled. Wage increases to economists tend to pull up the salaries of classicists.

The effect of such just wage considerations may be shown in Figure 8-13a by an increase in the wage received by uneducated workers to a minimum floor level (W_F), above the level that clears the market. In consequence unemployment rates will be higher for uneducated than for educated workers. Such unemployment will persist in spite of rapid increases in the average educational attainments of the labor force. As a result of this downward inflexibility at the lower end of the wage structure, the composition of labor demand does not match the composition of labor supply at existing prices and wages. This situation makes it difficult to achieve low unemployment rates for the economy as a whole.

APPENDIX: INDIFFERENCE ANALYSIS AND OBJECTIONS TO MARGINAL PRODUCTIVITY

Income and Substitution Effects of Wage Changes

The forces behind the short-run supply of labor by households may be analyzed by the use of indifference curves and the concepts of income and substitution effects. Leisure, defined as not working, may be treated as a good like any other good, whose price is equal to its opportunity cost, the wages foregone from not working.

This concept of leisure is shown in Figure 8-14, where income (all other goods) is measured on the vertical axis and leisure (hours per day) is measured on the horizontal axis. The hourly wage rate determines the slope of the consumption possibility line (PP). A rise in wage rates (e.g., from W_0 to W_1), has the effect of raising the price of leisure, as the amount of other goods that must be given up for an additional hour of leisure is increased.

In response to this change in relative prices, the *substitution* effect induces people to consume more of other goods and to reduce their consumption of the now relatively more expensive good leisure, i.e., to increase total hours worked. This increase is shown as the movement from A to B. Simultaneously the rise in wage rates raises workers real income. As workers become richer, they desire to purchase more of all goods, including leisure. The *income effect* will operate to reduce the number of

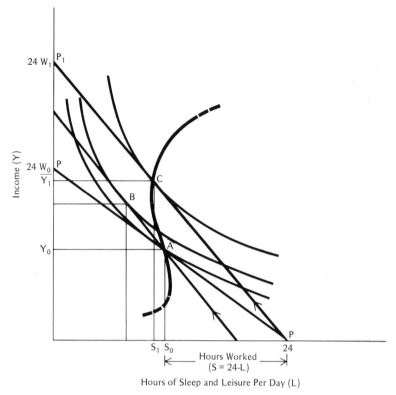

Figure 8-14 Income and Substitution Effects of a Change in Wage Rates

hours worked, provided that leisure is not an inferior good. This effect is shown as the movement from *B* to *C* in Figure 8-14.

At some sufficiently high wage rate, the income effect will dominate the substitution effect and the supply curve will bend backwards. Workers are so rich that they will buy more of everything, including the now more expensive leisure. Conversely, at some sufficiently low wage rate, the income effect will again dominate. Even though leisure is cheap, workers are so poor that they can afford very little of it.

Some Limitations of Marginal Productivity Theory

The demand for labor has been regarded as governed by its marginal revenue product. Although this is generally accepted by economists, there are severe difficulties with marginal productivity theory as an explanation of the distribution of income.

1. In an uncertain world, factor marginal-product curves become fuzzy bands made up of probability distributions rather than single-point estimates. Factors will then be paid a price governed by the anticipated certainty value of their marginal revenue product, which may be very much less than the actual *ex post* value, if substantial time and risk are involved in the production and marketing process. The

return to capital then becomes a residual claim after all other payments have been made and is only loosely related to the marginal productivity of capital.

2. An important question concerns whether, for the case in which each factor is paid a price equal to the value of its marginal product, total payments to all factors of production will be less than, equal to, or greater than the value of total output. This question is known as the *adding-up problem*.

It may be demonstrated by a simple mathematical proof (Euler's Theorem) that under conditions of constant returns to scale payment to each factor of a price equal to the value of its marginal product will exactly exhaust the total product. Constant returns to scale describes a production function relationship in which a change in each factor by a certain proportion P results in a change in total output by the same proportion: $PY = y(PL,PK)$.

This condition is satisfied in perfectly competitive equilibrium, as each firm is operating on the minimum point of its average cost curve, at which output average costs are (temporarily) constant and constant returns to scale occurs. If firms are producing under increasing returns to scale, the payment of a price to each factor equal to the value of its marginal product would more than exhaust total product. As this could clearly not occur, some factors would have to receive an income less than the value of their marginal product. Conversely, under decreasing returns to scale, the payment of a price to each factor equal to the value of its marginal product would be less than the value of total product. Some factors would necessarily receive an income greater than the value of their marginal product.

3. To the extent that fixed rather than variable proportions hold in the short run for particular factors, production isoquants are right-angled straight lines and no substitution of factors is possible. With fixed coefficients of production it is not possible to define the marginal product of a factor. Over some range its demand curve will be completely inelastic.

In the case of constant proportions between capital and labor, the concept of marginal product becomes undefined. With fixed factor proportions (zero elasticity of substitution), the demand for labor is perfectly inelastic. Its position is determined by the existing stock of capital and technology. The marginal product of labor curve may be regarded as tracing out a horizontal line up to full capacity utilization of capital, after which point it falls abruptly to zero. Such a demand for labor curve is shown in Figure 8-15.

The wage rate (W) and labor's share are still determinate so long as the supply of labor (S_{L_0}) is not perfectly inelastic. For the case in which the amount of labor as well as capital is completely fixed in the short run, the supply of labor curve becomes a vertical straight line. There is then no determinate market solution. (Strictly interpreted, the analysis indicates, as shown in Figure 8-15, that labor would receive a wage equal to labor's average product and so the entire income, or a zero wage and none of the income, depending on whether the fixed labor supply does [S_{L_1}] or does not [S_{L_2}] intersect the demand curve.)

Because for the economy as a whole some limited possibility of substituting labor for capital exists, even in the short run, and there is some elasticity in the supply of

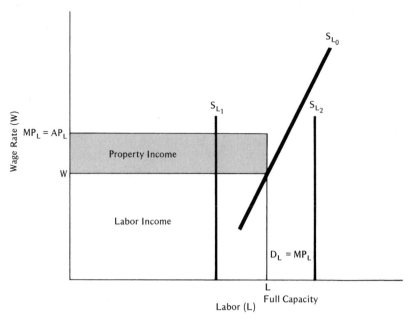

Figure 8-15 Labor and Property Income with Fixed Factor Proportions

labor, these extreme outcomes may be disregarded. Over the longer run, factors can always be substituted for one another, so that substantial variability of factor proportions exists. Even if all goods are produced with constant factor proportions, changes in the *mix* of goods will affect the relative demand for factors, provided only that different goods combine factors in different proportions.

competition and market power in factor markets II: capital

INTEREST TODAY rewards no genuine sacrifice any more than does the rent of land. The owner of capital can obtain interest because capital is scarce, just as the owner of land can obtain rent because land is scarce. . . . I see the rentier aspect of capitalism as a transitional phase which will disappear when it has done its work. The euthanasia of the rentier, of the functionless investor, will be nothing sudden, merely a gradual but prolonged continuance of what we have seen recently.

—JOHN MAYNARD KEYNES

INTEREST IS A TRIBUTE levied on present activity by past achievement. The dynamics of capitalism is postponement of enjoyment to the constantly postponed future—in Ruskin's words, "bulb issuing in bulb, never in tulip. . . ." What the elegant laws of supply and demand really describe is the antics of an animal which has confused excrement with aliment.

—NORMAN O. BROWN

This chapter considers the forces determining the return on capital and the share and composition of property income. Capital goods refer to those assets used in combination with labor in the production process. In developed capitalist economies these capital assets are for the most part owned by capitalists not directly but indirectly in the form of financial assets.

REAL AND FINANCIAL ASSETS

Real Assets

An economy's *real capital stock* refers to the total of all tangible assets in existence. Some of these assets are reproducible — plant, equipment, machines, houses, consumer durables, inventories — while others are nonreproducible — land, natural resources, and all "gifts of nature." Estimates of national wealth for the United States are presented in Table 9-1.

Table 9-1   NATIONAL WEALTH, 1900–68 (BILLIONS OF DOLLARS)

Year	All Tangible Assets	Reproducible Assets				Non-reproducible Assets		Net Foreign Assets
		Structures	Producer Durables	Consumer Durables	Inventories	Total	Land	
1900	88	35	7	6	10	31	27	−2
1929	439	190	38	42	38	113	96	12
1939	396	188	34	32	30	89	70	2
1945	576	286	49	46	53	122	99	−2
1950	1067	507	110	111	96	202	162	13
1958	1703	834	200	179	130	311	263	24
1968	3141	1536	330	234	216	727	716	50

Source: 1900–1958 — Raymond W. Goldsmith, The National Wealth of the United States in the Postwar Period, 1962, Table A-5. 1968 — Institutional Investors Study Report of the Securities and Exchange Commission (Washington, 1971), Supplementary Vol. 1, Table 3-4.

Capital goods are demanded for the services they yield. These services are of two kinds. Some capital goods are long-lived consumer goods yielding direct consumption services — houses, automobiles, consumer durables of all kinds. Other capital goods — plant, equipment, machines — are used by firms in the production of economic goods. Such producer durables are demanded because they increase the productivity of labor and so raise the productive capacity of the economy. Finally, because production takes time, it is necessary to hold inventories of raw materials and goods in process which are treated as a form of capital accumulation.

Investment is defined as expenditure on currently-produced tangible assets. Net investment is equal to the amount of capital accumulation undertaken in any period. Total output is measured as the sum of all consumption goods produced in the period, plus the accumulation of capital goods produced but not used up during the period. Goods produced but used up in the process of producing other goods are termed *intermediate* goods, as distinct from *final* goods. Capital assets thus represent long-lived intermediate goods, not yet used up in the production process.

This distinction between immediate and final goods reflects the belief that consumption is the end purpose of economic activity. Nevertheless, the services that assets yield are quite distinct from the question of whether the asset is used up or consumed in the period. Some assets, such as butter or machines, are used up with their services. But others, such as Old Masters, land, and financial assets, yield their services without depreciating in value and may even appreciate. Satisfaction is derived from asset ownership in addition to the satisfaction derived from current consumption or "using up." This fact is extremely important for an understanding of capitalist saving behavior, in which accumulation is often an end in itself.

Financial Assets

Financial assets, unlike tangible assets, are not part of an economy's real capital stock. The amount in existence does not increase the total physical productive capacity of an economy. Financial assets are simply pieces of paper that represent a promise to pay money or its equivalent in the future. For every financial asset owned by one economic unit, there is a corresponding financial liability owed by another economic unit. Financial assets thus represent claims of one economic unit against another, and so affect a transfer of income from debtors to creditors. While there are many different kinds of financial assets — currency, deposits in financial institutions, bills, notes, bonds, stocks — each represents a legally-enforceable promise on the part of the issuer to pay money, now or in the future, to the holder.

The Role of Financial Assets

In capitalist economies most of the real capital stock (producer durables) is directly owned and administered by business firms. But it is ultimately owned, through ownership claims to the firms themselves, by private capitalists. Financial assets and institutions have gradually evolved to fill a need arising from the institution of private property in a world where the future is uncertain.

Different economic units are faced with different expected opportunities from wealth ownership. The distribution of these opportunities is not identical to the distribution of wealth ownership. Financial assets perform two important economic functions, corresponding to their stock and flow dimensions.

First, financial assets permit the separation of *ownership* from *control* of real wealth. In capitalistic economies most wealth is privately owned. But there is no assurance that those who happen to own the wealth of society are those most capable and desirous of directly administering it. Scale economies are such that optimum firm size exceeds the wealth of most households. The existence of financial assets permits firms, by borrowing purchasing power, to administer more real wealth than they own; that is, to hold real assets in excess of their own net worth. Households with net worth in excess of their real assets specialize in holding financial assets. Financial assets affect a *transmutation* of wealth, as they are characterized by greater certainty, liquidity, convenience, and other properties compared to the real assets they represent. In socialist societies, where producer durables are publicly owned and administered, there is no separation of ownership and control and much less need for financial assets. This function of financial assets in permitting private capitalists to own the society's real wealth *indirectly* in the form of financial assets is shown diagramatically in Figure 9-1.

Financial assets similarly permit the *specialization of saving and investment by different economic units.* This is the flow aspect of the separation of ownership and administration of real wealth. Financial markets perform the function of allocating the current flow of saving among users and uses. Economic units with greater expected opportunities from wealth ownership, greater willingness to bear risk, or greater preference for present income are able to borrow and so acquire goods in excess of their current income. Other economic units with lower opportunities from real wealth ownership, higher aversion to risk, or greater preference for future income are able to purchase financial assets rather than tangible assets with their savings. Economic units are thus freed from the straitjacket of maintaining a balanced budget. They may invest (accumulate tangible assets) more or less than their current savings.

Balance sheets for the household and nonfinancial corporation sectors are presented in Table 9-2. Households hold about two thirds of their total wealth in the form of financial assets. These assets represent securities issued by, and claims against, other households and the business and government sectors. Nonfinancial business corporations, on the other hand, hold just about 70 percent of their total wealth in the form of tangible assets. Business net worth is represented in household portfolios by the value of corporate stock, plus household ownership of noncorporate business.

Most households hold a substantial portion of their wealth in assets such as real estate and automobiles for the direct consumption services that they yield. Such durable consumer goods and the value of the services-in-kind they yield will be ignored in the following discussion of property income. A value for rental services is imputed only to the housing stock in national income accounts, and it is extremely

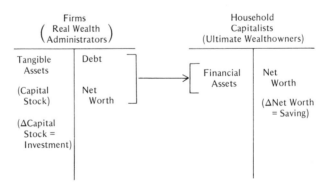

Figure 9-1 Indirect Ownership of Real Wealth through Financial Assets

Nonfarm Households

Financial Assets	1958 Dollars	1958 Percent of Total Assets	1968 Dollars	1968 Percent of Total Assets
Currency & Demand Deposits	61	4	107	3
Other Bank Deposits	141	9	355	11
Life Insurance Reserves	100	6	466	14
Pension and Retirement Funds	94	6	407	12
Mortgages, Bonds, and Notes	122	8	149	4
Common and Preferred Stock	343	21	828	25
Total	632	39	1052	31
Tangible Assets				
Structures	347	22	567	17
Land	92	6	251	7
Consumer Durables	165	10	234	7
Total	632	39	1052	31
Total Assets	1,602	100	3364	100

Liabilities	1958 Dollars	1958 Percent of Total Assets	1968 Dollars	1968 Percent of Total Assets
Consumer Debt	45	3 ⎫	161	5 ⎫
Loans	13	1 ⎬		⎬
Mortgages	117	7	241	7
Total	176	11	410	12
Net Worth	1,425	89	2954	88
Total Liabilities plus Net Worth	1,607	100	3364	100

Nonfinancial Corporations

Financial Assets	1958 Dollars	1958 Percent of Total Assets	1968 Dollars	1968 Percent of Total Assets
Currency and Demand Deposits	33	5	28	3
Trade Credit	83	12	213	19
Securities	22	3	18	2
Total	192	29	357	32
Tangible Assets				
Structures	181	26	272	24
Land	63	9	103	9
Producer Durables	145	21	233	21
Total	489	71	758	68
Total Assets	687	100	1115	100

Liabilities	1958 Dollars	1958 Percent of Total Assets	1968 Dollars	1968 Percent of Total Assets
Trade Debt	69	10 ⎫	222	20 ⎫
Bank Loans	26	4 ⎬	67	6 ⎬
Mortgages	30	4		
Bonds and Notes	70	10	137	12
Total	257	37	450	45
Net Worth	430	63	615	55
Total Liabilities plus Net Worth	687	100	1115	100

Source: Raymond Goldsmith, Robert Lipsey, Morris Mendelson, *Studies in the National Balance Sheet of the United States*, 1963, Vol. 2. 1968 — *Institutional Investor Study Report of the Securities and Exchange Commission* (Washington, 1971), Supplementary Vol. 1, Tables IB-2, IB-4.

difficult to estimate the value of property services yielded by the total stock of consumer durables. As shown in Chapter 4, upper income groups, who do most of the saving, hold the bulk of their wealth in the form of financial assets.

Investment in human beings will also be ignored. Human capital is not marketable as an asset, and it is conceptually and practically difficult to distinguish a property component of wages and salaries as the return to capital invested in education and training.

PROPERTY INCOME

With the exception of real estate and consumer durables, household capitalists own the economy's real capital stock indirectly rather than directly in the form of financial assets. As a result property income takes various forms according to the type of claim — rent, interest, dividends, profits, and capital gains. Each of these different types of property income received by owners of wealth is paid out of property income accruing to capital. They thus represent income transfer payments from wealth administrators to wealth owners.

Profits are defined as the residual of total revenues after deducting total costs. In addition to labor costs, other contractual expenses include rent and interest payments. Total property income, defined as all nonlabor income, is equal to the sum of rent, interest, and profits. The share of various forms of property income in the United States over the postwar period is presented in Table 9-3. Contractual property income (rent and interest) increased from 7 to 11 per cent of total personal income over the period, due entirely to the rise in interest payments. (Part of rental income includes estimated rents imputed as income to the owners of owner-occupied houses. Part of interest income represents a transfer from household borrowers to household lenders.) Corporate profits before taxes fluctuated cyclically between 10 and 17 percent of personal income, but averaged about 14 percent. Part of the reduction over the period was due to more liberal depreciation procedures, which reduce taxable profits.

As shown in Table 9-3 corporate profits, the residual property income remaining after all contractual costs have been met, were divided three ways. Between 40 and 50 percent was paid to the government in taxes. Of profits after taxes, about one half was paid out to stockholders as dividends and the remaining half retained in the business. Undistributed profits result in higher business assets and net worth, greater future business earnings and dividends, and higher share prices. The retained earning share of profits is thus received by wealth owners in the form of capital gains on corporate stock. Capital gains received by stockholders may exceed or fall short of retained earnings in any year, depending on the stock market's evaluation of corporate assets. As shown in Table 9-3, when the stock market is booming, capital gains may be as high as 30 percent of total personal income. Capital gains averaged about 8 percent of personal income over the period, nearly twice as much as retained earnings.

Table 9-3 PROPERTY INCOME AND PROPERTY SHARE, 1945–71 (BILLIONS OF DOLLARS AND PERCENT OF PERSONAL INCOME)

Year	Personal Rental Income $	%	Personal Interest Income $	%	Total $	%	Corporate Profits Before Taxes — Corporate Tax Liability $	%	Dividends $	%	Undistributed Profits $	%	Capital Gains on Stock $	%
1945	5.6	3.3	6.3	3.7	19.2	11.5	10.7	6.3	4.6	2.7	4.4	2.6	n.a.	n.a.
1946	6.6	3.7	6.8	3.8	19.3	13.8	9.1	5.1	5.6	3.1	9.9	5.5	−9.4	−5.3
1947	7.1	3.7	7.5	3.9	25.6	16.5	11.3	5.9	6.3	3.3	13.9	7.3	−3.4	−1.8
1948	8.0	3.8	7.9	3.8	33.0	16.7	12.5	5.9	7.0	3.3	15.6	7.4	−2.2	−1.0
1949	8.4	4.1	8.5	4.1	30.8	13.9	10.4	5.0	7.2	3.5	11.3	5.5	10.4	5.0
1950	9.4	4.1	9.2	4.0	37.7	18.7	17.8	7.8	8.8	3.9	16.0	7.0	24.3	10.7
1951	10.3	4.0	9.9	3.9	42.7	17.2	22.3	8.7	8.6	3.4	13.0	5.1	21.6	8.5
1952	11.5	4.2	10.6	3.9	39.9	14.3	19.4	7.1	8.6	3.2	11.0	4.0	13.0	4.8
1953	12.7	4.4	11.8	4.1	39.6	14.1	20.3	7.0	0.9	3.1	11.5	4.0	−9.3	−3.2
1954	13.6	4.7	13.1	4.5	38.0	13.2	17.7	6.1	9.3	3.2	11.3	3.9	76.4	26.4
1955	13.9	4.5	14.2	4.6	46.9	15.6	21.6	6.9	10.5	3.4	16.5	5.3	56.1	18.0
1956	14.3	4.3	15.7	4.7	46.1	14.7	21.7	6.5	11.3	3.4	15.9	4.8	17.2	5.2
1957	14.8	4.2	17.6	5.0	45.6	12.0	21.2	6.0	11.7	3.3	14.2	4.0	−42.9	−12.2
1958	15.4	4.3	18.9	5.2	41.1	11.5	19.0	5.3	11.6	3.2	10.8	3.0	115.1	31.9
1959	15.6	4.1	20.7	5.4	51.7	13.6	23.7	6.2	12.6	3.3	15.9	4.1	31.7	8.3
1960	15.8	3.9	23.4	5.8	49.9	12.4	23.0	5.7	13.4	3.3	13.2	3.3	−6.3	−1.6
1961	16.0	3.8	25.0	6.0	50.3	12.1	23.1	5.5	13.8	3.3	13.5	3.2	118.2	28.4
1962	16.7	3.8	27.7	6.3	55.7	12.5	24.2	5.5	15.2	3.4	16.0	3.6	−71.4	−16.1
1963	17.1	3.7	31.4	6.7	58.9	12.8	26.3	5.6	16.5	3.5	16.8	3.6	90.2	19.4
1964	18.0	3.6	34.9	7.0	66.3	13.4	28.3	5.7	17.8	3.6	20.6	4.1	83.6	16.8
1965	19.0	3.5	38.4	7.1	76.1	14.4	31.3	5.8	19.8	3.7	26.7	5.0	90.6	16.8
1966	20.0	3.4	43.1	7.3	82.4	14.3	34.3	5.8	20.8	3.5	29.1	5.0	−81.9	−13.9
1967	21.1	3.4	48.3	7.7	78.7	12.7	33.2	5.3	21.4	3.4	25.3	4.0	183.9	29.2
1968	21.3	3.1	54.0	7.8	84.3	12.9	39.9	5.9	23.6	3.4	24.2	3.6	142.1	20.6
1969	22.6	3.0	58.8	7.8	78.6	12.2	39.7	5.7	24.2	3.2	20.0	3.2	−118.6	−15.8
1970	23.3	2.9	64.7	8.1	70.8	10.3	34.1	4.7	25.0	3.1	16.2	2.4	−27.6	−3.4
1971	24.3	2.8	67.5	8.0	80.7	10.0	37.7	4.4	25.5	3.0	21.9	2.5	137.5	16.0

Source: Department of Commerce, Office of Business Economics; Federal Reserve Flow of Funds Accounts.

THE SHARE OF PROPERTY INCOME AND THE RATE OF RETURN ON CAPITAL

The Share of Property Income

As all income is either labor income or property income, the share of property income is the inverse of the share of labor income. The forces determining labor's share as discussed in Chapter 8 simultaneously determine property's share. In a world of perfect certainty, perfect competition in all markets, and homogeneous capital goods, the return to capital in equilibrium would measure the value of the marginal product of capital. If in addition the production function were characterized by constant returns to scale, payment to both labor and capital of a wage equal to their marginal product would add up exactly to the value of total income. Because none of these conditions are satisfied in practice, the return received by capital cannot be regarded as a measure of the value of capital's marginal product.

In a world of uncertainty and imperfectly competitive product and factor markets, total property income as discussed in the preceding chapter is the residual share of income remaining after all wages and salaries incurred in the productive process have been paid. The wage outcome and labor's share were there shown to depend on the relative bargaining power of labor and management, who may be regarded as the representatives of property owners.

The Rate of Return on Capital

The average rate of return actually received on capital in any period may be calculated as the ratio of property income to the value of the existing capital stock. Total profits represent the residual rents and quasi-rents earned on the existing stock of capital goods of various ages and efficiency. They will reflect the degree of monopoly (market power possessed by firms), transitory profits associated with the innovation of new techniques, and the risk and uncertainty of business ventures, as well as the productivity of the capital stock.

At any moment in time the size of the existing capital stock may be regarded as historically given. Although this assumption is not strictly true because in any finite period some net investment ordinarily occurs, the change is small relative to the previously existing capital stock. A more difficult problem is that it is impossible to measure the value of the economy's capital stock precisely. Capital goods are not homogeneous and malleable putty, but heterogeneous and highly specific tangible assets of different ages and efficiency. The amount that a capital good depreciates in any period can never be known precisely when technological change is occurring. Capital goods are usually measured at replacement cost or market value. As the cost of producing capital goods depends on the rate of profit, the analysis is to some degree indeterminate.

Differences Between the Rate on Capital and the Rate of Profit

The rate of return on capital does not correspond to profit rates as ordinarily reported and calculated for business firms. Profits in the accounting sense represent the residual of receipts over accounting costs. Profit rates are usually calculated by businessmen as a rate of return on invested (equity) capital.

Table 9-4 RATES OF RETURN IN ALL
MANUFACTURING INDUSTRIES, 1926–60
(PERCENTAGE RETURN ON BOOK VALUE
OF TOTAL ASSETS)

Year	Before Tax Return	After Tax Return	After Tax Return (5-Year Average)
1926	7.66	6.66	
1927	6.62	5.75	
1928	7.83	6.93	5.87
1929	8.21	7.36	
1930	3.19	2.67	
1931	−0.24	−0.54	
1932	−2.29	−2.50	
1933	1.60	1.17	0.96
1934	3.16	2.57	
1935	4.92	4.12	
1936	7.51	6.23	
1937	7.58	6.22	
1938	3.42	2.62	5.64
1939	7.26	6.00	
1940	10.05	7.12	
1941	16.36	8.56	
1942	17.93	7.30	
1943	19.49	7.30	7.04
1944	17.45	6.59	
1945	12.92	5.43	
1946	13.37	8.13	
1947	16.54	10.34	
1948	16.54	10.34	9.36
1949	12.77	7.93	
1950	18.13	9.97	
1951	16.86	7.34	
1952	13.21	5.96	
1953	13.46	6.05	6.50
1954	11.35	5.68	
1955	14.52	7.47	
1956	13.10	6.85	
1957	11.96	6.29	
1958	9.36	4.92	5.97
1959	11.82	6.30	
1960	10.40	5.48	

Source: George Stigler, *Capital and Rates of Return in Manufacturing Industries*, 1963 (Princeton, N.J.), Table 5, Errata Statement.

As previously emphasized, the meaning of costs differs in economic usage from ordinary business accounting usage. Interest paid is considered a cost in business accounting, but the opportunity costs of the firm's own capital, as of all resources owned by the firm, are ignored. The rate of return on capital represents business profits as reported, minus any labor costs of management calculated in the opportunity sense, plus all interest, rent, and other contractual property income payments, all expressed as a ratio of total assets (total debt and equity capital).

Table 9-4 presents estimates of the rate of return on capital in manufacturing in the United States. While exhibiting substantial cyclical variability, the *after-tax* return does not reveal any long-run trend. The secular rise and fall in before-tax rates of return reflects largely the change in corporate income taxes over the period.

These rates represent the average for all manufacturing industries. Because capital is heterogeneous and imperfectly mobile, at any time profit rates will differ substantially in different industries, though profits do tend to move upward and downward together in response to general market forces.

Expected Rate of Return on Investment

The return actually earned on the existing capital stock represents average rents and quasi-rents on machines of different ages and efficiency and is of little analytical value. Of more analytical importance is the expected rate of return on new investment. As long as the expected return on investment projects exceeds the marginal cost of funds, maximizing firms will desire to accumulate capital goods. The productivity of new capital goods plays an important role in determining their expected return and so the demand for investment. Technological change that increases the productivity of new capital goods will raise their expected rate of return. Capital accumulation, by raising the ratio of capital to output, will reduce the expected return, because capital goods like all other factors are subject to diminishing returns.

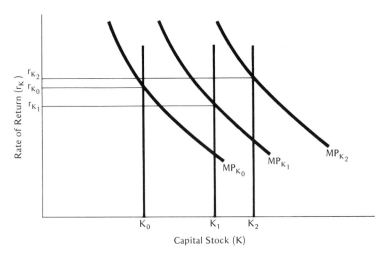

Figure 9-2 Rate of Return on Capital over Time

After firms have carried out their most attractive investment opportunities they must move on to projects of lower expected return, or not invest.

As shown in Figure 9-2, the behavior of the return on capital over larger periods of time will depend on the outcome of a race between technical change and growth of the labor force, both of which operate to raise the expected return on capital (a rightward shift of MP_K), and capital accumulation (a rightward shift of K), which lowers the expected return. Whether technical change is labor-saving or capital-saving will play an important role in influencing the demand for capital and its expected return.

Classical economists underestimated the force of technical progress, and believed that the accumulation of capital over time would gradually drive down the rate of profit. This hypothesis is shown in Figure 9-3, in which MP_K represents the expected rate of return on new investment for any given level of income and capital and S represents the economy's net saving function for any given level of (K). At some low but positive floor rate of return (r_S), they believed, net saving would fall to zero. Once this low rate of return had been reached, capitalists would no longer desire to accumulate but would be content to hold the existing stock of capital and consume all their income. At this point net capital accumulation would cease. With a zero population growth (as wages in the long run were expected to fall to subsistence) and zero technological change, the economy would cease to grow. This situation, shown at S in Figure 9-3, was termed the *stationary state*.

The famous English economist John Maynard Keynes also believed that capital accumulation would gradually drive down profit rates. But he did not believe that saving would fall to zero at some minimum floor return. As shown in Figure 9-4, Keynes argued that net saving and investment would continue even with very low expected rates of return. It was his belief that the capitalist system could be played with much lower profit rates than at present. Admittedly the stakes would be lower, but it was still the only game in town. As a result Keynes envisaged the eventual "euthanasia" of the rentier, not through revolution and appropriation, but through the shrinkage of property's share as profit rates fell. While Keynes' argument holds

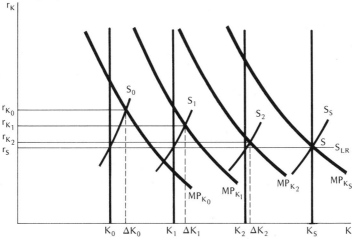

Figure 9-3 Classical View of the Rate of Return on Capital over Time

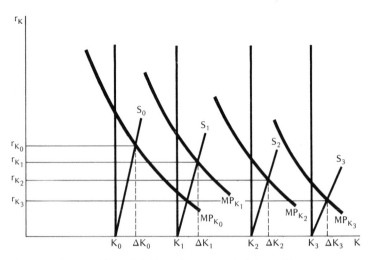

Figure 9-4 Keynesian View of the Rate of Return on Capital over Time

for a static economy, in a growing economy profit rates cannot be driven below the growth rate of the economy.

Capital Accumulation and the Supply of Saving

The critical variable governing the behavior of the return on capital over the long run is the rate of capital accumulation, which in turn depends on the return elasticity of the long-run supply of saving. Since in capitalist economies all business firms are ultimately owned by households, as reflected in the balance sheet relation liabilities or net worth must always increase to finance any accumulation of capital goods. The cost of funds to business firms and so the normal required rate of profit on new investment is the rate of return that must be paid to capitalists to induce them to accumulate.

Unfortunately little is known about the shape of the economy's long-run saving function. As shown in Table 9-4, the after-tax return on capital, while cyclically variable, exhibits considerable long-run stability. A classical economist would argue that this is attributable to a floor reservation price of savers (an elastic long-run supply-of-finance curve), while a Keynesian economist would attribute it to the fact the supply of saving has increased at the same rate as the demand for capital, since investment tends to create the saving necessary to finance it.

There is some evidence for the Keynesian interpretation, since both saving and investment are closely related to business profits. In developed economies a large proportion of saving is undertaken directly by business firms, rather than by households. As shown in Table 9-5, business saving currently accounts for about three quarters of total investment spending.

Retained earnings result in increased business assets, expected future profits, and capital gains income to stock owners. For tax reasons business managers save through retained earnings for their capitalist owners rather than pay out profits as dividends and borrow them back again. Stockowners have the possibility of "undoing" such saving by increasing their consumption expenditures out of capital gains income. But stock ownership is highly concentrated. In the United States the wealthiest 5 percent of households own about 95 percent of all stock held by the household sector. Most gains are unrealized and simply allowed to accumulate, so that consumption does not respond significantly to capital gains income. As long as capitalists are willing to let their capital gains accrue, their saving is undertaken automatically for them by business managers.

Because business saving and investment are closely related to business profits, there is an automatic mechanism operating to stabilize the return on capital over time. As expected profits rise, so will investment, actual profit, business saving, and the rate of accumulation. The law of diminishing returns acts to depress the return on capital. Similarly, with a fall in expected return there is a decrease in investment, profits, and business saving that sets in motion forces tending to raise the return on capital as the ratio of capital to output declines.

Table 9-5 BUSINESS AND HOUSEHOLD SAVING AND INVESTMENT, 1929–71 (BILLIONS OF DOLLARS AND AS PERCENTAGE OF GROSS INVESTMENT)

| | Personal Saving | | Gross Business Saving | | Gross Private Domestic Investment |
	Dollars	Percent	Dollars	Percent	Dollars
1929	4.2	25	11.2	66	17.0
1933	−.9	−56	3.2	200	1.6
1940	3.8	26	10.5	72	14.6
1945	29.6	325	15.1	166	9.1
1950	13.1	25	29.4	57	51.8
1955	15.8	24	46.3	69	66.9
1960	17.0	22	56.8	74	76.5
1965	28.4	25	84.7	75	112.2
1968	39.8	32	95.4	76	126.0
1969	37.9	20	95.6	69	137.8
1970	34.1	40	99.3	73	135.3
1971	60.5	41	117.1*	77	151.6

* Undistributed corporate profits $21.9
  Corporate Capital Consumption Allowances   61.9
  Noncorporate Capital Consumption Allowances 33.3
                                                                    ———
  Gross Business Saving   117.1

Source: Department of Commerce, Office of Business Economics.

FINANCIAL ASSET PRICES AND RETURNS

Financial assets represent a claim to a future income stream. Although there are many types of financial assets, they may be divided into two main categories, according to whether they represent a contractual or a residual claim to future income. *Debt* securities represent a legally enforceable promise by the issuer to pay a fixed interest and return of principal in some future period. *Equity* securities represent a share in the ownership of a business firm and entitle the owner to a pro rata share in any residual profits of the firm. As there is conflict over the share of total income going to labor and capital, so there is conflict over the share of property income going to bondholders and stockholders. As interest costs are contractual, higher interest rates will lower the residual remaining for distribution to stockholders if profit rates remain unchanged.

The price of financial assets is determined in competitive financial markets by the general forces of supply and demand. The price of a financial asset represents the market value of the future income stream to which the owner is entitled. The operations of compound interest and discount govern the relationship between present and future values. Once the price of an asset and its expected future income stream are known, it is possible to calculate the rate of return that can be earned from ownership of such an asset. The higher the price, the lower the rate of return from the purchase of any given stream. This rate of return is identical to the rate at which future income is discounted to determine the present market price.

Compound Interest

A dollar invested in the present will be worth more than one dollar in the future, depending on the rate of return and the distance in the future. At a 10 percent return per year, one dollar invested today will be worth $1.10 in one year's time. This

Table 9-6   TABLE OF COMPOUND INTEREST

Compound Amount of $1 Now at End of Specified Future Year

Year	4%	6%	8%	10%	15%	20%
1	1.04	1.06	1.08	1.10	1.15	1.20
2	1.08	1.12	1.17	1.21	1.32	1.44
3	1.12	1.19	1.26	1.33	1.52	1.73
4	1.17	1.26	1.36	1.46	1.74	2.07
5	1.22	1.34	1.47	1.61	2.01	2.49
6	1.27	1.41	1.59	1.77	2.31	2.99
7	1.32	1.50	1.71	1.94	2.66	3.58
8	1.37	1.59	1.85	2.14	3.05	4.30
9	1.42	1.68	2.00	2.35	3.52	5.16
10	1.48	1.79	2.16	2.59	4.05	6.19
11	1.54	1.89	2.33	2.85	4.66	7.43
12	1.60	2.01	2.52	3.13	5.30	8.92
13	1.67	2.13	2.72	3.45	6.10	10.7
14	1.73	2.26	2.94	3.79	7.00	12.8
15	1.80	2.39	3.17	4.17	8.13	15.4
16	1.87	2.54	3.43	4.59	9.40	18.5
17	1.95	2.69	3.70	5.05	10.6	22.2
18	2.03	2.85	4.00	5.55	12.5	26.6
19	2.11	3.02	4.32	6.11	14.0	31.9
20	2.19	3.20	4.66	6.72	16.1	38.3
25	2.67	4.29	6.85	10.8	32.9	95.4
30	3.24	5.74	10.0	17.4	66.2	237
40	4.80	10.3	21.7	45.3	267.0	1,470
50	7.11	18.4	46.9	117	1,080	9,100

represents the original amount, one dollar, plus the return on the investment, ten cents.

More generally, if P is the amount invested and r is the annual percentage rate of return, the value of the investment after one year will be $P + Pr$, or $P(1 + r)$. If P is invested for two years, the entire value of the investment after one year, $P(1 + r)$, will again earn a return of r, and its value after two years will be $P(1 + r)(1 + r)$ or $P(1 + r)^2$. After three years, the value of the investment will have grown to $P(1 + r)^3$. This process of adding interest is called *compound interest*. In general the formula for an amount P invested for n years at a constant annual rate of return r may be expressed $P(1 + r)^n$.

The value of this formula has been calculated for different values of r and n and is called a compound interest table. As presented in Table 9-6, it shows the amount that one dollar today will be worth at the end of the specified year compounded at different rates of interest. For example one dollar invested at 15 percent would have grown to \$4.05 in ten years and \$16.1 in twenty years.

Discounting

If P dollars invested at r percent will be worth \$$P(1 + r)$ in one year's time, it is also true that \$$P(1 + r)$ in one year's time will be worth P dollars today. This operation represents the reverse of compound interest and is called *discounting*. The present

Table 9-7 TABLE OF DISCOUNTED VALUE

		Present Value of \$1 at End of Specified Future Year			
Year	4%	6%	8%	10%	15%	20%
1	.962	.943	.926	.909	.870	.833
2	.925	.890	.857	.826	.756	.694
3	.890	.839	.794	.751	.658	.578
4	.855	.792	.735	.683	.572	.482
5	.823	.747	.681	.620	.497	.402
6	.790	.705	.630	.564	.432	.335
7	.760	.665	.583	.513	.376	.279
8	.731	.627	.540	.466	.326	.233
9	.703	.591	.500	.424	.284	.194
10	.676	.558	.463	.385	.247	.162
11	.650	.526	.429	.350	.215	.134
12	.625	.497	.397	.318	.187	.112
13	.601	.468	.368	.289	.162	.0935
14	.577	.442	.340	.263	.141	.0779
15	.555	.417	.315	.239	.122	.0649
16	.534	.393	.292	.217	.107	.0541
17	.513	.371	.270	.197	.093	.0451
18	.494	.350	.250	.179	.0808	.0376
19	.475	.330	.232	.163	.0703	.0313
20	.456	.311	.215	.148	.0611	.0261
25	.375	.232	.146	.0923	.0304	.0105
30	.308	.174	.0994	.0573	.0151	.00421
40	.208	.0972	.0460	.0221	.00373	.000680
50	.141	.0543	.0213	.00852	.000922	.000109

value, P, of $P(1 + r)$ in one year's time has been found by dividing by $(1 + r)$ or what is the same thing, by multiplying by $\frac{1}{1 + r}$. The present value of P dollars in one year's time is therefore $P(\frac{1}{1 + r})$ today. Similarly, the present value of P dollars in two years' time, discounted at the rate r, is $P(\frac{1}{1 + r})^2$. The general formula for the present value of P dollars in n years' time discounted at the rate r may be expressed by the formula $P(\frac{1}{1 + r})^n$.

The value of this formula calculated for different values of r and n is called a *discount table*. As presented in Table 9-7, it shows the present value today of a promise to pay one dollar at the end of a specified future year, when discounted at different rates of interest. For example, one dollar in ten years' time, discounted at 15 percent, is worth only 25 cents today, and one dollar in twenty years' time is worth only six cents today.

Tables 9-6 and 9-7 indicate the enormous power of even modest rates of compound interest and discounting when long periods of time are involved. The discounted present value of one dollar in fifty years is worth but a few pennies today. Conversely, one dollar invested today will be worth from tens to thousands of dollars in fifty years.[1]

Inverse Relationship Between Market Price and Return

The market price of a bond represents the present value of the expected future stream of interest and principal to which the owner is entitled. From this market price it is possible to calculate the *market rate of interest*, which represents both the market return on such an investment and the market rate of discount that equates the present value of the future income stream to its market price. Interest rates are conventionally defined as an annual percentage rate.

The market interest rate on a bond represents the expected rate of return to the owner, expressed in percent per year on the initial investment. The lower the market price for any given future income stream, the higher the rate of return and the rate of discount. The market price and the market rate of interest of any particular debt instrument are thus inversely related.

Consider the case of a promise to pay one dollar per year forever. If the interest rate were 10 percent, the value of this bond would be ten dollars, because one dollar represents a 10 percent return on an investment of ten dollars. In general, the market price (P) of a bond promising to pay A per year in perpetuity, yielding a rate of return r, is simply $r = \frac{A}{P}$ or, rearranging, $P = \frac{A}{r}$. In the case of a perpetuity the

---

1. As a useful short-cut, the number of years (n) it will take for a sum growing at a constant rate (r) to double in size is approximated by the expression $n = \frac{70}{r}$. This formula may be tested by comparison with the actuarially exact values in Table 9-6.

market price is simply the interest income divided by the market rate of interest.

It is important to distinguish the *coupon rate of interest* on a bond from the market interest rate, and the *face value* of a bond from the market value. Consider a bond with a face value of $100 and a coupon rate of 6 percent. The bond would then pay six dollars in interest income each year. The price of the bond would depend on the market rate of interest. For simplicity consider again the case of a perpetuity. If the market rate of interest were 6 percent, the market value would be $100. If the market rate of interest fell to 4 percent, the market price of the bond would rise to $P = \$150$. A return of 4 percent on an investment of $150 is exactly six dollars per year. If the market rate of interest rose to 8 percent, the market price of the bond would fall to $P = \$75$. A return of 8 percent on an investment of $75 is exactly six dollars per year.

The Price of Financial Assets in the Market Period

The price of any financial asset is determined in the market period by the demand of wealth owners to hold that asset in their portfolios relative to the existing stock of that asset. For portfolio equilibrium the price of different financial assets must adjust until wealth owners are content to hold exactly the existing stocks.

This equilibrium price of financial assets in the market period is illustrated in Figure 9-5. The stock of the financial asset existing at any moment of time is represented by the curve S_0, which represents the total stock of such securities that have been issued by economic units in the past. The demand for financial assets is represented by the demand curve D_0. The quantity demanded will be a function of total real wealth, the expected return on other financial assets and on capital goods, and wealth owner preferences for risk and for present versus future income, in addition to the price of the asset.

In equilibrium (E_M) the price of financial assets (P_{F_M}) has adjusted in such a way

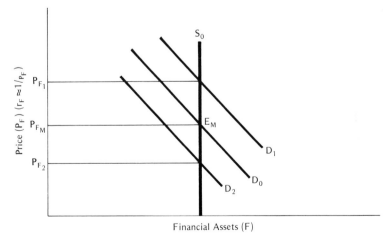

Figure 9-5 Determination of Financial Asset Prices in the Market Period

that wealth owners demand to hold exactly the stock of securities available. Individual wealth owners can change the quantity of securities held in their portfolios but wealth owners as a whole cannot, as in the market period the stock outstanding is given. As a result an increase or decrease in the demand for securities (e.g., to D_1 or D_2) leads to an increase or decrease in their market price and an inverse change in the market return.

For most financial assets existing stocks are large relative to net new issues even over a considerable period of time. As a result, the market-period analysis of Figure 9-5 applies over a long period of time. This is characteristic of asset markets in contrast to markets for most goods, where inventories are a small proportion of annual production, or for services, where inventories do not exist.

The Price of Financial Assets in the Long Run

Over time the stock of financial assets outstanding will gradually change due to net new issues or retirement of securities. The long-run supply of financial assets may be defined as the amount that debt issuers would desire to supply in complete portfolio equilibrium, after they have fully adjusted their real capital stock to the desired level. (The concept of a short-run supply of financial assets is less useful than in the case of commodities, as production conditions are very different and the market period is much longer.) In market-period equilibrium only asset holders are in portfolio balance. In long-run equilibrium, both asset holders and asset issuers are in portfolio balance.

Over the long run, new issues of securities by business firms depend on the differential between the expected rate of return on investment and the rate of return that must be paid for finance. The expected marginal revenue product of capital governs the demand for investment goods. The price of financial assets governs the cost of finance and so the normal rate of profit. Financial asset prices are determined by wealth owner demand to accumulate financial assets, which in turn depends on the long-run supply of saving.

This long-run equilibrium price of financial assets is illustrated in Figure 9-6. The long-run supply of securities (S_F) depends on the rate of investment and the rate of return on capital. The long-run demand for securities (D_F) depends on real income and wealth owner saving preferences. As discussed previously, considerable ignorance surrounds the return elasticity of these long-run functions. The long-run equilibrium price ($P_{F_{LR}}$) and return on financial assets, like the long-run price of commodities, represents a level toward which actual financial prices and returns are tending but never actually reach. It is sometimes termed the *natural* or *normal* rate of interest.

The market-period equilibrium price (P_M) of Figure 9-5, which is determined by portfolio preferences given stock relationships, may substantially exceed or fall short of (e.g., P_{F_1} or P_{F_2} in Fig. 9-5) the long-run equilibrium price ($P_{F_{LR}}$) of Figure 9-6, which is governed by the real rate of return on capital and saving preferences.

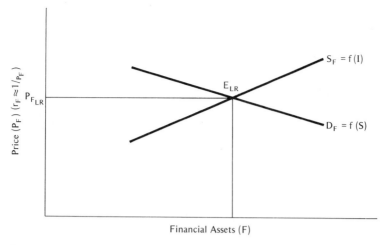

Figure 9-6 Determination of Financial Asset Prices in the Long Run

Changes in the market-period equilibrium price of financial assets relative to their long-run equilibrium price determines the rate at which business firms will desire to issue securities and add to their capital stock and so determines the level of planned business investment.

Money is one particularly important financial asset whose stock is controlled by the government. The manner in which changes in the stock of money affect the price and return of other financial assets, the cost of finance, and the volume of investment and consumption spending will be considered in a later chapter.

RENT

Economic rent is defined as the payment to any factor of production of a reward in excess of the amount necessary to call forth that supply of the factor. As shown in Figure 9-7a, some rent, the shaded area in the diagram, is paid to all owners of factors and commodities that are not in perfectly elastic supply. An increase in demand for a commodity ordinarily results in an increase in economic rent to the factors producing it, unless they are in perfectly elastic supply.

In the case of the factors whose supply is perfectly fixed, the total payment is economic rent, as shown in Figure 9-7b. This situation is not confined to rent on land. Beautiful women receive enormous nonpecuniary economic rents. Virtually all property income in the short run represents economic rent from the viewpoint of the economy. Due to the large nonpecuniary returns from wealth ownership in the forms of status, power, and achievement, most property income is rent in the long run as well.

The rent component of the price paid to a factor of production will vary depending on whether the viewpoint is the firm, the industry, or the entire economy. Alternatively expressed, the relevant opportunity cost is different in each case.

Consider an economist who receives a salary of $20,000 from his university. From

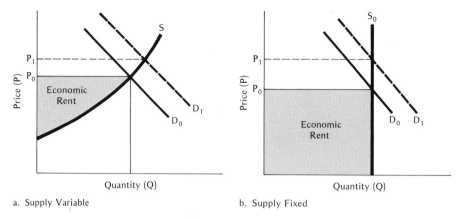

a. Supply Variable b. Supply Fixed

Figure 9-7 Economic Rent

the university's point of view there may be little or no economic rent involved, as the economist could command a salary of $20,000 from another university and would be willing to move. From the point of view of education as an industry, the economist's opportunity cost might be $10,000, the minimum academic salary that would induce him to leave university life and enter business. He thus receives a rent of $10,000 from the point of view of the industry, the excess of what he is paid in education over what would be necessary to induce him to offer his services as a teacher. Finally, from the viewpoint of the economy, he might be willing to supply the same amount of effort at all wages above some minimum income necessary for him to function effectively; for example, $5,000. From the economy's viewpoint, a rent of $15,000 is involved.

The rent component of the price paid to a factor will vary with the time period and institutional viewpoint considered. Factors whose short-run supply curve is inelastic but whose long-run supply curve may be considerably more elastic receive what is termed *quasi-rent*. Although it has a rent component in the short run, the price is required in the long run to induce that supply of the factor to be forthcoming. Although labor income includes large quasi-rents, virtually all property income is quasi-rents or rents on existing wealth.

Rent on Land

Land, defined broadly as all nonreproducible real capital goods, is the only factor of production completely inelastic from the viewpoint of society in the long run as well as the short run. All payments to unimproved land represent pure economic rent. A substantial part of actual land rent payments represents a return to capital invested in improving the land or natural resource. But the "original and indestructible powers of the soil" — for example, a particular site — would be supplied from society's point of view even in the absence of any payment.

Rent as the price paid for the use of land is determined by the demand for the services of the fixed stock of land in existence. The demand for the services of land in perfectly competitive markets will be equal to the value of land's marginal product. As the labor force, the reproducible capital stock, and the level of technology increase, the value of the marginal product of land rises. As shown in Figure 9-8, because the stock of land is fixed, as the marginal product of land increases (e.g., from D_0 to D_1), the rent paid will rise over time.

If technical change is land-saving, the value of marginal product curves in Figure 9-8 will rotate in a clockwise direction and become steeper. As shown by the dashed curve D_2, rent payments may fall. This process accounts in part for the decline in land rents as a proportion of total income as an economy develops.

The market value of a piece of land (P) with a rent of R_0, expected to grow at a rate g per year and discounted at a rate r, may be determined by the present value formula: $P = \dfrac{R_0}{(r - g)}$. A fall in the rate of discount or rise in the expected future rate of growth of rent income will result in an increase in land prices. The return on land cannot be reduced below the expected rate of growth of rental income. As $(r - g)$ approaches zero, as shown by the present value formula, land prices become infinite.

Assuming that the rate of discount and the growth rate remain unchanged, rent will increase by gR dollars per year and the value of land will increase by gP dollars per year. This *unearned increment* has long been regarded with disfavor by social reformers, because it is awarded to landowners as the economy grows without any corresponding contribution to output on their part. A tax on land rent by definition would not reduce the supply of land available and would permit this unearned increment to be transferred to the community. As land rent is capitalized in the price of land, a tax on rent would reduce land values.

This illustrates again the two functions of prices in a market economy. A positive rent is required to allocate scarce land among competing uses. If rent is reduced

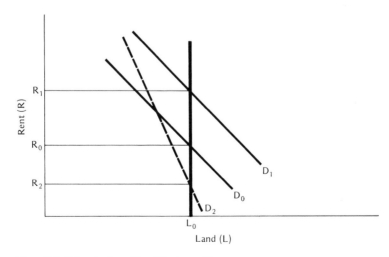

Figure 9-8 Determination of Land Rent over Time

to zero, misallocation will result (as occurred in Russia when land was treated as "free" for planning purposes). But a positive rent also serves to redistribute income to landowners, who in their role as owners make no contribution to production and so "deserve" no reward. The same argument may be applied more generally to all functionless property income.

Differential Rent

Units of land cannot be homogeneous, as they necessarily differ in their specific location. In addition, land is characterized by widely different fertility and natural resource endowment. As a result, the rental income and price of different units of land vary enormously.

This variation in land value is illustrated in Figure 9-9, which shows the value

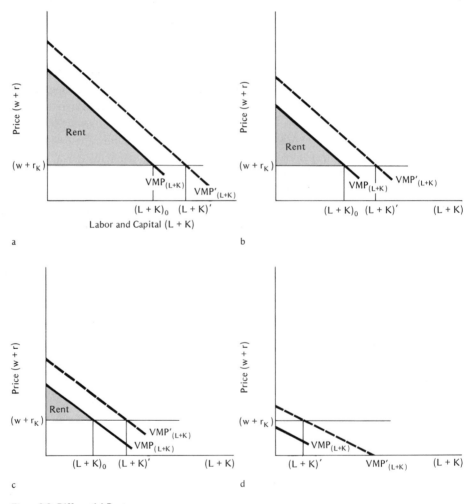

Figure 9-9 Differential Rent

of the marginal product (*VMP*) of the units of labor plus reproducible capital ($L + K$) applied to different units of land A, B, C, and D. Given the wage rate and the cost of capital ($W + r_K$), this formula will determine the amount of labor and capital applied to each unit of land. The total area under the value of marginal product curve is equal to the value of total product.

After payment of wages to labor and normal return to capital ($W + r_K$), the residual area, shaded in the diagram, represents the rent received by landowners. There may be some land (Figure 9-9d) whose productivity is so low that it is left uncultivated. While the rent of the submarginal land may be zero, its price may be positive due to the expectation that its rental income and value will appreciate in the future.

An increase in the price of goods and services produced with the aid of land will raise the value of labor and capital's marginal product (e.g., to *VMP'*) as shown in Figure 9-9. As a result, the derived demand for land will increase, rents will rise, and land will be cultivated more intensively. More labor and capital will be applied to each unit. As shown in Figure 9-9d, some previously submarginal land will now be brought into cultivation.

The value of land—like rent payments in general—is price-determined rather than price-determining. Rent for land may be high because the price of food is high or incomes are high, making the demand for land great relative to the supply. For an individual farmer the land rent he must pay is a cost that he must cover or go out of business. But it is a misunderstanding of the nature of rent to say that for the economy as a whole the price of food is high because high rents must be paid to landowners. Rents are a pure transfer payment, necessary to allocate a scarce and valuable factor. If only the American Indians had kept their title to Manhattan, their money troubles would be over.

APPENDIX: THE FAMILY OF FINANCIAL ASSET RETURNS AND THE DERIVATION OF PRESENT VALUE FORMULAS

Corresponding to the many types of financial assets, there are a whole family of asset prices and returns. Wealth owners have different portfolio tastes and prefer to hold wealth in different forms. Households, firms, and governments each issue their own various types of liabilities. Risk-adverse wealth owners will have some preferred diversified portfolio of assets. An increase in the relative supply of any asset will tend to lower its price and raise its rate of return.

The Structure of Interest Rates

Debt securities differ with regard to their maturity and in the risk that the future promise to pay will be honored. Table 9-8 presents interest rates on different types of debt instruments.

The shorter the maturity of the bond, the less will its market price be affected by changes in the market rate of interest. The longer the maturity of the bond, the greater the power of compound interest. As seen in Table 9-7 the present value of one dollar in one year is affected only slightly by changes in the rate of discount, but the present value of one dollar in ten or 20 years is effected enormously. As a result, the market price of long-term bonds varies much more than the market price of short-term bonds with changes in the rate of interest. Long-term bonds consequently have greater *capital uncertainty* than short-term bonds.

On the other hand, the income return from holding a long-term bond is highly certain over the life of the bond. If the investor were to consider holding short-term bonds over the same period and, reinvesting his money every time his bonds matured in other short-term bonds, he would be much less certain of the future interest income he would receive. Income would fluctuate with changes in the market rate of interest. Long-term bonds have lower *income uncertainty* than short-term bonds.

Competition among investors will ensure that the relative prices of various assets

Table 9-8 STRUCTURE OF INTEREST RATES, 1945–71 (PERCENT PER ANNUM)

	3-Month Treasury Bills	5-Year Average	U.S. Government 3–5-Year Issues	5-Year Average	Corporate Bonds (Moody's Aaa)	5-Year Average	Average Rate on Short-Term Bank Loans	5-Year Average
1945	0.4		1.2		2.6		2.2	
1946	0.4	.7	1.2	1.3	2.5	2.6	2.1	2.3
1947	0.6		1.3		2.6		2.1	
1948	1.0		1.6		2.8		2.5	
1949	1.1		1.4		2.7		2.7	
1950	1.2		1.5		2.6		2.7	
1951	1.6	1.5	1.9	2.0	2.9	2.9	3.1	3.3
1952	1.8		2.1		3.0		3.5	
1953	1.9		2.6		3.2		3.7	
1954	1.0		1.8		2.9		3.6	
1958	1.8		2.5		3.1		3.7	
1956	2.7	2.6	3.1	3.3	3.4	3.7	4.2	4.4
1957	3.3		3.6		3.9		4.6	
1958	1.8		2.9		3.8		4.3	
1959	3.4		4.3		4.4		5.0	
1960	2.9		4.0		4.4		5.2	
1961	2.4	3.0	3.6	3.8	4.3	4.4	5.0	5.0
1962	2.8		3.6		4.3		5.0	
1963	3.2		3.7		4.3		5.0	
1964	3.6		4.1		4.4		5.0	
1965	4.0		4.2		4.5		5.1	
1966	4.9	5.0	5.2	5.4	5.1	5.7	6.0	6.4
1967	4.3		5.1		5.5		6.0	
1968	5.3		5.6		6.2		6.7	
1969	6.7		6.9		7.0		8.2	
1970	6.5		7.4		8.0		8.5	
1971	4.3		5.8		7.4		6.3	

Sources: Treasury Department, Moody's Investors Service, Standard and Poor's Corporation.

will reflect their relative earning power. If one asset has a higher expected return over any particular holding period, investors will purchase more of it and its price will rise, reducing its expected return.

Long-term interest rates thus tend to reflect the average of expected future short-term interest rates. If interest rates are expected to rise in the future, present short-term rates will be below long-term rates. If interest rates are expected to fall in the future, present short-term rates will be above long-term rates. Because long-term rates represent an average of future rates, they do not fluctuate as much as short-term rates.

Equity Securities

The price of equities in the stock market similarly represents the present value of the expected future stream of income to which the stock owner is entitled. But dividends paid on stock, unlike interest payments on bonds, are not contractually fixed in amount. They depend on a corporation's earnings, which in a growing economy will be expected to grow in the future. As the value of the dividend paid in the future increases, so will the value of the stock. As a result, stockholders anticipate their future return to be in the form of dividend income plus capital gains. These gains will be related to the volume of retained earnings (i.e., business direct saving and investment), which will affect the rate of growth of business capital, profits, and dividends.

The expected value of future dividend payments is surrounded by much greater uncertainty than bond interest payments. Because households are averse to bearing risk, they will pay a lower price for a more uncertain future income stream. The rate at which future dividend and capital gains income from stock ownership is discounted is therefore higher than the rate of discount applied to interest income from bonds.

The uncertainty surrounding the level of future dividends and capital gains increases as dividends recede into the future. As a result, expected dividends and capital gains are discounted at a higher rate the more distant they are in the future. It is for this reason that corporations whose earnings are expected to grow more rapidly and so have a larger proportion of their income stream in the future are discounted at a higher rate and offer a higher return.

The present value P of an infinite income stream, with an initial value after one year of A, growing at the constant rate g and discounted at the constant rate r, is represented by the expression $P = A\left(\dfrac{1}{r-g}\right)$; or, rearranging, $r = \dfrac{A}{P} + g$.

With zero growth ($g = 0$), this equation reduces to the expression for the value of a perpetuity. The rate of return on a stock expected to grow at a constant rate is simply the existing dividend-price ratio $\dfrac{A}{P}$ plus the expected growth rate (g). The rate of return must therefore always exceed the expected growth rate.

If the dividend-price ratio remains constant, the price of the stock will grow at the same rate as the dividends. In this case, g will equal expected capital gains income, expressed as an annual percentage rate of return.

Table 9-9 presents average capital gains, dividend yields, and the rate of return on corporate stocks over the postwar period. These have been calculated on an index or average for 500 corporations, as the behavior of individual stocks vary widely. The return on equities averaged 13 percent over the period 1945–71. The very high rates of return in the 1950s were due to the rise in share prices that accompanied the doubling in price-dividend ratios from 15 to 30. If this period is excluded as exceptional, the average return on equity portfolios was about 10 percent.

The Derivation of Present Value Formulas

Bonds

With an interest rate of r percent per year, an investment of one dollar will have a value in one year of $\$1 \, (1 + r)$, in two years of $\$1 \, (1 + r)^2$, and in n years of $\$1 \, (1 + r)^n$. This may be expressed schematically:

0	1	2	3	n	time
1	1	1	1	1	(years)

$$1 \longrightarrow 1(1 + r) \rightarrow 1(1 +)^2 \rightarrow 1(1 + r)^3 \longrightarrow 1(1 + r)^n$$

Reversing the process, with a discount rate of r, a promise of $\$1 \, (1 + r)$ in one year will have a value of one dollar today. The present value has been found by multiplying by $(\frac{1}{1 + r})$. The present value of one dollar in one year is $\$1 (\frac{1}{1 + r})$, in two years is $\$1 \, (\frac{1}{1 + r})^2$ and in n years is $\$1 \, (\frac{1}{1 + r})^n$. This may be expressed:

0	1	2	3	n	time
1	1	1	1	1	(years)

$1 \longleftarrow 1(1 + r)$

$1(\frac{1}{1 + r}) \leftarrow 1$

$1(\frac{1}{1 + r})^2 \longleftarrow 1(\frac{1}{1 + r}) \leftarrow 1$

$1(\frac{1}{1 + r})^3 \longleftarrow 1$

$1(\frac{1}{1 + r})^n \longleftarrow 1$

The higher the rate of discount r, the lower is the present value $\$1(\frac{1}{1 + r})^n$ of a promise to pay one dollar in n years' time. Conversely, the lower the present price,

Table 9-9 EQUITY PRICES, DIVIDEND YIELDS, AND RATES OF RETURN, 1945-71

Year	Equity Price Index (Standard and Poor's 500 Common Stocks*) 1941–1943 = 10 Annual	Capital Gain or Loss (Percent Change in Equity Prices) $\left(\frac{\Delta P}{P}\right)$ Annual	5-year Average	Dividend Yield (Percent) $\left(\frac{D}{P}\right)$ Annual	5-year Average	Equity Rate of Return $\left(\frac{D}{P} + \frac{\Delta P}{P}\right)$ Annual	5-year Average
1945	15.2	21.6		4.2		25.7	
1946	17.1	12.7		3.8		16.5	
1947	15.2	-11.2	4.7	4.9	5.0	-6.2	9.7
1948	15.5	2.4		5.5		7.9	
1949	15.2	-1.9		6.6		4.7	
1950	18.4	20.8		6.6		14.2	
1951	22.3	21.4		6.1		27.5	
1952	24.5	9.7	14.6	5.8	5.9	15.5	17.8
1953	24.7	.9		5.8		6.7	
1954	29.7	20.1		4.9		25.0	
1955	40.5	36.4		4.1		40.4	
1956	46.6	15.1		4.1		19.2	
1957	44.4	-4.8	15.0	4.3	3.9	-.4	18.9
1958	46.2	4.2		4.0		8.2	
1959	57.4	24.1		3.2		27.3	
1960	55.8	-2.7		3.5		.8	
1961	66.3	18.7		3.0		21.6	
1962	62.4	-5.9	7.7	3.4	3.2	-2.5	11.1
1963	69.9	12.0		3.2		15.2	
1964	81.4	16.5		3.0		19.5	
1965	88.2	8.4		3.0		11.4	
1966	85.3	-3.3	3.9	3.4	3.2	0.1	7.0
1967	91.9	7.8		3.2		11.0	
1968	98.7	7.4		3.1		10.4	
1969	97.8	-1.0		3.2		2.3	
1970	83.2	-14.9		3.8		-11.1	
1971	98.3	18.3		3.1		21.4	

Source: Standard & Poor's Corporation.
* Average of monthly figures.

the higher is the rate of return earned on an investment promising to pay one dollar in the future.

More generally, the present value P of a promise to buy $\$x$ interest per year for n years, discounted at a constant rate r, may be represented as the sum of the following geometric progression (Equation 1):

1. $P = x/(1 + r) + x/(1 + r)^2 + x/(1 + r)^3 + \ldots + x/(1 + r)^n.$

In order to find an expression for the sum, first multiply both sides of equation 1 by $1/(1 + r)$, which gives:

2. $P/(1 + r) = x/(1 + r)^2 + x/(1 + r)^3 + x/(1 + r)^4 + \ldots + x/(1 + r)^n$
$$+ x/(1 + r)^{n + 1}.$$

Now subtract equation 2 from equation 1 to eliminate all the intermediate terms.

3. $P(\dfrac{r}{1 + r}) = x\left[(\dfrac{1}{1 + r}) - (\dfrac{1}{1 + r})^{n + 1} \right].$

Simplifying by dividing both sides by $(\dfrac{r}{1 + r})$, this becomes:

4. $P = x\left[\dfrac{1 - (\dfrac{1}{1 + r})^n}{r} \right].$

This formula represents the price or present value of a bond with a maturity of n years, paying $\$x$ per year interest, to yield a rate of return r. If after n years some principal $\$y$ is also to be repaid, the value becomes:

5. $P = x\left[\dfrac{1 - (\dfrac{1}{1 + r})^n}{r} \right] + y(\dfrac{1}{1 + r})^n.$

For the case of a promise to pay $\$x$ per year in perpetuity, $n \to \infty$ (where $\to$ means "approaches"). Providing that $r > 0, (\dfrac{1}{1 + r})^n \to 0$. The expression for present value than simplifies to:

6. $P = \dfrac{x}{r}.$

Equities

Similarly, the present value P of a future income stream with an initial value of $\$X_0$, expected to grow at the constant rate g per year and discounted at the constant rate r, may be represented as the sum of the following geometric progression:

0	1	2	3	n	time
1	1	1	1	1	(years)

X_0 $\qquad X_0(1 + g) \qquad X_0(1 + g)^2 \qquad X_0(1 + g)^{n-1}$

$X_0\left(\dfrac{1}{1 + r}\right) \longleftarrow$

$X_0\dfrac{(1 + g)}{(1 + r)^2} \longleftarrow$

$X_0\dfrac{(1 + g)^2}{(1 + r)^3} \longleftarrow$

$X_0\dfrac{(1 + g)^{n-1}}{(1 + r)^n} \longleftarrow$

7. $P = X_0\left(\dfrac{1}{1 + r}\right) + X_0\dfrac{(1 + g)}{(1 + r)^2} + \ldots + X_0\dfrac{(1 + g)^{n-1}}{(1 + r)^N}$.

In order to find an expression for the sum, multiply both sides of equation 7 by $\left(\dfrac{1 + g}{1 + r}\right)$.

8. $P\left(\dfrac{1 + g}{1 + r}\right) = X_0\dfrac{(1 + g)}{(1 + r)^2} + X_0\dfrac{(1 + g)^2}{(1 + r)^3} + \ldots + X_0\dfrac{(1 + g)^{n-1}}{(1 + r)^n} + X_0\dfrac{(1 + g)^n}{(1 + r)^{n+1}}$

Subtract equation 8 from equation 7.

9. $P\left(\dfrac{r - g}{1 + r}\right) = X_0\left[\left(\dfrac{1}{1 + r}\right) - \dfrac{(1 + g)^n}{(1 + r)^{n+1}}\right]$.

Simplifying by dividing both sides by $\left(\dfrac{r - g}{1 + r}\right)$ this becomes:

10. $P = X_0\left[\dfrac{1 - \dfrac{(1 + g)^n}{(1 + r)}}{r - g}\right]$

For the case of an income stream growing in perpetuity, $n \to \infty$. Providing that $r > g$, $\left(\dfrac{1 + g}{1 + r}\right)^n \to 0$. The expression for present value then simplifies to:

11. $P = X_0\left(\dfrac{1}{r - g}\right)$.

When $g = 0$ equation 11 reduces to the expression for the present value of a perpetuity (equation 6). From equation 11, note that as the expected rate of growth g rises toward the rate of discount r, the price of the asset approaches infinity. As a result, the discount rate must always exceed the growth rate if asset prices are to remain finite. This relationship implies that the rate of discount and therefore the cost of capital are higher for more rapidly growing corporations. It also suggests that the average rate of discount, and hence the average return on wealth, will be higher in more rapidly growing economies. Rearranging equation 11, we have:

12. $r = \dfrac{X_0}{P} + g.$

Equation 12 states that the rate of return on a claim to a growing income stream will equal the current income yield $\dfrac{X_0}{P}$ plus the expected growth rate g. If the income yield $\left(\dfrac{X_0}{P}\right)$ remains constant, the price of the asset will grow at the same rate as income. In this case, g will be equal to capital gains expressed as an annual percentage return $\left(\dfrac{\Delta P}{P}\right)$.

More rapidly growing income streams sell at higher prices and lower income yields. As the price-income ratio $\left(\dfrac{P}{X_0}\right)$ rises, the risk of capital loss from a reduction in the growth rate g, or an increase in the discount rate r, increases. A higher return r is therefore required by asset holders on more rapidly growing income streams.

the price system

MAN HAS ALMOST constant occasion for the help of his brethren, and it is in vain for him to expect it from their benevolence only. He will be more likely to prevail if he can interest their self-love in his favor, and show them that it is for their own advantage to do for him what he requires of them. Whoever offers to another a bargain of any kind, proposes to do this: Give me that which I want, and you shall have this which you want, is the meaning of every such offer; and it is in this manner that we obtain from one another the far greater part of those good offices which we stand in need of. It is not from the benevolence of the butcher, the brewer, or the baker that we expect our dinner but from their regard to their own interest. We address ourselves not to their humanity but to their self-love.

—ADAM SMITH

BRIEFLY, THEN, the universal basis of cooperation is the proportioning of benefits received to services rendered.

—HERBERT SPENCER

The previous chapters examined supply and demand forces for particular commodities in individual markets. The present chapter considers the fact that all markets in an economy are necessarily interrelated. In fact, if supply and demand relations in individual markets were independent, the economy would not work. There would be no forces operating to ensure that the total amount supplied and demanded in all markets would be feasible with what the labor force, given the capital stock and technology of the economy, is capable of producing.

GENERAL EQUILIBRIUM

Adam Smith, the father of modern economics, argued in 1776 in *The Wealth of Nations* that the free workings of competitive markets are more conducive to economic welfare than government intervention, direction, or regulation in the public interest. Each individual, in seeking his own self-interest is led "as if by an invisible hand" to a result that is in the interest of all. A more modern metaphor for the operations of the market system would be a giant computer, with an information storage and retrieval capacity of billions of units, and programmed to solve millions of equations simultaneously.

Partial Equilibrium Analysis

Partial equilibrium analysis studies a particular market, under the assumption that the price of one commodity can change without significant repercussions on the prices of other goods. For many kinds of decisions, the external effects on the rest of the economy are relatively small and the feedbacks from the rest of the economy negligible. Partial analysis is useful, and the *ceteris paribus* assumption with regard to other prices appropriate, where the sector considered is small relative to the rest of the economy. A reduction in the price of bicycles implies that if the demand for bicycles is inelastic, people have more to spend on other goods. Some other industries will find that their sales are higher, which may lead their owners and employees to travel more. Although this increase in travel may increase the demand for bicycles, the magnitude of such feedbacks are likely to be negligible and can be ignored without serious error of prediction.

General Equilibrium Analysis

Had the bicycle example concerned instead automobiles or labor, the interconnections would not have been negligible. Whenever the sector is large relative to the rest of the economy, its interrelation with other markets is likely to be substantial, and failure to consider feedbacks may lead to serious error. An analysis that takes into consideration the interconnections among prices is termed *general equilibrium analysis.* A general rise in wage rates, for example, will increase total labor income, the aggregate amount spent on goods and services and, in turn, the derived demand for labor itself. Failure to take such a feedback into account will lead to inaccurate predictions.

Nevertheless, generality in itself is not a virtue as, in the absence of sufficient empirical knowledge of all the interrelationships, all that a general theory is likely to predict is that anything can happen. To be useful, theories must be selective. The question is, What relationships are to be selected for analysis?

General Equilibrium

When prices are such that demand equals supply for every commodity, the economy is said to be in a position of general equilibrium. It is interesting to ask whether in principle there exists a set of nonnegative prices that satisfies general equilibrium and, if so, what its properties are. In addition to the existence of general equilibrium, there are also the problems of the *uniqueness* of this equilibrium and its *stability,* the power of the adjustment mechanisms.

The general equilibrium set of prices may be regarded as the solution of a set of simultaneous equations, each stating the conditions for equilibrium (zero excess demand) in the market for each good in the economy, where the equilibrium value for each price depends on the value of each of the others. The price system, like a gigantic computer, determines by an iterative process a solution to this interrelated system of equations.

The quantity of data required for coordination of a whole economy is intimidating. Billions and billions of processes are involved, far beyond the capability of the most ambitious computer. The price system solves this problem by changes in prices, which act as signals to individual market participants. Its great advantage is that it is not necessary for any single group of individuals to foresee and coordinate all changes and interactions.

When a problem is too vast to be comprehended as whole, the only expedient is an approach known among operations analysts as "suboptimization" and among economists as "decentralization." The problem is broken into pieces, and each piece is solved on the basis of assumed solutions for the others. As soon as each piece is solved, its results become data to be used in subsequent steps. Provided that the big problem is broken down into subproblems in the right way, this sequence of partial solutions will eventually produce the correct solution to the big problem.

The price system does just that. It divides the grand problem of economic coordination into the smaller problems of profit maximization for each firm and of balancing demand and supply in each market. When the small problems are all solved in ways that are consistent with one another, the big problem is solved, too. The human mind knows of no other way to deal with problems of such grand scale.[1]

1. Robert Dorfman, *The Price System* (New Jersey, 1964), p. 136.

The Adjustment Mechanism

General equilibrium in a market system is brought about by changes in market prices, which operate to disseminate economic intelligence to decision-makers and link all markets together.

The price system was not consciously created but evolved gradually. Its adjustment mechanism is far from perfect, and its rules are continually in a process of evolution. Firms and individuals differ in the alacrity with which they respond to economic signals. The resulting lags and frictions, which are particularly severe in imperfect markets in which business firms or labor unions possess considerable market power, impede the process of economic adjustment toward general equilibrium.

The configuration of this general equilibrium solution in a system where all markets are perfectly competitive will now be explored. These contours are important for comparative analysis, even though real-world economies never reach a position of general equilibrium where all markets are simultaneously cleared. It is, in fact, the existence of disequilibrium in particular markets that powers the continual process of economic change.

ALLOCATION AND DISTRIBUTION

As stated in Chapter 1, all economies, no matter how they are organized, must somehow decide the fundamental questions of allocation and distribution. It is now possible to show how the price system in a perfectly competitive economy provides answers to these questions.

With regard to *what* is produced, the price system will ensure that goods and services are produced in proportion to dollar votes, the price that consumers are willing to pay. A change in demand from one commodity to another will, in the short run, raise the price of the commodities for which demand is increased and lower the price of the commodities for which demand is decreased. This change will temporarily create excess profits in some industries and losses or below-normal profits in the others. Over the longer run, resources will flow to the industries where profits are above normal and flow out of the industries where profits are abnormally low. Profits function as a green or red signal to allocate resources in a market economy to those areas where demand is high relative to supply. Similarly, a change in technology that reduces costs in one area, or results in the innovation of a new product, will create above-normal profit opportunities which will induce existing firms to expand and new firms to move into these areas. Total supply will increase until profits are again normal.

Individual consumers are free to decide how they wish to spend their income among different goods. They allocate their purchases to maximize their utility. The market responds to their demands by adjusting the quantity offered. This process accords with the principle of *consumer sovereignty*. It is defended on the grounds that individuals are the best judges of their own interests and that freedom to choose and even to make mistakes is in itself desirable.

With regard to *how* goods are produced, competition forces producers to find the technique of production that represents the lowest cost. Firms that are not successful in cost minimization will be driven out of business by their more efficient competitors. Moreover, in perfectly competitive markets, each firm will move to the lowest point on its cost curve.

It is the threat of competition that compels each firm to produce at its lowest cost output with the most efficient techniques possible. In the absence of competition firms do not have the same incentive to minimize costs, because their survival may not be at stake and the inefficient may be sheltered from punishment. With downward-sloping demand curves, they will not operate with an output that represents the lowest point on their cost curves.

The question of *for whom* goods are produced is determined under the price system by the distribution of dollar votes. These votes in turn are based upon the distribution of ownership of labor and capital among households and upon the prices at which they are able to sell the services therefrom in factor markets. In competitive markets, firms pay for factors of production a price equal to the value of the marginal product of these factors, that is, in proportion to their contribution at the margin to the value of total output. As a result, individuals receive income according to what they and the factors of production that they own produce.

In imperfectly competitive markets property income represents *quasi-rents,* the residual income accruing to capital after all labor costs have been met. As property income is received by the owners of capital, who in their role as owners make no contribution, it was long termed *unearned income.*

The Role of Competition in Resolving Conflict

It is perfect competition rather than the market system per se that accomplishes the work of Adam Smith's "invisible hand." The pressure of competition assures that each producer is forced to produce at his most efficient factor combination and forced to adjust his output to his minimum long-run average cost. Producers are pushed by market forces to their most efficient production combination or are eliminated. The market, while impersonal, is not merciful.

Prices and profits perform a critical allocative role in competitive economies. High prices and high expected rates of profit act as a reward to signal resources into an industry, providing entry is free. Low prices and low expected rates of profits act as a goad to force resources out of an industry, providing exit is possible. Not all actual profits are functional in the sense of performing such allocative functions, and profits include a large component of economic rent. Yet opposition to nonfunctional profits and their effect on income distribution does not justify opposition to all profits or to the market system itself.

In spite of the huckstering, materialism, and hypocrisy that competition for private gain engenders (no salesman will easily admit that the good or service he is selling is inferior or inessential), there is a basic discipline that a competitive system imposes. It is difficult to hoodwink. Providing that competition exists, inefficiency will be punished and revealed in the income statement, in spite of the best public relations efforts.

The nature of the human situation is fundamental conflict between individuals. Goods are scarce and wants are unlimited. This conflict is reflected in the economic sphere in the divergence of goals between buyers and sellers. Sellers always prefer a higher price, buyers always prefer a lower price. Perfect competition ensures that no producer or factor owner is a price maker who can control the price at which he sells his product or factor. Price is determined solely by the impersonal market forces of supply and demand.

Perfect competition may thus be regarded as a form of social organization that eliminates conflict by dispersing and eliminating power. Individuals cannot achieve their own objectives at the expense of others. Only in perfectly competitive markets does no market power exist. As economic power is the most effective foundation for political power, the decentralization of economic decisions in competitive markets tends to be supportive of effective political democracy. Nevertheless, unequal distribution of wealth ownership leads to unequal political influence even under competitive markets. The outcome of a perfectly competitive economy merits examination not as a descriptive approximation of the real world but as a standard of comparison against which real-world results may be compared.

CHARACTERISTICS OF A PERFECTLY COMPETITIVE ECONOMY

Under certain restrictive conditions, it is possible to show that a perfectly competitive market economy results in an efficient allocation of resources. *Efficiency* is defined as a situation in which total output is at the maximum technically possible with given resources and level of technology, and the composition of output is such that it is impossible to make some individuals better off without making other individuals worse off.

It is important to note at the outset that *efficiency* in this special technical sense is not a synonym for *optimum* or even *desirable*. It is an analytic rather than a normative statement and implies no value judgment. The perfectly competitive outcome is efficient, but it is not the best of all possible worlds. It cannot be shown to maximize total economic welfare. In fact, as will be shown, there are in general an indefinite number of efficient outcomes, one for each distribution of ownership of productive factors.

Equality of Factor Price and Value of Marginal Product

In perfectly competitive markets, each firm will continue to hire factors until the value of the marginal product is equal to their price. For all factors, the ratio of their prices will be equal to the ratio of their marginal products, which ensures that each firm will operate with the lowest cost technique. As long as the ratio of factor prices does not equal the ratio of their marginal products, firms will substitute more of the factor with the greater marginal product per dollar of cost and so produce the same output at lower total cost.

Equality of marginal product with factor cost ensures that each firm is operating on its lowest total cost curve. As this rule also holds for firms in different industries hiring the same factor, total product could not be increased by shifting factors from one industry to another.

In a perfectly competitive market, each firm maximizes profits by producing at an output at which *price is equal to marginal cost.* As all firms in the market face the same price, the marginal cost of every firm is equal. Because of the law of diminishing returns, the marginal cost of every firm is rising. Equality of marginal cost, therefore, necessarily implies that total industry output is at a maximum from the given input of resources. The long-run equilibrium solution of each firm in a perfectly competitive economy is illustrated in Figure 10-1.

Any transfer of resources from one firm to another in such a situation will decrease total output because, given equality of marginal cost and rising marginal cost curves faced by each firm, the result of a transfer of resources from one firm to another would be to raise the output of the firm receiving additional resources by less than the reduction in output of the firm from which resources are taken. Conversely, so long as marginal costs of all firms are not equal, output could be increased by transferring resources from firms with higher marginal costs to firms with lower marginal costs.

This equality of price and marginal cost is similarly true in all markets in a perfectly competitive system. As a result, for all commodities produced in the economy, *the ratio of the prices at which they exchange will be equal to the ratio of their*

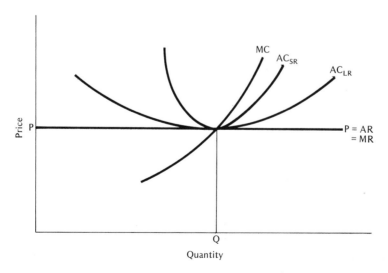

Figure 10-1 Long-Run Equilibrium in Perfect Competition

marginal costs. This fact implies that the value of total output for the economy as a whole is maximized, given the resource endowment and level of technology.

Equality of Price and Marginal Utility

Efficient allocation of resources results in least-cost production of goods to maximize the output from scarce resources. It also results in production of a *composition* of goods that reflects consumer preferences. In order to maximize total expected utility from consumption, consumers will equate the ratio of the prices of all goods to the ratio of the marginal utilities anticipated from consuming different goods.

Given technology, tastes, and the distribution of ownership of productive factors, the perfectly competitive solution is efficient in the sense that no individuals could be made better off without making others worse off. Only in perfect competition is the *opportunity cost of producing* one additional unit exactly *equal* to the *utility of consuming* an additional unit. Any other solution can be shown to be inferior, in the sense that some individuals could be made better off without making others worse off because for at least some commodities the marginal utility of consuming one more unit would exceed the marginal cost of production. As costs represent opportunities foregone, total utility could be increased by producing more of that commodity and less of others whose marginal cost equals or exceeds their marginal utility.

Conditions for Allocational Efficiency

Assuming for simplicity that utility is cardinal, the essence of an efficient solution is that for each good the marginal cost to all individuals in the society of producing one more unit (*marginal social cost*) is exactly equal to the marginal benefit to all individuals in the society from consuming one more unit (*marginal social benefit*): $MSC = MSB.$

Only if this equality is satisfied is it impossible to make someone better off without making someone else worse off. A number of conditions must be satisfied in order for the price system to obtain this efficient solution. These conditions may be shown by expanding the previous equation:

$$MSB \underset{6}{=} MPB \underset{5}{=} MU \underset{4}{=} P \underset{1}{=} MR \underset{2}{=} MC \underset{3}{=} MPC \underset{7}{=} MSC.$$

This expansion will now be explained.

1. *$P = MR$: Perfect Competition in Product Markets.* Perfect competition is necessary in order to equate price and marginal revenue. In the absence of perfect competition, the demand curve facing individual producers will slope downward; price will exceed marginal revenue, and too little will be produced relative to the perfectly competitive outcome. The efficient solution requires in particular *no economies of scale,* in order that the condition for perfect competition, that a large number of producers exist with no one producer able to affect market price, can be satisfied.

2. *MR = MC: Optimizing Behavior on the Part of Business Firms.* Profit maximization is necessary if producers are to produce at an output at which marginal cost is equal to marginal revenue, with least-cost production techniques.

3. *MC = MPC: Business the Best Judge of Its Own Self-Interest.* Business self-interest is necessary if marginal costs as viewed by business are to be equal to actual marginal private costs.

4. *MU = P: Optimizing Behavior on the Part of Consumers.* Utility maximization is necessary if consumers are to allocate their expenditures so that marginal utility is equal to price.

5. *MPB = MU: Consumers the Best Judge of Their Own Self-Interest.* Consumer self-interest is necessary if marginal utility as viewed by consumers is to be equal to actual marginal private benefits.

6. *MSB = MPB: Absence of External Benefits.* Individual consumers, acting in their own self-interest, will continue to consume up to the point at which price is equal to the marginal utility they derive from consumption. This private utility will equal the total gain to society *only* if the utility of other individuals is not affected, so that private benefits and social benefits are identical.

   The effects of one individual's behavior on the utility of others are termed *externalities* or *neighborhood effects.* While externalities are associated with virtually all behavior, for some actions they are particularly significant. In the case of drugs and alcohol for example, the utility of others is likely to be reduced as one man's utility of these goods is increased. With negative external benefits, marginal social benefit will be less than marginal private utility. The market, if left to itself, will result in *too much* production and consumption of such goods, in the sense that marginal social benefit will be less than marginal costs. For some goods—education and aesthetic design—external benefits are positive. *Too little* of such goods would be produced and consumed in a free market, as marginal social benefits would exceed marginal costs.

7. *MPC = MSC: Absence of External Costs.* There may similarly be *externalities on the cost side,* in which case the marginal private costs to the individual producers are not identical to marginal social costs for the economy as a whole. Techniques of production that result, for example, in water or air pollution result in costs to others in addition to the costs to the enterprise causing the pollution. *Too much* of such commodities would be produced, in the sense that marginal social costs would exceed marginal social benefits. Externalities such as environmental pollution tend to increase with the level of real income and population density.

   The existence of positive nonpecuniary rewards in different jobs will also mean that private costs to the firm are less than the total (pecuniary plus nonpecuniary) wage to the worker; too much of such commodities will be produced.

   These effects of externalities may be shown diagrammatically. In Figure 10-2 P_M and Q_M represent the price and quantity that will be produced and sold in perfectly competitive markets. Market supply and demand curves consider only private costs and benefits, whereas there are in fact externalities associated with all goods, in so far as someone else's behavior affects me. In Figure 10-2a

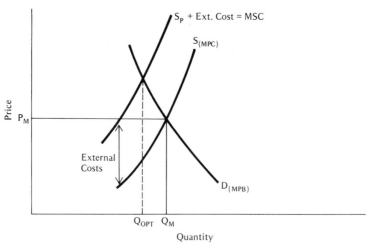

a. External Costs–Market Produces Too Much

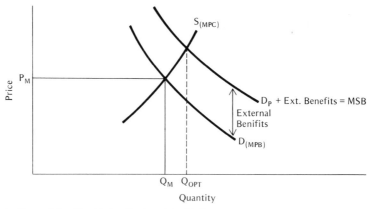

b. External Benefits–Market Produces Too Little

Figure 10-2 Effect of Externalities

a situation of external costs is illustrated, where marginal social costs exceed marginal private costs. Too much of such goods (Q_M) is produced by the market relative to the socially optimal amount (Q_{opt}). Conversely Figure 10-2b shows a situation where external benefits exist, and marginal social benefits exceed marginal private benefits. Too little of such goods is produced by the market relative to the socially optimum amount.

When any of these seven conditions is not satisfied the private market outcome will in general not be efficient. The appropriate price that would equate marginal social benefits and marginal social costs is sometimes termed the *shadow price.* Even in perfectly competitive markets, participants will consider only private benefits and costs; to the extent that externalities are important, some misallocation of resources will always occur with a market solution. But the resulting misallocation *may* be even greater if government planning is used to replace the market.

There are two important additional preconditions for an efficient allocation of resources through the price system implicit in the formal equality of marginal social benefit and marginal social cost by the private market; marginal costs must be greater than zero and the price mechanism must be feasible.

Nonzero Marginal Costs

Goods that can be produced with zero or near zero short-run marginal costs (a bridge or a beach) would never be produced privately at a price to satisfy the condition for efficient allocation. Private firms might provide a bridge, but they would charge a price greater than the marginal cost of using that bridge, which once it is produced is virtually zero. Equation of marginal cost and price would necessitate a zero price and zero revenue. This is related to the condition for perfect competition that economies of scale be absent, which result in marginal costs below average costs. This problem will be explored further in the next chapter.

Efficiency of Price as an Exclusion Principle

The price mechanism may itself be inefficient relative to other allocation and revenue systems. For some goods, externalities are so strong that it is not possible to use price to exclude those who choose not to pay. By their nature such goods, once produced, are available to everyone — for example, clean air or national defense.

For a larger class of goods, it may be technically possible to exclude those who choose not to pay, but it is more expensive to use the price system than to allocate resources and to raise revenue to another mechanism. It would be possible to charge people for the use of streets by putting a toll house at every corner, but the costs of collection would be high relative to collection by the tax system. When labor costs are lower relative to land rents (for example, in developing countries as compared to America), one finds many more parking attendants. In some less developed countries, the tourist is socially obliged to pay a boy to attend his car whenever and wherever he parks it.

The Theory of the Second Best

For presentational simplicity the relationships necessary for efficiency were formulated in terms of a single good for which it was necessary to posit cardinal utility. Had the argument been developed in terms of the ratio between any two goods, an assumption of ordinal utility would have been sufficient. For efficiency, the marginal rate of substitution between all goods would have to be equal to the ratio of their marginal costs.

Presentation of the argument in terms of the ratio between any two goods reveals that it is the *relative* existence of the given conditions rather than their absolute existence that is important. For example, if social benefits or costs exceed private benefits or costs *by the same proportion for all goods,* the market outcome will still be efficient. Similarly, if all goods are produced in markets with *the same degree of market power,* so that price exceeds marginal cost by an identical proportion for each good, an efficient allocation of resources will occur.[2]

This argument leads to an important insight. In an imperfect world, moving one market toward a more efficient price and output need not result in moving the economy toward a more efficient allocation, and could even result in a movement away from efficiency. For example, if all markets are imperfectly competitive by differing degrees, the attempt to increase competition in one market will only improve the allocation of resources if that market previously were less competitive than most, as reflected in a relatively higher ratio of price to marginal cost. If that market had previously been more competitive than most, increasing competition in that market will result in a greater misallocation of resources. Such considerations have been termed *the theory of the second best.* The general proposition is that the best solution in a perfect world is not necessarily the best solution in the *n*th best (real) world.

The conditions given here for an efficient allocation of resources are static, that is, they make no mention of time. Imperfectly competitive markets are frequently justified on the grounds that large firms possessing market power use part of their above-normal monopoly profits for research and development, with the result that cost-reducing technical change and product innovation occur more rapidly than they would under perfect competition. Similarly, subsidy or protection of certain industries is justified on the "infant industry" grounds that the resulting rate of growth and increase in efficiency will be more rapid.

In such cases, the disadvantages from the viewpoint of static resource allocation may be compensated for by the dynamic advantages of a more rapid fall in costs and greater choice over time. It is not possible to resolve these arguments analytically. The question is an empirical one — To what extent are these costs and benefits in fact associated with increased concentration and market power in particular markets? The answer presumably will not be the same in all cases.

Finally, once the future is introduced, general equilibrium requires not merely a present (spot) but also a future market for every good. Otherwise, producers do not have sufficient information on which to base decisions concerning the future.

These conditions for economic efficiency in a market economy will be reconsidered in the following chapter. One important economic function of government is to supplement the market whenever one or more of the conditions given here for efficient allocation is not fulfilled. But inefficiency of private market outcomes does not itself imply the desirability of government intervention, as government outcomes are also inefficient. It becomes an empirical question. The government has a potential role to play in capitalist economies whenever the invisible hand falters or fumbles.

---

2. This will strictly be the case only if factor supplies are given. If, for example, the supply of labor is not perfectly inelastic, a change in wage rates will affect the margin between work and leisure. Only perfectly competitive firms produce at the minimum point on their average cost curves.

THE DISTRIBUTION OF INCOME AND WEALTH

Under certain conditions a system of competitive markets has been shown to result in an efficient allocation of resources, in the sense that no one can be made better off without making someone else worse off. But the *particular* efficient solution generated will depend on the distribution of dollar votes, which in turn depend on the distribution of income and wealth. A change in the distribution of income would result in a different set of dollar votes. Prices and outputs would adjust in different markets until efficiency was again restored, with a different set of relative prices and a different allocation of resources. There are thus as many different efficient solutions as there are different distributions of income and dollar votes.

It is in this sense that a competitive market system may be compared to a giant computer. A change in preferences, or a change in income, is reflected as a change in market demand for goods and services. For each input of dollar votes, the computer calculates and provides an efficient solution of relative prices and outputs.

It may now be seen why a competitive outcome that is optimal in the sense of efficiency may be regarded as undesirable. It is quite consistent with efficiency that the market provide milk for the complexions of rich women, while poor children starve. It is even consistent with efficiency that all the wealth be owned by one person, while everyone else receives only a subsistence wage. One of the important economic goals of government in all capitalist countries is to reduce the degree of inequality in the distribution of income that results from the operation of market forces, primarily by raising the incomes of the very poor.

The Distribution of Income

In perfectly competitive markets all factors receive a price equal to the value of their marginal product. The distribution of income among households will thus depend on the price of productive factors as determined in factor markets and on the quantity of factors owned by each household, that is, the distribution of human and nonhuman capital.

Market power in factor and product markets alters the equation of marginal costs and marginal benefits of the previous section. The degree of market power will determine factor prices, factor shares, and dollar votes, which then become inputs in the determination of a particular efficient solution by competitive market forces.

The broad contours of the distribution of income deserve to be more widely known. The distribution of personal income by income level and by relative income class in the United States is summarized in Tables 10-1 and 10-2. As shown in Table 10-1, the proportion of families with income under $2,000 per year, after correction for changes in the price level, has fallen dramatically since 1929, from nearly one third of the population to one tenth. At the other end of the scale, the proportion of families with incomes over $10,000 has risen from one in twenty to more than one in three.

Table 10-1 DISTRIBUTION OF FAMILIES BY MONEY INCOME LEVEL, 1929-68

Family Personal Income Level	1929	1941	1947	1962	1966	1968
Under $2,000	31	27	16	12	11	10
$ 2,000-$3,999	39	29	28	19	16	14
$ 4,000-$5,999	15	22	26	21	14	13
$ 6,000-$7,999	7	12	14	18	18	14
$ 8,000-$9,999	3	4	7	11	13	13
$10,000-$14,999 ⎫	⎫	⎫	6	12	19	23
	5	6				
$15,000 and over ⎭	⎭	⎭	3	7	9	13
	100	100	100	100	100	100
Mean Family Income					$8,080	$9,220
Median Family Income					$6,930	$7,940

Sources: 1929–62—(1962 dollars), *Survey of Current Business,* Office of Business Economics, Department of Commerce.
1966–68—*Survey of Consumer Finances,* Survey Research Center, University of Michigan.

Table 10-2 DISTRIBUTION OF FAMILIES BY RELATIVE INCOME CLASS, 1929-68 (PERCENT DISTRIBUTION OF FAMILIES AND UNRELATED INDIVIDUALS)

Income Class	1929	1935–36	1941	1944	1962	1966	1968
Lowest Fifth	13 ⎰	4	4	5	5	4	4
Second Fifth	⎱	9	10	11	11	11	10
Third Fifth	14	14	15	16	16	17	17
Fourth Fifth	19	21	22	22	23	24	24
Highest Fifth	54	52	49	46	46	44	45
Top 5 Percent	30	27	24	21	20	29 *	30 *
Top 1 Percent	15	12	11	9		n.a.	n.a.

Source: 1929–62—Office of Business Economics; Department of Commerce; Bureau of the Census.
1966–68—*Survey of Consumer Finances,* Survey Research Center, University of Michigan.
1968 ⎰ Mean income of lowest decile: $1,210
⎱ Mean income of highest decile: $26,740
* Top 10 percent.

These changes have been due almost entirely to the rise in the level of per capita income as the economy has grown. As shown in Table 10-2, the relative distribution of income changed very slightly and has remained virtually constant over the postwar period. The top and bottom fifth together account for about one half of total personal income—the bottom fifth receives 5 per cent, and the top fifth 45 per cent. The richest 10 percent now receive 30 per cent of total income, more than the poorest half of the population (22 per cent). The greatest change in the relative distribution of income was the decline in the share of the top income groups from 1929 to 1944. These income figures do not include capital gains and business expense accounts, which are received primarily by upper income groups.

In all capitalist economies, the distribution of property income is much more unequal than the distribution of labor income. As shown in Table 10-3, the top 10 percent of the population receives more than one half of total property and business income. The top 5 percent earns 15 percent of wages and salaries but receives nearly one half of total property income. Nevertheless, the more unequal distribution of property income does not apply at the lowest levels. Because of the large number of retired people in this category, the poorest 40 percent receive 10 percent of business and property income but only 9 percent of wages and salaries.

Table 10-3   DISTRIBUTION OF PERSONAL INCOME BY TYPE OF INCOME, 1962 (PERCENTAGE OF TOTAL INCOME RECEIVED BY INCOME GROUP FROM SPECIFIED SOURCE)

		Wages and	Business and Property Income			Pensions and Annuities	Other Income (Transfers)
	Total	Salaries	Total	Business	Property		
Lowest Fifth	4	1	2	0	4	30	20
Second Fifth	10	8	8	7	8	33	37
Third Fifth	16	18	12	13	10	13	13
Fourth Fifth	24	28	15	17	11	11	16
Top Fifth	46	45	64	62	65	12	14
Total	100	100	100	100	100	100	100
Top 10 percent	30	27	51	49	53	8	5
Top 5 percent	20	15	44	42	47	6	1

Source: Survey of Financial Characteristics of Consumers, Board of Governors, Federal Reserve Board.

This disproportionate contribution of property income to the total income of the very rich is revealed more clearly in Table 10-4. The highest income class, those spending units with incomes over $100,000, received on the average $27,000 in wages and salaries and $130,000 in business and property income. Property income accounts for more than 80 percent of the total income of the very rich, not including capital gains.

The Distribution of Wealth

The unequal distribution of property income reflects the concentration of wealth ownership in all capitalist economies. It has been estimated that in the United States the wealthiest 1 percent of all families own about one third of total private wealth and that this concentration has been increasing in the postwar period. In England it has been estimated that more than one half of total wealth is owned by the wealthiest 1 percent of families.

The distribution of wealth by wealth level and by type of wealth in the United States is shown in Table 10-5. The poorest half of all consumer units own less than 5 percent of total wealth. At the other end of the scale, the richest 5 percent of consumers own more than half of total private wealth. These proportions would be but

Table 10-4 SHARE OF INCOME RECEIVED BY TYPE OF INCOME, 1962 (DOLLARS AND PERCENTAGE DISTRIBUTION OF MEAN AMOUNTS)

Income Class	Total Income		Wages and Salaries		Business and Property Income								
					Total		Business		Property		Pensions and Annuities		Other Income	
	Dollars	Per cent	Dollars	Per cent	Dollars	Per cent	Dollars	Per cent	Dollars	Per cent	Dollars	Per cent	Dollars	Per cent
All units	6,378	100	4,793	75	1,116	17	737	12	378	6	340	5	130	2
$0–$2,999	1,576	100	653	41	219	14	109	7	110	7	510	32	194	12
$3,000–$4,999	3,970	100	2,865	72	509	13	338	9	171	4	432	11	163	4
$5,000–$7,499	6,219	100	5,246	84	690	11	509	8	181	3	217	3	66	1
$7,500–$9,999	8,630	100	7,298	85	1,010	12	713	8	296	3	198	2	125	1
$10,000–$14,999	11,960	100	10,105	87	1,638	14	1,133	9	505	4	128	1	89	1
$15,000–$24,999	17,758	100	13,845	78	3,579	20	2,421	14	1,158	7	308	2	26	0
$25,000–$49,999	34,534	100	16,072	47	17,700	51	11,890	34	5,810	17	741	2	21	0
$50,000–$99,999	61,207	100	23,276	38	37,326	61	22,716	37	14,610	24	601	1	4	0
$100,000 and over	158,166	100	27,295	17	129,613	82	71,539	45	58,075	37	1,252	1	5	0

Source: Survey of Financial Characteristics of Consumers, Board of Governors, Federal Reserve System.

little altered if difficult-to-value and therefore omitted items such as consumer durables were included in the wealth measure.

In view of this inequality, another economic goal of governments in capitalist
economies is to reduce the degree of concentration of wealth ownership in the hands
of the very rich. A critical question here obviously concerns the influence of the rich
in the election process and in the councils of government. During the debate for
universal franchise in the nineteenth century, it was widely feared that the poor,
who were clearly in the majority, if given the vote would disappropriate the rich.
This has never happened, as yet.

Table 10-5 DISTRIBUTION OF WEALTH BY WEALTH LEVEL AND BY TYPE OF WEALTH,
1962 [1]

| | | | | | Percentage Share | | |
Wealth Class	Percent of All Consumer Units	Total Wealth	Own Home	Automobile	Business and Professional Wealth	Liquid Assets	Investment Assets
Zero–$999	25	*	*	5	*	1	*
$1,000–$4,999	19	2	4	13	*	5	*
$5,000–$9,999	16	5	12	15	3	7	1
$10,000–$24,999	23	18	36	30	9	22	7
$25,000–$49,999	11	18	24	19	18	25	11
$50,000–$99,999	4	14	11	10	19	17	15
100,000–$200,000	1	8	5	4	7	8	11
200,000 and over	1	33	8	5	44	13	53

*Less than ½ of 1 percent.
1. Assets are valued at market value. Equity in life insurance, annuities, retirement funds, household equipment, clothing,
sports equipment, boats, art collections, etc., are omitted. Debts secured by assets included in the wealth estimate, primarily
homes, automobiles, and marketable securities, are deducted from the values of the assets.
Source: Survey of Consumer Finances, Board of Governors, Federal Reserve System.

Property and Privilege

Prices serve two important functions in a market economy — to allocate resources
and to distribute income. This dual role of prices in a market system is the key to the
structure of privilege implicit in capitalism. All societies award to certain groups
disproportionate shares of wealth, power, and prestige. Ownership of property to be
used for private enrichment is the core institution of privilege under capitalism. Yet
the element of privilege in this institution, its operative result in favoring a very
small group with income, wealth, and power that allows a qualitatively different
style of life is largely hidden behind the functional aspects of the price system, the
efficient operation of the means of production, and the allocation of resources under
the discipline of impersonal market forces.

As privilege is limited under the law to advantages inherent in wealth ownership,
it is much less visible under capitalism than under other social systems. The privileges of wealth are open in theory to everyone, and the distribution of rewards is
exposed to the corrective scrutiny of the electorate. In all societies, the defense of

privilege is an active source of resistance to economic and social change. And in all societies, existing institutions come to be regarded as the natural order of things rather than a particular set of rules and conventions by which the economic game is played, rules that depend upon and may be changed by collective agreement.

From the viewpoint of economic analysis, the justification of any particular way of organizing economic behavior and of constituting economic institutions is pragmatic. Does it work? Or more accurately, does it work better (or less badly) than the best alternative? The development of such a rationalistic view of social institutions in modern societies, in part as a response to the continuous series of problems raised by population growth and new technology, has been an increasingly powerful solvent of existing practice and tradition.

APPENDIX: PARETO OPTIMALITY

The efficient outcome of a perfectly competitive economy is sometimes termed a *Pareto optimum*, after the Italian economist Vilfredo Pareto, who first formulated it. It is an optimum not in the general sense of best, but only in the special sense that no one can be made better off without making someone else worse off.

In the perfectly competitive outcome the ratio of the prices of all goods equals the ratio of their marginal costs. Similarly, the ratio of the prices of all factors is equal to the ratio of the values of their marginal products. This situation is an optimum in the sense that, whenever it does not hold, it would be possible to increase the total value of output with the same input of resources by the reallocation of resources among industries until equality of these ratios was established.

This condition for optimality may be demonstrated with a numerical example. Assume there are only two types of goods produced in the economy, "manufactures" (M) and "foodstuffs" (F). The price of M is 30, and the price of F is 10. The marginal cost of producing M is 20, and the marginal cost of producing F is 10. These conditions may be formulated:

$$P_M = 30 \quad MC_M = 20 \quad \frac{P_M}{P_F} = \frac{3}{1} \quad \frac{MC_M}{MC_F} = \frac{2}{1}$$

$$P_F = 10 \quad MC_F = 10$$

Good F is produced in competitive markets, and its price is equal to its marginal cost. Good M is produced in imperfectly competitive markets, and its price exceeds its marginal cost.

The value of total output could be increased by the transfer of resources to the production of good M, of which there is too little produced relative to the competitive solution. Assume that twenty units of resources are transferred from the production of F to the production of M. In consequence, two fewer units of F are produced, with a loss of output valued at 20. These twenty units of resources are now used to produce one additional unit of M, valued at 30. As a result of this reallocation of resources, the value of total output has increased by 10.

As this transfer of resources from F to M continues, the price of M will fall and the price of F will rise, given downward-sloping demand curves. Concurrently, the marginal cost of M will rise and the marginal cost of F will fall, assuming that cost curves are upward sloping. This process will continue to result in an increase in the value of total output until for each good *price is equal to marginal cost*, so that the ratio of the prices is equal to the ratio of the marginal costs:

$$P_M = 24 \quad MC_M = 24$$
$$P_F = 12 \quad MC_F = 12$$
$$\frac{2}{1} = \frac{P_M}{P_F} = \frac{MC_M}{MC_F} = \frac{2}{1}$$

Similarly, utility-maximizing households will adjust their purchases of different goods until *the marginal utility* of the last dollar spent in every direction is identical. Assume that this is not the case but that $\frac{P_M}{P_F} = \frac{2}{1}$ and $\frac{MU_M}{MU_F} = \frac{3}{1}$. Total utility would be increased by the purchase of one additional unit of M, yielding three "utils" of satisfaction, in place of two fewer units of F, resulting in the loss of two "utils" of satisfaction. Due to the principle of diminishing marginal utility, as this substitution continued, the marginal utility of M would fall and the marginal utility of F would rise. This process will continue until in equilibrium consumption has been adjusted so that the ratio of the marginal utilities is equal to the ratio of the prices:

$$\frac{P_M}{P_F} = \frac{2}{1} \quad \frac{MU_M}{MU_F} = \frac{2}{1}$$

As a result of profit maximization by firms and utility maximization by consumers, in perfectly competitive markets the ratio of the marginal costs of producing all goods is equal to the ratio of the marginal utilities from consuming them:

$$\frac{MU_M}{MU_F} = \frac{P_M}{P_F} = \frac{MC_M}{MC_F}.$$

Any other solution can be shown to be inferior, in the sense that some individuals could be made better off without making others worse off.

For example, if

$$\frac{30}{10} = \frac{MU_M}{MU_F} = \frac{P_M}{P_F} \frac{MC_M}{MC_F} = \frac{20}{10},$$ total utility could be increased by the production of more M and less F. As the marginal utility of M exceeds the marginal cost of M, and the cost of M represents two units of F foregone, total utility could be increased by transferring resources from the production of F to the production of M. As this transfer continued, the ratio $\frac{MU_M}{MU_F}$ would fall, and the ratio $\frac{MC_M}{MC_F}$ would rise, until in the competitive solution they were brought into equality.

These characteristics of a perfectly competitive economy may be shown diagrammatically. In Figure 10-3, units of good M are measured on the horizontal axis and

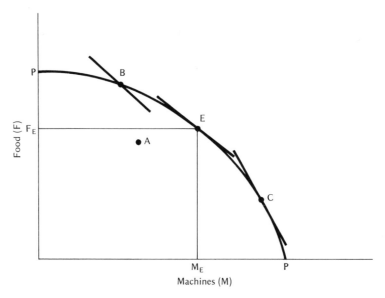

Figure 10-3 Pareto Optimality

units of good F are measured on the vertical axis. The production possibility curve PP shows the maximum amounts of the two goods that can be produced in the economy, given the existing resources of labor and capital and the level of technology. This curve is drawn concave to the origin to reflect diminishing returns and increasing costs of production for each commodity. The production possibility curve reveals the fundamental allocative nature of economic problems: More of one good implies less of another good. There is no such thing as a free drink, or even free love.

The condition that under perfect competition the ratio of the prices of all factors will be equal to the ratio of their marginal products ensures that all goods will be produced in the technically most efficient (least cost) way. This eliminates all points such as A in Figure 10-3 within the production possibility curve. As a result, the competitive outcome must lie somewhere on the *production frontier PP*.

The condition that for all goods the ratio of their prices must equal the ratio of their marginal costs ensures that the price ratio at which individuals can buy goods is equal to the slope of the production possibility curve, sometimes termed the *marginal rate of transformation*. The price ratio of the two goods may be represented by the slope of a straight line. Situations such as B in Figure 10-3 are eliminated, where the ratio of prices does not equal the ratio of marginal costs of production for that combination.

The condition that for all goods the ratio of their prices must equal the ratio of their marginal utilities to consumers determines the combination of goods produced, that is, where the economy is located along the PP curve. At the competitive outcome, shown as E in Figure 10-3, each consumer has adjusted his consumption of each good so that its marginal utility is proportional to its price, and at these prices the total amounts demanded equal the total amount supplied. At a lower relative price of F, for example, more of F would be demanded. But a lower relative price of

F would imply a steeper price line, which would be tangent to the production possibility curve, with a lower relative marginal cost of *F*, only at points to the right of *E* (e.g., *C*) where relatively lower amounts of *F* are produced.

The conditions for Pareto optimality are satisfied only at *E* and not at any other point within or on the *PP* frontier. At each of these other points, it is possible to reallocate resources to make some people better off without making others worse off. Point *E* is thus the only point where no conceivable reorganization could bring about an *unambiguous* reduction in scarcity or an unambiguous increase in the satisfaction of human wants. Movement away from *E* may in fact be toward a "better" allocation, but it will necessarily involve making some individuals better off at the expense of making others worse off.

It may now be seen how monopoly misallocates resources in comparison to the perfectly competitive optimum. Because price exceeds marginal cost, too little of monopolistically produced goods are produced. Consumers adjust their consumption until marginal utilities are proportionate to prices, but prices no longer reflect marginal costs. If good *M* were produced in imperfectly competitive markets while good *F* were produced competitively, the economy would locate at a position such as *B* in Figure 10-3, with too little *M* produced and too much *F* produced in comparison to the Pareto optimum allocation *E*. Monopoly also results in output at points such as *A* within the production possibility frontier by removing the external competitive stimulus to find the least-cost production technique and by producing with excess capacity at positions where average cost is falling and therefore above its minimum value.

Community Indifference Curves

The Pareto optimal allocation may be represented simply with the use of *social indifference curves*. In Figure 10-4 the production possibility curve *PP* represents the maximum amounts of the two goods *F* and *M* that the economy can produce, given its resource endowment and technology.

On the same diagram are drawn a set of community indifference curves, representing the tastes of individuals in the community. Each curve represents the alternative combinations of *F* and *M* that leave each individual in the community equally well off for any given distribution of income and wealth.

The point of allocative efficiency *E* is that point where the production possibility curve is tangent to the highest community indifference curve. At this Pareto optimal solution, the ratio of the prices of the two goods, represented by the slope of the price line at that point, is equal to the ratio of the marginal costs of producing the two goods, represented by the slope of the production possibility curve at that point (the marginal rate of transformation) and to the ratio of the marginal utility from consuming the two goods, represented by the slope of the indifference curve at that point (the marginal rate of substitution). Production at any other point on *PP* results in a lower level of total utility, as represented by a lower indifference curve.

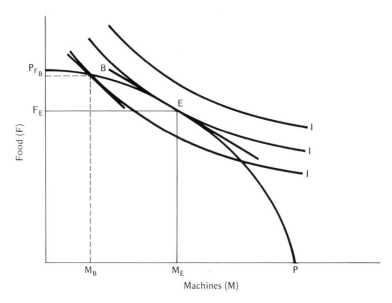

Figure 10-4 Pareto Optimality with Community Indifference Curves

At the point B, where the price ratio of the two goods does not equal the ratio of marginal costs, consumers have adjusted their consumption so that the price ratios equal the marginal rate of substitution. As seen, the community is on a lower indifference curve. The price of machines exceeds their marginal cost, and too few machines and too much food are produced relative to the Pareto optimum (F_E, M_E).

While elegant for presentation purposes, the concept of social indifference curves is extremely treacherous. Strictly speaking, the construction of community indifference curves requires that all individuals have the same tastes and preferences and that there are no externalities, so that the analysis can safely treat a representative consumer. When individuals have different tastes, a change in relative prices will affect different individuals differently, depending on how they value the goods that have fallen or risen in price. Some individuals may be made better off, others worse off: as interpersonal comparisons cannot be made, community indifference curves cannot be drawn.

The notion of preference for "society" is undefinable. Only individuals receive utility, not societies. There is, strictly speaking, no "national" interest or preference function.

the economic role
of government

THE DEMOCRATIC METHOD is that institutional arrangement for arriving at political decisions in which individuals acquire the power to decide by means of a competitive struggle for the people's vote.

—JOSEPH SCHUMPETER

FOR ALL MEN ARE BY NATURE provided of notable multiplying glasses, through which every little payment appeareth a great grievance; but are destitute of those prospective glasses to see far off the miseries that hang over them, and cannot without such payments be avoided.

— THOMAS HOBBES

Year	All Government Total Expenditures		All Government Purchases of Goods and Services		All Government Transfer Payments		Federal Government Purchases of Goods and Services		Federal Transfer Payments Grants, and Net Interest		State and Local Purchases of Goods and Services		State and Local Transfer Payments	
	$	%	$	%	$	%	$	%	$	%	$	%	$	%
1929	10.3	10.0	8.5	8.2	1.8	1.8	1.3	1.3	1.3	1.3	7.2	7.0	.5	.5
1933	11.2	20.2	8.0	14.4	3.2	5.8	2.0	3.6	2.0	3.6	6.0	10.8	1.2	2.2
1940	19.3	19.3	14.1	14.1	5.2	5.2	6.2	6.2	3.9	3.9	7.9	7.9	.13	1.3
1945	93.8	44.2	82.9	39.1	10.9	5.1	74.8	35.3	10.0	4.7	8.1	3.8	.9	.4
1950	63.9	22.6	42.1	14.8	21.8	7.8	23.2	8.1	19.1	6.7	18.9	6.6	2.7	.9
1955	99.8	25.0	75.8	19.0	24.0	6.0	46.6	11.7	21.6	5.4	29.2	7.3	2.4	.6
1960	146.1	29.0	99.6	19.8	46.5	9.2	53.5	10.6	38.5	7.6	46.1	9.2	8.0	1.6
1965	201.4	29.4	137.0	20.0	64.4	9.4	66.9	9.8	54.0	7.9	70.1	10.2	10.4	1.5
1968	296.8	34.3	199.6	23.1	97.2	11.2	98.8	11.4	82.8	9.6	100.8	11.7	13.3	1.5
1969	315.5	34.0	209.7	22.6	105.8	11.4	99.2	10.7	90.5	9.7	100.6	11.9	14.0	1.5
1970	341.8	35.0	219.4	22.5	122.4	12.8	97.2	10.0	107.9	11.1	122.2	12.5	14.5	1.6
1971	372.9	35.8	233.0	22.2	141.9	13.5	97.6	9.3	124.3	11.8	135.5	13.0	17.6	1.7

Source: Department of Commerce, Office of Business Economics.

Up to this point the analysis has been concerned with the behavior of 2 types of private economic units, households and firms. Governments represent the third important type of economic units. This chapter considers government economic behavior and outlines the economic functions of government in capitalist economies.

As seen in Table 11-1, government expenditures in the United States have increased dramatically since 1929, both absolutely and as a percentage of total income: Total government expenditures on goods and services rose from 8 to 22 percent of total income. In addition, government transfer payments increased from about 2 to 13 percent. Transfer payments, for example, old age pensions and unemployment compensation, do not represent a diversion of real resources from the private to the public sector but rather a redistribution of purchasing power among individuals within the private sector.

This growth of government expenditures has not been unique to the United States but has occurred in most countries. The share of the public sector rises as a proportion of total economic activity with the stage of a country's economic development. Table 11-2 presents an international comparison of the share of central government expenditures for selected countries. In developed countries, total spending by central governments typically accounts for between 20 and 30 percent of national income. In contrast, the share of government is much lower for less developed countries, between 10 and 20 percent.

Table 11-2 INTERNATIONAL COMPARISON OF CENTRAL GOVERNMENT EXPENDITURES, 1969

	Current Transfers to Household and Local Governments (Percent of GNP)	Current Outlays for Goods and Services (Percent of GNP)	Total Expenditures, (Percent of GNP)[*]
Nigeria[1]	1	3	8
Mexico[2]	1	3	7
Japan	6	2	12
Chile	6	7	22
United States	10	11	20
Italy	6	9	22
France	3	9	21
West Germany	15	16	39
Sweden[2]	12	9	27
United Kingdom	13	11	35

[*] Includes interest payments, public investment, subsidies, and other expenditures not included in the first two columns.
[1] 1966   [2] 1968
Source: United Nations, *Statistical Yearbook 1970.*

Table 11-3 presents the composition of government expenditure in the United States. Nearly one half of total federal expenditures are connected with defense, accounting for about three quarters of federal expenditures for goods and services. Health and welfare expenditures, primarily transfers, from the second largest component of the federal budget. About one half of state and local expenditures is devoted to education, with roads and highways accounting for the next largest share.

Table 11-3 COMPOSITION OF GOVERNMENT EXPENDITURES, 1968–70 (BILLIONS OF DOLLARS)

	Dollars		Percent of Total	
	1968	1970	1968	1970
Federal Total Expenditures	183.7	203.0	100	100
National Defense	80.5	80.3	44	40
International Affairs and Finance	4.6	3.6	3	2
Space Research and Technology	4.7	3.7	3	2
Agriculture	5.9	6.2	3	3
Natural Resources	1.7	2.5	1	1
Commerce and Transportation	8.1	9.3	4	5
Community Development and Housing	4.1	3.0	2	1
Education and Manpower	7.0	7.3	4	4
Health and Welfare	43.5	56.8	24	28
Veterans' Benefits and Services	6.9	8.7	4	4
Interest	13.7	18.3	7	9
General Government	2.6	3.3	1	2
State and Local (fiscal year)				
Total Expenditures	93.8	116.7	100	100
Education	38.2	47.2	41	41
Highways	14.0	15.4	15	13
Public Welfare	8.2	12.1	9	10

Sources: Department of Commerce, Bureau of the Census; Bureau of the Budget and Treasury Department.

Governments have assumed responsibility for these functions in virtually all countries.

On what basis can the observed concentration of government activity in these areas in all countries and the rise in government activity with increased economic development be explained?

GOVERNMENT ECONOMIC BEHAVIOR

A Utility Function for Government Decision-Makers

Household behavior has been interpreted as an attempt to maximize expected life-time utility: income, wealth, consumption, leisure, work, and security all enter into household utility functions. Business behavior was explained as the attempt to maximize a utility function that included profits, growth, and security. The utility function of business managers was derived from, but not necessarily identical to, the utility function of the ultimate household owners of business firms. The reflection of owner preferences in capital market valuations of individual business firms exercises a significant external discipline on manager freedom and discretionary power.

In a similar manner, it is possible to postulate a utility function for government decision-makers. This procedure may be applied to federal, state, and local governments, and to private nonprofit institutions generally — foundations, educational and religious institutions, hospitals, and community organizations of all types. The utility function of decision-makers in government and nonprofit institutions will be related to a particular institution's goals and objectives, which in turn are derived from the preferences of the individuals whom the institution purports collectively to represent and serve.

The goods and services provided by governments and nonprofit institutions are not sold for a profit and frequently are not exchanged on any market. As a result, it is difficult to assess the value of their programs. In the absence of a market price, there is no profit yardstick by which to judge success or efficiency. As competition is largely absent, though a kind of rivalry may exist, there is no assurance that the inefficient will be revealed, punished, or eliminated. Finally, no capital market exists on which the performance of governments and other nonprofit institutions are continually measured and evaluated. For all of these reasons, the relationship between the utility function of the decision-makers of governments and nonprofit institutions and the utility function of the individuals they represent or serve is likely to be extremely tenuous, more so than was the case of private business firms.

An Economic Theory of Government

Attempts have been made to develop a theory of government behavior based on the basic postulate that democratic governments may be regarded as attempting to maximize the length of their tenure in office. A democratic political system serves many of the functions of a market mechanism, enabling public preferences to be expressed periodically through votes cast for competing political parties. But the political system is a very imperfect substitute for the market mechanism. Instead of a large number of dollar votes distributed by consumers to reflect intensities of preferences among individual commodities, electors have ordinarily but a single vote and must choose among parties each offering an entire program of public goods. A single vote does not permit expression of intensities of preferences. Moreover, the rule of majority voting, 50 percent plus one, cannot reflect minority opinion. The problem of how political influence is distributed among different individuals and groups in different political decisions has proven extremely intractable to sociologists and political scientists because of the difficulty of measuring political power.

An additional explanation for the difficulty of developing operational models of government behavior lies in the fact that the behavior of large aggregates, to which the law of large numbers applies, may be predicted with greater confidence than the behavior of a single or a few economic units, in which a multiple of noneconomic factors — personality, leadership, tradition, ideology, tactics, and accident — interact to produce a highly particular historical event. To the extent that an outcome is unique, it is possible to speculate about its causes, but since the validity of any particular explanation cannot be refuted, a large number of competing interpretations may coexist.

Normative Rules for Government Behavior

In view of the extreme difficulty of developing a model of government that can serve to describe or predict government behavior in the real world, economists have fallen back on normative analysis of government operations. Rather than attempt to develop descriptive models of government behavior appropriate to different types of political systems, they have developed a set of normative rules describing the policy that a government would follow if it attempted to attain certain goals. These goals are concerned with aspects of the public interest, that is, the general welfare of all individuals in the economy. This is not to say that real-world governments actually behave in this way, but rather what their behavior would be if they acted to achieve these goals. The approach is similar to that earlier adopted for business managers, in which rules for share-price maximization were deduced that managers would follow if they act in the interest of the shareholders.

This approach is also not without pitfalls, in particular with regard to what constitutes policy "in the general interest." This goal is much more difficult to specify than the goals for a business firm. As described in the preceding chapter, it is possible to define an efficient solution, which states that situation A is preferable to situation B if nobody feels worse off in A than in B, and at least one person feels better off. "Better off" or "worse off" are measured by personal preferences. But there are an infinitely large number of efficient solutions, each corresponding to a different distribution of real income. To choose among them, it would be necessary to postulate a *social welfare function* that would permit the "best" of all the efficient optima to be selected. If the gainers in one situation are permitted to compensate the losers, a wider range of preferred states may be defined, but in the real world such compensation is ordinarily not feasible. The attempt to solve some of the problems involved in the moral judgment of various states of the world is known as *welfare economics*.

A fundamental limitation of welfare economics is the assumption that individual utility functions are independent. Individuals are assumed to derive utility from their own economic position but to be indifferent to the position of others. In fact, individual utility functions are highly *interdependent*. Envy, sympathy, benevolence, and malevolence are central modes of human experience. Although motives other than self-interest may be ignored as secondary for the analysis of market exchange, considerations in addition to self-interest become central when individuals are asked to choose among alternative government policies that affect many other members of the society. As stated by Reinhold Niebuhr,

> The finest task of achieving justice will be done neither by the Utopians who dream dreams of perfect brotherhood nor yet by the cynics who believe that the self-interest of nations cannot be overcome. It must be done by the realists who understand that nations are selfish and will be so till the end of history, but that none of us, no matter how selfish we may be, can be only selfish.

Because of the impossibility of making interpersonal comparisons of utility, the conclusions of welfare economics are extremely restrictive and have been of very limited significance for government policy. Virtually all real-world political decisions affect some individuals adversely. Where such conflict exists, welfare economics is of little use, as it is impossible to *prove* that the disutility of the losers does not exceed the utility of the gainers.

Nevertheless, if governments are to make policy, they cannot avoid making interpersonal utility comparisons. They must proceed as if they knew the social welfare function, even though such a function cannot be objectively derived. In practice, governments typically use broad aggregative and quantitative concepts of general welfare, per capita real income and gross national product, as measures of economic success. This usage is equivalent to the rule that the economic gains to some must exceed the losses to others, each measured at market value. The resulting degree of income inequality is then tempered by welfare and tax policy. Distributional effects of government policy are of paramount concern to particular groups and, to the extent that these groups possess political power, they attempt to shape policies in their own interest.

The Three Branches of Government

It is useful for purposes of analysis to regard governments as if they were divided into three separate branches. The *allocation branch* is concerned with the efficient allocation of resources in the economy with the goal of maximum total output. The *distribution branch* is concerned with the distribution of income among individuals and groups with the goal of equity. The *stabilization and growth branch* is concerned with the performance of aggregate output over time. Each branch is assumed to consider only its own objectives and to proceed on the assumption that the objectives of the other branches have been realized. In the real world, any particular government policy of course has allocation, distribution, and stabilization effects simultaneously. As will be shown, the formulation of rational social policy becomes extremely difficult, as allocation or stabilization policies are supported or opposed due to their distributional implications.

THE ALLOCATION BRANCH

In order for a private market economy to function, the government must set up and enforce certain constitutional rules of the game. These include the definition and enforcement of property rights, freedom of contract, and the exclusion of certain behavior with strong negative externalities, such as fraud and force. As will be seen, the government must also define and control the particular asset used as money, the medium of exchange. As these rules determine how the game is played, one of the most important and continuous functions of government is the redefinition of the rights and responsibilities of property ownership in response to changes in the economic environment associated with advances in technology, population growth, and capital accumulation.

The Conditions for Allocational Efficiency

As shown in the previous chapter, a competitive market system under certain highly restrictive conditions can be shown to establish an efficient allocation of resources, defined as a situation in which no one can be made better off without making someone else worse off. In this configuration, the ratio of the prices of all goods is equal to the ratio of their marginal costs of production. Because the economy is operating on its production possibility frontier, a greater quantity of output cannot be produced with the existing inputs of resources and technology. At the same time, as the allocation of resources is such that the ratio of all prices is equal to the ratio of their marginal utilities, consumers cannot achieve a higher level of satisfaction without making some other members of the community worse off. Resources are efficiently allocated when the following conditions hold. These ensure that for each economic good and service marginal social benefit equals marginal social cost:

$$MSB = MPB = MU = P = MR = MC = MPC = MSC.$$

As implied by the foregoing equation, seven conditions must be satisfied if this result is to occur:

1. $MSB = MPB$ Absence of external benefits.
2. $MPB = MU$ Consumers are the best judges of their own self-interest.
3. $MU = P$ Optimizing consumer behavior.
4. $P = MR$ Perfectly competitive markets; absence of economies of scale.
5. $MR = MC$ Optimizing producer behavior.
6. $MC = MPC$ Businesses are the best judges of their own self-interest.
7. $MPC = MCS$ Absence of external costs; absence of nonpecuinary returns.

In addition, use of the price system presupposes the following two initial conditions:

1. Nonzero marginal costs.
2. Efficiency of price as an exclusion principle.

These conditions taken together are extremely restrictive and in fact are never completely realized in practice. Whenever one or more of the above conditions necessary for market efficiency are not satisfied, *market prices* will not conform to efficiency *shadow prices*. The allocation branch of the government has a potential role to play whenever *allocational inefficiencies* exist. Although this role is very broad, the operative word is "potential." Government regulation or provision ordinarily creates its own inefficiencies. The "best" outcome will depend on a pragmatic trade-off of inefficient private solutions against inefficient government solutions. The real world is always the world of the second best.

Perfect Competition

In the absence of perfect competition, price will exceed marginal cost and too little of the goods and services will be produced relative to the competitive optimum. One important function of the allocation branch is thus to preserve and enforce competitive conditions and to prevent monopolistic misallocation of resources. This task is undertaken by antitrust and monopoly policy. In the United States, the government prohibits or requires government approval of behavior by individual firms such as merger, where the result is to reduce the degree of competition, any behavior whose effect is to create artificial barriers to entry or eliminate competition, and explicit price collusion.

In all countries, the effects of government intervention in many markets is to weaken competitive forces by, for example, the creation of entry barriers through tariffs and licensing or the prohibition of price competition through fair trade legislation. This result may largely be attributed to the distributional effects of allocation policy and the dominance of producer interests in the political process.

For goods whose production is subject to decreasing costs, a conflict exists between competitive markets and efficient production. Perfect competition is frequently not an alternative. Larger firms can produce at substantially lower average cost due to economies of scale, but this large size also results in the possession of market power. Policy must be decided for particular markets individually by a weighing of costs and benefits. Dynamic considerations of the behavior of costs over time, sometimes termed *infant industry* arguments, may justify interference.

In the extreme case of natural monopoly, governments typically either regulate the prices that may be charged by the monopolist or operate directly and provide the good or service collectively.

Business Optimizing Behavior and Sovereignty

It is the pressure of competition that forces businesses to be efficient and pushes them to maximize profits. In markets in which business firms have market power, managers may have considerable discretionary authority and may be content with a "satisfactory" level of profits and performance.

Through full disclosure, publicity, and the pressure of public opinion, government's attempt to dissuade firms from realizing excessive profits, insiders from taking advantage of valuable information, and in general to promote socially responsible behavior. Governments must also decide what behavior and expenses are to be considered as deductible for tax purposes. In the United States, the tax laws have played a role in encouraging the growth of advertising, corporate philanthropy, political contributions, and retained earnings.

Consumer Optimizing Behavior and Sovereignty

For some goods, the principle of consumer sovereignty is disregarded. Such cases are in part attributable to the existence of externalities, as in the prohibition of gambling, prostitution, and drugs, or the requirement and subsidization of universal schooling. Other cases appear to reflect primarily the belief that consumers are in fact not the best judges of their own self-interest, as when high excise taxes are placed on cigarettes and alcohol.

The market reflects the consumption preferences of existing market participants in proportion to their dollar votes. Governments may attach their own weights to the preferences of different groups. There is a widespread belief that private markets, if left to themselves, do not produce enough of certain goods from a social viewpoint (the creative and performing arts, natural wilderness areas), and government subsidy to supplement the dollar votes of the market is deemed necessary. Consumers may have an *option want* for the availability of these goods not expressed in current market purchases.

Governments also accept the responsibility to take a longer view than individual consumers and to consider the interests of generations as yet unborn. This responsibility is particularly important for decisions that concern the proportion of income to be saved, the rate of consumption of depleting resources, and long-lived or irreversible investment decisions.

Externalities

Externalities occur when consumption or production of a good or services affects the utility of others in addition to the consumer or producer. The existence of externalities or neighborhood effects is probably the most important single reason for government attempts to shape the outcome of the private market. Although externalities exist to a degree for all goods and services — no man is self-contained — for some goods these externalities are particularly important. Where externalities exist, the *shadow prices* that would result in efficient allocation ($MSB = MSC$) may diverge widely from existing market prices. Implicit behind consumer and producer sovereignty is the assumption that individuals should be allowed to decide freely how to make themselves better off, provided that they do not in the process make others worse off.

On the cost side, there are many activities in which social costs considerably exceed private costs, as in air and water pollution, congestion, location, deforestation, and employment damaging to the health or development of the worker. Too many of these goods will be produced by private markets ($MSC > MSB$). Governments may prohibit certain behavior or attempt to internalize these external costs, so that they will be borne and therefore taken into consideration by the private decision-maker.

On the benefit side, externalities may be positive or negative. Reforestation, urban planning, health, flood control, research, transportation, and education are all areas in which benefit to society exceeds the benefit to the private producer or consumer. Too few of these goods will be produced ($MSB > MSC$). Governments may attempt through subsidy or public provision to increase the output of such activities.

External benefits may also be negative. Prostitution, gambling, drugs, and alcohol are examples in which social benefits are held to be less than private benefits, as third parties receive disutility from such activities. Too many of these goods will be produced by the market ($MSC > MSB$).

As population density increases with the growth of urban environments, the proportion of externalities in private behavior increases and greater planning is required to shape the outcome of the market. People's utilities become increasingly interdependent. To the extent that art is a manifestation of order, aesthetically successful architecture and environmental design can never be the result of independent planning but can be created only within an aesthetic framework accepted by or imposed on all realty owners in the community. For this reason all cities have zoning codes. As the sprawling entrances of American towns and cities suggest, artistic harmony is one of the first casualties of an unplanned environment. The private market is concerned with efficiency, not aesthetics.

PUBLIC GOODS

For some goods, the marginal cost in the short run is zero. Such goods, once produced, can be made available to additional users at no extra cost. *Pure collective goods* are defined as goods that must be consumed by everyone equally, such as defense, justice, broadcasting, police protection, and roads. For many such goods, the price system is inefficient as a means of allocating resources and raising revenue. Once provided, the benefits cannot be denied to any individuals, whether they pay or not. In this case price as an exclusion principle breaks down.

Collective goods may be enjoyed by many once they are provided at all. No matter how important, how much they add to human satisfaction, they will not be provided by private enterprise if they cannot be sold on a market for a profit. Such goods must be provided by the allocation branch, and taxes must be levied to transfer resources from private to collective goods production.

The reason why collective goods must be provided through the political rather than the private marketplace, no matter how great their benefits relative to their costs, may be illustrated by the growing problem of air pollution. Suppose that there were one million individuals in the society and that each of them would be willing to pay $100 to be able to breath clean, pure air and (in some places) to see the sun and the stars again. Suppose further that air pollution came from furnaces and automobiles, and that a purification device available at a unit cost of $10 and attached to chimneys and exhaust pipes would catch all smoke particles.

Even though each individual valued clean air at $100, so that the total benefits from introducing the device would be $100 million while its total cost would be only $20 million (assuming each individual has one house and one car), such an antismog device would never be provided by private enterprise in private markets.

The difficulty may be illustrated by the payoff matrix faced by each individual prospective purchaser.

	No one else purchases public good	A few others purchase public good	All others purchase public good
I purchase public good	[1] Air is dirty. Payoff: −$20	[2] Air is dirty. Payoff: −$20	[3] Air is clean. Payoff: +$80
I don't purchase public good	[4] Air is dirty. Payoff: $0	[5] Air is dirty. Payoff: $0	[6] Air is clean. Payoff: +$100

Due to the nature of a public good as collectively consumed, behavior of others determines whether the air is clean or dirty. The individual's own decision has no perceptible effect on the amount of pollution. His strongly preferred outcome is represented in cell 6, and his second and nearly as strongly preferred preference in cell 3. But whatever estimate he makes of what everyone else will do, his expected payoff is always higher by not purchasing the antismog devices himself. Because whether the air is clean or dirty depends virtually entirely on what others do, it is always in his self-interest to be a freeloader.

If each device cleans the air by the proportion of the total smog that it eliminates, it would be worth only $.005 to each purchaser. But this means that it is also worth $.005 to him whenever *anyone else* buys a device, and that if everyone buys the total benefits will be $100 million. Because the benefits of public goods are consumed by all, no one will buy them for himself but everyone wants his neighbors to buy them. The private market, no matter how competitive, will not perform its allocative function efficiently.

One solution might be to attempt to educate everyone to stress his responsibility to the community and so include the utility of others to a greater extent in his own utility function. But even if through persuasion and propaganda the government succeeded in inducing each individual to value clean air at $1,000, because he sees its effects on others, the value of each device to the purchaser would still only be $.05. Everyone would have to become virtually selfless if individual action were to be relied on in the face of the self-interest temptation to be a freeloader. Selflessness is observed in small groups such as the family and in larger groups under exceptional conditions. But no utopian community based on selflessness has yet survived. The instinct of self-interest and self-love appear to be too strong.

Another alternative is to decide collectively to provide antipollution devices through the government. The government supplies such goods at zero cost and individuals pay the cost collectively in the form of taxes. This presupposes that the government has jurisdiction over the entire geographic area. A related alternative would be to pass a law forbidding anyone from polluting the air. Each individual is then required to purchase and install an antismog device.

Collective action always involves coercion. In this case, each individual is required to give up his freedom to pollute the environment, just as he is required to obey a large number of other rules and prohibitions as a member of a community. In return he receives assurance that all other individuals will also give up their rights to pollute the environment. The same argument applies, for example, to the prohibition of murder.

Negative freedom, in the sense of freedom from coercion of the individual by the state, is always reduced by increased government intervention. But *positive* freedom, in the sense of freedom to realize one's desires, in this case to breathe clean air, may be increased. Individuals may be free in the eyes of the law, yet unable to do what they want to do, because of irremediable or remediable coercion by the environment. No one will presumably ever be free to jump twenty feet in the air. But how really free is a deprived ghetto dweller or a peasant to realize his material or spiritual desires? The weighing of the trade-off between negative and positive freedoms is involved in virtually all decisions to alter the margin of collective versus individual authority.

The Quantity of Public Goods

The formal rule for the optimum provision of public goods and services is identical for the public sector and for the private sector: Continue to provide public goods until the marginal social benefit from increased government expenditures is equal to the marginal social cost of increased taxation. This rule is illustrated in Figure 11-1. Such a condition is purely formal until these magnitudes are known. A problem arises once it is admitted that different individuals prefer different public goods, so that the benefits will differ.

Consumer preferences for private goods are revealed by dollar votes that enable producers to determine the quantity of different goods and services to produce. As public goods are not sold on a market, the problem arises of how consumer preferences are to be revealed. What quantity of public goods do individuals want the government to supply? Were the government to ask individuals directly, the

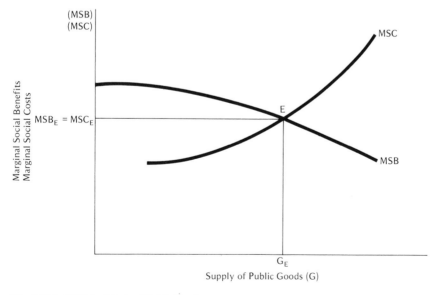

Figure 11-1 Optimum Supply of Public Goods

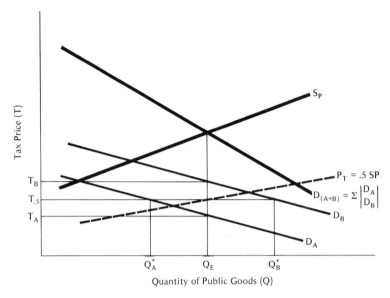

Figure 11-2 Differential Demand for Public Goods

question could be answered rationally only if a tax price were attached. Referenda are occasionally used for such purposes.

The determination of the efficient quantity of public goods is illustrated in Figure 11-2. Assume there are only two individuals in the economy, A and B. The tax price and cost of production of public goods is measured on the vertical axis, and the quantity of public goods supplied on the horizontal axis. The supply curve of producing public goods is represented by S_p, and the demand for public goods by the two individuals is represented by D_A and D_B, respectively. Because once the public goods are produced, each individual receives the same amount of them, the community demand curve $D_{(A + B)}$ must be represented by a *vertical* summation of the individual demand curves rather than a horizontal summation as is the case with private goods. Any given quantity produced is consumed by everyone.

The optimum quantity of public goods, where marginal social benefits equal marginal social costs, is represented by Q_E. At this point, the marginal cost equals the sum of the marginal utilities of all the individuals in the economy. In order for each individual to pay a tax price in proportion to benefit received, A would pay T_A and B would pay T_B.

Conflict and the Nonexistence of an Optimum Supply of Public Goods

The difficult problem now arises: How are true preferences for public goods to be revealed? If individuals know that they are to be taxed in proportion to benefits received, they would have an incentive to conceal and understate their true preferences. The amount of taxes each citizen pays would not perceptibly affect the total amount of public goods produced and enjoyed. As a result, true preferences would not be disclosed to the government, and it would not have the information to supply the optimum amount.

The government might decide to tax individuals on some other basis. Assume for simplicity that both A and B were taxed an equal amount. The tax price to each is then equal to half the total cost of providing public goods $(T_{.5})$. Given differences in tastes, neither A nor B would be satisfied with the amount P_E actually supplied, nor would both be satisfied with any other amount. Individual A would prefer less (Q_A^*) and individual B would prefer more (Q_B^*) than the quantity Q_E at the tax price $T_{.5}$. With any tax rule not equal to benefits received, conflict would be irreconcilable.

To summarize, different individuals have different tastes for public goods, as for private goods. But once the decision is made to supply a particular quantity of a public good, the same amount is available to all. As a result, individuals cannot adjust their consumption of individual public goods to make marginal utility proportionate to (given) relative prices as is the case for private goods: $\dfrac{P_A}{P_B} = \dfrac{MU_A}{MU_B}$. Given differing tastes, if all individuals must consume the same amount, marginal utilities could be made proportionate to tax prices only by charging different individuals a different tax for the same good: $\dfrac{T_A}{T_B} = \dfrac{MU_A}{MU_B}$. But if this were done, individuals could not be induced to reveal their true preferences for public goods.

It may be concluded that conflict is intrinsic in the formulation of the optimum supply of public goods. No efficient solution exists. Some individuals will always prefer more; others with differing tastes will always prefer less, whatever the amount supplied. On these grounds, it is in an individual's self-interest to locate in a community where others have similar tastes for public goods. It is similarly in his self-interest to freeload and to locate in a community or country where others have higher incomes.

If taxes are based on ability to pay, disagreement over the optimum allocation of public goods may be accentuated. The rich are then in effect charged a higher tax price for the same goods than the poor. Other things being equal, the rich as a result will prefer fewer and the poor more public goods. However, depending on the type of public good provided and its income elasticity of demand, the rich will prefer more of certain types of public goods, for example, airports, than the poor, even though they pay a higher tax price.

Benefit-Cost Analysis

The condition for an optimal supply of public goods such as shown in Figure 11-1, equality of marginal social benefit and marginal social cost, is purely formal unless these magnitudes are known. *Benefit-cost analysis* is an attempt to provide decision-makers with better information on which to base the supply of public goods. By enumerating, estimating, and evaluating the benefits associated with particular public programs and by estimating the costs of providing these public goods, total and marginal benefit-cost ratios can be calculated. This knowledge enables alternative programs to be evaluated and compared and the return at the margin on different programs to be estimated.

It is extremely difficult to evaluate the benefits of public expenditures such as defense, foreign aid, state department, space exploration, and research and development. But for many government programs, a rough sort of quantitative estimation of benefits can be attempted, as for education, highways, health, housing, environmental conservation, and manpower training.

Even if benefits cannot be measured directly, as in the case of defense, it may be possible to calculate the costs of realizing the same objective by different systems and techniques; for example, planes versus missiles for "first strike" or "second strike" capability. Such an analysis is termed *systems analysis.* To delineate the degree of uncertainty involved, it is useful to make high and low assumptions about various costs and benefits and then to look at the range over which the benefit-cost ratios vary as calculated under different assumptions, from the most favorable to the most unfavorable. This procedure is termed *sensitivity analysis,* since it reveals how sensitive or robust the conclusions are with respect to a change in the underlying assumptions.

With regard to public investment goods it is particularly important that future benefits and costs be discounted at an appropriate rate of discount, a rate similar to that applied in the private sector. Unless this is done resources will not be allocated correctly between the public and private sector, nor among public investment projects of differing duration.

Political Imperfections

In the real world, preferences for public goods are revealed through the political system by political votes rather than dollar votes for competing candidates and parties. Even democratic political systems are much less efficient than the market for the expression of preferences and the enforcement of efficiency. Although each man receives one vote, he cannot distribute his vote to reveal his preferences among different public goods but must chose between "packages" of public goods as proposed by competing parties. Moreover, party programs, in an attempt to capture as large a number of votes as possible, are typically framed in broad generalities to avoid offending anyone.

Majority rule is but one of a large number of possible collective decision rules. Different rules are likely to be appropriate for different decisions. There is nothing sacred about the rule of 50 percent plus one. For certain questions for collective choice, 20 percent or 80 percent plus one may produce a preferable result, for example, to protect intensely held feelings of minorities.

As there is rivalry but no competition among governments and departments in the production of public goods and services, inefficiency is difficult to eradicate. Absence of profits removes the criterion by which performance is measured in the private sector. The natural tendency of bureaucratic organization to expand due to the personal interests of bureaucrats (Parkinson's Law) is more difficult to resist in the absence of a quantifiable measure of output performance.

Allocation and distribution considerations are always combined in any particular policy. In the budgetary process by which taxes and expenditures are determined there is no comprehensive balancing of revenues and expenditures. Individual expenditure programs are considered separately, with the outcome being determined by bargaining among different political interest groups.

Equal political influence among citizens is an ideal goal rather than a description of democratic systems. In the real world, political power is not distributed equally. In a pluralistic society, different groups characteristically have a disproportionate influence in the formulation of public policy in areas where their interests are paramount.

THE DISTRIBUTION BRANCH

For any given distribution of dollar votes, the market under certain conditions has been shown to generate an efficient allocation of resources. Dollar votes reflect individual consumer preferences weighted by consumer income. Consumer income in turn is determined by the distribution of ownership of human capital and property, and the market price of their services. The share of property as the residual remaining after contractual labor costs reflects the degree of monopoly and the relative bargaining strengths of labor and capital. A change in the distribution of wealth or market power will result in a new distribution of income and a new composition of demand for goods and services, to which the market will respond with a new allocation of resources.

With regard to defining an optimum tax rate structure, governments are at sea without a compass or a rudder. In view of the impossibility of interpersonal utility comparisons, it is impossible even conceptually to define an optimum degree of tax progression or regression. Progressive tax rates cannot be justified on the basis of diminishing marginal utility. Redistribution can be based only on the ethical or aesthetic judgment that the existing degree of inequality is immoral, unfair, or unlovely.

Income Redistribution

As shown in the previous chapter, wealth ownership is highly unequally distributed in capitalist economies, with property ownership being much more highly concentrated than ownership of human capital. In most countries the government uses its coercive authority to redistribute income and wealth in the direction of greater equality.

Table 11-4 presents estimates of the proportion of federal income tax paid by different income groups and a comparison of the before-tax and after-tax distribution of income. While the top fifth of the population received 45 percent of total personal income, it paid an even greater proportion, 61 percent, of total federal income taxes. The top 5 percent paid more than one third of all taxes. Nevertheless, the net effect of the federal personal income tax on the relative distribution of income was not substantial. For each group except the upper fifth, the share of total income after tax was changed by less than 1 percent.

Table 11-4 DISTRIBUTION OF BEFORE- AND AFTER-TAX PERSONAL INCOME AND FEDERAL INCOME TAX LIABILITY, 1962 (MEAN AMOUNT IN DOLLARS AND PERCENT)

| | Family Personal Income | | Tax Liability | | After Tax Income | | Tax Rate |
	Dollars	Percent	Dollars	Percent	Dollars	Percent	Percent
Lowest Fifth	1,662	4.6	63	1.7	1,599	4.9	3.8
Second Fifth	3,966	10.9	238	6.3	3,727	11.5	6.0
Third Fifth	5,938	16.3	465	12.3	5,474	16.8	7.8
Fourth Fifth	8,241	22.7	711	18.8	7,529	23.1	8.6
Top Fifth	16,505	45.5	2,297	60.9	14,208	43.7	13.9
Total	7,262	100.0	755	100.0	6,507	100.0	10.4
Top 5 percent	28,482	19.6	5,451	36.1	23,020	17.7	19.1

Source: Survey of Current Business, Department of Commerce, Office of Business Economics; Current Population Reports, Bureau of the Census.

As shown in the final column of Table 11-4, the average effective tax rate paid was 10 percent, rising from 4 percent for the lowest fifth to 14 percent for the highest, and 19 percent for the upper 5 percent. This effective rate is in sharp contrast to nominal personal income tax rates, which in this period rose from 20 to 91 percent. This discrepancy between nominal and effective rates is due to the large number of exemptions, exclusions, and deductions written into the tax code. If capital gains were included in income the effective personal income tax rate would become regressive at upper income levels.

Table 11-5 presents one estimate of effective tax rates paid by income class to all levels of government. As may be seen, state and local taxes are regressive and fall proportionately more heavily on lower income groups. The total tax incidence of all levels of government appears U-shaped, with both the poor and the rich paying a higher proportion of their total income in taxes.

The net redistributive effect of all government operations can only be found by comparing the incidence of taxation by income class with the estimated incidence of government expenditure programs. For pure public goods, this incidence is extremely difficult to determine, and the estimates are sensitive to the assumptions made. As rich and poor do not benefit equally from public education, it is not appropriate to assume average benefits are measured by average costs of providing the public good. The most important public good quantitatively, defense expenditures, is probably best regarded as an intermediate good, a cost of maintaining the system, even though by convention all government expenditures are treated as final goods in the national accounts.

Table 11-5 EFFECTIVE TAX RATES BY INCOME CLASS, 1960 (PERCENT OF MONEY INCOME)

Tax Sources	Family Money Income							
	Under $2,000	$2,000–$2,999	$3,000–$3,999	$4,000–$4,999	$5,000–$7,499	$7,500–$9,999	$10,000 and Over	Total
Federal Taxes								
1. Individual Income Tax	3.9	7.0	7.9	6.6	6.7	8.1	15.6	10.4
2. Estate and Gift Taxes							1.2	0.4
3. Corporate Profits Tax	11.4	10.8	6.5	5.3	3.5	2.3	7.4	5.3
4. Federal Exercises and Customs	9.6	9.9	7.1	7.2	4.8	2.0	1.1	3.3
5. Social Security Contributions	12.9	14.3	12.0	9.0	5.7	3.4	1.4	4.4
6. Total Federal Taxes	37.8	42.0	33.6	28.1	20.8	15.7	26.6	23.9
State and Local Taxes								
7. Individual Income Tax	0.2	0.2	0.5	0.6	0.6	0.6	0.8	0.6
8. Estate and Gift Taxes							0.3	0.1
9. Corporate Profits Tax	0.6	0.6	0.4	0.3	0.2	0.1	0.4	0.3
10. Sales and Excise Taxes	11.2	11.7	8.6	8.7	5.8	2.5	1.4	4.0
11. Property Taxes	12.7	10.8	7.0	6.7	5.0	3.1	2.0	4.0
12. Social Security Contributions	1.6	1.8	1.6	1.1	0.8	0.8	0.4	0.8
13. Total State and Local Taxes	26.2	25.1	18.0	17.4	12.4	7.1	5.3	9.8
Total Taxes, Federal, State, and Local	64.1	67.2	51.6	45.5	33.2	22.8	31.9	33.7

Source: W. I. Gillespie, "Effect of Public Expenditures on the Distribution of Income," in R. Musgrave (ed.), *Essays in Fiscal Federalism* (Washington, 1965).

Studies of net incidence made for the United States suggest a substantial proportionate increase in real income for the lowest income classes, combined with a relatively small proportionate decline in real income of upper income groups. The size of the distribution branch as measured by net incidence is typically a small proportion (10 to 20 percent) of total budgetary expenditures and receipts. Alternatively expressed, by far the largest proportion of actual taxes paid by different income classes appear to be offset by benefits received, a *quid pro quo*. But benefits are estimated typically by average costs. Although this procedure may be unavoidable for national accounting, it is a much more dubious assumption for the question of distribution. The value of police protection, for example, varies widely by income class.

Principles of Taxation

There are two quite separate normative principles of taxation, the *benefit principle* and the *ability principle,* corresponding to the quite different objectives of the allocation and distribution branch. The benefit principle regards taxes as the price paid in exchange for public goods, a *quid pro quo* analagous to private market exchange. The goal of the allocation branch is that taxes ought to be in proportion to benefits received. The net result is to leave the distribution of real income unchanged. Although this situation can never be achieved on an individual basis for reasons developed in the previous section concerning the nature of public goods, it can be realized broadly by income class.

The *ability principle* regards taxes as an involuntary sacrifice that must be made to support the government. In this view, the ability to bear such sacrifices ought to determine the distribution of tax liabilities. This rule corresponds to the goal of the distribution branch to reach a more equitable distribution of income.

Types of Taxes

Taxes are levied on income, wealth, expenditures, and a number of miscellaneous transactions. Table 11-6 presents the chief sources of tax receipts for different levels of government in the United States. The federal government relies primarily on the personal and corporate income tax, while state and local governments receive most of their income from property and sales taxes. Sales and excise taxes are termed *indirect*, because they are not collected from the individuals who are intended actually to pay the tax.

The extent to which the corporate income tax is paid by the owners of the corporation in the form of lower profits or by the customers of the corporation in the form of higher prices is extremely difficult to determine. After-tax rates of return have not fallen over time as corporate income tax rates rose, which suggests that the tax has been passed on by corporations to consumers in higher prices and/or to labor in

Table 11-6 GOVERNMENT TAX RECEIPTS, 1968–70 (BILLIONS OF DOLLARS AND PERCENT OF TOTAL RECEIPTS)

	Dollars		Percent	
Federal Receipts	*1968*	*1970*	*1968*	*1970*
Total	153.7	193.7	100	100
Individual Income Taxes	68.7	90.4	45	47
Corporate Income Taxes	28.7	32.8	19	17
Employment Taxes and Contributions	29.2	39.1	19	20
Contributions for Other Insurance and Retirement	2.1	6.1	1	3
Excise Taxes	14.1	15.7	9	8
Estate and Gift Taxes	3.0	3.6	2	2
Custom Duties	2.0	2.4	1	1
Miscellaneous Receipts	2.5	3.4	2	2
State and Local Receipts (fiscal year)				
Total	91.6	114.5	100	100
Property Tax	26.3	30.7	29	27
Sales and Gross Receipts Tax	20.6	26.5	22	23
Individual Income Tax	5.8	8.9	5	8
Corporation Net Income Tax	2.2	3.2	2	3

Sources: Department of Commerce, Bureau of the Census, and Bureau of the Budget.

lower wages. But it is not known how much rates of return might have risen in the absence of the tax, and the question is still unresolved.

THE STABILIZATION AND GROWTH BRANCH

In addition to the allocation of resources among private and public goods and the distribution of income among individuals, governments are concerned with the behavior and performance of the economy as a whole. An unregulated private market economy, if left to itself, will not necessarily generate and maintain a level of aggregate demand equal to full employment aggregate supply. Prices do not adjust sufficiently rapidly to clear all markets simultaneously.

Investment, consumption, and saving decisions are made by millions of individual economic units. In the short run, market forces will not result in a general equilibrium situation in which total spending decisions by all units exactly equal the maximum total output that the economy can produce at constant prices. Investment decisions in particular are highly volatile. Investment expenditures are based on profit expectations rather than the level of investment consistent with full employment and stable prices. By the use of fiscal and monetary policy, the government attempts to manage the level of total spending to maintain a full employment level of output without inflation and to dampen fluctuations in the level of output.

Similarly, the rate at which the economy in the aggregate grows is determined by private decisions to save and invest and by the rate of technical change. The resultant rate of growth of the economy may be lower than that which individuals who make up the economy collectively regard as socially desirable, particularly in less-developed countries that desire to raise their income rapidly. In consequence, an additional goal of governments is to undertake measures to increase the rate of economic growth and encourage economic development.

These stabilization and growth goals will be considered in Parts IV and VI.

APPENDIX: TAXES AND INTERGOVERNMENTAL FISCAL RELATIONS

Types of Taxes

Taxes are imposed to reduce private spending and divert resources from the private to the public sector of the economy. Different types of taxes have different effects on private economic behavior, are paid by different individuals and are relied upon by different levels of government. The economic effects and incidence of the most important tax sources can be briefly summarized.

The Personal Income Tax

The personal income tax is largely borne by the individuals who pay the tax. The supply of labor appears to be inelastic, at least in the short run, and a number of empirical studies have concluded that, contrary to popular belief, the tax rate does not perceptibly affect work effort or incentives. The income and substitution effects operate in opposite directions. It should be noted that the substitution effect between work and leisure depends on the marginal tax rate, while the income effect operates through the average tax rate. As only monetary income is taxed and nonpecuniary rewards escape taxation, the existence of high rates may, at least over the longer run, affect occupational choice. A double taxation of saving is involved, as income is taxed when received and any income received from saving is again taxed. Income taxes expected to be temporary fall more heavily on current saving to the extent that consumption is a function of permanent income.

The definition of the tax base is a persistent problem. Because of deductions, exemptions, evasion, and tax avoidance, actual rates paid are much lower and less progressive than nominal rates. Capital gains are taxed at lower rates than regular income and in some countries escape taxation entirely, which encourages individuals to transform their income into capital gains form. In addition to reducing effective tax rates paid by the rich, corporations are induced to rely on internal financing through depreciation and retained earnings, so that owners receive a greater proportion of their return in the form of capital gains rather than dividends. This fact has important implications for the operation of capital markets.

Personal income taxation requires bookkeeping records and is difficult to administer where the level of literacy and taxpayer morality is low. For these reasons, the personal income tax is not a primary revenue source in less-developed countries. As individuals can move to escape the tax, potential migration of the tax base limits the extent that it can be relied upon by local and even state governments.

The Corporation Income Tax

The extent to which the corporate income tax is paid by business owners or passed on to consumers in higher prices depends on the time period considered, the tax rate, and the type of markets in which the corporation operates. In perfectly competitive industries in the short run, a tax on profits does not affect marginal cost. As a result, supply and therefore price remain unchanged, and the tax is paid entirely by the owners of business firms. In the longer run, the extent to which the after-tax real rate of return is lowered in competitive industries depends on the elasticity of the long-run supply of capital.

In imperfectly competitive markets, firms that were previously maximizing monopoly profits cannot pass on the tax, either in the short run or in the long run. The best-profit price and output before tax will still result in the largest after-tax profits.

Difficulty arises in the case of oligopolistic markets, where firms follow target-profit or average-cost pricing and do not utilize to the full their market power to achieve maximum profits. For such firms the corporate income tax may be treated like a rise in costs and passed on in higher prices to consumers.

Empirical studies indicate that after-tax profit rates in the United States have not fallen over the period in which the corporate income tax has been substantially increased, suggesting that the tax has been shifted either to consumers or to labor. But the evidence is inconclusive, as a large number of other valuables that affect profit rates have also changed over the same period, and in the absence of the tax profit rates might have risen.

The issue of who pays the corporation income tax is not yet settled, and the question is extremely important for distributional considerations. If not shifted, the corporation income tax is very highly progressive, falling predominantly on the wealthiest 5 percent of households who own most of the corporate stock. In this case, there is partial double taxation of property income, as the corporation pays the corporation income tax and the owners in addition pay the personal income tax on any dividend income received. If shifted, the incidence of the tax is regressive, as it falls primarily on consumers in the form of higher prices, and consumption expenditures fall as a proportion of income as income rises.

Taxes on Consumption

Taxes on consumption may take the form of a general sales tax, excise taxes on particular commodities, tariffs on imported commodities, a turnover or value-added tax on production, and a general expenditure tax on personal consumption. They are relatively easy to administer and are heavily relied on by less developed countries. The extent to which such taxes raise prices and reduce output, and so are divided between consumers and producers, depends on the relative elasticity of demand and supply curves. An expenditure tax on consumption expenditures avoids the double taxation of saving inherent in income taxation. It has the advantage of taxing individuals in proportion to what they consume and take out of the total output available, rather than in proportion to what they contribute.

All taxes on commodities drive a wedge between the price paid by the consumer and the revenue received by the producer. Price exceeds marginal cost and, unless supply or demand is perfectly inelastic, production of the taxed goods is reduced. As a result, specific taxes on particular commodities change the allocation of resources. They may be justified from the viewpoint of general welfare only on a second-best argument — for example, the existence of monopoly power, infant industries, or externalities — in which case private market prices do not equate marginal social costs and benefits.

Taxes on Wealth

Taxes on wealth may take the form of a property tax, net worth tax, estate, inheritance and gift taxes, and capital levies. Such taxes are typically more expensive to administer because, where no market transaction occurs, the value of the particular wealth forms that constitute the tax base must be assessed. In addition, certain types of wealth such as cash or diamonds may be hidden relatively easily. Local governments in most countries rely primarily on property taxation, largely confined to real estate.

Inheritance and estate taxation are widely accepted as socially desirable to temper the tendency of wealth ownership concentration to increase by intergenerational transfers and to reduce the inequality of opportunity and influence in a democratic society. Many economists and social reformers have argued for the desirability of substantial inheritance taxation, but it remains a small proportion of government tax revenues.

It is also frequently argued that wealth ownership represents a measure of ability to pay in addition to income received, as labor income in comparison to property income both depreciates and has no marketable capital value. In many countries, this argument is used to justify differentially higher tax rates on property income compared to labor income.

Taxes on property income are capitalized and so result in a lower market-value of property. Wealth represents the present value of a future income stream, net of taxes. As a result, total private wealth is reduced by taxes on property income. Assuming the capitalization rate remains unchanged, the value of the property falls in proportion to the tax rate. Taxes may thus be regarded as effecting a partial nationalization of private property. A fifty percent tax is equivalent to fifty percent nationalization. The government shares in the income from property as a silent partner, and although the control and administration of the property remains in private hands, its value is reduced by half. A 100 percent tax rate would be similar to complete nationalization as, except for the utility from status, control, and power, the market value of the private property right would fall to zero, since all income from the property would accrue to the government.

Tax Visibility

Direct personal income and personal wealth taxation have the important advantage that their incidence is visible. The political-technical question of determining the supply of public goods to match social benefits with tax costs and the purely political question of determining the desired degree of income redistribution can then be made on the basis of better information. On the other hand, indirect taxes such as corporation, sales, and excise taxes, whose incidence is hidden, may result in less disutility to taxpayers. Because of tax illusion, individuals are ignorant of the amount of taxes actually paid. While incompatible with rational collective decision-making, this consideration may be of paramount importance in countries where the sense of community cohesiveness or the degree of political stability is tenuous and fragile.

Intergovernmental Fiscal Relations

In the real world, there are not one but several levels of government. In addition to a central government and local or municipal governments, federations have an intermediate level of state or provincial governments. Central governments typically are responsible for national economic questions — for example, defense, international relations, currency, trade, and minimum national standards of welfare. State and local governments typically are responsible for the supply of those public goods produced and consumed locally, such as schools, roads, welfare, and police and fire protection. As shown, the tax sources of these various levels of government also differ substantially.

Different levels of government have different public expenditure responsibilities and revenue-raising resources. In the United States, the expenditure responsibility of state and local governments currently appears to exceed by a considerable margin their revenue capacities. Local governments are better able to judge the quantity and quality of public goods that individual communities prefer. At the same time, they are unable independently to raise tax rates or even to levy certain types of taxes because they fear the migration of their tax base. Individuals and businesses may leave a community if its tax rates exceed those elsewhere. The federal government has a comparative advantage in the collection of taxes while local governments have a comparative advantage in the provision of public goods.

This situation is illustrated in Figure 11-3. The marginal social benefits from local expenditures are drawn as exceeding those from central government expenditures. The rule just given still applies — the marginal social benefit from expenditures by all levels of government should equal the marginal cost of increased taxation of all levels of government. This situation is shown as $MSC^* = MSB^*$ in Figure 11-3. But with no transfers between governments, if each government deter-

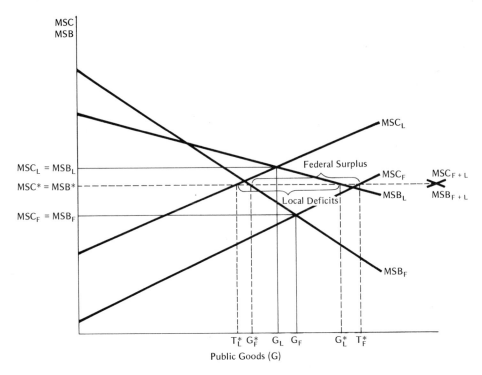

Figure 11-3 Supply of Public Goods with Multilevel Governments

mines its budget individually, a suboptimum allocation will result. Too much central government public goods (G_F) are provided and too little local government public goods (G_L).

In such a situation, total welfare could be increased by a transfer of resources from central to state and local governments, which could be achieved by tax and revenue sharing among levels of government or by grants and transfers from the federal to state and local governments. The goal would be to equalize marginal and social benefits and costs ($MSC^* = MSB^*$) for all levels of government. Federal spending would then be G_F^*, federal taxing T_G^*, and the federal government would subsidize local expenditures by the amount $(G_L^* - T_L^*) = (T_F^* - G_F^*)$.

BIBLIOGRAPHY OF SELECTED PAPERBACKS: PART THREE

Arnold, T. *The Folklore of Capitalism*, Yale University Press.
Batchelder, A. B. *The Economics of Poverty*, Wiley.
Bazelon, D. T. *The Paper Economy*, Random House.
Berle, A. A. *Power without Property: A New Development in American Political Economy*, Harcourt, Brace & World.
Budd, E. C. ed., *Inequality and Poverty*, Norton.
Eckstein, O. *Public Finance*, Prentice Hall.
Galbraith, J. K. *American Capitalism*, Houghton Mifflin.
———*New Industrial State*, New American Library.

Genovese, E. *The Political Economy of Slavery,* Vintage.

Goldman, M. *Controlling Pollution: The Economics of a Cleaner America,* Prentice Hall.

Haddad, W. and Pugh, G., *Black Economic Development,* Prentice Hall.

Haveman R. and Margolis J., ed., *Public Expenditures and Policy Analysis,* Markham.

Heady, E. O., *Primer on Food, Agriculture and Public Policy,* Random House.

Heilbroner, R. L. *The Limits of American Capitalism,* Harper & Row.

Hitch, C. J. and McKean, R. N. *Economics of Defense in the Nuclear Age,* Atheneum.

Jarrett, H., *Environmental Quality,* Johns Hopkins

Kain, J., *Race and Poverty, The Economics of Discrimination,* Prentice Hall.

Kolko, G. *Wealth and Power in America: An Analysis of Social Class and Income Distribution,* Praeger.

Miller, H. *Rich Man, Poor Man,* New American Library.

Monsen, R. J., Jr. *Modern American Capitalism: Ideologies and Issues,* Houghton Mifflin.

Phelps, E. S. ed., *Private Wants and Public Needs,* Norton.

Reagan, M. D. *Managed Economy,* Oxford University Press.

Schultze, C. L. *Politics and Economics of Public Spending: Gaither Memorial Lectures 1968,* Brookings Institution.

Sobel, R. *The Great Bull Market: Wall Street in the 1920's,* Norton.

Sutton, F. X., *et al, The American Business Creed,* Schocken.

Tabb, W., *The Political Economy of the Black Ghetto,* Norton.

Theobald, R. *The Rich and the Poor,* New American Library.

——ed., *Guaranteed Income: The Next Step in Economic Evolution,* Doubleday.

Thurow, L. C. *Poverty and Discrimination,* Brookings Institution.

Weisbrod, B. A., ed., *The Economics of Poverty: An American Paradox,* Prentice Hall.

Zeitlin, M., ed., *American Society, Inc.,* Markham.

PART FOUR

MACROECONOMICS

national income, national wealth, and flow of funds accounts

WHEN YOU CANNOT MEASURE what you are speaking about, when you cannot express it in numbers, your knowledge is of a meager and unsatisfactory kind.

—LORD KELVIN

WHEN YOU CAN MEASURE what you are speaking about, when you can express it in numbers, your knowledge is still of a meager and unsatisfactory kind.

—FRANK KNIGHT

This chapter is concerned with the problem of measurement of economic activity for the economy as a whole. The discussion proceeds in terms of a closed economy without foreign trade. Discussion of the complications introduced by trade with the rest of the world is deferred to Part Five.

Economic Statistics

The data by which an economy is measured are generated by millions of individual enterprises: households, farms, corporations, governments and semipublic agencies, each actively engaged in economic production. The supply and quality of these accounts, elaborate or skimpy, are largely a function of the needs and capacities of the economic units themselves. Households, for example, keep very incomplete accounts of transactions made and assets held.

Out of this vast sea of primary data, the statistical agencies must decide what information to request and collect, how often, and how to assemble and present it for wider use. This is a formidable task. The basic data with which an economic statistician must operate are frequently inaccurate, incomprehensive, biased and, above all, seldom or never the concepts and definitions relevant to theoretical understanding. Nevertheless, if economic analysis is to perform its function as a body of valid generalizations, it must have the empirical, preferably quantitative, counterparts to its basic theoretical concepts. Theory and data are intrinsically interrelated. The very development of economic knowledge has been described thusly:

> A process of continuous interaction between theory and measurement, where hypotheses originate from a preliminary observation and organization of data, indicate further extension and study of the data, and yield the next revision through the utilization of the extended body of systematized information.[1]

NATIONAL INCOME ACCOUNTING

The Circular Flow of Income and Output

Economic goods are exchanged among businesses, households, and governments in a circular flow of income and output. Households buy consumption goods from businesses in product markets in exchange for money, and they receive money income from the sale of the services of productive factors that they own in factor markets. Business units hire factors of production with the income they receive from selling goods and services. Some business units sell their output to other businesses rather than to households. Such goods are termed intermediate goods. This circular flow of income and output is shown diagramatically in Figure 12-1, which repro-

1. Simon Kuznets, "National Income: The Measure and Its Meaning," University Lecture, Johns Hopkins University, 1956.

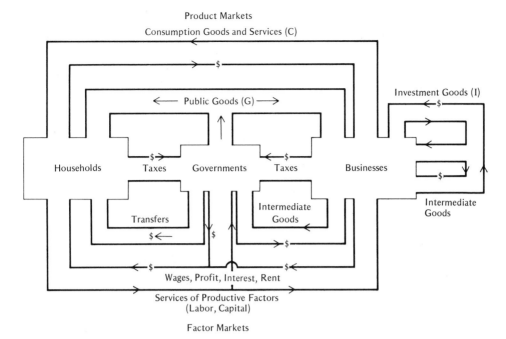

Figure 12-1 Circular Flow of Income and Output

duces the circular flow diagram of Chapter 1 with the addition of a government sector.

Governments participate in the circular flow of income and output by purchasing labor and capital services from households and goods and services from businesses. In return, governments provide, ordinarily at zero charge, public goods and services for households and businesses. Governments raise revenue from taxes levied on household and business income and on household and business expenditure. Government transfer payments are negative taxes and increase the income of the recipients in the private sector.

National output may be measured by estimating the value of the goods and services produced by an economy over some period of time, conventionally one year. As shown in Figure 12-1, the flow of final goods and services produced may be measured in two ways. The first is to monitor the flow of output through the upper loops and add up all the final goods and services produced in product markets, whether consumption or public goods, plus all intermediate investment goods produced but not used up in the current production of final goods. Alternatively, it is possible to monitor the flow of income through the lower loop and add up all the income received in factor markets.

As the total value of the goods and services currently sold or produced must be always identical to the total value of income currently received for production, these two approaches must yield the same total result; the top and bottom loops are identical. Profit is the residual that makes these approaches identical. For the firm's profit and loss statement, profit is defined as the difference between sales plus inventory change — the value of the upper loop — minus costs defined as all contractual payments to factors of production in the bottom loop. The top loop is termed *national product*; the bottom loop is termed *national income*.

National Product

On the product side, all the final goods and services produced by an economy may be classified as either consumption goods and services (C), investment goods (I), or public goods and services (G). This definition is exhaustive: All final goods and services produced must fall into one of these three categories. Therefore, $Y = C + I + G$.

Consumption goods and services are defined as all household expenditures for current output. Household purchases of durable goods, with the exception of houses, are treated as current consumption expenditures. Investment goods represent additions to the stock of intermediate goods purchased or retained by business units. All intermediate goods not used up in the production process are termed investment goods. Investment goods are used to increase the future production of other goods and are defined as business expenditures for plant, equipment, and inventory accumulation. Due to the operational difficulty of estimating their future lifetime, all business purchases of services are by convention regarded as intermediate goods rather than as investment expenditures. Public goods and services are defined as equal to all government expenditure for factors, goods, and services. No attempt is made to estimate intermediate government goods. In the United States' national accounts no distinction is made between public consumption and investment expenditures.

The definition of inventory accumulation as investment makes all private goods either consumption goods or investment goods. Goods intended for consumption that are currently produced but not consumed — like a can of beans that remains on the grocer's shelf — are defined as investment goods as they represent an addition to business inventory.

It is important to distinguish *investment* in the economic sense — the accumulation of physical assets, which in everyday language is sometimes termed *real investment* — from the accumulation of financial assets, which in everyday language is sometimes termed *financial investment*. In economic terminology the accumulation of financial assets is one form of saving. The term *investment* is used exclusively in economics to refer to the accumulation of real capital.

National Income

Alternatively, national income may be measured on the bottom loop by summing up all the payments to the owners of factors of production, wages (W) and salaries (S), rent (R), interest (i), and gross profits (P). This sum is sometimes called national income at factor cost: $Y_{FC} = W + S + R + i + P$.

Gross profits (P), the residual item that makes total factor payments identical to total receipts from goods and services produced, includes business direct taxes, dividends paid out, and business retained earnings.

The existence of government complicates the situation somewhat. Sales taxes and any other indirect business taxes (T_S) drive a wedge between total receipts to business firms and total market expenditures of households and firms. All indirect taxes thus have to be included in the income side if the lower loop is to equal the total value of the upper loop: $Y = W + S + R + i + P + T_S$.

Value Added

A third procedure to measure the value of total goods and services produced is termed the *value-added approach*. Final goods are produced typically by a number of different business firms, each operating at different stages in the production process. The total value of final goods is equal to the increase in value contributed by each firm involved in production and distribution, whether that firm produces goods in intermediate or final form.

The addition to total final value contributed by any one firm may be found by subtracting from the value of its sales the value of all intermediate goods and services that it purchases from other firms. Consider the case of a loaf of bread. The total sales of agricultural producers of wheat are primarily value-added, with the exception of the fertilizer and capital inputs they purchase from other businesses. The value added by the miller is the value of the miller's sales minus the value of the wheat that he purchased from farmers. The value added by the baker is the value of the bread that he sold minus the value of the flour that he purchased from the miller. The value added by the retailer is the value of his sales minus the value of his purchases. In this way, the total value of a loaf of bread can be broken down into the value added by the retailer, the baker, the miller, and the farmer, respectively.

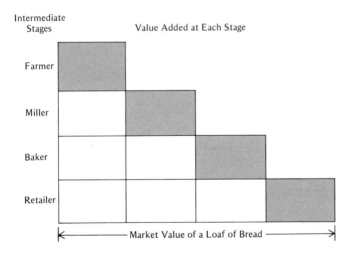

Figure 12-2 Value-Added Approach

These together must add up to the final price at which the bread is sold. This summation is illustrated in Figure 12-2.

National Income Accounts

It is desirable to be familiar with the most frequently used national accounting concepts. *Gross National Product* (GNP) is the term given to the aggregate money value of all final goods and services currently produced. Gross national product minus depreciation — the estimate of previously existing investment goods used up in production over the period — is termed *Net National Product* (NNP).

Net national product minus sales taxes, plus any government business subsidies, is called *National Income at Factor Cost*.

Personal Income may be derived from national income by subtracting corporate income taxes and business retained earnings and adding net government and business transfer payments. Interest paid by government and households, unlike interest paid by business, is by convention regarded as a transfer payment.

Personal income minus personal income taxes is termed *Personal Disposable Income*. Finally, personal disposable income minus consumption expenditures is equal to *Personal Saving*.

Table 12-1   RELATION OF GNP AND PERSONAL INCOME, 1950–71
(BILLIONS OF DOLLARS)

	1950	1960	1970	1971
Gross National Product	284.8	503.8	974.1	1046.8
− Depreciation	18.3	43.4	87.6	95.2
= *Net National Product*	266.4	460.3	886.5	951.6
− Indirect Business Taxes	23.3	45.2	92.9	102.1
− Business Transfer Payments	0.8	1.9	3.9	4.3
− Statistical Discrepancy	1.5	−1.0	−4.5	−4.7
+ Subsidies (less surplus of government enterprises)	0.2	0.2	1.7	0.9
= *National Income* (at Factor Cost)	241.1	414.5	795.9	850.8
− Corporate Profits	37.7	49.9	70.8	80.7
− Contributions for Social Insurance	6.9	20.7	57.6	65.2
+ Government Transfers to Persons	14.3	26.6	75.6	90.5
+ Interest Paid by Government (net) and by Consumers	7.2	15.1	31.7	31.9
+ Dividends	8.8	13.4	25.0	25.5
+ Business Transfer Payments	0.8	1.9	3.9	4.3
= *Personal Income*	227.6	401.0	803.7	857.0
Personal Income as Percent of GNP	79.9	79.6	82.5	82.0

Source: *Survey of Current Business*, Department of Commerce.

The relation of Personal Income to Gross National Product is presented in Table 12-1. In 1971, after depreciation allowances and indirect business taxes were deducted, each nearly 10 percent, national income was about 80 percent of GNP.

The subtraction of business retained earnings in the official derivation of personal income does not imply that this property income is lost to business owners. The effect of retained earnings is to increase the earning power of business corporations, future profits, and therefore personal disposable income of the owners of business firms in the form of capital gains on stock. Capital gains income in any one year may exceed or fall short of business retained earnings. Total capital gains received by stockholders fluctuate irregularly from year to year as the price of corporate shares rises or falls in response to changes in investor expectations of business earning prospects. Most capital gains are *unrealized* in the sense that they are saved and not turned into money by their owners. Capital gains are *realized* only when the stock is sold. Whether realized or unrealized, capital gains add to the value of stockholders' wealth.

Gross National Product, Net National Product, and National Income at Factor Cost tend to move together. Throughout the rest of this book *national income* or *national product* will be used loosely as a generic term to designate the set of these different measures of a country's total economic output.

Table 12-2 presents the various components of personal income. In 1971, about 70 per cent of personal income was made up of wages and salaries. Proprietors' income includes both labor and property income, which are difficult to separate. Rent, dividends, and interest accounted for about 15 per cent of personal income. Of gross corporate profits of approximately 80 billion, 35 billion was paid in corporate income taxes, and nearly half of profits after taxes were retained by corporations.

The behavior of national output and its components for the United States since 1929 is presented in Table 12-3. A striking characteristic is the tenfold growth in GNP over the period. Consumption expenditures rose at a relatively steady rate and exhibit a positive increase in every year. Business investment expenditures varied by a greater proportion from year to year than household consumption expenditures, and in a number of years decreased absolutely. Government expenditures grew most rapidly over the period. They increased sharply during the Korean War, leveled off somewhat, and then grew rapidly again during the war in Vietnam.

With regard to the composition of national output, the share of consumption expenditures fell over the period from 75 to 63 percent of GNP. Gross investment expenditures remained roughly constant at about 15 percent of GNP, although they varied between 3 and 19 percent from year to year. Government purchases of goods and services increased substantially from 10 to 22 percent of GNP.

The Rudiments of National Accounting

Individual households, businesses, and government units may spend more or less than their current income on currently produced goods and services. But for the economy as a whole, total income must necessarily always equal total output. From this necessary equality of income and output, it is possible to deduce some important national accounting identities.

Table 12-2 COMPONENTS OF PERSONAL INCOME, 1950–71

	1950		1960		1970		1971	
	Billions of Dollars	Percent of Personal Income	Billions of Dollars	Percent of Personal Income	Billions of Dollars	Percent of Personal Income	Billions of Dollars	Percent of Personal Income
Wages and Salaries	146.7	64.4	270.8	67.5	541.4	67.4	574.2	67.0
Other Labor Income	3.8	1.6	12.0	4.0	30.8	3.8	33.7	3.9
Proprietors Income	37.5	16.4	46.4	11.5	66.8	8.3	68.4	8.0
Rental Income of Persons	9.4	4.1	15.8	3.9	23.3	3.0	24.3	2.8
Dividends	8.8	3.8	13.4	3.3	25.0	3.1	25.5	3.0
Personal Interest Income	9.2	4.0	23.4	5.8	64.7	8.1	67.5	7.9
Transfer Payments	15.1	6.6	28.5	7.1	79.6	9.9	94.7	11.1
Less: Personal contributions for social insurance	2.9	1.2	9.3	2.3	28.0	3.5	31.2	3.6
= Personal Income	227.6	100.0	401.0	100.0	803.7	100	857.0	100
Less: Personal Taxes	20.7	9.0	50.9	12.7	115.9	14.4	115.8	13.5
= Disposable Personal Income	206.9	91.0	350.0	87.3	687.8	85.6	741.2	86.5
Less: Personal Consumption Outlays (Includes Interest Paid)	193.9	93.7*	333.0	95.1*	633.7	92.1*	680.8	91.9
= Personal Saving	13.1	6.3*	17.0	4.9*	54.1	7.9*	60.4	8.1

* Percent of Disposable Personal Income.
Source: Survey of Current Business, Department of Commerce, Bureau of Economic Analysis.

Table 12-3 COMPONENTS OF GROSS NATIONAL PRODUCT, 1929–71 (BILLIONS OF DOLLARS)

Year	Total GNP	Personal Consumption Expenditures	Percent of GNP	5-Year average	Gross Private Domestic Investment	Percent of GNP	5-Year average	Government Purchases of Goods and Services	Percent of GNP	5-Year average
1929	103	77	75		16.2	16		10.3	10	
1933	55	45	82		1.4	3		10.7	19	
1939	90	67	74		9.3	10		17.6	19	
1945	212	120	56		11	5		82	39	
1946	209	143	69		31	15		27	13	
1947	231	161	69	68.5*	34	15	15.5*	25	11	12.8*
1948	258	174	67		46	18		32	12	
1949	256	177	69		36	14		38	15	
1950	285	191	67		54	19		38	13	
1951	328	206	63		59	18		59	18	
1952	346	217	63	64.2	52	15	16.0	74	22	19.2
1953	365	230	63		53	14		82	22	
1954	365	237	65		52	14		75	21	
1955	398	254	64		67	17		74	19	
1956	419	267	64		70	17		79	19	
1957	441	281	64	64.2	68	15	15.8	86	20	19.8
1958	447	290	65		61	14		94	21	
1959	484	311	64		75	16		97	20	
1960	504	325	65		75	15		100	20	
1961	520	335	64		72	14		108	21	
1962	560	355	63	63.8	83	15	14.8	117	21	20.6
1963	590	375	64		87	15		123	21	
1964	632	401	63		94	15		129	20	
1965	685	433	63		108	16		137	20	
1966	750	466	62	62.2	121	16	15.4	157	21	22.0
1967	794	492	62		117	15		180	23	
1968	864	536	62		126	15		200	23	
1969	929	580	62		138	15		210	23	
1970	974	616	63		135	14		219	23	
1971	1047	662	63		152	14		233	22	

*Four-year average, 1946–49
Source: Survey of Current Business, Department of Commerce, Office of Business Economics.

In an economy without government and foreign trade, all final goods are by definition either consumption goods or investment goods:

1. $Y = C + I$.

Saving is defined as all current income that is not consumed:

2. $S = Y - C$.

Rewriting equation 2, in such an economy all income by definition is either consumed or saved:

2a. $Y = C + S$.

It follows from equations 1 and 2a that for an economy consisting only of households and business firms, actual savings must be equal to actual investment:

3. $S = I$.

This equality must always hold, even though for any individual unit current saving may exceed or be less than its current investment expenditures.

For the household sector, on balance its saving exceeds its current investment. For the business sector, on balance its investment spending exceeds its current saving. This relationship is illustrated for a two-sector model in Figure 12-3, assuming for simplicity that only business units invest. Household income is either spent on consumption goods or saved. Household saving represents demand for financial assets, which are purchased from business units in financial markets. Business investment expenditures are financed in part out of profits from current sales and in part out of borrowing by the sale of financial assets to households.

Once the government sector is introduced, all final goods and services produced are either consumption goods and services, investment goods, or public goods and services:

4. $Y = C + I + G$.

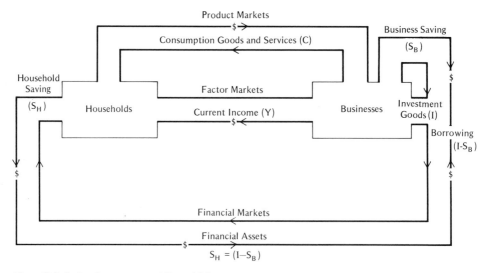

Figure 12-3 Saving, Investment, and Financial Assets

All incomes received are paid in taxes, spent on consumption goods, or saved. Private saving S_P is done by households and by business through retained earnings.

5. $Y = C + S_P + T.$

It follows from equations 4 and 5 that for the economy as a whole, actual private saving plus taxes always equals actual private investment plus government expenditure:

6. $S_P + T = I + G.$

Government saving is sometimes defined as the government's budget surplus, that is, tax receipts minus government expenditures on goods and services. This definition arbitrarily treats all government spending as consumption $(S_G = T - G)$.

Equation 6 may then be rewritten: $S_P + S_G = I$. Thus formulated, private saving plus public saving is identical to total private investment. Equation 6 is then formally identical to equation 3.

This relationship is illustrated in Figure 12-4, again assuming that all investment is undertaken by businesses. Household income is either paid in taxes, spent on consumption goods, or saved. Saving involves the purchase of financial assets. All final goods are either consumption, investment, or public goods and services. Government spending is financed out of taxes and borrowing, the issue of new financial assets. Business investment spending is financed out of retained earnings and borrowing. Recognition of household investment spending would mean that part of household saving takes the form of household accumulation of tangible assets, while only part is devoted to the purchase of financial assets from business and government.

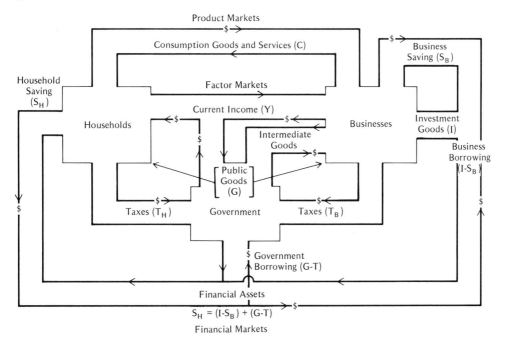

Figure 12-4 Saving, Investment, and Financial Assets with a Government Sector

NATIONAL WEALTH ACCOUNTING

Corresponding to the value of goods and services produced by an economy over some period of time, there is also some stock of wealth representing the value of all assets existing in the economy at any moment of time.

Wealth represents the present market value of expected future income. Future labor income is not capitalized in marketable wealth, as only the services of human capital can be bought and sold. As a result, wealth as measured by market value represents the capitalized value only of future property income. As described in Chapter 9, different types of income streams are discounted at different rates, depending primarily on the degree of uncertainty surrounding their future values.

Tangible Assets

In any consideration of the wealth of an economy it is critically important to distinguish between tangible assets and financial assets. Tangible assets represent the economy's stock of real capital goods, which are combined with labor in the production process to produce real output. With the exception of natural resources, they must themselves be produced with labor and capital. An increase in the proportion of real output devoted as investment to real capital accumulation implies a reduction in the proportion of real output in the form of final consumption goods from which utility is derived. The value of reproducible capital goods is ordinarily governed by their current cost of reproduction as reflected in their market price.

Financial Assets

Financial assets, in contrast, are not part of the economy's real wealth. They are not a factor of production in the production process, although, as will be shown, the types and characteristics of financial assets available, sometimes termed the level of financial technology, and their quantity can influence the amount of real goods and services produced in an economy.

Financial assets represent ownership rights to future income streams. As seen in Chapter 9, they permit the separation of ownership and control of an economy's real wealth. Income received from ownership of financial assets represents a transfer of property income from real wealth administrators, primarily business firms, to ultimate wealth owners, primarily households. This is shown schematically in a simplified form in Figure 12-5. The liabilities and net worth of business firms are represented as financial assets in the balance sheets of their ultimate household owners.

Alternatively expressed, for every financial asset there exists a corresponding financial debt or obligation. It follows from double-entry bookkeeping that the total value of all financial assets owned by all spending units in an economy is identically equal to the total value of all financial liabilities owed by all spending units in the

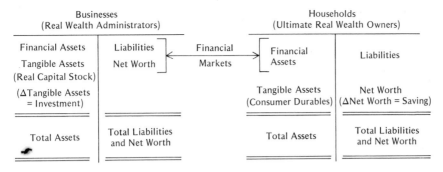

Figure 12-5 Indirect Ownership of Tangible Assets

economy. Providing they are equally valued in the balance sheets of debtors and creditors, financial assets and liabilities are identical for the economy as a whole, leaving national real wealth equal to the net worth of all the ultimate wealth owners in the economy.

National Wealth Accounts

National wealth accounts represent the total of all assets and liabilities existing in the economy at a moment of time. As such, they are simply an aggregation of the balance sheets of all the individual economic units in the economy: households, business firms, and governments.

National wealth accounts for the United States are currently being constructed by government statisticians, but unfortunately they are not yet regularly available. The total value of many tangible asset stocks and their distribution are extremely difficult to estimate, particularly where no market transactions are involved. Table 12-4 presents estimates of the United States National Balance Sheet for 1958 and 1968. Total assets outstanding were estimated at approximately $3,700 billion in 1958, and $7,500 billion in 1968.

Sector Holdings of Tangible and Financial Assets

As may be seen in Table 12-4, of the total tangible assets in the economy of approximately $3000 billion in 1968, $1000 billion were held by households directly, primarily in the form of houses and consumer durables. More than $1250 billion were held by business firms, including agriculture, and $700 billion were held by governments. Plant, equipment and inventories constituted less than half of total tangible assets in 1958, the rest being houses, land, and consumer durables. Households held more than one half ($2300 billion) of the total financial assets in existence in 1968 ($4350 billion), with the second largest share being held by financial institutions ($1400 billion).

Financial institutions are intermediate between the nonfinancial business, household, and government borrowers and the ultimate household lenders. They purchase

Table 12-4 NATIONAL BALANCE SHEET, 1958, 1968 (BILLIONS OF DOLLARS)

Balance Sheet Item	Nonfarm Households		Nonfarm Noncorporate Business		Agriculture*	
Year	1958	1968	1958	1968	1958	1968
Tangible Assets						
Residential Structures	347{	567	16{	100	20{	50
Nonresidential Structures	26}		26}		17}	
Land	92	251	23	29	88	153
Producer Durables	2		27	50	19	34
Consumer Durables	165	234			14	
Inventories			17	23	26	30
Total Tangible Assets	632	1052	108	203	182	266
Financial Assets						
Currency and Demand Deposits	61	107	13	12	6	6
Other Bank Deposits and Shares	141	355			3	
Life Insurance Reserves, Private	100{	466			7	
Pensions	93}				1	
Consumer Credit			5{	9		
Trade Credit			12}			
Bank Loans, n.e.c.						
Mortgages	27	35				
Securities: U.S. Government	59)	110			5	
Securities: State and Local	25}					
Securities: Other Bonds and Notes	11)					
Securities: Preferred Stock,						
Common Stock	333	828				
Equity in Noncorporate Business	Na.	392				
Total Financial Assets	970	2312	30	27	25	
Liabilities						
Currency and Demand Deposits						
Other Bank Deposits and Shares						
Life Insurance Reserves, Private						
Pensions						
Consumer Debt	45)	161	9}	25	1)	24
Trade Debt	2}				2}	
Bank Loans, n.e.c.	2)		12}		4)	
Mortgages	117	244	14	37	11	28
Bonds and Notes						
Total	176	410	41	61	21	51
Net Worth	1426	2954	97	168	187	224
Total Assets or Total Liabilities plus Net Worth	1602	3364	138	229	208	276

*Farm Business 1968.

Source: 1958 — Raymond Goldsmith, *Studies in the National Balance Sheet of the United States,* vol. II (1963).
1968 — *Institutional Investor Study Report of the Securities and Exchange Commission,* (Washington, 1971), Supplementary vol. 1, Tables IB-1-9.

the "primary" financial assets issued by households, businesses, and governments for their portfolios, and issue in exchange their "secondary" securities, primarily to household wealth owners. This intermediation of financial institutions is illustrated schematically in Figure 12-6.

Nonfinancial Corporations		Finance		State and Local Governments		Federal Government		Total	
1958	1968	1958	1968	1958	1968	1958	1968	1958	1968
21 } 181 }	272	1 } 5 }	12	6 } 133 }	376	1 } 35 }	103	411 } 423 }	1537
64	103	4	7	28	111	13	33	311	715
146	233	1	9	5	32	1	16	200 } 179 }	611
79	149					8	14	130	216
490	758	10	29	173	518	57	167	1653	3080
33	28	93	17	11	10	5	7	222	209
2	25	1	3	4	20			150	403
								106 } 94 }	466
8 } 83 }	213	33 } 4 } 54 }	326			2 }	67	46 } 100 } 54 }	621
		136	352		2	8 } 6 } 1 }	8	172	398
18 } 2 } 3 }	19	176 } 31 } 74 }	853	11 } 2 } 1 }	29		1	274 } 61 } 89 }	592
79		44	253					465	1107
									392
276	357	693	1432	30	62	58	92	2082	4349
		223	211			3	5	226	211
		152	412			1		153	412
		109 } 94 }	435					109 } 94 }	466
								46 }	
69 } 26 }	221	6		2	9	3 } 1 }	2	87 } 51 }	529
30	67		2					171	398
70	137	9	124	61	124	289	326	428	593
257	500	632	1282	63	133	298	333	1488	2791
508	615	71	179	140	448	−182	−75	2247	4637
766	1115	704	1461	203	580	116	258	3735	7428

As a result of this "layering" of financial assets, the value of total financial assets in the economy exceeds the value of total tangible assets. This is not the case in less developed economies, where financial claims and transactions are less important.

If valued in the same way, total financial assets and liabilities in the economy

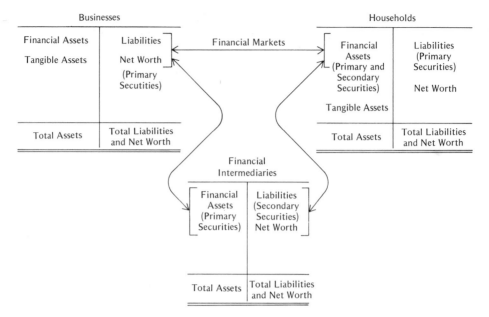

Figure 12-6 Indirect Ownership of Financial Assets

would be precisely offsetting. As may be seen in Table 12-4, in 1968, the total value of financial assets minus equity ownership was equal to the total value of liabilities ($2,800 billion). Net worth of the household sector was approximately equal to the value of all tangible assets in the economy ($3,000 billion). This represents the total real wealth of the economy. As G.N.P. more than doubled over the decade from 1958 to 1968, rising from $450 to $860 billion (Table 12-3), the total national wealth remained about 3½ times as large as G.N.P.

The federal government is shown in Table 12-4 with a negative net worth, since its total liabilities exceed its total assets. This reflects the difficulty of constructing a balance sheet for the public sector. The "assets" on which the central government relies for income are, for the most part, not marketable or capitalized. They rest on the real earning power and willingness to pay taxes of private households and firms. State and local governments have three times the real assets of the federal government.

FLOW OF FUNDS ACCOUNTING

Deficit and Surplus Spending Units

In the National Income Accounts, no mention is made of financial transactions. The accounts could equally well be describing a barter economy. Although saving and investment are always equal by definition for the economy as a whole, this is not the case for individual economic units. The issue or sale of financial assets permits some economic units to invest more than they save. The purchase of financial assets permits other economic units to save more than they invest.

The Flow of Funds Accounts are designed to supplement national income accounts by showing how the surpluses and saving of some economic units finance the deficits and investment of other economic units.

Economic units may be defined as *deficit-spending, balanced,* or *surplus-spending* units, according to whether their total current expenditure on goods and services exceeds, equals, or is less than their total current income received. For deficit-spending units, investment exceeds saving, which may be shown as follows. Total income (Y) is either consumed or saved: $Y = C + S$.

Total expenditures on current output (E) must be for either consumption or investment goods: $E = C + I$.

For deficit-spending units, current expenditures exceed current income: $E > Y$. Substituting, $C + I > C + S$ or $I > S$.

Conversely, for surplus-spending units, income exceeds current expenditure, and saving exceeds investment spending: $Y > E$ or $S > I$.

Sources and Uses of Funds

Deficit-spending units finance the excess of investment over saving by the issue or sale of financial assets. Surplus-spending units allocate the excess of saving over investment to the purchase of financial assets or the repurchase of debt.

Given the dual nature of financial assets, the purchase of financial assets by surplus-spending units must in the aggregate exactly equal the issue of financial assets by deficit-spending units. As total income and output are identical, if one unit spends more than his current income on current output, another must spend less on current output than his current income. This is another way of saying that for the economy as a whole total surpluses of some units must always exactly equal total deficits of other units.

Balance Sheet Changes

Uses of Funds	Sources of Funds
1. ΔFinancial Assets	3. ΔLiabilities (= Net Borrowing)
2. ΔTangible Assets (= Investment)	4. ΔNet Worth (= Saving)
ΔTotal Assets	ΔTotal Liabilities and Δ Net Worth

Flow of Funds Format

Saving (4)
Investment (2)
Net Surplus or Deficit (4-2)
Net Acquisition of Financial Assets (1-3)
Change in Total Financial Assets (1)
Change in Total Liabilities (3)
Statistical Discrepancy (3 + 4 −1 −2)

Figure 12-7 Sources and Uses of Funds

Sources of funds, that is, new command of purchasing power by economic units, come from current income, increases in liabilities (new borrowing), and sales of previously existing assets. Uses of funds, that is, new disposal of purchasing power by economic units, consist of current consumption, the acquisition of new assets, tangible and financial, and the repayment of previously existing debts. As shown in Figure 12-7, sources and uses of funds statements simply record changes in the balance sheet of an economic unit over a particular period.

By convention, instead of including current income and current consumption separately in the flow of funds accounts, they are netted out. Saving, the excess of current income over current consumption, which is also equal to the change in net worth, is listed as a source of funds. As shown in Figure 12-7, the net surplus or deficit of an economic unit on current account is exactly equal to its net acquisition of financial assets.

National Flow of Funds Accounts

National Flow of Funds Accounts ideally would record all financial transactions occurring in the economy over a particular period. Unfortunately, data on gross transactions are not available. The Flow of Funds Accounts, as currently constructed, estimate the net changes in financial assets and liabilities of all economic units in the economy. They also present estimates of saving out of current earned income. Like the National Wealth Accounts, they are grouped into sectors according to the nature of their activities, with greater detail reported for the financial sector of the economy.

Table 12-5 presents an abbreviated National Flow of Funds Accounts for the United States for 1970. As the Flow of Funds Accounts are not yet completely integrated with the National Income Accounts, a number of categories and classifications differ. Economic units are grouped by institutional type rather than by function. Unlike the National Income Accounts, household expenditure on consumer durable goods are treated as gross saving and investment, and depreciation of the stock of consumer durables is estimated.

As National Wealth Accounts are not yet compiled, the Flow of Funds Accounts cannot estimate the total change in net worth of individual sectors but only the change due to net saving out of current earned income. Capital gains and losses are not estimated and are not included in income, saving, and changes in net worth.

As may be seen in Table 12-5, gross saving was estimated at $228 billion for 1970, of which about 70 percent was accounted for by households. Net saving was $64 billion, of which more than 100 percent was due to the household sector. Gross private capital expenditures were $225 billion, of which approximately half were made by the household sector. Households acquired $67 billion of financial assets and issued $20 billion of debts. They had a current surplus of about $46 billion. The nonfinancial business sector issued $54 billion of new securities and acquired $24 billion of financial assets. It had a current deficit of about $30 billion.

Households primarily acquired demand deposits and currency, time and saving

Table 12-5   FLOW OF FUNDS, 1970 (BILLIONS OF DOLLARS)

Transaction	Private Domestic Nonfinancial Sector				Total	Financial Sector		Rest of the World	All Sectors
	Households	Business	State and Local Governments	U.S. Government		Commercial Banks	Nonbank Finance		
1. Gross Saving	160	82	-5	-13	4	3	1	-1	228
a. Capital Consumption	91	72		-13	2	1	1	0	165
b. Net Saving (1-1a)	69	10	-5	-13	2	2	0	-8	64
2. Gross Investment (3 + 4)	160	80	-5	-10	3	3	0	1	228
3. Private Capital Expenditure	113	110			2	1	1	0	225
4. Net Financial Investment (5-6)	46	-30	-5	10	1	2	-1	1	3
5. Net Acquisition of Financial Assets	67	24	8	5	108	42	51	6	217
a. Demand Deposits and Currency	3	1	1	2	1			-2	9
b. Time and Saving Deposits	35	13	9		1	2	1	-2	55
c. Life Insurance and Pension Funds	22								22
d. Credit Market Instruments (Bonds, Mortgages, Stocks, Loans)	7	2	-3	3	88	27	47	10	108
6. Net Increase of Financial Liabilities	20	54	13	15	106	40	52	5	214
a. Demand Deposits and Currency					9	6			9
b. Time and Saving Deposits					55	38	17		55
c. Life Insurance and Pension Funds				2	20		20		22
d. Credit Market Instruments (Bonds, Mortgages, Stocks, Loans)	21	33	12	13	13	-2	7	3	108
7. Statistical Discrepancy (1-2)	0	2	0	-3	1	0	1	-2	-1

Source: Board of Governors, Federal Reserve System.

deposits, and life insurance and pension fund reserves. They incurred debt primarily in the form of mortgages and consumer credit. Households were net sellers of corporate equities and withdrew resources from unincorporated businesses. Business units incurred a variety of liabilities: bonds, mortgages, bank loans, and trade credit being the most important.

The financial sectors issued liabilities approximately equal to the value of the financial assets they acquired. While their financial acquisitions were primarily credit market instruments issued by households, business, and government, their liabilities were primarily demand and saving deposits, life insurance, and pension fund reserves.

As capital expenditures and depreciation are not estimated for the government sector, saving by government is defined as its current surplus or deficit between expenditures and receipts.

PRICE INDEXES

The total value of goods and services produced in the economy may rise because the quantity of goods and services produced rises or because the price of goods and services produced rises, or because of some combination of the two. As it is goods and services and not prices that are relevant for welfare, the money value of current output must be deflated by a price index to determine the change in the quantity of output, that is, the change in real output as measured in constant prices and so in terms of money of constant purchasing power.

Prices of different goods do not move together. Typically some prices are rising and others falling at the same time. It is not meaningful to calculate a simple average of all prices in the economy, as a change in the price of one good, such as steel, may be much more important than a greater proportionate change in the price of another good, such as shoelaces. In order to handle this problem a weighted average must be developed in which the prices of steel, shoelaces, and all other goods are weighted by their relative importance in total output.

Consumer Price Index

The *consumer price index* is an attempt to measure the change in the level of prices of consumer goods. It is derived by first constructing a *representative market basket* made up of all the goods that consumers typically purchase in a particular period, containing a certain quantity of food, housing, clothing, and transportation. Changes in the general price level are then measured by (1) calculating the value of this basket at market prices prevailing in one period and (2) recalculating the value of the same basket of commodities as valued in the prices prevailing in another period.

Unfortunately, in a different period consumers always purchase a different market basket of commodities. The question then arises whether the weights used should be *initial* market period quantities or *final* market period quantities. The formulae for these two weighted averages for the general case of n commodities are:

Initial
period
weights (q_0)

$$\frac{\sum\limits_{i=1}^{n} p_1^i q_0^i}{\sum\limits_{i=1}^{n} p_0^i q_0^i}$$

Final
period
weights (q_1)

$$\frac{\sum\limits_{i=1}^{n} p_1^i q_1^i}{\sum\limits_{i=1}^{n} p_0^i q_1^i}$$

It can be shown that the former is biased upward and the latter biased downward. Consumers purchase more of those goods whose prices have fallen and less of those goods whose prices have risen. As a result, initial period quantities give too much weight to those goods whose prices have risen and too little to those goods whose prices have fallen.

One solution, and there is no ideal solution, is simply to average the quantities of both periods and use the averages as weights. This may be expressed:

Average
weights
$$\frac{(q_0 + q_1)}{2}$$

$$\frac{\sum\limits_{i=1}^{n} p_1^i \left(\frac{q_0 + q_1}{2}\right)^i}{\sum\limits_{i=1}^{n} p_0^i \left(\frac{q_0 + q_2}{2}\right)^i}$$

Quality Change

An even more difficult problem is that the goods and services in an initial market basket are not identical in quality to the goods and services in a later market basket. Because of technological change, a car or a doctor's services today are not the same commodities as a car or a doctor's services not long ago. Similarly, product innovation results in new commodities that previously were unavailable.

In practice, it is not possible to adjust precisely for quality change. How does one estimate the change in the quality of education, or of medical services, over the last ten years? To the extent that quality change is not adjusted for, it produces an *upward bias* in the price index.

It has been estimated that quality change in the American economy is on the order of 1 to 2 percent per year. This implies that an increase in the price index of 1 or 2 percent represents approximately constant prices in terms of goods of unchanged quality. An indication of the importance of this phenomenon may be seen by asking yourself whether you would prefer to purchase from the 1948 Sears Roebuck Catalog at 1948 prices or from the 1972 Sears Roebuck Catalog at 1972 prices, under the stipulation that you have to confine all your purchases to one catalog.

Inflation

Consumer price indexes by major categories are presented in Table 12-6. Inflation is defined as the annual percentage rate of change in the price index. Since 1955,

the consumer price index has never fallen on an annual basis, and the rate of inflation has accelerated since the mid-1960s.

Price indexes may be constructed for many different classes of goods. As may be
seen from Table 12-6, except for the immediate postwar period, the prices of services have increased more rapidly than commodities. This change in relative prices
is due primarily to lower rates of productivity growth in service industries. Prices
are based ultimately on average costs of production, adjusted upward by the degree
of market power. Productivity occurs at different rates in different industries, altering the relative cost of producing different goods. Goods for which productivity is
rising more rapidly can be produced at relatively lower cost, and their prices tend to
fall relative to other goods. Conversely, goods whose productivity gains are less
rapid can be produced only at relatively higher cost, and their prices tend to rise
relative to other goods.

Table 12-6   CONSUMER PRICE INDEXES, 1945–71

	All Items	Annual Percent of Change	5-Year Average	All Commodities	Annual Percent of Change	5-Year Average	All Services	Annual Percent of Change	5-Year Average
1944	52.7			54.7			47.5		
1945	53.9	2.3		56.3	2.9		48.2	1.5	
1946	58.5	8.5		62.4	10.8		49.1	1.9	
1947	66.9	14.4	6.4	75.0	20.2	7.7	51.1	4.1	3.7
1948	72.1	7.8		80.4	7.2		54.3	6.3	
1949	71.4	−1.0		78.3	−2.6		56.9	4.8	
1950	72.1	1.0		78.8	0.6		58.7	3.2	
1951	77.8	7.9		85.9	9.0		61.8	5.3	
1952	79.5	2.2	2.5	87.0	1.3	1.9	64.5	4.4	4.1
1953	80.1	0.8		86.7	−.3		67.3	4.3	
1954	80.5	0.5		85.9	−.9		69.5	3.3	
1955	80.2	−.4		85.1	−.9		70.9	2.0	
1956	81.4	1.5		85.9	0.9		72.7	2.5	
1957	84.3	3.6	1.6	88.6	3.1	1.1	75.6	4.0	3.0
1958	86.6	2.7		90.6	2.3		78.5	3.8	
1959	87.3	0.8		90.7	0.1		80.8	2.9	
1960	88.7	1.6		91.5	0.9		83.5	3.3	
1961	89.6	1.0		92.0	0.5		85.2	2.0	
1962	90.6	1.1	1.2	92.8	0.9	0.9	86.8	1.9	2.2
1963	91.7	1.2		93.6	0.9		88.5	2.0	
1964	92.9	1.3		94.6	1.1		90.2	1.9	
1965	94.5	1.7		95.7	1.2		92.2	2.2	
1966	97.2	2.9		98.2	2.6		95.8	3.9	
1967	100.0	2.9	3.4	100.0	1.8	2.8	100.0	4.4	4.5
1968	104.2	4.2		103.7	3.7		105.2	5.2	
1969	109.8	5.4		108.4	4.5		112.5	6.9	
1970	116.3	5.9		113.5	4.7		121.6	8.1	
1971	121.3	4.3		117.4	3.5		128.4	5.6	

Source: Department of Labor, Bureau of Labor Statistics.

Money Income and Real Income

The price index for all the goods and services produced in the economy, weighted by the quantities produced, is sometimes termed the *GNP price deflator.* A rise in national income measured at current market prices may be due in part to a rise in the price level and in part to an increase in the quantity of goods and services produced. Only the latter results in an increase in real income in the sense of more goods and services available.

To find the change in real income, money income must be deflated by the price index for GNP. For example, if money income increased from $1,000 billion to $1100 billion over the year while prices rose by 5 percent, the 10 percent increase in money income would be associated with only a 5 percent rise in real income. Real income represents income measured in constant prices, that is, in dollars of a constant purchasing power.

Per capita real income refers to real income divided by the population. It represents the amount of goods and services available to each individual in the population.

APPENDIX: PROBLEMS OF MEASUREMENT AND METHODOLOGY

The use of national income measures has become widespread during the last three decades by business, governments, and popular journals as well as in scholarly research. National income is widely used to compare the performance of a particular economy in different periods of time: in 1945 GNP in the United States amounted to $210 billion, in 1968 it was $860 billion. Per capita income, national income divided by population, is extensively quoted as an index of how well off inhabitants of a particular country are: in 1968 per capita income in the United States was approximately $3,000 per year; in India it was estimated at $50.

There are a number of fundamental qualifications and pitfalls that must be kept in mind in using any economic data. In view of the rudimentary nature of the National Wealth and Flow of Funds Accounts, some of these difficulties will be illustrated with reference to National Income measures. The same questions could be raised with regard to Wealth and Flow of Funds Accounts.

Inclusion

The first problem concerns the *scope* of activities to be counted as part of the national income and output. Economic goods have been defined as anything which is scarce and is generally bought and sold on a market. Activity that may generically be economic but does not involve a market transaction is very difficult to record and value, and for the most part is ignored in national accounting. The services of housewives, and more generally all activity that takes place in the home outside of the market sector, is not included in national output even though when the same activity is bought and sold in a market it is recorded. As a result, national income falls when a man marries his housekeeper, even though services received may increase.

With economic development, the market sector grows relative to the nonmarket sector as it encompasses activities formerly performed within the home. National income measures are thus likely to be biased upward over long periods of time with regard to the true rate of growth of real output, as households purchase goods and services that they previously provided for themselves—such as baking, laundering, cooking, and all do-it-yourself activities. With the rise in labor costs, the latter are likely to become increasingly important in the future, and the bias could be reversed.

As another example, illegal activities are not included. The income of gangsters and prostitutes are omitted, although they may involve market transactions. Such activities are difficult to record. It may be argued that they render no socially useful product, but this same argument could be (and has been) applied to many legal market transactions.

For the sake of consistency, a few nonmarket transactions are included. Goods produced and consumed on the farm are imputed as farmers' income and consumption in kind. Services from owner-occupied houses are also included in the form of imputed income and rent. That is, if you own your own home, an estimate is made of the rent that you would have paid on that house and this is added to your income and to your consumption.

Although rent is imputed on owner-occupied houses, no imputations are made for the services derived from other durable consumer goods, such as cars, appliances, furniture, and clothing. Such goods are real capital assets that yield a stream of direct consumption services over their lifetime until they are used up. But largely due to the empirical difficulties of estimating the outstanding stocks of such consumer durables and of valuing the services that they yield each year, they are by convention counted as consumption goods in the year in which they are produced and sold. When a car with an expected lifetime of ten years is purchased for $3,000, this is recorded as $3,000 of consumption in that year. More accurately, the purchase of the car represents an investment of $3,000 in the initial year, and consumption of automobile services of $300 a year for ten years, calculating depreciation on a straight line basis.

As stated above, all government expenditures for goods and services are included in national income. No attempt is made to distinguish public intermediate or investment goods. Government welfare expenditures and other transfer payments are not included in national income. Such expenditures redistribute income among individuals but do not add to the total value of current output produced.

Interest paid on the national debt is regarded by convention as a transfer payment and is not included in national income even though business interest payments are included. The justification for this is that historically most government debt arose in time of war, when government spending did not create a corresponding investment in the economy's real productive capacity. As a result, it is held that there are no services received from such past government expenditures that can be indirectly measured by the interest paid on government debt.

Netness

A second problem concerns the definition of *final* goods and services. Intermediate goods and services refer to all things used in the production of other goods. Flour sold to housewives is a final consumer good. But consider the same flour sold to bakeries for the production of bread. As the value of this flour is already included in the price of bread, to include both flour and bread in national income would involve double counting. Income would then depend upon the number of stages of production.

In practice, it is frequently difficult to distinguish final and intermediate goods. Many consumption expenditures, particularly in an advanced industrial economy, are necessary for earning a living or to offset the disadvantages of urban life. From the viewpoint of welfare, they might more properly be regarded as analogous to intermediate goods rather than as goods yielding final satisfaction. In the case of public goods, the distinction between final and intermediate goods is extremely difficult to draw, as the same good may be received by consumers and producers. By convention, all government expenditures for goods and services are arbitrarily regarded as final goods, including defense expenditures and government services provided to business firms.

A related issue concerns the question of investment goods. With the exception of final inventory accumulation, such goods are really a kind of intermediate good with a durability longer than one year. Due primarily to the difficulty of defining the duration of their effects, and therefore appropriate rates of depreciation, no business expenditures on services are considered final investments. There is a bias in favor of bricks and mortar. Research and development is treated as a current business expense, i.e., an intermediate rather than an investment expenditure.

Only household expenditure on new housing is considered investment, while all other consumer durable acquisition and purchase of investment services (e.g., education) is consumption. The depreciation of workers in current production is not considered in the adjustment of gross to net national product. The national income estimates implicitly assume that the provision of goods and services to consumers, present and future, is the ultimate purpose of economic activity. It is only by referring to this purpose that it is possible to determine what is a final product and what is a cost. Depreciation of physical capital goods is deducted but, as discussed earlier, it is a very rough estimate, heavily shaped by tax considerations.

Valuation

Perhaps the greatest difficulty in relating national income measures to economic welfare concerns the question of valuation. How should the various components of economic output be added together? National income is a measure of all final goods and services currently produced, using as weights for each good their *current market price*. Prices are used because they represent a measure of the economic importance of various goods. But the price weights do not provide an ideal reflection of total private or social importance.

If individuals adjust their consumption so as to maximize expected utility, the ratio of the marginal utilities anticipated from each private good or service will be proportional to the ratio of their prices. Valuation of goods and services at market price means measuring the area of the hatched rectangle, price times quantity, shown in Figure 12-8. The total utility or welfare derived from consumption of these goods is, however, not quantity times *marginal* utility but quantity times *average* utility. This is shown in Figure 12-8 and is drawn as equal to the total shaded area under the marginal utility curve.

The triangle under the marginal utility curve above price is sometimes termed *consumers' surplus*. It is a measure of what consumers would be willing to pay for the quantity of goods consumed over what they actually did pay.

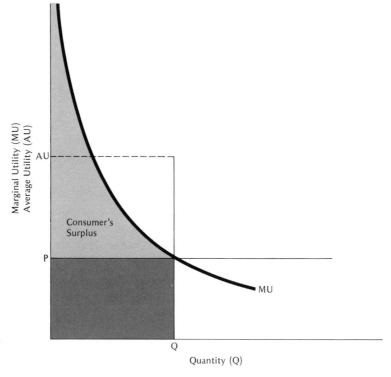

Figure 12-8 Consumer's Surplus

As it is impossible operationally to measure average utility, price must be used as an indirect measure of marginal utility. This creates the paradox that the greater the quantity of goods produced with any given demand curve, the lower the price and, after some point, the smaller the area of the rectangle.

In Paradise, where no goods are scarce, the consumption of all goods would be pushed to where their marginal utility is equal to zero; the prices of all goods would be zero; and the value of total output would be zero. Conversely, monopolistic restriction of output in markets where demand is inelastic would increase total revenue, the total compensation to productive factors, and the measured contribution of that good or service to national income, although total utility derived from that particular commodity would be reduced.

This argument holds *a fortiori* for a planned economy where prices are set by a central planning board. In this case, the rate at which measured total output grows will be dependent on the relative prices assigned to different goods and services by the planners. If capital formation is proceeding rapidly and capital goods are assigned a relatively high price, total output will grow more rapidly than would be the case with relatively lower prices for capital goods. Similarly, in comparing different economies with different relative prices, the size of their national incomes relative to one another will depend on which set of prices is selected as weights by which to value current output.

A final valuation question concerns government goods and services. Because public goods for the most part are not bought and sold on a market, it is not possible to determine a market price. By convention, public goods and services are valued at total cost of production. This cost is likely to differ greatly from the total utility received from such services by individuals in the economy. Different individuals will place different valuations on the same public good, and there is no direct process by which these valuations may be revealed and aggregated.

Caveat Consumptor

In using national income estimates, one must be aware of these problems. The answers given depend on the purpose for which the estimates are to be used. For year-to-year comparisons, the exclusion of housewives' services is not critical, but for longer periods the question requires explicit treatment.

National income estimates are based on the underlying assumption that the broad purpose of economic activity is to supply the material wants of consumers. The satisfaction or disutility received by individuals in their roles as producer or factor supplier is largely ignored, except as it is reflected in differential factor prices.

The concentration of governments and economists on measurable economic values may lead to neglect of more important criteria of social performances: the psychic, aesthetic, cultural. Nevertheless, their wide acceptance suggests that what they claim to measure, the volume of goods and services available for distribution, is of considerable interest to the groups comprising an economy. One of their great contributions to a democratic social order has been a widening of the area of agreement as to the facts. Nevertheless, it is necessary to be extremely cautious in interpreting changes in national income as a measure of changes in the economic welfare or satisfaction enjoyed by individuals in a society.

the determination of national income

WE SEE in almost every part of the world vast powers of production which are not put into action, and I explain this phenomenon by saying that from want of a proper distribution of the actual produce adequate motives are not furnished to continued production.

—ROBERT MALTHUS

PRODUCTIONS are always bought by productions or by services. Money is only the medium by which the exchange is effected. Hence the increased production being always accompanied by a correspondingly increased ability to get and consume, there is no possibility of overproduction.

—DAVID RICARDO

This chapter considers the forces determining the level of employment, income, and output in an economy. In the United States, during the Great Depression, unemployment rose from 3 percent of the labor force in 1929 to 25 percent in 1933. During those sad years, while people were looking in vain for work and families were starving in America and overseas, farmers were paid to paint potatoes blue, to destroy every fourth pig in the litter, to turn under every third row of cotton and wheat. When the United States entered the Second World War, unemployment was still above 15 percent. It was military spending that (fortuitously) pulled America out of the Great Depression.

What is the explanation for this economic and social catastrophe? It is important to understand the causes of the Great Depression so that such an event will never be allowed to happen again.

AGGREGATE DEMAND AND THE DETERMINATION OF NATIONAL INCOME

Assume for the moment that money wages are historically given and that involuntary unemployment of labor exists. Prices are some constant markup over variable costs. Credit is assumed to be available to potential borrowers at current interest rates in perfectly elastic supply, and money balances are sufficient to finance any change in spending. These assumptions are clearly not realistic, except in the special case of a depressed economy. But as will be shown the analysis also applies to disequilibrium situations in which wages and prices, though not constant but changing, do not adjust *instantaneously* so as to eliminate excess supply and demand in all markets. Under such circumstances, how is the equilibrium level of income determined?

Aggregate Demand

Aggregate demand for goods and services is the sum of the demand of households, businesses, and governments for currently produced economic goods. As seen in Chapter 12, aggregate demand may be broken down into demand for consumption goods, investment goods, and public goods. In Figure 13-1 aggregate demand (y) is measured on the vertical axis and aggregate money income and output $(P_0 Y)$ on the horizontal axis.

Household consumption expenditures are related to household current and lifetime income, wealth, the position of households in their life cycles, their willingness to spend, and a large number of other variables. All determinants of consumption expenditure except current disposable income will for the moment be assumed to be exogenous (determined by other factors). As developed in Chapter 4, household consumption expenditures (C) increase with current household disposable income in the short run, but by a smaller absolute amount. The consumption function is drawn in Figure 13-1 as a straight line, implying that the marginal propensity to consume $(\frac{\Delta C}{\Delta Y})$, the slope of the consumption function, is constant. A change in exogenous factors will shift the C curve up or down.

Household disposable income, as shown in Chapter 12, is derived from national income (Y). Shifts in the ratio of disposable income to national income will shift the consumption function of Figure 13-1.

For simplicity, business investment spending (I_0) and government spending on goods and services (G_0) are drawn as horizontal straight lines, on the assumption that all such spending is *exogenous* and invariant to the level of national income. A change in investment or government spending will shift these functions upwards or downwards.

The aggregate demand function $(C + I_0 + G_0)$ is shown as the vertical sum of planned consumption (C), investment (I_0), and government (G_0) expenditure at different levels of national income. The stock of wealth, the return on capital, financial asset prices, interest rates, technology, business expectations, household willingness to spend, and all other variables determining expenditures are exogenously determined. A change in any of these variables would shift the components and therefore the position of the aggregate demand function upward or downward. It is important to distinguish the *ability to spend,* which depends on current income, wealth, and borrowing opportunities, and the *willingness to spend* out of any given level of ability.

Aggregate demand is measured on the vertical axis and aggregate supply (money output) on the horizontal axis. At all points on the 45° line aggregate demand is

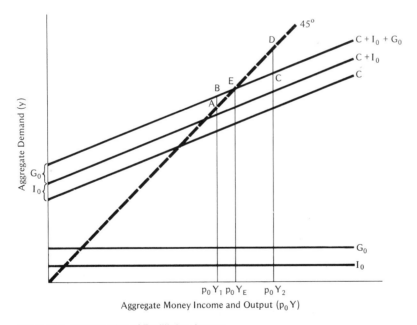

Figure 13-1 Determination of Equilibrium Income

equal to aggregate supply, as the vertical and horizontal coordinates are identical. So long as prices are constant (p_0) changes in money income ($p_0 Y$) are due entirely to changes in the quantity of real output produced (Y). At some point as full employment is approached, prices will begin to rise as demand increases. The nature of the aggregate supply function is considered in Chapter 14.

The Equilibrium Level of Income

The equilibrium level of national income is determined at the level $p_0 Y_E$ where aggregate demand is equal to aggregate supply. An upward or downward shift in the level of aggregate demand would result in a higher or lower level of equilibrium income and output.

Why is $p_0 Y_E$ an equilibrium level of income? Suppose the level of income and output were temporarily below $p_0 Y_E$—for example, $p_0 Y_1$. At this level of income and output, aggregate demand exceeds aggregate supply by the amount AB. Because prices are constant by assumption, households and governments can spend the amounts that they desire to spend and receive the real goods and services that they demand. Businesses will also be able to make the plant and equipment expenditure that they plan. But as aggregate demand exceeds aggregate supply, the total amount of goods produced in that period is less than the total amount of goods sold.

This excess of sales over current output implies that business inventories must have fallen by exactly the excess of aggregate demand over aggregate supply. As a result, actual total business investment is less than planned business investment by the amount BA, because of unintended running down of inventories. In the next period, businesses will attempt to restore their inventories to their desired level by hiring more workers and increasing production. As a result, the level of output and income increases. This process will continue until the economy has moved to the position $p_0 Y_E$, at which point there is no further tendency for the level of output to change.

Conversely, suppose the economy was initially at the level of income $p_0 Y_2$. At this level, aggregate demand for goods and services is less by the amount CD than aggregate supply of goods and services currently produced. Households and governments again purchase the amount of goods and services they desire. As aggregate supply exceeds aggregate demand, business inventories rise by the amount CD of excess supply of goods. Actual total business investment, including unintended inventory accumulation, exceeds planned business investment by the amount CD that the economy produces in excess of total sales. As a result, businesses reduce production by hiring fewer workers, and the level of output and income falls. This continues until the level of income and output is $p_0 Y_E$, at which point there is no further tendency to change.

In an economy in which there is involuntary unemployed labor and excess credit, money wages, and interest rates, and prices are constant, the level of national output is determined by the level of aggregate demand. Demand creates its own supply as long as an excess supply of labor exists.

Planned Saving and Planned Investment

In equilibrium, *aggregate demand equals aggregate supply* and *planned investment by business units is exactly equal to actual investment* by business units. When planned investment is less than actual investment, because of unintended and involuntary inventory accumulation, the level of income will tend to fall. Conversely, when planned investment exceeds actual investment, income will rise. An alternative way of stating the equilibrium condition for the level of income to remain unchanged is that *planned investment must equal planned saving* $(I_p = S_p)$.

As it is *unintended* inventory accumulation or decumulation that causes the system to adjust toward its equilibrium level, the determination of equilibrium income under such conditions may be termed the theory of the happy businessman. Only when businessmen are satisfied (are actually investing the amount that they had planned to invest) will they no longer adjust employment and output, so that there will be no further tendency for the system to change.

In such a situation, a reduced willingness to spend on the part of households or a reduced demand to invest on the part of business firms will result in a lower level of income. A planned increase in saving or reduction in investment shifts down the aggregate demand function at every level of income. Since long-term interest rates have been assumed constant and credit infinitely elastic, the increased saving does not get back into the income stream by financing an increase in planned investment expenditures. The reduced willingness to spend results rather in an increased demand to accumulate money balances (hoarding) and a fall in the velocity of money. If the money stock is constant, the level of income will fall, reducing planned saving. This process will continue until at some lower level of output planned saving again equals planned investment. In the new equilibrium, the money stock is again in the desired ratio to money income.

Planned Surpluses and Planned Deficits

The surplus of the household sector on current account must always be exactly offset by the deficits of the government and business sectors. One man's surplus is another man's deficit. But only at an equilibrium level of income are the *planned surpluses* of some sectors precisely equal to the *planned deficits* of other sectors.

Some economic units (primarily businesses) desire to spend more than their current income on goods and services; other economic units (primarily households) desire to spend less. These decisions are undertaken independently. Prices, wages, and interest rates do not adjust *instantaneously* to equate supply and demand in each market. During this transition period, which in a changing economy may be very long, there is no automatic adjustment mechanism to insure that aggregate demand by households, business firms, and governments will be exactly equal to the aggregate supply that the economy is potentially capable of producing.

Output and Demand Gap

National income in equilibrium will settle at that level of income and output where *planned saving* equals *planned investment* or, alternatively, where *planned surpluses* by surplus-spending units exactly offset *planned deficits* by deficit-spending units. The resulting equilibrium level of income may fall short of or exceed the full employment level of income.

In Figure 13-2, $p_0 Y_F$ represents full employment output. The aggregate demand function $(C + I + G)_1$ is less than the total volume of goods and services that the economy is capable of producing. Alternatively expressed, at full employment income planned saving by business and households exceeds planned investment spending by businesses plus planned government deficits. The deficiency by which aggregate demand falls short of aggregate supply at full employment is termed the *output gap*. The aggregate demand function must be shifted upward by this amount to produce equilibrium at full employment output.

Conversely, the aggregate demand function $(C + I + G)_2$ in Figure 13-2 exceeds the total volume of goods and services produced at full employment $(p_0 Y_F)$. In this situation, prices will rise as consumers bid up the price of final output and business firms bid up factor prices in an attempt to increase production. The excess of aggregate demand over full employment aggregate supply is termed the *demand gap*.

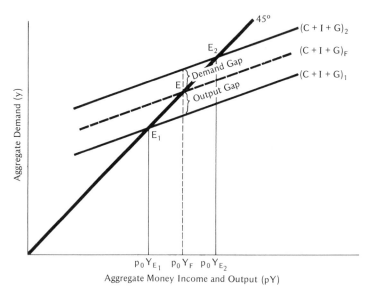

Figure 13-2 Output and Demand Gaps

THE CRITICAL ROLE OF INVESTMENT SPENDING

As long as unemployed resources exist and wages and prices are less than instantaneously flexible, aggregate demand creates its own supply. Changes in consumption, investment, and government spending or taxation result in a change in aggregate demand, which in turn determines the change in income and output.

The Great Depression

Table 13-1 presents the behavior of the components of aggregate demand in America during the Great Depression. Total GNP fell by nearly one half from 1929 to 1933. As government expenditures remained roughly constant, the fall in total output was due to the fall in consumption and investment spending. Consumption spending fell by about one third and so increased as a proportion of national income. It was investment spending which fell drastically, from $16 billion to $1 billion, declining from 16 to 2 percent of GNP.

As shown in Table 13-1, consumption spending remained a relatively stable proportion of total income through the period and was an even more stable proportion of personal disposable income. Investment spending was much more variable, falling or rising through the cycle with swings in investor optimism and pessimism concerning the profitability of new investment.

Table 13-1 CONSUMPTION, INVESTMENT, AND GOVERNMENT SPENDING, 1929–39

	GNP	*Personal Consumption Expenditures*		*Percent of Personal*	*Gross Private Domestic Investment*		*Total Government Expenditures*	
	Billions of Dollars	*Billions of Dollars*	*Percent*	*Disposable Income*	*Billions of Dollars*	*Percent*	*Billions of Dollars*	*Percent*
1929	103.1	77.2	75	93	16.2	16	10.3	10
1930	90.4	69.9	77	94	10.3	11	11.1	12
1931	75.8	60.5	80	95	5.6	7	12.4	16
1932	58.0	48.6	84	100	1.0	2	10.6	18
1933	55.6	45.8	82	100	1.4	3	10.7	19
1934	65.1	51.3	79	98	3.3	5	12.9	20
1935	72.2	55.7	77	95	6.4	9	13.4	19
1936	82.5	61.9	75	93	8.5	10	16.1	20
1937	90.4	66.5	74	93	11.8	13	15.0	17
1938	84.7	63.9	75	97	6.5	8	16.8	20
1939	90.5	66.8	74	95	9.3	10	17.6	19

Source: Department of Commerce, Office of Business Economics.

The Variability of Investment Spending

As developed in Chapter 6, business firms attempt to adjust their actual capital stock to some desired level, which is in turn related to the expected sales and rela-

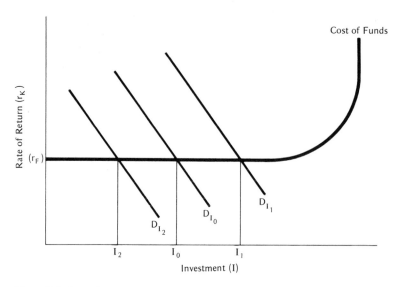

Figure 13-3 Determination of Investment Spending

tive factor costs. Actual investment spending represents the extent to which in any period firms choose to close the gap between desired and actual capital holdings.

Investment spending is determined as shown in Figure 13-3 by the investment opportunities available (the demand for investment), relative to the cost and availability of additional finance. An increase in profit expectations will shift the D_I curve rightward (e.g., to D_{I_1}) and increase the desired level of investment spending. The present discussion assumes that finance is always available in perfectly elastic supply, so that the intersection always occurs on the horizontal level of the cost of funds schedule. More pessimistic investment expectations will shift the D_I curve leftward, reducing the volume of planned investment expenditures.

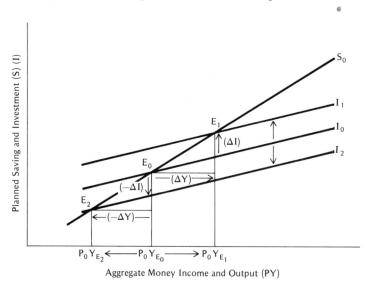

Figure 13-4 Investment Spending and Equilibrium Income

The variability of investment spending plays a crucial role in determining changes in the level of income. In equilibrium, planned saving is equal to planned investment. A rise in the level of planned investment will result in a much greater rise in the level of income and output. This relationship is shown in Figure 13-4, which presents planned saving (S_0) and investment (I_0) as two independent positive functions of the level of aggregate income and output. With an autonomous rise in planned investment spending (e.g., from I_0 to I_1), the level of output must rise. This increase will continue until, at some higher level of aggregate income $P_0 Y_{E_1}$, planned saving has risen sufficiently to offset the higher level of investment spending.

Conversely, a reduction in the level of planned investment (e.g., to I_2) will result in a fall in the level of output until, at some lower level of aggregate income $P_o Y_{e2}$ planned saving has fallen sufficiently to be again equal to the level of planned investment.

THE CLASSICAL VIEW OF THE DETERMINATION OF EMPLOYMENT, INCOME, AND PRICES

Before the Great Depression most economists believed that aggregate income and output in capitalist economies would tend toward an equilibrium level on the economy's production possibility frontier. They recognized that there would occur occasional temporary periods of crises, caused typically by monetary mismanagement, when goods remained unsold and workers were unemployed. But while they devoted considerable energy to the investigation and explanation of *business cycles,* they believed that these disturbances represented pathological fluctuations around an essentially fully employed equilibrium level of output. This position is now termed *classical,* as it corresponds loosely to the view of a body of nineteenth- and early twentieth-century economists called *classical* or *neoclassical.*

Since at least the eighteenth century a long line of critics have insisted that capitalist economies were subject to chronic stagnation and "underconsumption." But the classical economists were able to demonstrate that such views represented a misunderstanding of the workings of a competitive market economy. As long as wages and prices were flexible, they were able to demonstrate that the market mechanism would tend automatically to eliminate involuntary unemployment of labor and capital.

First, they were able to prove that total income must always be *sufficient* to purchase total output. This conclusion was essentially the recognition that total income received must be identically equal to the value of total goods produced, as developed in Chapter 12.

Second, they attempted to show that, apart from times of temporary crises, this income would always in fact be spent on currently produced goods and services. Every dollar of income earned must either be consumed (in which case it represents a demand for goods and services) or saved. If saved, it would be lent out at interest and thereby finance a demand for investment goods and services.

The Role of Flexible Interest Rates

The situation in financial markets is illustrated in Figure 13-5. Interest rates are measured on the vertical axis. The supply of finance (saving) and the demand for finance (investment) are measured as flows per period of time on the horizontal axis. Saving is drawn as positively related and investment as negatively related to the rate of interest, which is intended as a proxy for the average rate of return on financial assets. The saving and investment functions show what planned saving and investment would be at different rates of interest when the economy was at full employment.

In competitive financial markets, an increased desire to save (e.g., from S_0 to S_1) or a reduced demand to invest (e.g., from I_0 to I_2) in any period would result in a fall in interest rates. This drop would continue until at some lower level of interest rates (i_1 or i_2) saving and investment are again brought into equality, and equilibrium is restored.

Increased saving in this view results in a change in the *composition* rather than in the *level* of current output. Lower interest rates induce a greater demand for investment rather than consumption goods. Even though saving and investment decisions are made independently by different groups, the financial markets assure that there will never be a persistent excess of planned saving over planned investment. Saving is always returned to the income stream via the financial markets as demand for investment goods.

The classical economists recognized that this conclusion holds only so long as the equilibrium level of interest rates is positive. If saving were so large (S_3 in Figure 13-5) that the saving and investment functions at full employment intersected only at a negative interest rate (i_3), "oversaving" would occur. Interest rates would never fall below zero because wealth owners could always realize at least a zero return

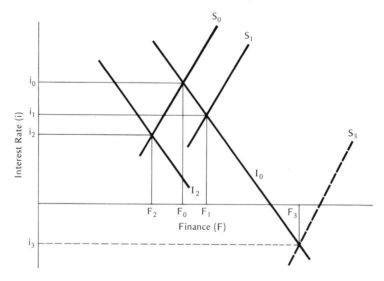

Figure 13-5 Saving and Investment with Flexible Interest Rates

from holding money. But as, in fact, profit rates and interest rates were observed always to be positive, this theoretical possibility could safely be ignored. Oversaving could occur only after interest rates had been driven down to zero.

In times of panic, people might *temporarily* prefer to hoard money rather than lend it out at interest. But as soon as confidence was restored, rational individuals would always prefer a positive interest rate on nonmonetary financial assets or on tangible assets to a zero return from hoarding money. Money was regarded as held only for transaction purposes, a medium of exchange with which to purchase other goods.

The Classical Role of Flexible Wage Rates

In competitive labor markets wages would similarly adjust in equilibrium to eliminate unemployment. The situation in the labor markets is illustrated in Figure 13-6. Wages are measured on the vertical axis and employment on the horizontal axis. The demand for labor is downward sloping and in competitive markets is determined by the value of labor's marginal product. The supply curve of labor is drawn as positively related to the real wage rate offered.

Money wage rates will fall in competitive markets as long as involuntary unemployment exists. Providing that wages are flexible downward, it was argued, as illustrated in Figure 13-6 that there is always some level of real wage rates $(W/P)_E$ at which all involuntary unemployment is eliminated. The absence of involuntary employment merely implies that equilibrium will lie at some position on the supply curve of labor. Full employment output is less than maximum employment and output as long as the supply curve of labor is positively sloped.

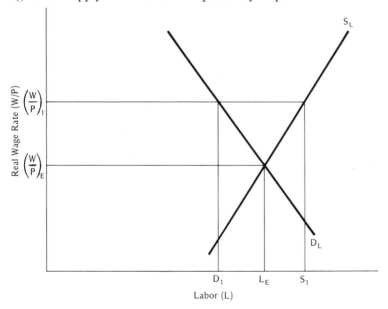

Figure 13-6 Full Employment with Flexible Wage Rates

The existence of involuntary unemployment is evidence that real wages are too high, e.g., $(W/P)_1$ for full employment. Workers and unions are unwilling to accept lower money wages. In this case, government policy to reduce unemployment should be directed at forcing a general reduction in money wage rates. The classical economists did not argue, though it would also follow logically from their model, that profits were too high and that more employment would result if firms accepted a lower rate of profit.

Say's Law

In this manner the classical economists were able to show that with competitive markets and flexible prices the economy would tend automatically toward a general equilibrium level of income and output on its production possibility curve, with no involuntary unemployment of capital or of labor. Under such conditions *supply creates its own demand.* The capacity of the economy to produce determines the amount of goods demanded.

This proposition that demand will always be sufficient to purchase all the goods and services produced at full employment is sometimes termed *Say's Law* after the nineteenth-century French economist J. B. Say. The market would tend automatically to eliminate excess supply of currently produced goods and services. If there were such overproduction and glut in some markets that production of some goods was unprofitable, there must be underproduction and profitable opportunities in other markets, because aggregate income is always sufficient to purchase all the goods and services produced. There could be particular gluts but no general glut.

THE KEYNESIAN VIEW OF THE DETERMINATION OF EMPLOYMENT, INCOME, AND INTEREST RATES

In a famous book, *The General Theory of Employment, Interest and Money,* published in 1936 in the depths of the Depression, the English economist John Maynard Keynes challenged the entire foundations and conclusions of the classical system. Keynes argued that the market price adjustment mechanism in capitalist economies was too weak to assure that the level of income would automatically tend in the short run toward the economy's production possibility frontier.

Less than Perfect Flexibility of Money Wages

In the face of the existence of massive involuntary unemployment, Keynes insisted that in practice the degree of downward money wage flexibility in labor markets was insufficient to assure full employment.

As illustrated in Figure 13-7 Keynes' position may be interpreted as the argument

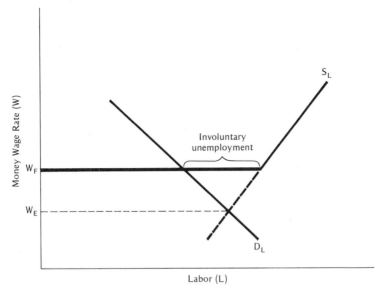

Figure 13-7 Unemployment with Inflexible Money Wage Rates

that in the short run there is some floor level to money wages (W_F). The resistance of workers and unions to a cut in money wages, even in the face of substantial unemployment, is the source of this downward *wage rigidity*.

A less restrictive interpretation of Keynes' argument is not that a floor level of money wages exists but merely that money wages do not adjust *instantaneously*. As a result, throughout the disequilibrium period the labor market is not cleared. In Figure 13-6, $(W/P)_1$ represents the current disequilibrium level of wages during the transition process.

As long as wages do not adjust instantaneously to the level that would clear the market (W_E), involuntary unemployment would persist. If the demand for labor (D_L) in Figures 13-6 or 13-7 is insufficient, involuntary unemployment occurs. Keynes argued that such a situation characterized real-world markets in which prices adjust sluggishly.

Table 13-2 presents the fall in money wages, prices, income, real output, and employment during the 1930s in the United States. Total money income fell by nearly half from 1929 to 1933, due roughly to a 25 percent decline in both real output and the average price level. There is little evidence that money wages fell less rapidly than prices from 1929 to 1932. But by 1932 money wages had reached something like a floor level. After this point they remained constant or increased, in spite of 10 million unemployed workers and very high persisting rates of unemployment. In the Great Depression wages did not adjust downward sufficiently rapidly so as to eliminate involuntary unemployment in the labor markets.

Unlike the classicists, Keynes did not believe that under these circumstances a general cut in money wages was the appropriate policy. What is true in partial equilibrium analysis for one employer — that a reduction in wage rates would lead to an

Table 13-2 MONEY WAGES, PRICES, INCOME, REAL OUTPUT, AND UNEMPLOYMENT, 1929–39

Year	Money Wage Rate (dollars/ hour)	Percentage Change in Money Wages	Consumer Price Index (1929 = 100)	Percentage Change in Consumer Price Index	GNP (in billions of dollars)	Percentage Change in GNP	Real Output (GNP in 1929 prices in billions of dollars)	Percentage Change in Real Output	Unemployment (in thousands)	Unemployment as Percent of Labor Force
1929	.56	1	100	0	103.1	6	104.4	6	1,550	3.2
1930	.55	−2	97	−3	90.4	−12	95.1	−9	4,340	8.7
1931	.51	−7	89	−9	95.8	−16	89.5	−6	8,020	15.9
1932	.44	−16	80	−10	58.0	−23	75.4	−15	12,060	23.6
1933	.44	0	75	−5	55.6	−4	74.2	−3	12,830	24.9
1934	.53	20	78	3	65.1	17	80.8	9	11,340	21.7
1935	.54	2	80	3	72.2	11	91.4	13	10,610	20.1
1936	.55	2	81	1	82.5	14	100.9	10	9,030	16.9
1937	.62	13	84	4	90.4	10	109.1	8	7,700	14.3
1938	.62	0	82	−2	84.7	−6	103.2	−5	10,390	19.0
1939	.63	2	81	−1	90.5	6	111.0	7	9,480	17.2

Source: Department of Commerce, Office of Business Economics; Department of Labor, Bureau of Labor Statistics.

increase in employment — is not true for the economy as a whole. In general equilibrium analysis, labor demand and the wage rate must be recognized as interrelated.

Keynes argued that even if money wages were forced downward, this would reduce worker money income. As a result, aggregate demand for goods and services would fall, pushing the level of output and prices further downward. In consequence, the demand for labor, which is derived from the demand for the goods and services that labor produces, would also fall. The result would be a painful downward spiral of wages and prices, with no assurance that full employment equilibrium would be achieved.

Less than Perfect Flexibility of Interest Rates

With regard to financial markets, Keynes argued that long-term interest rates may be above or below the level at which full-employment planned saving and investment are equated, because long-term interest rates do not adjust *instantaneously* to changes in saving or investment plans. In Figure 13-5, interest rates remain at i_0 even though the equilibrium rate has fallen to i_1 or i_2. This stickiness of interest rates is due primarily not to market imperfections but to *inelastic expectations* of lenders with regard to an uncertain future level of interest rates. As interest rates fall below their past historic norms, investors increasingly expect that they will rise again toward their long-term normal level sometime in the future. But interest rates and bond prices are inversely related. A fall in interest rates comes about by a rise in bond prices and a rise in interest rates by a fall in bond prices.

Individual savers faced with long-term bonds at relatively high prices and low interest yields expect interest rates to rise sometime in the future. They also expect bond prices to fall in the future and capital losses to be realized. Under such unfavorable prospects, rather than to purchase bonds at low interest rates with increasing risk of loss, savers prefer to stay liquid and increase their holdings of short-term debt and money.

The behavior of short- and long-term interest rates, the money stock, and the ratio of money to income during the 1930s in the United States is presented in Table 13-3. Short-term interest rates fell dramatically from 6 per cent to 2.5 per cent from 1929 to 1931 and, after some hesitation, continued to fall to the unprecedentedly low levels of about 0.5 per cent by 1939. In contrast, long-term interest rates remained virtually stable at about 4.5 per cent over the period from 1929 to 1933, in the face of a halving of total money income and a much greater fall in investment spending. Thereafter they fell gradually to about 3 per cent by the end of the decade.

As a result of the sluggish downward adjustment of *nominal* interest rates, the fall in the price level raised *real* interest rates. As shown in Table 13-3, short- and long-term interest rates in real terms doubled and tripled respectively between 1929 and 1933. A real interest rate of 10 to 15 percent made borrowing particularly unattractive. Deflation also increased the real return from holding money as the real value of money balances increased.

Table 13-3 SHORT-TERM AND LONG-TERM INTEREST RATES, MONEY STOCK, AND INCOME VELOCITY, 1929–39

Year	Short-term Interest Rate (Prime Commercial Paper, 4–6 months)	Real Short-term Interest Rate (nominal rate minus change in Consumer Price Index)	Long-term Interest Rate (Corporate Bonds: Moody's Aaa)	Real Long-term Interest Rate (nominal rate minus change in Consumer Price Index)	Money Stock (total commercial bank deposits adjusted and currency outstanding in billions of dollars)	Percentage Change in Money Stock	Ratio of Money to GNP
1929	5.9	6	4.7	5	54.8	−2	.53
1930	3.6	6	4.5	7	54.1	−1	.60
1931	2.6	11	4.6	13	52.4	−3	.69
1932	2.7	13	5.0	15	45.0	−16	.78
1933	1.7	7	4.5	10	40.8	−9	.73
1934	1.0	−2	4.0	1	44.2	8	.68
1935	.7	−2	3.6	1	49.1	11	.68
1936	.7	0	3.2	2	53.9	10	.65
1937	.9	−3	3.3	0	56.6	5	.63
1938	.8	3	3.2	5	56.0	−1	.66
1939	.6	2	3.0	4	60.2	7	.66

Sources: Department of Commerce, Office of Business Economics; Moody's Investment Service; Standard & Poor's Corporation.

As bank borrowers attempted to pay back their loans, the money stock (currency plus bank demand deposits) fell by about one quarter from 1929 to 1933. Because of the greater fall in money spending, the ratio of money to income rose from one half to nearly four fifths. Spending fell by nearly twice as large a proportion as the fall in the money stock.

Liquidity Preference

To explain this variability in the ratio of money to income, Keynes emphasized the role of money as an asset. In an uncertain world, individuals and firms would rationally demand money to hold as a wealth form, a liquid store of purchasing power. A *precautionary* and *speculative* demand for money was added to the quantity-theory *transactions* demand for money, which had been based solely on the role of money as a medium of exchange.

Any increased liquidity demand for money to hold (hoarding) breaks the Say's Law relationship between current income and total spending for currently produced goods and services. With a reduced willingness to spend, individuals may choose to save out of current income by the accumulation of money balances. But while individual households and firms can increase their money balances in this manner, households and firms in the aggregate cannot. The quantity of money is not privately produced like other goods but is fixed in amount by the government. In the Great Depression, the total of currency and bank deposits was permitted to decline. As a result, saving to accumulate money balances would not be returned to the income stream but would result in a fall in expenditures. Aggregate demand is then insufficient to purchase the aggregate supply of goods and services the economy was currently producing.

In Figure 13-8a, at a low but positive long-term rate of interest i_F, the demand for

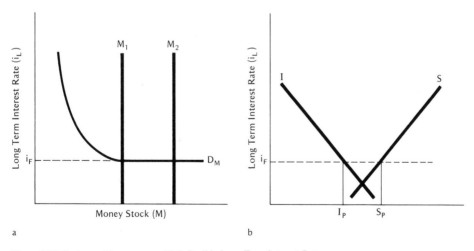

Figure 13-8 Saving and Investment with Inflexible Long-Term Interest Rates

money curve D_M becomes infinitely elastic. This elasticity was termed by Keynes the *liquidity trap*. There is an insatiable demand for liquidity. Under these conditions, an increased stock of money, e.g., from M_1 to M_2, would not result primarily in increased spending but would simply be hoarded because of an unsated demand for liquidity, with little or no effect on interest rates. Keynes argued that the money-income ratio was very unstable even in the short run, and might rise drastically with a low willingness to spend as the demand to hold money increased at low rates of interest.

While short-term rates of interest might fall to very low levels, long-term rates would not, because of the increasing risk of capital losses in the future should interest rates again rise. As the cost of finance for investment projects was regarded as dominated by the long-term rate of interest, as shown in Figure 13-8, planned saving at full employment (S_p) would exceed planned investment (I_p) without interest rates falling toward zero.

Keynes' Law

Under such circumstances, the classical conclusions are reversed. The equilibrium level of income is determined in the short run by the level of aggregate demand. *Demand creates its own supply.* In reversing Say's Law, Keynes argued that the aggregate supply of goods and services would adjust in the short run until equal to the aggregate quantity of goods and services demanded. It would be only an accident if this happened also to equal full employment output. In general it would not.

Whenever the downward price adjustment mechanism in labor, product, or financial markets is not instantaneous, the economy may remain stuck for a considerable transition period at a level of output well within its production possibility frontier. Shifts in the willingness to spend result in changes in output. The classical economists had conceded this possibility in the face of sticky wages and prices in imperfect markets. But they regarded such a disequilibrium situation as a temporary aberration from the final equilibrium position. Viewed in this light, the differences between Keynes and the classicists center on different meanings and time periods of equilibrium, stemming from different views of the rate of wage and price adjustment to market imbalance. Keynes' analysis represents an important attempt to recognize disequilibrium situations.

APPENDIX: THE MULTIPLIER AND THE ACCELERATOR

The Multiplier

As may be seen from Figure 13-4, the magnitude of the change in income resulting from any given autonomous change in investment spending will depend on the slope of the saving and investment functions. The steeper the saving function, the smaller will be the resultant change in income, as the volume of planned saving will respond rapidly to changes in the level of income. The steeper the investment function, the greater will be the resultant change in income, as additional investment spending will be induced at higher levels of income.

If the investment function in Figure 13-4 were steeper than the saving function, the system would be unstable. Planned saving and investment would diverge increasingly as the level of income and output rose or fell.

Saving and investment behavior are in fact interrelated. Most investment is financed internally by the savings of the economic unit undertaking the investment. But for the special case of a depressed economy — in which interest rates and money wages are at their floor level, credit is available to borrowers in elastic supply, and involuntary unemployment of labor exists — the saving and investment functions of Figure 13-4 may be regarded as independent of one another. In this case, so long as the saving and investment functions are stable, there will be a regular relationship between an autonomous change in the level of planned investment spending and the resultant change in income.

The ratio of the resultant change in income (ΔY) to the change in autonomous investment spending (ΔI) is termed the *multiplier*:

1. $M = \dfrac{\Delta Y}{\Delta I}$ or

2. $\Delta Y = M \Delta I.$

Its value will depend, as seen in Figure 13-4, on the slope of the saving and investment functions.

Consider the special case shown in Figure 13-9, in which the investment function is horizontal and therefore independent of the level of income. The value of the

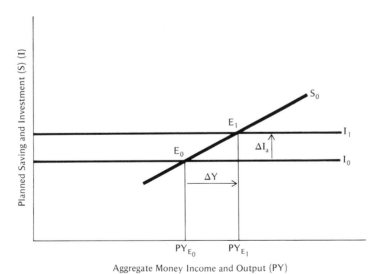

Figure 13-9 The Multiplier Effect of an Increase in Investment Spending

THE DETERMINATION OF NATIONAL INCOME   **347**

multiplier $(\frac{\Delta Y}{\Delta I})$ will then be simply the change in income (ΔY) divided by the induced change in saving (ΔS), which in equilibrium is equal to the autonomous change in investment (ΔI_a). But this ratio is the reciprocal of the marginal propensity to save $(\frac{\Delta S}{\Delta Y} = s)$. The value of the multiplier is then $M = 1/s$.

If the marginal propensity to save were for example 0.2, the multiplier would have a value of 5. An autonomous change in investment spending of one dollar would power a resultant multiplied change in the level of income of five dollars. Income must rise by five dollars for each one dollar increase in planned investment spending in order to generate an increase in planned saving of one dollar. At this point, planned saving and investment would again be equal, and equilibrium would be restored.

This relationship may alternatively be illustrated with regard to the aggregate demand and aggregate supply functions. Assume, as shown in Figure 13-10, that consumption spending is some stable linear function of aggregate income and that investment (I_0) and government expenditures (G_0) are autonomously determined by other factors and therefore independent of the level of income. The economy is initially in equilibrium at PY_{E_0}. Now say that, as a result of more optimistic business profit expectations or greater consumer willingness to buy, there is an increase in aggregate demand, so that the aggregate demand function shifts upward by the autonomous increase in spending (ΔA).

As aggregate demand now exceeds aggregate output, businessmen find that in the initial period inventories fall by the amount of the excess demand. As a result,

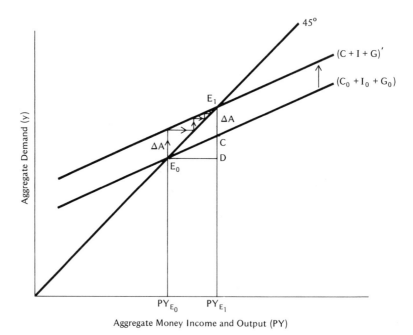

Figure 13-10 The Multiplier Effect of an Autonomous Increase in Spending

348 MACROECONOMICS

in the next period they increase output by hiring previously unemployed workers to replace the unintended inventory depletion. As shown in Figure 13-10, at this new higher level of income, aggregate demand again exceeds aggregate supply and the expansionary process continues. The new equilibrium level of income Y_{E_1} is reached when aggregate demand is again equal to aggregate supply and business planned investment is equal to business actual investment.

The multiple by which the change in income exceeds the change in autonomous spending is the ratio $M = \dfrac{\Delta Y}{\Delta A}$. As shown in Figure 13-10 the distance $DE_1 = DC + CE_1$. The change income is due to the change in autonomous spending plus the induced change in consumption spending. Therefore, ΔA can be written $\Delta Y - \Delta C$.

Substituting, $M = \dfrac{\Delta Y}{\Delta Y - \Delta C} = \dfrac{1}{1 - \dfrac{\Delta C}{\Delta Y}} = \dfrac{1}{1 - c}$.

The ratio $\left(\dfrac{\Delta C}{\Delta Y}\right)$ is the marginal propensity to consume (c), the change in consumption spending associated with a change in national income.

All disposable income is either consumed or saved: $Y = C + S$, or $\Delta Y = \Delta C + \Delta S$.

Dividing both sides by Y, $1 = \left(\dfrac{C}{Y}\right) + \left(\dfrac{S}{Y}\right)$ or $1 = \left(\dfrac{\Delta C}{\Delta Y}\right) + \left(\dfrac{\Delta S}{\Delta Y}\right) = c + s$.

As $s = (1 - c)$, the multiplier may be written $M = \left(\dfrac{1}{s}\right) = \left(\dfrac{1}{1 - c}\right)$.

The Time Dimension of the Multiplier

Given a constant marginal propensity to consume and save, the multiplier effect on income of an autonomous increase in spending can be regarded as the sum of the initial increase in autonomous spending plus the secondary chain of consumption spending generated by increases in the level of income.

Assume an initial increase in autonomous spending of ΔA. The owners of previously unemployed factors now employed to produce these goods find that their income increases by this amount. This results in a stable proportion of this increased income $(c\Delta A)$ being spent for consumption goods in the next income-expenditure period. This amount again gets into the income stream as income of the factors producing these additional consumption goods, the period of time again depending on the income-payments period; and the spending process continues.

The increase in the level of income is therefore the sum of the geometrical progression: $\Delta Y = \Delta A + \Delta A(c) + \Delta A(c)^2 + \ldots + \Delta A(c)^n$. Provided that c is less than unity, this series has a finite sum:

1. $\Delta Y = \Delta A(1 + c + c^2 \ldots + c^n)$.

In order to find the value of this sum, first multiply both sides by c:

2. $c\Delta Y = \Delta A(c + c^2 \ldots + c^n + c^{n+1})$.

Now subtract equation 2 from equation 1 in order to eliminate all intermediate terms

3. $\Delta Y(1 - c) = \Delta A(1 - c^{n + 1})$.

Simplifying further by dividing both sides by $(1 - c)$

4. $\Delta Y = \Delta A \ (\dfrac{1 - c^{n + 1}}{1 - c})$.

At the limit as n approaches infinity, $c^{n+1} \rightarrow 0$, equation 4 thus reduces to:

5. $\Delta Y = \Delta A \ (\dfrac{1}{1 - c})$.

This formula gives a value identical with that of the multiplier that was derived geometrically.

In this light, the multiplier effect is seen to be spread out over time. The lagged increase in income in response to a permanent change in autonomous spending at t_0 is shown in Figure 13-11a. Income will increase by the multiple amount not instantaneously but only after the passage of some period of time n, depending on the length of the income payments period. In a period of one year $(t + 1)$, only the first two or three terms of the expression will have occurred, and the value of the multiplier will be the truncated sum of the series to that point.

If income is to be maintained at this new higher equilibrium level, the level of autonomous spending must also be maintained at its new higher level. If autono-

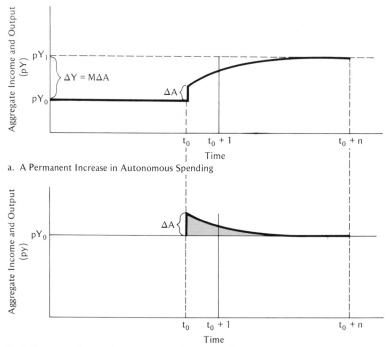

a. A Permanent Increase in Autonomous Spending

b. A Temporary Increase in Autonomous Spending

Figure 13-11 Multiplier Effect over Time

mous spending increased by the amount ΔA in the first period and then returned to its initial level, income would first rise and then fall back to its initial value. The multiplier would then be equal to the cumulative temporary increases in the level of income.

The effects on the level of income of a temporary increase in the level of autonomous spending are shown in Figure 13-11b. The sum of the temporary increases in income (shaded in the diagram) is equal to the permanent change in income $(M\Delta A)$.

The Supermultiplier

It is now appropriate to recognize that some investment spending is induced. An increase in current income leads to an expectation of even greater future sales and thereby shifts the demand for investment schedule shown in Figure 13-3 rightward. In this case, some investment spending, like consumption spending, will be positively related to the level of income.

If the marginal propensity to invest $\dfrac{\Delta I_i}{\Delta Y} = b$ is constant, the slope of the aggregate demand function in Figure 13-12 becomes $(c + b)$. The marginal propensity to spend out of income is equal to induced consumption (ΔC) plus induced investment spending (ΔI_i). An autonomous increase in investment spending from I_0 to I_1

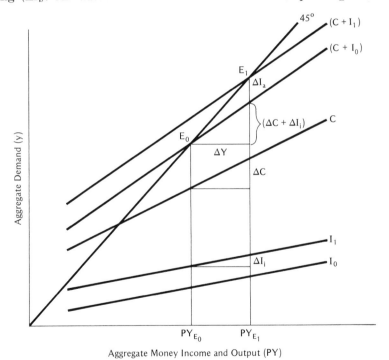

Figure 13-12 Supermultiplier Effect of an Increase in Autonomous Investment Spending

ΔI_a) will then result in a larger increase in the level of income and output ($\Delta Y = \Delta I_a + \Delta I_i + \Delta C$).

The ratio between the increase in income (ΔY) and the increase in autonomous spending (ΔI_A) now becomes $\dfrac{\Delta Y}{\Delta I_a} = \dfrac{\Delta Y}{\Delta Y - (\Delta C + \Delta I_i)} = \dfrac{1}{1 - (c + b)}$. This is termed the *supermultiplier*. Larger than the multiplier, it reflects the fact that a change in autonomous spending results in an induced change in consumption and in investment spending.

For a stable equilibrium to exist the value of $(c + b)$ must be less than one; otherwise, the system would explode or implode.

A Simple Macroeconomic Model

The model just described may be derived algebraically very simply. Assume that the marginal propensity to consume out of national income $(c = \dfrac{\Delta C}{\Delta Y})$ is constant and less than one. Consumption as a linear function of income may then be written:

1. $C = C_0 + cY$.

Assume that investment and government spending are entirely autonomous, that is, determined by forces outside the model and not functionally related to income:

2. $I = I_0$;
3. $G = G_0$.

The level of aggregate demand (y) is by definition the sum of consumption, investment, and government spending:

4. $y = C + I + G$.

Substituting equations 1, 2, and 3 in equation 4,

5. $y = C_0 + cY + I_0 + G_0$.

In equilibrium aggregate demand equals aggregate supply:

6. $y = Y$.

Substituting equation 6 in equation 5:

7. $Y = C_0 + cY + I_0 + G_0$.

Equation 7 may then be solved for the equilibrium level of income, where aggregate demand is equal to the aggregate output produced:

8. $Y = (C_0 + I_0 + G_0) \left(\dfrac{1}{1 - c}\right)$.

This represents another way of deriving the multiplier $M = \left(\dfrac{1}{1 - c}\right)$. The components $(C_0 + I_0 + G_0)$ represent total autonomous expenditures. For an equilibrium value of Y to exist, c must be less than one. If part of investment spending is induced and related to the level of income, the investment function may be rewritten as:

2a. $I = I_0 + bY$.

The autonomous component of investment is represented by I_0 and the induced component by bY, where b represents the marginal propensity to invest $(\frac{\Delta I}{\Delta Y})$.

Substituting in equation 4 and solving, the equilibrium level of income becomes:

8a. $Y = (C_0 + I_0 + G_0) \quad \dfrac{1}{1 - (c + b)}$

The expression $\dfrac{1}{1 - (c + b)}$ is the value of the supermultiplier. For an equilibrium solution to exist, $(c + b)$ must be less than one.

The Accelerator and the Business Cycle

As developed in Chapter 6, businessmen have some desired capital stock related to their expected level of sales. If the ratio of capital to output $(\frac{K}{Y})$ remains constant, net investment spending—the change in the capital stock—will be related not to the *level* but to the *rate of change* of expected sales and income. This is termed the accelerator relationship, as a change in sales results in an accelerated change in investment spending.

If the induced part of investment spending is related not to the level of income, but to the expected change in the level of income, the investment function may be rewritten:

2b. $I_t = I_0 + k(Y_{t + 1} - Y_t)$.

This is a simple formulation of the accelerator relationship, where k is equal to the capital-output ratio (K/Y). As $I = \Delta K$, if $\dfrac{\Delta K}{K} = \dfrac{\Delta Y}{Y}$ so as to maintain the capital-output ratio constant, $I = (\frac{K}{Y})\Delta Y = k\Delta Y$.

Substituting in equation 4, the system becomes:

8b. $Y_t = (C_0 + I_0 + G_0) (\dfrac{1}{1 - c}) + k(Y_{t + 1} - Y_t) (\dfrac{1}{1 - c})$

In stationary equilibrium $(Y_{t + 1} - Y_t) = 0$, and the system has the same solution as for autonomous investment. The existence of a stable equilibrium solution will depend on the magnitudes of k and c. If k or c are above certain values, no stable equilibrium will exist, and the interaction of the multiplier and accelerator will be explosive. For other values the system will result in damped or regular oscillations.

Actual investment spending is by no means simply related to the change in business sales. Because of the presence of unutilized capacity, unavailability of finance, changes in factor costs, and uncertainty, the capital-output ratio varies substantially in the short run. Businessmen adjust actual capital stocks toward their desired levels slowly, choking off the power of the accelerator. Nevertheless, the accelerator relationship provides a valuable insight into the observed instability of investment expenditure.

Fluctuations in investment spending then play an even greater role in producing fluctuations in the level of economic activity. An autonomous rise in investment spending will generate increased consumption spending and income through the multiplier relationship, which reacts back to increase the level of investment spending through the accelerator relationship, which in turn further raises the level of income. This upward interaction of the multiplier and the accelerator is characteristic of a boom. Widespread business optimism about the rate of growth of sales and profits may be self-sustaining.

As the economy increasingly presses toward full employment of labor and full utilization of capital capacity, the rate of growth of real output necessarily must decline. Prices and wages rise; the cost of finance increases; and the availability of funds declines. At such times, some planned investment projects are revised downward or postponed, and the growth of investment will decline.

A cutback in spending plans by some firms results in unintended inventory accumulation by others that may cause a further decline in production and revision of investment plans. If the cutbacks are sufficiently severe and widespread, pessimistic sales and profit expectations may become contagious and self-fulfilling. The multiplier and accelerator then interact downward. The level of income and spending contracts, unemployment and excess capacity rise, and the economy experiences a recession.

Autonomous disturbances in investment, consumption, or government spending play the role of external shocks to which the economic system responds according to its internal structure. This process has been compared to hitting a rocking horse with a hammer. Cyclical fluctuations of the economy exhibiting considerable regularity may result from random disturbances. Increased understanding of how the economy behaves has enabled governments to manage the level of aggregate demand so as to reduce the amplitude of cyclical fluctuations. The business cycle has been tamed, but as will be developed in the following chapters a new snake has reared its head.

the interrelation of real and financial variables

DECISIONS TO INVEST in private business of the old-fashioned type were, however, decisions largely irrevocable, not only for the community as a whole, but also for the individual. With the separation between ownership and management which prevails today and with the development of organised investment markets, a new factor of great importance has entered. . . . The Stock Exchange revalues many investments every day, and the revaluations give a frequent opportunity to the individual (though not to the community as a whole) to revise his commitments. . . . But the daily revaluations of the Stock Exchange, though they are primarily made to facilitate transfers of old investments between one individual and another, inevitably exert a decisive influence on the rate of current investment. For there is no sense in building up a new enterprise at a cost greater than that at which a similar existing enterprise can be purchased.

—JOHN MAYNARD KEYNES

THE WORLD WILL ALWAYS be governed by self-interest. We should not try to stop this, we should try to make the self-interest of cads a little more coincident with that of decent people.

—SAMUEL BUTLER

The present chapter develops a simple model of the economy to illustrate the inter-relation between real and financial variables. The classical and Keynesian theories of Chapter 13 are shown to be encompassed as a special case within a more general explanation. Each represents a simplification appropriate to different economic situations and time periods.

THE ROLE OF MONEY

The Classical View

The simple classical model assumes that a decision to save always results in the finance of an equal volume of investment expenditures. An increase in saving results in an increase in the supply of loanable funds, reducing the level of interest rates in financial markets and increasing demand for investment goods. Interest rates and financial asset prices are assumed to adjust rapidly to equate savers' demand to accumulate financial assets with borrowers' issue of financial assets to finance investment or consumption expenditures.

The classical model explains the *quantities* and *relative prices* of different goods and services, including interest rates. But it does not account for the determination of the general *level* of prices. The price level, the classicists argued, was determined by the stock of money, defining *money* as those assets generally accepted as a means of payment.

Households and firms were presumed to demand money normally only for trans-action purposes. Money was desired not for its own sake but for the real goods and services it could command, so that money balances were held as a temporary store of purchasing power in order to buy other things.

No one would rationally desire to hoard money in excess of transactions needs as long as it was possible to earn a positive income on bonds, equities, and other finan-cial assets or to enjoy the services from tangible assets. As a result, other assets with a positive income return dominate money as a permanent form of storing wealth.

In such a model all income received is either spent on consumption goods or is saved and finances investment spending. There is no break between the flow of income and expenditures. Aggregate demand is always exactly sufficient to pur-chase aggregate supply, no matter how productive the economy and how large the volume of goods and services produced at full employment. The total volume of expenditures for goods and services is directly proportional to the stock of money in existence. Because the economy was regarded as operating on its production possibility frontier, changes in the volume of spending due to changes in the stock of money would result in proportionate changes in the equilibrium level of prices and money wages.

The Quantity Theory

The proposition that the price level will vary proportionately with the stock of money has a long tradition in economics, having been first formulated by John Locke in the seventeenth century. It is known as the *quantity theory of money*. It may be expressed formally as

1. $MV = PY.$

M is the money stock, P is the price level, Y is the level of real output, which is assumed to determine the level of total transactions, and V is the income velocity of money, defined as the income–money ratio — total money spending on final goods and services divided by the stock of money in existence $\left(V = \dfrac{PY}{M}\right).$

By the definition of V, equation 1 is an identity that holds for all values of the variables. Whatever the values of P, Y, and M may be, V is by definition equal to the ratio of money expenditures (PY) to the money stock (M), the number of times on the average that a dollar circulates in the income stream.

The classical economists gave the quantity equation behavioral significance. They argued that V was relatively constant and not simply a residual identity. In any period of time, the velocity of money was determined primarily by historical and institutional factors that make up the payments habits of the community. The scope of market transactions, the frequency at which workers are paid, and the level of real income and wealth all affect the desired ratio of money to spending. These factors changed only slowly over the long run. It follows that in the short run V may be regarded as approximately constant.

Because with flexible wages the economy was believed to operate at full employment capacity, and the labor force, the capital stock, and technology also changed only slowly over time, in the short run the volume of real output (Y) could also be regarded as given. In this case, if V and Y are constant, the price level (P) must vary proportionately with the stock of money (M). The amount spent would not affect the level of real output; a doubling of the stock of money would result simply in doubling of the price level. Until prices had risen by this proportion, households and firms would have excess cash, which they would attempt to spend, forcing prices upward.

The quantity theory was also expressed as

2. $M = k(PY)$ or

3. $M/P = k(Y)$

where k is the inverse of V.

In this formulation, the quantity theory equates the stock of money (M) with the demand for money. Households and firms demand to hold money balances in some stable proportion *(k)* of their money income *(PY)*. Alternatively, real money balances *(M/P)* are demanded in some stable proportion *(k)* of real income *(Y)*. An increase or decrease in the stock of money *(M)* would create excess supply or excess demand for money. Spending would increase or decrease, and this process would continue until prices had changed sufficiently that money balances were again in the desired proportion *(k)* to money income, or real money balances were the desired proportion *(k)* of real income.

It was recognized that interest rates might temporarily be depressed or raised by money issue or withdrawal. But the events of the disequilibrium adjustment process were largely ignored as ephemeral by most classical economists. Their analysis was one of long-run comparative statics, comparing an initial and a final equilibrium position without regard to the transition period. In this view the long-run effects of monetary change are *neutral:* money does not affect any real variables in the economy but only the general level of prices.

The Keynesian View

It was Keynes' contribution to emphasize that economic units may save in order to accumulate money balances beyond transaction needs. An increased desire to save allocated to the accumulation of money balances may or may not result in an increase in loanable funds, lower interest rates, or greater investment spending, depending on whether the money stock is or is not increased, because the total stock of currency is controlled by the government. Unlike most other goods (exceptions being land, works of art, and other assets in fixed supply), the quantity of currency is not determined by the amount that private producers are willing to supply.

Individual economic units may increase their nominal money balances by spending less and saving a greater proportion of their income. But if the nominal stock of currency is held constant by the government, economic units *in the aggregate* cannot. The result of increased demand to hold money must then be a reduction in demand for other things. Aggregate demand for currently produced goods and services will be less than aggregate income and output. This disequilibrium will persist so long as households and firms in the aggregate desire to hold a greater total nominal quantity of money balances than the actual stock outstanding that the government permits to exist.

The Price of Money

An increased demand for any asset in fixed supply (land, bonds, equities) will drive up its price until the quantity demanded is equal to the total stock available. The same holds for money. But the difference between money and other assets is that *the nominal price of money is fixed.* Prices of all goods are quoted in terms of money, so that the money price of one dollar is always one dollar. It is only the real price or real value of one unit of money (what one dollar can buy of other things) that can vary, and it is inversely related to the money price of all other goods.

Because the money price of money is fixed, excess demand for money can drive up its real price only by driving down the price of all other goods, that is, by a general deflation. Similarly, an excess supply of money can drive down its real price only by driving up the price of all other goods, that is, by a general inflation. Because prices must adjust in all other markets, the price adjustment process to eliminate excess demand or supply of money takes much longer than is the case for other goods, where only one price must adjust.

Deflation

If as a result of excess demand for money balances there is an excess of aggregate supply over aggregate demand for currently produced goods and services, the price and wage level will gradually fall as sellers attempt to dispose of excess inventories and unemployed workers offer to work for lower money wages. This process will continue until prices have fallen sufficiently to increase the total real value of the stock of money balances to their desired level. After this point, saving will no longer be devoted to the accumulation of additional real money balances, and aggregate demand for goods and services will equal aggregate income and output.

So long as money wages and prices are not *instantaneously flexible* downward, a reduction in aggregate demand will induce a reduction in output, and create unemployment and excess capacity.

This will gradually force prices and wages to adjust downward. But the process may be extremely painful and drawn out, particularly if wages and prices are sticky. During this transition period, the economy can remain stuck far within its production possibility frontier. Rather than forcing down wages and prices in order to raise the real value of money balances, Keynes argued that it was preferable for the government simply to increase the nominal quantity of money.

Consumption and investment expenditures are a function not only of income but of the size, composition, and expected return on existing stocks of real and financial assets. As a result, changes in financial asset prices, returns, and quantities shift the aggregate demand function upward or downward and thereby affect the equilibrium level of income. The saving and investment functions of the simple Keynesian model can no longer be regarded as independent.

Keynes recognized that changes in the rate of interest will affect the level of aggregate demand. While he believed that saving plans were interest inelastic, he recognized that capital gains due to a change in long-term interest rates would affect consumption. Someone must own the economy's real capital stock, and wealth owners in the aggregate are made richer by a fall in the rate at which future income is discounted. He also acknowledged that changes in the cost and availability of long-term finance would affect the volume of investment expenditures, particularly for long-lived projects. Nevertheless Keynes was pessimistic as to the effectiveness of increases in the money stock alone to raise aggregate demand during a depression, primarily because he did not believe the monetary authorities could substantially affect the level of long-term interest rates on which investment depended.

Monetary Change

The causal sequence of monetary change in the Keynesian model is shown in Figure 14-1. Changes in the stock of money (e.g., from M_0 to M_1) relative to the demand for money determine changes in the level of interest rates (from r_{B_0} to r_{B_1}). These rates in turn affect the cost of finance and so the level of investment (from I_0 to I_1). Changes in investment through the multiplier relationship generate larger changes in the level of income and output (from Y_0 to Y_1).

Because the demand to hold money balances is a function of present and expected future levels of money income and expenditure, the one-way rightward causal description of changes in the money stock on the level of interest and income as shown in Figure 14-1 is unsatisfactory. Increases in the level of income in Figure 14-1c feed back to shift the demand for money function upwards to D_{M_1} in Figure 14-1a. Given the stock of money, higher levels of income ordinarily are associated with higher levels of interest rates. This in turn affects the saving and investment schedules and the level of income. This new level of income again reacts back on the demand for money. The level of interest rates and the level of money income are thus interrelated.

In Keynes' view, attempts by the government to control the stock of money would result primarily in changes in the liquidity of the economy and in the level of short-term interest rates. Unlike the classicists, he believed that the price level was largely determined by the existing level of money wage rates, which govern the variable cost curves and the supply price of business firms.

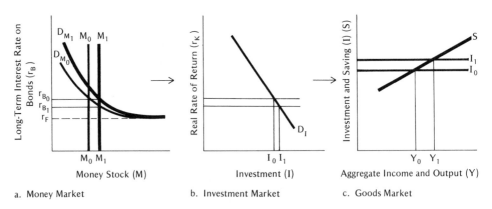

a. Money Market   b. Investment Market   c. Goods Market

Figure 14-1 Monetary Change and Its Effects

Desired Asset Stocks

As developed in Chapter 4, wealth-owner utility is positively related to expected return and negatively related to the risk of adverse outcomes. By diversifying their financial portfolios to allocate their wealth among a number of different assets, wealth owners are able to reduce the uncertainty associated with their total portfolio return, providing the returns on different assets are not perfectly positively intercorrelated. An unfavorable chance outcome on one investment is likely to be offset by a favorable chance outcome on another. As a result, the attractiveness of any particular asset will depend not only on its return but on how its risk varies with other assets and the amount of the asset previously held in wealth portfolios.

Depending on asset-holder aversion to risk, and the return and risk expectations on different assets, wealth owners may be regarded as having some preferred composition of financial assets and debts. Given tastes and risk expectations, the higher the return expected from holding a particular asset, the greater will be the share of that asset demanded in wealth portfolios and the smaller will be the share of that asset supplied as debt.

As each asset must have an owner, the prices and returns of those financial assets that are traded on competitive markets must adjust until in equilibrium wealth owners are content to hold exactly the existing asset stocks. This equilibrium situation, which must hold for each asset for general portfolio equilibrium, is shown in Figure 14-2.

If the price is below or above P_E, there will be excess supply or excess demand for the asset, and wealth holders will sell or buy additional amounts. The rate at

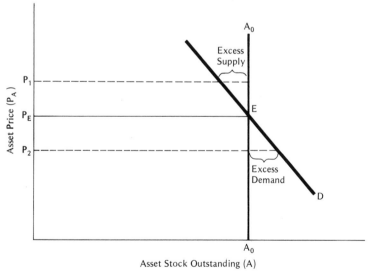

Figure 14-2 Equilibrium Price in Financial Asset Markets

which wealth owners adjust their asset stocks when they are in disequilibrium and the rate at which asset prices will change remain unspecified. It will differ for different assets, depending on the costs of transactions and the expected gains from portfolio adjustment.

The same principle applies to the demand for money. Given the services in kind (exchange convenience) and risk (capital certainty) characteristics of monetary assets relative to other wealth forms, the demand to hold money balances may be expressed as some function of an economic unit's expected transactions, wealth, and the rate of return expected from other assets, particularly those that are relatively close substitutes for money in wealth portfolios. Although only monetary assets are directly acceptable as a means of payment, other financial assets serve as a store of purchasing power (easily encashable with little cost and risk) and in addition yield a positive interest income.

The higher the return expected from nonmonetary assets, the greater will be the amount demanded in wealth portfolios and the smaller will be the share of money balances desired in total wealth. Financial asset stocks are largely given in the short run, as existing stocks are very large relative to current new issue flows. The supply of financial assets is determined by the preferences of asset issuers, and new issues of different assets are some function of their expected cost relative to the expected rate of return on real asset ownership. As will be shown in the next chapter the stock of currency, the non-interest-bearing debt of the government that serves as legal tender for the economy, is controlled by the central bank.

The general equilibrium relationship in financial asset markets is shown in Figure 14-3. Assume for simplicity there are only two financial assets, "money" *(M)*, bearing zero interest income, and "bonds" *(B)*, yielding a rate of interest of r_B percent. Variations in the return differential on the two assets, which in this case will be due

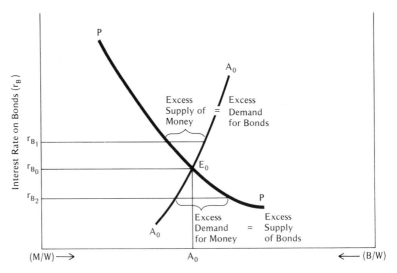

Figure 14-3 Portfolio Balance

solely to changes in the interest rate on bonds, are measured on the vertical axis. The services in kind on bonds and money are assumed given. Both are affected equally by changes in the general price level. If all financial asset prices vary proportionately, "bonds" may be regarded as representative of all nonmoney securities.

Total financial wealth (W) is equal to $M + B$. In Figure 14-3, the proportionate share of money in total financial wealth portfolios is measured from the left origin rightward, and the share of bonds from the right origin leftward. Holdings of tangible assets are for the moment considered to be in equilibrium.

The curve PP shows the proportion of money and bonds desired in wealth portfolios at different interest-rate differentials between money and bonds. Termed the *portfolio balance relationship*, it is negatively sloped, because at lower interest rates wealth owners hold a smaller proportion of bonds and a larger proportion of money in their portfolios.

The A_0 curve represents the value of the existing (historically given) stocks of money and bonds. It is positively sloped, as at lower interest rates bond prices rise, increasing their relative share in total wealth portfolios.

Given wealth-owner portfolio preferences *(PP)* and the historically determined stock of money and bonds outstanding (A_0), there is only one interest rate on bonds (r_{B_0}) at which assetholders are in portfolio balance (E_0). At higher interest rates — e.g., r_{B1} — there is excess supply of money and excess demand for bonds. Assetholders adjust to portfolio imbalance by buying bonds, which tends to drive up bond prices and lower interest rates. Conversely, at lower interest rates (r_{B_2}) there is excess demand for money and excess supply of bonds. This leads wealth owners to sell bonds to replenish their money balances, forcing bond prices downward and interest rates upward. Given existing stocks A_0, only at E_0 are wealth owners on their preferred portfolio balance relationship PP. The rate at which the price of different assets will adjust depends on their marketability and on the competitive nature of the markets in which they are traded.

THE MUTUAL INTERRELATION OF INTEREST RATES AND INCOME

The portfolio preferences of wealth owners together with the existing stocks of financial assets determine the price and return of financial assets in financial markets. Equilibrium in asset markets is reached when all wealth owners are in a position of portfolio balance and desire to hold exactly the existing stocks of assets and debts.

Changes in Income

As the level of aggregate income increases, the value of the exchange convenience services in kind of money increase. As larger money balances are demanded for

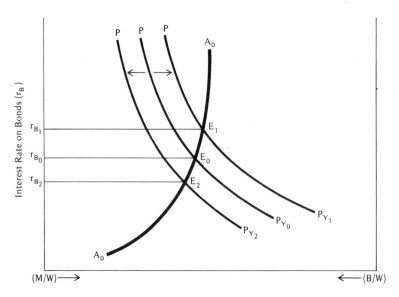

Figure 14-4 Effect of Changes in Money Income on Interest Rates

transaction purposes, the portfolio preference curve will shift rightward. Economic units will attempt to increase their holdings of money balances by running down and selling some of their other assets.

This situation is shown in Figure 14-4. If the stock of money and other financial assets remain fixed, the result of a rise in aggregate income from Y_0 to Y_1 will be a rightward shift of PP and a rise in interest rates to r_{B_1} (fall in security prices) in the new equilibrium. As the rise in the level of income continues, the money stock remaining unchanged, after some point the rise in interest rates will accelerate. As the money-income ratio falls with the increase in transactions, the value of the exchange convenience services of money over other assets will rise more sharply.

Conversely, a reduction in the level of income reduces the value of the exchange convenience services in kind from money balances. Individuals demand less money for transaction purposes, and the portfolio preference curve PP in Figure 14-4 shifts leftward. If the return and stock of other financial assets remain unchanged, the result of a fall in income from Y_0 to Y_2 will be a fall in interest rates to r_{B_2} (a rise in security prices) in the new equilibrium. After some point, as the money-income ratio rises, the decline in interest rates will moderate. As interest rates fall, asset-holders anticipate increased risk of capital loss in the future as current bond prices reach historically high levels.

The Interrelation of Interest Rates and Income

The interrelation of interest rates and income may be illustrated directly. In Figure 14-5, the level of interest rates (r_B) is measured on the vertical axis, and the level of aggregate money income (PY) is measured on the horizontal axis. Tastes, resources, technology, and stocks of financial assets and real capital are all assumed given.

The LM curve of Figure 14-5 illustrates the equilibrium points of Figure 14-4. It shows the combinations of interest rate and income that result in equilibrium in the financial markets, given the outstanding stocks of money, other financial assets, and real capital. Asset markets may not be in equilibrium, but at all disequilibrium points such as A and B in Figure 14-5 there will be a tendency for interest rates to change.

The demand for money balances is positively related to the level of income and negatively related to the rate of interest. With higher levels of money income, the quantity of money demanded rises. This demand must be offset by progressively larger increases in interest rates on bonds for portfolio equilibrium if the demand for money and bonds is to equal the existing stocks. Conversely, with lower levels of money income the quantity of money demanded in wealth portfolios falls. This lower demand must be offset by progressively smaller reductions in interest rates on bonds for portfolio equilibrium.

As may be seen from an examination of Figure 14-4, the effect of an increase in the stock of money is to shift the LM curve of Figure 14-5 rightward. A lower level of interest rates is then consistent with portfolio equilibrium at any given level of money income. Conversely, the effect of a decrease in the stock of money is to shift the LM curve leftward.

Similarly, the effect of an increase in the stock of bonds is to shift the LM curve leftward. A higher level of interest rates is then required for portfolio balance at any given level of money income. The effect of a decrease in the stock of bonds is to shift the LM curve rightward.

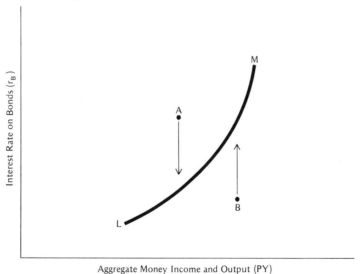

Figure 14-5 Combination of Interest Rates and Income Consistent with Equilibrium in Financial Markets

Interest Rates and Aggregate Demand

Now consider the situation in the markets for current output. As seen in Chapter 13, the equilibrium level of national income was defined as the point at which aggregate demand equals aggregate supply, or planned saving equals planned investment, or planned surpluses equal planned deficits.

In Figure 14-6 the *IS* curve shows the combinations of interest rates and income that are consistent with equilibrium in the markets for current output. At all points on the *IS* curve, the conditions for equilibrium in the goods markets are satisfied. Tastes, resources, technology, financial and real asset stocks, the return on real capital, and thus the consumption and investment functions of households and business are assumed constant. While markets for current output may not be in equilibrium, at all disequilibrium points such as *A* and *B* in Figure 14-6 there will be a tendency for the level of money income to change.

The *IS* curve is drawn as downward sloping, on the assumption that planned saving rises more rapidly than planned investment as the level of income increases. As a result, lower rates of interest, to raise investment and deter saving, are required for planned saving to equal planned investment at higher levels of output.

The downward slope of the *IS* curve can alternatively be explained in terms of aggregate demand and supply. Aggregate demand, which is the sum of consumption and investment spending, is negatively related to the level of interest rates. As the marginal propensity to spend is assumed to be less than one, higher levels of aggregate demand, equal to higher levels of aggregate output, can be sustained only with lower rates of interest.

If the marginal propensity to spend were greater than one, so that as income increased planned investment exceeded planned saving, the *IS* curve would be upward sloping.

Increases in the real rate of return expected from tangible assets will raise

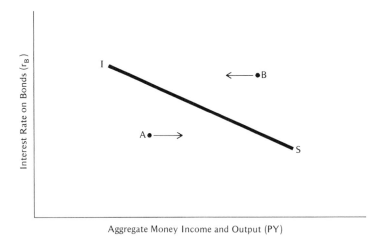

Aggregate Money Income and Output (PY)

Figure 14-6 Combination of Interest Rates and Income Consistent with Equilibrium in Output Markets

planned investment spending and thereby shift the *IS* curve rightward. The magnitude of the rightward shift in response to any change in autonomous investment spending will depend on the value of the multiplier, that is, the marginal propensities to consume and invest. An increase in the value and the liquidity of financial asset portfolios will also shift the *IS* curve rightward, depending on the importance of these variables in the consumption and investment functions of households and business firms. Conversely, a reduction in autonomous spending or in the value and liquidity of wealth portfolios will shift the *IS* curve leftward.

General Equilibrium in Financial and Output Markets

It is at last possible to look at the conditions required for general equilibrium. The *LM* curve of Figure 14-5 shows the combinations of interest rates and income levels consistent with *equilibrium in financial markets.* At all points off the *LM* curve, there will be a tendency of interest rates to move toward the *LM* curve. The *IS* curve of Figure 14-6 shows the combinations of interest rates and income levels that are consistent with *equilibrium in the markets for current output.* At all points off the *IS* curve, there will be a tendency for the level of income to move toward the *IS* curve.

These two curves are superimposed in Figure 14-7. Only at their intersection at *E* is there no tendency for either interest rates or income to change. The point *E* therefore represents a position of general equilibrium in financial and output markets. The economy will not ordinarily be operating in equilibrium, but at all disequilibrium points there will be a tendency for interest rates and money income to change as shown. To the extent that financial asset prices and returns adjust more rapidly than the general price level and aggregate output, there will be a

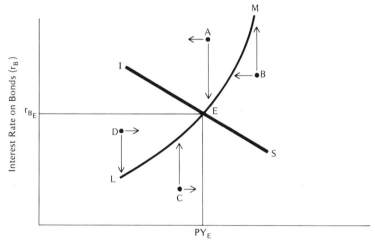

Figure 14-7 Interrelation of Interest Rates and Income for General Equilibrium in Financial and Output Markets

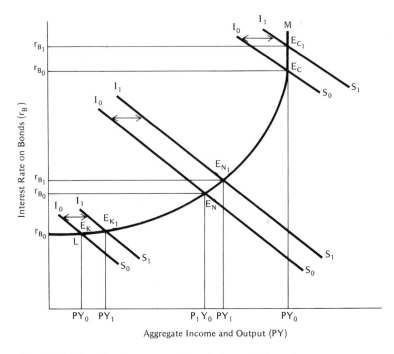

Figure 14-8 Effect of an Autonomous Change in Aggregate Demand

stronger tendency to move towards points on the *LM* curve, and indicated by the lengths of the vertical arrows in Figure 14-7.

An autonomous increase in investment or consumption demand will shift the *IS* curve rightward (from $I_0 S_0$ to $I_1 S_1$ in Figure 14-8). At any level of interest rates, aggregate demand now equals aggregate supply only with a higher level of income and output. The new equilibrium position will be characterized by a higher level of income and interest rates. For the case of a reduction in investment or consumption spending the effects are reversed, and the *IS* curve shifts leftward.

At the normal intersection position (E_N), where the *LM* curve is positively sloped, a change in aggregate demand results in a change in both interest rates and income levels. As seen in Figure 14-8, the extent to which interest rates and income are affected by a change in aggregate demand will depend on the initial equilibrium position.

If the intersection point were initially along the horizontal portion of the *LM* curve (E_K), changes in investment and consumption behavior would result solely in shifts in the level of money income, while interest rates would remain constant. This is the *extreme Keynesian case.* Income would increase by the value of the multiplier times the increase in autonomous spending.

If the intersection point were initially on the vertical section of the *LM* curve (E_C), changes in investment and consumption behavior would result solely in changes in the level of interest, with no change in the level of money income. This is the *extreme classical case.* Shifts in planned investment and spending plans are brought into equality in the capital markets by changes in the rate of interest, while the level of money income remains constant.

Monetary Change

An increase in the stock of money (or reduction in the stock of bonds) shifts the *LM* curve rightward: (from LM_0 to LM_1 in Figure 14-9). A lower level of interest rates is then consistent with equilibrium in the financial markets at every level of income. The effect of an increase in the money stock may again be seen to depend on the initial equilibrium position.

If the economy were operating in the classical range (E_C), the effect would be a reduction in interest rates and a rise in aggregate money demand. With full employment, prices would rise, reducing the real value of the money stock and pushing interest rates again upward. In the new equilibrium, providing real output remained constant, prices would have changed by the same proportion as the money stock, and interest rates would have returned to their initial level.

If the economy were operating in the Keynesian range (E_K), the effect of an increase in the money stock on both interest rates and income would be slight. Increases in the stock of money would be largely hoarded, provided that the demand for money is at such times interest elastic. Aggregate demand and money income would not increase, and the income velocity of money would fall. The effects of a reduction in the money stock (or rise in the stock of bonds) are exactly reversed, and result in a leftward shift of the *LM* curve.

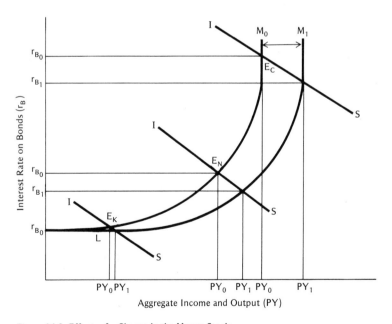

Figure 14-9 Effects of a Change in the Money Stock

Classical and Keynesian Ranges

The classical and Keynesian views may now each be seen to be roughly appropriate for different situations. In a period of extreme depression or in the short run before prices have adjusted, the analysis of the Keynesian model is more correct. Changes in the stock of money are largely hoarded, aggregate demand is unaffected by monetary change, and the money-income ratio rises or falls. Changes in saving or investment behavior result in changes in the equilibrium level of income as predicted by the multiplier, so long as interest rates remain unchanged.

At the other extreme, when the money-income ratio has reached its lower limit or in the long run after all prices have fully adjusted, the classical conclusions are more correct. The effect of a change in saving or investment behavior is primarily to change the level of interest rates, while the level of money income is determined by the stock of money in existence.

Neither of these extreme positions are likely to occur in the real world. The economy will ordinarily operate in a disequilibrium position, as represented by the points off both the *IS* and *LM* curves in Figure 14-7.

Up to this point the analysis has not distinguished whether the change in aggregate money income and output (PY) on the horizontal axis is due to a change in the price level (P) or to a change in real income (Y). This problem must now be considered.

THE PRICE LEVEL

If individuals have no "money illusion" and always base their consumption and investment decisions solely on real income and real rates of return, a change in the price level will simply cause a proportionate horizontal shift in the *IS* relationship. To the extent that changes in the price level affect the real value of financial assets and debts, changes in the value and composition of total wealth will shift the *IS* and *LM* functions. In addition changes in the price level typically lead to expectations of a further change in prices and so affect the differential real return between financial assets whose return is fixed in money terms (money and debts) and equities and real assets whose return is expected to increase with the general level of prices. What forces determine the levels of commodity prices?

The equilibrium price of an individual good or service in a perfectly competitive market was defined as the price at which the quantity that buyers desire to purchase is equal to the quantity that sellers desire to supply. Neither buyers nor sellers have any incentive to change their behavior.

A similar principle may be applied to the total of all goods and services produced in the economy as a whole. Equilibrium in the goods market may be defined as that price level at which planned aggregate demand for final goods and services equals planned aggregate supply of final goods and services currently produced. As long as this equality does not hold, there will be a tendency for the price and/or quantity of current output to change.

The determination of equilibrium in the goods market at the intersection of aggregate demand and aggregate supply relationships is illustrated in Figure 14-10. Real income and output (Y) is measured on the horizontal axis, and the price level (P) is measured on the vertical axis. As long as relative prices remain unchanged, real output can be treated as a single good with a single price.

The money value of planned aggregate demand is represented by the constant money expenditure curve D_0. As aggregate money expenditure (PY) may be decomposed into price times quantity, this curve is a rectangular hyperbola. The area under its coordinates is constant and equal to any particular money level of aggregate demand, the sum of consumption, investment, and government spending.

The aggregate supply relationship S_0 shows the short-run supply price of real goods and services, given the level of money wage rates and the real capital stock. The horizontal section of the aggregate supply curve applies to the range of output over which, given existing wage rates, firms are producing at constant costs and do not raise their profit margins as demand increases. Because of the operation of the law of diminishing returns, as more and more workers are employed with a given capital stock, after some point average variable costs rise even with a constant money wage rate. As maximum capacity output Y_{FK} is approached, the supply price at which goods are sold must rise if price is to cover average variable costs of production. Once the output Y_{FK} is reached, the economy has attained its maximum

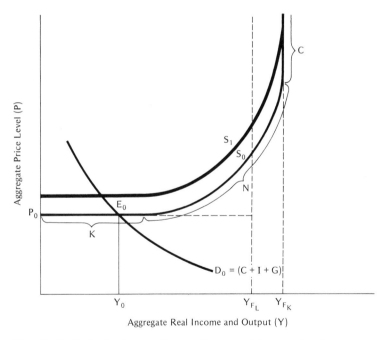

Figure 14-10 Equilibrium between Aggregate Demand and Aggregate Supply

output with the given stock of capital, and the aggregate supply function becomes vertical.

Three phases of the aggregate supply curve of Figure 14-10 may be distinguished. The horizontal section K, which will be termed *Keynesian*, refers to the range of output in which the price level remains constant, so that shifts in the aggregate demand function result solely in changes in the level of real output. In economies operating with substantial excess capacity, the price level in the short run is largely invariant to the level of aggregate demand.

The vertical range C, in which real output is at its maximum value, will be termed *classical*. It describes the situation in which the effects of a change in aggregate demand in the short run are reflected entirely in a change in the price level, as firms are operating at full capacity.

The section N may be termed the *normal range*, in which shifts in the aggregate demand schedule result in changes in both the level of real output and the level of prices. The rise in the price level in response to an increase in aggregate demand may be due to increasing costs as the marginal productivity of labor falls with a given capital stock and/or to rising profit margins as firms raise their markup over costs in response to a rise in demand for their products. If money wages rise in response to a rise in prices, the effect is to shift the entire supply curve vertically upwards, e.g., to S_1.

Only if the aggregate supply function remained horizontal up to full employment output Y_{FL}, as shown by the dashed line in Figure 14-10, would the price level remain constant until the economy had reached its full employment output. As shown in Figure 14-10 full employment output (Y_{FL}) will be below full capacity (maximum) output (Y_{FK}) from a given capital stock, if the latter is defined as the point at which total output is at a maximum, at which point the marginal product of labor will have fallen to zero.

financial intermediation, money, and banking

IT IS PREOCCUPATION with possession, more than anything else, that prevents men from living freely and nobly.

—*BERTRAND RUSSELL*

THE NOTION OF PROPERTY, as it has developed over centuries and as it is embodied in our legal codes, has become so much a part of us that we tend to take it for granted, and fail to recognize the extent to which just what constitutes property and what rights the ownership of property confers are complex social creations rather than self-evident propositions.

—*MILTON FRIEDMAN*

This chapter examines those assets that serve as money, and the institutions that issue them. Because money is but one financial asset among many, it is first necessary to consider the general process by which financial assets are created.

FINANCIAL INTERMEDIATION

Business firms administer most of the economy's real capital stock. But in capitalist economies firms are themselves owned by household capitalists, through ownership of financial assets issued by businesses. Households hold some tangible assets such as houses, land, and consumer durables, but they hold the greater portion of their wealth in the form of financial assets.

Direct and Indirect Finance

Financial assets, the claim of one economic unit against another, are created by the act of borrowing. The purchase and sale of newly issued financial assets enables the saving of surplus-spending units to be mobilized to finance the investment of deficit-spending units.

Finance may occur *directly,* in which case surplus-spending units purchase directly the financial assets issued by deficit-spending units, for example, household purchases of new issues of business or government securities. Ultimate lenders then own real wealth indirectly through their ownership of financial assets, which permit the separation of ownership and control.

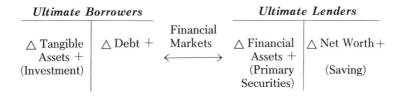

As an economy develops, *financial intermediaries* find it profitable to occupy an intermediate role between ultimate household lenders and business, government, and other household borrowers. It is convenient to distinguish *primary securities,* the financial assets issued by nonfinancial units, and *secondary securities,* the financial assets issued by financial intermediaries.

With indirect finance, intermediaries acquire the primary securities of ultimate borrowers and issue their own secondary securities for the portfolios of ultimate lenders. Secondary securities permit the *indirect ownership of primary securities* by ultimate wealth units. In addition to bringing borrowers and lenders together, financial intermediaries *transmute* the primary securities issued by nonfinancial units into secondary securities possessing greater liquidity, convenience, lower risk, and other properties attractive to wealth owners.

		Financial			
Ultimate Borrowers		*Intermediaries*		*Ultimate Lenders*	
△ Tangible Assets + (Investment)	△ Debt + ↔	△ Financial Assets + (Primary Securities)	△ Debt + ↔	△ Financial Assets + (Secondary Securities)	△ Net Worth + (Saving)

Types of Financial Intermediaries

Because of scale economies in lending and borrowing, intermediaries specialize in the type of secondary security they provide. Financial intermediaries offer a rich menu of different types of secondary securities, catering to the diverse tastes of different wealth owners. The primary securities they demand are in general related to the maturity and liquidity of the secondary securities they supply.

Table 15-1 presents the growth of the main groups of financial intermediaries in the American economy. As may be seen, different intermediaries grew at very

Table 15-1 GROWTH OF FINANCIAL INTERMEDIARIES, 1900–70 (TOTAL ASSETS, BILLIONS OF DOLLARS)

	1900	1929	1933	1945	1952	1960	1965	1970
I. Banking System								
Federal Reserve Banks	—	5.5	7.0	45.1	51.9	52.2	63.1	85.1
Commercial Banks	10.0	66.2	46.1	160.3	186.6	226.0	337.6	503.3
Total Bank System	10.0	71.7	53.1	205.4	238.5	278.2	400.7	588.4
Percent of Total	66	59	49	58	49	39	37	39
II. Insurance								
Private Life Insurance	1.7	17.5	20.9	44.8	73.4	115.9	154.1	199.1
Nonlife Insurance	0.5	4.7	3.5	7.7	15.9	27.1	39.8	51.7
Private Pension Funds	—	0.5	0.7	2.9	9.0	36.9	72.6	105.9
Total Insurance	2.3	23.5	26.2	57.2	100.7	179.9	266.5	356.7
Percent of Total	15	19	24	16	21	25	25	24
III. Miscellaneous Financial Intermediaries								
Savings and Loan Associations	0.5	7.4	6.2	8.6	22.5	71.5	129.6	176.6
Mutual Savings Banks	2.4	9.9	10.8	17.0	25.2	40.6	58.2	78.9
Investment Companies	—	3.0	1.3	2.7	6.1	17.0	35.2	47.6
Other	0.0	4.8	4.6	6.6	15.7	41.0	63.4	96.5
Total Miscellaneous	2.9	25.1	22.9	34.9	69.5	170.1	286.4	399.6
Percent of Total	19	20	21	10	14	24	27	26
IV. Government Agencies								
Lending Institutions	—	0.4	2.8	32.6	29.9			
Pension Funds	—	1.5	2.9	25.6	48.5			
Total Government	—	1.9	5.7	58.2	78.4	118*	122.5*	175.9*
Percent of Total		2	5	16	16	13	11	12
Total	15	122	108	356	487	746	1076	1522

* Total holdings of credit market instruments by federal, state, and local governments and their agencies, excluding the Federal Reserve System.

Source: 1900–52 — Raymond Goldsmith, *Financial Intermediaries in the American Economy Since 1900* (Princeton, 1958); 1960–70 — Flow of Funds, Board of Governors, Federal Reserve System; Total Financial Assets only.

different rates. With the innovation of new forms of financial assets and institutions the share of the banking system fell from two thirds to about 40 percent of total intermediary assets over the period.

The Relative Volume of Financial Intermediation

The relative size of different financial intermediaries in the long run is determined by the portfolio preferences of asset holders and asset issuers. All financial institutions exist on the profit they earn by lending at a higher rate than that at which they borrow. Financial firms will increase the volume of their intermediation so long as such expansion is profitable.

This situation for a particular intermediary is shown in Figure 15-1. The volume of intermediation is measured on the horizontal axis, and rates of return on the vertical axis. For presentational simplicity intermediary net worth and cash reserves are ignored the total earning assets assumed to equal total liabilities. The curve D_S represents the demand for the intermediary's secondary securities (sources of funds). Given asset-holder preferences, the return on other assets, and the level of wealth and income, an intermediary can increase the volume of its secondary securities only by offering higher rates of return (r_S), either in money or additional services.

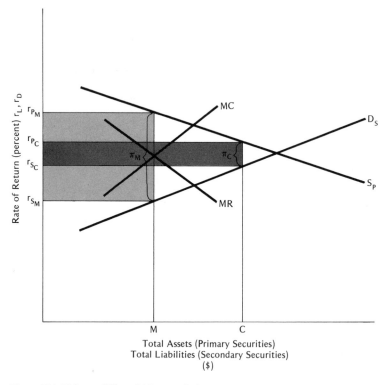

Figure 15-1 Volume of Financial Intermediation

Similarly it is faced by some supply of primary securities (S_P) (uses of funds), and in general is able to increase its lending only by lowering the average return earned (r_P), either by lowering the rate charged or by accepting more risky loans. The slope of the supply and demand for funds schedules will depend on the competitive nature of the markets for different financial assets. They will be flatter for individual firms than for the industry as a whole.

The volume of intermediation will depend on the degree of competition and the policy goals of management. Average costs of providing intermediation in addition to explicit interest costs are included in the cost of funds curve (D_S).

For competive intermediaries the volume of intermediation established (C) will be where the average return earned on primary securities (r_{P_C}) just exceeds by some normal profit margin (π_C) the average cost of funds (r_{S_C}). The required profit markup will vary positively with the intermediary's capital (net worth) — asset ratio.

A noncompetitive intermediary will not expand beyond the point where marginal costs equal marginal revenues, with a volume of output (M) and the profit margin (π_M). Intermediaries are typically closely regulated by public agencies. Depending on the nature of such regulation and the goals of management, intermediaries with some market power will operate with a volume of intermediation and a profit spread somewhere within these two limits. In the case of mutual institutions, if borrowers or lenders control the intermediary's policy they may be able to capture these profits for themselves in the form of lower rates paid for loans or higher rates received on claims.

An increase in wealth owner demand to hold the intermediary's secondary securities (a rightward shift in D_S), or an increase in borrower demand for credit (a rightward shift in S_P) will raise the volume of intermediation. The higher the return offered by any intermediary, whether in income or in services-in-kind, the larger will be the proportion of its secondary securities that it is able to lodge in wealth owner portfolios and the greater its relative volume of intermediation.

The Money Volume of Intermediation

Portfolio preferences and relative asset returns determine the composition of wealth portfolios and thereby, in long-run equilibrium, the relative size of different financial intermediaries. Given preferences and asset returns, the real volume of intermediation will be a function of total real wealth and income. Similarly, the total money volume of intermediation will depend on the money value of total wealth and income.

The stock of currency *(fiat money)* or the noninterest-bearing debt of the government plays a key role in determing the money value of total income and of wealth. Thus it is sometimes termed *high-powered money*. Given tastes, technologies, and opportunities, households and firms demand high-powered money in some proportion to their total money income and wealth. An increase in the stock of high-powered money results in excess supply of currency and increased demand for other assets and for currently produced goods and services.

MONEY AND BANKING

Money

In addition to their role in the wealth ownership and saving-investment process, certain financial assets perform the important function of facilitating economic exchange. Barter, the exchange of one good for another, requires a *dual inverse coincidence of wants* if exchange is to occur. Money, which may be defined generically as *all assets generally acceptable as a means of payment for settlement of debt*, permits the act of purchase and the sale of goods to be separated into two different transactions. As these transactions may be separated over time, there is no longer the necessity of a dual coincidence of wants. Over this time interval, money assets provide a vehicle for storing wealth.

In the past, the assets generally accepted as a medium of exchange were valuable real commodities such as cattle, gold, or silver. In all economies today financial assets, which can be produced at much lower real cost, constitute the bulk of the money stock. The two chief financial assets that serve as money are *currency* (high-powered money) and *demand deposits* of commercial banks. Such assets typically bear no interest income (although demand deposits in some countries are interest-bearing). Nevertheless, they yield a nonpecuniary return in kind to the holder in the form of exchange convenience over other assets for transaction purposes. Monetary assets in common with many other wealth forms also offer a low risk form of storing wealth.

Currency—notes or coin—is now in all countries *the non-interest-bearing debt of the government* (although commercial banks used to be permitted to issue private bank notes). Governments are able to confer general acceptability upon fiat money by making it the exclusive legal tender for the settlement of private and public debts.

Demand deposits are *the debt of commercial banks* (although in some countries other financial institutions also accept demand deposits). Demand deposits *represent a promise to pay currency on demand* and are typically transfered by check without encashment. Banks offer convenient safekeeping, bookkeeping, and a host of other services to depositors not available from the holding of currency. As long as wealth owners have confidence that bank deposits can be turned into currency on demand, deposits themselves are directly acceptable as a means of payment and dominate currency for most transactions. Wealth owners hold a small proportion of their money balances in the form of currency for cash transactions and deposit the rest in their bank. The major proportion of wealth-owner money balances are held in the form of bank deposits.

The Central Role of High-Powered Money

Money, the assets used as means of payment, consists of currency and commercial bank demand deposits. But only currency is autonomously determined outside the private sector as the debt of the government. Central governments alone have the authority to determine by fiat what shall be acceptable as legal tender and how much shall be issued.

The central role of high-powered money is illustrated schematically in Figure 15-2. Households, firms, and financial institutions each desire to hold some proportion of their total asset portfolios in the form of currency balances. For simplicity, each sector is shown to have the same desired cash ratio. An expansion in the stock of high-powered money, as shown by the dashed line, will lead to excess supply of currency and excess demand for other assets and goods.

Although any single private economic unit can reduce its holdings of high-powered money by spending, all units in the aggregate cannot. In the new final equilibrium, the total money value of other assets and goods will have increased, as shown by the dashed line, so that the proportion of high-powered money in total wealth portfolios and the ratio of money to income will have returned to the desired level. Precisely the opposite behavior would apply for a reduction in the nominal money stock.

The argument applies the reasoning of the quantity theory to the money value of wealth as well as income. As long as portfolio tastes and relative asset returns remain unchanged, an increase in the high-powered money stock would result in a

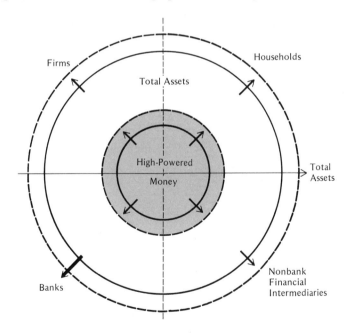

Figure 15-2 Central Role of High-Powered Money

proportionate increase in all prices, assets, and liabilities, which would return all real magnitudes to their initial levels in the final equilibrium position.

Table 15-2 presents the amount of high-powered money held by the banking system and the rest of the economy. As may be seen the total stock of high-powered money has grown primarily during wars: by 100 percent during World War II, 10 percent during the Korean War, and 25 percent during the Vietnam War. The ratio

Table 15-2   STOCK OF HIGH-POWERED MONEY, 1867–1971 (BILLIONS OF DOLLARS, YEAR'S END)

Year	Total High-Powered Money[1] (3 + 5)	Total Commercial Bank Deposits	Reserves Held by Member Banks[2]	Ratio of Member Bank Reserves to Total Bank Deposits (Percent) (3 ÷ 2)	Currency Held by Public	Ratio of Currency to Total Bank Deposits (Percent) (5 ÷ 2)
1867	.9	.7	.3	42.9	.6	85.7
1900	2.0	5.7	.8	14.0	1.2	21.1
1929	6.6	42.9	2.8	6.5	3.8	8.9
1933	8.0	27.0	3.2	11.9	4.8	17.8
1945	42.6	107.0	16.4	15.3	26.2	24.5
1946	43.5	115.7	17.0	14.7	26.5	22.9
1947	45.4	121.8	18.9	15.5	26.5	21.8
1948	47.3	121.9	21.4	17.5	25.9	21.2
1947	42.8	122.2	17.6	14.4	25.2	20.6
1950	42.9	127.6	18.0	14.1	24.9	19.5
1951	47.0	133.9	21.0	15.7	26.0	19.4
1952	48.1	140.7	20.9	14.9	27.2	19.3
1953	48.8	145.2	21.0	14.5	27.8	19.1
1954	47.8	152.8	20.4	13.4	27.4	17.9
1955	47.6	157.2	19.8	12.6	27.8	18.2
1956	48.1	160.2	20.1	12.5	28.1	17.6
1957	48.3	164.9	20.0	12.1	28.3	17.2
1958	48.0	177.4	19.5	11.0	28.5	16.1
1959	48.1	180.9	19.2	10.6	28.9	16.0
1960	48.3	184.1	19.3	10.5	29.0	16.0
1961	49.5	197.6	20.1	10.2	29.4	14.9
1962	50.4	212.7	20.0	9.4	30.4	14.3
1963	53.0	231.5	20.7	8.9	32.3	14.0
1964	55.7	249.9	21.6	8.6	34.1	13.6
1965	58.8	274.9	22.7	8.3	36.1	13.1
1966	62.0	289.5	23.8	8.2	38.2	13.2
1967	65.4	325.3	25.3	7.8	40.4	12.4
1968	70.3	358.8	27.2	7.6	43.4	12.1
1969	74.0	352.3	28.0	7.9	46.0	13.1
1970	78.1	396.1	29.1	7.4	49.0	12.3
1971	83.8	445.6	31.3	7.0	52.5	11.8

1. Currency outside Treasury and Federal Reserve, plus (after 1914) member bank deposits at Federal Reserve.

2. Commercial bank vault cash, plus (after 1914) member bank deposits at Federal Reserve.

Source: Columns 2 and 5, 1867–1968, M. Friedman and A. Schwartz, *Monetary Statistics of the United States* (New York, 1970); 1969–71, Board of Governors, Federal Reserve System; Column 3, 1929–55, P. Cagan, *Determinants and Effects of Changes in the State of Money, 1875–1960* (New York, 1965); 1956–71, Board of Governors, Federal Reserve System, Banking and Monetary Statistics.

of bank cash reserves to total commercial bank deposits and the ratio of currency to bank deposits held by the public have both declined substantially over the postwar period. Since 1965 their rate of decline has decreased, and they are currently at a level of 7 and 12 percent respectively.

The disequilibrium adjustment process by which changes in the stock of high-powered money spill over into other markets to affect the demand and price of other goods forms the centerpiece of monetary control over the economy. The previous comparative static analysis does not specify the *speed* at which different economic units adjust their holdings of different assets to a disturbance in the stock of high-powered money. Changes in the stock of high-powered money affect the nominal volume of total assets and liabilities of different financial intermediaries at very different rates. Changes in the stock of currency affect first the demand for its closest substitute, demand deposits of commercial banks. The volume of bank total assets and deposits responds much more rapidly than that of other financial intermediaries to changes in the stock of high-powered money. The bank sector shown in Figure 15-2 expands outward most rapidly, changing the composition of total assets in disequilibrium.

Bank deposits constitute the major share of money balances in the public's wealth portfolios and dominate currency as a means of payment for large transactions and as a temporary store of value for large amounts. So long as the public desires to maintain its currency-deposit ratio stable, an increase in the supply of currency leads almost immediately to an increase in the quantity of bank deposits demanded. In the short run the total stock of high-powered money and total bank deposits move closely together. This is not true for nonbank intermediaries. In order to understand the dynamics of this relationship, it is necessary to look more closely at the nature of bank intermediation.

Commercial Banking

Commercial banking originated with the money lenders and goldsmiths of Renaissance Italy. Individuals storing their gold with the goldsmith for safety found it convenient, rather than to transfer gold physically, to write on a piece of paper directing the goldsmith to pay the stipulated amount to a particular party. These slips of paper themselves gradually circulated in place of gold. These early bank notes were the first forms of paper gold.

Bankers soon observed that only a small proportion of the gold stored with them for safekeeping was actually used to make transactions. As the remainder was simply gathering dust in their strong boxes, they took the strictly dishonest step of lending out other people's gold at interest.

Even though it was someone else's gold, this system worked well so long as depositors had no reason to suspect that the bank did not hold enough gold to cover all their outstanding deposits. For this reason, it was very important that the banker cultivate and retain his depositors' confidence in him as a man of the highest integrity. Once confidence was broken and a run on the bank commenced, the bank was doomed, as its available gold reserves were in fact less than 100 per cent of its deposits. The result would be bankruptcy, a term etymologically derived from the fact that resentful creditors would literally break the bench at which the money changer conducted his business.

Cash Reserve Requirements

Through experience, bankers gradually discovered that it was necessary always to keep a certain minimum proportion of total deposits in the form of non-income-earning gold or currency reserves. They were forced to balance considerations of profitability against considerations of prudence and liquidity if they were to remain in business. Much later governments *required* that banks maintain a stipulated minimum gold or cash reserve ratio. This was initially done in order to ensure a minimum degree of bank liquidity and thus to protect depositors from unsound banking behavior. But it was gradually realized that the maximum amount of bank deposits that could be created by the banking system was directly related to the amount of gold and currency available in bank reserves.

For liquidity purposes all financial intermediaries, like all nonfinancial units, hold money balances in some proportion to their total assets for transactions needs. Non-banks and nonfinancial units hold most of their money balances in the form of bank deposits. But bank demand deposits are generally acceptable as a means of payment only so long as they can be converted into cash on demand. As a result, commercial banks must hold most of their money balances in the form of legal tender, either as currency or as deposits with the central bank.

Commercial banks, like other financial institutions, realize a profit by earning a higher rate on their total assets than they must pay on their total liabilities. As cash reserves do not earn income, banks have an incentive to maintain their cash reserves as low as prudently possible. Unlike other financial institutions, commercial banks are legally required by the government to maintain a minimum ratio of cash to total deposit liabilities. This ratio exceeds that which banks would desire to maintain on liquidity grounds to ensure the convertibility of their deposits into legal tender. As a result banks do not normally hold cash reserves in excess of those legally required, but invest all excess cash immediately in earning assets. To the extent that their reserve-deposit ratio is stable, the government can predict the level of bank deposits that will be associated with any particular level of bank reserves.

Reserve requirements raise the amount of high-powered money demanded by the commercial banking system. For any level of money income and wealth, the amount of currency demanded is increased. Reserve requirements represent a legally-created increase in the demand for currency, imposed only on commercial banks. The amount of existing high-powered money available for the asset portfolios of other sectors is thus reduced.

In this sense the banks are maintained in a disequilibrium position. They would nearly always prefer to hold less cash reserves than they actually hold. With a reduction of required reserve ratios, the volume of bank intermediation would expand. The same stock of high-powered money would then support a higher level of money income and wealth.

The Volume of Bank Intermediation

The situation for an individual bank is shown in Figure 15-3. For simplicity bank net worth is again ignored. As the top rate that a bank can pay on its deposits $(\bar{r}_D)$ is fixed by law, a bank can increase the demand for its deposits only by advertising and offering nonpecuniary services. The amount of cash lent to it is determined by the amount received by its depositors and so is largely beyond its control. As a result, given the current interest and servicing costs of deposits $(\bar{r}_D)$, its supply of funds schedule (the demand for its deposits) is horizontal up to some quantity determined by depositor preferences and the supply of high-powered money, and then becomes sharply upward sloping. The dashed demand curve D_D shows the quantity of deposits that would be demanded if banks were permitted to vary the interest rate on deposits.

The amount of earning assets that the bank can purchase is less than its deposits by its required cash reserves (R). As shown in Figure 15-3, given the demand for loans (supply of primary securities) with which it is faced, the reserve determines the amount of loans the bank will grant (L) and the rate charged on loans that will clear the loan market (r_L). In response to excess demand for loans banks typically resort to credit (non-price) rationing. Depending on the demand for loans relative to the supply of high-powered money, the interest rate on loans $(\bar{r}_L)$ is frequently

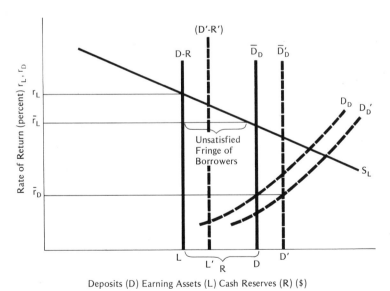

Figure 15-3 Volume of Bank Intermediation

below the rate that will clear the loan market (r_L), and there is a fringe of unsatisfied borrowers.

An increase in the stock of high-powered money results in an increase in the demand for bank deposits, shifting the D_D curve rightward in Figure 15-3, e.g., to D'_D, as the excess cash of the public is deposited with the banking system. The banks, finding themselves with excess cash reserves, purchase securities and grant additional loans. These earning assets are purchased with cash, *most of which is immediately redeposited with and so reloaned to the banking system,* further shifting the demand for bank deposits rightward.

DIFFERENCES BETWEEN BANK AND NONBANK INTERMEDIATION

Monetization of Debt

All financial intermediaries transmute primary securities into secondary securities with characteristics more attractive to wealth owners. Demand deposit liabilities of commercial banks are unique in that they are directly acceptable as means of payment. Banks alone can transmute debt into money.

Because deposits are preferred to currency as a form of holding money balances, an increase in the stock of high-powered money results in an increase in the public's demand for bank deposits. Any excess supply of currency is thus deposited with the banking system. So long as the average cost of providing and servicing demand deposits (typically 1 to 2 per cent) is low relative to the interest rate earned on primary securities, banks have a profit incentive to lend out all excess cash by the purchase of securities and the granting of loans. As a result, the volume of bank intermediation expands. This process will continue until bank assets and deposits have risen to such a level that bank required cash reserves are equal to actual cash reserves. At this point banks no longer have an excess supply of cash and are unable to purchase additional earning assets.[1]

Assetholders will be willing in equilibrium to hold a larger amount of bank deposits, like any other asset, in their portfolio only if the relative return paid is increased. But they will be willing to borrow from the banks and to accept in return additional deposits, even at a constant rate of return, as long as they have all the currency balances that they desire and can use these deposits to purchase other goods. As bank deposits are the chief means of payment, an increase in the quantity of bank deposits will result in an increase in spending for other financial assets and for currently produced goods and services. Increased supply of deposits results in increased demand for other things.

Increased lending to nonbank institutions is financed primarily by saving out of

1. If the demand for bank credit is such that the return on earning assets falls to the cost of providing bank deposits, banks will prefer to hold excess cash. In this case, the equilibrium volume of bank intermediation will be reached at a position where desired cash reserves exceed required cash reserves. This situation existed in the United States in the late 1930s, when banks voluntarily held excess reserves.

current income or, if the yield differential is attractive, by the reduction of other assets. Such lending involves a contractual postponement in the exercise of purchasing power that wealth represents. As a result, a higher income rate of return is demanded by wealth owners to compensate for this loss of liquidity. Increased lending to banks is financed primarily by borrowing currency from banks. Convenience lending of currency to a bank imposes no postponement of the use of purchasing power by the depositor. Expansion of bank intermediation will ordinarily raise aggregate demand by a much greater amount than an equal expansion of nonbank intermediation.

Government regulations prevent nonbank financial institutions from offering checking and transfer privileges on their liabilities and convertibility into currency on demand. Demand deposits represent the lowest-cost form of borrowing. A number of secondary securities — commercial-bank time and saving deposits and deposits in some thrift institutions — while not directly transferable by check can be turned into cash quickly, easily, conveniently, and without cost. For this reason they are a closer substitute for the exchange convenience function of money than other assets, and are sometimes termed *near money.*

Direction of Causality

Although banks and other financial institutions are identical as to *function* in intermediating between borrowers and lenders, the direction of causality in their expansion process is reversed.

Both banks and nonbanks lend only the currency entrusted to them by their depositors and creditors. The lenders to a bank as to a nonbank are its depositors and creditors, who lend currency in return for deposits or other claims.

But nonbank secondary securities are not themselves means of payment. As a result, nonbank borrowers do not *accept* nonbank deposits or claims when they receive a loan, but demand bank deposits. Nonbanks must therefore first induce surplus units to purchase more of their secondary securities *before* they can increase their lending to borrowers. Nonbank securities are held primarily as a store of wealth and are purchased generally out of *current saving.* As a result, total nonbank claims do not vary directly in the short run with changes in the stock of high-powered money, but only with changes in the level of money income, saving, and asset returns.

Borrower		*Nonbank*		*Lender*	
△ Money +	← ——————— △ Debt +	△ Money + △ Primary Security +	← ——————— △ Debt +	△ Money + △ Secondary Security +	△ Net Worth +

In the case of commercial banks, the direction of causality is typically reversed. With excess supply of high-powered money, the volume of lending *by* the banking system directly determines the volume of lending *to* the banking system. Bank borrowers or their creditors do accept bank deposits rather than currency as payment. Economic units borrow from the bank and simultaneously increase their lending to the bank whenever they do not take their loan out as currency but leave it in the bank as a deposit.

Borrower and Lender		*Bank*	
$\triangle$ Currency $+$	$\leftrightarrows$	$\triangle$ Currency $-$	
		$+$	
$\triangle$ Deposits $+$	$\triangle$ Debt $+$	$\triangle$ Primary Security $+$	$\triangle$ Deposits $+$

As bank loans are spent, the newly created deposits are transferred to other economic units who in turn, as long as they hold deposits, become *temporary lenders* to the bank. *Convenience lending* of currency to a bank involves no postponement of the use of purchasing power by the depositor, as bank deposits are themselves money. Increased convenience lending to the banking system, in the form of the holding of more deposits, is thus financed not out of current saving but by increased borrowing from the banking system. As a result, commercial banks expand their volume of intermediation much more rapidly in response to a change in high-powered money than do nonbank intermediaries. The volume of lending by the banking system governs the volume of lending to the banking system.

Speed of Adjustment

A change in the stock of high-powered money affects first the demand for bank deposits, as the public deposits its excess supply of currency in the banking system. The banks, finding themselves with excess cash reserves, increase the volume of their lending and their purchases of earning assets. While one bank can lend out its excess cash reserves, banks in the aggregate cannot, as the public continually redeposits any excess currency with the banking system. The expansion of bank intermediation continues until total deposits and required reserves have risen to eliminate bank excess reserves, and the banks are again in a position of equilibrium.

The increase in the share of money in wealth portfolios is only acceptable to the public at a lower rate of return on other financial assets. The rise in the money stock and in financial asset prices induces wealth owners to increase their accumulation of tangible assets, buy more consumption goods, and issue more debt. The resultant rise in money income, whether due to a rise in output or in prices, generates larger money saving and over a much longer period increases the money volume of nonbank intermediation. The process continues until in the final equilibrium the money value of income, wealth, and the level of financial intermediation of all types has increased in proportion to the change in the high-powered money stock.

THE RESERVE-DEPOSIT RELATIONSHIP

The commercial banking system is unique in the rapid adjustment of its total assets and liabilities to changes in the stock of high-powered money. For purposes of monetary control, required cash reserves are set by the government to exceed the amount of reserves that banks themselves would desire in order to maintain convertibility of their deposits into currency on demand. Each bank attempts to manage its cash in such a way as to hold no more cash than is required and to loan out all excess reserves.

In a multibank system, the attempt of one bank to reach portfolio balance by adjusting its cash affects the deposits and cash position of other banks and propels them into disequilibrium. They in turn purchase additional earning assets in order to operate with zero excess reserves. The process continues until the banking system's total assets and deposits have adjusted in such a way that no bank is in disequilibrium. As a result there is a close relationship in the short run between the quantity of high-powered money and the level of bank intermediation.

This relationship is shown graphically for the entire banking system in Figure 15-4. Bank deposits and reserves are measured on the vertical axis, and bank earning assets on the horizontal axis. For a given stock of high-powered money, the curve DD shows how bank deposits (D) are related to bank earning assets (L). As some cash reserves are lost to the public as deposits expand, the slope of DD will be less than unity.[2]

The distance between DD and the line RR represents *required reserves* as some fixed proportion of deposits. *Actual reserves* are represented by the shaded distance between DD and the 45-degree line, which follows from the balance sheet identity $(R + L) = D$ or $R = (D - L)$.[3]

The equilibrium position of the banking system is represented at E_0. Only at this point do actual reserves equal required reserves (R_0). At all lower levels of deposits and earning assets, actual reserves exceed required reserves and banks will purchase securities. At all higher levels, actual reserves fall short of required reserves and banks will be forced to sell securities.

The deposit demand curve DD in Figure 15-4 represents the fundamental behavioral relationship between bank earning assets and deposits for any given level of high-powered money. An increase in the stock of high-powered money will increase the public's demand for bank deposits. As a result, the DD curve will shift upward and a new larger equilibrium level of bank intermediation will be attained. A change in portfolio tastes or relative asset returns will also shift the position of the DD curve.

2. If C is the proportion of total money balances held in the form of currency by the public, the slope of DD for the banking system as a whole is equal to $(1 - C)$. Even if there is no cash drain to the public, so that DD has a slope of 45 degrees, required reserves will rise as deposits expand, ensuring a determinate level of intermediation.

3. Bank capital (K) is assumed to be zero, but it could easily be added to the model. Since $R + L = D + K$ or $R = (D - L) + K$, capital could be measured downward from the origin on the vertical axis, in which case the 45-degree line would go through K.

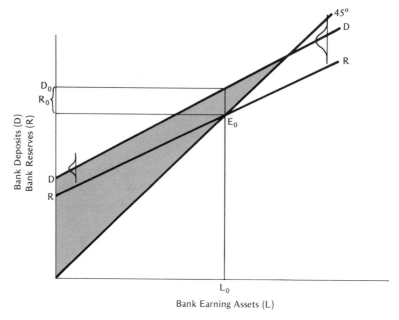

Figure 15-4 Volume of Bank Deposits and Earning Assets

Figure 15-4 may also be used to describe the relationship between earning assets and deposits for a single bank. In this case, the *DD* curve will be much flatter. To an individual bank in a multibank system, the *DD* curve will appear nearly horizontal, as new deposits and thus cash reserves are lost to other banks when earning assets are purchased. For such a bank, the volume of loans does not determine the volume of its deposits.[4]

Table 15-3 presents the growth and composition of commercial bank assets and liabilities. Time deposits, on which interest is paid, have increased relative to demand deposits. (See pages 390–391.)

APPENDIX: THE RESERVE-DEPOSIT MULTIPLIER

The total volume of deposits the banking system can create depends on the total amount of cash reserves deposited with the banking system and the required minimum ratio of reserves to deposits. A change in the cash reserve base will result ordinarily in a multiple expansion in the amount of deposits held with the banking system. This process is known as the *bank reserve-deposit multiplier.*

---

4. Because of the bank borrower-depositor relationship, the position and slope of the *DD* curve for an individual bank will depend on the types of earning assets acquired. It will, for example, be flatter for an open-market purchase of securities than for increased local loans. Banks can never be certain of future cash drains and the size of their deposits. For any individual bank each point on the *DD* curve may be regarded as the mean of some expected probability distribution of deposits associated with a particular level and composition of earning assets.

If C_B represents cash reserves held by the banking system, D is the volume of deposits, and R is the required minimum cash reserve ratio, then:

$R = C_B/D$ or

$D = C_B(1/R).$

Provided that these ratios remain constant, a change in bank cash reserves (ΔC) would then result in a predictable multiple change in the volume of deposits (ΔD), such that:

$\Delta D = \Delta C(1/R).$

Now let C_P represent cash reserves owned by the public, and L the ratio of cash to deposits desired by the public:

$L = C_p/D.$

Total high-powered money (M) is then held between the banks and the public:

$M = C_B + C_p.$

Substituting, we find that

$M = DR + DL = D(R + L)$ or

$D = \left(\dfrac{1}{R + L}\right) M.$

Provided that these ratios remain constant, a change in high-powered money (ΔM) would result in a predictable multiple change in bank deposits (ΔD):

$\Delta D = \left(\dfrac{1}{R + L}\right) \Delta M.$

The division of the total stock of high-powered money between the banking system and the public is determined by the cash reserve ratios maintained by each sector:

$\dfrac{C_B}{C_p} = \dfrac{R}{L}.$

A Numerical Example

This multiple expansion of deposits to cash reserves occurs for the banking system as a whole, even though any individual bank in a multibank system can only lend out some proportion of the cash deposited with it. An individual banker cannot create deposits by some multiple of the cash deposited with him.

This process may be illustrated by an arithmetic example. Assume that all banks maintain a minimum required reserve ratio of cash to deposits of 20 percent and that all new cash is deposited by the public in the banking system. The reserve-deposit

Table 15-3 ALL COMMERCIAL BANKS: PRINCIPAL ASSETS AND LIABILITIES, 1929–70 (BILLIONS OF DOLLARS AND PERCENT OF TOTAL ASSETS)

	1929	%	1933	%	1941	%
Assets						
Cash	9.0	14.4	7.4	18.3	26.6	33.6
Loans	36.0	57.7	16.2	40.0	21.7	27.4
Investments						
U.S. Government	4.9	7.9	7.5	18.5	21.8	27.6
Other	8.7	13.9	6.5	16.0	7.2	9.1
Total Assets	62.4	100	40.5	100	79.1	100
Liabilities and Net Worth						
Deposits						
Interbank	4.7	7.5	3.5	8.6	11.0	13.9
Demand					{44.3	56.0
Time	}46.5	74.2	29.1	71.9	{16.0	20.2
Borrowing	1.7	2.7	0.5	1.2	0.0	0.0
Capital Accounts	8.8	14.1	6.2	15.3	7.2	9.1
Total Liabilities and Net Worth	62.4	100	40.5	100	79.1	100
Number of Banks	24,026		14,440		14,278	

Source: Board of Governors, Federal Reserve System.

multiplier is then five. Now consider the consequences of a new deposit of $100 in cash in one bank in the system. Its balance sheet is affected:

Bank A

Cash Reserves	+$100	Deposits	+$100

The bank finds itself with excess cash reserves of $80 above its required reserves. Rather than hold non-interest-earning cash, it can lend $80 out at interest. If the borrowers withdraw their loans in cash, the bank's final balance sheet position will appear:

Bank A

Reserves	+$20	Deposits	+$100
Loans and Securities	+$80		

The result of this process has been to increase the total money stock by $80, because there are now $100 of deposits, plus $80 of cash circulating outside the banking system.

But the expansion process is not yet complete. The borrowers from the bank will ordinarily deposit their $80 in another bank, or pay them to someone else who will in turn make such a deposit. The original bank lost $80 of cash reserves, but the same amount was gained by other banks in the system. Their balance sheets will initially be affected:

1945	%	1950	%	1960	%	1965	%	1970	%
34.8	21.7	41.1	24.3	52.1	20.2	61.9	14.2	93.6	16.2
26.1	16.3	52.2	30.9	117.6	45.6	246.9	56.7	313.3	54.4
90.6	56.5	62.0	36.7	61.0	23.7	65.0	14.9	61.7	10.7
7.3	4.6	12.4	7.3	20.9	8.1	50.4	11.6	86.1	14.9
160.3	100	168.9	100	257.6	100	435.5	100	576.2	100
14.1	8.8	14.0	8.3	18.9	7.3	19.4	4.5	32.6	5.7
105.9	66.1	104.7	62.0	139.3	54.1	166.4	38.2	217.3	37.7
30.2	18.8	36.5	21.6	71.6	27.8	199.4	45.8	231.1	40.1
0.2	.1	0.1	.1	0.2	.1	4.6	1.1	19.4	3.4
8.9	5.6	11.6	6.9	21.0	8.2	34.9	8.0	43.0	7.5
160.3	100	168.9	100	257.6	100	435.5	100	576.2	100
14,011		14,121		13,472		14,309		13,686	

Banks B

Cash Reserves	+$80	Deposits	+$80

They similarly find themselves with excess reserves and will loan out these excess reserves at interest. In equilibrium the change in their balance sheets will appear:

Banks B

Cash Reserves	+$16	Deposits	+$80
Loans and Securities	+$64		

The result of their operations has again been an increase in the money stock, this time by $64, as there are now $180 of deposits plus $64 of cash in wealth-owner portfolios.

The expansionary process is not yet complete, as the $64 loaned out will again be deposited in other banks that will initially have excess reserves of four-fifths of $64, or $51, which will again be lent out at interest. The process of loan and deposit expansion will thus continue until no bank in the system has excess reserves.

As long as all new cash received is redeposited in the banking system, in the final equilibrium position the banking system as a whole will have increased deposits by $500, the value of the reserve-deposit multiplier (five) times the initial increase in cash reserves ($100). This $500 is exactly the sum of the increase in deposits at each stage of the expansion process: $100 + $80 + $64 + $51 + $41 + $33 + ... = $500.[5]

The final equilibrium balance sheet position for the system as a whole is then:

All Banks

Cash Reserves	+$100	Deposits	+$500
Loans and			
Securities	+$400		
	+$500		+$500

With an initial withdrawal of $100 in cash from the banking system, a multiple contraction of earning assets and reserves would occur. Each bank would find itself with insufficient reserves and would be forced to sell securities in order to bring its reserves up to the minimum legally required level. The final equilibrium balance sheet position of all banks is then:

All Banks

Cash Reserves	−$100	Deposits	−$500
Loans and			
Securities	−$400		
	−$500		−$500

In practice, all banks ordinarily expand or contract deposits simultaneously rather than sequentially as in the example. A one-bank system would immediately make loans and investments of $400, confident that it would not lose reserves to other banks.

There is nothing mechanical about this adjustment process. Portfolio preferences depend on relative asset returns, and stable portfolio preferences do not imply constant portfolio ratios. If banks do not find it profitable to adjust their loan and security portfolios, excess cash deposited with the banking system will simply result in an increase in bank cash reserves. The initial position of the banking system will also be its final equilibrium position, and there will be no multiple credit or deposit creation. The desired ratio of cash reserves to deposits will have increased.

Conversely, if banks initially hold excess reserves, a reduction in the stock of high-powered money or a withdrawal of currency by the public will lead to no multiple reduction of credit and deposits. Banks ordinarily find it profitable to lend out excess reserves at interest rather than hold non-interest-bearing cash reserves. But this is not always the case. Similarly, if the public changes its desired portfolio composition

5. This sum is found as the sum of the following infinite geometric progression:

$$\Delta D = 100 \left[1 + .8 + (.8)^2 + (.8)^3 + \ldots + (.8)^n\right] \quad \text{as } n \to \infty$$

$$\Delta D = 100 \left[\frac{1}{1 - .8}\right] = 100 \left(\frac{1}{.2}\right) = 100 \times 5 = 500$$

between cash and deposits, it will affect the amount of reserves available to the banking system and the volume of bank intermediation.

In the long run not merely bank deposits but income, wealth, and all other assets will vary with the stock of high-powered money. Provided that these ratios remain constant, it would be possible to calculate a cash-liabilities multiplier for all types of financial intermediaries.

central banking and monetary policy

FROM JULY 1927 to March 1933, the money stock in the United States fell by one third, and over two thirds of the decline came after England's departure from the gold standard. Had the money stock been kept from declining, as it clearly could and should have been, the contraction would have been shorter and far milder. It might still have been relatively severe by historical standards. But it is literally inconceivable that money income could have declined by over one half and prices by over one third in the course of four years if there had been no decline in the stock of money. I know of no severe depression in any other country or any time that was not accompanied by a sharp decline in the stock of money and equally of no sharp decline in the stock of money that was not accompanied by a severe depression. . . . [But] however consistent may be the relation between monetary change and economic change, and however strong the evidence for the autonomy of the monetary changes, we shall not be persuaded that the monetary changes are the source of the economic changes unless we can specify in some detail the mechanism that connects the one with the other.

— *MILTON FRIEDMAN*

EVERY SHORT STATEMENT about economics is misleading, with the possible exception of my present one.

— *ALFRED MARSHALL*

Individual actions lead to unintended social outcomes. A widely accepted objective of modern governments is to manage the level of aggregate demand to avoid both unemployment and inflation. An important tool toward these goals is monetary policy.

Monetary policy refers to central bank control of the supply and demand for the nominal stock of high-powered money. Changes in the stock of or demand for high-powered money initiate, as described in the previous chapter, a drawn-out adjustment process encompassing changes in the volume of bank intermediation, the price and supply of financial assets, saving, investment, and consumption plans, and the level and composition of aggregate spending in money terms. The central bank attempts to use its knowledge of these relationships to provoke disequilibrium and propel aggregate economic activity in some desired direction.

TECHNIQUES OF MONETARY CONTROL

Open Market Operations

Central banks have a variety of techniques to control the volume of commercial bank intermediation. The most important is *open market operations,* which refers to the buying and selling of government securities in the bond market. As the central bank is part of the government its debts are legal tender (high-powered money). A change in central-bank security holdings results in an identical change in central-bank liabilities.

When the central bank purchases securities it pays with checks drawn against itself. These checks are deposited by the sellers of the security in the commercial banking system and are then deposited by the commercial banks in the central bank. Claims against the central bank are high-powered money and constitute the reserves of the banking system. Conversely, sale of securities held by the central bank means that the central bank receives a check from the public drawn upon the commercial banking system. When cleared, this reduces the public's deposits with the commercial banks and reduces the commercial banks' deposits with the central bank by an identical amount.

Providing that commercial banks operate with a stable ratio of reserves to deposits, changes in bank cash reserves due to open-market operations induce equal proportionate changes in the volume of commercial bank loans and deposits as banks attempt to restore their desired reserve ratio. This response is indicated by the balance sheet transactions below the dashed line.

By changing the liabilities of the central bank and so the stock of high-powered money, open-market operations change the amount of currency that the public deposits with the banking system. As a result the demand for bank deposits and the relationship between bank earning assets and bank deposits shift upward or downward. As shown in Figure 16-1, open-market purchases result in an equal upward shift in the DD relationship to D_1D_1. The result is a new equilibrium position for the

Central Bank		Banking System		Public	
Securities +	Deposits +	Reserves +	Deposits +	Deposits + Securities −	
		Securities + Loans +	Deposits +	Securities − Deposits +	Debt +

OPEN-MARKET SALES

Securities −	Deposits −	Reserves −	Deposits −	Deposits − Securities +	
		Securities − Loans −	Deposits −	Securities + Deposits −	Debt −

banking system (E_1), with larger reserves (R_1), a higher level of deposits (D_1), and greater earning assets (L_1). Open-market sales have exactly the opposite effects.

The government ordinarily holds deposits with both the central bank and the commercial banking system, which enables the Treasury to affect the stock of high-powered money and the amount of commercial bank reserves by shifting its outstanding deposits between the central bank and the commercial banks.

Reserve Requirements

A second technique of central bank control is changes in the level of reserve requirements. Required reserves represent a legislated increase in the demand of the banking system for high-powered money. A reduction in the required reserve ratio provides commercial banks with excess reserves, which will be lent out to expand their assets and liabilities. Conversely, an .increase in the required reserve ratio forces banks to reduce their assets and deposits outstanding by selling securities and calling in loans.

Changes in required reserve ratios may be represented by an upward or downward shift in the position and slope of the *RR* curve for any given demand for deposits curve *DD*. As shown in Figure 16-2, an increase in reserve requirements from R to R_1 reduces the level of bank deposits from D to D_1.

Reserve requirement variation is an extremely direct and powerful technique. Paradoxically, this is the very reason given in most countries for its infrequent use. There is in principle nothing to prevent reserve requirement changes from being very small, in order not to be too unsettling in impact. But changes in reserve requirements, by changing the proportion of earning assets to total assets, affect the profitability of the commercial banking system. A reduction in required reserves increases the proportion of earning assets in bank portfolios and in the short run will raise bank profits. Over the longer run, competitive pressures tend to distribute part of these windfall gains to depositors and borrowers. As a result, bankers are always in favor of lower reserve requirements and opposed to an increase in required reserve ratios.

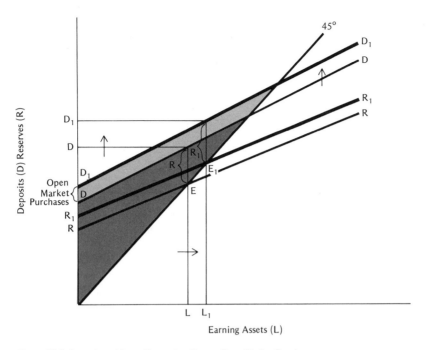

Figure 16-1 Deposit and Loan Expansion Due to Open Market Purchases

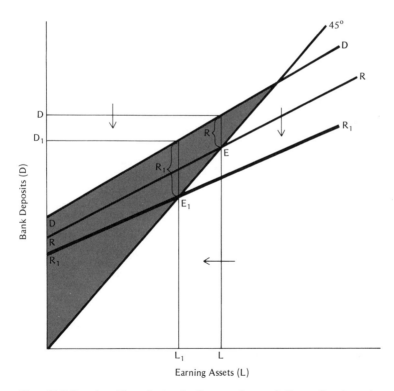

Figure 16-2 Deposit and Loan Contraction Due to an Increase in Reserve Requirements

Discount Rate

A third technique of central bank control is changes in the *discount rate*, the rate at which the central bank is willing to lend to the commercial banks. In the United States, member banks may borrow temporarily from the Federal Reserve System to meet short-run reserve deficiencies. A change in the discount rate frequently acts as a signal of the direction in which the central bank expects or intends the level of interest rates to move. In some countries, interest rates on bank loans are tied formally to the central bank discount rate.

Commercial bank borrowing from the central bank is equivalent to a variation in marginal reserve requirements, at the initiative of the commercial banks, but with some positive cost. A variable interest rate paid or charged by the central bank on cash reserves has sometimes been suggested as an alternative control tool.

Regulation of Bank Borrowing and Lending Rates

In a competitive banking system, individual banks have an incentive to pay interest and offer other services on deposits in order to increase their output and profits as long as the marginal cost of deposit funds is less than the marginal rate earned on their asset portfolios. The interest rate on deposits would then be equal to the interest rate on loans, minus the cost of servicing deposits and including some profit margin sufficient to yield a normal rate of return on bank capital.

In the United States the central bank sets a ceiling rate that banks are permitted to pay for deposits and restricts the entry of new banks into the market. The historic rationale for this policy, which was introduced in the Great Depression when nearly half the banks in the country failed, was to prevent price competition for deposits and so protect the profits of existing banks. The central bank is concerned to ensure the solvency of the banking system. When a bank fails its depositors may lose part of their money and be unable to exchange their deposits for cash until the bank is wound up. Deposit insurance has since reduced this risk to deposits, but the policy remains.

The effects of deposit rate regulation are analyzed in Figure 16-3. The dashed curve D_D represents the demand for bank deposits as the deposit rate is increased. At a ceiling deposit rate ($\bar{r}_D$) the amount of bank deposits demanded is equal to $\bar{D}$, given the high-powered money stock. Deposit rate ceilings thus result in a lower level of bank intermediation, a higher lending rate on loans (r_L) and higher bank profits than would occur (D_C) if banks were permitted to compete for deposit funds. (The competitive unregulated volume of intermediation is the intersection of the dashed D_D and S_L curves, including normal profits in the average cost of deposit funds.)

Frequently, in order to restrain bank profits or to favor borrowers, the maximum rate of interest on bank loans is also controlled. As shown in Figure 16-3, a ceiling loan rate ($\bar{r}_L$) reduces bank profits and creates excess demand for bank credit. The

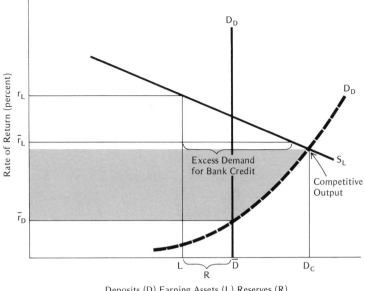

Figure 16-3 Regulation of Bank Borrowing and Lending Rates

unsatisfied fringe of borrowers who desire but cannot find lending accommodation at the controlled rate is increased. Banks must ration credit on nonprice criteria such as borrower character, credit worthiness, collateral, wealth, or purpose of the loan.

A rise to the ceiling rate of interest paid on bank deposits would result in an increase in the quantity of deposits demanded, given the stock of high-powered money. This increase would cause the D_D curve of Figure 16-1 and 16-2 to shift upward and steepen, resulting in a larger equilibrium volume of bank intermediation. As may be seen from Figure 16-3, lending rates will fall with the expansion of bank credit, other things being equal, unless a ceiling on lending rates was previously in force. By offering various extra services to depositors and by reducing the rate charged to borrowers, individual banks competing for depositors can circumvent to some degree the interest rate ceiling on deposits. Competition for borrowers by offering lower loan rates will reduce bank profit margins.

Ceilings on deposits and loans represent a hidden subsidy from lenders to borrowers equal to the difference between the controlled rate and the rate that would occur in the absence of government price-fixing. In Figure 16-3, the cost of the subsidy to bank depositors is equal to the shaded area. Part of this is received by those bank borrowers able to find accommodation, part accrues as profits to bank share owners, and part is a net social loss to everyone.

Moral Suasion

A fifth monetary control technique is *moral suasion,* sometimes disrespectfully termed open-mouth policy. The central bank may be able by direct request to persuade or cajole the commercial banks to restrict lending to all or to specific groups of borrowers. In the United States this is enforced by the threat to apply more stringent requirements in the amounts the Federal Reserve is willing to loan to commercial banks at the discount window.

Moral suasion is more effective in countries where branch banking is permitted and the number of commercial banks is therefore small. In Canada, England, and most European countries the three to five largest banks account for from 50 to nearly 100 percent of all deposits. The United States has a unit banking system. Branch banking is permitted only in certain states and is not permitted across state lines. There are approximately 13,000 commercial banks in America, 6,000 of which are members of the Federal Reserve System and account for nearly 90 percent of all bank deposits. Nevertheless, the 100 largest banks account for approximately one half of total deposits in all commercial banks.

Selective Controls

Central banks have a number of direct weapons to influence financial behavior. One of these is *selective control* of lending or borrowing by particular groups. In many countries, central banks regulate the minimum proportion of short-term government securities that commercial banks must hold in their portfolio, so-called *secondary reserve requirements*. The terms at which consumers may purchase credit, the collateral for bank loans, and the margins that must be put up to purchase equities are frequently controlled by central banks.

THE EFFECTS OF MONETARY CHANGE

Portfolio Disequilibrium

As developed in the previous chapters, households and firms desire to hold wealth in some preferred portfolio composition. Given portfolio preferences and anticipated return opportunities, financial-asset prices must adjust until wealth owners are content to hold exactly the existing asset stocks. Until this is the case there will be a tendency for financial-asset prices to change.

Figure 16-4 reproduces the portfolio balance diagram of Chapter 14. Postulating that all asset holders and issuers are initially in a position of full portfolio equilibrium at E, an increase in the stock of high-powered money will shift the A_0 curve rightward to A_1.

Initially, before prices have changed, households and firms are at position B. They have been pushed into disequilibrium and are holding greater currency balances than the desire by the amount EB. These currency balances are almost immediately deposited with the banking system, resulting in excess bank cash reserves. The banks are then in a position of portfolio disequilibrium. Depending on their speed of adjustment, they will spend these excess money balances to purchase

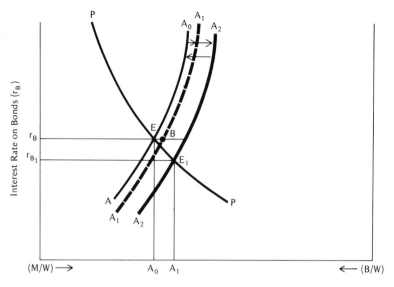

Figure 16-4 Portfolio Adjustment to Monetary Disturbance

earning assets. Any excess cash is again lent to the banking system. As banks adjust their portfolios to eliminate excess reserves, the stock of money shifts rightward, e.g., to A_2. In the process interest rates are forced downward. With the increased proportion of money balances in wealth portfolios, the new temporary equilibrium position E_1 which clears the financial markets is characterized by higher prices and a lower expected rate of return (r_{B_1}) on financial assets.

The banking system is now in portfolio equilibrium. But households and firms are not. As a result of lower interest returns and costs, greater portfolio liquidity, higher financial asset prices, and greater wealth, at E_1 desired holdings of real assets and debt now exceed actual holdings. This induces firms and households to increase their investment expenditures and to issue debt to finance real asset accumulation. Expenditures for present consumption goods also respond to the higher liquidity and value of wealth portfolios.

Over time, the rise in money income and the issue of new debt shifts the A_2 curve leftward, causing interest rates to move upwards. The rise in interest rates reduces planned deficits and raises planned surpluses. This process continues until asset holders and issuers are again in a position of full portfolio equilibrium, where actual asset stocks and liabilities are at their desired levels.

This sequence occurs in reverse for a reduction in the stock of money. Interest rates will initially rise and then gradually fall as deficit spending and debt issue is reduced throughout the adjustment process.

The Transmission Process

The transmission process by which a change in monetary variables affects real behavior is summarized in the flow chart of Figure 16-5. A change in the stock of

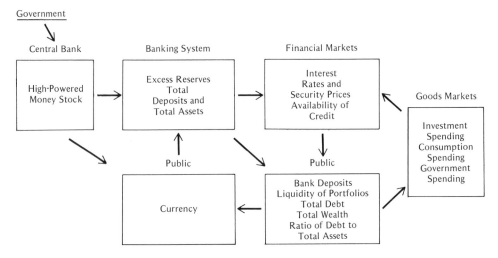

Figure 16-5 Transmission Process of Monetary Change

high-powered money affects bank total deposits and earning assets, the level of interest rates and security prices, the availability of credit (including all noninterest terms of borrowing the collateral and maturity conditions), the ratio of money balances in total wealth, and the value of total wealth itself. These in turn affect the quantity of real capital that wealth owners wish to hold and thus business, government, and household spending behavior. Changes in deficit or surplus spending for currently produced goods and services affect the supply and demand for financial assets, and so spill back into financial markets. In this manner excess supply or demand for money spills over into other financial markets, and then into the markets for current output.

Economists are now agreed on the general outlines of this stock-adjustment process in response to monetary change. But the shape and stability of portfolio preferences, the speed at which different assetholders adjust, and the magnitude of the effects on the level and composition of aggregate demand have not yet been determined.

Monetary Injection

Money does not come from mysterious, untraceable sources. The effects of monetary change depend on how a given increase in the money stock is injected into the income stream: government deficit-spending for goods, transfer payments, financial assets (lending), bank loans, or bank purchases of existing securities.

While the stock of money and the supply of credit are logically quite distinct, they happen to be bound together for institutional reasons in modern economies. Commercial bank deposits make up the bulk of the money stock, and commercial banks operations are legally restricted to the purchase of certain types of financial assets.

As a result an increase in the money stock is ordinarily associated with an increase in total bank credit which may finance to a greater or lesser extent an increase in borrowing and deficit spending by debtor units, depending on whether banks purchase existing securities or grant additional loans as they expand their assets.

Money introduced into the system by bank loan operations will be associated with a greater increase in aggregate demand than money introduced through bank purchases of existing securities. Open-market operations by the central bank may induce commercial banks to acquire investments; but if there is no demand by economic units to borrow and deficit spend, the result will be primarily a bidding up of bond prices, a fall in interest rates, and a piling up of liquidity by firms and households, with a resulting rise in the money-income ratio.

The effects of changes in financial variables on income variables will vary over time with regard to both speed and magnitude, depending on the stage of the business cycle. For example, in a boom, when investment demand has shifted outward and businessmen are operating near the vertical section of their cost of finance schedule, shifts in the availability of credit (horizontal shifts in the cost of finance schedule) will be more important. Conversely, in periods of depressed activity when investment demand has shifted leftward and businessmen are operating along the horizontal section of their cost of finance schedules, shifts in the availability of credit are unlikely to result in large changes in expenditures, while lower interest rates will make attractive certain long-term real investment projects.

The effect of monetary change thus depends on the choices of private economic units to acquire currently produced investment and consumption goods and services or to raise the liquidity of their wealth portfolios. As a result the relationship between changes in the money stock and the flow of income and expenditure is quite unstable and irregular in the short run.

PROBLEMS OF MONETARY POLICY

Governments gradually learned that they could influence the level of private spending by controlling the stock of high-powered money. The purpose of aggregate demand management by the monetary authorities is to achieve certain broad social goals, most importantly price stability, full employment, balance of payments equilibrium, and rapid growth.

In periods of recession and rising unemployment central banks act to increase the stock of money, primarily by open market purchases of securities. This action provides banks with excess cash reserves, inducing them to purchase securities. They thereby increase the stock of deposits and lower the level of interest rates. By increasing the stock of money and lowering the return on financial assets relative to real assets, central banks attempt to generate controlled portfolio disequilibrium to push wealth owners toward greater capital accumulation and increased aggregate spending for current output.

Conversely, in periods of inflation and rising prices central banks act to reduce the stock of money, primarily by open-market sales of securities. This action reduces bank cash reserves and forces banks to sell securities to raise their cash reserves up to their required level. The result is to reduce the stock of deposits and raise the level of interest rates. By creating portfolio imbalance and raising the return on financial assets relative to real assets, central banks attempt to depress the level of aggregate demand and discourage wealth owners from investment spending on real capital goods.

Countercyclical monetary policy thus represents an attempt to fight fire with fire. In response to exogenous shifts in private spending, central banks purposely generate portfolio disequilibrium by altering the size and composition of existing stocks of money and securities in the portfolios of private economic units, in an attempt to alter the level and composition of aggregate demand in some desired direction.

Lags

Because a considerable and variable period of time may be encompassed by the process of adjustment to monetary change, the achievement of the goals of countercyclical policy requires that the government both know the effects of its policy actions and be able to forecast the future course of the economy. It is convenient to distinguish three different types of lags involved in stabilization policy. These lags are illustrated diagramatically in Figure 16-6.

The recognition lag (R) refers to the period of time that lapses before changes in the level of economic activity are recognized by the stabilization authorities. It is always difficult to know when a turning point in the business cycle has occurred, as different indices are typically moving in opposite directions. It has been estimated that in the past the recognition lag has varied between one to six months and has been longer at the peak than at the trough.

The *administrative lag* (A) refers to the period of time that occurs between the date at which the need for a change in policy controls is recognized and the date

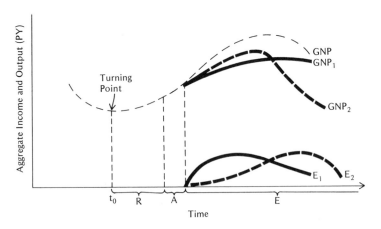

Figure 16-6 Lags in Stabilization Policy

when a policy control variable is actually changed. The length of the administrative lag varies widely with the type of stabilization policy being considered and the decision-making process of the appropriate government agency.

The administrative lag is likely to be short for monetary policy. The central bank can and frequently does change the directives to the manager of its open-market operations every week and thereby alters the stock of commercial bank reserves. As the banking system ordinarily allocates its portfolio between excess reserves and earning assets in a stable and known relationship, the central bank can control with considerable precision the total stock of money and bank credit.

The *effects lag* (E) refers to the period of time between when the policy change is initiated and when the effects of the policy on private spending are felt. The previous two lags are sometimes termed *inside lags,* because they occur within the government, while the third is termed an *outside lag.* It is of a different nature from the first two lags, both of which refer to discrete periods of time. The effects of a change in government policy on national income and expenditure do not occur all at once but are distributed gradually over some period of time. They typically increase to some maximum value and then decline.

The effects lag may be defined as the period of time necessary for a certain proportion of the total effects (e.g., 90 percent) to be realized. Depending on the particular policy change and the stage of the business cycle in which it occurs, the effects lag has been estimated to be as short as a few months, or as long as several years. Figure 16-6 shows two alternative hypothetical impact paths, E_1 and E_2. The *GNP* curve represents the hypothetical course of national income in the absence of any policy change. GNP_1 represents its course under a policy change with the effects lag structure E_1, and GNP_2 its course under a policy change with the lag structure E_2. The effects lag for monetary control is likely to be highly variable over different

Table 16-1   ESTIMATED LAG BETWEEN TURNING POINTS IN GROWTH OF MONEY STOCK AND IN THE LEVEL OF ECONOMIC ACTIVITY

Troughs (dates of)			Peaks (dates of)		
Trough in Date of Change of Money Stock Series	Trough in Economic Activity Series (Reference Cycle)	Lead of Money Stock Series in Months (before upturns)	Peak in Rate of Change in Money Stock Series	Peak in Economic Activity Series (Reference Cycle)	Lead of Money Stock Series in Months (before downturns)
October, 1931	March, 1933	17	November, 1927	August, 1929	21
October, 1937	June, 1938	8	April, 1936	May, 1937	13
January, 1949	October, 1949	9	June, 1943	February, 1945	20
September, 1953	August, 1954	11	November, 1951	July, 1953	20
December, 1957	April, 1958	4	February, 1955	July, 1957	29
December, 1959	February, 1961	14	June, 1958	May, 1960	23
December, 1969	November, 1970	11	July, 1968	November, 1969	16
		Average 10.6			Average 20.3

Source: 1927–1959 — Milton Friedman and Anna Schwartz, "Money and Business Cycles," *Review of Economics and Statistics* February, 1963).
    1968 – 1970 — B. W. Sprinkel, *Money and Markets: A Monetarist View* (New York, 1971).

stages of the business cycle. If restrictive monetary policies with the effects lag E_2 are undertaken to restrain a current expansion, they may have their primary impact in aggravating next year's recession. As a result the net effects may at times actually be disstabilizing.

Table 16-1 presents one estimate of the lag between turning points in the growth of the money stock and in the level of economic activity. As may be seen, the lag of economic activity behind the money stock is highly variable. It appears to be greater for peaks than for troughs.

Limitations of Countercyclical Monetary Policy

In view of the experience of the 1930s, monetary control was long held to be more effective as a restrictive technique than as an expansionary technique. A reduction in the amount of money and credit available and a rise in the interest costs of borrowing *must* eventually operate to reduce planned spending of households and business firms. Increases in the amount of money and in the availability of credit and reductions in the cost of borrowing do not *force* households and business firms in the same way to increase spending, and they need not do so when they are pessimistic about the future course of the economy. Nevertheless, as shown in Table 16-1, the average lag of spending behind monetary turning points was shorter for troughs than for peaks. Movements in economic activity for a time are self-reinforcing.

Monetary policy has redistributional consequences between debtors and creditors, borrowers and lenders. Financial institutions are typically net creditors, who tend to gain from higher interest rates and to lose from inflation. Net debtors lose from higher interest rates.

Even though nonbank financial intermediaries are not directly controlled by the central bank, they normally operate to reinforce central bank monetary policy. The volume of nonbank intermediation responds, positively though with a greater lag than bank intermediation, to changes in the stock of high-powered money. But if banks are restricted by a ceiling rate on deposits, a rise in market interest rates may enable nonbank intermediaries to pay higher rates on their secondary securities. As a result, they may be able to bid funds away from the banking system that they can in turn lend out, increasing their share of intermediation and in the process total spending and the value of total wealth. A given nominal stock of high-powered money may then support a higher level of total wealth and income, as the share of bank intermediation has declined, even though the nominal quantity of bank deposits remains constant.

This relative growth of nonbank intermediation will occur only if commercial banks are prohibited from paying interest on demand deposits and are restricted by an effective ceiling on the interest rates they can pay on time deposits. Commercial banks have an important advantage over most thrift institutions in that their assets are shorter-term. As a result, they are able to pay higher interest rates for deposits in periods of rising interest rates, as their total interest earnings respond rapidly to a rise in the level of market interest rates. In such periods commercial banks are able to bid deposits away from thrift institutions holding portfolios of longer-term securities, which then yield an average rate of return much lower than current market rates. An additional explanation for the ceiling on bank deposits is that it protects the size and solvency of thrift institutions, whose share of intermediation would be much lower if bank deposit rates were not artificially kept low. As lenders value liquidity highly, banks can borrow at lower cost than virtually all nonbank institutions. With anticipated inflation the real rate of return on deposits is even lower, further reducing asset holders' desired money-income ratio.

In summary, the stock of currency and demand deposits and the flow of spending do not exhibit a close and stable relationship in the short run. The lag between money and spending is long and variable. Restriction of the growth of demand deposits and a rise in interest rates will induce firms and households to economize on demand deposits and hold smaller money balances for the same volume of transactions. If portfolio preferences are elastic, or economic units have ample portfolio liquidity, very large changes in deposits may be necessary in order to affect private spending substantially.

Because the monetary authorities have sadly incomplete information about the structure of the economy and its response to monetary disturbance, they are forced to look at a number of *indicators* of monetary policy — such as the money stock or market interest rates — to interpret the effects of their past policy actions. Unfortunately as each of these monetary indicators may also change for other reasons, the task of countercyclical monetary control is extremely difficult and complicated.

Some economists have even argued that, because of the choice of misleading indicators and to the long and variable effects lag, monetary policy has in the past on balance been disstabilizing. Central bankers sometimes describe their job as "leaning against the wind." But as the effects of their policy actions are distributed over a variable and distant future, it is very difficult to discern *now* the direction that economic winds will be blowing at some future date.

A BRIEF HISTORY OF MONETARY POLICY

Once upon a time, when all currencies were fully convertible into gold, a country's money stock increased or decreased according to whether its balance of trade was favorable or unfavorable. A favorable balance of trade means an excess of merchandise exports over imports. So long as all currencies were convertible into gold, the excess of sales to foreigners over purchases from foreigners would be paid for by shipment of gold. A country with a favorable balance of trade would find that its gold reserves would rise. Its banks would then increase their loans and deposits, generating a rise in expenditure, income, and prices. This increase would operate to depress exports and stimulate imports, and forces were automatically set in play to restore the balance of payments toward equilibrium.

Conversely, with an unfavorable balance of trade the excess of imports over exports would result in a gold outflow and a reduction of a country's monetary base. Its banks would be forced to contract loans and reduce deposits. Prices and income would fall, tending to increase exports and reduce imports. This gold-based system was known as the international *gold standard,* and it operated from early in the nineteenth century until the Great Depression of the 1930s.

The gold standard contained a self-regulating adjustment mechanism to eliminate imbalances in trade between nations. At the same time it made a country's domestic money supply and the level of domestic spending, output, and prices dependent on its foreign trade balance and thus on the behavior of other countries. A country that played the rules of the gold standard game was forced into a domestic inflationary process whenever its exports exceeded its imports. Conversely, it was forced to watch a deflationary process force down prices and increase unemployment whenever its imports exceeded its exports. Only short-term international capital flows in response to interest-rate differentials (that is, lending and borrowing between countries) served to loosen this iron discipline.

It is not surprising that as governments gradually developed an understanding of what was occurring and a responsibility for domestic prosperity, they attempted to insulate their domestic economy from the rest of the world whenever it was regarded as being in the national interest by breaking the link between a country's domestic money stock and the amount of gold reserves it possessed. An outflow of gold would not lead to a restriction of bank loans, bank deposits, and deflation if the loss of gold reserves were offset by increased domestic currency. Similarly, gold inflows would not be inflationary if they were sterilized by being acquired by the government or offset by greater reserve requirements imposed on the banking system. The development of central banks to manage the domestic money supply thus led to the breakdown of the gold standard, as the automatic adjustment mechanism was no longer allowed to operate.

In addition to changes in the size of the high-powered money stock, shifts in the demand for high-powered money also proved disstabilizing. Before the existence of central banks, seasonal or cyclical increases in the public's demand for currency would force commercial banks to raise interest rates and sharply contract credit in an attempt to protect their cash-reserve position. If the banks could not meet all demands for cash they could not maintain the instant convertibility of their deposits on demand. In these circumstances, a run might develop in which many banks might fail, or a bank holiday be declared during which convertibility would be suspended.

Such banking panics occurred with disconcerting regularity in all countries. The chief function of central banks was thus originally to act as "lender of last resort." In times of a liquidity crisis, the commercial banks could borrow additional cash from the central bank by *rediscounting* certain eligible securities in their portfolios. In this way, a more elastic supply of high-powered money was provided in response to changes in the demand for currency.

Required cash-reserve ratios were instituted originally to protect depositors and insure bank solvency. With increased understanding, their primary function came to be to provide a fulcrum by which the central bank could control the amount of bank deposits. As long as commercial banks maintain a stable reserve-deposit ratio, control of commercial bank cash reserves means control of the total stock of bank deposits. Central banks have now been created in virtually all countries.

The Federal Reserve System

The central bank in the United States is called the Federal Reserve System. It was set up in 1914 as a private central bank and is still in part owned by all commercial banks that are members of the Federal Reserve System. This arrangement was chosen to ensure the central bank's independence from the government. It was believed that governments would be tempted to abuse the privileges of fiat money issue to finance public expenditures, with government deficits and inflation as the consequences.

Although traces of its earlier history remain, the Federal Reserve is now a public agency, though it retains considerable more policy independence than most other government departments. In the United States, it is still independent from the government for its budget, as it more than covers its expenses by the interest earnings on its asset portfolio. In most countries, the central bank is no longer privately owned but simply a branch of the government.

The composition and growth of the Federal Reserve's assets and liabilities are presented in Table 16-2. Nearly three quarters of its total assets are now held in the form of federal government securities, and nearly two thirds of its liabilities are Federal Reserve Notes, that is, currency outstanding. Currency is also issued by the Treasury. Almost one third of Federal Reserve liabilities are in the form of

Table 16-2 FEDERAL RESERVE SYSTEM, PRINCIPAL ASSETS AND LIABILITIES, 1929–71 (BILLIONS OF DOLLARS, YEAR-END FIGURES)

Assets, Liabilities, Net Worth, and Capital	1929	1933	1941	1945	1950	1960	1965	1970	1971
Gold and Foreign Exchange	3.0	3.8	20.5	17.9	21.5	17.5	14.3	10.9	10.3
Loans to Member Banks	0.6	0.0	0.0	0.2	0.0	0.0	0.1	0.3	0.0
U.S. Government Securities	0.5	1.9	2.3	24.3	20.8	27.4	40.8	62.1	70.2
Bills	0.1	0.4	0	12.8	1.2	2.9	9.1	26.0	30.1
Notes	0.2	1.1	.8	2.1	12.5	12.5	24.8	33.2	35.6
Bonds	0.1	0.4	1.5	.9	4.6	2.5	6.6	2.9	3.3
Total Assets	5.5	7.0	24.4	45.1	47.2	53.0	62.7	85.8	94.6
Liabilities and Net Worth									
Federal Reserve Notes	1.9	3.1	8.2	24.6	23.6	28.4	37.1	50.3	53.8
Deposits									
Member Bank Reserves	2.4	2.7	12.4	15.9	17.7	17.1	18.5	24.1	27.8
U.S. Treasury	0.1	0	0.9	1.0	0.7	0.5	0.7	1.2	2.0
Capital Accounts	0.4	0.4	0.4	0.6	0.9	1.2	1.1	1.4	1.5
Total Liabilities and Capital	5.5	7.0	24.4	45.1	47.2	53.0	62.7	85.8	94.6

Source: Board of Governors, Federal Reserve System.

deposits, primarily held by commercial banks. These deposits, plus member bank holdings of currency, constitute the cash reserve base of the commercial banking system.

Table 16-2 shows the rapid increase in Federal Reserve assets and liabilities that occurred from the depths of the depression in 1933 to the end of the Second World War in 1945. In the postwar period, central-bank total assets and liabilities grew much more slowly.

For several decades after the experience of the 1930s it was widely believed that monetary policy was ineffective in stimulating demand. You can lead a borrower to credit, but you can't make him drink. There are three points at which the transmission process might be truncated.

First, at existing levels of interest rates and demand for credit the monetary authorities might be unable to increase the stock of money. This would occur if banks do not find it profitable to make additional loans or investments, but instead hold increases in cash as excess reserves. The monetary authorities would then be "pushing on a string."

Second, even if the money stock is increased, long-term interest rates might not fall if they were already low relative to expected future rates, a phenomenon termed the *liquidity trap*. Keynes believed that given some expected normal range for future interest rates based on past experience, as current long-term interest rates were driven increasingly below this normal range by increases in the ratio of money to wealth, more and more individuals would anticipate that interest rates would rise in the future toward their old normal levels. As a result, given the inverse relation between long-term bond prices and interest rates, wealth owners increasingly expect capital losses because of holding long-term bonds. This process offers increasing resistance to any fall in long-term interest rates. At some level of interest rates, wealth owners would prefer to accumulate money rather than to invest in long-term bonds. Long-term rates would not fall further unless expectations about the future were changed. Short-term interest rates could fall to very low levels, but investment plans are based on long-term rates. In this liquidity trap situation, increases in the stock of money do not result in increased expenditures but are simply held in idle balances, and the ratio of money to income rises.

Third, even if long term interest rates fall, investment might not increase if the demand to invest by business firms were interest inelastic. In the face of excess capacity and depressed demand, business firms would be unlikely to respond to lower long-term interest rates by significantly increasing investment expenditures.

Monetarism and Causality

Recently, monetary policy has experienced a resurgence. Table 16-3 presents the growth of the money stock, GNP, prices, and interest rates over the postwar period. There is no close year-to-year relationship between money and income. In the immediate postwar period, in the early fifties, and in the middle fifties, large changes in

Table 16-3 GNP, MONEY STOCK, PRICES, AND INTEREST RATES, 1945–71

Year	Money Stock (Commercial Bank Demand and Time Deposits Plus Currency Outstanding)	GNP in Billions of Dollars	Ratio of Money Stock to GNP	Percent Change in Money Stock (annual)	Percent Change in GNP (annual)	Percent Change in Consumer Price Index (annual)	Interest Rates Short-Term[1]	Interest Rates Long-Term[2]	Real Interest Rates Short-Term Interest Rate—Percent Change in CPI	Real Interest Rates Long-Term Interest Rate—Percent Change in CPI
1945	132.5	211.9	.63	15.7	.9	2.3	.75	2.62	−1.55	.32
1946	143.8	208.5	.69	8.5	−1.6	8.5	.81	2.53	−7.69	−5.97
1947	148.5	231.3	.64	3.3	10.9	14.4	1.03	2.61	−13.37	−11.79
1948	147.6	257.6	.57	−.6	11.4	7.7	1.44	2.82	−6.36	−4.98
1949	147.6	256.5	.58	0.0	−.4	−1.0	1.49	2.66	2.49	3.66
1950	152.9	284.8	.54	3.6	10.9	1.0	1.45	2.62	.45	1.62
1951	160.8	328.4	.49	5.2	15.3	8.0	2.16	2.86	−5.74	−5.04
1952	168.6	345.5	.49	4.8	5.2	2.2	2.33	2.96	.13	.76
1953	173.3	364.6	.48	2.8	5.5	0.8	2.52	3.20	1.72	2.40
1954	180.6	364.8	.50	4.2	.1	0.4	1.58	2.90	1.08	2.40
1955	185.2	398.0	.47	2.5	9.1	−0.3	2.18	3.06	2.58	3.46
1956	188.8	419.2	.45	1.9	5.3	1.5	3.31	3.36	1.81	1.86
1957	193.3	441.1	.44	2.4	5.2	3.5	3.81	3.89	.21	.29
1958	206.6	447.3	.46	6.9	1.4	2.8	2.46	3.79	−.24	1.09
1959	210.0	483.7	.43	1.6	8.1	0.8	3.97	4.38	3.17	3.58
1960	214.6	503.7	.43	2.2	4.1	1.6	3.85	4.41	2.25	2.81
1961	228.7	520.1	.44	6.6	3.3	1.1	2.97	4.35	1.97	3.35
1962	245.9	560.3	.44	7.5	7.7	1.2	3.26	4.33	3.16	3.23
1963	265.8	590.5	.45	8.1	5.4	1.2	3.55	4.26	2.35	3.06
1964	273.8	632.4	.43	3.0	7.1	1.3	3.97	4.40	2.67	3.10
1965	298.1	684.9	.43	8.9	8.3	1.7	4.38	4.49	2.44	2.79
1966	314.0	747.6	.42	5.3	9.5	2.9	5.55	5.13	2.65	2.23
1967	345.7	793.9	.44	11.0	5.9	2.9	5.10	5.51	2.20	2.61
1968	378.0	864.2	.44	9.3	8.9	4.2	5.90	6.18	1.70	1.98
1969	386.8	929.1	.42	2.3	7.5	5.4	7.83	7.03	2.43	1.63
1970	418.2	974.1	.43	8.1	4.8	5.9	7.72	8.04	1.82	2.14
1971	464.7	1046.8	.44	11.1	7.5	4.3	5.11	7.39	0.81	3.04

Source: Department of Commerce, Board of Governors, Federal Reserve System.

1. Prime commercial paper, 4–6 months.
2. Moody's Corporate Aaa.

aggregate spending occurred in many years with small increases in the money stock. They are reflected in the fall in the ratio of money to GNP over these periods. During the 1960s the money-income ratio remained fairly stable, and the change in GNP was closer to the change in the stock of money, with the important exception of 1969 and 1970.

From the observation of this association between money and income has grown the new policy of *monetarism:* money matters, but the government must not attempt to "fine-tune" the economy. If only the money stock were increased at a constant rate, for example 3 or 5 percent per year, money income would also grow at this rate, and fluctuations in the level of activity would be smaller. Inflation can be defeated simply by restraining the growth of the money stock.

As shown in Table 16-3, there is both theoretical and empirical evidence of a rough longer-run stability in the relationship between spending and changes in the money stock. But this observed regular association between changes in money and income does not prove that the direction of causality runs from money to income. Increases in the money stock, even though under the control of the central bank, respond to increases in the demand for money and credit.

This influence occurs because the central bank is unwilling to permit the large and rapid procyclical fluctuations in the level of interest rates that would result from stable monetary growth. The central bank fears ensuing disorderly conditions and even liquidity crises in the financial markets. In the face of an increase in spending and a rise in the demand for credit, interest rates tend to rise sharply. The central bank has the choice of accommodating this demand and permitting the stock of money and credit to increase, or of doing nothing. In this case it must be asked to sit as a spectator at a wake of increasing credit crises, and watch a wave of firms unable to obtain additional short-term financing slide into bankruptcy. The resulting impact on the stock market and investor confidence may be difficult to reverse.

Even if a credit crisis is avoided, there is no assurance that the reduction in spending and money income which will follow a restriction of monetary growth will halt the rate of inflation. If money wages and costs continue to increase, so will prices. The reduction in spending will then cause primarily a fall in real output, with a resulting increase in unemployment rates and excess capacity. This occurred in 1969, when for the first time the stock of money was reduced, but the rate of inflation nevertheless continued to accelerate.

In view of these alternatives, it is not surprising that increases in the money stock became endogenous, as the money supply responds to increases in the demand for money required to finance a higher money level of transactions. In response to the higher unemployment rates, the money stock was increased rapidly in 1970.

As shown in Table 16-3, the level of interest rates rose sharply over the postwar period. This rise accompanied the fall in the ratio of money to income to 1960. Movements in the level of interest rates are characteristically inversely related to changes in the money stock and positively related to the increase in GNP. During the late sixties a large rise in interest rates occurred while the ratio of money to income remained relatively stable. This rise in interest rates after 1965 was associated with the rapid rise in prices. Anticipated inflation drives up nominal interest rates as lenders demand a higher return to compensate for expected inflation and a lower real purchasing power of money in the future, while borrowers are willing to pay a higher return since they anticipate being able to repay in dollars of lower real value.

Nominal interest rates do not adjust sufficiently in the short run to compensate fully for increases in the price level. Real interest rates typically fall as the rate of inflation accelerates. As seen in Table 16-3, real interest rates were quite low throughout the period and exceeded 3 percent in only a few years.

APPENDIX: THE VARIABILITY OF MONETARY CHANGE

The variability of the consequences of monetary change is illustrated in Figure 16-7, which reproduces the *IS-LM* diagram of Chapter 14. The effects of a change in the stock of money on interest rates, prices and real output can be seen to depend on

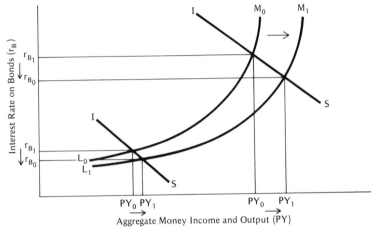

a. Expansionary Monetary Policy

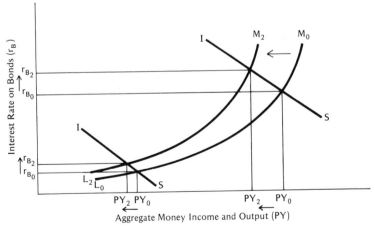

b. Restrictive Monetary Policy

Figure 16-7 Differing Effects of Monetary Policy

where the *IS* and *LM* curves initially intersect and on where the aggregate demand function intersects the aggregate supply function in output markets.

An increase in the stock of money (or reduction in the stock of bonds) shifts the *LM* curve rightward, as a lower level of interest rates is now consistent with equilibrium in the financial markets at any level of money income. Conversely, a reduction in the money stock (or increase in the stock of bonds) shifts the *LM* curve leftward, raising interest rates at any given level of money income.

If interest rates are low relative to past levels and if portfolios are already liquid, the level of interest rates will be insensitive to a change in the money stock. As shown in Figures 16-7a and b, over the Keynesian range, where interest rates are at or near their floor level and the stock of money is large relative to wealth and income, expansionary or restrictive monetary policy has little effect on either the level of aggregate spending and income or on interest rates. In addition in periods of recession the *IS* relationship will slope downward relatively steeply, as the demand to invest will be interest inelastic.

Expansionary monetary policy will eventually be effective even in this Keynesian range by increasing portfolio liquidity, the real value of private wealth, and so aggregate demand, thus shifting up the *IS* curve. A restrictive monetary policy, which shifts the *LM* curve leftward, if carried far enough must eventually always become effective in reducing spending.

Over the normal and classical range changes in the money stock affect both the level of interest rates and aggregate money demand, depending on the slope of the *IS* relationship. Both expansionary and restrictive monetary policy are likely to be effective over the normal range, and even more effective if the economy is in the classical range. In periods of prosperity, the *IS* relationship will be flat or even upward sloping as the demand to invest will be strongly responsive to the level of income. If the *IS* relation is upward sloping in a boom, an increase in the stock of money will result in a rise in interest rates, while a restrictive monetary policy will cause interest rates to fall.

Figure 16-7 does not specify how a change in aggregate spending is divided between changes in the price level (P) and changes in the volume of real output (Y). This proportion will depend, as described in Chapter 14, on the intersection of the aggregate demand and aggregate supply function, and on how close the economy is operating to its capacity ceiling. At low rates of utilization prices are stable in response to shifts in aggregate demand, and the supply response occurs primarily in real output (Y). But as full capacity is approached, the change in prices (P) accounts for a larger and larger component of the total change in money expenditure and income (PY).

fiscal policy
and the public debt

IF THE TREASURY were to fill old bottles with bank-notes, bury them at suitable depths in disused coal-mines which are then filled up to the surface with town rubbish, and leave it to private enterprise on well-tried principles of laissez-faire to dig the notes up again . . . there need be no more unemployment and, with the help of the repercussions, the real income of the community, and its capital wealth also, would probably become a good deal greater than it actually is. It would, indeed, be more sensible to build houses and the like; but if there are political and practical difficulties in the way of this, the above would be better than nothing.

JOHN MAYNARD KEYNES

WE MUST REDUCE expenditures drastically, but we must be careful not to affect anyone's constituents.

—UNKNOWN

Fiscal policy refers to all government budgetary and tax operations undertaken to manage the level of aggregate demand. Debt policy refers to changes in the quantity and composition of outstanding government debt undertaken for the same purpose. As high-powered money is but one form of government debt, fiscal, debt and monetary policy are necessarily interrelated.

FUNCTIONAL FINANCE

Government in the National Accounts

Government spending for goods and services is similar to investment and consumption expenditure as constituting one component of aggregate demand. Government taxes are similar to saving in that they reduce the proportion of current income devoted to current expenditure.

The inclusion of government fiscal operations in the national accounts may be shown as follows. Total income received is either paid out in taxes, consumed, or saved (transfer payments are considered as negative taxes).

$Y \equiv T + C + S$ (where $\equiv$ means "is identical to").

Total output consists of consumption goods, investment goods, and public goods: $Y \equiv C + I + G$.

Equating: $S + T \equiv I + G$

This formula states that taxes plus saving are always identically equal to investment plus government spending. Taxes are similar to saving as a *leakage* in the multiplier process, reducing aggregate demand. Government spending is similar to investment as an *injection* into the multiplier process, increasing aggregate demand. In equilibrium, planned saving plus taxes must be equal to planned investment plus government spending.

Disposable income is equal to total income received minus taxes paid. As a result a change in taxes will affect private consumption and investment spending, depending on which tax rates are changed and whose disposable income is altered.

The Need for Aggregate Demand Management

If the level of income is not to change, aggregate demand must equal aggregate supply. Aggregate demand consists of the sum of consumption, investment, and public expenditures undertaken independently by millions of individual households, businesses, and governments.

Investment decisions must be undertaken in the present with regard to an uncertain future. Because future prices, sales, and the investment plans of other firms cannot be known in advance, firms never have enough information to ensure that their investment projects will later turn out to be appropriate. Market forces

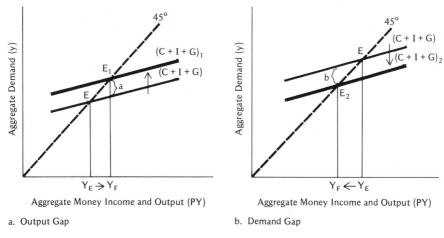

Figure 17-1 Demand Management

alone are insufficient to ensure that the investment plans of firms will always be compatible with both the saving plans of households *and* the real productive potential of the economy. As a result aggregate demand in any period is likely to exceed or fall short of aggregate output at full employment and stable prices.

Consider first a situation in which aggregate spending is insufficient to purchase all the goods and services produced at full employment. The extent of this deficiency, shown as a in Figure 17-1a, is termed the *output gap*. As a result, the economy will tend toward the equilibrium income level Y_E where aggregate demand $(C + I + G)$ is equal to a lower level of aggregate supply, as indicated by the intersection with the 45-degree line. An increase in government spending *ceteris paribus* will raise aggregate demand. A reduction in government taxes *ceteris paribus* will raise disposable income and therefore private consumption and investment spending. The goal of fiscal policy in such a situation is therefore by some combination of expenditure increases and tax reductions to raise the aggregate demand function to $(C+I+G)_1$, so that the new equilibrium level of income (E_1) is at full employment output.

Conversely, aggregate demand may exceed aggregate supply at full employment. The extent of this excess, as shown as b in Figure 17-1b, is termed the *demand gap*, because the equilibrium level of income Y_E will now be above full employment. The goal of fiscal policy is by some combination of tax increases and expenditure reductions to reduce aggregate demand to $(C + I + G)_2$, at which point the equilibrium level of income (E_2) is at full employment output.

Functional Finance

Until the Keynesian revolution in economics, economists and statesmen agreed that governments, like individuals, had an economic as well as a moral obligation to live within their means. Fear of the consequences of inflation and of an ever-increasing government debt was the specter behind the traditional view that governments must operate at all times to balance their budgets. It was this hold of fiscal orthodoxy that prevented governments from increasing expenditures or cutting taxes in the Great Depression of the thirties. In fact, in a desperate attempt to balance the budget, exactly the opposite policy was pursued in most capitalist countries, with the salient exception of Nazi Germany.

This policy of orthodox finance was bitterly attacked by Keynes and his followers. They insisted that the orthodox rule of public finance — that the government must balance its budget like any other economic unit — was desperately inappropriate in the Great Depression. They had great fun pointing out that there was no intrinsic reason for the government's budget to be balanced over an hour, a week, a year, or even a business cycle as a goal in itself.

Keynesians argued that decisions to change the level of taxes and expenditures ought to be judged by their *effects* on the economy, not by any predetermined rules of fiscal morality. The government should increase expenditures or cut taxes in a depression in order to raise aggregate demand. Conversely, the government should reduce expenditures or raise taxes in an inflation in order to lower aggregate demand. These simple rules were termed *Functional Finance*. While controversial when first formulated in the early forties, they have now become widely accepted in both government and business circles.

Whether the government "ought" to have a surplus or a deficit thus depends on the saving and spending decisions of households and businesses. If, as shown in Figure 17-1a, aggregate spending was insufficient to purchase all the goods and services provided at full employment (Y_F), the government should run a deficit either by increasing spending or by cutting taxes to increase aggregate demand and eliminate this output gap. Similarly, if aggregate demand exceeds full employment output (Y_F) as shown in Figure 17-1b, the government should run a surplus to reduce aggregate demand and eliminate the demand gap.

The Effects of Government Expenditure and Taxation, *Ceteris Paribus*

In Figure 17-2 Y_E represents an initial equilibrium position of less than full employment. An increase in government expenditures, tax receipts being held constant, raises the government expenditures component of the aggregate demand function. Provided that the consumption and investment functions remain unchanged, the aggregate demand function will shift upward to $(C + I + G')$. Alternatively, the government could keep public expenditures constant and raise the disposable income of households and businesses by reducing taxes. Depending on which type of taxes are cut, and again provided that the expenditure functions out of disposable income remain unchanged, consumption and investment spending will increase, shifting the level of aggregate demand upward to $(C' + I' + G)$. A similar effect occurs as a result of an increase in government transfer payments, which increase private disposable income and may be regarded as negative taxes.

Whether government expenditures should be increased or taxes cut depends on

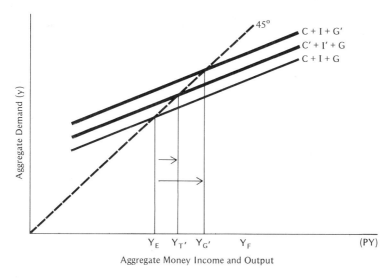

Figure 17-2 Effect of Increasing Government Spending or Cutting Taxes, <u>Ceteris Paribus</u>

whether the allocation goals of the government are to shift the composition of aggregate output toward public goods or private goods. The desired mix of output between the private and public sector is largely a political decision. As the benefits of public goods are extremely difficult to measure, and these benefits are shared unevenly among different groups, there is always a difference of opinion as to whether more public goods or lower taxes are preferable.

The Fiscal Multiplier

The effects of an increase in government spending or a reduction in taxes on the equilibrium level of income under such circumstances will depend on the value of the multiplier, that is, the slope of the aggregate demand function in Figure 17-2 representing the marginal propensity to spend out of disposable income.

The effects of an increase in government expenditure on aggregate demand *ceteris paribus* will always be greater than the effect of an equal reduction in taxes, because an increase in government spending raises the level of aggregate demand in the initial period by the full amount of the increase in government expenditure on goods and services. A reduction in taxes or an increase in transfer payments results in a smaller initial increase in private spending, depending on the value of the marginal propensity to spend, so long as it is less than one.

Full Employment Equilibrium

For full employment equilibrium, aggregate demand must equal aggregate output at full employment. If household saving exceeds business investment at full employ-

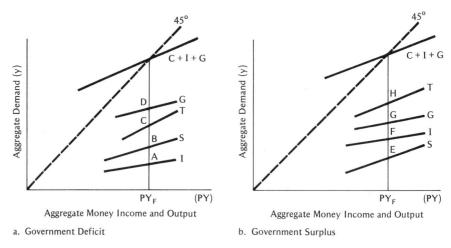

a. Government Deficit

b. Government Surplus

Figure 17-3 Full Employment Equilibrium

ment levels of income, government spending must exceed government tax receipts by the same amount. Alternatively stated, the surplus spending of the household sector at full employment must be offset exactly by the deficit spending of the business and government sectors. As surpluses and deficits must necessarily balance, if one sector runs a surplus it must be offset by the deficits of other sectors if national income is not to fall.

This balanced situation is shown in Figure 17-3a, which corresponds to the output-gap situation of Figure 17-1a. Planned saving exceeds planned investment at full employment by the amount AB. This excess of private saving over investment is exactly offset by government deficit spending of DC. The surplus of the household sector is exactly offset by the deficits of the business and government sector. Equilibrium could have been reached with a lower level of government spending (shifting down the G function) and a lower level of taxation (shifting down the T function). Lower taxes would result in more consumption and investment spending, increasing the proportion of private to public goods at full employment.

In Figure 17-3b, private investment exceeds private saving by EF at full employment, corresponding to the demand gap situation of Figure 17-1b. The excess of business deficit spending over household surpluses at full employment must be exactly offset by a government surplus of GH. Only when total planned surpluses and deficits are equal is there no tendency for the level of income to change.

Fiscal Drag

Government tax receipts are more responsive in the short run to changes in the level of income than are government expenditures. With a progressive tax rate, taxes may rise more than proportionately to the increase in national income. Many expenditure programs in contrast are independent of the level of income. In Figure 17-4, G and T show how government expenditures and tax receipts vary with the level of national income. As income increases from PY_1 to PY_F, the government's budget deficit (BA) falls and becomes a government budget surplus (EF).

The economy may be unable to attain full employment because, as national income increases, the tendency of tax revenues automatically to rise operates to depress aggregate demand. Such a situation has been termed *fiscal drag*. What appears to be an expansionary fiscal policy, if judged by the current deficit, is actually restrictive, as a large surplus would be generated at full employment. The effects of government spending and taxation on the economy thus cannot be judged merely by looking at the *actual* budget deficit or surplus. It is more revealing to look at what the budget deficit or surplus would be in a position of *full employment*. As shown in Figure 17-4, the actual budget deficit BA at the low level of income Y_1 is consistent with the potential budget surplus EF at full employment (PY_F).

Paradoxically, if the interaction of the multiplier and accelerator effects in response to a rise in demand is sufficiently strong, a reduction in tax rates or a rise in government spending may stimulate such a rise in the level of income that sufficient additional tax revenue is generated to reduce the government's deficit. In Figure 17-4, if the lower tax rate structure T' results in a rise in the level of income from pY_1 to pY_2, it will reduce the deficit from BA to DC. Cutting taxes may then be consistent with reducing the government's deficit.

Different types of taxes, as well as the same tax under different conditions, have very different effects on private spending and saving decisions. A temporary change in personal income taxes will result in a relatively small alteration in aggregate demand, as household consumption plans are largely based upon lifetime or permanent income and wealth. On the other hand, a change in an expenditure or sales tax may result in a large reduction in aggregate demand, particularly if the tax is believed to be temporary, in which case households and businesses can avoid the tax by postponing expenditures. The willingness to spend decreases. As a tax cut

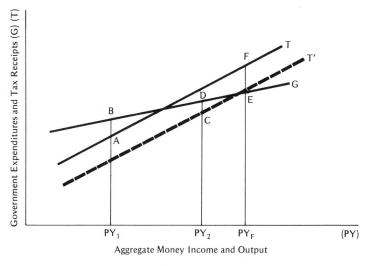

Figure 17-4 Actual and Full Employment Budget Surplus or Deficits

and a tax increase often have different results, the effects of tax changes are not reversible.

As a result the level of the government's deficit or surplus, even at full employment, does not represent an accurate measure of the net expansionary or restrictive effects of government operations. With a given tax structure, increases in the government's budgetary deficit are expansionary and increases in the government's budget surplus restrictive. But a given surplus or deficit can have different expansionary or restrictive effects on the economy, depending on how the tax revenues are financed and how they are spent.

Secular Stagnation

Government deficit spending during a depression was termed *pump-priming*. In addition to making such a policy politically more palatable, this term indicated a hope that once prosperity was regained, private investment spending would recover and government deficit spending would no longer be necessary.

In view of the unprecedented length and depth of the Great Depression, many economists and social critics came to believe that mature and rich capitalist economies were likely to generate a persistent excess of saving over investment at full employment. With such a tendency toward underconsumption, oversaving, and secular stagnation, governments would be forced continually to run a deficit in order to maintain aggregate demand equal to aggregate supply at full employment.

Marxist critics argued that this reinforced the imperialist tendencies of capitalist governments, as government deficit spending for military purposes abroad was politically the easiest way to maintain full employment at home. More sanguine critics argued that there was no intrinsic reason why democratic governments could not provide socially desired public works such as schools, houses, and roads rather than tanks and missiles. Most were agreed that the size of government expenditures required to stabilize the economy was likely to increase. To the delight of some and the chagrin of others, the future for capitalism appeared bleak.

FINANCIAL AND BALANCE-SHEET EFFECTS OF FISCAL POLICY

The conclusions of the foregoing analysis of the effects of a change in government expenditure and taxes depend on the assumption that the consumption and investment propensities of the private sector out of disposable income remain unaffected. As this *ceteris paribus* assumption is never exactly satisfied in practice, the conclusions of the simple Keynesian model may be regarded as a kind of first approximation.

Changes in government expenditures or taxation cause an equal change in the government's deficit or surplus, which must somehow be financed. Alternatively expressed, fiscal policy also affects financial markets and the balance-sheet position of the private sector, which in turn react back to affect private consumption and investment propensities out of disposable income. The manner in which fiscal changes are financed affects the position of the consumption and investment functions in Figure 17-2 and thereby the magnitude of the resulting change in aggregate demand.

An increase in government spending must somehow be financed if taxes are to remain unchanged. Similarly, a reduction in government tax receipts requires that other sources of finance be relied on to finance an existing level of expenditures. Government deficits may be financed by the issue of debt, or by printing high-powered money, the non-interest-bearing debt of the government. Similarly, government surpluses result in the reduction of government debt, either bonds or high-powered money. These effects of government deficits or surpluses on the balance sheet of the private sector are shown as follows:

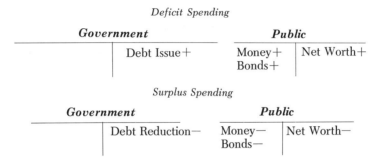

Deficit Spending

Government		*Public*	
	Debt Issue+	Money+ Bonds+	Net Worth+

Surplus Spending

Government		*Public*	
	Debt Reduction−	Money− Bonds−	Net Worth−

Although an increase in taxes is similar to an increase in saving in reducing current expenditure on goods and services, its balance-sheet effects are very different. Saving results in an increase in private assets and net worth, while taxes reduce private assets and net worth. Money is transferred to the public sector through the coercive power of the government. Transfer payments are negative taxes; private assets and net worth are increased through the largess of the government.

The effect of government budgetary operations thus depends on how the accompanying government deficit or surplus is financed, and on the response of private economic units to changes in financial variables and their balance sheet position. If the government borrows by the issue of bonds to the public to finance a deficit, the result is to increase the demand for loanable funds and raise interest rates. As the money stock is unaffected, the increased proportion of securities in wealth portfolios will be held only at higher interest rates.

If the government finances its deficits by printing high-powered money or, what is the same thing, by the sale of bonds to the central bank, the result is to increase bank reserves. Bank credit and bank deposits will then increase by the same proportion. The increased proportion of money balances in wealth portfolios will cause security prices to rise and interest rates to fall. If the government finances its deficit by selling bonds to the banking system and the central bank provides the banks with sufficient reserves, bank deposits and therefore the money stock are increased by an amount equal to the government deficit.

The effects of a government surplus are exactly the reverse, depending on whether it results in redirection of government debt or a reduction in the money stock.

The Relation Between Monetary and Fiscal Policy

Monetary policy was defined in Chapter 16 as government control of the high-powered money stock to achieve certain stabilization goals. It is now possible to see the manner in which monetary and fiscal policy are related. Government budgetary deficits financed by printing money or by the sale of bonds to the central bank or to the commercial banks must result in an increase in the total money stock. Conversely, government budgetary surpluses not allocated to the retirement of debt or the purchase of new financial assets must result in a reduction in the money stock.

The Treasury affects the high-powered money stock by running a deficit or surplus between its cash receipts and its cash expenditures. The central bank affects the high-powered money stock by the purchase and sale of existing securities for money and so shifts the composition of money and bonds in wealth-owner portfolios.

Government deficits financed by sales of bonds to the public and government surpluses devoted to the purchase of private debt or the retirement of government debt both leave the high-powered money stock in the hands of the private sector unchanged. But by changing the stock of securities outstanding, they affect financial asset prices, the level of interest rates, and the demand for loanable funds.

Once these balance-sheet effects of fiscal policy are acknowledged, all the old fears of secular stagnation may be put to rest. Increases in the money stock will raise private consumption and investment spending and permit a full-employment equilibrium level of income even with no government deficit spending. An increase in the high-powered money stock — whether through currency issue or government borrowing from the banking system and whether injected by government deficit spending for goods and services, transfer payments, or central bank purchase of outstanding securities — raises the money balances and net worth of the private sector.

Stagnation, in the sense of an excess of planned saving over planned investment at full employment, need never be a serious problem under capitalism, no matter how mature and rich the economy, how concentrated the distribution of income and wealth, or how low the expected return on real investment. It can always be avoided simply by the government's raising the ratio of high-powered money to income and thereby increasing the net worth of the private sector. The huge rise in the money-income and liquidity ratio of the private sector following the Second World War was responsible for the inflation experienced in virtually all countries in the postwar period.

If the government finances a change in expenditure or taxes by issuing money, it reinforces the stabilization effects of the simple Keynesian model. But deficits or surpluses financed by debt issue have the opposite effect on private spending and may even completely offset the simple Keynesian effects. Increased government spending financed by debt issue drives up interest rates and reduces the amount of loanable funds available, so that private deficit spending declines. Similarly, increased taxes and government surpluses used to repurchase government debt permit greater private deficit spending, as money withdrawn from the private sector by taxation is returned to it again by debt reduction.

Underestimation of the importance of the accompanying financial changes explains in part the unsatisfactory record of government fiscal policy in combatting inflation over much of the postwar period. While deficits were financed largely by bank borrowing and increases in the money stock, surpluses were used largely to retire the national debt, so that the amount of money in the hands of households and firms was not reduced.

LIMITATIONS OF FISCAL POLICY

There are serious obstacles to the successful use of fiscal policy for stabilization purposes. It is extremely difficult to adjust expenditures and tax rates flexibly in response to cyclical changes in aggregate demand. The three types of lags described for monetary also apply to fiscal policy. Although the recognition lag is similar and the effects lag is shorter, the administration lag is very much longer for fiscal policy. Because government expenditures and taxes have distributional and allocational effects, even if there is a consensus with regard to the desirability on stabilization grounds of changing the government's surplus or deficit, the fight remains on what expenditures or whose taxes should be increased or decreased.

Changes in tax rates and expenditure programs in most countries require legislative approval, which may or may not be rapidly forthcoming in response to executive requests. In parlimentary systems of government the executive branch typically has the authority to initiate discretionary changes rapidly, as it controls the legislature. This is not the case in the American system.

Because it is politically unpopular to cut expenditure programs, and even more unpopular to raise tax rates, the decision lag in the direction of fiscal restraint is likely to be particularly long. This has resulted in an inflationary bias to fiscal policy in most countries. Governments find it politically much more attractive to run a deficit than a surplus. The central bank, which is more shielded from the political arena, is then assigned the unpleasant job of restricting the growth of the money stock and raising interest rates.

Expenditure Policy

The executive branch of the government ordinarily has some authority and flexibility to speed up or slow down the rate of disbursement of certain expenditures. With many government expenditure programs, considerable time is required even after a policy decision has been made for preliminary planning and organization before the programs can be put into effect. For this reason it has long been argued that the government should prepare a shelf of public works projects, on which all preparatory work has been completed and disbursements can occur rapidly. Granting the executive a discretionary standby authority to vary tax rates, at least within a certain range, would also reduce the administration lag and increase the flexibility of fiscal policy.

Table 17-1 presents the change in government expenditures and rates of unemployment and inflation in the postwar period. As may be seen, government expenditure changes were on balance disstabilizing. The largest increases and decreases were associated primarily with the Korean war in 1951 and the Vietnam war in 1966. Notable exceptions were the peacetime increases in government spending in 1958, 1961 and 1962, in the face of substantial unemployment. These increases are evidence that the old fiscal orthodoxy has lost its hold.

Table 17-1 CHANGE IN FEDERAL GOVERNMENT
EXPENDITURES, CHANGE IN GNP, AND
UNEMPLOYMENT RATES, 1945–71
(BILLIONS OF DOLLARS)

Year	Change in Federal Government Expenditures on Goods and Services	Change in GNP	Unemployment Rate (Percent of Labor Force)
1945	3.4	1.8	1.9
1946	−38.0	−3.4	3.9
1947	−5.8	22.8	3.9
1948	5.1	26.3	3.8
1949	6.4	−1.1	5.9
1950	−0.5	28.3	5.3
1951	17.0	43.6	3.3
1952	13.2	17.1	3.0
1953	6.0	19.1	2.9
1954	−7.3	0.2	5.5
1955	−1.6	33.2	4.4
1956	3.8	21.2	4.1
1957	7.7	21.9	4.3
1958	9.3	6.2	6.8
1959	2.1	36.4	5.0
1960	2.0	20.0	5.5
1961	9.1	16.4	6.7
1962	8.2	40.2	5.5
1963	3.6	30.2	5.7
1964	4.2	41.9	5.2
1965	5.4	52.5	4.5
1966	18.9	62.7	3.8
1967	23.3	42.1	3.8
1968	19.5	71.0	3.6
1969	10.1	64.9	3.5
1970	9.7	45.0	4.9
1971	0.4	72.7	5.9

Source: Treasury Department: Board of Governors, Federal Reserve System.

Tax Policy

Different taxes differ widely in the extent to which the revenues they bring in are responsive to changes in the level of income. Personal and corporate income taxes are ordinarily proportional or even progressive with regard to their revenue yield, depending on the structure of rates and exemptions, so that these tax receipts increase by the same or greater proportion than national income. Other taxes — for example, inheritance taxes, property taxes, excise taxes — have yields that are relatively insensitive to changes in the level of income.

Taxes whose yields are highly elastic to changes in the level of national income are sometimes termed *built-in stabilizers*, as their effect is to dampen fluctuations in the system to exogenous shocks. Unemployment compensation, welfare payments, and

Table 17-2   CHANGE IN GOVERNMENT TAX RECEIPTS, TRANSFER PAYMENTS, AND GNP, AND RATES OF UNEMPLOYMENT, 1945–71 (BILLIONS OF DOLLARS)

Year	Change in Federal Government Tax Receipts	Change in Federal Government Transfer Payments	Change in GNP	Unemployment Rate (Percent of Labor Force)
1945	0.8		1.8	1.9
1946	4.7		−3.4	3.9
1947	4.1	−0.4	22.8	3.9
1948	0.1	−1.2	26.3	3.8
1949	−4.4	1.1	−1.1	5.9
1950	11.0	2.1	28.3	5.3
1951	14.1	−2.3	43.6	3.3
1952	3.2	0.3	17.1	3.0
1953	2.8	0.7	19.1	2.9
1954	−6.2	2.0	.2	5.5
1955	8.3	0.9	33.2	4.4
1956	5.5	1.0	21.2	4.1
1957	4.0	2.3	21.9	4.3
1958	−2.9	3.8	6.2	6.8
1959	11.0	0.7	36.4	5.0
1960	6.8	1.2	20.0	5.5
1961	1.8	3.2	16.4	6.7
1962	8.1	1.6	40.2	5.5
1963	8.1	1.4	30.2	5.7
1964	0.5	1.0	41.9	5.2
1965	9.7	0.7	52.5	4.5
1966	18.3	3.9	62.7	3.8
1967	8.2	5.0	42.1	3.8
1968	25.7	5.6	71.0	3.6
1969	26.3	5.9	64.9	3.5
1970	6.0	6.2	45.0	4.9
1971	7.2	12.5	72.7	5.9

Source: Treasury Department; Board of Governors, Federal Reserve System.

agricultural subsidies are example of built-in stabilizers on the expenditure side. Such government transfer payments tend to fall when the level of national income rises, and conversely.

Table 17-2 shows the change in federal government tax receipts and transfer payments in the postwar period, as well as changes in GNP and the unemployment rate. The failure of tax receipts to rise in 1964 was due to tax reduction undertaken to stimulate demand. Tax receipts fell in the recessions of 1949, 1954, and 1958, and rose sharply in the expansions of 1951, 1959, and 1966 to 1969. In the absence of such built-in stabilizers, the fluctuations in aggregate demand would have been even greater.

THE PUBLIC DEBT

Government spending may be financed by taxation, by the issue of debt, or by the issue of high-powered money. On what principles ought these financing decisions to be made?

Allocation

All government policies have allocational and distributional implications. From the allocation point of view taxes may be viewed as the price paid for public goods. The *benefit principle* as a maxim of public finance states that taxes ought to be paid in proportion to benefits received.

In order to realize the benefit principle intertemporally — to assure that individuals in each period pay only for the public goods they receive in that period — it is necessary to distinguish consumption and investment components of public expenditure. Expenditure for public goods currently consumed, together with current consumption of the stock of past investment goods, should be paid by current taxpayers and financed out of current tax receipts. Government investment expenditures should be financed by borrowing. Repayment of government debt out of future tax receipts should be tailored to the time distribution of future services provided by government investment. In this manner each generation of taxpayers would pay only for the government services currently received and consumed. A new school would be financed not out of current tax revenues by taxpayers during the period of construction but by future taxpayers over the entire expected lifetime of the school.

On allocation grounds it may therefore be concluded that if the benefit principle is accepted the government should borrow only to finance public investment spending. As for a business firm, it should continue to borrow and to deficit spend only as long as the estimated marginal return from the public investment projects exceeds the marginal cost of finance. Government expenditure for current consumption goods must be financed entirely out of taxation.

In practice it is extremely difficult to distinguish the consumption and investment components of government expenditures and the time path of returns from public investment services. Investment expenditure is not confined to the accumulation of physical assets such as bricks, mortar, machines, and roads. It also comprises investment in human capital, health, education, and the production and distribution of knowledge, and so includes the salaries of teachers, doctors, and researchers. For these reasons, the criteria for intertemporal allocation are extremely difficult to apply. Present taxpayers enjoy the services of existing public capital goods paid for by past taxpayers and, in turn, pay for new capital goods whose services will be enjoyed by future taxpayers. In this way, it could be argued, a rough intergenerational equity is realized, similar to that between parents and children.

Stabilization and Money Issue

Government deficits or surpluses undertaken for stabilization purposes should be financed by money issue or withdrawal. As long as unemployed resources exist, the opportunity cost of increased present spending is zero. Whether the public or the private sector should increase spending is an allocation decision. The effective restraint on money issue is the danger of inflation. As the money stock increases, the aggregate demand function rises to obviate the need for further stabilization deficits.

Fiscal policy thus includes monetary policy as a special case. Whether the money stock is changed by the purchase of goods and services, taxes and transfers, or financial assets (monetary and credit policy) depends on the allocation and distributional goals of the government. Governments cannot avoid affecting the level of interest rates and thereby the price of present versus future goods by whatever policy they follow, protestations of central bankers notwithstanding. They have no choice but to choose.

Coordination of Government Policy

The agencies that determine government expenditure, taxation, debt, and monetary decisions are typically uncoordinated. They do not have separate responsibility for nor do they separately distinguish allocation, stabilization, and distribution goals. Government deficit spending may be undertaken for stabilization considerations, have distributional and allocational effects, and be financed out of bond issues. The effects of such contradictory policy combinations on aggregate demand will largely offset one another in a fully employed economy. Much public disagreement over stabilization policy (tax increase versus expenditure reduction versus tighter money) is due to anticipated distributional effects, and particular policies are supported or opposed largely on grounds of special interest.

For rational collective choice, government interest-bearing debt should be issued only when the expected returns on public investment exceed the interest cost, and be paid off over time only as the benefits from public investments are realized. The composition of government debt between money, short-term bonds, and long-term bonds should be determined by the desired structure of returns on financial assets, which affects the price of future goods relative to present goods, the rate of investment, and the rate of growth.

The Burden of the Public Debt

Most existing central-government public debt arose during wars. Military spending may be regarded as a kind of intermediate good, a cost of maintaining the economy, resulting in no future stream of utility-producing services. Fear of the consequences of continual public debts issued under such circumstances formed the basis for the traditional view that governments must balance their budgets. Deficit spending continues to be regarded by many as a profligate weakness by irresponsible governments, creating inflation, raising interest rates, and shifting the "burden" of current expenditures to future generations.

The issue of bonds does shift the cost of present government expenditure from present taxpayers to those future generations who are taxed to repay the debt. But if the debt is never repaid, this transfer will not occur. Borrowing to pay for present expenditures will not shift the burden onto our grandchildren and posterity, as long as they also choose never to repay the debt but to shift it on to their grandchildren. The process can continue like a kind of intergenerational chain letter; as long as it never comes to an end no generation will ever pay. But can this process continue indefinitely? Are there no debt limits? Will not such a perpetual growth of public debt lead to eventual government bankruptcy?

Stable Debt–Income Ratios

As human lives are all too finite, individuals cannot plan continually to spend more than their current income. At death all their outstanding debts must be repaid. As a result, after some point they will no longer be able to borrow at any interest rate, as lenders will not believe that additional loans can be repaid.

Households that borrow may find themselves in a state of bankruptcy in which they are unable to fulfill their debt obligations. In earlier centuries, the legal power of creditors over debtors was much greater, and debtors could be thrown into debtor's prison or indentured. The law currently provides that their assets may be taken over by their creditors. In this manner households are forced to live within their means over their lifetime horizon. Thrift, whether the provision of a nest egg for one's retirement or a legacy for one's heirs, is still regarded as desirable and morally commendable individual behavior in our society, a touchstone of the Protestant ethic. Individual households maintain a fairly stable ratio of debt to income, so that aggregate household debt continually increases with income over time.

Business corporations must also live within their means over their lifetime horizon. But as business corporations, unlike individuals, have typically *unlimited* life expectations, *they may persist forever in being deficit spenders,* that is, in spending more than their current income on investment goods and services.

In fact, all large business firms characteristically do exactly that. Businesses borrow in order to acquire plant, equipment, and other earning assets. Persistent deficits and borrowing for investment purposes by business firms are not regarded as morally reprehensible but as good business, as long as the expected return on investment exceeds the interest cost of borrowing.

As a corporation's income, output, and assets grow over time, so do its debts, in order to maintain its preferred debt ratio. While all interest and principal on *individual* loans and bonds are repaid on time, *total* corporate debt outstanding continues to grow to finance continuous corporate asset acquisition. It can safely be predicted that the total debt outstanding of AT&T or General Motors will continue to increase so long as these corporations continue to grow. Corporations like households over time maintain a fairly stable ratio of debt to income, so that corporate debt in the aggregate continually rises with total income.

Government deficit spending similarly must be financed by borrowing. Like households or businesses, governments should borrow only to finance public investment spending as long as the expected return on investment exceeds the cost of borrowing. Persistent government deficits result in continual growth in government debt outstanding. A continuous growth of government debt may involve increased taxes in order to pay the interest on the debt. But tax *rates* need not increase, even with a growing debt, unless interest payments grow more rapidly than the growth of national income. It is the ratio of interest payments to income that determines the average tax rate that must be levied in order to finance the debt.

Growth in the level of national income permits a rise in government debt without increasing the ratio of interest payments to income. In a growing economy the government may persistently run a deficit and increase its debt outstanding without increasing the tax burden, as long as the growth of the national debt does not exceed the rate of growth of national income.

Governments even more than corporations have unbounded life expectations. The government's estate is never closed. As a result governments never have to pay back all their debts at some future time, as does a private individual. Government debt can continue to grow indefinitely, providing national income and the assets of the public sector grow proportionately. Stable debt-income ratios imply in a growing economy that the debt of all sectors will grow at the rate of growth of income. Governments, unlike households and firms, never die. The government is a continuing collective and thus analogous to the household and business sectors.

Because increases in government debt also increase private wealth, the effect of a rise in the ratio of debt to income will be a rise in the ratio of wealth to income. This change will increase private spending and reduce the size of the government's deficit required for stabilization purposes. Rather than issuing bonds, governments should finance stabilization deficits by money issue, in which no interest burden is involved.

Domestic Debt

Increased domestic debt implies at the same time increased holdings of bonds by the individuals and firms that purchased them. It is in this sense that we owe the debt to ourselves. As cartoonists used to delight in putting it, "Every baby is born with a $2,000 per capita national debt burden on his back." Yet there must at the same time be another baby born with a silver spoon of $2,000 of government debt as assets in his inheritance portfolio.

The burden of domestic debt is the *frictional* cost of imposing taxes to pay the interest and then of paying the tax receipts out again as income to bondholders. In addition to the costs of administration, collection, and payment, taxes levied to pay the interest on the debt have distorting effects on the supply of labor and capital and affect the amount of effort, investment, and saving undertaken.

In addition to this frictional burden, the existence of a domestic debt affects the distribution of income. All financial assets transfer income from debtors to creditors. The effect of government debt will be to redistribute income toward greater inequality whenever the distribution of ownership of government bonds is more highly concentrated than the distribution of tax liabilities. If these redistributional effects of an existing debt are undesirable, the debt could always be reduced or eliminated by a once-and-for-all capital levy on wealth owners.

Empirical studies for the United States indicate that the net redistributional effect is slight. However, for other countries and other times (as in England in the nineteenth century), the net effect of government domestic debt has been strongly regressive. Indirect taxes were collected disproportionately from lower-income classes, while bondholders were higher-income individuals with higher marginal propensities to save. The result of such a redistribution of income was forced saving through the government as fiscal intermediary, a reduction in interest rates, and a rise in the ratio of saving and investment to national income.

External Debt

When a government borrows from other countries these conclusions must be revised. External borrowing, unlike internal borrowing, results in a greater supply of goods and services in the present to the economy as a whole. External debt has some similarities to one individual or corporation borrowing from another. Internationally, governments do not have the power of taxation or money issue.

When external debts are repaid or when interest is paid on external debts, the result is a reduction in goods and services available to nationals, as such payments are made to foreigners. As a result, it is particularly important that government borrowing from abroad be undertaken only if the return on the government investment expenditure is expected to exceed the interest cost of borrowing. Only in this case will future generations be better off, as they will be able to pay these external servicing costs of the debt out of larger future income.

The creation of internal debt due to domestic borrowing can never result in a national bankruptcy. As seen, such debt is owed to citizens of the country. Increased debt of the government is always exactly offset by increased wealth of bondholders, who are also taxpayers and who can always be paid in newly issued currency. These conclusions do not hold for external debt. Excessive or unwise borrowing from foreign countries can result in national bankruptcy. The country may be forced to default, because of its inability to meet contractual payments of interest and principal to foreign creditors. It may then be unable to borrow further even at very high interest rates.

APPENDIX: THE NET EFFECTS OF FISCAL POLICY

The Classical View

The classical economists believed that changes in the level of government expenditures or taxes would be completely ineffective in combating cycles in the level of economic activity. They argued that an increase in government spending or a reduction in taxes, if financed by borrowing, would simply raise interest rates and reduce the funds available to finance private investment. If financed by printing money, such expenditures would be inflationary.

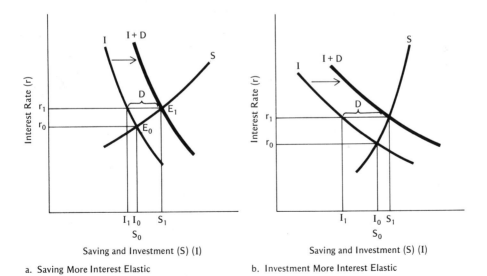

a. Saving More Interest Elastic
b. Investment More Interest Elastic

Figure 17-5 Classical View of Fiscal Deficits

Government expenditures were implicitly regarded as wasteful and likely to be less productive than private expenditures. This is probably objectively accurate when government budgets are decided by and for an aristocracy or a plutocracy. The best of all taxes under such circumstances may well be those that are least in amount.

These classical effects of an increase in government deficit spending financed by government borrowing are illustrated in Figure 17-5. For any given level of income the saving function (S) is positively related to the level of interest, and the investment function (I) is negatively related. Government deficit spending (D) financed by borrowing increases the demand for loanable funds.

If saving is more interest elastic than investment, government deficit spending will result primarily in an increase of planned saving (S_1) and reduction of private consumption expenditures, as shown in Figure 17-5a. If investment is more interest elastic than saving, as was held likely to be the case, government deficit spending will result primarily in a reduction of private investment spending (I_1), as shown in Figure 17-5b. The classical view thus represents the exact opposite of the simple Keynesian analysis.

A Reconciliation

The classical and simple Keynesian views may be reconciled by the use of the *IS-LM* diagram developed in Chapter 14, which permits the net effects of government expenditure, taxes, and financing on the level of income and interest rates to be analyzed.

In Figure 17-6 the *IS* relationship shows the combination of interest rates and

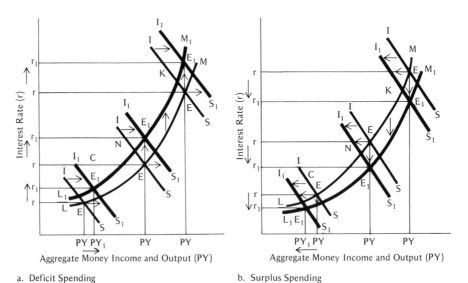

a. Deficit Spending

b. Surplus Spending

Figure 17-6 Pure Fiscal Policy

income that result in aggregate demand equal to aggregate supply in the markets for current output, including government spending and taxation. An increase in government spending like an increase in private spending shifts the *IS* relationship rightward, by an amount equal to the change in government spending times the multiplier ($\Delta Y = M\Delta G$). Similarly, a reduction in government taxes shifts the *IS* relationship rightward, by an amount equal to the initial change in private spending times the multiplier.

Conversely a reduction in government spending, like a reduction in private spending, shifts the *IS* relation leftward. Similarly, an increase in government taxes shifts the *IS* relation leftward, by an amount equal to the initial change in private spending times the multiplier.

The effect of expansionary or restrictive fiscal policy in the financial markets will depend on how the concurrent government deficit or surplus is financed and on the initial equilibrium position of the economy.

Pure Fiscal Policy

Consider initially the *pure* fiscal policy case, in which the stock of money remains unchanged, and government deficits are financed entirely by the sale of bonds to the public. This increases the stock of bonds outstanding and the *LM* relationship shifts upward, as shown in Figure 17-6a. With a larger stock of bonds in wealth-owner portfolios, a higher interest rate is required for portfolio balance for any given stock of money.

Government surpluses result in the retirement of bonds held by the public. This action reduces the stock of bonds outstanding, and the *LM* relationship shifts downward, as shown in Figure 17-6b. With a smaller stock of bonds in wealth-owner portfolios, a lower interest rate is required for portfolio balance for any given stock of money.

As seen in Figures 17-6a and 17-6b, expansionary or restrictive pure fiscal policy may be expected to have very little effect on the equilibrium level of income when the economy is operating in the normal range. The increase in government spending or reduction in taxes tends to raise aggregate demand, but the rise in interest rates required to finance the deficit tends to reduce total private spending. This is consistent with the classical argument .

In the classical range, pure fiscal policy has no effect on the equilibrium level of income and results solely in a change in interest rates. The classical analysis is correct.

It is only when the initial equilibrium position of the economy lies in the Keynesian range that pure fiscal policy will substantially affect the equilibrium level of income. In this case, interest rates are at their floor level and remain relatively unaffected by the sale or purchase of government bonds. As a result, the change in government spending is not offset by an induced change in private spending.

As described in Chapter 14, Keynesian analysis also applies to the short-run disequilibrium period before prices and interest rates adjust. As may be seen, the initial impact effects of pure fiscal policy are to change aggregate demand as predicted by the Keynesian analysis.

Mixed Fiscal-Monetary Policy

Now consider the *mixed* fiscal-monetary policy case, in which government deficits or surpluses result in equal opposite changes in the stock of money, while the stock of bonds remains unchanged.

Government deficits are financed by an equal increase in the money stock, which shifts the *LM* relationship rightward as shown in Figure 17-7a. A higher level of money spending is then compatible with any given level of interest rates. Conversely, government surpluses result in an equal reduction in the money stock. This action shifts the *LM* relationship leftward, as shown in Figure 17-7b, because a lower level of money spending is compatible with any given level of interest rates.

As seen in Figures 17-7a and 17-7b, both expansionary and restrictive mixed fiscal-monetary policies are effective in altering the equilibrium level of aggregate income and output. The expansionary effects of a government deficit are due both to the increase in government spending or reduction in taxes and to the rise in the stock of money, which offsets the rise in interest rates associated with the increased level of aggregate demand.

The restrictive effects of a government surplus are due both to the decrease in government spending or increase in taxes and to the reduction in the stock of money, which offsets the fall in interest rates associated with the reduced level of aggregate demand. The net change in interest rates will be slight and may be in either direction, depending on the extent of the shift in the *LM* curve.

The effectiveness of mixed fiscal-monetary policy on money income holds what-

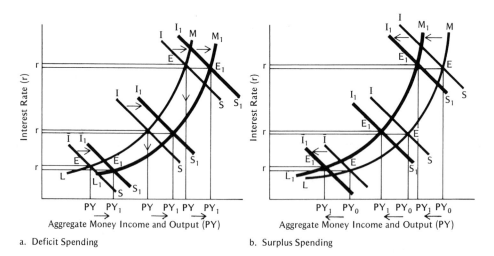

a. Deficit Spending b. Surplus Spending

Figure 17-7 "Mixed" Fiscal Monetary Policy

ever the initial equilibrium position of the economy. As both occur simultaneously it makes little sense to inquire whether the fiscal or the monetary effect is more important. While their relative contribution will vary depending on the initial configuration of the economy, their combined effect is always greater than the effect of either in isolation.

unemployment versus inflation

THE PHILOSOPHERS have only interpreted the world in various ways; the point, however, is to change it.

—*KARL MARX*

JUDGMENTS ARE BASED on experience, and experience is interpreted by each individual in terms of his own enculturation. . . . In every culture change is less difficult to effect in certain aspects than others, though the element of culture most susceptible to change will vary from people to people. In our own society, the centers of sanctioned change lie in the fields of material culture and technology. But, to take only one instance, equal receptivity to change certainly does not characterize our attitude toward the intangibles of our economic organization.

—*MELVILLE HERSKOVITS*

Full employment and price stability are the two most important stabilization goals of government. Since World War II governments in all countries have assumed increasing responsibility for steering the economy between the Scylla of unemployment and the Charybdis of inflation. Balance of payments equilibrium and the growth rate as important additional goals of economic policy are considered in Parts V and VI. In an open economy where imports and exports form a substantial share of total income, inflation and unemployment may be imported.

THE AGGREGATE SUPPLY RELATIONSHIP

In Figure 18-1 an economy's aggregate supply function (S_0) relating real output and prices is drawn for a given level of money wage rates (W_0). Aggregate demand is drawn as a rectangular hyperbola to represent any given level of money expenditure (PY).

If an economy's aggregate supply function were horizontal up to full employment of labor and vertical beyond this point, as shown by the dashed curve in Figure 18-1, no problem of conflict between full employment and inflation would exist. The objective of stabilization policy would be to manage aggregate demand so that it intersected the aggregate supply function at its corner solution (D_F). With lower levels of *aggregate demand* (D_U), unemployment would result, and monetary-fiscal policy must be used to raise the level of money expenditures and income. With higher levels of aggregate demand (D_I), prices would rise, and monetary-fiscal policy must be used to reduce the level of money expenditures and income.

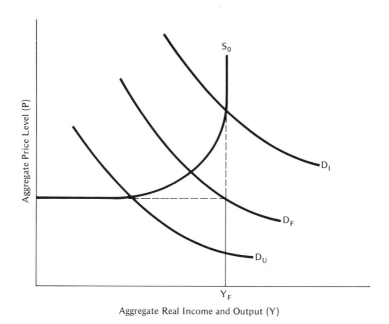

Figure 18-1 Aggregate Demand and Aggregate Supply

Unfortunately prices tend to rise before full employment of labor and full utilization of the capital stock is reached. As shown in Figure 18-1, the aggregate supply function typically has an initial horizontal segment, a rising segment, and a vertical segment. Changes in aggregate demand will result in changes in both real output and prices, in a proportion depending on where aggregate demand intersects the aggregate supply curve.

The aggregate supply function for the economy is the summation of the supply functions of all the individual firms in the economy. As described in Chapter 5, firm supply price is based on average variable costs (sometimes termed prime costs) and on the degree of profit markup over variable costs. Variable costs in turn are governed by the existing capital stock, technology, and the prices of the variable factors of labor and intermediate goods.

Average Variable Costs

In Figure 18-2 average variable costs are drawn as constant and then rising as plant capacity is approached. As employment increases beyond a certain point, the marginal productivity of labor will fall in accordance with the law of diminishing returns. If money wages are constant, average variable costs will rise. To the extent that quality differences in labor are imperfectly reflected in wage rates, less productive workers will be hired last, an additional reason why labor's marginal productivity may fall and average variable costs rise as output expands. A rise in money wage rates will shift the cost curve upward, e.g., to AVC_1.

Surprisingly, there is little empirical evidence that average labor productivity falls as output increases. The data suggest in contrast that average labor productivity typically rises with output. One explanation would be that because a large proportion of labor costs are fixed, there is less underutilization of labor as output increases,

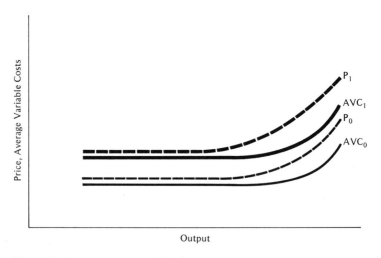

Figure 18-2 Firm Cost and Supply Price Curves

and unit labor costs fall. In a world where sales are uncertain, firms build a certain amount of reserve capacity into their operations to be able to take advantage of unforeseen increased demand for their products.

Profit Margins

The other component of supply price is the average profit markup. Firms' supply price may rise more rapidly than unit variable costs, as indicated by the dashed curves P_0 and P_1 in Figure 18-2, to the extent that market power increases in periods of buoyant demand.

There are a number of reasons why an increase in demand will operate to raise firm profit markups. As shown in Figure 18-3, an outward shift in demand will ordinarily raise the profit-maximizing price (from P_{M_1} to P_{M_2}) even when average variable costs remain constant. Prices may be increased in response to the increased market power. In the face of shortages and delays some customers will be willing to pay higher prices to assure a supply, and some prices will rise in response to demand increases even if no market power exists.

Rather than profit maximization, firms possessing market power characteristically set a price (P_T) to yield some target rate of profit at normal levels of utilization. At higher levels of output profits will exceed this target level, even when the administered price remains constant, as average costs fall with output.

For all industries where fixed costs are substantial, as shown in Figure 18-3, average total costs (unit costs) will fall with sales as fixed costs are spread over a larger

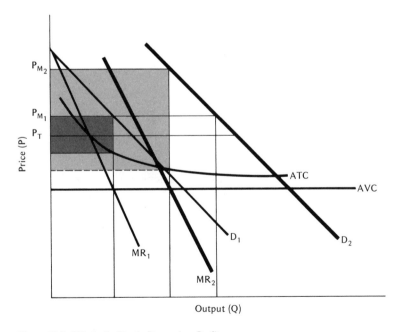

Figure 18-3 Effect of a Rise in Demand on Profits

volume of output. This drop is consistent with the observed rise in average labor productivity as output expands for firms that treat a part of their labor costs as fixed. In industries where scale economies are important, average variable costs will fall with output.

In all such cases profits will rise as sales expand unless prices fall with average costs. Even if prices are not increased, the share of sales going to profits and the return to capital will rise. Workers in such industries will demand money wage increases in an attempt to defend their share of receipts and will point to the higher profits and higher labor productivity as evidence that management could well afford to pay higher wages. Unions in such industries may successfully negotiate higher money wages even in the face of substantial unemployment in the economy. Unions in other industries may then also demand higher wages to maintain parity. Higher wages raise firm cost curves and lead in turn to higher prices to maintain profit margins. In this manner profits, wages, and prices dynamically interact to create a persistent rise in prices, even without any continual increase in the degree of market power possessed by firms and unions.

Wage–Price Spiral

Figure 18-4 reproduces the aggregate demand and supply curves of Figure 18-1. When the aggregate demand function intersects the aggregate supply function on its horizontal segment (E_0), a rise in demand will not operate directly to raise prices. When the aggregate demand function intersects the aggregate supply function on its rising segment (E_1), a rise in demand will result in a higher level of prices unless profit margins are reduced. But this higher level of prices will not lead to a continuing rate of inflation unless money wages rise. The effect is simply to raise the ratio of prices to wages.

At some output the existing supply of labor will be fully employed (Y_{F_L}). A rise in demand beyond this point (E_2) will directly induce a rise in money wages, as firms attempt to bid workers away from other firms. Any rise in money wages will cause the aggregate supply curve to shift upward (e.g., to S_1), with a subsequent higher level of prices necessary to maintain existing profit margins. The rise in money incomes will simultaneously increase disposable income and cause a responsive upward shift in the aggregate demand function. There is no determinate solution as supply and demand interact in a continuing wage-price spiral. Figure 18-4 is then of little analytical use, as the two curves are interrelated and shift upward by unspecified amounts.

Money Wage Rates

The behavior of money wages is critical for the inflation process. If profit margins increase before full employment is reached, because prices fail to fall with falling average costs, the profit share will increase without any rise in prices. Even if real

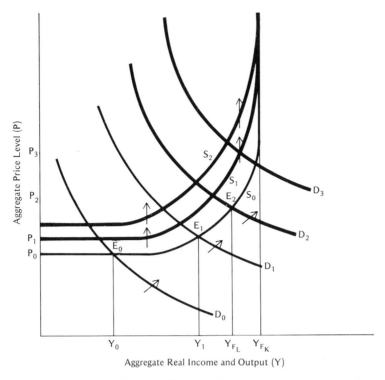

Figure 18-4 Interaction of Aggregate Demand and Supply

wages do not fall, workers possessing market power will bargain for higher money wages, shifting the supply curve upward in an attempt to maintain their share of total income. If prices increase before full employment is reached (Y_{L_F}), whether because of increasing costs or rising profit margins, real wages will fall. The fall in real wages will reinforce the rise in profits in inducing workers with market power to bargain for higher money wages, shifting the supply curve upward even in the face of existing unemployment.

Only if money wages do not respond to a rise in aggregate demand is full employment consistent with price stability. The very concept of a supply curve of labor independent of a demand curve for labor is appropriate only for competitive markets. As shown in Chapter 8, when both sides possess market power under collective bargaining, money wages may rise in response to any change in labor demand, profits, prices, or unemployment rates that affects labor's relative bargaining position vis-a-vis management. A wage bargain consistent with price stability at lower levels of employment may be inflationary at full employment.

Demand and Cost Inflation

A rise in prices due to an upward shift in the aggregate demand function is termed *demand* inflation, and a rise in prices due to an upward shift in the aggregate supply function is termed *cost* inflation. Some types of inflation are clearly demand inflation, as typically occurs during wartime with a large increase in government expenditures and deficits financed by money issue. If money income is to increase persistently, it always requires an increase in the money stock. But changes in the money stock are likely to be related to the level of unemployment. As shown in Figure 18-4, the level of output consistent with full employment of labor (Y_{F_L}) may not coincide with the level of output consistent with full employment of capital (Y_{F_K}).

In peacetime conditions, with a wage-price spiral in process, it is ordinarily of little meaning to ask whether the rise in wages "caused" the rise in prices (cost-push) or whether the rise in prices "caused" the rise in wages (demand-pull). In the conflict over distributive shares, wages and prices chase one another upward. An initial rise in wages need not cause inflation if profits are reduced. Conversely an initial rise in prices need not cause a rise in money wages if labor is willing to accept lower real wages. The pursuers and the pursued, each acting in his own self-interest, attempt to increase or maintain their share of the economic cake. And why not? That is what capitalism is all about.

Market Power

Possession of market power typically results in inflexibility of wages and prices. This inflexibility is particularly evident in a downward direction. Suppliers who are able to set the price at which they sell their services are characteristically unwilling to reduce this administered price quickly in response to a fall in demand. But in a market system price changes are the adjustment mechanism by which markets are cleared. As a result, with wage and price inflexibility all markets will not be simultaneously cleared. Instead of price reductions there occur unemployment and excess capacity in response to a decline in demand; real income and output fall in addition to the price level. Similarly, with a rise in demand before output can be increased, queues, shortages, and a rise in prices occur.

Downward Wage Inflexibility

Because of the rise in average labor productivity over time, money wage increases up to this amount will not increase average labor costs. The same number of workers can produce a greater volume of output. If average money wages increase more rapidly than the average rate of productivity growth, average costs will rise. Such wage increases will be inflationary unless employers accept lower profit margins.

In those sectors where output is rising more rapidly than average, workers may receive wage increases greater than the national average. Such increases may be justified on allocation grounds if relatively higher wages are required to attract labor. In the long run workers tend to leave those sectors where relative wages fall and to be attracted to those sectors where relative wages rise. As long as the average level of money wage rates is increasing, downward inflexibility of wages need not inhibit relative wage adjustments. A rising level of money wages may ameliorate social conflict, in the sense that no group's wages are forced to fall absolutely to permit a change in relative wages to occur.

Relative wage differentials are only one of the factors affecting labor mobility. Workers also move in response to differential employment opportunities. Relative wage differentials frequently reflect differential market power where entry is restricted. The large wage increases recently negotiated by craft unions in construction trades, and by automobile and steelworkers where total employment has been growing slowly or even declining, can hardly be justified as necessary on labor allocation grounds.

Unions are concerned to keep up with the wage gains of other unions and of unorganized workers. The relative wage structure remains roughly stable over time. As a result, any wage increases in excess of national average-productivity gains are likely to be inflationary. Even if they do not cause costs and prices for the *produced* commodities to rise, workers in other areas possessing market power will demand wage increases based on the gains received by workers in these key leading sectors.

Downward Price Inflexibility

Although downward wage inflexibility in labor markets need not be inflationary as long as average money wage increases do not exceed national average gains in labor productivity, this rule does not apply to downward price inflexibility in product markets. Inflation refers to the increase in the price index for goods and services, not for labor.

In a competitive economy prices are governed in the long run by average costs of production. In imperfect markets prices are based on average costs plus some profit markup. Relative price changes in product markets play the critical central role of allocating demand among industries and firms.

In economies where productivity is increasing at different rates, the *relative* cost of those commodities whose productivity is increasing more rapidly than average will fall and the *relative* cost of those goods and services experiencing lower rates of productivity increase must rise. This explains why the prices of goods with a larger labor service component — household help, haircuts, restaurants, theater — are, to the astonishment and delight of tourists, relatively so much lower in less developed than in more developed countries.

If the price of those goods with lower productivity growth does not increase relatively, wages and profits in these areas must fall relative to other sectors. Workers and capital will leave the industry, and supply will decrease. This movement will continue until prices have risen sufficiently that income in these sectors are comparable to those earned elsewhere in the economy.

The fundamental difficulty may be stated as follows: In an economy where productivity gains are occurring at disparate rates in different sectors, relative prices must change. But stability of the price index, which is an *average* level of prices, logically necessitates that some prices must fall *absolutely*, in those areas where productivity is rising more rapidly, in order for a change in relative prices to occur. Prices of commodities sold in competitive markets do fall absolutely in response to productivity increase. But prices of goods produced in concentrated markets are frequently inflexible downwards, even if their rates of productivity increase are in excess of the national average.

THE TRADE-OFF BETWEEN UNEMPLOYMENT AND INFLATION

A critical variable determining the course of inflation is the behavior of money wages. To what extent do wage rates rise before full employment is reached? Annual observations for the rate of increase of money wages, prices, and the unemployment rate in the United States since 1952 are presented in Table 18-1. The relationship between the change in money wages and unemployment rates is plotted in Diagram 18-1.

Table 18-1   INFLATION, UNEMPLOYMENT
AND WAGE RATES, 1952–71

Year	Change in Consumer Price Index (Percent)	Unemployment Rate (Percent)	Change in Average Hourly Earnings (Percent)
1952	2.2	3.0	4.8
1953	.8	2.9	5.9
1954	.5	5.5	2.5
1955	−.4	4.4	3.6
1956	1.5	4.1	5.3
1957	3.6	4.3	5.0
1958	2.7	6.8	3.2
1959	.8	5.0	3.6
1960	1.6	5.5	3.5
1961	1.0	6.7	2.4
1962	1.1	5.5	3.8
1963	1.2	5.7	2.7
1964	1.3	5.2	3.5
1965	1.7	4.5	3.8
1966	2.9	3.8	4.5
1967	2.9	3.8	4.7
1968	4.2	3.6	6.3
1969	5.4	3.5	6.7
1970	5.9	4.9	5.9
1971	4.3	5.9	6.2

Source: Department of Commerce.

As indicated by the looseness of the scatter, a large number of factors in addition to the level of unemployment affect money wage gains. Nevertheless, a strong negative relationship is discernable, summarized by the curve drawn through the center

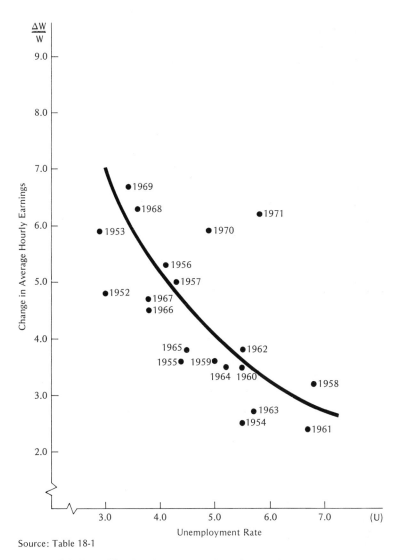

Source: Table 18-1

Diagram 18-1 Money Wage Rate Increases and Unemployment Rates, 1952-71

of the scatter. Up to 1970, only in years when unemployment rates were 4.5 percent or higher was the rise in money wage rates less than 4 percent per year. As unemployment rates fell below 4 percent, money wage increases tended to rise more rapidly.

As worker productivity on the average in America has been rising by nearly 3 percent per year, money wage increases of this magnitude would be roughly consistent with constant average variable costs and so, with no change in profit margins, with constant prices. With a stable price level both wages and property income would then increase on the average by 3 percent per year. The distribution of income between labor and capital would remain constant. Money wage increases in excess of 3 percent per year would increase average costs and so result in rising prices with constant profit margins, or if prices remained constant, in a falling share of profits.

Diagram 18-1 suggests that when unemployment rates are low, labor's bargaining power increases and it is able to negotiate higher money-wage bargains. But many other forces in addition to the level of unemployment affect the rate at which money wage rates rise. Movements in money wage rates in different industries are related to the cost of living index, profit rates, changes in demand, productivity growth, union strength, the degree of market concentration, and collective bargaining agreements in key industries. These other forces account for the loose scatter in Diagram 18-1, the location of individual observations away from the underlying relationship. The large rise in money wage rates since 1969 reflects the high rate of inflation. Workers build expected cost of living increases into their money wage demands because they are concerned to increase their *real* wages.

The Relation Between Wage and Price Increases

To what extent are increases in money wage rates passed on in higher prices? To what extent do increases in money wage rates keep up with the rate of inflation?

Diagram 18-2 presents the association between annual money wage increases and increases in the price level for the United States in the postwar period. As expected, a strong positive relation exists, summarized by the line drawn through the center of the scatter. But on a year-to-year basis, the association is not particularly close, as

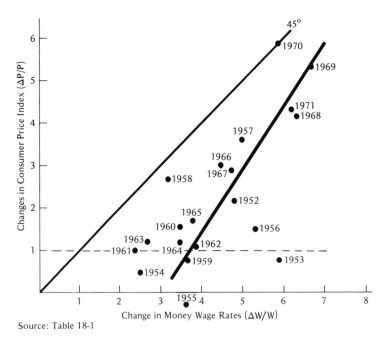

Source: Table 18-1

Diagram 18-2 Rate of Increase of Prices and Money Wages, 1952-71 indicated by the loose scatter of points off the central relationship. This scatter indicates that many other forces are at work. In individual years price increases may considerably outstrip money wage increases, and conversely.

The relationship appears to be linear, with a slope slightly greater than one. The linearity indicates that price and wage increases tend to move roughly proportionally. The slope, slightly greater than one, indicates that money wage increases tend to fall behind price increases as the rate of inflation increases.

The positive intersect of the line with the horizontal axis at about a 3-percent per year increase in money wages indicates that money wage increases of about 3 percent per year are consistent with price stability. With average productivity increasing at about 3 percent per year, money wage increases of this amount are consistent with roughly constant average costs per unit of output.

Because of quality changes, which are not caught in the price index, the price index is biased upward. A 1 percent increase in the price index, indicated by the dashed line in Diagram 18-2, is consistent with approximate price level stability.

Combining the results of Diagrams 18-1 and 18-2, the rate of inflation and the rate of unemployment are plotted in Diagram 18-3. The resulting negative relationship is summarized by the curve drawn through the center of the scatter. Similar curvilinear relationships between inflation and unemployment may be observed for

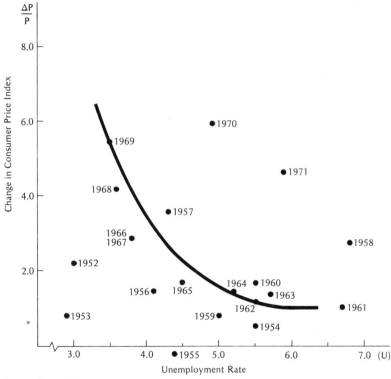

Source: Table 18-1

Diagram 18-3 Inflation and Unemployment, 1952-71

most countries. Although their distances from the origin and their slopes differ greatly, they all show the characteristic negative association between inflation and unemployment.

As long as the future is like the past, this observed association may be expected to hold in the future. By managing the level of aggregate demand, the government can move the economy to different feasible combinations along the curve. But it cannot move the economy to the origin. Lower unemployment involves accepting greater inflation. Greater price stability necessitates accepting higher levels of unemployment. There is a conflict between these two stabilization goals, and a difficult tradeoff must be faced. More of one goal implies less of the other.

As even inaction leads to some outcome, whatever the government does represents a policy. It must choose. As long as this tradeoff represents the alternatives available, the choice is properly a political decision, not one that can be made by experts. There are costs associated with unemployment and costs associated with inflation. These costs are borne by different groups of individuals. In view of the impossibility of making interpersonal utility comparisons, economic analysis cannot define a "best" solution but can only show as accurately as possible the costs involved.

In an effective two-party system, one party will prefer a position along one range of the curve and the other party along the other. In the United States, the Republican and Democratic parties have in the past offered a choice between a more northwest and a more southeast location on the curve.

For intelligent social decisions it is necessary to have information on the tradeoff and on the costs associated with each alternative. Why are full employment and price stability desirable social goals? What are the costs of unemployment and inflation?

The Costs of Unemployment

The costs of unemployment are threefold:

1. First is the opportunity cost of unemployment in terms of the goods and services that the unemployed would have been capable of producing. An economy with unemployed labor is operating within its production possibility frontier. The labor services of the unemployed are being wasted and can never be recaptured. These opportunity costs are absolutely very considerable. Unemployment means operating with a significantly smaller per capita real income.
2. Second, there is the loss of happiness and the psychic destruction from the fact of unemployment itself — the despair, desolation, rage, and hatred that it breeds in a worker unable to find a job.
3. The third cost of unemployment is the social cost external to the unemployed worker associated with higher unemployment rates: higher crime rates, greater need for police and welfare services, civil disorder, and embitterment of class

conflict and alienation. This cost includes any effects on the state of mind of the prosperous due to awareness that others are in poverty because of inability to find a job. Few Americans could live unaffected in Bombay, where thousands of homeless sleep on the streets every night, and children are crippled to make them more successful beggars. When the poverty of the unemployed is largely hidden in tenements, ghettos, rural slums, and old-age homes, the power of sympathy is reduced. Man can get used to many things.

These costs are borne overwhelmingly by the unemployed themselves. The reduction in aggregate real income falls primarily on the unemployed, who no longer receive a pay check, while the rest of society makes a much smaller sacrifice. As unemployment rates differ greatly by type of worker, the costs of greater unemployment fall disproportionately on minority groups, the uneducated and the unskilled, the very old, and the very young. These are not groups that possess large amounts of political power.

The Costs of Inflation

Inflation is defined as a general increase in the price level. The consumer price index is the price of a market basket of goods and services bought by a representative consumer. The wholesale price index is based on a basket at wholesale prices, and the GNP deflator includes all goods weighted by their proportion of the GNP. These different indices yield slightly different rates of inflation, depending on the goods included and the weights chosen. The rate of inflation is not unambiguous.

Because of the difficulty of taking quality changes into account, price indexes tend to be biased upward in economies experiencing technological change and product innovation. Unmeasured quality change has been estimated to occur at a rate of 1 to 2 percent a year in the United States.

The costs of inflation are more widely distributed and more difficult to measure than the costs of unemployment. The short-run costs of moderate rates of inflation are primarily redistributional. It is not the real value of total output so much as who receives it that is affected.

Distribution Effects

Inflation results in an arbitrary redistribution of wealth and income. Inflation aids debtors by reducing the real value of their debt obligations, thus raising their net worth. Conversely, creditors whose assets are fixed in money terms suffer a decline in net worth. These redistributive effects of inflation fall particularly heavily on unsophisticated savers, whose wealth is concentrated in fixed money form. A lifetime's skimping and self-denial for retirement may be cruelly eroded.

In addition to redistributing wealth between debtors and creditors, inflation operates to redistribute income according to the relative ability of different groups to raise their money income in response to a rise in the general price level. It is convenient to distinguish *passive* and *active* sectors according to their ability to protect their real income from inflation. Active sectors typically include profit recipients and labor union members. These groups are able to raise their money incomes rapidly and more or less in proportion to experienced rises in prices to maintain their real purchasing power intact.

Passive sectors, unable to adjust fully or rapidly their money incomes to a rise in the price level, are forced to suffer a fall in real income and in the share of total output. Such recipients include retired individuals living on a fixed money income, who may be unable to adjust at all, rentier groups living on interest income that adjusts upward only incompletely and slowly to anticipated inflation, civil servants, teachers and all salary groups whose money incomes are traditionally inflexible and are renegotiated only infrequently in the face of continuing rises in the cost of living.

Allocation Effects

In addition to redistributive effects, rapid rates of inflation over the longer run may reduce the size of total output and its rate of growth by distorting the allocation of resources. Changes in the price level increase the uncertainty attached to economic decisions. Economic units are no longer able to calculate and contract with a constant measuring rod of money.

Over time, as inflation becomes more widely anticipated, wealth owners shift to asset forms that offer protection against inflation. The nominal level of interest rates rises in response to anticipated inflation, which tends to reduce somewhat its redistributional force against creditors. But inflation distorts the allocation of resources. Flight into equities, land, inventories, real estate, and consumer durables reduces the amount of saving allocated to the accumulation of assets that increase future productive capacity.

Nominal financial-asset yields historically have not risen sufficiently to offset fully the rate of inflation actually experienced, so that the real return on lending falls. This phenomenon may operate to reduce the funds available for investment. Offsetting this effect is the possibility that increased debtor investment expenditures, made attractive by lower real costs of borrowing and lower debt-income ratios, may be financed out of new bank credit. This practice has sometimes been termed *forced saving.*

Cross-section studies of different countries at one period of time and time series studies of one country over a number of different periods suggest that over a considerable range the rate of inflation does not substantially affect the rate of growth of the economy. As shown in Diagram 18-4, high rates of growth have been achieved with both high and low rates of inflation. Similarly, low rates of growth have occurred in countries experiencing both high and low rates of inflation. Extremely

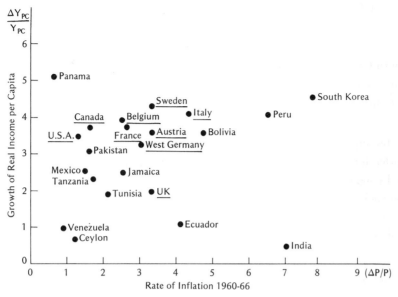

Source: Statistical Office of the United Nations

Diagram 18-4 Rates of Growth and Inflation in Developed and Less Developed Countries, 1960-66 (Average Rates for Period — Developed Countries <u>Underlined</u>)

rapid rates of inflation and deflation do however tend to be associated with lower rates of growth or real output.

THE DILEMMA–INCOMES POLICY

Inflation and unemployment are at least as old as the pyramids. Inflation, interrupted by periods of falling prices, has been characteristic of all economies over their entire recorded history. What is new is the assumption of responsibility on the part of governments for managing the economy to avoid both of these undesirable outcomes.

Inflation in the past was associated largely with autonomous increases in the money stock, due to gold discoveries, or gold imports, and to government money issue to finance increased wartime expenditure. Modern cost inflation is the outcome of a struggle over distributive shares by sellers possessing the power to affect the price of their product or service. The lower the rate of unemployment, the greater the relative bargaining power of labor and the higher the money wage increases that it can negotiate. To protect their profit margins, firms pass on these cost increases in the form of higher prices. For any given rate of expected inflation the position of the tradeoff relationship — its shape and distance from the origin — will depend on the extent to which existing shares are accepted as fair, and the degree of market power possessed by labor and management.

In the long run, it may be possible to reduce the market power involved in price and wage determination in an economy, to shift the tradeoff curve down toward the origin. But breaking up large corporations and large unions to achieve perfect competition in all markets is not a feasible alternative. Due largely to the requirements of modern technology, big business, big unions, and big bureaucracies are a fact of modern economic life. Raising the skills, work habits, and productivity of those at the bottom of a heterogeneous labor queue has in practice proven extremely intractable.

The dilemma arises when the level of unemployment compatible with approximate price level stability is regarded as unacceptably high. Faced with a Hobson's choice, by aggregate demand management the government chooses a compromise position such as A in Figure 18-5, with a target of 4 percent unemployment. It then resigns itself to accepting a moderate level of price inflation (3.5 percent) as the lesser of two evils.

The Development of Inflationary Expectations

Unfortunately, this is not the end of the story. With the growth in government responsibility and ability to manage the economy, a new factor has been added. Households and firms for the first time come to believe that the government can in

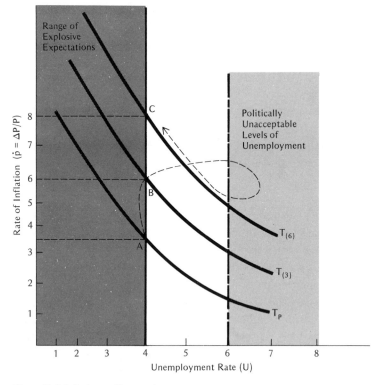

Figure 18-5 Inflationary Expectations

fact manage the economy to peg the level of unemployment at 4 percent. As a result the future will no longer be like the past. There is a critical change in expectations and in behavior.

The curve T_P in Figure 18-5 is the trade-off appropriate to widespread expectations that the future course of prices and unemployment over the long run will be similar to the *past*, when prices and employment rose and fell over the business cycle. The government chooses and effectively maintains the point A. Gradually, households and firms come to expect that the government is able and determined to hold the economy at point A. But this implies that they will now also gradually come to expect prices to increase continually at 3 percent per year and unemployment not to exceed 4 percent.

Given this change in expectations, both workers and employers will build them into their demand and supply offers. With the same rate of unemployment, workers will now demand higher money wage increases to compensate for the now higher expected future rise in prices. Workers bargain for *real* wages, since they are no

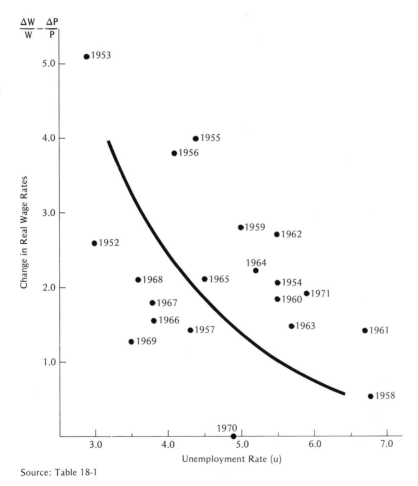

Source: Table 18-1

Diagram 18-5 Real Wage Rate Increases and Unemployment 1952-71 longer under the illusion that prices will remain constant. Similarly, business increasingly expects prices to increase steadily at 3 percent and is willing to pay higher money wages, confident that they will also be able to charge higher prices. Both labor and capital become confident that the government will manage aggregate demand and increase the money supply in order not to permit unemployment to rise above the tolerable level. As a result, they can raise prices with some assurance that the government will bail them out and not permit widespread unemployment and excess capacity to develop.

As shown in Diagram 18-5, the ability of workers to increase their real wages is also inversely related to the level of unemployment. While the relationship is loose, higher increases in real wages are associated with lower levels of unemployment.

The Dilemma

Anticipated inflation thus tends to displace the entire tradeoff curve upward, as expectations of future price increases are continually revised. The tradeoff relationship between inflation and unemployment becomes increasingly unfavorable. As may be seen from Diagrams 18-1 and 18-3, such shifts in expectations have occurred several times in the past twenty years, the last and most dramatic in 1969–71. At all levels of unemployment less than for example 4 percent the rate of inflation tends to accelerate, as shown by the shaded area in Figure 18-5. The trade-off relationship shifts upward to $T_{(3)}$, consistent with an expected rate of inflation of 3 percent. But the actual rate of inflation will then become 6 percent, and once this is anticipated the trade-off relationship will again shift upward $(T_{(6)})$.

In response to the higher rate of inflation, for example from A to B Figure 18-5, the government by restrictive monetary-fiscal policy may attempt to restrain the growth of aggregate money demand. But if inflation is widely expected to continue at a higher rate, the effect will primarily be to increase unemployment. With an expected rate of inflation of 6 percent, much higher levels of unemployment would be required to force workers to accept noninflationary money wage increases of 3 percent.

As a result of restrictive monetary-fiscal policy the economy will follow the dashed path. For a time the government has the worst of both worlds. Unemployment and inflation increase simultaneously. Although sufficiently high rates of unemployment would eventually cause the growth of money wages to decline, and so break the back of inflationary expectations, such high unemployment rates are not politically tolerable. With unemployment rates above (for example) 6 percent, the government finds itself forced to take steps before the next election to reduce the level of unemployment, if it is to survive in office. As a result the authorities give in, and the money stock is increased to accommodate a higher level of aggregate demand and money income. The process thus proceeds anew by a kind of ratchet effect, as indicated by the dashed path in Figure 18-5.

Given the structure of the economy, there is a whole family of tradeoff curves

lying one above the other, each corresponding to a higher level of expected inflation. As long as the government provides enough high-powered money, any rate of
inflation can be sustained.

After You, Alphonse

The inflationary process once started is extremely difficult to halt. If money wage
increases were to be held in fact to the average rate of productivity growth, it is true
that prices would eventually stop rising. But this would require labor to absorb the
entire initial adjustment. In the new equilibrium its share of income would have
fallen. If prices were in fact to be held constant it is true that wage increases would
eventually fall to the average rate of productivity growth. But this would require
capital to absorb the full burden of stabilization. In the new equilibrium its share of
income would be lower. What is required is a *mutual deescalation* of demands, in
which labor accepts less than the sum of productivity increases plus past cost-of-
living increases, and business absorbs part of past cost of production increases in
setting its current prices. But as the bargaining is over real wages, any formula for
deescalation involves the political problem of how income ought to be distributed.

In economies in which market power exists in product and factor markets, money
wages within wide limits are determined by the relative bargaining strength of labor
and management. Under these circumstances inflation may be viewed as the indirect result of a struggle on the part of both capital and labor to increase or defend
their shares of total income, where total claims exceed the value of total output at
constant prices. The blame for inflation cannot be attributed meaningfully to labor
or to capital in isolation. It is the side-effect of a conflict over distributive shares.
Both groups desire to increase their shares, and both are willing to use their market
power to this end.

Once inflation is viewed as the outcome of a political struggle over the distribution
of income, the question whether inflation is "caused" by increases in the money
stock or by increases in money wages is of little meaning. If the money-income ratio
is stable, there will be a close statistical association between changes in the money
stock and the level of money income.

$$k_1 = PY/M \qquad P = k_1 \left(\frac{M}{Y}\right)$$

If the share of income between labor and property is stable, there will be a
close statistical association between prices, money wage rates, and average labor
productivity.

$$k_2 = \left(\frac{WL}{PY}\right), \quad P = k_2 \left(\frac{W}{Y/L}\right)$$

Although the observed stability of k_1 and k_2 may be of interest for predicting the
future course of inflation, it says nothing about the question of causality. Only if the
increases in the money stock or in money wages could be shown to be *autonomous*
could it be concluded that they caused the observed rate of inflation. But as de-

scribed above, higher prices both lead to higher wages and require a higher money stock with any given level of unemployment.

Incomes Policy

Modern inflation (in countries where governments have accepted the goal of full employment) is the outcome of a struggle over distributive shares by groups possessing market and political power. With the increasingly unfavorable alternatives between inflation and unemployment, as future inflation becomes anticipated and the tradeoff relationship shifts upward, governments have been pushed toward direct participation in price and wage decisions to achieve their stabilization goals. Such attempts are termed *incomes policy*.

In the United States, guidelines were set up in the early 1960s by the Council of Economic Advisors. They stated that money wages on the average should not increase more rapidly than the rate that average labor productivity is increasing, about 3 percent per year. At the same time, firms and industries enjoying more rapid rates of productivity increase were expected to reduce the prices of their goods and services, while those sectors in which productivity increases are less than average were permitted to increase their prices. In 1971, for the first time in peacetime, price and wage controls were enacted for a 90-day freeze. A pay board and a price commission were then created to rule on allowable increases in prices and wages, with the full coercive authority of the government behind them.

Wage and price freezes, norms, and direct government controls, although new in the United States, have been attempted by a large number of governments in the postwar period. The one thing that is known definitely about incomes policies is that they have never yet been more than temporarily successful in halting inflation. For a time they can reduce the level of actual and expected inflation. But the suggested normal rate of wage increase tends to become a minimum rate in wage negotiations, to be adjusted upwards in special circumstances. Incomes policy tends to flatten out the trade-off relationship but not prevent it from shifting upwards. Average wage increases may actually be higher in periods of depressed demand and unemployment than they would otherwise have been.

Detailed control over prices requires a substantial input of information and resources, even if confined to the largest corporations. Such an extension of government control renders its political feasibility slight. But it could be done. The more central problem concerns not the extension of government regulation and bureaucracy, but the policy that is to be pursued. For the first time the question of what *ought* to be the income of various groups has somehow to be decided as a political decision rather than as the outcome of market forces over which no one has conscious control or responsibility. Because it is a distribution decision over relative shares, no neutral rules can be designed by economic experts.

Consider the widely suggested rule that money wage gains are noninflationary if they increase at the same rate as average productivity. Such a rule results in the share of income received by labor and property being frozen at its existing level. But there is no general agreement that the initial level is equitable. With changes in capital-output ratios, such a rule could lead to substantial changes in the rate of return on capital. Perhaps more important, at any point in time some workers are attempting to catch up with past increases in prices and wages of other groups. Many workers would thus argue that on equity grounds their wages ought to increase more than the rule permits. Unions with strong market power are unlikely voluntarily to accept less than average wage increases in order to admit the claims of the weaker to catch up. One historic purpose of unions has been to raise the share of total income going to their members.

Rather than stabilize prices, it would technically be much easier to stabilize money incomes. Prices in the long run are based on average costs. In an economy where productivity increases are occurring at different rates, relative prices must change. If wages are increased by the average rate of growth of productivity, while the average price level can remain stable, all individual prices must change, some up, some down, as well as all wages, except for those few commodities where productivity gains are exactly equal to the national average. A goal of stable money incomes would be much easier to realize. Once relative incomes are agreed upon, wage rates could remain constant, except for any changes that might be required to reallocate labor among occupations, adjustments which could easily be made. The prices of all those goods where no productivity change occurred could then stay constant. Prices would fall absolutely only for those goods whose average costs were decreasing. The essential point is that once *all* relative incomes are agreed upon, including property income, there is no longer any need to look at prices.

Modern capitalist economies appear to have reached the point where the market can no longer serve to distribute income without inflation, unless the goal of full employment is relaxed. Groups possessing market power are able to raise the price of their services. The government, once having accepted responsibility that unemployment will not increase beyond a certain level, has no choice but to permit the money stock to accommodate to higher levels of prices and incomes. More and more voices are being raised that perhaps we must just learn to live with inflation.

But it would be possible to decide collectively on what relative wages ought to be — how much a blue-collar worker ought to receive relative to a white-collar worker or a professional. Public opinion surveys indicate both that fairly widespread consensus exists on equitable wage and salary differentials, and that these are smaller than observed market differentials. Once these questions have been taken out of the market and into the political arena, it is a short and natural step to ask what the share of property ought to be, what ought to be the levels of unearned incomes? An incomes policy successfully carried out might lead to very large changes in the rules of the economic game. The day that relative incomes are decided in advance by truly democratic debate will be a day in which the degree of exploitation inherent in economic organization has been significantly reduced. A just society is one that free and rational persons would accept as fair, as seen from an initial hypothetical position of equality. Injustice in the distribution of income, wealth, and other social values such as opportunity, liberty, and the bases of self respect, is simply an inequality that cannot be justified, that it is agreed is not to the benefit of all.

APPENDIX: FULL EMPLOYMENT

Unemployment

How much unemployment is compatible with full employment? To what extent do inefficiencies in the labor markets account for the levels of unemployment observed and the position of the tradeoff relationship?

An unemployed worker is operationally defined as someone who was not working but was actively looking for work in the period under consideration. Unemployment figures are estimated from sample surveys and from the number of individuals

Table 18-2 COMPOSITION OF THE UNEMPLOYED, 1960–70

	1960		1965		1970	
	Number	*Percent*	*Number*	*Percent*	*Number*	*Percent*
Total	3.9	100	3.4	100	4.1	100
By Color and Sex						
White	3.1	80	2.7	79	3.3	80
Male	2.0	52	1.6	47	1.9	46
Female	1.1	28	1.1	32	1.5	37
Nonwhite	.8	20	.7	20	.8	20
Male	.5	13	.4	12	.4	10
Female	.3	7	.3	9	.4	10
By Age and Sex		100				
16 to 19 yrs.	.7	18	.9	26	1.1	27
Male	.4	11	.5	15	.6	15
Female	.3	7	.4	12	.5	12
20 to 24 yrs.	.6	15	.5	15		22
Male	.4	10	.3	9	.5	12
Female	.2	5	.2	6	.4	10
25 to 44 yrs.	1.4	37	1.1	32	1.1	27
Male	.9	24	.6	18	.6	15
Female	.5	13	.5	15	.5	12
45 to 64 yrs.	1.0	26	.8	26	.8	20
Male	.7	18	.5	15	.4	10
Female	.3	8	.3	9	.4	10
65 years and over	.1	3	.1	3	.1	2
Percent w/o Work for						
4 Weeks or Less		45		48		52
5 to 10 Weeks		21		21		23
11 to 14 Weeks		9		8		8
15 to 26 Weeks		13		12		10
Over 27 Weeks		12		10		6
Total		100		100		100

Source: Department of Labor, *Manpower Report of the President.*

registered with unemployment offices. Part-time unemployment refers to individuals who would have preferred at current wage rates to work full time but are only holding part-time jobs. Underemployment, defined as individuals employed at a lower-level job or at a lower level of work effort than their maximum capacity, may be quantitatively most important of all, but is virtually impossible to measure.

The composition of the unemployed in 1960 and 1970 is presented in Table 18-2. Nonwhites form about 20 percent of the unemployed. The proportion who are women increased from about one third to one half over the period, as did the proportion who are under 25 years of age. About one half had been out of work for 4 weeks or less. The proportion unemployed 15 weeks or more varies with the total amount of unemployment.

Frictional Unemployment

Short-term unemployment due to workers changing jobs and new workers entering the labor force is termed frictional unemployment. The volume of frictional unemployment depends on the rate of labor mobility or turnover between different jobs, and the efficiency of the labor market in providing information about job opportunities, as reflected in the average period of time it takes a worker to find a new position. If one man in ten changed jobs each year and was unemployed for an average of five weeks, the frictional unemployment rate would be 1 percent. The level of frictional unemployment will depend in addition on the proportion of new entrants to the total labor force and the strength of seasonal factors.

It is impossible to define precisely the proportion of total unemployment that is frictional. One operational criterion is by duration of unemployment. Workers who have been unemployed for less than for example four weeks consist primarily of those who are changing jobs plus new entrants to the labor force. Frictional unemployment has been estimated at between 1 and 2 percent per year in the American economy.

As frictional unemployment is related to change and growth in the economy it is not necessarily undesirable. In an economy in which demand and technology are changing rapidly, labor mobility is important. In the interest of maximum output, labor must be allocated where its productivity is highest. From the viewpoint of workers, labor mobility offers one means of getting information about different jobs in choosing a vocation, and the satisfaction to be received from work.

Information Costs

Information in an uncertain world is not free. It can be obtained only with some effort and expenditure of time. Because of the heterogeneity of labor and imperfections of the labor market, a worker is never sure of the opportunities available to him at any time. Rather than reducing his wage demands immediately and taking the first job that comes along, an unemployed worker will search for and explore other wage offers. He is always uncertain of how general market conditions may have changed.

A rational worker will search as long as the expected incremental gain exceeds the marginal cost of continued search. The incremental gain diminishes as the period of time devoted to information collection increases. The employee in this manner gradually gets a better idea of his potential market price and may be willing to lower his supply price. The greater the costs of collecting information and of moving, the greater will be the dispersion among job opportunities at any moment of time and the greater the gain from more extended search. Persons or resources engaged full-time in this search process of acquiring additional information are frictionally unemployed.

The level of frictional unemployment and so the position of the tradeoff curve could be reduced substantially by improving the efficiency of the labor market, particularly with regard to improving the quality and use of the employment services, making general labor-market information more available, and reducing the costs of mobility. Improved counseling of new entrants to the labor force would reduce the number of times they change from job to job until they find satisfactory employment.

Much frictional unemployment is caused by differentials between the rate of growth of job opportunities and the rate of growth of the labor force in different professions and in different geographic areas. Transportation subsidies to workers moving from one labor market area to another one can considerably increase labor mobility. The financial and psychic costs of pulling up one's roots and moving to an unknown city are considerable, even if one has information concerning the job opportunities that exist there. Employer subsidies to locate in areas of labor surplus also reduce the level of frictional unemployment.

Structural Unemployment

Structural unemployment refers to geographic and occupational pockets of unemployment relatively unaffected by a rise in aggregate demand. As wages are not instantaneously flexible, the composition of demand for labor does not match the composition of supply of labor. As a result, while there may be no excess supply of labor in the aggregate, there will exist excess supply of particular types of workers or in particular areas and excess demand for other types of workers and in other areas.

Unemployment rates vary greatly by level of educational attainment, age, skill category, geographic area, and race. Selected differential unemployment rates are presented in Table 18-3. As may be seen, unemployment rates are higher for non-whites than for whites, for blue-collar workers than for white-collar workers, for young workers than for older workers. Unemployment rates are also higher for primary and high school drop-outs rather than for university graduates and for workers in Appalachia and other depressed areas. These relative differentials in unemployment rates are maintained in the face of changes in the level of aggregate demand, while the absolute level of unemployment rises or falls.

Table 18-3   DIFFERENTIAL UNEMPLOY-
MENT RATES, 1960–70

	1960	1965	1970
All Workers	5.5	4.5	4.9
White	4.9	4.1	4.5
Nonwhite	10.2	8.1	8.2
Male			
White	4.8	3.6	4.0
Age 16–17	14.6	14.7	15.7
20–24	8.3	5.9	7.8
35–44	3.3	2.3	2.3
65 and over	4.0	3.4	3.2
Nonwhite	10.7	7.4	7.3
Age 16–17	22.7	27.1	27.8
20–24	13.1	9.3	12.6
35–44	8.2	5.1	3.9
65 and over	6.3	5.2	3.8
Female			
White	5.3	5.0	5.4
Age 16–17	14.5	15.0	15.3
20–24	7.2	6.3	6.9
35–44	4.2	4.1	4.3
65 and over	2.8	2.7	3.3
Nonwhite	9.4	9.2	9.3
Age 16–17	25.7	37.8	36.9
20–24	15.3	13.7	15.0
35–44	8.6	7.6	4.8
65 and over	4.1	3.1	1.9
By Occupation			
White Collar Workers	2.7	2.3	2.8
Professional & Technical	1.7	1.5	2.0
Blue Collar Workers	7.8	5.3	6.2
Nonfarm Laborers	12.6	8.6	9.5
Service Workers	5.8	5.3	5.3

Source: Department of Labor, *Manpower Report of the President.*

Some types of unemployed — for example, older workers skilled only in an obsolete craft, ghetto youths and other disadvantaged groups, and Indians on reservations — are insensitive to changes in the level of aggregate demand. Such structural unemployment must be attacked directly by government and industry programs of worker retraining. To date such retraining has proven both expensive and applicable only to a small and select minority of the unemployed. At present rates it would take many decades for retraining programs to eliminate all current structural unemployment.

Full Employment

Full employment may be defined as an unemployment rate equal to the sum of frictional plus structural unemployment. As such, it will vary widely from region to region and from country to country.

Table 18-4 presents unemployment rates for selected developed countries from 1960 to 1970. This evidence suggests that full employment is associated with rates of unemployment between 1 and 4 percent in different countries. Part of the differences are due to differences in measurement. But countries with a more homogeneous labor force, lower labor turnover, and better organized labor exchanges have much lower levels of frictional and structural unemployment. In most less developed countries, in contrast, unemployed workers are typically 10, 20 and even 30 percent of the labor force.

Table 18-4   INTERNATIONAL COMPARISON OF
UNEMPLOYMENT RATES, 1960–70

	1960	1963	1965	1967	1969	1970
United States	5.5	5.7	4.5	3.8	3.5	4.9
Canada	7.0	5.5	3.9	4.1	4.7	5.9
France	2.5	2.1	2.0	2.7	2.6	3.0
West Germany	0.8	0.5	0.3	1.0	.07	.06
Great Britain	2.0	3.5	2.2	3.8	3.7	3.9
Italy	4.3	2.7	4.0	3.8	3.7	3.5
Japan	1.7	1.3	1.2	1.3	1.1	1.1
Sweden	n.a.	1.4	1.2	2.1	1.9	1.5

Source: Handbook of Labor Statistics; U. S. Dept of Labor. Figures adjusted to U.S. concepts.

All unemployment above this full employment level may be regarded as due to deficiency in the level of aggregate supply. At going money wage rates there are not enough job opportunities available to provide all workers who would accept a job with employment.

If accurate data were available, this insufficiency in the demand for labor could be measured by the excess of total unemployed individuals over total job vacancies. But the total volume of unemployment and of vacancies are extremely difficult to measure, as each includes an active and a passive component. The latter consists of those workers who at going wage rates would accept a job, or employers who would hire a worker, but are not *actively* in the labor market because they do not believe that opportunities or workers are available and so regard active search as fruitless. Labor force participation rates vary positively with the level of aggregate demand. As a result, counting active unemployment understates the true volume of unemployment by a varying amount throughout the business cycle.

Labor is heterogeneous, and wage rates do not fully reflect differences in labor productivity. In every occupation workers may be viewed as arranged in a queue, with the most able, most highly motivated, and best trained at the top, and the least skilled and most discriminated against at the bottom. Employers first pick the workers from the top of the queue and go further down the queue only as total demand for labor rises. The workers at the bottom tend to be the last hired and the first fired. They are employed continuously only in periods of tight labor demand.

Structural unemployment is positively related to variations in the level of aggregate demand. During World War II, unemployment which had been regarded as hopelessly structural dissolved under the pressure of buoyant demand, as hard-core unemployables found work in the face of ample job opportunities.

Such a queuing model of labor markets suggests that a high level of aggregate demand is sufficient to reduce most structural unemployment. Black workers experienced on the average an unemployment rate roughly twice that of whites. This difference can be explained in part as due to the fact of racial discrimination, so that blacks are last hired and first fired. Black workers are concentrated in unskilled occupations where employment is more sensitive to cyclical factors. To the extent that this relationship is maintained over the cycle, every reduction in the general level of unemployment by 1 percent reduces black unemployment rates by approximately 2 percent. Conversely, an increase in general unemployment rates from 4 to 6 percent is associated with an increase in black unemployment rates from 8 to 12 percent.

BIBLIOGRAPHY OF SELECTED PAPERBACKS: PART FOUR

Friedman, M. & Heller, W. W., *Monetary vs. Fiscal Policy: A Dialogue*, Norton.
Friedman, M. & Schwartz, A. J., *The Great Contraction, 1929–1933*, Princeton University Press.
Galbraith, J. K., *The Great Crash, Nineteen Twenty-Nine*, Houghton Mifflin.
Galenson, W. P., *Primer on Employment and Wages*, Random House.
Goldsmith, R., *Financial Institutions*, Random House.
Lebergott, S., *Men without Work: Economics of Unemployment*, Prentice-Hall.
Lekachman, R., *Keynes and the Classics*, Heath.
———, ed., *Keynes' General Theory: Reports of Three Decades*, St. Martin.
Mayer, M., *Wall Street: Men and Money*, Macmillan.
Mayer, T., *Elements of Monetary Policy*, Random House.
Okun, A., ed., *The Battle against Unemployment*, Norton.
Phelps, E. S., ed., *Problems of the Modern Economy*, Norton.
Ritter, L., and Silber, W., *Money, a Guide for the 1970's*, Basic.
Shannon, D. A., *The Great Depression*, Prentice-Hall.
Slesinger, R. E., ed., *National Economic Policy: The Presidential Reports*, D. Van Nostrand.
Technology and Economic Developments: A Scientific American Book, Random House.
Theobald, R., *The Challenge of Abundance*, New American Library.
Thurow, L. C., ed., *American Fiscal Policy: Experiment for Prosperity*, Prentice-Hall.
Tobin, J., *National Economic Policy*, Yale University Press.
Wolfbein, S. L., *Employment, Unemployment and Public Policy*, Random House.

PART FIVE

INTERNATIONAL ECONOMICS

international trade

THANK GOD I am not a free trader. In this country pernicious indulgence in the doctrine of free trade seems inevitably to produce fatty degeneration of the moral fibre.

— *THEODORE ROOSEVELT*

"EVERY MAN for himself, and God for all of us," said the elephant as he danced among the chickens.

— *CHARLES DICKENS*

THE BENEFITS FROM INTERNATIONAL TRADE

The previous chapters have treated the case of a closed economy not engaged in trade with the rest of the world. In addition to producing goods for domestic consumption and investment directly, some firms find it profitable to produce goods that buyers in other countries demand, or to purchase goods produced in other countries. This chapter considers the principles of international trade.

Advantages of Specialization

Within a domestic economy, total output will be higher if individuals specialize in the production of those goods and services for which they and the factors they own are relatively most efficient. This result is assured domestically by self-interest, to the extent that information, mobility, and competition exist. Individuals sell the services of the factors they own to the highest bidder. Productive factors make a greater contribution to total output, the income of their owner is higher, and everyone benefits. Imperfections in information, mobility, and competition operate to reduce efficiency and so real income and output.

The same principle holds for the international economy. If different countries specialize in the production of those goods in which they are relatively most efficient, total world output will be greater and each country will be able to consume a larger quantity of goods than in the absence of trade. In order for trade to be mutually profitable, all that is required is that a country have a *comparative advantage* in the production of some commodities as reflected in a *difference in the price ratio at which goods are exchanged* between different countries. An absolute advantage in production is not necessary. Differences in relative prices of goods may be due to diversity in conditions of supply, as reflected in differences in relative factor costs and productivity, and to diversity in conditions of demand among the trading partners.

The effect of trade in permitting a country to move beyond its domestic production-possibility curve is shown diagramatically for a simple two-good competitive economy in Figure 19-1. For a particular country, the maximum amounts of food (F) and machines (M) that can be produced, given the country's factor endowment and level of technology at a particular point in time, are shown by the production possibility curve PP.

Let the slope of the straight line TT represent the ratio of the price of machines to the price of food as determined in international markets. As the price of machines rises relative to food, the price line TT would become steeper. More units of food must then be exchanged for one machine. By producing machines and food domestically in the combination $(F_T M_T)$ at the point T^* on the production possibility curve and then exporting machines in exchange for food or food in exchange for machines at the international price ratio, the country is able to move along the exchange pos-

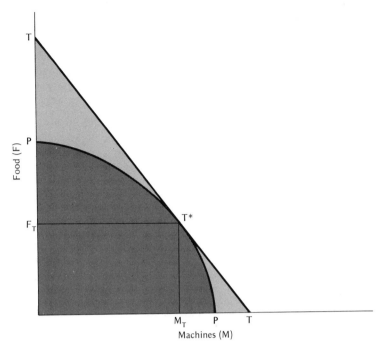

Figure 19-1 Benefits from Trade

sibility curve *TT*. It will always be better off as long as its domestic price ratio in the absence of trade differs from the international price ratio, that is, if it was not initially at the point *T** on its production possibility frontier.

As seen in Figure 19-1, the exchange possibility curve (*TT*) at all points except *T** lies *outside* the domestic production possibility curve (*PP*). *It follows that with trade* the *consumption possibility* frontier becomes the exchange line *TT*. This will lie outside the domestic *production possibility* frontier *PP* whenever the domestic price ratio differs from the international price ratio.

Comparative Advantage

The principle of comparative advantage holds for all countries, *irrespective of their size or of their level of per capita real income and productivity.* One country may be *absolutely* more productive in the production of all commodities, as reflected by a much higher production-possibility curve. Nevertheless, as long as some relative prices differ between it and the rest of the world, it can always increase its consumption possibilities beyond its own production possibilities by exporting those commodities that it produces relatively more efficiently and by importing those commodities that it produces relatively less efficiently in comparison to other countries. This rule is termed the principle of *comparative advantage.*

It should be apparent from Figure 19-1 that it is only the existence of comparative advantage (that is, differences in *relative* price ratios) and not absolute advantage or disadvantage (that is, differences in the absolute level of productivity) that is necessary for trade to be mutually advantageous.

Consider the case of a professor who hires a student to do some computing. Suppose that the professor is twice as efficient in terms of productivity per hour in the computer laboratory as the student but ten times as efficient as the student would be in the classroom as a teacher. If wages are earned in proportion to productivity, it will be in the self-interest of the professor to hire the student. For even though the professor is twice as productive as the student in computing, he is ten times as productive in teaching. As a result, if he specializes in teaching in the classroom and pays the student with his earnings, he will be better off than if he were to have spent his own time in the computer laboratory. The student also benefits by earning an income in proportion to his highest productivity rather than in his next best job on the grounds crew.

It follows that individuals in a very rich country such as the United States can benefit from trading with very poor countries, even though an American worker may be able to produce more of everything in one day than his poorer foreign counterpart. Similarly, individuals in poor countries can also benefit. The poor country where wages are very low will not be able to undersell America in everything but only in those things for which its cheap labor is relatively less inefficient.

As will be shown in Chapter 20, the exchange rate between the two currencies will adjust or can be adjusted so that total exports and imports for each country are approximately in balance.

The Extent of Specialization

Table 19-1 presents the ratio of exports and imports of goods and services to gross national product (GNP) for a number of selected countries. As may be seen, the ratio of trade to income varies widely. It will be smaller for larger countries, as a large country can to a greater extent specialize regionally and so trade with itself. The world as a whole is self-sufficient.

Given the size of the political boundaries, which determines what is considered "foreign" trade, what governs the amount of trade and specialization that will occur? Differences in relative prices may be due to differences in production conditions or to differences in demand conditions.

The extent to which a country will specialize thus will depend first on the *curvature* and *slope* of its production possibility frontier, which reflect the extent to which relative costs change as more and more of the export commodities are produced. The slope of the production-possibility curve represents the ratio of the marginal costs of production of the two goods, the amount of one that must be given up to get more of the other.

In the extreme case of constant costs, the production-possibility curve is represented by a straight line. This situation is shown in Figure 19-2. If a country pro-

Country	Exports of Goods and Services	Imports of Goods and Services
Australia	16	16
Brazil	7	8
Canada	24	23
Denmark	29	31
France	14	15
Germany, Fed. Rep.	23	16
Israel	29	36
Japan	12	11
Pakistan	5	9
Sweden	23	24
Thailand	19	24
Trinidad	72	65
U.S.A.	4	4
U.S.S.R.	2*	
United Kingdom	21	20

* Net exports of goods and services.

Source: Statistical Office of the United Nations.

duced under conditions of constant cost, there would be complete specialization whenever the international price ratio differed from the domestic price ratio in the absence of trade. The country would always locate at a corner position.

Given the degree of curvature of the production-possibility curve, the extent of specialization will depend on differences in taste, which govern the location of the country on its production-possibility curve. Its position determines the difference between the international price ratio and the domestic price ratio that would have

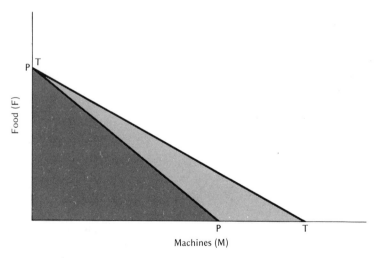

Figure 19-2 Complete Specialization with Constant Costs

occurred in the absence of trade. The greater the differences in taste among countries, the greater the difference in relative prices and the more trade that will occur, to the mutual advantage of both parties.

DISTRIBUTION OF THE GAINS FROM TRADE

The previous discussion showed that *total* income will always be greater if trade is permitted than if trade is prohibited, whenever relative prices differ among countries. But it did not consider how the *gains from trade are distributed* among different trading countries.

The world as a whole gains from free trade among countries, in the sense that the value of total world output is increased. But it does not follow that each country gains proportionately. Which countries gain the most will depend on the difference between what a country's domestic price ratio would have been in the absence of trade and the resulting international price ratio when trade occurs.

Even though trade may be voluntary, indicating that both parties are made better off, one partner may gain much more from the exchange than the other. This fact is at the basis of the concept of imperialism. Historically, the desire to make money has frequently been followed by the assertion of a right to govern or control others to protect one's interests.

Determination of the Price of Internationally Traded Commodities

For the world as a whole, total exports must equal total imports. Exports of a particular commodity by all exporting countries must exactly equal imports of the same commodity by all importing countries. Prices on the world market will adjust until for each commodity the total quantity supplied by exporters is equal to the total quantity demanded by importers.

This balance is shown in Figure 19-3. For the world market, total demand is the sum of the demand curves of each country, and total supply the sum of the supply curves of each country. If transportation costs were zero, the world price would be identical in all countries.

As in the real world transportation costs are not zero, prices will differ in the two countries by the cost of transport (T). As shown in Figure 19-3, the effect of added transport cost is to reduce the amount of trade that occurs. Very substantial transportation costs prevent bulky or perishable commodities from being traded at all. At the other extreme, the market for gold or diamonds is international and price differences among countries small.

There is always conflict between buyer and seller. A reduction in the world price is beneficial to the real income of an importing country. The amount of real goods and services it can command with a given volume of exports then increases. Conversely, a reduction in the world price is detrimental to the real income of an export-

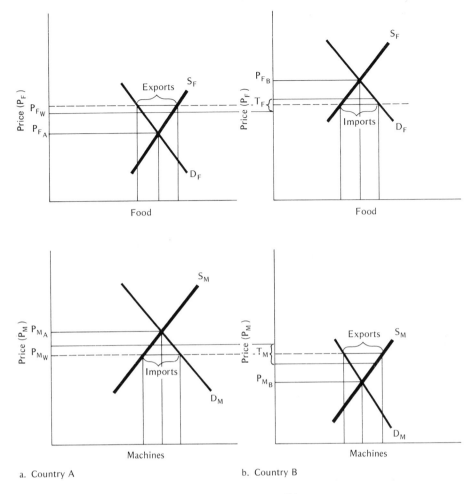

a. Country A b. Country B

Figure 19-3 Equilibrium Price of Internationally Traded Commodities

ing country. With the same level of exports, it is then able to command a smaller real quantity of imports.

The ratio of the price index of exported goods to the price index of imported goods is termed a country's terms of trade $(\frac{P_x}{P_M})$. When this ratio falls, it is said that the "terms of trade" have turned against the country.

THE EFFECTS OF PROTECTION

All countries protect some of their domestic producers from international competition by restricting the free movement of goods, services, and factors of production between countries. Tariffs are taxes levied on the value of imported goods. Quotas are restrictions on the quantity of goods that may be imported. Both tariffs and quotas reduce the volume of international trade and so the degree of mutually profitable division of labor. Immigration restrictions represent a quota on the movement of labor.

Tariffs

Tariffs have the effect of raising the price that domestic consumers have to pay and increasing the price received by domestic producers. As such, they may be viewed as a kind of indirect subsidy from domestic consumers to domestic producers, with the additional unfortunate indirect effect of lowering average productivity and real income for the country at large. The amount of the subsidy to domestic producers is effectively hidden from the public.

In Figure 19-4, the world supply of imports S_M is represented for simplicity as perfectly elastic. The supply curve to domestic consumers, as represented by the heavy line, is made up of the combined least-cost supply from domestic and foreign producers. With free trade the domestic price is P_W, equal to the world price, and the quantity demanded is Q_0. The total amount supplied is divided between imports (M_0) and domestic production (S_0).

The imposition of a tariff of T per unit may be shown by a vertical upward displacement of the supply of imports schedule by the amount T. The result is an increase in the price to domestic consumers to P_1, a reduction of imports to M_1, and a rise in domestic production to S_1. The hatched area (TM_1) represents government

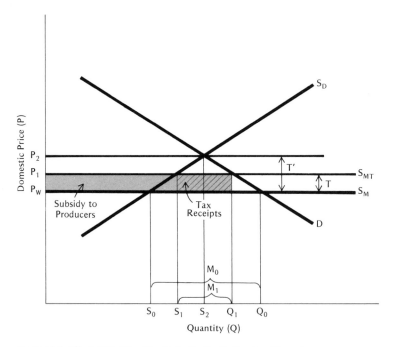

Figure 19-4 Effect of Tariffs with a Perfectly Elastic Supply of Imports

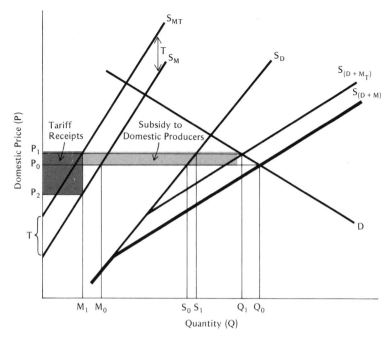

Figure 19-5 Effect of Tariffs with an Upward-Sloping Supply of Imports

total tax receipts. The larger shaded rectangle (TS_1) represents the subsidy to domestic producers, which is the increase in price paid by consumers to producers as a result of the tariff. In the case of a horizontal supply of imports, the domestic price rises by exactly the amount of the tariff.

If tariffs are set high enough to eliminate imports entirely (T') no tariff revenue is received by the government. In this case, the domestic price is P_2 and the subsidy $(T'S_2)$ goes entirely to domestic producers.

If the world supply of imports schedule (S_M) is upward sloping, the domestic price will rise by less than the amount of the tariff. This increase is shown in Figure 19-5 as a rise in price from P_0 to P_1. The supply curve to consumers is again the combined least-cost supply from domestic and foreign producers $S_{(D + M)}$. In this case, part of the tariff receipts are paid by foreign producers in the form of a lower price (P_2) received for their exports. The subsidy from domestic consumers to domestic producers is lower as a result. In the extreme case of a perfectly inelastic supply of imports there will be no change in the domestic price, and the entire tariff will be paid by the foreign producers.

Quotas

The effect of quotas is shown in Figure 19-6. The government restricts the amount of imports from M_0 under free trade to the quota amount M_Q. The supply curve to domestic consumers now becomes the heavy line S_Q. This is again the combined

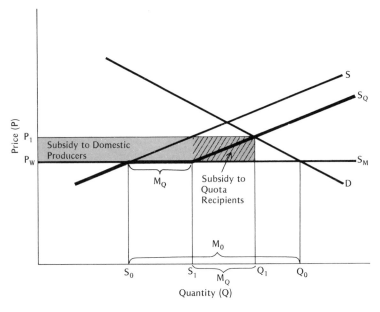

Figure 19-6 Effect of Quotas

least-cost supply from domestic and foreign producers, except that foreign supply is now limited to the amount of the quota. As a result of the quota, the domestic price rises from P_W to P_1.

The implicit subsidy to domestic producers is again equal to the quantity produced times the increase in price paid. But the hatched area now represents the hidden subsidy received by recipients of quota permits. These importers are now able to sell in the domestic market at a price (P_1) which exceeds their cost (P_W).

Quota permits have an economic value equal in total amount to the hatched area in Figure 19-6. The government could capture these scarcity rents by taking advantage of the market system and selling quotas by auction to the highest bidder, but this practice is not typically followed. As a result, importers have an incentive to spend money in other ways such as contributions to political campaigns, lobbying, and bribery in order to secure such valuable favors. The oil quota policy currently followed in the United States, where quotas are simply awarded to distributors in proportion to their share of the domestic market, is an egregious example of such hidden subsidies.

Direct Subsidies

Due to the hidden nature of the subsidy implicit in tariff and quota protection, economists have long argued that *if* protection of an import-competing industry is held to be desirable in the general interest, then an *explicit* direct subsidy to domestic producers from the government is preferable. The subsidy would then be paid by taxpayers as a whole rather than by consumers of the protected product. Just as important, the total costs of the protective policy would be fully revealed in the government's budget, so that rational social decisions may be made by a comparison of costs with benefits.

In the case of both tariffs and quotas the costs to society are hidden and extremely difficult to estimate, while the benefits of protection to recipients are highly visible. It is, of course, precisely because the costs of explicit subsidies through the budgetary system would be fully disclosed, and so be subject to critical scrutiny and probable reduction over time as a result of their high visibility, that such procedure is characteristically adamantly opposed by domestic producers of the protected commodities. This parallels exactly the case of agricultural policy. Farmers in most countries have been opposed to explicit government subsidies as "handouts," preferring to earn their income "honestly" under price support schemes involving import quotas, output restriction, or government stockpiling.

THE COSTS OF INTERNATIONAL TRADE AND ARGUMENTS FOR PROTECTION

Tariffs and quotas, by restricting the volume of international trade, reduce the degree of mutually profitable international specialization and division of labor. In this sense they resemble in their effects an artificial increase in transportation costs between countries. They may be viewed as similar to the invention of the steamship or the airplane, only in reverse, an almost unmitigated social catastrophe. In view of this, the on-the-surface astonishing fact that virtually all countries impose tariffs or quotas demands explanation.

The previous analysis assumed implicitly that countries always operate on their production-possibility frontier, so that resources are fully employed. This is, of course, not in general the case. It also ignored all adjustment problems associated with the immobility of labor and capital as resources are shifted from one industry to another. These transition costs may be substantial in the short run. Thirdly, the argument proceeded as if the market outcome were always efficient.

The analysis did not consider possible effects of changes in the composition of output on the growth of the economy and the resultant outward shift of the production-possibility curve over time. Alternatively stated, the argument was static throughout. It did not consider any dynamic effects of trade and specialization on the rate of technological advance, and on the supply of labor and capital, the forces that underlie the growth process.

Rates of Protection

Estimates of rates of protection in the most important trading countries are presented in Table 19-2. As may be seen, the existence of tariff barriers raised the price of traded goods by 7 to 16 percent compared to what their price would have been under free trade. The effective rate of protection, which relates only to domestic value added after all imported raw materials have been subtracted, is much higher

Table 19-2 RATES OF PROTECTION IN SELECTED COUNTRIES, 1962

Country	Nominal Average Tariff Rate [1]	Effective Average Tariff Rate [2]
United States	11.6	20.0
United Kingdom	15.5	27.8
Common Market	11.9	18.6
Sweden	6.8	12.5
Japan	16.2	29.5

1. Tariff averages are calculated by weighting with the combined imports of the areas.
2. Effective tariff rates indicate the excess of domestic value added because of tariff protection as a percentage of domestic value added under free trade.

Source: Bela Balassa, "Tariff Protection in Industrial Countries: an Evaluation," *Journal of Political Economy* (December 1965). Data from national tariff schedules and United Nations.

—on the order of 15 to 30 percent. Most less developed countries have even higher effective rates of protection.

Table 19-3 presents some evidence on the degree of protection in the United States. Tariff rates have fallen dramatically since the Great Depression, from 50

Table 19-3 TARIFF RATES IN THE UNITED STATES, 1926–66

Year	Duty Paid as Percent of Dutiable Imports	Dutiable Imports as Percent of Total Imports	Duty Paid as Percent of Total Imports
1926–1930 average	40.1	34.2	13.7
1931–1935 average	50.1	36.9	18.5
1936–1940 average	37.9	39.5	15.0
1941–1945 average	32.1	34.0	10.9
1946–1950 average	16.1	41.5	6.7
1951–1955 average	12.1	44.3	5.3
1956–1960 average	11.4	55.6	6.3
1961–1965 average	11.8	62.6	7.4

Duty as Percent of Dutiable Imports for Selected Commodities, 1966.

All Items	12
Food and Live Animals	9
Beverages and Tobacco	17
Crude Materials	10
Mineral Fuels and Related Materials	4
Chemicals	17
Machinery and Transport Equipment	11
Other Manufactured Goods	16
Glassware including Imitation Gemstone and Beads	29
Pottery	37
Woolen Fabrics, Broad Woven	47
Clothing	26
Clocks and Watches	41

Source: Department of Commerce, Bureau of the Census.

percent to about 12 percent, as the country has moved substantially toward a lowering of tariff walls. Dutiable imports have, however, increased as a percentage of total imports, so that duty paid as a percent of imports first fell and then increased slightly in the postwar period.

As may be seen, individual commodities have widely different tariff rates. The lower the comparative advantage, the higher the rates of duty required to protect domestic producers from foreign competition.

Conflict Between Buyer and Seller

Most of the support for protection follows from recognition of the following proposition. Just as the gains from trade are not shared equally among different trading countries, within any country the gains from trade are not distributed equally among different groups. Moreover, unlike the case among countries, some groups within an economy lose *absolutely* from a movement toward free trade, unless they are compensated by the rest of the society, and gain *absolutely* from greater restrictions on trade.

In all countries pressure for protection comes from domestic producers of imported goods who, in the short run at least, always benefit from tariffs or quotas at the expense of domestic consumers. This follows from the central conflict between buyer and seller. Each individual is a producer and also a consumer. But his activity as a producer is much more specialized, and his preferences and interests with regard to a particular commodity are far more intensely felt. As a result, the gains and losses from protection are not symmetrical.

A reduction in protection, by reducing the price of imported goods, raises the real value of goods and services that may be commanded by consumers for any given money income. In this manner, the gains from trade are distributed widely throughout the economy, as all individuals in their role as consumer find their real income slightly increased. An increase in protection, on the other hand, raises the real income and employment of a few domestic producers of the protected goods a great deal, as the demand for and price of their product is increased. Prices allocate resources, but they also distribute income.

Political Considerations

These differences in the distribution and intensity of gain and loss are reinforced by differences in political influence due to the institutional structure of most political systems. In virtually all countries, individual political representatives are elected on the basis of geographic constituencies. Producer groups are typically, although not always, located in particular areas because of the advantages of specialization. Consumers are spread more evenly throughout the population. As a result, producer groups are likely to have special political representatives from their localities, while consumers, who form no one's particular geographic constituency, characteristically have their interests less well represented in government.

The domestic producers of any one commodity constitute only a small proportion of all the individuals in the economy. Representatives of different special-interest producer groups may, however, be able to gain a majority coalition by log-rolling and lobbying techniques within government committees. Consumers, on the other hand, seldom create an effectively organized special-interest lobby to influence political decisions. Everyone's interest is no one's interest.

There are, however, two important counteracting forces. Export industry interests are aware of the consequences that movements toward greater protection are likely to result indirectly in lower export sales. Foreign countries characteristically retaliate in kind to tariff increases and, in any case, will have lower foreign exchange earnings with which to purchase domestic goods. Tariff reductions are for this reason likely to be politically more successful when negotiated reciprocally and marshal additional political support from export interests.

The second force is the recognition by enlightened public opinion that the community as a whole tends to gain from freer trade, even if some individuals do not.

Thus armed, it is now appropriate to consider the chief arguments offered to justify protection, recognizing that frequently they may serve as a guise for special interests. Patriotism is the last refuge of the scoundrel.

Cheap Foreign Labor

One fallacious argument may quickly be dispensed with, even though in many peoples' minds it is regarded as the most important. Protection is frequently called for because of the alleged impossibility or inequity of requiring domestic workers and producers to compete with "cheap" foreign labor. If such competition were permitted, it is argued, this would eliminate domestic producers and drive down the wages of domestic workers.

The latter part of this conclusion is clearly false. As has been shown, the benefits of trade in raising real income derive from comparative advantage, independent of the existence of absolute advantage. Producers in poor countries could and do similarly request protection against unfair competition from mass-produced goods, which are produced with the modern technology and "cheap" capital of developed countries.

What is true is that if foreign goods can be imported more cheaply, the domestic demand for these goods and so the incomes of their domestic producers will fall. Capital and labor will be forced to relocate in other industries where foreign countries do not have a comparative advantage. The market is not merciful. But this same process occurs in the domestic market whenever producers are driven out of an industry by a change in tastes or technology. These costs of change are inherent in progress. The appropriate response is not to restrict technical progress or free trade but to cushion the costs involved to the losers and to control the rate at which tariffs are reduced.

Market Power

There are a number of nonfallacious arguments that under certain circumstances may be held to justify protection. If a country is faced with an inelastic supply of imports, the imposition of a tariff will drive down the price that foreign exporters receive. As a result, the foreigner pays most of the tariff, while the tariff receipts are enjoyed by the government and taxpayers of the tariff-imposing country.

Small countries are typically faced with an elastic world supply of most imported goods, so that for them this argument is unlikely to be persuasive. On self-interest grounds, they are likely to be in favor of cutting tariffs reciprocally.

Large countries that do possess market power in international markets may by means of a selective tariff barrier succeed in turning the terms of trade, the ratio of the price of their exports to the price of their imports, in their favor. Like any monopolist, they then gain. As total world income is lower as a result of the reallocation of resources due to trade restrictions, it necessarily follows that other countries will always lose more than the countries with the stronger bargaining position will gain.

Domestic Employment

Another argument is that an increase in exports increases domestic employment, while an increase in imports operates to reduce domestic employment. Thus a "favorable" balance of trade—an excess of current exports over current imports of goods and services—will operate to increase the level of employment.

The excess of exports over imports of goods and services represents the net amount of financial assets, including gold, purchased from foreign countries plus grants given to them. In double-entry bookkeeping, every transaction represents both a sale and a purchase. Foreign countries, if they do not pay for their imports with the foreign exchange earned by exports, must pay either in gold, borrow (that is, sell short- or long-term financial assets), or receive grants or transfers of foreign exchange. For this reason, the balance of exports minus imports $(X - M)$ is termed *net foreign investment,* as it may be regarded as the amount of real goods and services invested or given to foreign countries.

Net foreign investment has a similar affect on domestic aggregate demand and employment as does an increase in domestic investment, with the important difference that it does not increase domestic productive capacity. In a depression, an increase in net foreign investment as in domestic investment will result in a multiplied increase in the level of national income, an effect called the *foreign trade multiplier.* A policy of raising tariffs, if it increases net foreign investment, will result in an increase in the level of domestic income and employment. To the extent that domestic employment is increased, higher tariffs may be regarded as a means of exporting domestic unemployment. But as aggregate demand can always be increased by increasing the money stock, a beggar-my-neighbor tariff policy makes little economic sense.

Another difficulty with this policy is that other countries are certain to reciprocate by raising their tariff barriers in return. The result, as in the Great Depression, is a downward escalation of the world economy to increasingly suboptimum positions. Economists have long argued that monetary and fiscal policy are preferable methods to raise the level of domestic aggregate demand toward full employment output.

It is important to note that transition costs, in the form of unemployment and excess capacity, resulting from a change in resource allocation due to tariff reduction are much higher in an economy where aggregate demand is depressed. In such economies, opposition to tariff cuts and pressure for tariff increases are likely to be much stronger. The identical argument applies to the attitude of domestic workers and unions to restrictive labor practices and the acceptance of labor-saving technology.

Risk and Autonomy

There are two important economic arguments for protection that concede the fact that a country's real income at every moment in time will be lower as a result of trade restrictions but hold this to be offset by other considerations.

The first argument follows from the presence of uncertainty and the principle of diversification in reducing risk. A country that specializes in exporting a small number of commodities in which it has a comparative advantage will be exposed to variations in world price and demand, over which it ordinarily has no control. As a result, the risk involved in international specialization, as measured by the variation in its export earnings over time, may be substantial. This risk is particularly likely for primary commodities, such as foodstuffs and raw materials, whose prices vary more than those of manufactured commodities.

It has also happened that over longer periods of time the prices of primary commodities have fallen relative to manufactured commodities, as the growth of supply exceeds the growth of demand. When this occurs, the terms of trade will shift against a country specializing in primary products. The development of protected import-competing industries, while less productive and so resulting in a lower real income, may permit a more stable rate of growth of domestic income and consumption over time. A country does not have so many eggs in the foreign-trade basket.

The second argument is based on noneconomic considerations. Self-sufficiency may be desired per se for reasons of national security. Greater international specialization, the result of greater free trade, results in individual countries being more dependent economically on one another. As is the case for individuals in a domestic economy, this greater dependence reduces their individual freedom of behavior. In a hostile world, autarchy is desired for its own sake, even when the economic outcome is known to be second best.

As long as the costs of such policies are known and accepted, economists have no quarrel with such arguments.

The Dynamics of Development

Probably the most powerful case for protection is *dynamic* rather than static and so does not meet the comparative advantage argument head on. It concerns the relationship between the composition of domestic output and the rate of growth of future productive capacity, and is sometimes termed the *infant country* argument.,

Less developed countries can never initially have a comparative advantage over developed countries in manufactured goods. As a result, international specialization will at first necessarily result in their providing primarily agricultural goods and industrial raw materials. But to the extent that the development process is centrally linked to the emergence of a manufacturing sector and to the skills and attitudes formed within an urban way of life, such specialization may inhibit their transition toward a modern developed economy.

The forced development of a protected import-competing industrial sector would, it is frequently argued, assist in a more rapid transformation of the economy from primitive to developed capitalistic forms of productive organizations and so accelerate the take-off to development. In terms of Figure 19-1, the country at every moment in time could consume a lower value of goods and services than would be the case under free trade, but the production possibility curve (*PP*) will shift outward more rapidly. Over time such a policy would result in a larger total consumption for future generations.

This case is frequently combined with the infant industry argument that in the protected industries — once sufficient experience, externalities, and economies of scale are developed — the country will eventually develop a genuine comparative advantage. The weakness of this argument is that protection itself will not necessarily lead the domestic producers to strive to reduce costs. Depending on how the duties are calculated, they may have little or no incentive to seek greater efficiency.

The argument is also frequently combined with a not-strictly economic argument concerning a country's way of life and the quality of the culture and society that it can sustain. Less developed countries are understandably unwilling to be confined to the role of "hewers of wood and drawers of water," which specialization in primary commodity exports often seems to imply (for field research on this question visit any Canadian mining town). The choicest fruits of civilization — literature, the arts, science, cultural sophistication, political democracy — all have developed and ripened in urban environments. In addition, the world has a long history of imperialism, and there is a deep suspicion of the political influence that follows trade and investment.

In general, whenever market failure shows that the private market outcome is not efficient, most importantly when externalities of various sorts exist, the community may find the free trade solution suboptimal. In the face of insufficient knowledge, economists are hotly divided as to the extent that protectionist restrictions can be an effective strategy to economic development. The argument is largely academic. Virtually all less-developed countries currently are attempting to develop industry behind high tariff walls.

Traditionally, economists ideologically committed to free trade have been highly critical of all of these arguments for protection, regarding them essentially as a cover for special interests. For all its faults free international trade in the nineteenth century was a powerful engine of growth. The essential spirit of economics is a constant questioning of the relationship between the costs and benefits expected from any action. Political decisions about economic development matters are frequently bad decisions. A politician, primarily responsible to his immediate electorate, is likely to be concerned with snatching local benefits. The result not infrequently is a tremendous waste of scarce resources in grandiose industrial monuments, local monopolies doing inefficiently what the foreigner could do efficiently, and a transfer of income to the politically powerful. There are good reasons to expect that a country would do better to concentrate its development efforts in what it is already able to export, where it therefore has a comparative advantage, instead of in import-substitution industries where the foreigner can do better. Modern development effects have been described as a "Maginot Line" strategy — find out where the enemy is strongest and then attempt to overwhelm him at that point.

Self-interest is a powerful thing. As John Stuart Mill put it more than a century ago, "While there are occasional valid arguments for tariffs, politicians can seldom be trusted to know when to use them." Development policy has enabled local educated business and political elites to survive and prosper. But self-interest cuts two ways. Awareness of income inequalities stemming from property ownership and political power rather than from evident differences in productive contribution has created a widespread latent threat of revolution in many countries against the local establishment of capitalists and politicians.

APPENDIX: INDIFFERENCE CURVES AND THE GAINS FROM TRADE

In the absence of trade the amounts of food and machines produced (F_E, M_E) are determined by the country's preferences, as represented by the community indifference curve $I_0 I_0$ in Figure 19-7. The slope of the tangent at E represents the domestic price ratio of machines to food.

Now let trade be introduced. Maximum welfare will be reached at the trading position F, where the exchange possibility line TT is tangent to the community indifference curve $I_1 I_1$. This represents the highest indifference curve that can be attained. At the point F the country exports ($M_T - M_F$) of machines, in return for imports $(F_F - F_T)$ of food. It now has more of both goods (F_F, M_F) than were available in the absence of trade (F_E, M_E).

The distribution of the gains from trade is shown for the two-country two-commodity case in Figure 19-8. For simplicity transportation costs are assumed to be zero, so that the TT ratio is identical for both countries. If a country could produce traded goods domestically in the absence of trade at very nearly the same relative prices as they are traded internationally (Country A), then its gains from trade will be slight.

However, if the international price ratio differs substantially from a country's domestic price ratio in the absence of trade (Country B), the gains from trade in that commodity will be large. This advantage will accrue for imported goods that a country could produce domestically only with extreme difficulty and so at a very high cost and for exports that could be sold in the domestic market only at much lower prices.

In the two-country case the international price ratio will adjust until exports and imports of each commodity are equal. Exports of machines by country B are equal to imports of machines by country A. Similarly, exports of food by country A are equal

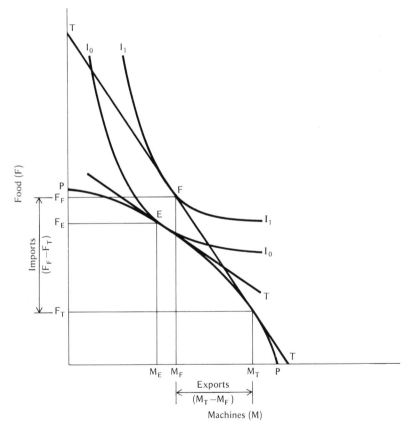

Figure 19-7 Gains from Trade

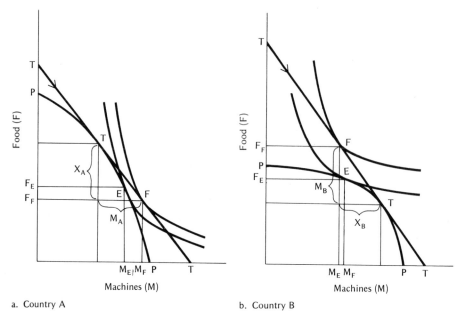

a. Country A   b. Country B

Figure 19-8 Distribution of Gains from Trade

to imports of food by country B. As imports are paid for with exports, in the absence of international capital movements for each country the value of its imports must exactly equal the value of its exports. This comes about through changes in the country's *exchange rate,* the price of its currency in terms of foreign currencies.

the international economy

IMPERIALISM IS CAPITALISM at that stage of development at which the dominance of monopolies and finance capital is established; in which the export of capital has acquired pronounced importance; in which the division of the world among the international trusts has begun; in which the division of all territories of the globe among the biggest capitalist powers has been completed.

—*V. I. LENIN*

THE IDEAS OF ECONOMISTS and political philosophers, both when they are right and when they are wrong, are more powerful than is commonly understood. Indeed the world is ruled by little else. Practical men, who believe themselves to be quite exempt from any intellectual influences, are usually the slaves of some defunct economist. Madmen in authority, who hear voices in the air, are distilling their frenzy from some academic scribbler of a few years back. I am sure that the power of vested interests is vastly exaggerated compared with the gradual encroachment of ideas. Not, indeed, immediately, but after a certain interval; for in the field of economic and political philosophy there are not many who are influenced by new theories after they are twenty-five or thirty years of age, so that the ideas which civil servants and politicians and even agitators apply to current events are not likely to be the newest. But, soon or late, it is ideas, not vested interests, which are dangerous for good or evil.

—*JOHN MAYNARD KEYNES*

International trade permits countries to achieve a higher level of real consumption than they could achieve if they were to produce all goods themselves. The present chapter examines the relationships between a country's foreign transactions and its domestic economic activity, the interrelationships between the economies of different trading countries, and the international financial assets and institutions that serve to facilitate and impede trade among nations.

THE BALANCE OF PAYMENTS

A country's balance of payments refers to a double-entry listing of all international transactions during a year. All goods and services sold must be either paid for or given away (sold at a zero price). Both sides of every transaction are recorded in the balance of payments, so that it must always balance in total. An item is entered as a *credit* if it results in foreign currency being received and as a *debit* if it results in foreign currency being paid out.

Alternatively expressed, a credit represents a claim against other nations' currencies. A debit represents a claim of other countries against the domestic currency.

The Balance of Payments Accounts

There are many different types of international transactions that enter into the balance of payments. As shown in the presentation of the U.S. balance of payments in Table 20-1, it is customary to distinguish current account transactions, capital account transactions, and gold and foreign exchange movements.

Private current account transactions are composed of merchandise exports and imports and so-called invisible items. These include shipping and insurance services, tourist receipts and expenditures, earnings on foreign investments, and private gifts and transfers, primarily remittances that immigrants send back to their families. Government current account transactions consist primarily of grants to foreign countries and economic and military expenditures abroad.

Capital account transactions are made up of private and government short-term and long-term loans to, and borrowing from, foreigners. The difference between the net balance on current and capital accounts is made up of gold and foreign currency outflow or inflow. The balance on liquidity basis depends on what types of capital flows are included in the liquidity statement. The fact that short-term transfers of funds into the United States are excluded in Table 20-1 exaggerates the size of the liquidity deficit.

Net Foreign Investment

A surplus (+) or deficit (−) on current account must be accompanied either by capital movements (foreign lending (−) or borrowing (+)) and/or by an inflow (−) or

Table 20-1 UNITED STATES BALANCE OF PAYMENTS, 1967–70 (BILLIONS OF DOLLARS)

	1967	1968	1969	1970
1. *Current Account Transactions*				
Exports of Goods and Services				
Merchandise	30.5	33.4	36.5	42.0
Military Sales	1.2	1.4	1.5	1.5
Transportation	2.7	2.9	3.1	3.7
Travel	1.6	1.8	2.0	2.3
Investment Income Receipts	6.8	7.7	8.9	9.6
Other Services	2.8	3.1	3.3	3.8
Total	45.7	50.2	55.4	62.9
Imports of Goods and Services				
Merchandise	−27.0	−33.3	−35.8	−39.9
Military Expenditures	−4.3	−4.6	−4.9	−4.8
Transportation	−3.0	−3.2	−3.5	−4.0
Travel	−3.2	−3.1	−3.4	−4.0
Investment Income Payments	−2.3	−2.8	−4.4	−5.1
Other Services	−1.2	−1.4	−1.4	−1.5
Total	−41.0	−48.2	−53.3	−59.3
Balance on Goods and Services	4.8	2.0	2.1	3.7
Remittances and Pensions	−1.3	−1.2	−1.2	−1.4
Balance on Current Account	3.5	.8	.9	2.3
2. *Capital Account Transactions*				
U.S. Government Grants and Capital Flow, Net	−4.2	−4.0	−3.9	−3.2
U.S. Private Capital Outflow, Net	−5.5	−4.9	−5.0	−6.4
Foreign Capital Inflow, Net (Excluding change in liquid assets in U.S.)	3.2	8.4	3.9	3.9
Errors and Unrecorded Transactions	−.5	−.2	−3.0	−1.3
Balance on Capital Account	−7.1	−.6	−7.9	−7.0
Balance of Payments on Liquidity Basis (1 + 2)	−3.6	.2	−7.0	−4.7
Change in Liquid Liabilities (All foreign accounts)	3.5	.7	8.2	1.4
3. *Change in U.S. Official Reserve Assets*				
Gold	1.2	1.2	−1.0	.8
Convertible Currencies	−1.0	−1.2	0.8	2.2
IMF Gold Branch Position	−.1	−.9	−1.0	.4
Total	.1	−.9	−1.2	3.4

Source: Board of Governors, Federal Reserve System.

outflow (+) of foreign currencies or gold. As the total balance of payments statement must always balance, any net balance on current account must be exactly offset by the net balance on capital and gold accounts. Foreign goods received, if not matched by earnings from goods exported or gifts, must be owed or paid for by the shipment of gold.

For this reason, the excess of exports over imports of goods and services is termed *net foreign investment,* as it permits a country to acquire foreign assets of equal amount. Unlike domestic investment, net foreign investment may be represented by the accumulation of financial assets as well as by direct investment in real capital goods. A surplus of exports over imports enables a country to export capital and so to build up its overseas investments.

The international investment position of the United States is presented in Table 20-2. Although American total assets abroad are about double foreigners' total assets in the United States, American direct private investments abroad are six times as large as foreigners' direct private investments in the United States. Foreigners in contrast held large amounts of short- and long-term financial claims against the United States. This reflects the position of the American dollar as an international currency and the high state of development of American financial markets, which make American securities attractive to foreign investors.

Table 20-2   U.S. INTERNATIONAL INVESTMENT POSITION
1960–70 (BILLIONS OF DOLLARS)

	1960	1965	1970
Total U.S. Assets and Investments Abroad	85.6	120.4	166.6
Nonliquid Assets	66.2	103.2	139.7
U.S. Government	16.9	23.3	32.2
Private Long term	44.5	71.4	104.8
Short term	4.8	8.4	12.8
Liquid Assets	19.4	17.2	16.9
Total Foreign Assets and Investments in U.S.	40.9	58.8	97.5
Nonliquid	19.9	29.7	54.3
Private	19.8	29.2	50.5
Foreign Official Agencies	0.1	0.5	3.8
Liquid	21.0	29.1	43.2
Private	9.1	12.9	22.6
Foreign Official Agencies	1.9	16.2	20.6
Net International Investment Position of the U.S.	44.7	61.6	69.1

Source: Department of Commerce, Office of Business Economics.

THE BALANCE OF TRADE

The net balance of exports minus imports of merchandise is sometimes referred to as the *balance of trade*. An excess of merchandise exports over imports was traditionally termed a *favorable balance of trade, while an excess of merchandise imports over exports was termed an unfavorable* balance of trade. Countries with an unfavorable balance of trade must have a positive "invisible" balance, borrow from other countries, or ship out gold to pay for their excess of imports over exports. Countries with a favorable balance of trade must have a negative invisible balance, lend to foreigners, or import gold.

This choice of terms is unfortunate, as a so-called unfavorable balance of trade may be very desirable for a country, and conversely. It is always in a country's interest per se to be able to enjoy valuable imported foreign good without having to pay for them by exporting valuable domestic goods. An excess of merchandise imports over exports financed by borrowing may be used to finance current consumption. But it may also be used to build up a country's future productive capital stock. Provided that the return on domestic investment projects exceeds the external cost of borrowing, the larger stream of future interest, dividend, and principal repayment obligations associated with higher indebtedness can be paid out of an even larger stream of future domestic income. A development policy of export taxation and import substitution is likely to lead to a chronic balance-of-payments problem if the domestic investment projects yield a low return.

An excess of merchandise imports over exports may alternatively be financed by invisible earnings from past foreign investments. This is typically the case for developed creditor countries. An unfavorable balance of trade is undesirable only when it reflects a country's persistent inability to pay for current imports of consumption goods with current export earnings.

Disequilibrium in the Balance of Payments

Given the exchange rates, tastes, and productivity among trading partners, a country's volume of imports in the short run is positively related to the level and growth of domestic aggregate demand, which determines its income and price levels. When the growth of domestic aggregate demand exceeds domestic supply, demand for imports is likely to rise dramatically.

A country's volume of exports in contrast is related in the short run to the level and growth of income of its trading partners and thus only indirectly, through the effect of its import purchases on foreign income, to the level and growth of its own income. As represented in Figure 20-1, imports and exports are a function of national income, and the marginal propensity to import is higher than the marginal propensity to export:

$$(\frac{\Delta M}{\Delta Y} > \frac{\Delta X}{\Delta Y}).$$

Two important conclusions follow. Rapid expansion of domestic economic activity in the short run ordinarily provokes a worsening of a country's balance of trade, as imports rise more rapidly than exports. If the country is unable to finance the resulting imbalance on current account from its existing foreign exchange reserves, it will

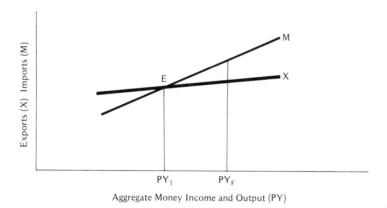

Figure 20-1 Imports and Exports as Related to National Income

attempt to borrow from other countries and international institutions. If such credit is not forthcoming in sufficient quantity, the government will be forced to impose import restrictions, to restrain the growth of domestic demand, or to devalue its exchange rate. *Devaluation* refers to a reduction in the price of one country's currency in terms of other currencies.

Second, there is no assurance that full employment levels of domestic income (PY_F In Figure 20-1) will coexist with balance of payments equilibrium. If at full employment imports substantially exceed exports at existing price levels and exchange rates, as illustrated in Figure 20-1, there will be a conflict between the two goals of full employment and balance of payments equilibrium.

The government may feel forced to sacrifice its full employment objectives to protect its foreign balance and to depress aggregate demand through fiscal and monetary policy so as to restrict the level of income toward Y_1. This must be the case if it has exhausted its gold and exchange reserves, cannot borrow additional amounts, and is not willing to devalue its currency. Restrictive monetary policy is likely to be more effective than fiscal policy with regard to balance of payment objectives. Higher interest rates attract foreign capital inflows, restrict domestic capital outflows, and thus increase the supply of foreign exchange. Fiscal policy, on the other hand, may selectively tax imports, subsidize exports, and restrict the inflow or outflow of capital funds.

Foreign Trade in the National Income Accounts

In an economy with foreign trade, the national income identity becomes

$$1. \quad Y = C + I + G + (X - M)$$

where $(X - M)$ represents the excess of exports (X) over imports (M), or net foreign investment.

Equation 1 may alternatively be written as

$$1a. \quad Y = (C - C_M) + (I - I_M) + (G - G_M) + X$$

This states that national income equals domestically produced consumption, investment, public and export goods, where $(X_M + I_M + G_M) = M$.

The saving-investment identity now becomes

$$2. \quad (S + T + M) = (I + G + X)$$

or

$$3. \quad (S - I) + (T - G) + (M - X) = 0.$$

Equation 3 states that total sectoral surplus and deficits must equal zero.

Alternatively,

$$4. \quad S + (T - G) = I + (X - M).$$

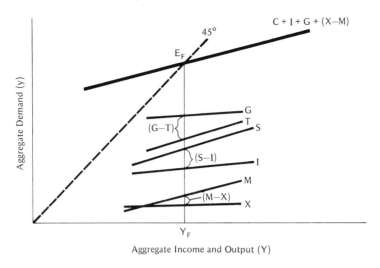

Figure 20-2 Aggregate Deficits Equal Aggregate Surpluses

Private plus net public saving equals private domestic plus net foreign investment. Although this relationship necessarily holds *ex post,* it is again an equilibrium condition when expressed *ex ante.*

These *ex ante* relationships are illustrated in Figure 20-2. In equilibrium, aggregate demand equals aggregate supply. At full employment, whether the government's budget is in surplus or deficit depends on the shape and position of the other functions. Total deficits and surpluses must cancel out. If, as shown in Figure 20-2, planned saving exceeds planned investment at full employment, the government must either run a deficit or permit a deficit in the balance of payments if full employment is to be maintained. An attempt to reduce the deficit $(M - X)$ in the balance of payments may be incompatible with full employment, given existing import and export preferences, unless government policy is itself responsible for the existing foreign deficit or surplus.

FOREIGN EXCHANGE RATES

International trade, like domestic trade, is facilitated and constrained by the stage of development of financial technology and the availability of credit and financial assets. Exporters must exchange foreign sales receipts into domestic currency in order to pay domestic factors of production and suppliers of intermediate goods. Importers must exchange domestic sales receipts into foreign currency in order to pay foreign exporters. Similarly international lenders, borrowers, and transferrers of capital demand and supply foreign currency. For this purpose there exists in all countries a foreign exchange market of some sort on which foreign currencies can be bought and sold for domestic currency.

Foreign exchange rates refer simply to the price of a unit of foreign currency in terms of domestic currency, stated in a regrettably confusing terminology. The higher the price of foreign currencies in the foreign exchange market, the lower the value of the domestic currency in terms of other currencies. The term *a rise in a country's exchange rate* is used to refer to a general fall in the price of other foreign currencies. Conversely, *a fall in the exchange rate* denotes a general rise in the price of foreign currencies in terms of domestic currency. A rise (fall) in the exchange rate is so termed because it is associated with a rise (fall) in the price of the domestic currency in terms of foreign currencies.

The Demand and Supply of Foreign Currencies

The demand for foreign exchange is based on the demands of importers and capital investors for foreign currencies, while the supply of foreign exchange is based on the supply of foreign currencies by exporters.

This relationship is shown diagramatically in Figure 20-3. Assume that there is only one foreign currency, pounds (£). The exchange rate P £, the price of pounds in terms of domestic currency, is measured on the vertical axis. Total export receipts and import expenditures of foreign exchange are measured on the horizontal axis.

As the price of the foreign currency rises, the value of domestic currency depreciates. To receive any given price in domestic currency, exporters can sell their product for a lower price in the foreign country, so that the volume sold will increase. Providing foreign demand is elastic, total sales receipts will also increase. The export

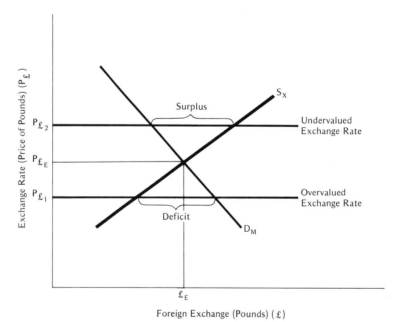

Figure 20-3 Determination of Exchange Rates

receipts curve is drawn upward sloping in Figure 20-3, on the assumption that, as the price of the foreign currency rises, export receipts increase in value.

The import receipts curve is drawn downward sloping, on the assumption that demand for imports is elastic. As the price of the foreign currency falls, imports become cheaper domestically. Total purchases of imports will increase in value only if the demand for imports is elastic. To the extent there are domestic substitutes for imported goods, the total demand for imports in each country is likely to be elastic.

Free Exchange Rates

When the price of foreign currency is determined in the foreign exchange market by market forces of supply and demand, it is termed a *floating* or *freely fluctuating* exchange rate.

A fall in the price of foreign currency in the foreign exchange market is termed an *appreciation* of the domestic exchange rate, and a rise in the market price of foreign currency is termed exchange rate *depreciation*.

In Figure 20-3 the equilibrium exchange rate for current account balance is shown as $P \pounds_E$. If the country were the recipient of net long-term capital inflows or transfers, the equilibrium domestic exchange rate would be higher. The price of foreign currency would then be lower, as such investment flows would be accompanied by a increased supply of foreign exchange.

What determines the equilibrium value of a country's exchange rate? As shown in Figure 20-3 it depends on the supply and demand for foreign currency. In the absence of trade restrictions, the volume and growth of exports and imports will vary with the level and change in productivity, tastes, prices, and incomes between the trading partners. If productivity gains and product innovation are occurring more rapidly in one country, *ceteris paribus* its exchange rate will tend to rise, as it becomes increasingly successful in selling its goods to others.

Similarly, if the price level in one country rises more rapidly than in another, *ceteris paribus* its exchange rate will tend to depreciate by a similar proportion. This rough relationship between exchange rates and purchasing power is sometimes termed the *purchasing power parity* doctrine. The volume of private and public real and financial investment and transfers to and from other countries also affect the equilibrium exchange rate.

Fixed Exchange Rates

At the other extreme from a floating exchange rate is the policy of a *fixed exchange rate,* when the government fixes or pegs the price of gold and foreign currencies, by selling or buying gold and foreign exchange to prevent their domestic price from deviating beyond very narrow limits. These limits are termed the gold "points," as historically they were accounted for by the transportation costs of shipping gold from one country to another. An increase in demand for a country's currency (supply of foreign exchange) cannot drive up its price beyond the upper gold point. The central bank will simply supply unlimited amounts of currency (demand foreign exchange) at that price. An increase in supply of a country's currency (demand for foreign exchange) cannot drive down its price below the lower gold point. The central bank will buy currency (supply foreign exchange) at that price. But the amount it can buy will depend on its reserves of gold and foreign currencies. When its foreign exchange reserves are exhausted, it has no longer the means to support the price and must devalue the currency.

Devaluation is defined as a reduction of the value of a currency fixed in terms of gold, that is, a rise in the official price of gold. *Revaluation* refers to an increase in the value of a currency pegged in terms of gold, that is, a fall in the price at which the government undertakes to buy and sell gold.

Even when a fixed exchange rate is initially established at the free market equilibrium rate, over longer periods of time the equilibrium value is likely to change with diverse movements in underlying factors in the two countries. If the price of foreign currency is fixed below the free market equilibrium level (e.g., $P_{\pounds_1}$ in Figure 20-3) the domestic exchange rate is said to be *overvalued*. In such situations the government will be forced to take steps to restrict imports and capital exports in order to avoid the depletion of its foreign exchange reserves. The effects of such measures may be represented in Figure 20-3 by a leftward shift of demand curve for foreign exchange.

Conversely, if the price of foreign currencies is set above the free market level (e.g., $P_{\pounds_2}$) the exchange rate is said to be *undervalued*, and the country will accumulate foreign exchange reserves. With a fixed exchange rate and trade restrictions no one knows exactly what the free market equilibrium exchange rate would be. As a result it is difficult to determine the extent a currency is undervalued or overvalued.

THE FLEXIBILITY OF EXCHANGE RATES

There has recently been a heated discussion as to whether fixed or floating exchange rates are preferable. Central bankers and government officials typically prefer fixed exchange rates, while academic economists have argued for flexible rates.

Stable exchange rates have the advantage of reducing uncertainty and so increasing the volume of trade between countries. Businessmen are able to calculate with greater confidence the future price and profit from foreign sales and purchases. But if the exchange rate is overvalued — fixed at a level too high to maintain current account balance — the country will persistently lose reserves. The government must then take steps to protect its gold and foreign exchange reserves by restricting merchandise and invisible imports through tariffs and quotas, by restricting capital outflows (tending to shift the D_M curve leftward), and by subsidizing exports (tending to shift the S_X curve rightward). When a country's current balance is fundamentally in disequilibrium, the benefits of a stable exchange rate in terms of increasing international trade are thus increasingly offset by the restrictive measures to reduce imports that the government is forced to impose in order to protect its foreign exchange reserves. An example of this was the temporary 10 percent surcharge on all imports into the United States instituted in 1971 to reduce the U.S. deficit.

The case against flexible rates is the opposite side of the argument for fixed rates. Flexible rates increase the degree of uncertainty involved in world trade. Traders cannot be sure what currency values will rule in the future. This uncertainty is reinforced by the possibility that private speculation may cause large and disorderly fluctuations in the market exchange rate in response to small temporary changes in underlying conditions. Buying and selling future foreign exchange in the forward markets is one way such uncertainty is reduced, and speculators will also operate to iron out such fluctuations over time.

An exchange rate is a two-edged instrument, as every exchange rate is shared by two countries. On these grounds it is often argued that unilateral action affecting exchange rates is unacceptable in principle. The determination of exchange rates is properly a subject for international consultation and agreement.

The Frequency of Exchange Rate Adjustment

It is important to emphasize that truly "fixed" exchange rates have never existed. All countries have in fact adjusted their exchange rate over longer time periods as such fundamental changes in underlying conditions occurred as differential rates of inflation, productivity increase, and income growth. In consequence, rather than considering as opposites the alternatives of fixed versus floating exchange rates, it is more fruitful to ask how frequently exchange rates ought to be altered. Seen in this light the argument loses most of its ideological heat. After some point a country's exchange rate becomes so overvalued that the costs of maintaining that rate, in terms of restrictions that reduce international trade, outweigh the costs of flexibility in moving to a lower rate.

Devaluation or depreciation always increases the physical volume of exports and decreases the physical volume of imports. Exports are cheaper from the point of view of other countries, while imports are dearer at home. But the critical question concerns its effect on the value of exports and imports. Providing that the sum of the elasticity of demand for exports and the elasticity of supply of imports exceeds one, a fairly weak condition likely to be satisfied in practice, the effects of devaluation will be to improve the balance of trade, that is, to increase the value of exports and/or to reduce the value of imports. In terms of Figure 20-3, this condition assumes that the demand curve for foreign currency does not intersect the supply curve from below, and that a stable equilibrium exists.

At the same time, devaluation is unpleasant, as it operates to reduce the real income of the country by worsening its terms of trade. Devaluation reduces the price at which goods are sold to others and increases the price that a country must pay for the goods that it purchases from others. This is one explanation of why many countries maintain as a matter of policy an overvalued exchange rate and then rely on trade restrictions to keep down the size of their foreign exchange deficit.

Another important reason is national prestige. The value of exchange rates, for no good economic reason, often becomes an important symbol of national pride. Heads of state become emotionally committed and personally identified with the maintenance of an overvalued or even an undervalued exchange rate.

Unfortunately the appropriate amount of devaluation for an overvalued exchange rate is subject to a very high degree of uncertainty. Governments do not know in advance what response other countries will make to devaluation by one country. If the country is large, there may be a general round of devaluations in response. All countries may reduce the value of their currency in terms of gold, so that the relative value of different currencies may remain largely or completely unaffected. The effect is simply to increase the world price of gold. Devaluation by a small country is less likely to provoke general devaluation by others. A country can never publicly admit in advance that it is even considering devaluation or revaluation. If they suspect devaluation, creditors and speculators will immediately unload all their asset holdings of the country's currency, while in the case of revaluation there will be a huge capital inflow. There is thus a built-in credibility gap.

A compromise solution is a *sliding or adjustable peg exchange rate*. This method involves setting stable exchange rates in the short run, with some provision for greater flexibility through widening of the upper and lower prices at which a government commits itself to sell and buy gold. It is then announced in advance that these upper and lower limits could be altered by some formula by a small amount — for example, a maximum of 1 or 2 percent per year. This method discourages speculators, yet at the same time over the longer run prevents a fundamental disequilibrium in the balance of payments from developing.

Optimum Currency Areas

Economists recently have devoted a great deal of attention to the concept of the geographic area over which exchange rates are fixed. This is another recognition of the fact that alternatives are a spectrum rather than a dichotomy, in this case over space rather than over time. All countries with a single currency have in effect a fixed rate internally. But it would be conceivable for different cities, states, or regions within one country to have separate floating exchange rates. There is nothing economically sacred about national boundaries. Is it possible to define an *optimum currency area?*

For small areas, fixed exchange rates are desirable, as foreign trade makes up a large proportion of their total economic activity. For such areas or countries a fall in the exchange rate that results in a roughly proportionate rise in the price of imports and exports will result in a relatively large change in the country's domestic price level. If the domestic price level were to change in proportion to the devaluation of the exchange rate, all benefits from devaluation in improving a country's balance of payments would be eliminated. To be successful, devaluation must operate to reduce a country's domestic consumption and force a reallocation of resources into export- and import-competing industries.

For larger economic areas, countries, or groups of countries, where foreign trade makes up a smaller proportion of total income and output, flexible exchange rates are likely to be much more effective in inducing a reallocation of resources into export industries. In this case the effect of devaluation on domestic price levels will be much smaller because import and export goods, whose prices rise, form a much smaller proportion of total output. This has been termed the *degree of openness* of an economy.

Fixed exchange rates also operate in a more satisfactory manner where there is a relatively free flow of capital among the areas concerned. Imbalance on current account will then be offset by an outward or inward flow of foreign investment in response to changing return differentials, giving the area more time to adjust to a temporarily unfavorable fluctuation in its trade balance. It is thus not forced to cut back on its purchases from outside in response to transitory declines in its export earnings.

Fixed exchange rates similarly are much more satisfactory when labor as well as capital mobility is high, as is usually the case within a country, and explains why fundamental payments disequilibrium for a particular internal area do not develop. As labor as well as capital will move in response to differential return and opportunity, fixed exchange rates do not necessitate unemployment or deflation in those areas where productivity is increasing relatively slowly.

This is not the case in the absence of capital and labor mobility. If workers in the United States had been prevented from leaving the southern states or Appalachia, such states would have experienced much higher unemployment rates, and wage rates and prices would have been forced downward in these areas. Rather than forcing a drastic downward adjustment of wages and prices, which is ordinarily extremely difficult and accompanied by severe transition costs of unemployment and foregone production, it would be preferable under these circumstances simply to change the exchange rate when fundamental conditions change. As an analogy, in the summer and winter, as days become longer or shorter, instead of adjusting the timing of our daily behavior to the fundamental change in external circumstances, it is more convenient to adjust our watches.

These considerations suggest that there may be advantages to having relatively stable exchange rates among smaller economic areas, for example, individual states and countries in North America, individual countries in the European Common Market, South America, or Africa. These might then be combined with freely fluctuating exchange rates among larger economic areas, for example, the continents of North America, Europe, South America, Asia, and Africa.

International financial difficulties stem fundamentally from the fact that, for the world economy as a whole, there exists no central bank to provide a supply of international currency and credit appropriate to the level of international transactions. In the absence of an international currency, countries hold and borrow reserves of gold and the currencies of other countries to meet their future international payment obligations.

Reserves of gold and foreign exchange provide a buffer against unsynchronized short-term fluctuations in the flow of current receipts relative to current expenditures. A government is then not forced to borrow at desperately unfavorable terms, or to restrict its current imports, or to change its exchange rate in response to a temporary fall in its current export earnings. With ample reserves and credit, a longer period of time is available to make adjustments to correct a fundamental disequilibrium in the balance of trade. Individual countries may be regarded as having a demand to hold a reserve of foreign exchange in some proportion to their wealth, to the volume and time-shape of their international transactions, to the return on reserves, and to the availability and cost of credit, for reasons similar to the reasons that individual households or firms demand money balances.

The Gold Standard

Unlike the case of domestic economies, countries have not as yet been able to agree on the creation and regulation of an international currency. Historically this role was by default largely filled by gold, which as a commodity was generally accepted in settlement of international payments. For nearly a century before World War I, gold was used as the predominant international medium of exchange. Under the *gold standard* each country's currency was freely convertible into gold at a fixed rate to both nationals and foreigners.

The gold standard's great virtue was that it required no international authority for its operation. A country with a favorable balance of trade would experience a gold inflow and, through the bank deposit-reserve multiplier, an increase in its domestic money supply and a fall in interest rates. The resulting increase in spending would tend to raise the level of income and prices, reducing exports and raising imports. Capital would flow out in response to higher returns in foreign countries. The system thus operated in an *automatic manner* to reduce the favorable trade balance. Conversely, a country with an unfavorable balance of trade would experience a gold outflow, a reduction in its domestic money supply, a rise in interest rates, and a fall in income and prices. This would operate to raise exports and reduce imports, attract foreign capital inflows, and so automatically to reduce the unfavorable trade balance.

The gold standard collapsed in this century chiefly because governments became increasingly unwilling to abide by the rules of the gold standard game. Reluctant to let the foreign tail wag the domestic dog, they broke the link between gold inflows and outflows and the domestic money supply by "sterilizing" gold inflows or using the printing press to offset gold outflows. A government could then protect the domestic economy from a fortuitous improvement in its external balance leading inexorably to inflation, or a deterioration in its balance of payments provoking a deflation or depression.

Adjustment to Payments Imbalance

Unfortunately, greater domestic autonomy was achieved only at the cost of greater international instability. There was no longer an automatic mechanism to push countries toward foreign balance. All countries desire a favorable balance of payments. Yet this is not possible for the world as a whole, unless total world international reserves increase. Only if reserves are provided by an international central bank or by gold is it possible for all countries simultaneously to increase their net foreign exchange balances.

One country's surplus on current account necessarily implies an equal deficit for other countries. In practice most of the burden of adjustment falls on debtor countries. Creditor countries are not forced to take steps toward restoring current account balance but may simply sit back and watch their gold and foreign exchange reserves accumulate.

This is not the case for debtor countries. A country with a persistent unfavorable balance of trade must somehow reduce its domestic consumption and allocate more resources to export production and import substitution. It may attempt to do so by restrictions on imports through increased use of tariffs and quotas, subsidization of exports, controls over capital outflows, deflation on the level of domestic demand through restrictive monetary and fiscal policy, and devaluation.

Devaluation has the initial effect of raising the demand for exports and the price of imports, many of which may be used as intermediate goods in the production of exported and domestic goods. In order to result effectively in a reallocation of resources, the expansionary effects of devaluation must be offset by restrictive monetary and fiscal policy. To the extent that demand is not restrained and domestic prices are permitted to rise, the effectiveness of exchange rate devaluation in inducing the necessary reallocation of resources is dissipated.

The Role of Gold

World stocks of gold available for monetary purposes have grown much less rapidly than the volume of international trade. As gold reserves have fallen increasingly below world demand for international liquidity, countries have been forced to hold a growing proportion of their total foreign exchange reserves in the form of certain key currencies believed firmly pegged to gold, the most important being the American dollar and the British pound. This practice is sometimes termed the gold exchange standard, as these currencies are convertible into gold on demand.

A general rise in the price of gold has been suggested by some as a means of increasing the stock of international reserves. The result would be to increase the real purchasing power in terms of goods and services of total gold stocks and so to increase the quantity of international liquidity. Overnight the world would be made wealthier, not in terms of the real goods and services it could produce, but in terms of the real goods and services each country could command. Until prices rose proportionately the ratio of wealth to income would increase.

A legislated increase in the price of gold has three undesirable aspects. The first is the inequitable distribution of benefits from such a policy. The main gainers from a rise in the price of gold would be the chief gold-producing and -exporting countries, which happen to be South Africa and the Soviet Union, precisely the countries that many governments do not wish to assist in this manner. The other chief beneficiaries are the countries that hold relatively large gold stocks. These are the rich creditor countries that have chosen to accumulate international reserves but not to hold them in the foreign exchange of other countries — at present, France, Italy, and Switzerland. As some of these countries have refused to play according to the rules of the gold exchange game but have turned in foreign currencies for gold, the key currency countries are reluctant to reward them in this manner.

The second is due to the fact that by raising the price of gold, more of the world's resources will be allocated to digging gold out of the ground, only in order to bury it again somewhere else, while the services of gold as a commodity cannot be enjoyed. As these scarce resources could have been allocated to the production of utility-providing goods and services and fiat money can perform equally well all of the monetary functions of gold, it is clearly desirable on economic grounds to move away from the use of gold as an international means of payment. Gold is an economic anachronism, whose monetary use is an open confession of failure on our part to agree on how and at what rate the stock of international money should be created.

The third general argument against using gold as money is that the supply of new gold, and hence the growth of gold stocks, is determined not by the amount of gold demanded for transactions purposes at existing prices and trade levels but by the supply conditions surrounding the discovery and production of new gold. In the nineteenth century, because of important gold discoveries, gold stocks increased much more rapidly than during the twentieth century. As a result, the ratio of the stock of gold to the volume of international transactions has fallen substantially over the present century.

Key Currency Countries

As gold stocks have not grown as rapidly as international trade, countries have found it necessary to supplement their gold reserves by holdings of certain currencies that may be exchanged into gold on demand and are considered as good as gold. These key currencies are primarily the American dollar and to a much lesser extent the British pound. As foreigners increase their holdings of dollars and pounds as world trade and the demand for foreign exchange reserves increases, the key currency countries, which are playing in part the role of an international central bank, find that the value of their liabilities owed to foreigners (foreign holdings of their currency) rise relative to their own holdings of gold.

Alternatively expressed, as foreign exchange holdings have increased with the increase in trade more rapidly than gold stocks, the ratio of gold reserves to dollars and pounds outstanding has necessarily fallen. These trends are summarized in Table 20-3. As may be seen, the ratio of monetary gold stocks to the total value of international trade has fallen from about 60 percent in 1950 to 14 percent in 1970. United States gold stocks fell from two and one-half times imports in 1950 to less than one-third of imports in 1970.

The total value of dollars and pounds held by foreigners increasingly exceeds the total amount of gold reserves held by America and England. As a result, it becomes more and more difficult to maintain confidence on the part of foreign creditors that dollars and pounds will in fact be convertible into gold on demand. If all foreign short-term claims were to be presented for collection, gold reserves would be insufficient.

This is, of course, also the case for a domestic banking system, whose reserves cover only a small proportion of total deposit liabilities. But, unlike the case of a domestic banking system, there is no international central bank to assume the critical role of lender of last resort. If creditors and speculators have the slightest suspicion that a country cannot fulfill its promise to exchange its currency into gold at a fixed rate but may be forced to devalue and so raise the price of gold, they will attempt to turn their dollar and pound holdings into gold before this event occurs.

Key currency countries benefit from their role as international banker by what is in effect a low-interest loan from creditor-holders of their currency. They are able to purchase current goods and services from other countries and to buy control of their industries, in return for which the other countries hold low-interest-bearing liquid deposits. But there are also considerable costs to this role of a key currency country, which become accentuated as the ratio of gold stocks to total short-term currency obligations outstanding continues to decline. To sustain confidence in convertibility, key countries may be forced to take drastic steps to protect their gold reserves, including sacrifice of the goal of domestic full employment. The foreign tail again wags the domestic dog.

This deterioration in the reserve position of the United States is presented in Table 20-4. The ratio of the United States gold stock to short-term liabilities to foreigners fell from 1.6 in 1955 to .26 in 1970. Large shifts in international confidence, leading to the demand by private foreign holders to convert short-term claims into gold, could be extremely embarrassing. The United States has attempted to buttress its exposed position by negotiating a series of contingency currency-swapping arrangements with other central banks. Although these arrangements left it better able to ride out waves of speculative pressure, there have been occasions in

Table 20-3 GOLD RESERVES AND INTERNATIONAL TRADE, 1950–70

	1950			1960			1965			1970		
	Gold Reserves	Total Imports of Goods and Services	Ratio: Gold/ Imports	Gold Reserves	Total Imports of Goods and Services	Ratio: Gold/ Imports	Gold Reserves	Total Imports of Goods	Ratio: Gold/ Imports	Gold Reserves	Total Imports of Goods	Ratio: Gold/ Imports
World	35.3	59.7	.59	40.2	135.5	.30	43.2	174.9	.25	41.3	291.9	.14
United States	22.8	9.0	2.53	17.8	15.1	1.18	13.8	21.3	.65	11.1	39.8	.28
France	.7	3.1	.23	1.6	6.2	.26	4.7	10.3	.46	3.5	18.8	.19
Germany	—	2.7	—	3.0	10.1	.30	4.4	17.5	.25	4.0	29.8	.13
Italy	.3	1.4	.21	2.2	4.7	.47	2.4	7.4	.32	2.9	14.9	.19
Switzerland	1.5	1.0	1.50	2.2	2.2	1.00	3.0	3.7	.81	2.7	6.5	.41
United Kingdom	3.3	7.3	.45	3.2	12.6	.25	2.3	15.6	.15	1.3	21.7	.06
India	.2	1.2	.17	.2	2.3	.09	0.3	2.9	.10	0.2	2.1	.09

Source: Board of Governors, The Federal Reserve System; International Monetary Fund; Statistical Office of the United Nations.

the past few years when the entire system appeared extremely fragile. In 1971, the United States permitted its exchange rate to fluctuate by ceasing to buy and sell gold at a fixed price. This decision takes the world a long step towards the demonetization of gold. It also encouraged surplus countries to revalue, since they could no longer exchange their reserves of dollars for gold.

Table 20-4   U.S. RESERVE ASSETS AND SHORT-TERM FOREIGN LIABILITIES, 1955–70 (BILLIONS OF DOLLARS)

	1955	1960	1965	1968	1970
U.S. Reserve Assets					
U.S. Gold Stock	21.8	17.8	13.8	10.9	11.1
Foreign Currency Holdings	—	—	.8	3.5	0.6
Reserve Position IMF	1.6	1.6	.9	1.3	1.9
S.D.Rs.					0.9
Total	23.4	19.4	15.5	15.7	14.5
Short-term Liabilities to Foreigners					
International Monetary Fund	.2	.8	0.8	1.0	0.6
Official Foreign Institutions	6.9	11.1	15.4	12.5	20.1
Banks and Other Foreigners	4.8	7.6	11.5	19.6	21.8
Total	13.6	21.0	29.1	33.9	43.3
Short-term Claims on Foreigners	1.5	3.6	7.6	8.7	10.8
Ratio of Gold Stock to Short-term liabilities to Foreigners (Percent)	160	85	47	32	26

Source: Board of Governors, The Federal Reserve System; International Monetary Fund.

Toward an International Central Bank

The obvious economic solution is to create an international institution that can provide international currency. The creation of international liquidity by the purchase of securities by an international central bank would increase the supply of international credit and so tend to lower interest rates. It could also provide a politically attractive means of financing development loans.

Because of political differences among countries, such an institution has not yet been achieved. Just as conflicts arise within a country concerning the appropriate monetary policy to pursue, largely because of distributional effects, there are conflicts among countries. Debtor countries prefer more expansionary monetary policy with inflation, easy credit, and low interest rates. Creditor countries prefer a more restrictive monetary policy with stable prices, tighter credit, and high interest rates.

No final agreement has as yet been reached as to how voting control over the policy of an international central bank would be shared among different countries. At what rate ought such a bank to increase the supply of international money? Because international money would be the liability of an international central bank, it must be decided how this liability would be created. To whom would such a bank lend and on what terms? Would international money originate in the bank's purchase of securities from private individuals or from governments? Should such loans be made on market considerations or distributed by some formula — for example, in proportion to the size of a country's existing reserves, trade, income, or population?

There are two international institutions that already exist to form the nucleus of a world central bank. The first is the International Bank for Reconstruction and Development, or the World Bank as it is frequently called. The capital stock of the World Bank is subscribed by all member countries according to a quota system. The bank is empowered to use its capital to make medium and long-term loans to developing countries. It also issues bonds in the capital markets of developed countries, backed by the credit of its members, in order to raise additional credit to finance economic development. The World Bank plays an important role in financing the development projects of less developed countries, but its lending potential is currently very small relative to the total development needs and expectations of the Third World. Its loans are intended to be made on sound commercial principles, while an affiliated organization, the International Development Association, makes "softer" loans.

The second institution is the International Monetary Fund, which was created at the end of World War II to provide a means by which stable exchange rates could be maintained by voluntary international cooperation, in place of the automatic but harsh workings of the gold standard. Countries in payments imbalance are first expected to seek to restore their foreign balance by adjustments in their domestic economic policies. All member countries are pledged to maintain stable exchange rates except in circumstances of fundamental disequilibrium. Member countries are permitted to initiate a depreciation of their currency of up to 10 percent and, after consultation, the Fund may accede to further devaluation.

Each country deposits gold and its own currency with the Fund by a predetermined quota related to its national income and trade volume. Twenty-five percent of a country's quota must be paid in gold, while the rest is payable in the country's own currency. In return, the Fund undertakes to provide short-term credit on request to any member country experiencing foreign exchange deficits. These drawing rights are set for each country as determined by its quota with the Fund.

The Fund may also make recommendations for remedying a longer-term or *fundamental disequilibrium* in a member country's balance of payments. Additional short-term Fund credit beyond the quota is discretionary and ordinarily contingent on a country's agreement to carry out Fund recommendations.

In addition to the IMF, the central banks of the largest trading countries have arranged a standby system of short-term credits and swaps of currency to central banks of countries experiencing temporary balance of payments deficits or surpluses. A country losing or gaining foreign exchange may swap it right back again and so maintain its desired exchange reserves. This practice has prevented private speculators from forcing an individual country to devalue or revalue its currency due to a temporary flood of "hot money."

The Group of Ten, made up of the ten most important developed trading countries, has taken an historic step toward the demonetization of gold by agreeing to refuse to purchase gold on private markets for monetary purposes. This move has resulted in a two-price system for gold: the official rate at which the central banks of these countries buy and sell gold among themselves, and a free market price determined by private supply and demand.

Provided that these countries do not purchase any additional gold except from one another, their aggregate monetary gold stocks cannot increase. The gold reserves of these ten countries, if they in fact are used only to keep accounts with one another, have become totally atavistic. They might as well not exist as, if they disappeared, no one would notice their absence. One is irresistibly reminded of the stone money on the Island of Yap, resting peacefully at the bottom of its lagoon.

Growth of international reserves is to be provided by Special Drawing Rights from the International Monetary Fund. These reserves are simply Fund credits, distributed to countries in proportion to their Fund quotas. These SDR's represent the first movement toward an international fiat money or "paper gold." It is at this date still unknown whether SDR's will be created in sufficient volume to replace gold completely as a true international currency. Nothing could be less certain than a forecast of future developments in the international financial system. But there appears more reason for optimism at this time than there has been for several decades. To spite the cynics, progress does occur.

BIBLIOGRAPHY OF SELECTED PAPERBACKS, PART FIVE

Cohen, B., *American Foreign Economic Policy,* Harper & Row.

Hayter, T., *Aid as Imperialism,* Penquin.

Ingram, J., *International Economic Problems,* Wiley.

Janeway, E., *The Economics of Crisis: War, Politics and the Dollar,* Weybright.

Kennen, P., *International Economics,* Prentice-Hall.

Landes, D. S., *Bankers and Pashas: International Finance and Economic Imperialism in Egypt,* Harper & Row.

Magdoff, H., *Age of Imperialism: The Economics of U.S. Foreign Policy,* Monthly Review Press.

Ranis, G., *The United States and the Developing Economics,* Norton.

Triffin, R., *Our International Monetary System: Yesterday, Today and Tomorrow,* Random House.

PART SIX

ECONOMIC GROWTH AND DEVELOPMENT

economic growth and development

AT THE HISTORICAL DAWN of capitalist production — and every capitalist upstart has personally to go through this historical stage — avarice, and desire to get rich, are the ruling passions. . . . Accumulate! Accumulate! That is Moses and the prophets. . . . Accumulation for accumulation's sake, production for production's sake.

— *KARL MARX*

THE AMERICAN ECONOMY presents us with a spectacle of growing resources pressing against limited wants. Expanding markets in conditions of material abundance depend upon men's dissatisfaction with their lot being perpetually renewed. Whether individual campaigns are successful or not the institution of commercial advertising accentuates the materialistic tendencies in society and promotes the views that the things that matter most are the things money will buy.

A short visit to the U.S. is enough to convince one that wealth, competition and free institutions provide no safeguards against the prevalence of appalling standards.

— *EZRA MISHAN*

Economic growth may be defined as an increase in the total quantity of real goods and services produced in an economy. This increase is usually expressed as an annual percentage rate of change in per capita terms, as that is the relevant concept from the point of view of welfare. Table 21-1 presents estimates of the growth rate of per capita real income in selected countries. As may be seen, growth rates varied widely, from about zero to more than 10 percent per year.

Table 21-1 GROWTH RATES OF PER
CAPITA REAL INCOME
FOR SELECTED
COUNTRIES, 1955–68

Country	Average Annual Growth	
	1955–60	1960–68
Australia	1.9	2.3
Bolivia	−2.6	3.2
Brazil	3.2	1.1
Canada	.7	3.6
Dominican Republic	2.1	−0.6
France	3.7	4.4
Germany	6.0	3.4
India	N.A.	0.4
Indonesia	N.A.	−0.2
Israel	5.5	4.2
Japan	10.2	9.2
Morocco	−2.3	0.9
Pakistan	1.2	3.5
Sweden	3.1	3.8
Thailand	1.9	3.0
U.S.S.R.[1]	8.3	5.8
United Kingdom	2.1	2.3
U.S.A.	.4	3.7
Venezuela	4.2	1.3
Yugoslavia[1]	8.0	4.9

1. Net material product.

Source: Statistical Office of the United Nations.

The Production Function

The output of economic goods and services (Y) produced in an economy is directly related to the factors of production involved: labor (L), real capital including natural resources (K), and the technology (T) by which these inputs are combined to produce output. This may be summarized in simplified form by the production function: $Y = T(L, K)$. Growth of real output (Y) must be due to increases in the factor inputs L and K and/or to a rise in the level of technology T, i.e., an increase in output from the same inputs.

To what extent have experienced rates of growth been due to these different causes? What are the form and characteristics of the production function? Aside from academic curiosity, this is an extremely important question. A government that desires to increase the economy's rate of growth can do so successfully only if it knows the contributions made by various factors to the growth process.

Capital accumulation, resource discovery, and technological change operate to raise total output, and so the average product of labor and per capita real income. Ordinarily they will also raise the marginal product of labor, and so real wage rates. But to the extent that technological change is predominantly labor-saving rather than capital-saving, the demand curve for labor will become steeper. As shown in Chapter 8, the real wage rate may fall even though average productivity rises.

The Race Between Labor, Capital, and Technology

The course of real wages and per capita income over time is the outcome of a race between increases in the supply of labor that operate to reduce real wages and per capita income, and increases in the capital stock and the level of technology that operate to increase real wages and per capita real income.

The classical economists recognized that capital, like labor, was subject to diminishing returns unless offset by technological change. For this reason they believed that profit rates would fall as the amount of capital per worker increased. As investment and saving are positively related to the rate of return, at some very low but presumably still positive rate of profit on capital, net saving and investment would cease. Total income would then remain constant and the economy would have reached the *stationary state*.

We can now see with hindsight wisdom that the classical economists underestimated the power of technological change in the development of capitalist economies. Over the last fifty years, per capita real income in America has increased at between 2 and 3 percent per year, capital per worker risen substantially, and profit rates remained roughly stable. While 2 percent sounds like a modest figure, the power of compound interest is such as to make a 2 percent increase in per capita income very powerful on an accumulated basis. From the compound interest formula given in Chapter 9, the number of years required for a quantity growing at the constant rate g percent to double in amount is approximated by the expression $(\frac{70}{g})$. For example with a rate of growth of 7 percent, income doubles every ten years; with a rate of 3.5 percent, every twenty years; with a rate of 2 percent, every thirty-five years.

If the future is similar to the past, per capita real income in developed countries may be expected to double roughly every generation. The implications of such a rate of growth over the longer run are staggering. For an economy such as the United States poverty, in the sense of *absolute* material deprivation, within a historically relatively short period of time will no longer be a major social problem. Some individuals will always be relatively poor, compared to the national average, as long as income is not equally distributed. But provided that the distribution of income does not become more unequal, the absolute income of the poor will increase dramatically. By the year 2000 average incomes will be about $20,000 a year in 1970 dollars.

The critical qualification in the above passage is the phrase, "if the future is like the past." The earth's supply of natural resources is not infinite. There must therefore be some finite limit to the level of economic output and population that can be sustained. No one really knows what that limit is or when it will be reached. People delight to tell economic ghost stories, and there is a long tradition of doomsday literature. Nevertheless we do live on Spaceship Earth, and a balance must be maintained between its life-support capability and the demands made by its inhabitants. We cannot continue to grow indefinitely at our past rate. Some have argued that we have in fact already exceeded the point at which all of the world's present population could live at the standard achieved by the average American or European family, given current levels of resource intake and waste output.

To put it bluntly, if we take as the price of a first-class ticket the resource requirements of those passengers who travel in the Northern Hemisphere of the Spaceship, we have now reached a point at which the steerage is condemned to live forever — or at least within the horizon of the technology presently visible — at a second class level; or at which a considerable change in living habits must be imposed on first class if the ship is ever to be converted to a one-class cruise.[1]

Population Growth

The outlook for the less-developed countries is much less optimistic. Rates of population increase for selected countries are presented in Table 21-2. Growth of population at rates equal to or exceeding the growth of total output has resulted for many countries in constant and even declining levels of per capita real income. The emergency nature of this problem has led to a revival of neo-Malthusian theories of population increase.

Population growth is affected by a large number of noneconomic forces that influence family formation, fertility rates, and death rates. The rapid rates of population growth of 2 and 3 percent currently experienced in most less-developed countries have been due to the fact that death rates, in particular infant mortality rates, have fallen rapidly and dramatically from forty and fifty to fifteen and twenty per thousand, while birth rates have fallen much more slowly from their high initial levels of forty and fifty per thousand. In the developed countries, birth rates have followed the gradual decline in death rates with a long and variable lag, as real incomes have risen. Less developed countries currently have death rates equivalent to those in Europe of only a few decades ago, combined with birth rates equivalent to medieval Europe.

1. R. Heilbroner, "Ecological Armageddon." Reprinted in *Between Capitalism and Socialism* (New York, 1970), p. 271.

Table 21-2 RATES OF POPULATION INCREASE IN SELECTED COUNTRIES, 1958–69

Country	Annual Rate of Change (Percent)	
	1958–63	*1963–69*
Australia	2.1	2.0
Brazil	3.1	3.0
Canada	2.0	1.8
France	1.3	0.9
Germany	1.3	1.0
Ghana	2.7	2.7
India	2.3	2.5
Israel	3.5	2.9
Japan	0.9	1.1
Kenya	2.9	2.9
Pakistan	2.1	2.1
Sweden	0.5	0.8
Thailand	3.0	3.1
U.S.S.R.	1.7	1.1
United Kingdom	0.7	0.6
United States	1.6	1.2

Source: Statistical Office of the United Nations.

Current rates of population growth are clearly transitory. Applying the previous formula for compound interest and extrapolating, in a few hundred years there would be standing room only. It has been estimated that if population growth continued at present rates, in about 1,000 years the mass of people on the earth's surface would be expanding physically at the speed of light, which represents an absolute upper limit of sorts.

Current rates of population growth must decline, if not as the result of voluntary private decisions, then as the result of government policy, famine, war, or disease. With modern technology it is now possible for the first time in human history that no unwanted child be born. While birth control programs are becoming increasingly central as a means of bringing the population "explosion" under control, determination of the desired rate of population growth by government policy appears still a long way off. But this outlook could change rapidly. Before it was perverted by Nazi Germany, eugenics policy had attained wide acceptance among progressive groups in all countries.

AN OPTIMUM RATE OF GROWTH?

Unlike the rate of growth of population, the rate of growth of the capital stock and of technological change are variables upon which government economic policy can explicitly operate. For this reason, economists have long focused upon the effects of investment in capital goods, human beings, research, and development in contributing to the rate of growth of an economy.

Rapid growth has become a widely adopted goal of government economic policy. It is frequently suggested that a mix of easy money policy with low interest rates to encourage investment and tight fiscal policy with a budget surplus to restrain demand and generate public saving is the appropriate combination of stabilization techniques to achieve the goal of more rapid growth. But is more rapid growth always good? Is it possible to define an optimum growth rate? The question of the costs and benefits of economic growth must now be considered.

Alternative Growth Paths

Consumption of economic goods and services, including leisure, is ordinarily regarded as the point of economic activity, the reason why the economic game is played. But an economy that consumes all of its current output will have no goods left over to maintain or add to its capital stock. Its future income will then fall. The greater the proportion of its current output that an economy allocates to investment in assets and services that increase future productive capacity, the smaller will be the level of its current consumption. But the higher will be the growth of real output and thus its potential level of future consumption.

This relationship is shown in Figure 21-1. Consumption goods and services (C) are measured on the horizontal axis, and investment goods and services (I) on the

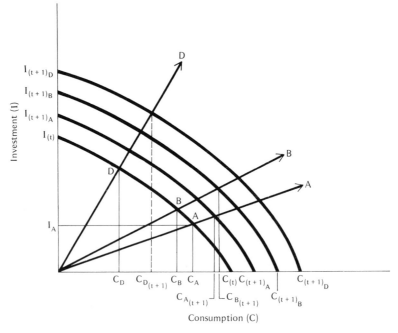

Figure 21-1 Alternative Growth Paths

vertical axis. Investment is defined broadly to include all expenditures that increase future productive capacity, including education, training, research and development as well as the accumulation of physical capital goods. Given the labor force, natural resource endowment, initial capital stock, and level of technology, the production transformation relationship between consumption and investment goods in period t is shown as curve I_tC_t. This curve represents the production frontier in the sense that with unemployed resources or inefficiency the economy may operate well inside the CI curve.

If the economy is located at the point A on its production possibility frontier, its present consumption would be higher (C_A) than if it produces at the point $B(C_B)$. But increasing the amount of output currently devoted to investment will result in a more rapid rise in the economy's future productive capacity. Growth in the economy's productive capacity is represented in Figure 21-1 by an outward shift in the production possibility curve, as shown by the curves $IC_{(t+1)_A}$ and $IC_{(t+1)_B}$.

Depending on the rate at which increases in investment shift out the production possibility curve over time, there exists some optimum investment ratio that must be followed to maximize growth. What mix should the government select?

If the economy moves outward on the investment-consumption ray B, it will have lower consumption in the present but higher consumption in the next period ($t + 1$) than if it moves out on the ray A. However, it is possible to save and invest too much. Capital is subject to diminishing returns and once built must be maintained and replaced when it wears out. An economy that raises its investment ratio to D and grows outward on the ray D has less consumption both in the present and in the next period than if it follows either of the other alternative growth paths.

The rates of growth of consumption over time along these alternative growth

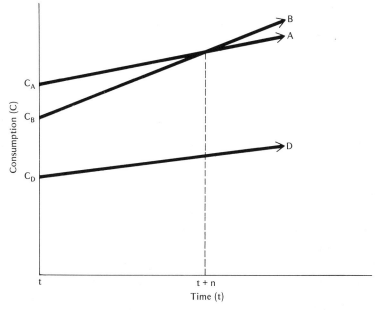

Figure 21-2 **Alternative Growth Paths over Time**

paths are plotted in Figure 21-2. Assuming that consumption is desirable, paths *A* and *B* clearly both dominate *D*, as they always provide higher levels of consumption. But whether *A* or *B* is preferred depends on the economy's preference for present versus future income. Path *A* provides higher consumption from the present up to the point *n*, while path *B* provides higher consumption in all future periods after *n*.

Intertemporal Redistribution of Income

Income in the future is valued less highly than income today. Whether path *A* or *B* is preferable will depend on the time period considered and the rate of discount applied to future consumption. Given some social rate of time preference, it might appear possible to find the present value of the consumption streams *A* and *B* and simply select the larger. But present discount rates can reflect the preferences only of present economic units. It is difficult to see how the preferences of generations as yet unborn can be taken into account today, although presumably they would always prefer a larger to a smaller future income.

Because of the impossibility of making interpersonal comparisons of utility, it is not possible to define an optimum growth path. It becomes a redistribution question over time. One might argue that path *B* ought to dominate *A*, as future generations will enjoy higher incomes forever after the period *n* is passed, and forever is a very long time. On the other hand, advocates of path *A* could argue that future generations will be wealthier than present generations (the power of compound interest).

Reducing present consumption in order to increase investment to raise future consumption thus results in a regressive redistribution of consumption intertemporally from the poor present to the rich future. If the period *n* lies in the very near future, it may be that most of the present generation would prefer to consume less now in order to be able to consume more in the future. But some members of the present generation would not, particularly if they do not expect to be alive in period *n*.

The Raising of a Surplus

If the choice is determined democratically by majority voting, the preferred growth rate will depend on how much an increase in current investment increases future productive capacity. For both present and future, it will always be desirable that investment expenditures be allocated to those projects whose effect on increasing future capacity is greatest. The surplus of present income over consumption devoted to growth will also depend on the initial level of consumption, the expected level of future consumption, and the concern of the present for the future.

Russia under Stalin's leadership launched a policy of rapid economic growth by drastically reducing consumption. The surplus was raised by force from the peasantry by the device of the collective farm and used by the state to feed an urban population engaged in producing capital goods. Stalin was pitiless in carrying out this policy of "starving to glory." It could not conceivably have been pursued by a democratically elected government.

Poor countries whose population is growing more rapidly than real income so that per capita income is falling enjoy very little luxury of choice. Given their rate of population growth, they have to grow faster to keep from getting poorer. Somehow a surplus has to be raised to support growth-producing activities.

Shifts in the relative productive capacity of nations in the past have been accompanied by a parallel shift in their international power and sphere of influence. For this reason, governments mistrustful of their rivals may be driven into a growth race as an unintended result of nationalist and military posture. In such situations, the costs of more rapid material growth may widely exceed the benefits. Nevertheless, like arms control, it may be difficult for one country acting unilaterally to deescalate, without adversely threatening its national self-interest.

Figure 21-3 presents estimates of feasible upper and lower limits of United States and Russian growth rates. Even if most citizens would prefer the lower paths, with their higher present consumption, governments, fearing the future shift in power that might occur if their rivals chose to grow along their upper boundary, choose to grow along their upper paths.

GROWTH WITH FIXED FACTOR PROPORTIONS

As seen in the previous section, a country can raise its rate of growth by increasing the proportion of its output devoted to growth-producing activities.

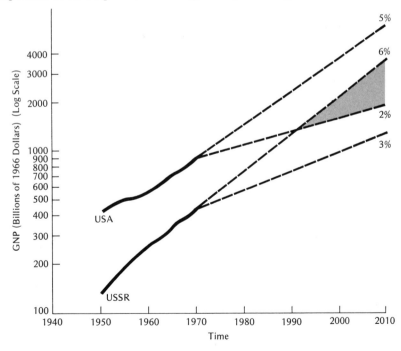

Figure 21-3 Feasible Growth Paths: United States and Russia, 1970-2000

The Capital-Output Ratio

Given the level of technology and the supply of labor, the economy's capital-output ratio $(K/Y = k)$ describes the average amount of capital goods required to produce a given output. The ratio of capital to annual output varies widely among different industries. It is relatively high in capital-intensive industries such as hydroelectric power and relatively low in labor-intensive industries such as services. It also differs among different countries. But, for a particular country, the value of k typically changes only slowly. In the United States, it has been estimated that the ratio of capital stock to annual output has fallen over the last fifty years from about 2.2 to 1.5. The particular value is clearly sensitive to the manner in which capital is defined and measured.

From the definition, $K = kY$. This formula states simply that, for example, with a capital-output ratio of 2, the capital stock must be twice the value of output in every year. Providing that k is constant, this holds in period t: $K_t = kY_t$ and in period $t + 1$: $K_{t+1} = kY_{t+1}$. Subtracting: $K_{t+1} - K_t = k(Y_{t+1} - Y_t)$ or $\Delta K = k\Delta Y$. As long as k is constant, the average capital output ratio equals the marginal capital output ratio:

$$\left(\frac{K}{Y}\right) = \left(\frac{\Delta K}{\Delta Y}\right) = k.$$

This implies that in order to attain an increase in output of $100 with a capital-output ratio equal to two, the capital stock must increase by $200.

The change in the capital stock (ΔK) is also by definition identical to net investment (I) over the period $(I = \Delta K)$. It follows that with a constant capital-output ratio the *level* of net investment demand will be some constant multiple of the *change* in output: $I = k\Delta Y$.

The Dual Function of Investment Spending

As earlier discussed, for a particular economy average saving behavior is relatively stable over time. Let the proportion of income saved $\left(\frac{S}{Y}\right)$ be represented by s. If this proportion remains constant, the average propensity to save (s) equals the marginal propensity to save: $S = sY$, $\Delta S = s\Delta Y$. From the multiplier relationship $(1/s)$, it is possible to determine the level of aggregate demand associated with every level of investment: $I\left(\frac{1}{s}\right) = Y$. Alternatively expressed: $I = sY = S$. This equation simply states that because investment is equal to saving, if net saving is a constant proportion of income, then net investment will also be a constant proportion of income as long as $S = I$.

These formulations reveal the *dual function* of investment activity. The level of investment through the multiplier relationship, assuming the proportion saved is constant, determines the *level* of aggregate demand. At the same time, the level of investment, through its capacity-creating powers, determines the *increase* in aggregate supply.

A Fixed-Proportions Growth Model

It is then natural to inquire what is the rate of growth of investment and income at which aggregate demand and aggregate supply both grow at the same rate. In equilibrium growth, planned saving (sY) must exactly equal planned investment $(k\Delta Y)$.

Equating: $sY = k\Delta Y$, or $\dfrac{\Delta Y}{Y} = \left(\dfrac{s}{k}\right)$.

The equilibrium rate of growth of output $\left(\dfrac{\Delta Y}{Y}\right)$ is thus equal to the savings ratio divided by the capital-output ratio. With a constant capital-output ratio and a constant savings ratio, the equilibrium rate of growth of output is also equal to the rate of growth of the capital stock and the rate of growth of investment. This rate has been termed the *warranted* rate of growth, in the sense that only this particular rate of growth of investment is warranted by the economy's savings ratio and capital-output ratio. If an economy saved 10 percent of its income and its capital-output ratio were equal to 2, its warranted growth rate would be 5 percent per year.

This formulation of the growth process has been termed the *Harrod-Domar model* after its discoverers. If for the moment the assumptions of a constant s and k are accepted, the model suggests two important implications.

The Instability of Growth Under Capitalism

The first is the innate *instability* of full employment growth in a capitalist economy where the volume of investment is determined primarily by profit expectations. Should the rate at which investment expenditures increase exceed the warranted rate, aggregate demand will exceed aggregate supply of output. This result follows because investment determines the *level of aggregate demand,* $Y = I\left(\dfrac{1}{s}\right)$, but only the *change in the level of aggregate supply* $\left(\Delta Y = \left(\dfrac{I}{k}\right)\right)$. The level of aggregate supply is determined by the capital stock $\left(Y = \dfrac{K}{k}\right)$. In the face of excess demand for goods and services, business investment demand will tend to be even larger in the next period. Thus a rate of growth in excess of the warranted rate leads to an unstable ever-increasing upward expansion of spending, greater than the economy's ability to raise real output.

Conversely, if investment expenditures grow at a rate below the warranted rate, aggregate demand $\left(I\left(\dfrac{1}{s}\right)\right)$ will fall short of aggregate supply $(Y + I/k)$. As a result, excess capacity will appear and investment expenditures will grow even more slowly in the next period.

A fixed-proportions model thus has the "knife-edge" property that, whenever the growth of investment diverges from the warranted rate, the system is unstable and explodes upward or downward into inflation or depression. This property provides some insight into the characteristic cyclical development of capitalist economies.

The Importance of Saving

The second implication is that the rate at which the economy grows is critically dependent on the proportion of current income that the economy is able to save and invest. If a country desires to grow more rapidly, it must somehow raise its savings ratio. With a capital-output ratio, for example, of 3, and a net savings ratio of 6 percent, which approximates that of many poor countries, total output will grow at a rate of only 2 percent. If the population is growing more rapidly than 2 percent, per capita income will fall.

The proportion of income consumed and invested in selected countries is presented in Table 21-3. Developed countries have in general both higher net saving ratios and lower capital-output ratios than less developed countries. This explains in part their higher growth rates. As the capital-output ratio was regarded as largely technologically determined, it was concluded that the key to the development process lay in raising an economy from a 5 percent saver to a 15 percent saver.

Table 21-3 CONSUMPTION AND INVESTMENT EXPENDITURES IN SELECTED COUNTRIES (PERCENTAGE OF GNP)

| Country | Year | Consumption | | Investment Fixed Capital Formation |
		Private	Government	
Australia	1968	61	13	27
Brazil	1967	75	11	14
Canada	1969	58	17	21
France	1968	61	13	25
Germany, Fed. Rep. of	1969	55	16	24
Israel	1968	66	30	20
Japan	1966	55	10	31
Pakistan	1967	81	7	14
Sweden	1969	54	22	23
Thailand	1967	66	9	25
U.S.A.	1968	61	21	17
U.S.S.R.	1968	64	8	14*
United Kingdom	1968	63	18	18

* Net fixed capital formation.

Source: Statistical Office of the United Nations.

GROWTH WITH VARIABLE FACTOR PROPORTIONS

The Instability of Marginal Capital-Output Ratios

The use of the fixed-proportions model by underdeveloped countries attempting to raise their rate of economic growth led to disappointment and disillusion. Even if the government of a poor country succeeded by heroic and unpopular measures in holding down real consumption and raising the savings ratio, real output did not rise as predicted. The marginal capital-output ratio did not stay put at its average historical level but rose concurrently with the increase in investment. If the country's average capital-output ratio were three, then the marginal capital-output ratio relating new capital investment to increases in output was observed to be five, ten, or higher. Instead of one hundred of new capital resulting in an increase in productive capacity of thirty-three, the increase in output was twenty, or ten, or even zero.

Further studies of developed and less developed countries revealed, as indicated by the scatter in Diagram 21-1, that some countries with high saving and investment ratios grew relatively slowly, while other countries with low saving and investment ratios grew relatively rapidly. Virtually no positive relationship within developed or underdeveloped countries is evident in Diagram 21-1. Clearly, other factors are at work in determining the growth of output. Higher levels of investment alone do not necessarily lead to higher rates of growth of output. Marginal capital-output ratios

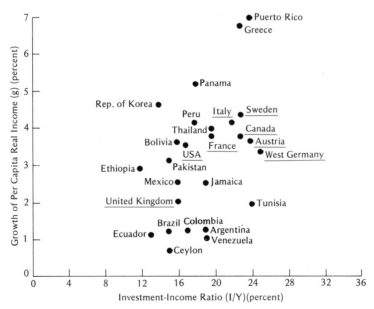

Source: Statistical Office of the United Nations

Diagram 21-1 Growth Rates and Investment Ratios in Developed and Less
Developed Countries, 1960-1966. (Average Rates and Ratios
for Period. Developed Countries Underlined.)

and average capital-output ratios may and do differ enormously. It is not merely the amount but also the productivity of new investment that is important.

The assumption in the Harrod-Domar model of a constant marginal capital-output ratio as investment is increased appears on the surface to be in conflict with the law of diminishing returns. As the capital stock increases and labor and technology remain constant, the marginal product of capital will fall. As a result, the marginal capital-output ratio will rise.

The assumptions of fixed factor proportions and constant returns to scale implicit in a constant capital-output ratio thus appear to require a particular set of conditions. The labor force and the level of technology must increase in an accommodating fashion to offset the law of diminishing returns. The observed historical stability of a country's capital-output ratios and profit rates over time must therefore have been due to the following fact: population growth and technological change must have occurred at just such a rate as roughly to offset the tendency of the marginal product of capital to fall as capital was accumulated.

Business firms seeking to reduce costs substitute one factor for another in response to a change in relative factor prices or productivity. While for many individual processes the proportion in which factors are combined is largely fixed, this is not true for commodities in the aggregate, as the same goods may ordinarily be produced by different techniques. Similarly, with technological change embodied in new capital goods, it is unreasonable to assume constant returns to scale. Improvements in technology result in a change in output greater than the proportionate increase in capital and labor inputs.

A Variable Proportions Growth Model

The recognition of the variability of marginal capital-output ratios and the attempt to include the effects of both labor and capital in the growth process led economists to variable-proportions models, which take into account the fact of diminishing returns as one factor is increased disproportionately. These models are termed *neoclassical,* in view of their similarity to the view of the growth process held by nineteenth-century economists.

Under the assumption that labor and capital can be combined in variable proportions and both are subject to diminishing returns, the growth of output, assuming temporarily that technological change is absent, is attributable to the growth of capital, plus the growth of labor inputs. This may be expressed: $\frac{\Delta Y}{Y} = a\left(\frac{\Delta K}{K}\right) + b\left(\frac{\Delta L}{L}\right)$ where a and b are weights reflecting the relative contribution of capital and labor to the growth of output.

If the further heroic assumption is made that each factor is paid the value of its marginal product, these weights are simply the relative shares of each factor in total income.[1] In the American economy, labor's share is approximately 70 percent and property's share 30 percent, so that $a = 0.3$ and $b = 0.7$. In contrast to the fixed-proportions model, this formulation suggests that less than one third of the growth in output is attributable to capital accumulation alone.

As long as the marginal product of capital is positive, output per worker is greater as the quantity of capital per worker increases. If new entrants to the labor force are to be given the same amount of capital as existing workers, part of current output must be saved and invested in any year simply to equip the new workers. Otherwise average capital per man will fall over time. As a result, the greater the rate of growth of the labor force, the greater the proportion of current income that must be diverted from current consumption to investment, merely to equip new workers with the existing level of capital per man.

This important insight reveals that countries in which population is growing very rapidly will find it extremely difficult to raise per capita consumption, because they must devote a large proportion of existing output to investment expenditures merely to stay even.

The Importance of Technological Change

In the very long run, the amount of capital investment has no effect on an economy's per capita rate of growth. The investment rate simply determines some long-run equilibrium amount of capital per man. Income per man will be higher with greater capital per man, but capital per worker will not continue to increase indefinitely. In such long-run growth models, the rate of growth of income is dependent solely on the rate of growth of the labor force and the rate of technological change.

Technological change operates to raise output from a given input of factors, as if a magic wand were waved over the economy. It may be represented formally in the given expression as follows: T is the rate of technological change such that:

$$\frac{\Delta Y}{Y} = T + a(\Delta K/K) + b(\Delta L/L).$$

1. This may be shown as follows: Total income (Y) is allocated to labor (wL) and capital (rK) where w is the average wage rate, L the number of workers, r the average return on capital, and K the capital stock:

1. $Y = wL + rK$

Increases in income are similarly due to increase in factor inputs, depending on each factor's marginal product.

2. $\Delta Y = w\Delta L + r\Delta K$

Dividing both sides by Y:

3. $\dfrac{\Delta Y}{Y} = \dfrac{w\Delta L}{Y} + \dfrac{r\Delta K}{Y}$

Multiplying numerator and denominator of each fraction by L and K respectively:

4. $\dfrac{\Delta Y}{Y} = (\dfrac{wL}{Y})(\dfrac{\Delta L}{L}) + (\dfrac{rK}{K})(\dfrac{\Delta K}{K})$, so that $a = (\dfrac{wL}{Y})$ and $b = (\dfrac{rK}{Y})$

The rate of technological change is extremely difficult to measure, so that very little is known about its contribution to the growth process. Attempts have been made to estimate the contribution of increases in the labor force, the capital stock, investment in human capital due to education and training, and all other quantifiable factor inputs to the rise in productive capacity. All these factors appear to account for less than half the experienced increase in productivity per worker in the United States. The residual is then attributed to "technological change," which becomes a catchall phrase for everything else. There is some evidence that the rate of technical change is influenced by the level of investment as new techniques become embodied in more productive modern equipment.

ECONOMIC DEVELOPMENT

Economic development refers to the entire process by which less developed countries with relatively low levels of per capita income become developed countries with relatively high levels of per capita income. Economic development occurs through a broad, cumulative, and circular interaction of economic, social, and political change, in which events in one sphere react upon and influence changes elsewhere.

Underdevelopment and Poverty

Because *underdevelopment* refers to a total condition pervading an entire society, focusing on economic variables alone provides only a partial explanation and in isolation may well be misleading. Even the concept of rational behavior, the foundation on which all economic analysis is based, varies widely in content as farmers and entrepreneurs in diverse environments respond differently to changes in incentives, institutions, and controls.

The common and defining characteristic of less developed countries is a low level of per capita income and output. More than half the world's current population of 3.5 billion has a per capita income of less than $100 a year. Table 21-4 presents estimates of per capita income in selected countries. The data speak for themselves most eloquently. The Chinese word for peace is *ho-ping*. Translated literally, it means "food for all."

Noneconomic Variables

The process by which an economy is transformed or "takes off" from a primitive subsistence economy toward a modern developed economy, or from stagnation to sustained growth, is extremely complex and difficult to formulate with precision. A large number of noneconomic variables play a critical role.

Table 21-4   PER CAPITA INCOME IN
            SELECTED COUNTRIES,
            1958–68 (AT MARKET PRICE
            CONVERTED INTO U.S.
            DOLLARS)

Countries	1958	1965	1968
Australia	1,126	1,640	1,991
Brazil	250	212	263
Canada	1,503	1,824	2,247
France	1,003	1,448	1,940
German, Fed. Rep. of	838	1,455	1,726
Ghana	150	251	198
India	64	91	73
Israel	454	1,076	1,185
Japan	284	694	1,122
Kenya	81	90	110
Pakistan	62	95	122
Sweden	1,342	2,248	2,905
Thailand	80	109	116
U.S.A.	2,361	3,240	3,569
U.S.S.R.	951	1,296	1,700*
United Kingdom	1,014	1,467	1,457

* Estimate
Source: Statistical Office of the United Nations.

Income and wealth ownership are typically very unequally distributed, with most of the small surplus that the economy does produce above subsistence going to the traditionally dominant or ruling groups. The power of these groups is generally based on an economic fact, concentrated land and property ownership, reinforced by a class or caste system of social values. These privileged groups offer strong resistence to change; yet without a radical transformation in the existing structure of power and control economic development has proven extremely difficult. Under some land tenure systems, for example, neither tenant nor landlord has an incentive to improve the property. While the relationship of tenure systems to agricultural productivity is not yet well understood, observers all agree on the political difficulty of land reform.

If the elite groups do not possess entrepreneurial skills, the saving that does occur may be channeled not toward productive investment but directed to the accumulation of assets that do not increase future productive capacity — for example, residences, personal durables, land, jewelry, and gold — or to the maintenance of retinues of servants and dependents.

The Structural Transformation

When the average level of productivity per worker is low, one man can produce enough food only for himself and his family, with a very small surplus left over for others. As a result, a large proportion of the labor force, from two thirds to 90 percent in very poor countries, must be employed in agriculture. Development is centrally a matter of raising productivity. As the bulk of the population is in agriculture, this initially refers to agricultural productivity. With the process of development, as per capita productivity rises, the proportion of the labor force in agriculture falls. A structural transformation of the economy occurs, and the proportion of the labor force in manufacturing and services rises. This decline of the labor force in the agricultural sector, when coupled with high rates of population growth, combine to produce a very rapid rise in the nonagricultural labor force, and typically results in mass urban unemployment.

Table 21-5 presents the share of agriculture in selected countries. As seen, the proportion of the labor force in agriculture declines from 90 to less than 10 percent in more developed countries. Even in Denmark, New Zealand and Australia, which are highly specialized and major food exporters, the proportion of the labor force in agriculture is less than 20 percent. In the United States, which is also a major food exporter, one man can, on the average, provide enough food for himself and twenty other families.

Table 21-5   THE SHARE OF AGRICULTURE IN
SELECTED COUNTRIES, 1965

Country	Percent of Labor Force	Percent of Net National Product	Per Capital Net National Product in U.S. Dollars
Nepal	94	66	70
Ivory Coast	86	44	220
Nigeria	60	65	80
India	73	50	90
Brazil	52	—	240
Taiwan	47	26	230
Portugal	42	19	399
Japan	27	12	860
Denmark	17	10	2,246
New Zealand	13	—	1,930
Australia	10	11	1,840
U.S.A.	6	3	3,250
United Kingdom	4	3	1,620

Source: Statistical Office of the United Nations.

Table 21-6 presents sector shares of GNP in selected countries. The share of manufactures and services rises with development.

As a result of low productivity and low income, savings ratios are very low. Most of the population must spend most of their income on food and other necessities. With a low savings ratio, investment is low, and there is a shortage both of tangible capital and of investment in human capital in the form of education and training. This situation in turn tends to keep productivity and real income low. Finally, the poverty and ignorance of those on the lower rungs of the social system make it difficult to transform the social order so that sustained development and modernization

Table 21-6 SECTOR SHARES OF GNP IN SELECTED COUNTRIES

	Year	Agriculture	Industry	Construction	Transportation and Communications	Wholesale and Retail Trade	Other Services
Australia	1967	9	34	8	8	15	26
Burma	1967	34	10	2	7	29	17
Canada	1966	7	33	6	9	13	32
Chile	1966	11	39	6	5	16	23
France	1968	7	38	10	5	11	33
Germany	1968	4	44	7	6	13	26
India	1967	52	15	4	4	10	15
Israel	1968	8	25	8	9	18	33
Japan	1968	10	31	8	8	17	26
Pakistan	1968	46	12	5	7	12	18
Phillipines	1968	34	20	4	4	11	28
South Africa	1968	10	36	4	9	14	27
Sudan	1966	54	6	6	14		19
Thailand	1968	30	16	6	7	20	21
U.S.A.	1968	3	32	5	6	16	39
U.S.S.R.	1968	21	52	10	6	11	
U.K.	1968	3	40	7	8	11	33
Zambia	1967	9	45	7	7	13	20

Source: Statistical Office of the United Nations.

can occur. This structure, by which the factors making for low incomes are self-reinforcing, has been termed the *vicious circle of development.*

The reduction in death rates combined with high birth rates has resulted, as discussed above, in a worldwide population explosion. Many underdeveloped countries have rates of population increases of 3 percent and more, which approach and even exceed their rates of growth of output. As a result, per capita income has increased very slowly and in some cases has actually fallen over the postwar period. Saving is simply not available to provide these new workers with capital and training. Combined with the structural transformation of the economy, insufficient jobs are available and unemployment rates are explosively high.

Development Plans

In this desperate situation, the governments of these countries have been forced by pressures largely beyond their control to take an increasingly active role in planning a strategy of development. In an attempt to raise the savings ratio, governments have attempted to increase the proportion of tax receipts in national income. This involves of necessity taxation of the rural sector, usually based on primary agricultural production for export. The result has frequently been a loss of export revenue, exacerbating the balance of payments problem.

Less developed economies typically are heavily dependent on the export of a few primary commodities to provide foreign exchange with which to purchase imports of capital goods critically necessary for the growth process. For small countries exports are frequently a large share, from one quarter to over one half, of GNP. The development process is then constrained by the ability of the country to raise its export production and by the price on the world market for primary commodities. All too characteristically, rapid growth of income leads to an even more rapid growth of imports and a subsequent foreign exchange crisis. The development boom then has to be choked off by restrictive monetary and fiscal policy and a battery of quantitative controls.

Socialization of savings is characteristically accompanied by a socialization of investment. Tax revenues are used to finance government investment expenditures in those key projects regarded as a precondition if economic growth is to occur. Investment in power, irrigation, transportation, communication, and education are sometimes termed *social overhead capital.* Such services frequently require a large scale of investment if indivisibilities are to give rise to scale economies. Because they are characterized by important external benefits to society at large, private industry is unlikely to undertake them in sufficient quantity.

Unfortunately there is frequently a yawning discrepancy between a government's intentions and its ability to carry out its development plans. Such softness is characteristic of governments in most developing nations. Resources are wasted, bureaucracies are created, bribery and cynicism is widespread, and the economy fails to grow. Rather than an increase in productive capacity, the development plan results primarily in private profits at public expense, and a transfer of the proceeds of taxation from the rural poor to the educated elite.

Under such circumstances the success of the struggle to escape from poverty may require some revolutionary movement to carry through a program of mass awakening and modernization. Economic development involves changing an entire society in a way that is bound to shake its existing social order of power and prestige. To date there has been a striking lack of success in most countries' efforts to accelerate their rates of economic growth. Almost nowhere in Latin America, Africa, or Southeast Asia does per capita output show a strong, steady, upward trend. What one sees instead is a terrible changelessness that seems impossible to affect. A central achievement of the Russian, Chinese, Mexican, Yugoslav, and Cuban revolutions was in overcoming the sapping inertia of a despairing and torpid peasantry and bringing that release of energies which is borne with hope and enthusiasm for the future.

Even more hopeless, corrupt, and miserable than Russia, China was the source of endless horror stories of peasants eating mud when the crops failed, of the sale of daughters into prostitution to ward off starvation, of the subhuman degradation of the "coolie," the ricksha boy, the city homeless. China, in a word, was like India. But that too has changed. In China, we no longer find the homeless on the street, or forced prostitution, or children deliberately mutilated to become appealing beggars, although we still find all of these things in India. Nor do we find corruption in government, or an inability to distribute food supplies in bad times so as to provide a fair ration for all. More significant, we see an all-important redirection of

Chinese life away from the endlessly static past to a new future. . . . China is a nation in a paroxysm of change that has brought much that is ugly, cruel, and mean. And yet, before we condemn it for its very obvious evils, let every reader ask himself into which society he would take his chances as an anonymous human being today — India or China?[2]

Foreign Assistance

The developed countries can strategically assist the development process by foreign aid in the form of grants, loans, and technical assistance. Foreign investment, whether public or private, provides foreign exchange that permits a developing country to import goods of a greater value than it exports and to raise domestic investment above domestic saving. Provision of technical assistance in the form of personnel to assist in the education and training of the labor force is also critically important, as the absence of a skilled and productive labor force is generally the greatest single bottleneck to acceleration of the development process.

The climate surrounding foreign aid programs is now heavy with disillusion and distrust. In 1971 the United States Senate took the astonishing action of refusing to pass the foreign aid bill. It has become very clear that the impact made by outside resources depends on the efficiency with which they are used by the recipient. Over the last decade, the developed countries have not recorded a particularly splendid record of assistance to their desperately poor neighbors. In the United States, foreign aid has fallen from 1.5 percent of GNP in 1948 to less than 0.4 percent today. This drop is in part attributable to the increased concern for poverty and disparity of standards of life and opportunity at home. More important, foreign aid has no domestic constituency in the political decision-making process.

Governments in the developed countries somehow have to be convinced of the political advantages to themselves of aid to the growth of other economies. In a world where imperialism is no longer tolerated, some alternative way of gaining political advantage to donor nations appears necessary. The link to an assisting country's enlightened self-interest in a more prosperous world at present often appears tenuous. This is particularly the case when its aid alone is very small relative to the needs of the Third World, and it has no assurance that its rich neighbors will match its own contribution. The United Nations has pleaded for a foreign aid target equal to 1 percent of each developed country's GNP. This has rarely been achieved in practice. Official aid flows of about $7 billion are dwarfed by developed countries' military expenditures, which exceed $150 billion per year. The United States' defense budget alone currently exceeds the total income of the poorest third of the world's population!

In the absence of more effective international institutions, with their corollary of

2. R. Heilbroner, *Between Capitalism and Socialism*, 1970, pp. 66–7.

self-imposed limitations on the area of national sovereignty, the chief reliance for some time to come must probably be placed on the sympathy and altruism of individuals and leaders in the richer countries, and on fear. Yet charity alone is certain to be insufficient, as the glow of righteousness comes to the giver long before the needs of the recipient are satisfied. The developed 20 percent of the world's population (North America, Northern Europe, Australia, and Japan) receive about 80 percent of the world's income. The annual *increase* in income of these developed countries (currently approximately $60 billion) exceeds the *total* income of each of the continents of Africa, Asia, and South America. Can Americans (and others) comfortably live in a world with the knowledge that the average amount spent on an American dog compares favorably with the average income of one-third of the men, women, and children living in the world?

Even more ominously, the mathematics of compound interest suggest that absolute income differentials between rich and poor will widen dramatically in the near future. With per capita income growing at a rate of roughly 2.5 percent in America, per capita income doubles every 27 years or approximately every generation. Suppose optimistically that the poor countries were able to bring their population increase under control and to carry out a successful development effort, so that their per capita income grew at the same rate. With an initial level of per capita income in America of $3,000 and in underdeveloped countries of $100, the existing differential is $2,900. In one generation, if the future resembles the past, per capita income in America will have grown to $6,000. But in the underdeveloped countries, per capita income will have risen only to $200, so that the differential has become $5,800.

Even if the poor countries somehow succeeded in raising their per capita income growth to 5 percent, a rate never experienced historically in any country for extended periods, their per capita income in one generation would grow only to $400 and the absolute gap would still have widened dramatically.

Once these conditions become more widely known, there is perhaps hope for an awakened conscience and a rediscovery of the inner truth that "it is more blessed to give than to receive." But this is probably too naïve. For a strong and continuing aid motivation, developed countries must see their political and economic fortunes as intrinsically dependent upon the growth and security of developing countries. More than the whiff of revolution may be needed to awake jaded social consciences and produce effective international institutions. As a distinguished recent report eloquently concluded,

In short, we face an essential need and an unprecedented opportunity. International development is a great challenge of our age. Our response to it will show whether we understand the implications of interdependence or whether we prefer to delude ourselves that the poverty and deprivation of the great majority of mankind can be ignored without tragic consequences for all.[3]

3. *Report of the Commission on International Development*, Lester B. Pearson, Chairman (1969).

APPENDIX: BALANCED GROWTH, GOLDEN AGES, AND GOLDEN RULES

Balanced Growth

In order to investigate the contributions of capital, labor, and technological change to the rate of growth of output, it is a convenient analytical simplification to postulate a condition of *balanced growth*, in which all factors and output grow at the same (constant) rate. This concept of balanced growth is a counterpart to the concept of stationary equilibrium in static analysis. Real-world economies do not, of course, move along a balanced growth path but are always in unbalanced growth.

Because capital (K), labor (L), and output (Y) all grow at the same rate in balanced growth, the ratio of capital to output $(\frac{K}{Y})$, labor to output $(\frac{L}{Y})$ and capital to labor $(\frac{K}{L})$ all remain constant. With a constant output-labor ratio (average productivity per man), the rate of growth of total output (g_Y) would be equal to the rate of growth of population (g_L), and per capita income would remain constant. This is sometimes termed the "natural" rate of growth, that is, the rate determined by the natural forces of population increase, provided that full employment is maintained.

If technological change were increasing productivity per worker autonomously at a certain rate (g_T), the rate of growth of output (g_Y) would equal the population growth rate (g_L) plus the rate of technical progress (g_T), $g_Y = (g_L + g_T)$, again assuming that full employment is maintained. Output per worker would grow at the rate g_T. If the capital-output ratio remained constant, then the capital-labor ratio would also increase at the rate g_T.

A Simple Neoclassical Growth Model

The presentation of a simple neoclassical growth model is shown in Figure 21-4. The output-labor ratio (income per capita) (Y/L) is measured on the vertical axis, and the capital-labor ratio (capital per worker) (K/L) is measured on the horizontal axis. The production function Y shows how output per worker rises as the amount of capital per worker is increased. To avoid the complications of depreciation, assume that income is measured in net terms, after all provisions to maintain the capital stock. Again temporarily assuming a given level of technology, greater and greater additions of capital per worker are subject to diminishing returns, as shown by the declining slope of the production function Y in Figure 21-4. Assume again for simplicity that the proportion of income saved (s_0) remains constant. The S_0 curve, drawn as a constant fraction of Y, then indicates the amount the economy would save per worker at different levels of per capita income.

Golden Age Growth Paths

What level of net investment is required to maintain different capital-labor ratios? Let the rate of growth of the labor force be represented by g_L, (for example, 2 percent). With a capital-labor ratio equal to one, 2 percent of current income must then be saved and invested in order to provide new workers with the amount of capital per man equal to that of existing workers. The level of net investment necessary to maintain capital per man constant is therefore simply the rate of growth of the labor force times the particular capital-labor ratio to be maintained. This is represented by the straight line I drawn through the origin with a slope of g_L, so that the amount of investment required at any point is $g_L(K/L)$.

The intersection of the savings and investment functions at E shows the long-run balanced growth path that an economy, given its production function, savings preference, and rate of population growth, would eventually approach. At all capital-labor ratios below the value $(K/L)_E$ (e.g., $(K/L)_1$), current saving and investment would exceed the level of investment required to maintain that capital-labor ratio constant. As a result, capital per man would gradually increase over time until E was eventually attained. Conversely, at all capital-labor ratios greater than $(K/L)_E$ (e.g., $(K/L)_2$), current saving and investment would be less than the investment required to maintain capital-labor ratio constant. As a result, capital per man would fall, and this process would continue until E was eventually reached.

Such balanced growth configurations, in which capital, labor, and output all grow at the rate g_L so that capital per man remains constant, have been termed *golden age* growth paths. This term emphasizes that such paths would be reached only in the

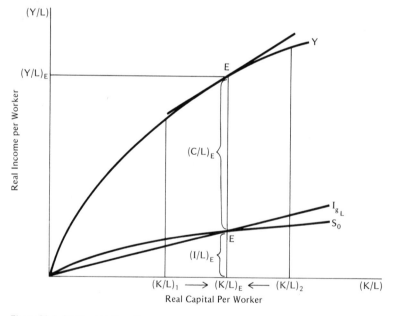

Figure 21-4 Golden Age Growth

very long run, assuming that saving ratios, labor force growth rates, and technology remain constant.

Consumption per man is represented in Figure 21-4 by the vertical distance $(Y/L - S/L)$. Once the golden age growth path was achieved, consumption per capita would remain constant $(C/L)_E$ and income and capital would grow at the rate of growth of the labor force (g_L). As this is true for all balanced growth paths, irrespective of the particular savings ratio, it suggests the important conclusion that *in the very long run, the amount of capital investment has no effect on an economy's rate of growth,* which is dependent solely on the rate of growth of the labor force, as is shown in Figure 21-5. Income is measured on a log scale on the vertical axis, and time on the horizontal axis. In all golden-age balanced-growth paths, income grows at the rate of the labor force (g_L). A change in the level of investment can change the rate of growth of the economy only while it moves the economy from one growth path to another, for example, during the period *nm* as the economy moves from path A to path B.

One plausible type of technical change may be introduced easily into the growth path diagram. Technical change is classified as neutral, labor saving, or capital saving according to whether it leaves the proportion of income going to labor and capital unchanged, reduces labor's share, or reduces capital's share. As previously stated, income shares in many countries appear to have remained roughly stable over considerable periods of time.

"Neutral" technical change, which leaves the capital-output ratio and the return on capital constant, may be represented in Figure 21-4 by an upward shift of the production relation of g_T per cent per year. Alternatively, as one worker next year

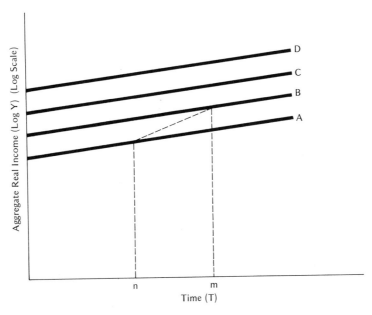

Figure 21-5 Alternative Long-Run Growth Paths

can produce as much as $(1 + g_T)$ workers this year, the growth of labor in *efficiency units,* that is, in units of constant productivity, may be measured in the diagram as $(g_L + g_T)$. The investment ratio then has the slope $(g_L + g_T)$, and output and capital stock in balanced growth both grow at the rate $(g_L + g_T)$. Income, consumption, and capital per worker then grow at the rate g_T. In the long run, the amount of capital formation again has no effect on the growth rate, which is determined by the natural growth of labor and the rate of technical change.

The Golden Rule

There now arises the question whether, if the economy alters its savings ratio and thus its investment and long-run capital-labor ratio, there exists some growth path that is optimal in terms of yielding *highest per capita consumption* $(\frac{C}{L})$, even though in the very long run, as seen, the growth *rate* is solely determined by natural forces.

Consumption, the difference between income and investment, will be maximized when the slope of the production relation is equal to the slope of the investment line $(g_L + g_T)$. This maximum could be achieved by the economy raising the savings function to S^*, as shown in Figure 21-6. As a result, in this golden age path the capital-labor ratio is $(K/L)^*$, per capita income is $(Y/L)^*$, and consumption per head $(C/L)^*$ is the distance $(\frac{Y}{L})^* - (\frac{I}{L})^*$.

Such a growth configuration has been termed the *golden rule* path. An economy

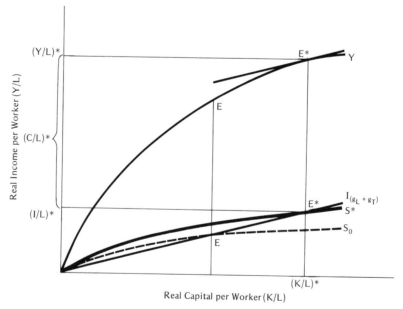

Figure 21-6 Golden Rule Growth

that selected such a saving and investment ratio would maximize the consumption per head of all future generations. It may thus be regarded as *the amount of savings and investment that all future generations would desire each present generation to do unto them.* As may be seen by inspection, with any other saving ratio, consumption per head is lower.

The slope of the production function represents the marginal product of capital, that is, the rate of return on investment. The golden rule thus requires that investment be increased so long as the marginal efficiency of investment exceeds the growth rate of the economy $(g_L + g_T)$.

At the initial equilibrium E in Figure 21-6 the return on investment (i.e., the marginal product of capital) exceeds the growth rate of the economy, which appears to be the case for most capitalist economies. Business firms cease investing well before the rate of return on capital has been driven down to the rate of growth of the economy. Capitalist economies therefore presumably operate and grow on a path well below their golden rule savings ratio.

As any increase in the savings ratio toward S^* necessitates lower present per capita consumption in order to achieve for all time greater future per capita consumption, as previously discussed, it cannot be concluded that even the golden rule path is best in any normative sense. Such a decision again necessarily involves an intergenerational comparison of utility. Present generations are asked to consume less so that the future can consume more.

As seen from Figure 21-6 it is possible for savings to be too large (for example, any savings ratio above S^*). This may be the case in some planned economies, where saving has been pushed too far. In such a case, although per capita income will be higher, the greater proportion of that higher income that must be saved and invested

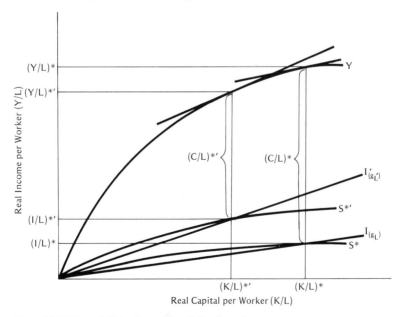

Figure 21-7 Effect of Higher Rate of Population Growth

in order to equip the labor force with the higher quantity of capital per worker results in a lower level of per capita consumption.

This geometric presentation of the neoclassical model permits a demonstration of the effects of rapid rates of population growth in depressing the maximum sustainable level of per capita consumption. In Figure 21-7 assume that the rate of labor force growth rises, e.g., to g_L. The amount of net investment required to equip new workers increases as a proportion of Y, as shown by the steeper slope of the investment function I' (g_L). As a result, in the new golden rule path capital per worker $(K/L)^{*\prime}$ and per capita consumption $(C/L)^{*\prime}$ will both be lower the higher the rate of population increase.

Per capita consumption is greatest with zero population growth. In this case, net investment and saving is zero, even though capital per worker is very large, and the marginal product of capital has been pushed down to zero in the golden rule path. This rule reveals that saving must be higher in economies with more rapid population growth just to maintain the level of capital per worker.

BIBLIOGRAPHY OF SELECTED PAPERBACKS: PART SIX

Baldwin, R., *Economic Development,* Wiley.

Balogh, T., *The Economics of Poverty,* Free Press.

Baran, P. A., *The Political Economy of Growth,* Monthly Review.

Dobb, M., *Economic Growth and Underdeveloped Countries,* International Publishing Company.

——, *An Essay on Economic Growth and Planning,* Monthly Review.

Drake, M., *Population in Industrialization,* Barnes & Noble.

Frank, A. G., *Capitalism and Underdevelopment in Latin America,* Monthly Review Press.

Furtado, C., *Development and Underdevelopment,* University of California Press.

—— *Obstacles to Development in Latin America,* Doubleday.

Galbraith, J. K., *Economic Development,* Houghton Mifflin.

Galeano, E., *Guatemala: Occupied Country,* Monthly Review.

Gill, R. T., *Economic Development: Past and Present,* Prentice-Hall.

Heilbroner, R. L., *The Great Ascent: The Struggle for Economic Development in Our Time,* Harper & Row.

Hirschman, A. O., *The Strategy of Economic Development,* Yale University Press.

Johnson, H., *Economic Policies Toward Less Developed Countries,* Praeger.

Kuznets, S., *Toward a Theory of Economic Growth,* Norton.

Maddison, A., *Economic Growth in the West: Comparative Experience in Europe and North America,* Norton.

Mishan, E., *Technology and Growth: The Price We Pay,* Praeger.

Myrdal, G., *Approach to the Asian Drama: Methodological and Theoretical Selections from Asian Drama,* Random House.

—— *The Challenge to Affluence,* Random House.

North, D. C., *Economic Growth of the United States,* Norton.

Pincus, J. A., *Trade, Aid and Development: The Rich and Poor Nations,* McGraw-Hill.

Shonfield, A., *The Attack on World Poverty,* Random House.

Sweezy, P., *Theory of Capitalist Development,* Monthly Review.

index

HB
171.5
· M674